WARPLANES·OF·THE
Luftwaffe

WARPLANES·OF·THE
Luftwaffe

Editor: David Donald

Aerospace Publishing London
AIRtime Publishing USA

Published by
Aerospace Publishing Ltd
179 Dalling Road
London W6 0ES
England

Published under licence in USA and
Canada by
AIRtime Publishing Inc.
10 Bay Street
Westport, CT 06880
USA

Aerospace **ISBN: 1 874023 56 5**
AIRtime **ISBN: 1-880588-10-2**

Distributed in the UK,
Commonwealth and Europe by
Airlife Publishing Ltd
101 Longden Road
Shrewsbury SY3 9EB
England
Telephone: 0743 235651
Fax: 0743 232944

Distributed to retail bookstores in the
USA and Canada by
AIRtime Publishing Inc.
10 Bay Street
Westport, CT 06880
USA
Telephone: (203) 226-3580
Fax: (203) 221-0779

US readers wishing to order by mail,
please contact
AIRtime Publishing Inc. toll-free at
1 800 359-3003

Publisher: Stan Morse

Editor: David Donald

Associate Editors:
Jon Lake
Robert Hewson
Sophearith Moeng

Sub Editor:
Karen Leverington

Authors: David Donald
Bill Gunston
Jon Lake
David Mondey

Artists: Keith Fretwell
Ichiro Hasegawa
John Weal
Iain Wyllie

The editor would like to express his
gratitude to Mr John Weal for his
invaluable help in the production of
this book.

Typesetting by SX Composing

Printed in Singapore

WORLD AIR POWER JOURNAL
is published quarterly and
provides an in-depth analysis
of contemporary military
aircraft and their worldwide
operators. Superbly produced
and filled with extensive colour
photography, World Air Power
Journal is available by
subscription from:

UK, Europe and
Commonwealth:
Aerospace Publishing Ltd
FREEPOST
PO Box 2822
London, W6 0BR
UK
Telephone: 081-740 9554
Fax: 081-746 2556
(no stamp required if posted in
the UK)

USA and Canada:
AIRtime Publishing Inc.
Subscription Dept
10 Bay Street
Westport, CT 06880
USA
Telephone: (203) 226-3580
Toll-free number in USA:
1 800 359-3003

CONTENTS

ARADO AR 68	6	HEINKEL HE 50	96
ARADO AR 95	6	HEINKEL HE 51	96
ARADO AR 196	7	HEINKEL HE 59	97
ARADO AR 232	15	HEINKEL HE 60	97
ARADO AR 234 BLITZ	15	HEINKEL HE 100	98
ARADO AR 240	23	HEINKEL HE 111	98
BACHEM BA 349 NATTER	23	HEINKEL HE 114	107
BLOHM UND VOSS BV 138	24	HEINKEL HE 115	108
BLOHM UND VOSS HA 139	26	HEINKEL HE 162 SALAMANDER	113
BLOHM UND VOSS BV 141	26	HEINKEL HE 177 GREIF	120
BLOHM UND VOSS BV 142	27	HEINKEL HE 219 UHU	128
BLOHM UND VOSS BV 222 WIKING	28	HEINKEL HE 274/277	135
BLOHM UND VOSS BV 238	28	HEINKEL HE 280	135
DFS 230	29	HENSCHEL HS 123	136
DORNIER DO 17/215	30	HENSCHEL HS 126	138
DORNIER DO 18	34	HENSCHEL HS 129	140
DORNIER DO 24	36	HENSCHEL HS 130	147
DORNIER DO 26	38	JUNKERS JU 52	148
DORNIER DO 217	38	JUNKERS JU 86	156
DORNIER DO 335 PFEIL	46	JUNKERS JU 87	158
FIESELER FI 103	54	JUNKERS JU 88	168
FIESELER FI 156 STORCH	54	JUNKERS JU 188	180
FIESELER FI 167	60	JUNKERS JU 252	188
FLETTNER FL 282 KOLIBRI	61	JUNKERS JU 287	188
FOCKE-ACHGELIS FA 223 DRACHE	61	JUNKERS JU 290	189
FOCKE-WULF FW 56 STÖSSER	62	JUNKERS JU 352 HERKULES	195
FOCKE-WULF FW 58 WEIHE	62	JUNKERS JU 388	195
FOCKE-WULF FW 187	63	MESSERSCHMITT BF 109	196
FOCKE-WULF FW 189 UHU	63	MESSERSCHMITT BF 110	210
FOCKE-WULF FW 190/TA 152	71	MESSERSCHMITT ME 163 KOMET	222
FOCKE-WULF FW 200 CONDOR	85	MESSERSCHMITT ME 261	229
FOCKE-WULF TA 154 MOSKITO	93	MESSERSCHMITT ME 262 SCHWALBE	229
GOTHA GO 145	93	MESSERSCHMITT ME 321/323	238
GOTHA GO 229 (HORTEN HO IX)	94	MESSERSCHMITT ME 410	245
GOTHA GO 242/244	94		
HEINKEL HE 46	95	INDEX	252

Arado Ar 68

Development of the Arado Ar 68, which was to be the last biplane fighter to enter front-line service with the Luftwaffe, followed on from the sole Ar 67. Reaching contemporary standards of aerodynamic efficiency, the aircraft had an oval-section fuselage of steel tube construction, with metal panels covering the rear decking and forward sections. The single-bay wings were of wood, with plywood and fabric covering. The distinctive fin, which was to be used almost without exception in subsequent single-engined Arado designs, was introduced on the Ar 68, which also featured spatted landing gear.

The prototype **Ar 68a** flew for the first time in 1934, powered by a BMW VId 12-cylinder Vee engine which provided a maximum continuous output of 410 kW (550 hp), resulting in disappointing performance. The problem was partially overcome

in the **Ar 68b** second prototype, which was powered by a supercharged 455-kW (610-hp) Junkers Jumo 210 12-cylinder inverted-Vee engine, which both improved forward vision from the cockpit and provided full power at higher altitudes. Three more prototypes followed.

Initial deliveries were made of the BMW VI-powered **Ar 68F-1** to the Luftwaffe in the late summer of 1936, commencing with II/JG 134 'Horst Wessel'. Deliveries of the Jumo 210Ea-powered **Ar 68E-1** followed in

the spring of 1937, this variant being able to carry six small bombs on an underfuselage rack.

By the outbreak of World War II, most surviving Ar 68s had been relegated to advanced fighter trainer status with the Jagdfliegerschulen (fighter pilot schools), where they operated for some while. However, a few Ar 68Es were serving as night-fighters with 11./JG 2 and 5./JG 52 along the French border, while 10. (Nachtjagd)/JG 53 had Ar 68Fs at Heilbronn. These units quickly re-equipped during the winter of 1939-40.

During the winter of 1939-40, a few Ar 68F-1s were used in the night-fighting role by 10. (Nacht)/Jagdgeschwader 53 'Pik As'. This aircraft carries the wing's famous ace of spades badge.

Specification
Arado Ar 68E-1
Type: single-seat fighter
Powerplant: one 515-kW (690-hp) Junkers Jumo 210 Da inverted inline piston engine
Performance: maximum speed 305 km/h (190 mph) at sea level; service ceiling 8100 m (26,575 ft); range 415 km (258 miles)
Weights: empty 1840 kg (4,057 lb); maximum take-off 2475 kg (5,457 lb)
Dimensions: span 11.00 m (36 ft 1 in); length 9.50 m (31 ft 2 in); height 3.28 m (10 ft 9 in); wing area 27.30 m² (293.86 sq ft)
Armament: two fixed forward-firing 7.92-mm (0.31-in) MG 17 machine-guns, 500 rounds per gun; wing racks for six SC 10 10-kg (22-lb) fragmentation bombs

Arado Ar 95

Dipl Ing Walter Blume designed the Arado Ar 95 in 1935 for service in the coastal patrol, reconnaissance and light attack roles. A two-seat twin-float seaplane, it was of all-metal construction, with parallel-chord wings which were attached to centre-sections of unequal chord and thickness. This unusual feature was intended to provide easier access to the cockpits from the lower wing-root, which was thicker and of wider chord, and improved upward visibility was to result from the thinner and narrower upper surface. The single-step floats were strut-braced to the fuselage and wing centre-section. The twin cockpits were enclosed by a sliding canopy, the rear end being left open to permit the use of a 7.92-mm (0.31-in) machine-gun, supplementing the similar

Arado Ar 95A-1 of 3./SAGr 125, Baltic Sea, summer 1941.

3. Staffel/Seeaufklärungsgruppe 125 was the main Ar 95 operating unit, flying the type along the Baltic coast in support of the German advance through Estonia and Latvia. This aircraft is armed with SC 50 bombs.

forward-firing weapon mounted in the upper fuselage.

In 1937 the first prototype was flown, powered by an 656-kW (880-hp) BMW 132De 9-cylinder engine. The second was fitted with the 515-kW (690-hp) Junkers Jumo 210 12-cylinder engine, and both machines were evaluated competitively with two prototypes of the Focke-Wulf Fw 62 single-float seaplane. Although the BMW-powered version was adjudged worthy of further development, and a batch of six prototype and pre-production aircraft served a trial period with the Condor Legion during the Spanish Civil War, the Ar 95 was not immediately adopted for German military use.

Undaunted, Arado offered the

design for export as the **Ar 95W** floatplane, ordered by Turkey in 1938, and as the **Ar 95L** with fixed, spatted landing gear, which was the subject of a Chilean order. The latter was fulfilled prior to the beginning of World War II, but the frustrated Turkish aircraft were instead diverted to the Luftwaffe under the designation **Ar 95A**, seeing wartime service on coastal reconnaissance work. They were initially assigned to 3./Seeaufklärungsgruppe 125 operating in the Baltic, and in 1941 participated in operations off the coast of Latvia and Estonia. The aircraft then operated in the Gulf of Finland, and were reassigned to SAGr 127. The **Ar 195** was an unsuccessful attempt to provide a

carrierborne torpedo bomber and patrol aircraft.

Specification
Arado Ar 95A-1
Type: two-seat coastal patrol and light attack aircraft
Powerplant: one 656-kW (880-hp) BMW 132De radial piston engine
Performance: maximum speed 310 km/h (193 mph) at 3000 m (9,840 ft); cruising speed 255 km/h (158 mph) at 1200 m (3,935 ft); service ceiling 7300 m (23,945 ft); range 1100 km (683 miles)
Weights: empty 2450 kg (5,402 lb); maximum take-off 3560 kg (7,870 lb)
Dimensions: span 12.50 m (41 ft 0 in); length 11.10 m (36 ft 5 in); height 3.60 m (11 ft 9¾ in); wing area 45.40 m² (488.70 sq ft)
Armament: one fixed forward-firing 7.92-mm (0.31-in) MG 17 machine-gun and one flexible 7.92-mm (0.31-in) MG 15 in rear cockpit; an underfuselage rack accommodated an 800-kg (1,764-lb) torpedo or a 500-kg (1,102-lb) bomb

Arado Ar 196

Although it exerted only a minor influence on World War II, the **Arado Ar 196A** was nevertheless an important type. Possessed of quite a useful performance, and remarkably heavily armed – typically with two cannon and three machine-guns – it served all round the coastal areas of Hitler's Europe and was also the standard aircraft carried aboard major surface warships of the German navy, the biggest battleships (*Bismarck* and *Tirpitz*) carrying four each.

The first shipboard aircraft of the resurrected German navy was the Heinkel He 60, a conventional biplane. All such aircraft had to be stressed for catapult launching, possibly while the ship was rolling or pitching in a heavy sea, and for subsequent recovery by crane after alighting on the open ocean, possibly with severe waves. The main purpose was short-range reconnaissance, but coastal patrol, rescue of downed aircrew and even local close support of ground forces (for example in anti-partisan operations) were all to become important secondary duties.

By 1936 it was clear that the He 60 was becoming outdated. Heinkel was invited to produce a successor, but the resulting He 114 proved to have extremely poor hydrodynamic and seakeeping qualities and to be deficient in other respects. After prolonged testing and modification of the He 114, it was decided in about October 1936 to issue a fresh specification and see if Arado Flugzeugwerke or the Focke-Wulf company could offer a better product. Focke-Wulf produced a conventional biplane in the Fw 62, but the Arado offering was a monoplane, with (surprisingly) a low-mounted wing.

The Kriegsmarine and Reichsluftfahrtministerium agreed that the aircraft should be powered by a BMW 132K nine-cylinder radial engine of 716 kW (960 hp) (virtually the same as the engine of the He 114). It was further stipulated that prototypes had to be produced with twin floats and with a single central float and small stabilising floats under the wingtips. The two rival companies quickly submitted drawings and costings and the Ar 196 was judged to be the more attractive. Two prototypes of the Fw 62 were ordered as an insurance, but four were ordered of the Arado. With works numbers 2589-2592, the first two (**Ar 196 V1** and **V2**) were **A-series** aircraft with twin floats, while **V3** and **V4** were the **B-series** machines with a central float. All were registered as civil aircraft (respectively D-IEHK, IHQI, ILRE and OVMB).

A pair of Arado Ar 196A-3s of 2./SAGr 128 flying from their Brest base during the late summer of 1943. Ar 196-equipped Seeaufklärungs-gruppen operated in the Mediterranean, Norway and on the Eastern Front. The Ar 196A-3 was the most numerous of the aircraft's sub-types, and incorporated a number of structural improvements.

In some respects the prototypes were interim aircraft. Their engines were 657-kW (880-hp) BMW 132Dc type, driving a Schwarz two-bladed propeller. As originally built the first aircraft had twin exhaust pipes which were led round under the left side of the fuselage. Later the standard arrangement was twin shorter pipes discharging equally to left and right of the ventral centreline. The cowling fitted the engine tightly, with blisters over the valve gear, and cooling was controlled by trailing-edge hinged gills. Overall the aircraft needed very little modification, the only visible change between the first two prototypes

In many ways the 'eyes of the Kriegsmarine', the Arado Ar 196 had superb water and flight handling characteristics. During its early career its heavy armament made it the scourge of lumbering enemy maritime patrollers, although this was steadily reversed as the war progressed.

being elimination of the balance horn at the top of the rudder and a slight increase in fin area. The V1 was also later fitted with the three-bladed VDM constant-speed propeller that was made standard. Very small modifications were made to the floats, the water rudders being modified.

Thus, V2 and V3 were similar apart from the latter's different float arrangement. V4, however, was fitted with more streamlined stabilising floats, with a simpler arrangement of struts. It also was the first Ar 196 to be fitted with armament, comprising a 20-mm MG FF cannon in each wing, fed from a 60-round drum which left a blister in the underside, plus a single 7.92-mm MG 17 machine-gun in the right side of the forward fuselage with its muzzle firing through the forward ring of the engine cowl (at about '8 o'clock' seen from the front), and a small container on the underside of each outer wing, just outboard of the cannon, for a single SC 50 (50-kg/110-lb) bomb.

The four seaplanes were carefully evaluated at Travemünde in 1937-38, but it proved difficult to decide which was the preferred float arrangement. The central float was considered preferable in operations from choppy water, but the stabilising floats of the version could easily dip into the sea during take-off, resulting in pronounced asymmetric drag and causing tricky problems. In the event, although a further B-series prototype was built (the **V5**, D-IPDB), it was decided to standardise on the twin-float arrangement and this was used on the 10 **Ar 196A-0** pre-production aircraft which were delivered from the Warnemünde factory from November 1938.

Conventional design

Structurally the Ar 196 was conventional to the point of being traditional. While the wing was a two-spar all-metal stressed-skin component, the fuselage was constructed around a strong framework of welded steel tubes with light formers and stringers supporting a skin which was light alloy from the engine firewall to the rear cockpit and fabric from thence to the tail. The tail was a stressed-skin structure but with the movable surfaces covered with fabric. The floats were Alclad light alloy. Fuel was carried in two 300-litre (66-Imp gal) tanks, one in each float, with the feed pipes passing up the forward struts. The latter also incorporated protecting rungs forming a ladder with which the crew or servicing personnel could climb up to the engine or cockpit. Each wing carried slotted flaps and Flettner tabbed ailerons, and was arranged to fold to the rear, undersurface outermost, about a skewed hinge very close to the root. Folding the wings necessitated disconnecting the wing/float bracing struts.

The crew comprised a pilot and an observer/gunner. The latter normally faced aft, and as there was no fuselage tank the seats were close together. A continuous glazed canopy covered the cockpits, the pilot having a section sliding to the rear and the observer a sliding portion which originally could be completely closed. In the production versions the rear cockpit could not be totally enclosed, but wind deflectors avoided any discomfort and the definitive arrangement made it easier to aim the rear armament, which in the initial **Ar**

The first and second prototypes of the Ar 196 had conventional twin floats, while the third, fourth and fifth prototypes (for the B-series) had a single main float on the centreline, with stabilising floats under the wings. The unarmed second aircraft is shown here undergoing a catapult launch.

This view of the prototype Ar 196 shows the twin-float layout that became the standard. The horn balance on the rudder was discarded for the V2, which was similar apart from this and changes to the water rudders. Both aircraft flew in the summer of 1937.

196A-1 version comprised a single 7.92-mm MG 15 machine-gun with seven 75-round saddle-type magazines. The forward-firing armament was omitted, the two SC 50 bombs were retained. The engine was changed for the definitive BMW 132K, driving a Schwarz three-bladed propeller with no spinner. A great deal of operational equipment was added in the production A-1 version, including catapult spools (the structure being locally strengthened), large smoke canisters in the floats, and also emergency rations, extra ammunition and flares in the aft part of the floats.

From the start the Ar 196A was extremely popular. Its performance was adequate, handling was superb both on the water and in the air, its reliability was excellent and the view from the cockpits very good despite the low-mounted wing.

Deliveries of the first 20 of the A-1 version started in June 1939. All this batch were assigned to Bordfliegerstaffel 1/196 and 5/196, one of the first to go to sea being mounted on the catapult of the pocket battleship *Admiral Graf Spee*. This sailed for the south Atlantic in mid-August 1939, and on 13 December of that year encountered three (much less powerful) cruisers of the Royal Navy. Captain Langsdorff perhaps should have launched his brand-new seaplane, which could then have directed the fire of his 28-cm (11-in) guns, while he steamed out of range of the British cruisers. Instead he closed with the British vessels, soon suffering crippling damage. As luck

The Ar 19C V3 (illustrated) and V4 tested the single main float arrangement. Although this and the twin-float arrangement had many advantages, the overall water handling of the twin system was deemed to be more important than the choppy water handling characteristics of the single.

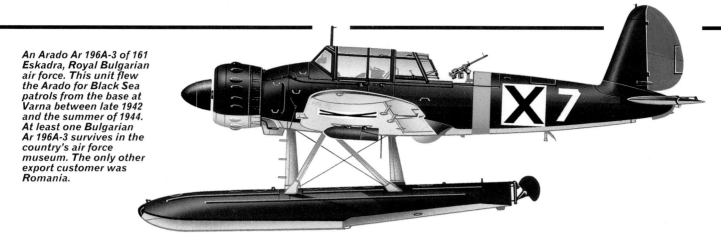

An Arado Ar 196A-3 of 161 Eskadra, Royal Bulgarian air force. This unit flew the Arado for Black Sea patrols from the base at Varna between late 1942 and the summer of 1944. At least one Bulgarian Ar 196A-3 survives in the country's air force museum. The only other export customer was Romania.

would have it, the very first salvo from the British ships struck the *Graf Spee*'s catapult and destroyed the Ar 196A-1 that might have turned the tables.

Subsequently, additional seaplanes replaced the He 60 in shore units as well as aboard all the Kriegsmarine's major surface warships. The very severe winter of 1939-40 delayed flight testing from Warnemünde, but the 20 A-1s were followed from November 1939 by the **Ar 196A-2** version. This was intended for a wider spectrum of duties than shipboard reconnaissance. Operating from shore bases it was expected to range over the North Sea and Baltic looking for shipping to harass and hostile aircraft to destroy, and it was fitted with the forward-firing armament. The MG 17 was installed in the right side of the nose, as in the V4 prototype, and two MG FF cannon were also fitted, installed in an improved way which left the wing undersurface undisturbed, the ammunition drum causing only a modest blister in the top of the wing. The pilot could elect to use the MG 17 only. Though they were not expected to be used very much, the cannon also gave the pilot a feeling of moral superiority, with the knowledge that the Arado could probably shoot down any hostile aircraft it was likely to encounter over the open ocean.

Ar 196s were active over most European waters, from Norway to the Mediterranean. This Ar 196A-3 belonged to 4./Bordfliegergruppe 196 operational in the Adriatic in 1943. The aircraft often scouted ahead for warships, spotting targets at long range and warning of danger.

Above: Ar 196A-1s were delivered for the shipborne patrol mission, 20 of which were followed by the Ar 196A-2 (illustrated). Intended for the coastal patrol mission, these were the first aircraft to feature the forward-firing armament for nuisance attacks against vessels.

Arado Ar 196

Inevitably the empty and gross weights kept rising, but the Ar 196 never became sluggish or difficult to handle. In 1940 the factory delivered 98, this total including the first few of 24 of a version designated **Ar 196A-4**. This replaced the A-1 aboard the warships, differing in having the forward-firing armament and also the additional FuG 16Z radio. A further change was that the Schwarz propeller was replaced by a VDM pattern with a spinner, as fitted to the modified V1 prototype. The V4 was also slightly stronger, for harsh shipboard use. On 26 May 1941 the great battleship *Bismarck* launched her Ar 196A-4s in an attempt to destroy or drive away the RAF Coastal Command Catalina flying-boat that was looking for the battleship as it raced for a home port. They did not succeed, and the 'Cat' called up Swordfish torpedo aircraft which, by crippling Bismarck's steering gear, sealed the ship's fate (it was sunk on 28 May).

On the other hand, on 5 May 1940 two A-2 seaplanes from 1/Küstenfliegergruppe 706, based at recently occupied Aalborg in Denmark, spotted a British submarine, HMS *Seal*, which had been damaged by a mine in the Kattegat. Unable to dive, the British submarine had to lie helplessly on the surface while an A-2 flown by Lt Günther Mehrens attacked with cannon and two bombs. When a second A-2 joined in the submarine surrendered. Mehrens alighted and took on board the submarine's commanding officer, taking him back to Aalborg.

Definitive A-3 variant

Production in 1941 comprised 97 Ar 196s, almost all being of the definitive **Ar 196A-3** sub-type, which incorporated a few further structural changes and additions to the equipment. Production in 1942 totalled 94 A-3s, and between July 1942 and March 1943 a further 23 were delivered from SNCA du Sud-Ouest at Bougenais (St Nazaire). The parent factory delivered 83 seaplanes in 1943, nearly all being of the final main production model, the **Ar 196A-5**. This had a much more effective rear armament, comprising an MG 81Z twin-gun installation, with automatic mass balance and no fewer than 2,000 rounds in a continuous pair of belts. The MG 81 fired at 1,800 rounds per minute per gun. Other changes included the FuG 25a, and later the FuG 141, as well as the FuG 16Z radios. Cockpit instrumentation was improved and there were other minor changes.

In summer 1943 the Fokker works at Amsterdam was brought in to build the A-5 version, producing 69 by termination in August 1944.

Bordfliegerstaffel 1./196 and 5./196 were the two units responsible for providing aircraft for naval vessels, based initially at Wilhelmshaven and Kiel-Holtenau. This aircraft is seen on board the Prinz Eugen heavy cruiser.

The Ar 196 was designed to meet a requirement to replace floatplanes aboard large ships of the Kriegsmarine. Here one of the prototypes is tested aboard a ship. In operation the aircraft was catapulted into the air for take-off, and hoisted back on board the ship after a sortie.

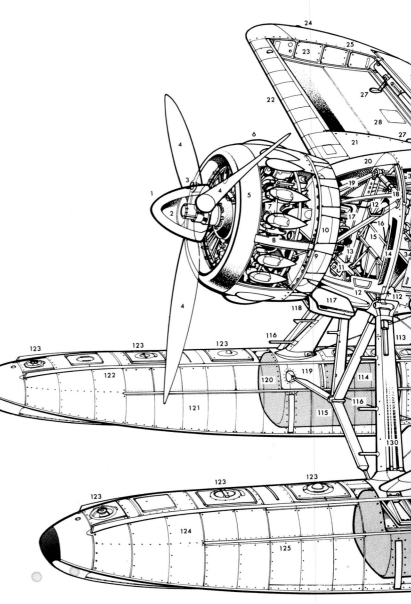

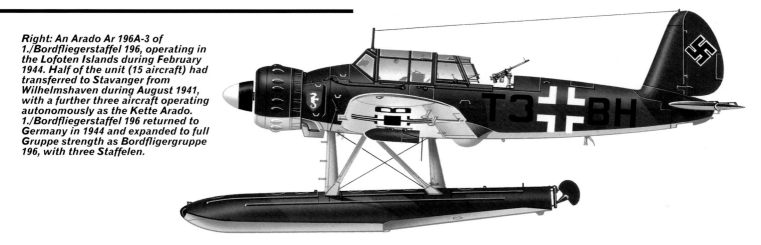

Right: An Arado Ar 196A-3 of 1./Bordfliegerstaffel 196, operating in the Lofoten Islands during February 1944. Half of the unit (15 aircraft) had transferred to Stavanger from Wilhelmshaven during August 1941, with a further three aircraft operating autonomously as the Kette Arado. 1./Bordfliegerstaffel 196 returned to Germany in 1944 and expanded to full Gruppe strength as Bordfligergruppe 196, with three Staffelen.

1 Spinner
2 Propeller hub
3 Starboard fuselage fixed 7.9-mm MG 17 gun port
4 Schwarz adjustable-pitch three-bladed propeller
5 Cowling ring
6 Cylinder head fairings
7 BMW 132K nine-cylinder air-cooled radial engine
8 Cowling panel frame
9 Quick-release catch
10 Cowling flaps
11 Engine lower bearers
12 Handholds
13 Engine accessories
14 Air louvre
15 Firewall bulkhead frame
16 Oil tank
17 Starboard MG 17 trough
18 Fuselage frame/engine support bearer attachment
19 Engine upper bearers
20 Forward fuselage decking
21 Starboard wing skinning

22 Leading-edge rib stations
23 Starboard outer rib
24 Starboard navigation light
25 Starboard wingtip
26 Starboard aileron
27 Aileron mass balance
28 Underwing access panel
29 Aileron control linkage
30 Windscreen
31 Instrument panel
32 Forward fuselage upper frame
33 Sea rudder lever
34 Handhold
35 Sea equipmenl locker (incl. drag-line and anchor/heaving-line)
36 Rudder pedal assembly
37 Seat support frame
38 Entry footstep
39 Seat adjustment handwheel
40 Armrest and seat harness
41 Control column
42 Pilot's seat
43 Sliding canopy
44 Rear-view mirror
45 Aerial mast

46 (Starboard) wing fold position
47 Pilot's headrest
48 Support frame
49 Canopy aft section
50 Aft canopy lock/release
51 First-aid kit
52 Observer/gunner's sliding seat
53 Entry footstep
54 Flare cartridge stowage
55 Chart table
56 Radio equipment
57 Fuselage frame/aft spar attachment
58 Wingroot fillet
59 Observer's sliding seat port
60 Ammunition box
61 Dorsal gun swivel mounting
62 Wind deflector plate
63 Ammunition feed
64 Ring sight
65 Twin 7.9-mm MG 81 flexible machine-guns
66 Flare bomb stowage
67 Gun support bracket
68 Fuselage aft frame

69 Master compass access
70 Fuselage skinning
71 Stringers
72 Elevator control cable linkage
73 Rudder controls
74 Tailfin/fuselage support/attachment bracket
75 Tailfin root fillet
76 Starboard tailplane section
77 Elevator mass balance
78 Starboard elevator section
79 Tailfin leading-edge
80 Rudder internal mass balance
81 Rudder tab linkage
82 Tailfin structure
83 Aerial
84 Aerial stub attachment
85 Rudder upper hinge
86 Rudder frame
87 Rudder post
88 Rudder tab
89 Elevator tab
90 Tab hinge
91 Elevator frame
92 Elevator mass balance

93 Tailplane structure
94 Elevator attachment
95 Rudder control linkage
96 Tailplane attachment
97 Elevator cable/rod link
98 Tie-down lug
99 Catapult attachment
100 Control lead
101 MG 81Z counterbalance
102 Wing attachment strengthening plate
103 Wing fold line
104 Gun charging cylinder
105 Ammunition drum 60 rounds
106 Port wing fixed 20-mm MG FF cannon
107 Cannon aft mounting bracket
108 Cartridge collector box
109 Cannon barrel support sleeve
110 Watertight muzzle cap
111 Forward spar attachment
112 Float forward strut/fuselage attachment
113 Tubular strut fairing
114 Inner Vee-strut

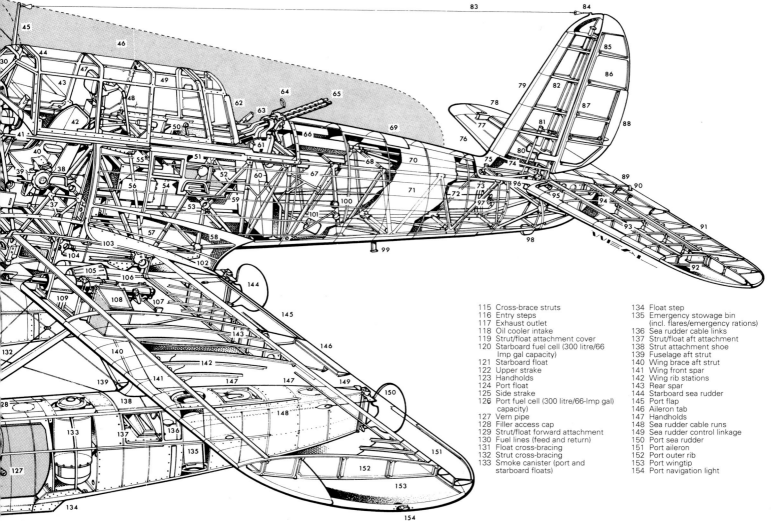

115 Cross-brace struts
116 Entry steps
117 Exhaust outlet
118 Oil cooler intake
119 Strut/float attachment cover
120 Starboard fuel cell (300 litre/66 Imp gal capacity)
121 Starboard float
122 Upper strake
123 Handholds
124 Port float
125 Side strake
126 Port fuel cell (300 litre/66-Imp gal capacity)
127 Vern pipe
128 Filler access cap
129 Strut/float forward attachment
130 Fuel lines (feed and return)
131 Float cross-bracing
132 Strut cross-bracing
133 Smoke canister (port and starboard floats)

134 Float step
135 Emergency stowage bin (incl. flares/emergency rations)
136 Sea rudder cable links
137 Strut/float aft attachment
138 Strut attachment shoe
139 Fuselage aft strut
140 Wing brace aft strut
141 Wing front spar
142 Wing rib stations
143 Rear spar
144 Starboard sea rudder
145 Port flap
146 Aileron tab
147 Handholds
148 Sea rudder cable runs
149 Sea rudder control linkage
150 Port sea rudder
151 Port aileron
152 Port outer rib
153 Port wingtip
154 Port navigation light

Arado Ar 196

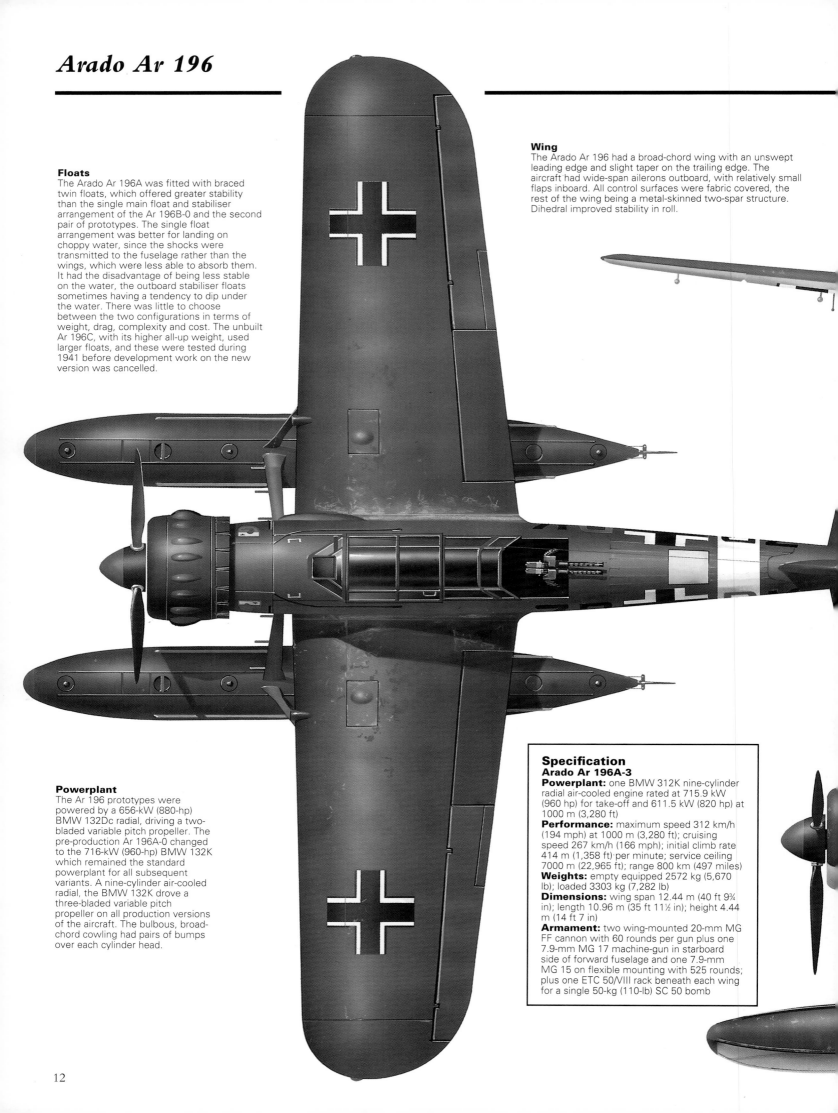

Floats
The Arado Ar 196A was fitted with braced twin floats, which offered greater stability than the single main float and stabiliser arrangement of the Ar 196B-0 and the second pair of prototypes. The single float arrangement was better for landing on choppy water, since the shocks were transmitted to the fuselage rather than the wings, which were less able to absorb them. It had the disadvantage of being less stable on the water, the outboard stabiliser floats sometimes having a tendency to dip under the water. There was little to choose between the two configurations in terms of weight, drag, complexity and cost. The unbuilt Ar 196C, with its higher all-up weight, used larger floats, and these were tested during 1941 before development work on the new version was cancelled.

Wing
The Arado Ar 196 had a broad-chord wing with an unswept leading edge and slight taper on the trailing edge. The aircraft had wide-span ailerons outboard, with relatively small flaps inboard. All control surfaces were fabric covered, the rest of the wing being a metal-skinned two-spar structure. Dihedral improved stability in roll.

Powerplant
The Ar 196 prototypes were powered by a 656-kW (880-hp) BMW 132Dc radial, driving a two-bladed variable pitch propeller. The pre-production Ar 196A-0 changed to the 716-kW (960-hp) BMW 132K which remained the standard powerplant for all subsequent variants. A nine-cylinder air-cooled radial, the BMW 132K drove a three-bladed variable pitch propeller on all production versions of the aircraft. The bulbous, broad-chord cowling had pairs of bumps over each cylinder head.

Specification
Arado Ar 196A-3
Powerplant: one BMW 312K nine-cylinder radial air-cooled engine rated at 715.9 kW (960 hp) for take-off and 611.5 kW (820 hp) at 1000 m (3,280 ft)
Performance: maximum speed 312 km/h (194 mph) at 1000 m (3,280 ft); cruising speed 267 km/h (166 mph); initial climb rate 414 m (1,358 ft) per minute; service ceiling 7000 m (22,965 ft); range 800 km (497 miles)
Weights: empty equipped 2572 kg (5,670 lb); loaded 3303 kg (7,282 lb)
Dimensions: wing span 12.44 m (40 ft 9¾ in); length 10.96 m (35 ft 11½ in); height 4.44 m (14 ft 7 in)
Armament: two wing-mounted 20-mm MG FF cannon with 60 rounds per gun plus one 7.9-mm MG 17 machine-gun in starboard side of forward fuselage and one 7.9-mm MG 15 on flexible mounting with 525 rounds; plus one ETC 50/VIII rack beneath each wing for a single 50-kg (110-lb) SC 50 bomb

Defensive guns
The MG 81Z installation, mounted in the rear cockpit of the Ar 196A-5, paired two MG 81 7.9-mm (0.31-in) machine-guns on a single mount, with a maximum load of 2,000 rounds.

Shipborne operations
The Ar 196 was designed from the start for shipboard operation, and was equipped with catapult spools and had an airframe strong enough to withstand the rigours of catapult launches. Ar 196A-1s replaced He 60 biplanes on the *Graf Spee*, the *Scharnhorst*, the *Gneisenau*, the *Lutzow*, the *Admiral Scheer* and the *Prinz Eugen*.

Arado Ar 196A-5
2./SAGr 125
Eastern Mediterranean
1943

The definitive Ar 196A-5, which featured improved radio equipment and improved defensive armament in the form of the MG 81Z installation. Fixed forward-firing armament remained two 20-mm MG FF cannon in the wings and one MG 17 7.9-mm (0.31-in) machine-gun in the starboard cowling. In the anti-shipping role the Ar 196 had underwing racks for a pair of SC 50 bombs. This Ar 196A-5 served with 2./Seeaufklärungsgruppe (SAGr) 125 in the eastern Mediterranean and Aegean Seas during 1943, alongside the Blohm und Voss BV 138. The unit later became 4./SAGr 126 under the control of Luftwaffenkommando Südost.

Structure
The rectangular section steel tube fuselage was faired to an oval using former ribs and was covered by metal skinning forward and fabric aft. The single-step floats were all metal, and consisted of seven watertight compartments which accommodated 300 litre (66 Imp gal) as well as ammunition and food containers.

Arado Ar 196

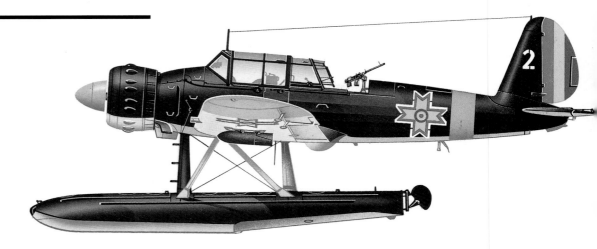

These colourful national markings help to identify this Arado Ar 196A-3 as an aircraft of the Romanian Escadrila 102, Flotila de hidroaviatie. This unit operated from Odessa in late 1943 under the Aufklärungsführer Schwarzes Meer West. The Ar 196A was also operated by Romania's Escadrila 101, Flotila de hidroaviatie. The Ar 196s were usually escorted by Romanian fighters, usually the IAR 80s of the 46th fighter squadron.

At Warnemünde production was terminated in March 1944 after the delivery of 22 of the A-5 version, bringing the total production of all versions to 541, including the 10 A-0s and five prototypes.

Almost all this considerable total operated from shore bases, mainly with Seeaufklärungsgruppen, often in units partly equipped with the BV 138 flying-boat. Two of the chief units were gruppen of SAGr 125, based first in the Baltic and later from Constanza for operations over the Black Sea, and SAGr 126 based on Crete and other locations for operations over the eastern Mediterranean and Balkans. Other units included SAGr 128, which operated over the western part of the Channel and the Bay of Biscay, and SAGr 131 which operated off the west coast of Norway until the autumn of 1944. Further Ar 196 seaplanes flew over the Black Sea with the 101st and 102nd coastal reconnaissance squadrons of the Royal Romanian air force, as well as the 161st coastal squadron of the Bulgarian air force. Most of these operations ceased by the late summer of 1944 as a result of the westward movement of the Eastern battlefront.

In 1940-41 Arado also built a small number of **Ar 196B-0** seaplanes with the single central float configuration. Otherwise similar to the A-2, the B-series was for a time on the strength of Bordfliegerstaffel 1/196 at Wilhelmshaven. There was also a project for an Ar 196C, which would have been improved in equipment and in streamlining, but it was never built.

An Ar 196 in flight, carrying a 50-kg (110-lb) SC 50 bomb under each wing. The aircraft also had two 20-mm MG FF cannon and a 7.9-mm MG 17 machine-gun firing forward, and a 7.9-mm MG 17 in the rear cockpit.

The crew of a 2./SAGr 125 Ar 196A-3 prepares for launch from their Crete base in the summer of 1943. As the war neared its end, the Ar 196 gradually disappeared from service, although a few served right through. It was to be the last fighting floatplane built in Europe.

Arado Ar 232

Early in 1940, work began on the design of a transport aircraft to augment and ultimately replace the venerable and ubiquitous Junkers Ju 52/3m. A twin-engined design, the Arado Ar 232 was to feature a pod-and-boom fuselage with a hydraulically-operated rear loading door. It had a novel arrangement of 11 pairs of small wheels used to support the fuselage during loading and unloading operations, the tricycle main landing gear having been partially raised by means of two hydraulic rams.

The first two prototypes, flown in 1941, were each powered by two 1193-kW (1,600-hp) BMW 801MA radial engines, but the insatiable demands of the Focke-Wulf Fw 190 production lines necessitated a change of engine for subsequent aircraft. The selection of the lower-powered BMW-Bramo 323R-2 meant that four engines were needed, and the third aircraft introduced a 1.70-m (5-ft 7-in) increase in wing centre-section span to accommodate them. Both the **V1** and **V2** prototypes were operated by the Luftwaffe into Stalingrad, one aircraft being

the last transport to leave the beleagured garrison. Some 20 **Ar 232B-0** production aircraft were delivered, serving with the Ergänzungs-Transport Gruppe and then Transportfliegerstaffel 5 (later redesignated 14./TG 4). This unit flew many special missions into Soviet territory. Survivors were passed to III/KG 200 in March 1945, but only one aircraft survived the end of hostilities.

Specification
Arado Ar 232B-0
Type: heavy transport
Powerplant: four 895-kW (1,200-hp)

The twin-engined Ar 232 V2 is seen in flight. The type was nicknamed the 'Tausendfüssler' (Millipede) on account of its unusual undercarriage.

Arado Ar 232A-0 serving with Transportfliegerstaffel 5 on special transport duties in late 1944.

BMW-Bramo 323R-2 radial piston engines
Performance: maximum speed 340 km/h (211 mph) at 4600 m (15,090 ft); cruising speed 290 km/h (180 mph) at 2000 m (6,560 ft); ceiling 8000 m (26,245 ft); range 1060 km (658 miles)

Weights: empty 12802 kg (28,224 lb); maximum take-off 21135 kg (46,595 lb)
Dimensions: span 33.50 m (109 ft 10¾ in); length 23.52 m (77 ft 2 in); height 5.69 m (18 ft 8 in); wing area 142.60 m² (1,535 sq ft)
Armament: one 13-mm (0.51-in) MG 131 machine-gun in the nose; one or two similar weapons at the rear of the fuselage pod and one 20-mm MG 151/20 cannon in a power-operated dorsal turret

Arado Ar 234 Blitz

In November 1940, many British officials thought the de Havilland company mad as it began flight testing a new reconnaissance and bomber aircraft that was thought to have such a high performance that it needed no defensive armament. How amazed they would have been had they been able to travel eastwards to the German company Arado Flugzeugwerke, where engineers Walter Blume and Hans Rebeski were beginning the design of an unarmed reconnaissance aircraft planned to fly even faster and higher than the famous Mosquito. It was to be able to do this because its engines were to be turbojets, revolutionary new engines then in the early stages of testing at the BMW and Junkers companies.

They submitted to the Air Ministry technical staff their E 370 proposal in early 1941. With it came various more radical schemes, but it was the relatively conventional 370 that was to be accepted and awarded the '8 series' type number **234**.

Predictably, it was an extremely clean and straightforward aircraft of all-metal stressed-skin construction, with a smooth flush-riveted exterior skin. The tapered wing was mounted on top of the slender fuselage, and the two engines were underslung below the wing in near nacelles about the same distance from the centreline that one might have expected with a piston engine. In the extreme nose was the single-seat cockpit, the entire nose being glazed with Plexiglas. The pilot got aboard by pulling down a retractable step on the left side, clambering up kick-in steps up the left side and entering via the roof hatch. This hatch could be jettisoned, but there was no ejection seat and emergency escape was a doubtful proposition. The cockpit itself,

however, was roomy, comfortable and well laid out, and was pressurised by engine bleed.

The challenging demand for a combat range of 2200 km (1,367 miles) meant that almost the entire fuselage aft of the cockpit had to be occupied by fuel, the tanks being filled through the top of the fuselage. All flight controls were manually operated and conventional, the ailerons being of the sharp leading-edge Frise type and the elevators and rudder having prominent mass balances plus a combined balance weight in the fuselage. The tailplane incidence could be varied for trimming purposes by a large lever in the cockpit, driving a screwjack. Inboard and outboard of the engines were hydraulically actuated plain flaps with a maximum of 45° for landing. It was planned that the big reconnaissance cameras would be carried in the rear fuselage.

The one feature that was truly unconventional was the landing gear. With the benefit of hindsight one can see that there should have been no serious problem, but the Arado design team could see no way

The Luftwaffe's second jet in service, the Arado Ar 234, was also the world's first jet bomber. This captured aircraft is an Ar 234B-2, the definitive production variant that was capable of flying bombing or reconnaissance missions. The projection above the cockpit is a persicopic sight which could serve the optional rearward-firing armament, as well as giving the pilot his only view aft.

Arado Ar 234 Blitz

to fit a normal undercarriage. With the slim fuselage full of fuel there was no room for retracted main gears as well, nor could landing gears be accommodated in the jet nacelles or wing, the high wing meaning that ordinary wing-mounted gears would have to be very long. The company therefore proposed various unconventional arrangements, and the Air Ministry staff selected one of the most unusual. On take-off, the **Ar 234** was to ride on a large three-wheeled trolley. It would land on a central skid, with small stabilising skids under the engine nacelles.

Engine trouble

The engine selected was the 109-004A being developed by Junkers. Construction of the **Ar 234 V1** first prototype began in the spring of 1941, Junkers having promised delivery of engines in about 10 months. Work at Arado's Warnemunde factory went ahead rapidly, but the engine suffered very serious delays and did not even begin flight testing until March 1942. What is very curious is that, whereas two 004As powered the first Me 262 in July 1942, Arado did not receive a single engine until February 1943, and could not fly the 234 V1 until 15 June 1943. By this time, the engineless airframe had been waiting for 18 months. Arado considered beginning flight testing using piston engines, but there was inadequate propeller ground clearance. If a conventional landing gear had been adopted this problem would not have arisen; and if Junkers had delivered engines much earlier, this outstanding aircraft would have been available up to a year earlier and in greater numbers.

As it was, the flying qualities of the 234 proved to be delightful. Based at Rheine, under chief test pilot Selle, the programme unearthed hardly any shortcomings, and from the start every pilot who flew the 234 had nothing but praise for its handling (although it took up to 10 test flights with each aircraft before the ailerons could be judged properly rigged). In contrast, the take-off/landing gear gave endless trouble. On the first flight, the big trolley was correctly jettisoned at 60 m (200 ft) but the parachute failed to deploy and the trolley was destroyed on hitting the ground. The same thing happened on the second flight. After this, it was decided to let the aircraft rise clear, leaving the trolley on the ground, but even so both the trolley and the skid gear gave trouble. Often the skids failed to retract, pitching and porpoising on landing was severe, and on several occasions one side skid would collapse and let the wingtip drag over the ground. Moreover, the aircraft could not taxi on its high-drag skids, and it was

For take-off, the Ar 234A sat on a large trolley that featured a steerable nosewheel and mainwheel brakes for taxiing. During the first flights of the V1, the trolley was jettisoned at altitudes, but subsequently was released on the runway.

realised that on mass operations the airfield would quickly become filled with immobile Ar 234s which would obstruct following aircraft and present helpless targets to strafing aircraft. In the late summer of 1943 it was wisely decided to change to conventional landing gear. The planned Ar 234A production version was cancelled, but seven further **A-series** aircraft had already been built and **V2**, **V3**, **V4**, **V5** and **V7** all flew in rapid succession (**V6** and **V8** were set aside for fitting with four engines). In the closing months of 1943, the prototypes tested pressurisation, take-off booster rocket packs that hung under the wings, the lighter and more powerful 004B engine and, in some aircraft, an ejection seat.

Dubious debut

While this work was going on at Rheine a major factory at Alt Lonnewitz was tooled up to produce the **Ar 234B** – popularly named the **Blitz** – with conventional landing gear. The first B-series prototype, the **V9**, was flown on 10 March 1944, the pilot being the very experienced Joachim Carl who had succeeded Selle on his predecessor's death in the crash of V7 due to engine fire. **V10** introduced the RF 2C periscopic sight and racks for bombs or drop tanks under the engines and a bomb under the fuselage. **V11** flew on 5 May 1944,

Landing the Ar 234A was accomplished on a grass strip, the aircraft resting on a central main skid and two outrigger skids which were housed in the engine nacelles. These skids were also deployed for take-off, being used as supports to which the trolley was attached.

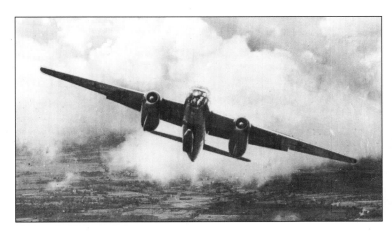

An early Arado Ar 234 in flight reveals landing skids extended beneath the slender fuselage and engine nacelles. Clean, the Arado Ar 234 had a limiting Mach No. of 0.78, giving the aircraft enough performance to escape from any opposing fighter, if seen in time.

Fitted with Rauchgeräte take-off booster rockets and carrying an SC 500J 500-kg bomb under the centre fuselage and under each engine nacelle, the 10th prototype begins its take-off run. The type began flying operationally in the summer of 1944.

followed by the first pre-production **Ar 234B-0** on 8 June. Carl had been told to make the first flight of the B-0 before 400 important guests. He insisted on making a quick test flight beforehand and was horrified to find this hastily completed machine nothing like the hand-built prototypes. Almost everything went wrong and Carl had no idea how he managed to regain the airfield with both engines flamed out and no idea whether the landing gears were up or down. Frantic work ensured that the 'official first flight' in the afternoon went off without a hitch.

Design features

Arado built 20 B-0s, 13 going at once to Rechlin test centre. The production line went straight on with a limited run of **B-1** reconnaissance aircraft, followed by the standard production model, the **B-2**. Arado managed to fit normal landing gear by removing the centre fuselage tank, making the front and rear tanks bigger so that the total capacity of 3800 litres (835 Imp gal) was only slightly affected. Each leg with a big low-pressure tyre retracted forwards and inwards, the wheel being stowed upright. The nosewheel, fitted with spring-cam centring, retracted, all units being moved hydraulically. A braking parachute was housed in a box under the rear fuselage, its cable being attached to the rear of the tail bumper. In practice, this device was seldom used.

The B-2 was able to fly reconnaissance or bombing missions, and most aircraft were fitted with aft-firing defensive armament, another curious choice because the installation was heavy and the Ar 234 was virtually immune to interception by Allied fighters except in the vicinity of its airfield. The armament comprised two 20-mm MG 151 cannon, mounted horizontally and parallel in the rear fuselage, and

each fed with 200 rounds from a magazine overhead. The guns could be sighted by the aft-facing optics of the RF 2C periscope above the cockpit. The centreline attachment, in a fuselage recess, could take a PC 1400 (1400-kg/3,000-lb) bomb, and that under each engine could take an SC 500J (500-kg/1,100-lb) bomb or a 300-litre (66 Imp-gal) drop tank. Normal maximum bomb load was 1500 kg (3,300 lb). In the reconnaissance role, various cameras could be fitted, such as two Rb 50/30 or 73/30, or one of each.

Hi-tech cockpit

The cockpit was well arranged, the only problem being that of escape in emergency. Standard equipment included a Patin PDS three-axis autopilot, with course-setting control twistgrip on the right handgrip of the pilot's control yoke. Rudder pedals were out in front, with clear Plexiglas giving a view in all forward directions. Between the pilot's legs was the complex Lofte 7K tachymetric bombsight. At the start of the bombing run the pilot would swing the control yoke clear and fly the aircraft on the bombsight control knobs, looking through the optical sight. Alternatively, he could fly the aircraft in the normal way and use the periscope sight and associated BZA bombing computer for a dive attack.

Handling was beautiful at all speeds, though of course a heavy bomb load made the aircraft sluggish and reduced speed by some 96 km/h (60 mph). Limiting Mach number was about 0.78, and the

Several Ar 234Bs were captured intact by the Allies at the war's end. Naturally, they became the subject of much interest and were extensively tested in both Britain and the United States, although the type's limited engine life (and a high level of sabotage) proved a major handicap.

Arado Ar 234 Blitz

The Ar 234 used a similar engine installation to the Messerschmitt Me 262 fighter, with long, narrow-throated nacelles slung below the inboard part of the wing. The adoption of a tricycle undercarriage on production aircraft left the engine nacelles free for weapons carriage, and bomb shackles were incorporated to take up to 500 kg (1,100 lb) of bombs beneath each wing. A third bomb shackle was located under the centreline, capable of carrying weapons of up to 1400 kg (3,000 lb), including the 1000-kg SC 1000 'Hermann', with which Ar 234s unsuccessfully attacked the bridges at Remagen during early 1945.

Arado Ar 234B-2/lr Blitz cutaway key

1 Port elevator hinge
2 Tailplane skinning
3 Port elevator
4 Tab actuating rod
5 Elevator trim tab
6 Geared rudder tab (upper)
7 Rudder hinges
8 Tail navigation light
9 Plywood fin leading edge
10 T-aerial
11 Re-transmission aerial
12 Aerial matching unit
13 Tailfin structure
14 Rudder construction
15 Rudder post
16 Rudder tab (lower)
17 Lower rudder hinge
18 Rudder actuating rods
19 Parachute cable
20 Cable anchor point/tailskid
21 Starboard elevator tab
22 Elevator construction
23 Tailplane construction
24 Elevator control linkage
25 Tailplane attachment potnts
26 Elevator rod
27 Port side control runs
28 Internal mass balance
29 Parachute release mechanism
30 Main FuG 16zy panel (BZA computer)

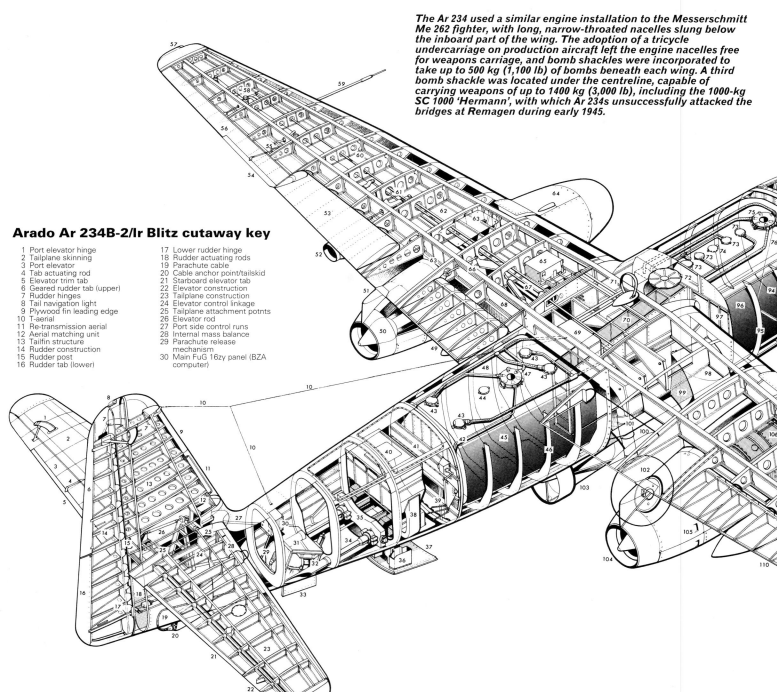

31 Brake parachute container
32 Starboard MG 151 cannon muzzle
33 Brake chute door (open)
34 Mauser MG 151/20 cannon (rearward firing)
35 Cannon support yoke
36 Spent cartridge chute
37 Access panel (lowered)
38 Ammunition feed chute
39 Tail surface control rods (starboard)
40 Ammunition box
41 Bulkhead
42 Fuel vent pipe
43 Fuel pumps
44 Fuel lever gauge
45 Rear fuel cell (2000-litre – 440-Imp gal capacity)
46 Fuselage frames
47 Fuel filler point
48 Fuel lines
49 Inner flap construction
50 Exhaust cone
51 Nacelle support fairing
52 RATO exhaust
53 Outer flap section
54 Aileron tab
55 Tab actuating rod
56 Port aileron
57 Port navigation light
58 Aileron control linkage
59 Pitot tube
60 Front spar
61 Outer flap control linkage
62 Wing construction
63 Nacelle attachment points (front and rear spar)
64 Detachable nacelle cowling
65 FuG 25a IFF unit
66 Inner flap control linkage
67 Control rods and hydraulic activating rod
68 Rear spar
69 Hydraulic fluid tank (18-litre – 4-Imp gal capacity)
70 Centre section box
71 FuG 25a ring antenna
72 Suppressed D/F antenna
73 Fuel pumps
74 Fuel level gauge
75 Fuel filler point
76 Fuel lines
77 Bulkhead
78 Port control console (throttle quadrant)

79 Pilot entry hatch (hinged to starboard)
80 Periscopic sight
81 Periscopic head (rearview mirror/gunsight)
82 Clear vision cockpit glazing
83 Instrument panel
84 Rudder pedal
85 Swivel-mounted control stick
86 Lotfe 7K tachometric bombsight mounting
87 Pilot's seat
88 Starboard control console (oil/temperature gauges)
89 Radio panel (FuG 16zy behind pilot's seat)
90 Oxygen bottles
91 Nosewheel door
92 Nosewheel fork
93 Rearward-retracting nosewheel
94 Nosewheel well centre section
95 Fuselage frames
96 Forward fuel cell (1800-litre – 385-Imp gal capacity)
97 Bulkhead
98 Mainwheel door
99 Starboard mainwheel well
100 Mainwheel leg door
101 Starboard mainwheel leg
102 Forward-retracting mainwheel
103 SC 1000 "Hermann" bomb beneath fuselage
104 Engine exhaust
105 Auxiliary cooling intakes
106 Starboard Jumo 004B turbojet
107 Annular oil tank
108 Riedel starter motor on nose cone
109 Auxiliary tank (300-litre/66-Imp gal) beneath nacelle (not carried with SC 1000 bomb)
110 Flap outer section construction
111 Walter HWK 500A-1 RATO unit
112 RATO recovery parachute pack
113 Aileron tab
114 Starboard aileron construction
115 Wing skin stiffeners
116 Starboard navigation light

The wheeled undercarriage gave the Ar 234B better flexibility of operations. This is the second B-series prototype (Ar 234 V10), which first flew on 2 April 1944 and lacked cabin pressurisation. It could be fitted with Rauchgeräte rocket-assisted take-off units under the wings.

clean aircraft was fully aerobatic, although pilots were warned that, should they by some mischance be intercepted, they should use speed rather than manoeuvres to escape. Surprisingly, in view of the tall fin and narrow track, crosswinds were no problem, nor was an overshoot, but brakes tended to burn out after two or three landings and engine failures were common, time between engine overhauls being 10 hours.

Plugging the intelligence gap

In July 1944 two early prototypes, V5 and V7, had joined 1 Staffel of Versuchsverband Oberefehlshaber der Luftwaffe at Juvincourt, France, and following indoctrination flying formed the core of Sonderkommando Gotz based at Rheine in September with four B-1s. Strength built up and from early October operational reconnaissance missions were being flown over the Allied area of north-west Europe and the British Isles. In November, SdKdo Hecht and Sperling began operations, followed by Sdkdo Sommer at Udine to cover the Italian front. In each case, the arrival of the Arados transformed the situation, good photo coverage having previously been perilous and almost impossible to achieve.

From October 1944, KG 76 began to convert to the B-2 bomber, beginning with II Gruppe. This began flying bombing missions during the push through the Ardennes. Later, in March 1945, III/KG 76 at last succeeded in collapsing the Remagen bridge over the Rhine, but by this time the loss of the bridge had little effect. Almost all surviving

With only 8.3 kN (1,850 lb) of thrust available from each Jumo 004B jet, the Ar 234A was short on take-off power, particularly when loaded to the maximum weight of 8000 kg (17,600 lb). Rauchgeräte take-off rocket units were added to improve the thrust, these being jettisoned after climb-out and descending to earth by parachute.

Arado Ar 234B-2 Stabs-Staffel, Kampfgeschwader 76 Karstedt, 1945

The staff squadron of KG 76 was the first recipient of the Ar 234B-2 bomber version, receiving its first aircraft in October 1944. Pilots converted to the type at a training unit at Alt-Lonnewitz before moving west to join the fight against the Allies. II Gruppe/KG 76 converted in November, in time to join the Ardennes counter-offensive in December-January. I Gruppe started work-up in January, followed swiftly by III Gruppe, although neither attained full status. III/KG 76 expended most of its efforts against river crossings, including the famous Remagen bridge across the Rhine. By the end of March the Ar 234 units had virtually ceased operations.

Bombsight
The Ar 234B-2 had a complex bomb-aiming system. For shallow dive attacks the PV1B sighting head was used, this being situated in the RF2C periscope above the cockpit, which could also be rotated aft to sight for the defensive cannon. The correct sighting angle was fed to the PV1B by the BZA 1 bombing computer. For level-bombing some Ar 234B-2/1 aircraft had a Lofte 7K tachometric sight located between the pilot's feet. With the aircraft on autopilot, the pilot disconnected the control column and swung it to the side to allow him to operate the Lofte 7K. After bomb release the control column was reconnected.

Powerplant and fuel
The Junkers Jumo 004B Orkan turbojet ran on J2 fuel, housed in two tanks in the fuselage either side of the wing. The forward compartment held 1800 litres (396 Imp gal) and the rear 2000 litres (440 Imp gal). A Riedel two-cylinder starter motor span the turbines up to 3,000 rpm, at which time the combustion chambers were electrically ignited. Petrol was used for the start-up sequence, fuel supply automatically switching to J2 at 6,000 rpm when the pilot activated the thrust levers.

Arado Ar 240

The development of the FA-13 armament system (guns in remotely controlled barbettes, aimed periscopically) prompted the Reichsluftfahrtministerium to request proposals for a fast twin-engined aircraft to carry two such installations. The contenders were Ago with its Ao 225 design, and Arado with the Hans Rebeski-designed E.240, redesignated **Ar 240** when awarded a contract. In fact, as a result of development problems, the barbettes were not fitted to the first two prototypes, which were mid-wing monoplanes powered by two 802-kW (1,075-hp) Daimler-Benz DB 601A engines. The second aircraft was armed, but only with two forward-firing 20-mm MG 151120 cannon in the nose and two 7.92-mm (0.31-in) MG 17 machine-guns in the wingroots.

As a result of instability problems with the first two Ar 240s, the third appeared after major redesign incorporating a 1.25-m (4-ft 1½-in) fuselage 'stretch'. The pressurised cockpit was also moved forward and a new tail-cone, with small fins replaced the original tail-mounted dive-brake. Flown in spring 1941, this was the first Ar 240 with the FA 13 barbettes – one above and another below the fuselage behind the cockpit. Each carried a pair of 7.92-mm (0.31-in) MG 81 machine-guns. The barbettes were removed during the summer of 1941, when two cameras were fitted for a period of operational evaluation with a reconnaissance unit (3./Aufklärungsgruppe Oberbefehlshaber der Luftwaffe). The fourth prototype was fitted with two 1305-kW (1,750-hp) DB 603A engines.

A number of pre-production machines were completed and the Ago factory at Oschersleben was tasked with the manufacture of 40 production Ar 240s. In December 1942, however, the programme was discontinued as a result of continued teething problems with this ambitious project. A handful of pre-production aircraft did fly with service units, notably JG 5 in northern Finland, and reconnaissance units in Russia and Italy. Variants were the DB 605-powered **Ar 240B**, the **Ar 240C** with longer wings and a variety of armament options, and the **Ar 440** with longer fuselage. Prototypes of all were finished and flown.

Combat use of the Ar 240 was very limited, but a handful served unofficially with front-line units. This is the second Ar 240A-0, seen while being flown by JG 5 'Eismeer' in northern Finland. Together with the first A-0, this aircraft flew recce missions along the Murmansk railway.

Specification
Arado Ar 240A
Type: multi-role aircraft
Powerplant: two 877-kW (1,175-hp) Daimler-Benz DB 601E inverted inline piston engines
Performance: maximum speed 620 km/h (385 mph) at 6000 m (19,685 ft); cruising speed 555 km/h (345 mph) at 6000 m (19,685 ft); climb to 6000 m (19,685 ft) in 11 minutes; service ceiling 10500 m (34,450 ft); maximum range 2000 km (1,242 miles)
Weights: empty 6200 kg (13,669 lb); maximum take-off 9450 kg (20,833 lb)
Dimensions: span 13.33 m (43 ft 9 in); length 12.80 m (42 ft 0 in); height 3.95 m (12 ft 11½ in); wing area 31.30 m² (336.9 sq ft)
Armament: two fixed forward-firing 7.92-mm (0.31-in) MG 17 machine-guns in wingroots and two FA 13 barbettes each with two 7.92-mm (0.31-in) MG 81 machine-guns in ventral and dorsal positions

Bachem Ba 349 Natter

Selected to fill an RLM requirement for a point defence fighter to attack Allied bombers, the **Ba 349** was a comparatively crude airframe, emphasis being placed on ease of manufacture by unskilled woodworkers. Roll control was exercised by differential use of the elevators. The fuselage housed a Walter 109-509A-2 sustainer rocket capable of producing 16.68 kN (3,748 lb) thrust for 70 seconds at full power but also able to run at outputs as low as 1.47 kN (331 lb) for increased endurance. The aircraft was to be launched vertically, by four Schmidding 109-533 solid-fuel rockets, two on each side of the fuselage, and each producing 11.77 kN (2,646-lb) thrust for 10 seconds before being jettisoned.

The first of 15 Natters manufactured for the test programme became available in October 1944 and was used for unpowered handling trials, towed aloft behind a Heinkel He 111. Unmanned flights using the booster rockets only followed. The first vertical launch with booster and sustainer rockets firing, still without a pilot, took place on 23 February 1945. Just a few days later, test pilot Lothar Siebert was killed when, in making the first and almost certainly the only piloted vertical launch, the cockpit cover became detached in flight and the aircraft dived into the ground from about 1525 m (5,000 ft).

Operational tactics evolved for the Natter involved a vertical launch on autopilot, the pilot assuming manual control when positioned above the approaching bombers. Placed in a shallow dive, the Natter would have been armed by jettisoning the nosecone to expose its battery of rockets. Having fired these unguided missiles, the aircraft was flown clear of the battlezone, and the pilot would then bale out. The entire nose section was to be jettisoned by uncoupling the control column, moving it forward to release the safety catches, and then releasing mechanical catches to separate the nose from the rest of the fuselage. The pilot was effectively ejected by the deceleration of the rear section as it streamed a braking and recovery parachute. The rear fuselage was to be salvaged.

The **Ba 349A** was the initial production version, of which 50 were ordered for the Luftwaffe and 150 for the SS. About 36 Natters were completed but not used operationally, despite about 10 being set up for launch at Kirchheim. Allied tanks approached too closely to the base, so the interceptors were destroyed on the ramps before they could be captured or used. The **Ba 349B** was an improved version with increased tail unit area and more powerful Walter 109-509C rocket which provided maximum thrust of 19.62 kN (4,410 lb) and more effective throttle control down to 1.96 kN (441 lb). Only three were finished.

Specification
Bachem Ba 349A Natter
Type: single-seat fighter
Powerplant: one 16.67-kN (3,748-lb) thrust Walter 109-509A-2 rocket motor and four 11.75-kN (2,640-lb) thrust Schmidding 109-533 booster rockets
Performance: maximum speed 800 km/h (497 mph) at sea level; initial climb rate 11100 m (36,415 ft) per minute; service ceiling 14000 m (45,920 ft); radius of action at 12000 m (39,360 ft) 40 km (24.8 miles)
Weight: maximum take-off 2200 kg (4,850 lb)
Dimensions: span 3.60 m (11 ft 9¾ in); length 6.10 m (20 ft 0 in); wing area 2.75 m² (29.60 sq ft)
Armament: 24 Fohn unguided rockets

An example of the remarkable Ba 349 shows the nosecone removed to reveal the unguided rocket armament. A combat debut was just hours away when the Allied land forces came too close to the launch site.

Blohm und Voss BV 138

The first flying-boat design to be built by Hamburger Flugzeugbau GmbH, under the direction of chief engineer Dr Ing Richard Vogt, was the **Ha 138**. Three prototypes of the original twin-engined design were each to have been powered by a different manufacturer's 746-kW (1,000-hp) engine for comparative evaluation, but development delays necessitated redesign to accept three 485-kW (650-hp) Junkers Jumo 205C engines. Almost two years after the completion of the mock-up, the first prototype (**Ha 138 V1**) took off on its maiden flight, the date being 15 July 1937. A second prototype (**Ha 138 V2**), with a modified hull design, joined the test programme at the Travemunde centre in November but the aircraft were quickly proved to be unstable, both hydrodynamically and aerodynamically. Modifications to the vertical tail surfaces failed to improve the performance adequately and radical redesign was undertaken.

The result was the **BV 138A**, adopting the designation system of the Blohm und Voss parent company. The hull was much enlarged, its planing surfaces were improved, and the revised tail surfaces were carried by more substantial booms. The prototype first flew in February 1939, and was followed by five more pre-series **BV 138A-0** aircraft. Testing confirmed that there were still shortcomings in the aircraft's structure, and the BV 138A-04 was returned for further strengthening to become the first of 10 **BV 138B-0**s. Meanwhile, a batch of 25 **BV 138A-1**s was constructed, as the need for coastal transport aircraft was pressing. The first two rapidly entered service with KGzbV 108 See for service in the Norwegian campaign, and soon after 1./KüFlGr 506 equipped for service in the Bay of Biscay from October 1940, being rapidly joined by 2./KüFlGr 906. The BV 138A-1s proved troublesome in service, problems surfacing with the structure, engines and bow armament. Most of these were attended to in the **BV 138B**, which was fitted with more powerful Jumo 205D engines to overcome the weight increase.

The first **BV 138B-1** flew in December 1940, and was a much better machine than its predecessor. Bow armament consisted of a 20-mm MG 151 cannon, and there was an MG 15 in an open position behind the central engine nacelle. A factory conversion (**BV 138B-**

1/U1) increased the weapon load to six bombs or depth charges. The **BV 138C-1** which followed had further airframe strengthening, a four-bladed propeller on the central engine (retrofitted to BV 138B-1s), an additional gun in the starboard side, fired by the radio operator, and a 13-mm MG 131 in the central nacelle position. The **BV 138C-1/U1** was also available with extra armament capability. During 1942-43 a handful were converted to **BV 138 MS** standard, with a circular degaussing loop for mine-sweeping, with onboard field-generating equipment and all armament deleted. These became known as '*Mausiflugzeug*' (mouse-catching aircraft).

In addition to operating from shore bases, BV 138s operated from seaplane tenders, some being modified with catapult points for launch. All aircraft could be fitted with assisted take-off rockets, and several sprouted FuG 200 Hohentwiel radar for shadowing convoys. The standard crew was five (six in the C-1), and the gun positions offered excellent fields of fire. Despite its early teething troubles, the BV 138 became an outstanding maritime patroller, offering long endurance and able to withstand a great amount of damage from either the enemy or the elements.

In early 1941 the two France-based BV 138A-1 units were withdrawn to Germany for conversion to the BV 138B-1 and were later reassigned to the Baltic. Meanwhile, Norway was becoming a principal operating location for the type, with the establishment of 2./KüFlGr 406 (later designated 3.(F)/SAGr 130), 3./KüFlGr 906, 1.(F) and 2.(F)/SAGr 130, and 1.(F) and 2.(F)/SAGr 131. From Norwegian bases the BV 138s ranged over the North Atlantic and Arctic Oceans, shadowing and attacking convoys bound for Russia. In the course of such activities BV 138s shot down a Catalina and a Blenheim. In northern waters BV 138s refuelled at sea from U-boats, and in a remarkable three-week deployment in the summer of 1943 operated from a base established on Novaya Zemlya (Soviet territory) by crews from two U-boats.

Left: A BV 138C-1 of Seeaufklärungsgruppe 130 makes a rendezvous with a U-boat in the Arctic Ocean. Note the hastily-applied white distemper for Arctic camouflage, the four-bladed propeller on the central nacelle, and the Hohentwiel search radar antennas on the wing leading edges.

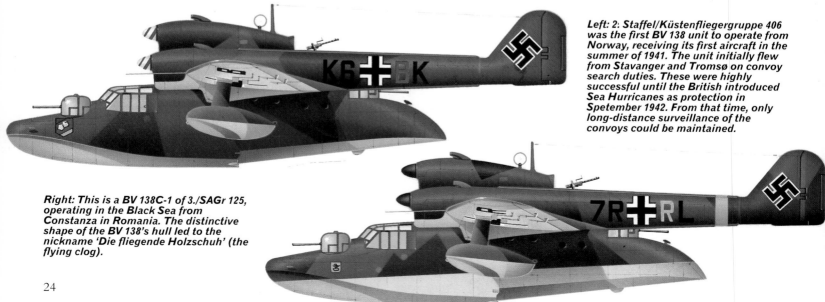

Left: 2. Staffel/Küstenfliegergruppe 406 was the first BV 138 unit to operate from Norway, receiving its first aircraft in the summer of 1941. The unit initially flew from Stavanger and Tromsø on convoy search duties. These were highly successful until the British introduced Sea Hurricanes as protection in September 1942. From that time, only long-distance surveillance of the convoys could be maintained.

Right: This is a BV 138C-1 of 3./SAGr 125, operating in the Black Sea from Constanza in Romania. The distinctive shape of the BV 138's hull led to the nickname 'Die fliegende Holzschuh' (the flying clog).

Right: Operating in the Trondheim region in April 1944 were the BV 138C-1s of 1.(F)/SAGr 130, this aircraft featuring a disruptive pattern which proved highly effective along northern coastlines.

Below: This BV 138C-1 came south from Norway in mid-1944 to operate on the Black Sea, based at Varna in Bulgaria with 1.(F)/SAGr 131.

Below: A few BV 138 MS mine-sweepers were operated by the Luftwaffe's Minensuch-gruppe to clear rivers, canals and coastal waters, this variant featuring a dural degaussing loop for exploding magnetic mines. The armament was deleted, a simple fairing replacing the bow turret, underneath which was an auxiliary motor for the field-generation equipment.

Further areas of operations included the Black Sea, where the BV 138C-1s of 3.(F)/SAGr 125 flew missions from Constanza until late 1944. In 1943 the type was assigned in numbers to the Biscay and Mediterranean theatres. 3./KüFlGr 406 (later 1.(F)/SAGr 129) operated from Biscarosse until 1944, while 3.(F)/SAGr 126 operated from Crete. This unit was transferred to the Baltic, and surrendered at the end of the war in Denmark. A few BV 138s were still serving in Norway to the end, including the aircraft of 3.(F)/SAGr 130, one of which was charged with flying Hitler's last will and testament out of Berlin on 1 May 1945. Despite landing on a Berlin lake under heavy shellfire, the BV 138 commander would not let the couriers on board as they did not have identification. Instead, he picked up 10 wounded men and flew back to Copenhagen.

Specification
Blohm und Voss BV 138C-1
Type: reconnaissance flying-boat
Powerplant: three 656-kW (880-hp) Junkers Jumo 105D inline piston engines
Performance: maximum speed 285 km/h (177 mph) at sea level; cruising speed 235 km/h (146 mph); service ceiling 5000 m (16,405 ft); maximum range 5000 km (3,107 miles)
Weights: empty 11770 kg (25,948 lb); maximum take-off 17650 kg (38,912 lb)
Dimensions: span 27.00 m (88 ft 7 in); length 19.90 m (65 ft 3½ in); height 5.90 m (19 ft 4¼ in); wing area 112 m² (1,205.6 sq ft)
Armament: one 20-mm MG 151 cannon in the bow turret, one 13-mm (0.51-in) MG 131 machine gun in the position at the rear of the centre engine nacelle, and one 7.9-mm MG 15 firing through starboard hatch; three 50-kg (110-lb) bombs under starboard wingroot or (BV 138C-1/U1) six 50-kg (110-lb) bombs or four 150-kg (331-lb) depth-charges

Blohm und Voss BV 138 MS of 6. Staffel/Minen-suchgruppe 1, based at Grossenhode in 1944-45.

Above: Whereas most BV 138s operated in the harsh environment of the northern oceans, the BV 138C-1s of 3.(Fern)/Seeaufklärungs-gruppe 125 patrolled the balmy Black Sea. Note the gunner in the central nacelle position, which offered an excellent field of fire to the rear.

Blohm und Voss Ha 139

For its newly-established transatlantic postal service, Lufthansa in 1935 issued a specification for a new marine aircraft. This was required to take off and land in rough water, to be suitable for catapult launching, and to be capable of carrying a 500-kg (1,102-lb) minimum payload for at least 5000 km (3,107 miles) at a cruising speed of 250 km/h (155 mph). The Hamburger Flugzeugbau subsidiary of Blohm und Voss evolved a number of design studies, including the **P.15** project which later became the subject of an order for three prototypes. The selected power-plant was the specially-developed Junkers Jumo 205 diesel, offering a specific fuel consumption almost 25 per cent lower than comparable petrol engines.

The first prototype **Ha 139 V1** made its maiden flight in the autumn of 1936, and by March 1937 the first two aircraft had been delivered to Lufthansa, to operate between Horta, in the Azores, and New York. The slightly enlarged and heavier third aircraft, designated **Ha 139B**, joined the programme in mid-1938.

Late in 1939 the three Ha 139s and their crews were absorbed into the Luftwaffe, the third prototype being modified for reconnaissance duties. A lengthened

glazed nose was fitted to accommodate an observer, and to compensate for this the vertical tail surfaces were again enlarged. An Ikaria glazed mounting for a single MG 15 gun was added to the nose, and a similar weapon was provided in a hatch in the flight deck roof, to be fired by the radio operator. Two further MG 15s could be fired through openings in the lower sides of the fuselage. Designated **Ha 139B/U** (Umbau), this machine flew in its new form for the first time on 19 January 1940 after taking off from the catapult of the Luft Hansa support vessel *Friesenland*. After trials the Ha 139B/U was delivered to 1./Küstenfliegergruppe 406, which flew it alongside other seaplanes on transport and Arctic weather reconnaissance missions during the

Norwegian campaign. The other two prototypes underwent similar conversions, and were also used in Norway. Flying with Kampfgruppe der besondere Verwendung 108 See, the aircraft were primarily employed on transport duties, taking supplies to ground units stationed along isolated fjords.

A lack of spares hindered the Luftwaffe career of the Ha 139s, but the V3 was reworked in 1942 as the **Ha 139B/MS** (Minensuche) for minesweeping duties. A large degaussing loop stretched from the nose to the wingtips and then back to the tailplane. There is no record of the aircraft ever being delivered to an operational minesweeping unit and it was later scrapped, along with the other two machines.

This is the Ha 139 V3 seen in its final form as the Ha 139B/MS. The enormous degaussing loop required considerable bracing. This configuration was never used operationally.

Specification
Blohm und Voss Ha 139
Type: long-range mail, mine-sweeping and reconnaissance floatplane
Powerplant: four 447-kW (600-hp) Junkers Jumo 205C diesel engines
Performance: maximum speed 315 km/h (196 mph); cruising speed 260 km/h (162 mph); service ceiling 3500 m (11,485 ft); maximum range 5300 km (3,293 miles)
Weights: empty 10360 kg (22,840 lb); maximum take-off 17500 kg (38,581 lb)
Dimensions: span 27.00 m (88 ft 7 in); length 19.5 m (63 ft 11¾ in); height 4.8 m (15 ft 9 in); wing area 117 m² (1,259 42 sq ft)
Armament: (Ha 139B/U) four 7.92-mm (0.31-in) MG 15 machine-guns, mounted one each in nose, dorsal and twin beam positions

Blohm und Voss BV 141

In 1937 the Reichsluftfahrtministerium issued a specification for a single-engined three-seat short-range reconnaissance and observation aircraft, the emphasis being placed on good all-round visibility. The requirement drew responses from Arado and Focke Wulf, in addition to the novel approach of Hamburger Flugzeugbau's Dr Ing Richard Vogt. This unorthodox design featured an asymmetric layout, the 645-kW (865-hp) BMW 132N radial engine being installed at the forward end of a port-side tail boom, with the extensively-glazed crew nacelle mounted to starboard. Official preference was for the Focke-Wulf Fw 189, but Hamburger Flugzeugbau built a private venture **Ha 141-0** prototype which flew on 25 February 1938. This featured a fuselage nacelle with a stepped cockpit and nose glazing. Two further prototypes appeared in the autumn of 1938, both slightly

larger than the first and with an extensively-glazed nacelle similar to the fuselage of the Fw 189. The third aircraft, with wider track landing gear, was armed with two fixed forward-firing 7.92-mm (0.31-in) MG 17 machine-guns, plus two MG 15s of similar calibre firing to the rear. It was also able to carry a camera and racks for four 50-kg (110-lb) bombs, and was sufficiently successful in initial trials to extract from the RLM an order for five examples of the pre-production Blohm und Voss **BV 141A-0**. These aircraft featured an increase in wing span and area and were powered by a 746-kW (1,000-hp) BMW-Bramo 323 radial engine

Evaluation at the Erprobungsstelle Rechlin was completed satisfactorily, but plans for production were terminated in April 1940 as the type was officially considered to be underpowered. In reality, the main stumbling block was fear of the type's unusual configuration. Five pre-

production **BV 141B-0** aircraft were then built with the BMW 801 radial and extensive redesign, including equal-taper outer-wing panels and an asymmetric tailplane to improve the rear gunner's field of fire. These proved markedly inferior to their predecessors, and despite the delivery of one BV 141B-0 to Aufklärungsschule 1 for service trials in the autumn of 1941, and

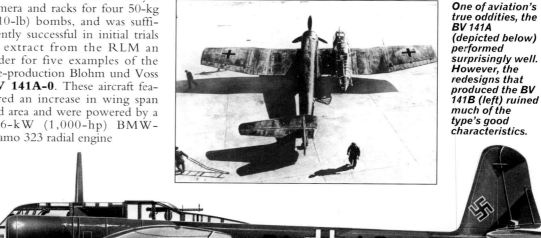

One of aviation's true oddities, the BV 141A (depicted below) performed surprisingly well. However, the redesigns that produced the BV 141B (left) ruined much of the type's good characteristics.

plans for the production of enough aircraft to equip one *Staffel* on the Eastern Front, development was delayed and finally discontinued in 1943.

Specification
BV 141B-0
Type: short-range reconnaissance and observation aircraft
Powerplant: one 1163-kW (1,560-hp) BMW 801A radial piston engine
Performance: maximum speed 370 km/h (230 mph) at sea level; service ceiling 10000 m (32,810 ft); range 1200 km (746 miles)
Weights: empty 4700 kg (10,362 lb);

maximum take-off 5700 kg (12,566 lb)
Dimensions: span 17.46 m (57 ft 3½ in); length 13.95 m (45 ft 9¼ in); height 3.6 m (11 ft 9¾ in); wing area 53 m² (570.51 sq ft)
Armament: two fixed forward-firing 7.92-mm (0.31-in) MG 17 machine-guns and two aft-firing flexibly-mounted 7.92-mm (0.31-in) MG 15 machine-guns, plus provision for four SC50 50-kg (110-lb) bombs

The V9 was the first of the BV 141B-0 aircraft, this version being readily identified by the tailplane offset to port. The A-0 had a conventional tailplane (if anything about the BV 141 could be described in such terms).

Blohm und Voss BV 142

The Hamburger Flugzeugbau Ha 139 long-distance floatplane had proved highly successful during its early flight trials in 1937, and the company was naturally encouraged to develop a land-based version, mainly for over-land mail carriage. Using as many of the floatplane components as possible was desirable, both to keep development costs down and to maintain quality as much as possible.

Consequently, when the **Ha 142 V1** emerged in 1938 it featured a similar slender fuselage and the inverted-gull wings of the Ha 139. These were very thick, thanks to a single tubular spar, but contained 5295 litres (1,165 Imp gal) of fuel. Twin wheels replaced both of the floats, and a twin-wheel retractable tailwheel was added. The flight deck had accommodation for a crew of four, comprising pilot, co-pilot, navigator and radio operator. In the fuselage was a small mail compartment.

Proudly registered D-AHFB in honour of the manufacturer, the Ha 142 V1 took to the air on 11 October 1938, followed a short time later by the **V2**. In the intervening period, the company had changed its name to Blohm und Voss, and the aircraft to **BV 142**. By the summer of 1939, four prototypes were involved in the flight test programme. In the event, only the V1 was to serve Luft Hansa. After some modifications, it was delivered to the airline for exploratory flights. Christened 'Kastor' and reregistered D-ABUV to reflect its manufacturer's new name, it made a few flights before returning to Blohm und Voss. By this time any thoughts of using the aircraft in commercial service had been abandoned.

Shortly after the start of World War II, it was proposed to convert the four aircraft to serve as long-range maritime surveillance aircraft, and to this effect the V2 was chosen for trial modification. Dubbed the **BV 142 V2/U1**, its main feature was an elongated nose with glazed panels. Operating far from friendly fighters, it had defensive armament incorporated for protection, with a small cabin in the aft compartment for two gunners, and the mail compartment was converted into a small weapons bay. Extensive radio and navigation equipment was fitted, known as 'Transozean-Funkanlage'.

Coded PC+BC, the V2/U1 was delivered in the spring of 1940 to 2./Aufklärungsstaffel, Oberbefehlshaber der Luftwaffe, being attached directly to the headquarters of Luftflotte 3. The first prototype was similarly converted (PC+BB) and the **V3** and **V4** should have followed suit. However, serious long-range

Derived directly from the Ha 139, the BV 142 had similar inverted-gull wings. It was not successful in the maritime patrole role for which it was modified.

transport shortages necessitated their use during the invasion of Denmark and Norway. The pair served with Kampfgruppe zur besonderen Verwendung 105 under Fliegerkorps X alongside a miscellany of large types (Ju 89, Ju 90, Fw 200 etc.) and their ultimate fate is uncertain.

The two maritime patrollers were disappointing in service, their performance with weapons being considerably less than expected. Despite their defensive armament, they were considered extremely vulnerable and consequently few sorties were mounted. By 1942 they had both been withdrawn from service. Plans existed to use the pair for

launches of the Blohm und Voss GT 1200C guided torpedo, but these were not implemented.

Specification
Blohm und Voss BV 142 V2/U1
Type: long-range maritime reconnaissance aircraft
Powerplant: four 656-kW (880-hp) BMW 132H-1 radial piston engines
Performance: maximum speed 375 km/h (233 mph) at sea level; cruising speed 325 km/h (202 mph); service ceiling 9000 m (29,525 ft); maximum range 3900 km (2,423 miles)
Weights: empty 11000 kg (24,251 lb); maximum take-off 16500 kg (36,376 lb)
Dimensions: span 29.53 m (96 ft 10½ in); length 20.45 m (67 ft 1 in); height 4.44 m (14 ft 6¾ in); wing area 130 m² (1,399.35 sq ft)
Armament: one 7.92-mm (0.31-in) MG 15 machine-gun each in the nose, twin beam positions and ventral cupola, and power-operated dorsal turret; provision for four 100-kg (220-lb) or eight 50-kg (110-lb) bombs in former mail bay

Blohm und Voss BV 222 Wiking

Blohm und Voss BV 222A-0 of LTS See 222, based at Petsamo in Finland, early 1943.

The largest flying-boat to achieve operational status during World War II, the Blohm und Voss BV 222 was designed originally by Dr Ing Richard Vogt and Herr R. Schubert, to meet a 1937 Lufthansa requirement for a long-range passenger transport.

Three aircraft, each powered by six 746-kW (1,000-hp) BMW-Bramo Fafnir 323R radials, were ordered in September 1937, and work on the first began in January 1938. There were a number of notable features incorporated in the design, including an extensive unobstructed floor area, made possible by a beam of almost 3.05 m (10 ft), and an absence of intermediate bulkheads above floor level. The wing incorporated a tubular main spar that served also to contain fuel and oil tanks (a feature of Vogt designs), and the outboard stabilising floats each split into halves to retract sideways into the wing.

On 7 September 1940 Flugkäpitan Helmut Rodig made the first flight with the prototype, which clearly had military potential. Indeed, soon afterwards it was fitted with enlarged doors for transport duties with the Luftwaffe, undertaking its first sortie on 10 July 1941. After initial service on the route to

Norway it was transferred to the Mediterranean theatre, being used to carry supplies for German forces from Greece to Libya.

Armament was introduced with the second and third prototypes, flown on 7 August and 28 November 1941, respectively. The third carried only a 7.92-mm (0.31-in) MG 81 machine-gun in the bow, but the second was fitted additionally with a similar weapon in each of four waist positions and in two upper turrets, plus a pair of 13-mm (0.51-in) MG 131 guns in two gondolas located beneath the centre-section. The first prototype was retrospectively equipped with similar bow and waist armament, and with an MG 131 in each of the upper turrets. On 10 May 1942 it was delivered to Luftverkehrsstaffel 'C' (later redesignated Lufttransportstaffel See 222). It was joined by the second prototype in August of that year, after the aircraft had been provided with a

modified bottom to the hull.

In addition to the three prototypes, there were five **BV 222A-0**s (**V4** to **V8**) and five **BV 222C-0**s (**V9** to **V13**), the latter being powered by Jumo 207C diesel engines and featuring revised defensive armament and rockets for assisted take-offs. The **BV 222B** was a proposed Jumo 208-powered version for Luft Hansa, while the **BV 222D** was to have been a military model with Jumo 207Ds. Unavailability of this engine led to the proposed **BV 222E**, which would have featured six Bramo Fafnir 323 radials.

Transport operations in the Mediterranean built up during 1942, but the V6 and V8 were shot down by the RAF. Operations switched to night, and continued until early 1943, when the surviving Wikings moved to Biscarosse for maritime patrol duties with Aufklärungsstaffel See 222 (subordinate to 3./KüFlGr 406). For their new-

found role, the BV 222s were fitted with FuG 200 Hohentwiel radar and long-range communications equipment. The V3 and V5 were sunk at their moorings, but the force was augmented by further deliveries. It redesignated as 1. (Fern)/Seeaufklärungsgruppe 129 in October 1943, and continued to support U-boat operations far out in the Atlantic. A further loss was the BV 222C-010, shot down by the RAF, but one of the Wikings dispatched a Lancaster. In July 1944 the unit disbanded, and the BV 222s returned to transport duties. Seven survived hostilities, and three were captured and evaluated by the Allies.

Specification
Blohm und Voss BV 222C
Type: long-range transport/maritime reconnaissance and patrol aircraft
Powerplant: six 746-kW (1,000-hp) Junkers Jumo 207C inline diesel engines
Performance: maximum speed 390 km/h (242 mph) at 5000 m (16,405 ft); cruising speed 345 km/h (214 mph) at 5550 m (18,210 ft); service ceiling 7300 m (23,950 ft); range 6095 km (3,787 miles)
Weights: empty 30650 kg (67,572 lb); maximum take-off 49000 kg (108,027 lb)
Dimensions: span 46.00 m (150 ft 11 in); length 37.00 m (121 ft 4¾ in); height 10.90 m (35 ft 9 in); wing area 255 m² (2,744.89 sq ft)
Armament: (BV 222C-09) three 20-mm MG 151 cannon (one each in forward dorsal and two over-wing turrets) and five 13-mm (0.51-in) MG 131 machine-guns (one each in bow position and four beam hatches)

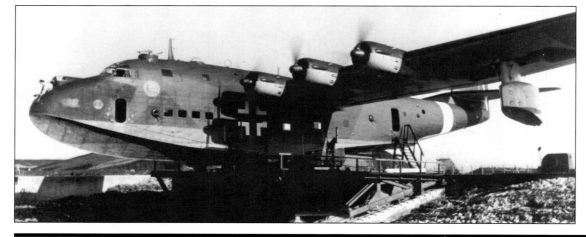

The BV222A-0 V8 runs its engines on a launching ramp. This aircraft was shot down by RAF Beaufighters over the Mediterranean in December 1942.

Blohm und Voss BV 238

In early 1940, Dr Richard Vogt began work on the design of a series of flying-boats to undertake both long-range maritime patrol and transport duties, mainly as a successor to the BV 138 which was entering service at the time. Water tank work showed that the flying-boat's planing bottom could be far more slender than was traditional, allowing the con-

struction of a much larger aircraft. Armed with these results, Vogt's team began work on a new design in November, the result being designated the Blohm und Voss **BV 238**. Power was to have come from four 24-cylinder Jumo 223 engines, consisting of four 6-cylinder rows in a box arrangement. By July 1941 it was obvi-

ous that the Jumo would not be available, so Vogt redesigned the aircraft with six engines.

In late 1941 three **BV 238A** prototypes were ordered with DB 603 engines, and one **BV 238B** with BMW 801 radials. Soon after, Blohm und Voss proposed the **BV 238-Land**, later redesignated **BV 250**. This was a landplane version with bomb

bays replacing the planing bottom, and having sufficient range to reach the US coast in the strategic reconnaissance role. Four prototypes of this version were ordered, and assembly of three was begun, although not finished.

As the BV 238/250 programme was on an enormous scale, it was decided to build a research replica of approximately quarter-scale, to be powered by six 15.7-kW (21-hp) engines. Built near Prague, the resulting

FGP 227 proved a complete financial loss, refusing to take off when fitted with wheeled undercarriage, being deliberately damaged by French prisoners of war when being transported to Travemünde for trials as a flying-boat, and then having all engines seize on its first flight, resulting in further damage. This first flight occurred in September 1944, some months after the full-scale aircraft had flown.

Flight trials with the **BV 238 V1** began in April 1945, and although it was not the world's largest aircraft in terms of dimensions (the Tupolev ANT-20 had that distinction), it was certainly the heaviest, and at its full take-off weight it would need rockets to assist take-off. The aircraft was sunk at its moorings on Lake Schaal by USAAF P-51 Mustangs in late 1944, by which time the DB 603-powered **V2** and **V3** were virtually complete. The **V4** (with BMW 801s) and **V5** (pre-production aircraft for BV 238A) were well advanced, as were the three BV 250s, but with the loss of the only flying aircraft, and the

more pressing needs of the Luftwaffe at the time, the programme was terminated.

Specification
Blohm und Voss BV 238 V1
Type: long-range multi-role flying-boat
Powerplant: six 1417-kW (1,900-hp) Daimler-Benz DB 603G inline piston engines
Performance: maximum speed at AUW of 60000 kg (132,277 lb) 425 km/h (264 mph) at 6000 m (19,685 ft); range approximately 7850 km (4,878 miles)
Weights: empty 54780 kg (120,769 lb); maximum take-off (overload) 100000 kg (220,460 lb)
Dimensions: span 60.17 m (197 ft 4¾ in); length 43.36 m (142 ft 3 in); height 12.80 m (42 ft 0 in); wing area 360 m² (3,876.84 sq ft)
Armament: (projected) four 13-mm MG 131 machine-guns in each of nose and tail turrets, and in turrets on rear of each wing, pairs of MG 131 in fuselage

The V1 was the only example of the monster BV 238 to fly. It did not have armament fitted, and was still undergoing initial flight tests when it was sunk and the programme cancelled.

beam stations and two 20-mm MG 151 cannon in dorsal turret; wing bays for 20 250-kg (551-lb) bombs and external racks for four LD 1200 torpedoes, four 1000-kg (2,250-lb) bombs, four Hs 293 missiles or four BV 143 glide bombs

DFS 230

Following military interest in a research glider developed by DFS, a contract was awarded for the construction of three prototypes. Demonstrated successfully during 1937, following a pre-production batch of **DFS 230A-0s**, it was ordered into limited production as the **DFS 230A-1** operational version and **DFS 230A-2** with dual controls for training. These and subsequent versions totalling more than 1,000 aircraft were built by several factories, becoming the Luftwaffe's standard assault glider. A braced high-wing monoplane of mixed construction, the DFS 230 provided accommodation for a crew of two and eight fully armed troops. Towable by a variety of Luftwaffe aircraft, the DFS 230 used jettisonable landing gear for take-off, and landing was accomplished on a central skid mounted beneath the fuselage. The **DFS 230B-1** and dual-control **DFS 230B-2** introduced air-deployable brake parachutes to allow the glider to dive steeply if it came under attack. An MG 15 was fitted behind the cockpit for a measure of self-defence and for suppressive fire once the glider was on the ground. Some

DFS 230 gliders often worked with Ju 52s on assault and transport operations. Usual tugs for the glider were the He 45, He 46 or Hs 126.

units field-modified their gliders with twin MG 34 guns in the nose.

The DFS 230 mounted the world's first operation by glider-borne troops when the Belgian fort of Eben Emael was captured on 10 May 1940. DFS 230s were used also in the invasion of Crete and on many other airborne operations. Most often, they were used as transports, and in this role they flew their last mission in March 1945. In order to achieve very short landing runs, one fuselage was delivered to Focke-Achgelis for modification with a three-bladed autogyro rotor, being designated the **Fa 225**. This demonstrated very short landing runs but was difficult to control. A more practical solution was the use of forward-thrusting Rheinmetall-Borsig brake rockets strapped to the nose. These could stop a DFS 230 in just 15 m (50 ft) while producing a cloud of white smoke which disguised the aircraft and its occupants. A force of rocket-equipped gliders, designated **DFS 230C-1**, was used in the daring rescue of Benito

Mussolini from his mountain-top prison. An improved rocket nose section was proposed for the production **DFS 230D-1**, which in the event did not materialise. The **DFS 230 V7** was an entirely new design which would have been built as the **DFS 230F-1**. Only one prototype was built.

Specification
DFS 230B-1
Type: assault transport glider
Performance: maximum gliding speed 290 km/h (180 mph); normal towing speed 180 km/h (112 mph)
Weights: empty 860 kg (1,896 lb); maximum take-off 2100 kg (4,630 lb)
Dimensions: span 21.98 m (72 ft 1½ in); length 11.24 m (36 ft 10½ in); height 2.74 m (9 ft 0 in); wing area 41.3 m² (444.56 sq ft)
Armament: one 7.9-mm (0.31-in) MG 15 machine-gun

A cloud of smoke envelops a DFS 230C-1 during trials of the powder rocket brakes. Combined with the brake chute which allowed a steep approach, the rockets could stop the glider in a very short distance.

Dornier Do 17/215

Inevitably dubbed the 'Flying Pencil' due to its long slender fuselage, the **Do 17** was actually designed purely as a commercial aircraft, primarily a high-speed mailplane but capable of carrying six passengers. In this guise, the **Do 17 V1** first flew in late 1934, being passed to Lufthansa for evaluation with the second and third prototypes in 1935. The airline found the passenger accommodation (a single two-seat cabin behind the flight deck, and an equally cramped four-seat cabin aft of the wing) completely impractical, and the prototypes were returned to Dornier. The type was saved from what seemed certain oblivion by a Lufthansa pilot, a former Dornier test pilot acting as liaison between airline and air ministry, who flew the aircraft and suggested it had potential as a bomber, although he felt it lacked keel area. A fourth prototype was commissioned, with a bomb bay in the lower fuselage and with new twin endplate fins and rudders. This was followed by five similar prototypes, three of which introduced a glazed tip and bottom to the standard long nose and the last three of which had an aft-facing gun position, with a single 7.9-mm (0.31-in) MG 15 fired by the radio operator, behind the flight deck. The seventh and the ninth aircraft also had a shortened, but more extensively glazed nose, which was adopted on production versions.

The initial production model was the **Do 17E-1**, which was produced alongside the almost identical **Do 17F-1**, which was a dedicated long-range reconnaissance aircraft. Both aircraft had provision for a downward-firing MG 15 in a hatch just ahead of the bomb bay. In the E-1 this could accommodate up to 750 kg (1,650 lb) of bombs, although 500 kg (1,100 lb) was a more usual load, while in the F-1 it carried a pair of cameras. To make the aircraft suitable for licensed manufacture and dispersed production, the Do 17 was designed in modular components, which had the added benefit of allowing major items to be replaced at unit level.

The Luftwaffe rapidly formed four new *Kampfgeschwader* with the new type, and Do 17F-1s equipped an *Aufklärungsgruppe*. Do 17F-1s

The original 'Flying Pencil': Dornier's Do 17 V1 fast mailplane caused much anxiety in Britain and France when it appeared in late 1934, as its military potential was both obvious and frightening.

were sent to Spain with the Légion Condor in the spring of 1937, 15 aircraft from Aufkl.Gr.(F)/122 joining 1.A/88. They proved able to evade enemy fighters, as did the 20 Do 17E-1s which joined them in Spain with 2.K/88.

The **Do 17M** and **Do 17P** were developed in parallel as replacements for the earlier Do 17E-1 and Do 17F-1. The 562-kW (750-hp) BMW VI 7,3 12-cylinder engines were to have been replaced by the same 746-kW (1,000-hp) Daimler Benz DB 600As that powered the Do 17 V8, which participated in the 1937 International Military Aircraft Competition at Zürich, outrunning all the fighters present. Unfortunately, production of the DB 600A was slow and engines were reserved for fighter production, so the Do 17M bomber emerged with 675-kW (900-hp) Bramo 323A-1 Fafnir nine-cylinder air cooled radials, while the Do 17P had the 648-kW (865-hp) BMW 132N, which gave the reconnaissance aircraft the required range. Armament was increased by the addition of a forward-firing MG 15, which could be clamped fore-and-aft and aimed by the pilot using a ring-and-bead sight, or used as a free gun by the navigator/bomb-aimer. Do 17Ms and Do 17Ps still in service in 1940 often had an extra pair of MG 15s added. Both versions had a bomb bay that was extended aft and housed up to 1000 kg (2,205 lb) of bombs. The provision of a dinghy resulted in a change of designation to **Do 17M/U1**, while tropical filters resulted in the **Do 17M-1/Trop** and **Do 17P-1/Trop**.

Dornier Do 17Ms were exported to Yugoslavia as **Do 17Kb-1** bombers, and **Do 17Ka-2** and **Ka-3** reconnaissance aircraft. All were powered by Gnome-Rhône 14 Na/2 radials and all had FN-Browning machine-guns (and some also had 20-mm Hispano Suiza 404 cannon) as defensive armament. They also had the original long glazed nose of the Do 17 prototypes. Twenty German-built aircraft were supplied, and licence-production began at the State Aircraft Factory in 1939. When German forces invaded in 1941, Yugoslavia had 70 Do 17Ks on strength, 26 being destroyed in the initial assault. Some survivors fled to Egypt (two briefly entering RAF service) and others were passed to Germany's new-formed ally, the Croatian air force, along with some surplus Do 17E-1s. The **Do 17L** designation

Above: The Do 17P-1 still equipped many reconnaissance units on the outbreak of war, and the similar Do 17M-1 bomber was also on charge. Note the slim fuselage of these early aircraft.

Below: Seen on their way to a strike in Poland during the opening days of the war, these Do 17Zs served with KG 2, which partnered KG 3 in the northern sector of the attack.

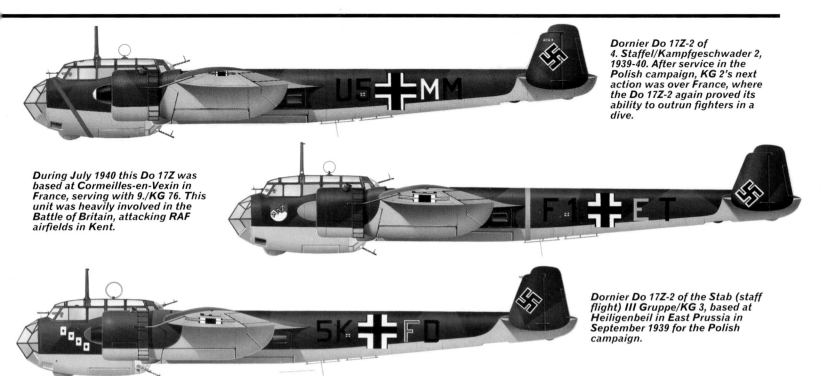

Dornier Do 17Z-2 of 4. Staffel/Kampfgeschwader 2, 1939-40. After service in the Polish campaign, KG 2's next action was over France, where the Do 17Z-2 again proved its ability to outrun fighters in a dive.

During July 1940 this Do 17Z was based at Cormeilles-en-Vexin in France, serving with 9./KG 76. This unit was heavily involved in the Battle of Britain, attacking RAF airfields in Kent.

Dornier Do 17Z-2 of the Stab (staff flight) III Gruppe/KG 3, based at Heiligenbeil in East Prussia in September 1939 for the Polish campaign.

was allocated to a pathfinder equivalent to the Do 17M, which only reached prototype status.

The Spanish Civil War showed that the Do 17 was vulnerable from below, and the cockpit had proved too cramped. The **Do 17S** (a high-speed reconnaissance aircraft that did not go beyond the proto-type stage) and the **Do 17U** (a pathfinder version of which three proto-type **Do 17U-0**s and 12 production **Do 17U-1**s were completed) introduced a redesigned forward fuselage which increased the height of the cockpit, allowed the carriage of a five-man crew (two radio operators in the Do 17U) and a new lower-hemisphere machine-gun in a flexible mounting firing back from the step where the new deep cockpit met the original shallow fuselage. The Do 17S and Do 17U were powered by the DB 600, but the **Do 17Z-1** bomber, which shared the same forward fuselage, retained Bramo 323A-1 Fafnir radi-als. Underpowered with its full bomb load, the aircraft was refined into the **Do 17Z-2** by the introduction of 746-kW (1,000-hp) Bramo 323P engines with two-speed superchargers. The **Do 17Z-3** was a dual-role reconnaissance bomber, with provision for a camera in the entry hatch, while the **Do 17Z-4** was a dual-control trainer ver-sion, and the **Do 17Z-5** a long-range over-water recconnaissance air-craft with flotation bags and extra survival equipment.

Some 212 of the 370 Do 17 bombers on strength on the outbreak of war between Britain and Germany were Do 17Z-1s and Z-2s, the rest being Do 17M-1s and a handful of Do 17E-1s. These aircraft equipped nine *Kampfgruppen* with four *Kampfgeschwader*. There were also 262 Do 17s serving with 23 *Staffeln* in the long-range reconnais-sance role. A handful of Do 17Ms served with a variety of other units, three being on charge with the *Stab* of each *Stukagruppe*, for example. The Do 17 participated in the invasions of Poland and France (but not of Norway), and played a major part in the Battle of Britain, where it proved able to outrun most fighters in a shallow dive. Nonetheless,

Illustrating the broad slab wing of the Do 17 is this early Z-1, the first bomber variant with a redesigned cabin. This version was markedly underpowered and had a reduced bomb load to compensate.

losses were heavy and defensive armament proved inadequate. The Do 17s made a number of spectacular low-level terrain-following mass raids, but several units began converting to the much superior Ju 88 even before the battle was over and, by the time Hitler launched Operation Barbarossa, only KG 2 remained fully equipped with the Do 17. Three *Gruppen* initially flew the Do 17 on the Eastern Front, the last being III/KG 3 which handed its aircraft on to the Croatian IV/KG 3 (a *Staffel*-strength unit), which continued to operate the type until transferred to anti-Partisan duties in Croatia in November 1942. Another 'foreign operator' was Finland, which received 15 Do 17Z-2s

Fitted with BMW-Bramo 323P Fafnir engines rated at 746 kW (1,000 hp) for take-off, the Dornier Do 17Z-2 appeared in 1939, capable of carrying a 1000-kg (2,205-lb) bomb load. These examples were some of the last in front-line service, fighting on the Eastern Front in 1942 with 15.(Kroat)/KG 53.

Dornier Do 17/215

Many of the Do 17s surviving into 1941 served with KG 2, and this Do 17Z-2 flew with that unit's I Gruppe based at Tatoi, Greece, in May 1941. Do 17Zs could undertake shallow diving attacks at speeds up to 595 km/h (370 mph) on account of their sturdy structure.

Deployed to Vitebsk on the central sector of the Eastern Front in December 1941 was this Do 17Z-2, flown by Croatian volunteers as 10.(Kroat.)/KG 3. After a disastrous start to operations, the unit returned to Croatia for a few months.

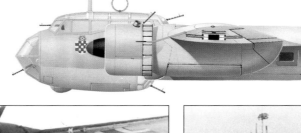

Left: Apart from the Croatian-staffed unit, the last Do 17Z front-line operator was III/KG 3, which flew on the Eastern Front. Here an aircraft of 7. Staffel is bombed up by traditional methods. The unit left the fray to convert to Ju 88s in early 1942.

Above: Photographed in the winter of 1939, this Do 17Z-2 served with the Stab/KG 3, the wing's staff flight (as denoted by the last 'A' in the code). KG 3's I and II Gruppe converted to the Ju 88A in late 1940 after participating in the Battle of Britain.

in early 1942, using the aircraft to replace Blenheims and keeping them operational until mid-1944.

Production of the Do 17Z, which lacked the speed of the Ju 88 or the bomb load of the He 111, had finally been terminated in 1940, after 522 Do 17Zs had been delivered. The end of production did not spell the end for the Do 17, however. The single **Do 17Z-6 Kauz** was a dedicated night intruder created by grafting the cannon-nose of a Ju 88C-2 to the airframe of a Do 17Z-3. This gave the aircraft a forward-firing armament of three MG 15 machine-guns and a 20-mm MG FF cannon. The similar **Do 17Z-10 Kauz II** had an entirely new, purpose-designed nose with four MG 15s and a pair of MG FFs, as well as a Spanner Anlage IR detector. The crew of the Z-6 and Z-10 was reduced to three, with the engineer loading the MG FFs

and the radio-operator firing the aft-facing machine-guns. The last nine Do 17Z-3s on the production line were completed to Do 17Z-10 standards and were allocated to 4./NJG 1 at Deelen, which scored its first kill by despatching a Wellington into the Zuyder Zee on 18 October 1940. The unit also had some success in infiltrating RAF airfield circuits as bombers returned to base. The small number of aircraft produced remained active until early 1942.

The **Do 215** designation was applied to the Do 17Z on the orders of the Reichsluftfahrtministerium to cover a proposed export version for Yugoslavia. Prototypes were demonstrated with Gnome-Rhône (**Do 215 V2**)and DB 601A (**Do 215 V3**) engines, the DB 601-powered version attracting a Swedish air force order as the **Do 215A-1**. Embargoed before delivery, the 18 aircraft were modified on the pro-

Do 17/215 variants

Do 17 V1, **V2** and **V3**: original prototypes with single fin and BMW VI Vee-12 engines
Do 17 V4: prototype for military trials with twin fin, radio operator's compartment and bomb bay: **V6** similar, while **V5** powered by Hispano-Suiza 12Ybrs engines; **V7** introduced single aft-firing MG 15
Do 17 V8: prototype for Do 17M series, also known as **Do 17M V1**; powered by DB 600A; **V2** and **V3** similar apart from having Bramo 323A-1 radial engines
Do 17 V9: production bomber prototype with shortened nose and extensive glazing for bombardier; enlarged vertical tail surfaces; later used for high-speed communications work
Do 17 V10: prototype used for engine development
Do 17E-1: first production bomber

with BMW VI 7,3 engines and second MG 15 firing down through hatch in floor of cabin
Do 17F-1: parallel version of E-1 for reconnaissance with auxiliary fuel tank and vertical cameras in bomb bay
Do 17K: export version of Do 17M/P for Yugoslavia
Do 17L: two prototypes of pathfinder version of Do 17M with accommodation for fourth crew member
Do 17M-1: major bomber version with Bramo 323A-I engines and lengthened bomb bay; forward-firing MG 15 added; modifications included addition of emergency dinghy pack on roof of cockpit (**Do 17M-1/U1**), two more MG 15s and fitment of sand filters (**Do 17M-1/Trop**)
Do 17P-1: reconnaissance version of M-1; powered by BMW 132N engines; known as **Do 17P-1/Trop** with sand filters fitted
Do 17R: two prototypes for trials programme

Do 17S-0: DB 600G-powered reconnaissance model with accommodation for five in a new deepened crew compartment; three prototypes only
Do 17U-0 and **Do 17U-1**: three pre-production and 12 production pathfinder aircraft with seating for five in deepened cabin; DB 600A engines
Do 17Z-0: pre-production model of four-seat bomber with deepened cabin
Do 17Z-1: production variant; similar to Do 17M apart from forward fuselage; additional MG 15 in nosecone; bomb load reduced due to weight considerations
Do 17Z-2: version of Z-1 with Bramo 323P engines which restored bomb load to 1000 kg (2,205 lb); field modifications resulted in **Do 17Z-4** dual-control trainer and **Do 17Z-5** with flotation equipment
Do 17Z-3: reconnaissance variant of Do 17Z-2
Do 17Z-6 Kauz: night-fighter

version which married Z-3 airframe to nose and forward-firing armament of Ju 88C-2; crew reduced to three; one completed with aft bomb bay retained
Do 17Z-10 Kauz II: definitive night-fighter with newly-designed nose housing four MG 17s and four MG FF cannon
Do 215 prototypes: export demonstration aircraft based on Do 17Z; **V1** powered by Bramo 323A-1, **V2** by Gnome-Rhône 14N and **V3** by DB 601A
Do 215A-1: DB 601A-powered reconnaissance bomber ordered by Sweden but delivered to Luftwaffe as **Do 215B-0** and **Do 215B-1**
Do 215B-2: unbuilt bomber variant
Do 215B-3: two examples supplied for trials to Soviet Union
Do 215B-4: Luftwaffe production variant similar to B-1 but with revised camera options
Do 215B-6 Kauz III: night-fighter version of B-4 using Do 17Z-10 nose

In early 1941 KG 2's Do 17Zs were sent south to support the push through the Balkans and Greece, and flew anti-shipping operations until June, when I and III Gruppe were deployed on the Eastern Front.

duction line for the long-range reconnaissance role and were delivered to the Luftwaffe as **Do 215B-0**s and **Do 215B-1**s. Dornier was ordered to continue production of the aircraft for the Luftwaffe, and produced a succession of sub-variants. The unbuilt **Do 215B-2** was a bomber, while the **Do 215B-3** designation covered two aircraft supplied to Russia. The **Do 215B-4** had different camera equipment and was converted to night-intruder configuration as the **Do 215B-5**. Unlike the original Kauz II, the Do 215B-5 was adapted to carry the FuG 202 Lichtenstein BC AI radar, paving the way for the fitting of radar to the Bf 110 and Ju 88 night-fighters. The Do 215 had disappeared from front-line service by the middle of 1942, although four were transferred to Hungary, serving on until the end of the year.

The last Luftwaffe 'Flying Pencils' served as glider tugs for the DFS 230 until the last days of the war, despite steady replacement by more powerful He 111s towing larger Gotha Go 242 gliders. They participated in one of the *Schleppgruppen*'s final operations, the resupply of Budapest in early 1945. In early 1943, the Do 17 glider tugs had enjoyed their finest hour (and perhaps had written the proudest chapter in the type's history) towing DFS 230 gliders of I/Luftlandegeschwader 1 (I Gruppe of Air-Landing Group 1) to resupply and eventually evacuate German forces in the Kuban bridgehead. By the end of the war, however, numbers had dwindled to the extent that only one captured Do 17 was taken on charge by the Allies for evaluation.

Croatian pilots of 10.(Kroat.)/KG 3 plan a mission in front of their hastily snow-camouflaged Do 17Z-2. The Croats returned to Russia in July 1942 as 15.(Kroat.)/KG 53, although they had left again by November.

The DB 601 engines and prominent undernose fairing identify this as a Do 215B-4 reconnaissance aircraft. The fairing housed an Rb 50/30 camera, behind which was the window for an Rb 20/30.

This Do 215B-1 was converted on the production line for Luftwaffe use. It was configured for long-range reconnaissance and served with 3.Aufkl. St./Ob.d.L. at Stavager in April 1940.

Specification
Dornier Do 17Z-2
Type: four-seat medium bomber
Powerplant: two BMW-Bramo 323P Fafnir nine-cylinder radial engines, each rated at 746 kW (1,000 hp) for take-off and 701 kW (940 hp) at 4000 m (13,120 ft)
Performance: maximum speed 410 km/h (255 mph); service ceiling 7000 m (22,965 ft); range 1160 km (720 miles); standard tactical radius 330 km (205 miles)
Weights: empty 5209 kg (11,484 lb); empty equipped 5962 kg (13,145 lb); maximum overload 8837 kg (19,481 lb)
Dimensions: wing span 18.00 m (59 ft 0½ in); length 15.79 m (51 ft 9⅗ in); height 4.56 m (14 ft 11½ in); wing area 55.00 m² (592 sq ft)
Armament: two forward-firing 7.9-mm (0.31-in) MG 15 machine-guns, either fixed or free-mounted, two MG 15s firing from side windows, one MG 15 firing aft from dorsal and ventral positions in forward compartment; maximum internal bomb load of 1000 kg (2,205 lb)

This Do 17Z-10 Kauz II was based with I/NJG 2 at Gilze-Rijen in October 1940. It was used in the night intruder role over southern England and East Anglia.

This Do 215B-5 Kauz III served with Stab II/NJG 2 based at Leeuwarden in the summer of 1942, and was the personal mount of Gruppenkommandeur Helmut Lent. It has FuG 202 Lichtenstein BC radar fitted and a ventral tray with MG FF cannon.

Dornier Do 18

The **Do 18** was designed as a successor to military versions of the Do 15 Wal (whale) flying-boat, an aircraft always intended as a military flying-boat but which was perhaps better known as a South Atlantic mail carrier for Lufthansa. Thirty Militar-Wal 33s (also known as the '10 Tonnen-Wal') were delivered to the Luftwaffe, serving in the long-range maritime reconnaissance role from 1933 until 1938. Dornier designed the Do 18 to replace Do 15s belonging to Lufthansa and the Luftwaffe, beginning work on four prototypes during early 1934.

The Do 18 retained the same basic configuration as the Do 15, with a typical Dornier two-step hull, with the rear step fairing into a vertical knife-edge and water rudder. The hull was formed from seven compartments, all of which were watertight, and any two of which could be filled with water without the aircraft sinking or losing its stability. Compartmentalised sponsons (known as *Stümmel*) provided lateral stability on the water, contributing to lift in the air.

The Do 18 introduced an enclosed cockpit, housing pilot and co-pilot side-by-side and radio operator and navigator immediately aft. A compartment over the rear step provided space for a defensive gunner, with another open gun position in the nose. Jumo 205 six-cylinder, two-stroke compression ignition engines, which used diesel heavy oil and were each rated at 447 kW (600 hp) (eventually 656 kW/880 hp in later versions) for take-off, were mounted in tandem above the high-set wing.

The **Do 18a** prototype first flew on 15 March 1935, and later served with Luft Hansa, along with the **Do 18c** third prototype and two other early boats. The four began services in 1935, and were operated by the auirline under the designation **Do 18E**, making many record-breaking long-distance flights before settling into routine operations on the South Atlantic route. The initial military *Seefernaufklärer* aircraft was the **Do 18d**, which was actually the second aircraft to fly. The **Do 18b** second prototype was completed as the production prototype of the **Do 18D** series. Deliveries to the Luftwaffe began in 1936, initially from Dornier's own Friedrichshafen factory, but then (as Do 17 production was stepped up) from the Weser company's Einswarden and Nordenham plants. All but the first few **Do 18D-1**s were fitted with twin water rudders and controllable

Showing the open bow position to advantage, this aircraft was the pre-production Do 18D-01. The **Stümmel** *sponsons were a Dornier trademark.*

radiator flaps, were powered by 447-kW (600-hp) Jumo 205Cs, and had two 7.9-mm (0.31-in) MG 15 machine-guns in open positions in the nose and above the rear step, with two ETC 50 bomb racks below the starboard wing for carriage of a pair of 50-kg (110-lb) bombs. By the summer of 1939, five *Staffeln* were equipped with the survivors of the 75 Do 18Ds built, but the type's poor performance and limited defensive armament rendered it clearly on the verge of obsolescence. The Do 18D's designated successor, the Blohm und Voss BV 138, was severely delayed, and it was clear that a new version of the Do 18 would need to be pressed into service to fill the gap. Minor equip-

Right and below: The pre-war **Küstenfliegergruppen** *usually had three squadrons.* **1. and 3. Staffel** *had short-range types, while* **2. Staffel** *operated Do 18Ds in the long-range reconnaissance role. Five such squadrons were so equipped.*

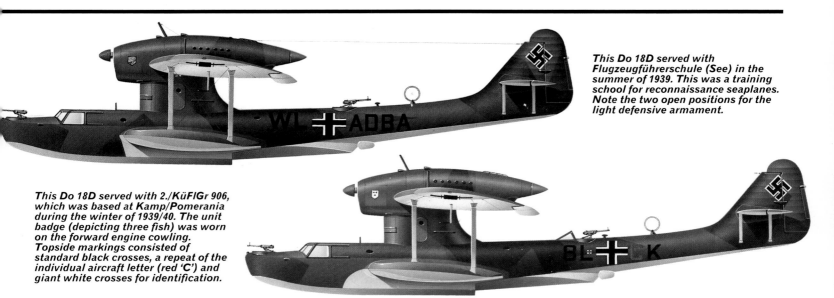

This Do 18D served with Flugzeugführerschule (See) in the summer of 1939. This was a training school for reconnaissance seaplanes. Note the two open positions for the light defensive armament.

This Do 18D served with 2./KüFlGr 906, which was based at Kamp/Pomerania during the winter of 1939/40. The unit badge (depicting three fish) was worn on the forward engine cowling. Topside markings consisted of standard black crosses, a repeat of the individual aircraft letter (red 'C') and giant white crosses for identification.

ment changes resulted in the **Do 18D-2** and **Do 18D-3** variants.

The **Do 18G-1** introduced uprated Jumo 205D engines, rated at 656 kW (880 hp), with performance being further enhanced by aerodynamic improvements that included sharper bow contours. Take-off performance could be further enhanced since there was provision for *R-Geräte* take-off booster rockets. Defensive armament was also improved, with a 13-mm MG 131 in the open bow position, and a power-operated mid-upper turret over the rear step housing a 20-mm

MG 151 cannon. The **Do 18H-1** was an unarmed version for crew training. Seventy-one of these aircraft were delivered to the Luftwaffe before production ceased in the early summer of 1940. Do 18G-1s supplanted the Do 18Ds of the remaining four fully-equipped *Staffeln* of the *Küstenfliegergruppen* (2./KüFlGr 106, 2./ and 3./KüFlGr 406, and 2./KüFlGr 906), and with a handful of units that included the antiquated Dorniers within their inventories (including 1./KüFlGr 406, 1./KüFlGr 506 and 3./KüFlGr 906). The Do 18Ds were transferred to *Seenotdienst* (air-sea rescue) duties. The last front-line Do 18G-1s were withdrawn from operational use by Norway-based units (3./KüFlGr 406 and 3./KüFlGr 906) in August 1941, but many continued to be used, having been modified for the *Seenotdienst* role as **Do 18N-1**s.

Specification
Dornier Do 18G-1
Type: four-seat maritime patrol and air-sea rescue aircraft
Powerplant: two Junkers Jumo 205D six-cylinder piston engines rated at 656 kW (880 hp) for take-off
Performance: maximum speed 267 km/h (166 mph); long-range cruising speed 164 km/h (102 mph); service ceiling 4200 m (13,800 ft); range 3500 km (2,175 miles)
Weights: empty equipped 5978 kg (13,180 lb); maximum loaded 10795 kg (23,800 lb)
Dimensions: wing span 23.70 m (77 ft 9 in); length 19.38 m (63 ft 7 in); height 5.32 m (17 ft 5½ in); wing area 98.00 m² (1,054.86 sq ft)
Armament: one 13-mm MG 131 machine-gun on D 30/131 mount in open nose position and one 20-mm MG 151/20 in HD 151/1 dorsal turret; wing racks for two 50-kg (110-lb) bombs

Above: The Do 18G differed by having a power-operated dorsal turret, although the type remained very vulnerable to enemy fighters. This 6. Seenotstaffel Do 18G-1 is being hoisted on to a launching trolley, which is wheeled down the slipway into the water.

Right: A Do 18D displays the Junkers-style 'double-wing' flap and aileron arrangement. The type's front-line career lasted until August 1941.

Right: The Do 18 served well in the air-sea rescue role, although it was slowly displaced by the far better Do 24. This is a Do 18G-1, serving with 6. Seenotstaffel in the central Mediterranean during 1941/42.

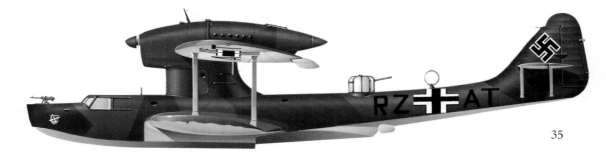

Dornier Do 24

The **Dornier Do 24** was designed to meet a Royal Dutch navy (MLD) requirement for a replacement for the Wal, primarily for use in the Dutch East Indies. Of broadly similar configuration to the Do 15 and Do 18, the Do 24 was designed with three side-by-side tractor engines, and had a similar structure to the earlier aircraft. The crew complement was raised to six, and armament was increased to two 7.9-mm (0.31-in) FN-Browning machine-guns in enclosed nose and tail turrets, with a 20-mm Solothurn cannon in the mid-upper position. Living and sleeping quarters were provided amidships to allow the aircraft to operate away from base for extended periods. To ensure compatibility with the newly delivered Martin 139 land-based bomber, the MLD specified that the new flying-boat should be powered by the same Wright Cyclone radial engines, and completion of the first two prototypes (which were powered by the Jumo 205 Diesel) was delayed while the first two production machines, with Cyclones, were completed. The first of these made its maiden flight on 3 July 1937. Twelve **Do 24K-1**s were built for the Netherlands, before the Dutch planned to licence-assemble 48 more under the designation **Do 24K-2**.

Work on the Jumo-engined first and second prototypes was resumed, and the first flew on 10 January 1938. The Luftwaffe displayed little interest in the aircraft, since the BV 138 was felt to meet its flying-boat needs. The two prototypes languished until 1940, when they were hastily fitted with defensive armament consisting of a 20-mm MG 151 cannon in an HD 151/1 turret amidships, and single 7.9-mm (0.31-in) MG 15 machine-guns in open bow and stern positions. Delivered to the Kampfgeschwader zur besonderen Verwendung 108 See, the aircraft were used in support of the invasions of Denmark and Norway, the second being lost on a resupply mission to Narvik.

Into battle

Despite the aircraft's impressive performance, no effort was made to begin production until after the invasion of Holland, when the Germans overran the licence-manufacturing plants for the aircraft. Twenty-five Do 24K-2s had been delivered to the East Indies, where they fought against the invading Japanese (the survivors of these aircraft, with five surviving Do 24K-1s, went on to fight in Allied hands, eventually in RAAF service), but three were complete, awaiting dismantling for shipment, and 20 more were in stages of completion.

The three completed aircraft were evaluated for the *Seenotsdienst* role, the elderly He 59 seaplane and Do 18 having already been shown to be somewhat wanting. With its high cruising speed, superb seaworthiness and high internal capacity, the Do 24 was tailor-made

The V3 (right) was the first Do 24 to fly, and acted as the prototype for the Dutch Do 24K contract. The Jumo-powered V1 (below) did not fly until 1938.

for the role, and the Dutch production organisation was resurrected under supervision by the Weser Flugzeugbau. Aviolanda resumed hull production, and De Schelde continued producing wings, with Fokker responsible for assembly and flight test. The aircraft were fitted with German instruments and radios, and MG 15s replaced the Brownings in the nose and tail turrets, with captured French Hispano Suiza 404 20-mm cannon in the mid-upper turret. Eleven aircraft were delivered as **Do 24N-1**s in the autumn of 1941, before stocks of the Wright Cyclone were exhausted. With 746-kW (1000-hp) nine-cylinder BMW-Bramo 323R-2 Fafnir radials fitted, 170 **Do 24T-1**s were delivered from the Dutch line by the end of 1944, with 48 more produced by the former CAMS factory at Sartrouville before it was abandoned in 1944. It resumed production soon after, producing 22 Dorniers for the Aéronavale.

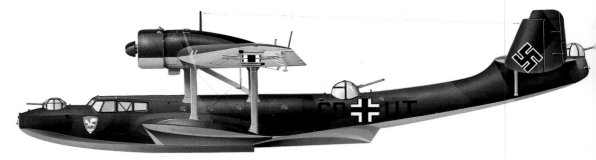

The Do 24 V1 and V2 prototypes remained unwanted at Friedrichshafen until 1940, when they were hastily fitted with gun armament and dispatched to Norway for service with KGzbV 108 See, which operated a motley collection of seaplanes for resupplying German troops along the Norwegian fjords during Operation Weserübung. The two Do 24s performed excellently in this harsh environment, although this aircraft, the V2, was shot down during a resupply mission into the northerly Narvik Fjord. Both aircraft retained their Jumo 205C diesel engines.

This Do 24T-1 served with 3. Staffel/Seenotgruppe, Seenotbereichskommando III, based at Bordeaux-Wimereux in the summer of 1942. The 3.Staffel badge on the nose depicted a seagull holding a lifebelt.

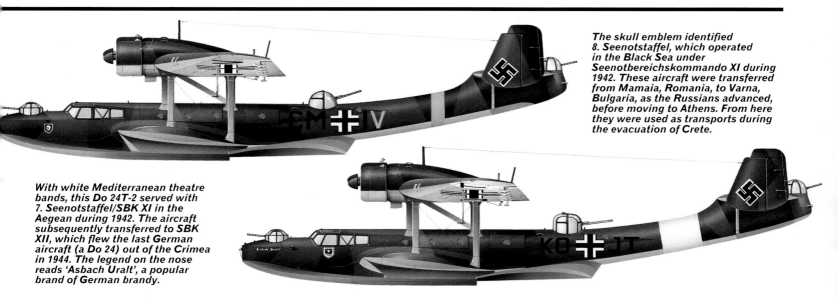

The skull emblem identified 8. Seenotstaffel, which operated in the Black Sea under Seenotbereichskommando XI during 1942. These aircraft were transferred from Mamaia, Romania, to Varna, Bulgaria, as the Russians advanced, before moving to Athens. From here they were used as transports during the evacuation of Crete.

With white Mediterranean theatre bands, this Do 24T-2 served with 7. Seenotstaffel/SBK XI in the Aegean during 1942. The aircraft subsequently transferred to SBK XII, which flew the last German aircraft (a Do 24) out of the Crimea in 1944. The legend on the nose reads 'Asbach Uralt', a popular brand of German brandy.

The **Do 24T-2**, introduced in 1943, replaced the French 20-mm cannon with a German MG 151, and had improved radio equipment. Do 24s served with Luftwaffe *Seenotstaffeln* on every front, initially augmenting and then replacing Heinkel He 59s and Do 18s. When not performing in the air-sea rescue role, the Do 24s undertook troop transport, resupply and even convoy escort and maritime reconnaissance duties. During March 1943, when the thaw made it impossible for land-based aircraft to resupply the Kuban bridgehead, 22 Do 24Ts carried in 1000 tonnes (1,102 tons) of supplies, evacuating the wounded on their return journeys. Later in 1943, Do 24s evacuated the German garrisons from various Greek islands, including Crete, flying 24 men each with 30 kg (66 lb) of equipment on each flight.

In the rescue role, Do 24Ts served in the Arctic, the Mediterranean, the English Channel, the North Sea and the Atlantic, epic rescues including the recovery of a fighter pilot who ditched just off the Scillies, and the rescue of the crew of a meteorological aircraft 563 km (350 miles) out into the Atlantic. Perhaps the Dornier's greatest strength was its ruggedness, which enabled it to operate in terrible sea states. On one occasion, a Do 24T lost its entire tail unit and part of the rear fuselage after landing to pick up survivors, but taxied back to the Kjølle Fjord after sealing all the watertight bulkheads and crowding everyone into the bows to compensate for the lost tail.

During the last months of the war, the rescue organisation formed its own defence unit with Me 410s following increasing losses to enemy fighters. The aircraft slowly withdrew to northern Germany, the survivors congregating at Sylt, where most were captured and scrapped by the Allies. One aircraft was used as a gunnery target by the RAF, but refused to sink and had to be scuttled by charge, an indication of the type's considerable ruggedness. Variants were few, but included the experimental **Do 318 V1**, which tested a boundary-layer control system in 1944, and a very small number of **Do 24MS** aircraft with a degaussing loop and onboard field generators for the mine-sweeping role.

Specification
Dornier Do 24T-1
Type: air-sea rescue and transport flying-boat
Powerplant: three BMW-Bramo 323R-2 Fafnir nine-cylinder radial engines, each rated at 746 kW (1,000 hp) for take-off
Performance: maximum speed 331 km/h (206 mph); service ceiling 7500 m (24,605 ft); range 4700 km (2,920 miles)
Weights: empty 9400 kg (20,723 lb); maximum overload 18400 kg (40,565 lb)
Dimensions: wing span 27.00 m (88 ft 6⅞ in); length 22.05 m (72 ft 4 in); height 5.75 m (18 ft 10⅛ in); wing area 108 m² (1,162.5 sq ft)
Armament: one 7.9-mm (0.31-in) MG 15 machine-gun in bow and stern turrets and one 20-mm Hispano Suiza 404 cannon in dorsal turret

The Do 24T-1 excelled in the rescue role. Two hatches were cut into the port side at roughly dinghy level, while the cabin had six bunks for survivors and emergency medical equipment was carried.

Twelve **Do 24T-3**s (similar to the Do 24T-2) were also supplied to Spain in June 1944. These aircraft were destined to enjoy a long and productive life, finally being retired in 1970. A single aircraft was used as an aerodynamic testbed for a new wing design by Dornier under the designation **Do 24TT**, first flying in its new configuration on 24 April 1983, paving the way for the high-technology SeaStar.

Above: Most, but not all, Do 24T-2s were fitted with a 20-mm MG 151 cannon in the dorsal turret in place of the French-built weapon of the T-1. The stern and bow turrets retained the ubiquitous MG 15 free-firing gun.

Right: It is believed that only two aircraft were modified to Do 24MS standard for mine-sweeping, fitted with a dural hoop and onboard field-generating equipment. These may have served operationally with the Minensuchgruppe.

Dornier Do 26

Aerodynamically the cleanest of the Dornier flying-boats, the all-metal Dornier **Do 26** was developed for transatlantic mail services, designed to carry a crew of four and 500 kg (1,102 lb) of mail between Lisbon and New York. The mid-span stabilising floats retracted completely into the wings, and the rear pair of the two tandem pairs of Junkers Jumo 205 diesel engines could be given an upward tilt of 10° on take-off so that the three-bladed metal propellers were clear of the spray from the hull. Three Do 26s, stressed for catapult launching from support ships, were ordered by Deutsche Lufthansa in 1937, and the first of these was flown on 21 May 1938. Two of the three (**V1** and **V2**) were completed before the outbreak of World War II and were delivered to the airline under the designation **Do 26A**. They were never used as intended, across the

The V6 was the last Do 26 to be built, seeing service in the Norwegian campaign as a transport.

North Atlantic, and made just 18 crossings of the South Atlantic. The **V3** was intended to be the prototype for the **Do 26B** with a cabin for four passengers and VDM propellers, while the **V4**, **V5** and **V6** were intended to be **Do 26C**s with accommodation for eight passengers. However, with the outbreak of war, all four boats were completed to Luftwaffe specifications as **Do 26D-0**s.

These featured Jumo 205D engines and were armed with three 7.92-mm (0.31 in) MG 15 machine-guns in two beam positions and a watertight position in the rear hull, and a bow turret containing a 20-mm MG 151b cannon. Along with the V2, the four Do 26Ds were assigned to 1./Küstenfliegergruppe 406 (later

1./KüFlGr 506) for transport and maritime reconnaissance duties. The unit took part in the Norwegian campaign, flying troops and supplies into fjords. Two were shot down by RAF Hurricanes on 28 May 1940, one managing an emergency landing only to be captured by Norwegian forces. The remaining three continued on transport work until the fall of Norway, when

they were withdrawn from front-line use and emplyed on communications work until spares difficulties forced their total retirement.

Specification
Dornier Do 26D-0
Type: coastal patrol and transport flying-boat
Powerplant: four 656-kW (880-hp) Junkers Jumo 205D diesel engines
Performance: maximum speed 323 km/h (201 mph); long-range cruising speed 257 km/h (160 mph); service ceiling 4500 m (14,765 ft); maximum range 7100 km (4,410 miles)
Weights: empty 11300 kg (24,912 lb); maximum overload 22500 kg (49,600 lb)
Dimensions: span 30.00 m (98 ft 5 in); length 24.60 m (80 ft 8½ in); height 6.85 m (22 ft 6 in); wing area 120.00 m² (1,291.71 sq ft)
Armament: one 20-mm MG 151 cannon in bow turret; two 7.9-mm (0.31-in) MG 15 machine-guns firing rearwards from beam turrets and a similar weapon firing from rear lower fuselage

An unusual feature of the Do 26 was the raising of the rear engines for take-off.

Dornier Do 217

In 1937 the RLM had called for an enlarged Do 17Z with much heavier bomb load and considerably greater fuel capacity, able to accept any of a range of engines, and equally capable at level or dive bombing. First flown in August 1938, the **Do 217 V1** was powered by 802-kW (1,075-hp) DB 601A engines but, despite its similar appearance to the Do 17/215, it was a totally new design. It soon showed that it was less pleasant to fly, and in fact crashed, but development continued. Prototypes flew with Junkers Jumo 211A and BMW 139 engines before the big BMW 801 was used in the **Do 217 V9** prototype of January 1940. By this time handling was acceptable, the leading edges of the fins being slotted, but the unique dive-brake, which opened like a giant cross at the extreme tail, caused endless difficulty. In mid-1941, after wing brakes had been tried and several aircraft lost, the RLM abandoned its stance that the heavy Do 217 had to be a dive-bomber.

The first aircraft into service was the batch of eight **Do 217A-0**s, built for the reconnaissance role and serving with Aufklärungsgruppe Ob.d.L. Delivered to this special unit in the spring of 1940, the aircraft undertook clandestine reconnaissance missions in the winter over the Soviet Union, in preparation for the invasion of that country. The equivalent **Do 217C** bomber did not enter service, and the A-0s remained the only examples of the 'thin-body' 217s to see service.

In early 1940 the V9 prototype appeared, this being a radically

The Do 217 V4 illustrates the early thin-body configuration of the bomber. It was the first prototype with armament.

modified bomber with a much deeper fuselage throughout its length. Entering service in late 1940, the **Do 217E-1** was the first 'deep-body' model, able to carry the massive bomb load of 4000 kg (8,818 lb), of which 2517 kg (5,550 lb) was inside the bomb bay. A handful to fly, but still a most effective bomber, the Do 217E-1 had a hand-held 20-mm MG FF in the nose, used by KG 40 against ships in the Atlantic, and seven MG 15s. The **Do 217E-2** introduced the EDL 131 electric dorsal turret with the excellent MG 131 gun, a hand-aimed MG 131 being in the ventral position, a fixed MG 151/15 firing ahead and three hand-aimed MG 15s completing the defence, although R19 (the 19th in the *Rustsätze* series of field kits) added twin or quadruple MG 81 machine-guns firing aft from the tailcone. Other *Rustsätze* added barrage cable cutters and various weapon kits, by far the biggest of which hung two Hs 293 anti-ship missiles under the wings, with Kehl/Strassburg radio command guidance link. The first operational missile carrier was the **Do 217E-5**, flown by II/KG 100,

Dornier Do 217

Above: Seen in late 1942, this aircraft is a Do 217E-4 of II Gruppe/Kampfgeschwader 40. This group had been the first to put the Do 217E into action, employed on anti-shipping duties against the British. Note the lateral-firing MG 15 in the aft portion of the flight deck.

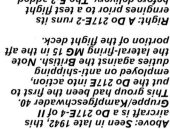

Right: A Do 217E-2 runs its engines prior to a test flight before delivery. The E-2 added an MG 131 in an electrically-operated dorsal turret in the rear of the flight deck, greatly enhancing defensive armament. A similar weapon was housed in the ventral step position.

change in the Do 217J night-fighter was the nose. Instead of a multi-pane Plexiglas nose for a bomb aimer, the J-1 had a 'solid' nose in which were installed four 20-mm MG FF cannon and four 7.92-mm MG 17 machine-guns. The E-2's aft defensive armament, comprising an MG 131 dorsal turret and a hand-aimed MG 131 in the ventral position, was retained unchanged. The J-1 was operational from February 1942. Crews liked its firepower and endurance, but found it a rather heavy brute which was sluggish when fast manoeuvres were called for (not often) and needed bigger airfields than most of those that were available. More serious was the lack of airborne radar, although in 1941-42 most Luftwaffe night-fighter pilots were far from convinced that such new gimmicks were worth having.

Radar fighter

Dornier has no record of the first flight of a **Do 217J-2**, with FuG 202 Lichtenstein BC radar, but it was probably in the spring of 1942. The J-2 was a definitive night-fighter, not an intruder, the bomb bays being eliminated. The J-2 was lighter than previous Do 217 versions, and despite the 'mattress' of radar antennas Do 217J performance was almost the same as before. Only small numbers were built, and few combat missions were flown before 1943.

Despite its later suffix letter, the corresponding Daimler Benz night-fighter, the **Do 217N**, flew as early as 31 July 1942, the DB 603 engine installation having been designed in 1941. Production **Do 217N-1** began to reach the Luftwaffe in January 1943. By this time, critical feedback about the 217J had been going on for many months, and the NJG crews were disappointed to find the N-1 incorporated none of their mostly obvious recommendations. This was largely because the RLM, and Erhard Milch in particular, disallowed any modifications that would reduce output or increase costs. By mid-1943, however, Dornier had switched to the N-2, and also produced the U1 conversion set with which existing night-fighters could be modified. The chief changes were to remove the dorsal turret and lower rear gun gondola and add wooden fairings. The reduction in drag and removal of some weight of some 2 tonnes (2.2 tons) of

which went into action with increasingly devastating effect against British ships from 25 August 1943.

Kampfgeschwader 2 was the only wing to be totally equipped with Do 217Es, and for most of its career operated from bases in the Netherlands against Britain, taking part in the 'little Blitz' in 1944. KG 40 had been the first operator of the Do 217E, beginning anti-ship operations in the spring of 1941 but giving up its Dorniers in 1943. In April 1943, II/KG 100 equipped with the Do 217E-5/Hs 293 combination, while III/KG 100 operated the Do 217K-2/FX 1400. Other units which operated the type were I and III/KG 66 for bomber operations, and Versuchskommando/KG 200, which flew the type's last operational sortie on 12 April 1945 when Do 217E-5s launched Hs 293 glide bombs against bridges over the Oder.

With the Do 217E sub-types, Dornier got the much heavier Do 217 family into service; and all subsequent models proved adequate but generally (and, in the case of the Do 217K-2, severely) underpowered. Despite this, and the absence of the 1491-kW (2,000-hp) engines that were needed, Dornier proposed in early 1941 to develop a night intruder fighter version. The main, and obvious,

A complete reworking of the basic design introduced the Do 217E, with a much deeper fuselage to allow the carriage of large bomb loads. This aircraft is the sixth pre-production Do 217E-0.

An important aircraft in the development of the Do 217 was this Do 17M-1, which tested the strange cruciform tail airbrake. The arrangement worked well here, but not on the 217.

Left: This Do 217E-2/R19 of 9./KG 2 has two remotely-controlled 7.9-mm (0.31-in) MG 81 machine-guns in the tailcone.

With a redesigned nose packed with guns, the Do 217J was the night-fighter/intruder version of the Do 217E. This example, the Do 217J-2, differed from the J-1 by having radar fitted and the bomb bay deleted.

Above: To safeguard against non-delivery of the BMW engines, Dornier adapted the K-model to take the DB 603A engine. This example being similar in performance and produced in parallel. This example belly-landed in good condition during a 1944 attack on London, and was subsequently repaired.

Above: A marshall waves out a III/KG 2 Do 217E-4 for a mission. Visible in the nose glazing is the MG 15 operated by the navigator/bombardier, and below the glazing is the barrel for the fixed MG 151/15 cannon, aimed by the pilot. Do 217s intended primarily for the anti-shipping mission had this latter weapon replaced by a 20-mm MG FF.

Left: Ground crew manhandle a bomb towards the waiting bay of a Do 217E-1. The aircraft wears a crude Wellenmüster scheme, indicating a primary overwater role. The Do 217E had a long bomb bay which reached from the ventral step to the fuselage cross marking. Normal internal loads consisted of eight 250-kg (551-lb) bombs, four 500-kg (1,102-lb) bombs or a combination of two 1000-kg (2,205-lb) and two 250-kg (551-lb) weapons.

Below: The combination of the dorsal turret and lateral-firing weapons gave a good field of fire, but all were operated by just the radio operator.

performance to a useful level, maximum speed at medium heights exceeding 500 km/h (310 mph). With the devastating armament of four MG 151s and four MG 17s firing ahead, and four more MG 151s firing at 70° upwards, the **Do 217N-2** was a vast improvement over the J-1, and soon appeared with the FuG 220 Lichtenstein SN-2 radar. By 1944, 217Js and Ns were scattered over a vast area of Germany and the occupied countries, as well as serving with I/NJG 100 on the Eastern Front. Only 364 Do 217Js and Do 217Ns were delivered, and they had faded from the NJG (night-fighter wings) front line by mid-1944.

The next major bomber version was the **Do 217K-1**, which began to come off production in about October 1942. It was similar to the later E-series, and it was likewise intended for night bombing. The only significant changes were fitting BMW 801D engines, giving a maximum power of 1268 kW (1,700 hp), and a redesign of the forward fuselage. There had been nothing particularly wrong with the original cockpit of the Do 172/215/217E, but Dornier – influenced by Junkers' development of the Ju 88B/188 – developed a nose similar to that of the He 177, with the front glazed part continued up to the top of the fuselage. This had the slight drawback of making the pilot look ahead through distant Plexiglas on which he tended to mis-focus his eyes, especially when the panes reflected lighted parts of the cockpit. Initially, the K-1 had twin MG 81Z twin 7.92-mm guns in the nose, two single MG 81s firing to the sides/rear, an MG 131 in the dorsal turret and another MG 131 in the rear ventral position. Later, two more MG 81s were added firing to the sides. It was possible to fit the R19 installation of one or two MG 81Z firing astern from the tailcone, but it was more common to have the R25 installation of a Perlon dive-bombing parachute. Not many K-1s were built, and at least one was fitted with underwing racks for no fewer than four LT F5b torpedoes.

Dornier Do 217

Dornier Do 217 variants

Do 217 V1: first prototype of new bomber, based on Do 17 but enlarged; powered by DB 603A

Do 217 V2 and V3: second and third prototypes with Jumo 211

Do 217 V4: fourth prototype with Jumo 211 and defensive armament fitted

Do 217 V1E: fifth prototype produced as replacement for V1 which was lost in single-engined testing accident; V1E fitted with rod and pulley controls in place of cables

Do 217 V5 and V6: similar to V1E and used for various trials during 1939

Do 217 V7 and V8: two prototypes powered by BMW 139 radial

Do 217 V9: prototype for Do 217E series

Do 217A-0: pre-production long-range reconnaissance aircraft with forward fuselage bulge extended aft to house cameras; powered by DB 601A; eight were built, seeing service with special reconnaissance units

Do 217C V1: single Jumo 211-powered prototype for bomber version, lacking extended fuselage bulge with fully bomb bay fitted

Do 217C-0: DB 601A-powered pre-production bomber (four built) with additional defensive armament including nose-mounted MG 151/15 cannon

Do 217E-0: pre-production bomber with BMW 801MA radials and deepened fuselage throughout

Do 217E-1: production bomber with five 7.9-mm (0.31-in) MG 15 machine-guns firing through the sides and rear

Do 217E-2: improved bomber with turret in rear of cockpit for single 13-mm MG 131 machine-gun, and a similar weapon replacing the ventral 15-mm MG FF; two further MG 15s added to cockpit glazing and free-mounted 20-mm MG FF cannon added in nose for anti-shipping role; fixed 15-mm MG 151 often replaced by 20-mm MG FF; various *Rüstsätze* (field conversion sets) available for this and other variants, including R1 for carrying a 1800-kg (3,968-lb) bomb, R2 external bomb racks, R4 torpedo carrier, R5 for adding a 30-mm MK 101 cannon in lower port side of fuselage, R6 bomb bay camera installation, R7 emergency dinghy pack, R8, R9, R13, R14 and R17 auxiliary fuel tanks, and R25 for HS 293 missiles, R19 which added an MG 81Z twin-gun installation in the tail

Do 217E-3: bomber with BMW 801ML powerplant with revised propellers

Do 217E-4: similar to E-2/3 but with BMW 801C engines and *Kuto-Nase* balloon cable-cutters set in the wing leading edges

Do 217E-5: built as dedicated launchers for the HS 293 stand-off missile, with ETC 2000/XII carrier under each wing, FuG 203b Kehl III transmitter and *Knüppel* joystick for the bombardier to guide the missile

Do 217H: single conversion of Do 217E with DB 601 engines and experimental turbo-chargers for high-altitude trials

Do 217J-1: night-fighter/intruder version of Do 217E-2 with 'solid' nose housing four 7.9-mm MG 17 machine-guns and four 20-mm MG FF cannon; MG 131 upper turret and aft-firing MG 131 retained

Do 217J-2: similar to J-1 but with FF cannon; MG 131 upper turret and aft-firing MG 131 retained

Do 217K-1: standard bomber version returning to twin-fin configuration with twin MG 81 machine-gun installation in nose, two (later four) more firing from cockpit beam positions, dorsal turret with single MG 131 and similar weapon in ventral position

Do 217K-2: specialist version for carriage of Fritz X glide bomb; extended-span wings and carriage between fuselage and nacelles, FuG 203a Kehl I guidance equipment

Do 217K-3: similar to K-2 but with FuG 203c or d Kehl IV transmitter for guiding both Fritz X and HS 293

Do 217M-1: parallel version of Do 217K-1 but with DB 603A engines

Do 217M-5/11: two aircraft for carriage of HS 293 (M-5) or either Fritz X or HS 293 (M-11) in semi-recessed bay in fuselage

Do 217N-1/U1: 20-mm MG 151/20 cannon replacing MG FF, and both aft-firing MG 131s removed; some aircraft modified as Do 217N-1/U1 later, FuG 212 radar introduced

Do 217N-2: embodied improvements of Do 217N-1/U1; later added FuG 220 Lichtenstein SN-2 radar, but continued to carry FuG 202 Lichtenstein BC radar and *Matratzen* antenna array; powered by BMW 801ML engines

Do 217P V1: prototype of high-altitude bomber with two DB 603B engines and single DB 605T in an HZ-*Anlage* arrangement, the DB 605 being mounted in the fuselage (with underside airscoops) to supercharge the main engines; four-man crew in pressure cabin

Do 217P V2 and V3: similar to V1 but with extended-span wings

Do 217R: designation of five Do 317A aircraft completed without pressurisation for use as HS 293 carriers for KG 100

Do 317 V1: Dornier contender for 'Bomber B' contest, based closely on Do 217 but with pressurised cabin and triangular tailfins

Do 317A: intended production version, six DB 603A engines, of which five used as Do 317Rs built;

Do 317B: more ambitious version with DB 610 coupled engines, extended wing and remotely-controlled defensive gun barbettes; not built

Running a few weeks later in timing, the **Do 217K-2** was the heaviest of all production 217s, at 16850 kg (37,147 lb). It was specifically developed to carry the FX 1400 radio-controlled heavy bomb, the He 111H having been found not really suitable for the task. The massive bombs, also known as 'Fritz X', were slung on special racks under the inner wings. An extra fuel tank of 1160-litre (255-Imp gal) capacity was fitted into the forward bomb bay. To carry the greatly increased weight, the outer wings were extended in span from 19 to 24.8 m (62 ft 4 in to 81 ft 4 in), and handling and overall performance remained satisfactory. Almost all K-2s had the R19 fitting of twin MG 81Z guns (four in all) in the tail, and some even had an MG 81Z firing aft from the tail from the tail of each engine nacelle.

KG 2 became the only *Geschwader* to be completely equipped with the Do 217. Originally beginning replacement of the Do 17Z in 1941, KG 2 pulled back from the Russian Front and relocated to the Netherlands for bombing and anti-shipping strikes over the North Sea. The wing stayed there until September 1944, taking part in numerous cross-Channel operations, including *Operation Steinbock*, the so-called 'little Blitz' of January 1944 mounted by Hitler as a reprisal for the RAF's nightly bombing raids. Here, Do 217Es of III./KG 2 taxi out from Gilze-Rijen in March 1942. Other KG 2 aircraft were at Eindhoven.

Right: Do 217E-5 of II./KG 100, carrying the Henschel Hs 293 guided bomb under the ETC 2000/XII wing racks.

Above: Do 217E-2 of 6./KG 40, based at Bordeaux-Mérignac for anti-shipping duties.

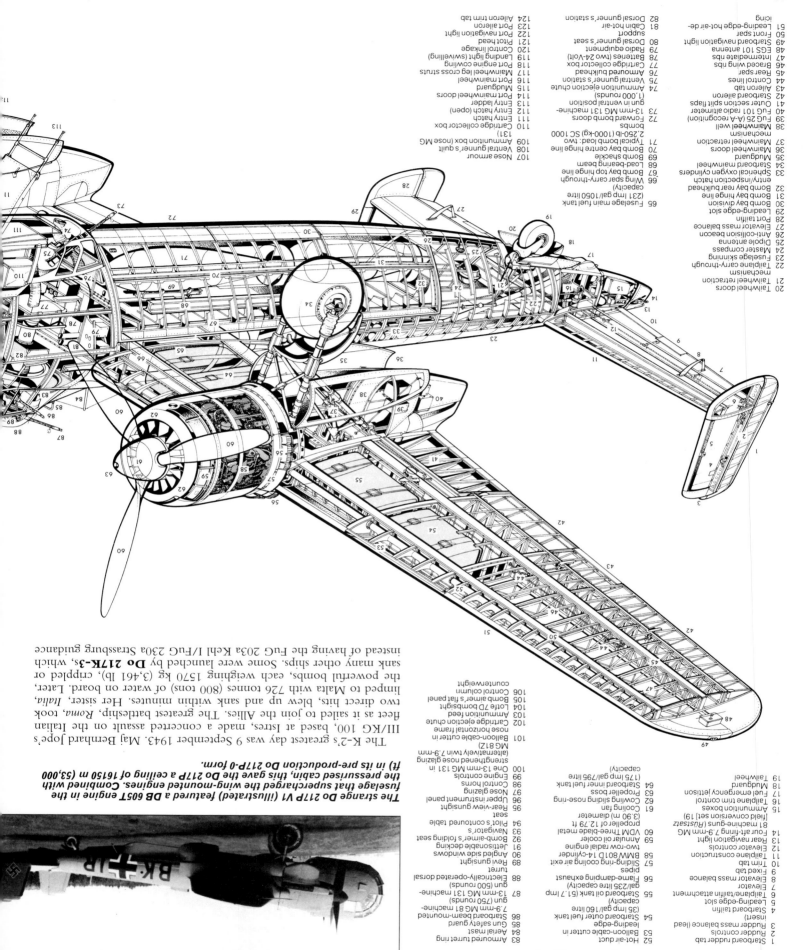

Dornier Do 217

Dornier Do 217K-1 cutaway drawing key

1 Starboard rudder tab
2 Rudder controls
3 Rudder mass balance (lead insert)
4 Starboard tailfin
5 Leading-edge slot
6 Tailplane/tailfin attachment
7 Starboard tailplane
8 Elevator mass balance
9 Fixed tab
10 Trim tab
11 Tailplane construction
12 Elevator controls
13 Rear navigation light
14 Four aft-firing 7.9-mm MG 81 machine-guns (Rüstsatz field conversion set 19)
15 Ammunition boxes
16 Tailplane trim control
17 Fuel emergency jettison
18 Mudguard
19 Tailwheel
20 Tailwheel doors
21 Tailwheel retraction mechanism
22 Tailplane carry-through mechanism
23 Fuselage skinning
24 Master compass
25 Dipole antenna
26 Anti-collision beacon
27 Elevator mass balance
28 Port tailfin
29 Leading-edge slot
30 Bomb bay division
31 Bomb bay hinge line
32 Bomb bay rear bulkhead entry/inspection hatch
33 Spherical oxygen cylinders
34 Starboard mainwheel
35 Mudguard
36 Mainwheel doors
37 Mainwheel retraction mechanism
38 Mainwheel well
39 FuG 25 (A-A recognition)
40 FuG 101 radio altimeter
41 Outer section split flaps
42 Starboard aileron
43 Aileron tab
44 Control lines
45 Rear spar
46 Braced wing ribs
47 Intermediate ribs
48 EGS 101 antenna
49 Starboard navigation light
50 Front spar
51 Leading-edge hot-air de-icing

52 Hot-air duct
53 Balloon-cable cutter in leading-edge
54 Starboard outer fuel tank (35 Imp gal/160 litre capacity)
55 Starboard oil tank (51.7 Imp gal/235 litre capacity)
56 Flame-damping exhaust pipes
57 Sliding-ring cooling air exit
58 BMW 801D 14-cylinder two-row radial engine
59 Annular oil cooler
60 VDM Three-blade metal propeller of 12.79 ft (3.90 m) diameter
61 Cooling fan
62 Cowling sliding nose-ring
63 Propeller boss
64 Starboard inner fuel tank (175 Imp gal/795 litre capacity)
65 Fuselage main fuel tank (231 Imp gal/1050 litre capacity)
66 Wing spar carry-through
67 Bomb bay top hinge line
68 Load-bearing beam
69 Bomb shackle
70 Bomb bay centre hinge line
71 Typical bomb load: two 2,250-lb (1000-kg) SC 1000 bombs
72 Forward bomb doors
73 13-mm MG 131 machine-gun in ventral position (1,000 rounds)
74 Ammunition ejection chute
75 Ventral gunner's station
76 Armoured bulkhead
77 Cartridge collector box
78 Batteries (two 24-Volt)
79 Radio equipment
80 Dorsal gunner's seat
81 Cabin hot-air support
82 Dorsal gunner's station

83 Armoured turret ring
84 Aerial mast
85 Gun safety guard
86 Starboard beam-mounted 7.9-mm MG 81 machine-gun (750 rounds) capacity
87 13-mm MG 131 machine-gun (500 rounds)
88 Electrically-operated dorsal turret
89 Revi gunsight
90 Angled side windows
91 Jettisonable decking
92 Bomb-aimer's folding seat
93 Navigator's seat
94 Pilot's contoured table
95 Rear-view gunsight seat
96 Upper instrument panel
97 Nose glazing
98 Control horns
99 Engine controls
100 One 13-mm MG 131 (175 Imp gal/795 litre capacity)
101 Balloon-cable cutter in nose horizontal frame
102 Cartridge ejection chute
103 Ammunition feed
104 Lotfe 7D bombsight
105 Bomb-aimer's flat panel
106 Control column counterweight
107 Nose armour
108 Ventral gunner's quilt
109 Ammunition box (nose MG 131)
110 Cartridge collector box
111 Entry hatch
112 Entry hatch (open)
113 Entry ladder
114 Port mainwheel doors
115 Mudguard
116 Port mainwheel
117 Mainwheel leg cross struts
118 Port engine cowling
119 Landing light (swivelling)
120 Control linkage
121 Pitot head
122 Port navigation light
123 Port aileron
124 Aileron trim tab

The strange Do 217P V1 (illustrated) featured a DB 605T engine in the fuselage that supercharged the wing-mounted engines. Combined with the pressurised cabin, this gave the Do 217P a ceiling of 16150 m (53,000 ft) in its pre-production Do 217P-0 form.

The K-2's greatest day was 9 September 1943. Maj Bernhard Jope's III/KG 100, based at Istres, made a concerted assault on the Italian fleet as it sailed to join the Allies. The greatest battleship, *Roma*, took two direct hits, blew up and sank within minutes. Her sister, *Italia*, limped to Malta with 726 tonnes (800 tons) of water on board. Later, the powerful bombs, each weighing 1570 kg (3,461 lb), crippled or sank many other ships. Some were launched by Do 217K-3s, which instead of having the FuG 203a Kehl I/FuG 230a Strassburg guidance

Intended primarily as a night-bomber, the Do 217K-1 introduced BMW 801D radials and a redesigned forward fuselage, giving the aircraft a bulbous look by eliminating the stepped cockpit. This aircraft wears the badge of Luftflotte 2 on the nose.

link, had the FuG 203c or 203d Kehl IV with which the bomb aimer could guide either FX 1400 or the smaller Hs 293A winged bomb.

The other production Do 217 family was the M bombers. Structurally, these were similar to earlier versions; in fact, the first **Do 217M** was merely a K-1 fitted with Daimler Benz DB 603A liquid-cooled engines, each of 1380 kW (1,850 max hp). The **M-1** went into production almost straight away, being very similar to a K-1 except for having slightly better performance at high altitude. Not many were built, the need for night-fighters being more pressing, but one achieved notoriety on the night of 23 February 1944 when it made a perfect belly landing near Cambridge (and was soon flying in RAF markings), the crew having baled out over 100 km (62 miles) away, near London.

Even at light weights, height could not be maintained on one engine and, as with all the Do 217s, the feeling was that there was too much aeroplane for the available wing area and power.

Various related aircraft which never entered service were all intended for flight at high altitudes. First to be started, as an entry in the 1939-40 Bomber B requirement, was the **Do 317**. This was to be basically a 217 with DB 604 engines, each with four banks totalling 24 cylinders and giving a maximum power of 1984 kW (2,660 hp) each, and with a four-seat pressurised cabin in the nose. In 1940 this was dropped and some of its features used to assist development of the **Do 217P**, which had a similar pressure cabin but was powered by two DB 603B engines supercharged by a large two-stage blower and intercooler in the rear fuselage, driven by a third engine, a DB 605T. The first 217P flew in June 1942, and there were plans for a production **Do 217P-1** reconnaissance aircraft with almost the same extended outer wings as the K-2 (raising service ceiling to an estimated 16154 m/53,000 ft), but this was abandoned.

Meanwhile, in late 1941, the Do 317 was resurrected, and in early 1943 the first 317 began flight testing. This was planned in two versions. The **Do 317A** was a broadly conventional high-altitude bomber with DB 603A engines, outwardly having much in common with the 217M apart from an odd tail with triangular vertical surfaces. The next-generation **Do 317B** was to have had extended wings of 26 m (85 ft) span, huge DB 610 double engines each of 2141 kW (2,870 hp), and defensive armament comprising a remotely-controlled 20-mm MG 151 in the tailcone and three twin-gun turrets, two of them remotely controlled. Eventually the 317 also ground to a halt, but five of the 317A series prototypes were modified as unpressurised launch aircraft for the Hs 293A radio-controlled missiles. Redesignated as Do 217Rs, they saw combat duty with III/KG 100 at Orléans-Bricy in 1944. At 17770 kg (39,021 lb), they were the heaviest of the whole 217/317 family to fly, although, had they gone ahead, the 317A and 317B would have been much heavier still.

Total Do 217 production amounted to 1,541 bombers and 364 night-fighters.

The Do 317 was an advanced extension of the Do 17/217 line, featuring a pressurised cabin. No real increase in performance over the Do 217P was found and, apart from the Do 317 V1 (illustrated), the other five prototypes were completed without pressurisation and used by KG 100.

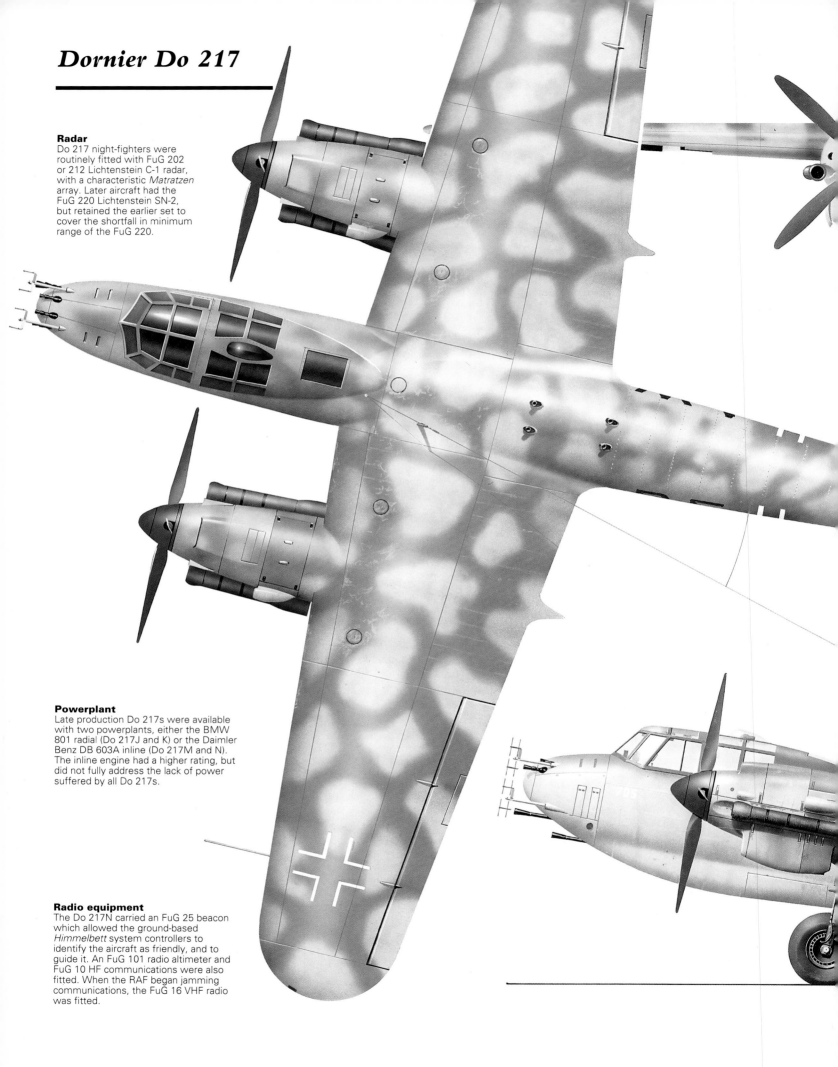

Dornier Do 217

Radar
Do 217 night-fighters were routinely fitted with FuG 202 or 212 Lichtenstein C-1 radar, with a characteristic *Matratzen* array. Later aircraft had the FuG 220 Lichtenstein SN-2, but retained the earlier set to cover the shortfall in minimum range of the FuG 220.

Powerplant
Late production Do 217s were available with two powerplants, either the BMW 801 radial (Do 217J and K) or the Daimler Benz DB 603A inline (Do 217M and N). The inline engine had a higher rating, but did not fully address the lack of power suffered by all Do 217s.

Radio equipment
The Do 217N carried an FuG 25 beacon which allowed the ground-based *Himmelbett* system controllers to identify the aircraft as friendly, and to guide it. An FuG 101 radio altimeter and FuG 10 HF communications were also fitted. When the RAF began jamming communications, the FuG 16 VHF radio was fitted.

Operations
The N-2 was the best of the Do 217 night-fighter variants, but it remained underpowered and its high wing loading did not confer much agility. Nevertheless, it was a stable gun platform and very hard-hitting. During the early days of the night war, the type often operated with Messerschmitt Bf 110s in a hunter-killer team, using its radar to direct the more nimble fighters into the attack.

Dornier Do 217N-2/R22

In production from the spring of 1943 until late in that year, the Do 217N-2 embodied as standard all the production developments, made to the N-1. Many aircraft were modified like this one to Do 217N-2/R22 standard, with the four *schräge Musik* cannon in the fuselage. As well as subsequently gaining Lichtenstein SN-2 radar, the Do 217N-2 also later featured the FuG 227 Flensburg set, which homed in on the emissions of the RAF's Monica tail-warning radar, and the FuG 350 Naxos tuned to H$_2$S bombing radar frequencies.

Markings
This aircraft wears typical night-fighter markings, consisting of mottled light greys. It wears factory codes (used as radio call-signs) prior to delivery to an operational unit.

Specification
Dornier Do 217N-2/R22
Type: four-seat night-interceptor and intruder-fighter
Powerplant: two Daimler Benz DB 603A 12-cylinder liquid-cooled engines, each rated at 1305 kW (1,750 hp) for take-off and 1380 kW (1,850 hp) at 2100 m (6,889 ft)
Performance: maximum speed 425 km/h (264 mph) at sea level; 500 km/h (310 mph) at 6000 m (19,685 ft); maximum cruising speed 465 km/h (289 mph) at 5400 m (17,716 ft); economical cruising speed 420 km/h (261 mph) at 5400 m (17,716 ft); time to 4000 m (13,123 ft) 11 minutes; time to 6000 m (19,685 ft) 17 minutes; service ceiling 8400 m (27,559 ft); normal range 1755 km (1,090 miles)
Weights: empty equipped 19780 kg (43,607 lb); loaded 13700 kg (30,202 lb)
Dimensions: wing span 19.0 m (62 ft 4 in); length (including aerials) 18.90 m (62 ft 0 in); height 5.0 m (16 ft 5 in); wing area 57 m^2 (614 sq ft)
Armament: four 7.9-mm MG 17 machine-guns in fuselage nose; four 20-mm MG 151 cannon in lower nose; four 20-mm MG 151 cannon firing upwards from central fuselage, tilted forward 70°

Armament
The Do 217N-2 dispensed with the rearward-facing armament (with a considerable weight-saving), and relied on the four-gun, four-cannon nose armament and the *schräge* Musik installation. The original MG FF cannon were very reliable, but were replaced by MG 151/20s offering a much higher muzzle velocity and better rate of fire

Iain Wyllie

Dornier Do 335 Pfeil

No-one can accuse the World War II German aircraft designers of conservatism and, while the majority of combat aircraft were of conventional design, there were many others which pushed the forefront of aeronautics. Unhampered by tradition, German designers sought fresh means to solve old problems, and in so doing provided the Allies in both East and West with a wealth of advanced research material following the end of hostilities. One of the most famous of the bizarre shapes which took to the air over Germany was the **Dornier Do 335 Pfeil**, a brave attempt to provide the Luftwaffe with a potent fighter-bomber, night-fighter and reconnaissance platform.

Prof Dr Claudius Dornier was the genius behind the famous company of Dornier-Werke GmbH, and he had established a long line of successful aircraft, notably in the field of flying-boats. For most of the late 1930s and World War II, Dornier was primarily concerned with the production of bombers for the Luftwaffe. Since the end of World War I, Claudius Dornier had been interested in the field of centre-line thrust, whereby two engines shared the same thrust line – one pulling and one pushing. Benefits of this system were obvious over a conventional twin layout, with only the same frontal area as a single-engined aircraft, the wing left clean of engine nacelles and attendant structures, and no asymmetric pull if one engine cut out. However, problems did exist in the area of the drive shaft which drove the rear propeller.

Dornier's extensive flying-boat experience gave him a wealth of knowledge in simple centreline thrust arrangements, where two engines were mounted back-to-back over the centreline of many of his designs. By the mid-1930s, he saw the possibility of using this concept to power a high-speed fighter, but first the rear engine extension shaft arrangement had to be proved. To that end Ulrich Hutter was commissioned to design a small testbed for the arrangement. Designated the **Göppingen Go 9**, and built by Schempp-Hirth, the testbed featured a pencil-slim fuselage contained a 59.6-kW (80-hp) Hirth HM 60R engine mounted at the centre of gravity beneath the shoulder-set wing. Stalky main undercarriage units retracted into the wing, while a nosewheel unit retracted forward into the extreme nose. Behind the wing a long and slender tail boom hid the drive shaft, which extended past a cruciform tail to a four-bladed wooden propeller.

Fighter or bomber?

Flying for the first time in 1940, the Go 9 proved that the rear pusher principle was both efficient and safe, which gave Dornier new impetus to his fighter designs taking shape on the drawing boards. However, the Technische Amt of the RLM decreed that Dornier abandon his work with fighters and return to the main job in hand of producing bombers and flying-boats, despite some initial interest in his

The Do 335 V1 first prototype first flew on 26 October 1943, and is seen here during an early flight. It differed from subsequent prototypes in having an external oil cooler intake, and single-piece circular mainwheel covers in addition to the oleo door. Later aircraft had more conventional undercarriage doors, and an enlarged annular cowling.

The second production Do 335A-0 wears werk-nr 102 on its tail. To the RLM (the German air ministry), the aircraft was known as Projekt 231, and to its test pilots it was the Pfeil (Arrow) but its prominent nose saw it dubbed 'Ameisenbär' ('ant eater') by its crews. This aircraft was eventually shipped to the USA for evaluation.

Do 335 V1 differed most obviously from subsequent prototypes in having an extra oil cooler intake underneath. The first aircraft (CP+UA) took to the air on 26 October 1943. The unusual circular mainwheel covers were unique to this aircraft.

Designed by Ulrich Hutter, the all-wooden Göppingen Go 9 was the testbed for the Do 335's aft-mounted prop design. Built by Schempp-Hirth and powered by a Hirth HM 60R engine mounted below the wing, the Go 9 attained a speed of 220 km/h (137 mph).

radical designs. Nevertheless, in 1942 the Technische Amt issued a requirement for a high-speed unarmed intruder aircraft, and Dornier submitted his **Projekt 231** design, incorporating the tractor-pusher engine arrangement. After evaluation, Dornier was awarded a development contract in the face of opposition from Arado and Junkers, and the designation **Do 335** was assigned to Projekt 231.

As design got underway, the RLM issued a new directive to redesign the Do 335 as a multi-purpose day fighter, night-fighter, fighter-bomber, *Zerstörer* and reconnaissance platform, which caused a delay in production of the prototype. By the autumn of 1943 the Do 335 was ready for flight.

Dornier's concept had emerged as a fearsome looking aircraft, appearing as purposeful as a fighter could. In the forward fuselage a Daimler-Benz DB 603 featured an annular-ring cowl, while exhaust

The first prototype Dornier Do 335 displayed remarkably good handling characteristics despite its unconventional appearance and configuration and its turn radius, in particular, was significantly better than had been expected. The aircraft did porpoise and snake at high speed, however, but not sufficiently to dampen the enthusiasm of the Rechlin test pilots. Development was remarkably rapid, but production was slow to get started.

stubs just aft of the trailing edge belied the position of the rear engine. Underneath the rear fuselage a large airscoop aspirated the second unit, which powered a three-bladed propeller mounted behind a cruciform tail. Under the centre-section of the wing were doors for a small weapons bay, capable of carrying a single 500-kg (1,100-lb) or two 250-kg (550-lb) bombs. The undercarriage was a tricycle arrangement, with the wide-track main units retracting inwards into the wing and the nosewheel retracting backwards (following a 90° rotation) into the area beneath the cockpit.

Remarkable shape, remarkable performance

The broad wing was set well back, and although the name **Pfeil** was used semi-officially, the service pilots who became acquainted with this extraordinary machine soon dubbed it 'Ameisenbär' (ant-eater), thanks to its long nose. A Dornier pilot was at the controls for the first flight from Oberpfaffenhofen, this taking place on 26 October 1943 with the **Do 335 V1** first prototype (CP+UA). After initial Dornier trials, it moved to Rechlin to begin extensive official trials. Reports from Oberpfaffenhofen and Rechlin were favourable, with only slight longitudinal stability problems encountered. Most pilots were surprised at the speed, acceleration, turning circle and general handling of the type, and development continued smoothly. Further prototypes joined Dornier and Rechlin trials, introducing new im-

provements such as redesigned undercarriage doors and blisters in the canopy accommodating mirrors for improved rearward vision.

By the fifth prototype armament had been installed, this comprising two MG 151 15-mm cannon in the upper fuselage decking and a single MK 103 30-mm cannon firing through the forward propeller hub. Subsequent prototypes were used for further flight trials and engine tests, culminating in the **Do 335 V9** built to pre-production standards. The first **Do 335A-0** pre-production aircraft (VG+PG) followed shortly in mid-1944, with full armament and ready to start operational evaluation. The Erprobungskommando 335 was established in September 1944 to conduct tactical development using many of the 10 Do 335A-0s built. Service trials began with the V9 with the Versuchsverband des Oberfehlshabers des Luftwaffe.

By late autumn in 1944, the **Do 335A-1** full production model appeared at Oberpfaffenhofen, this introducing the definitive DB 603E-1 engine and two underwing hardpoints capable of carrying fuel or 250-kg (550-lb) bombs. Similar in airframe details to the Do 335A-1 was the **Do 335A-4** unarmed reconnaissance version. Only one was completed, adapted from a Do 335A-0 with two Rb 50/18 cameras in the weapons bay and increased external fuel. DB 603G engines were to have been fitted with higher compression ratio and more powerful superchargers.

Two-seat night-fighter

Next in the line of Pfeil variants was the **Do 335A-6** (prototype **Do 335 V10**), which was the night-fighter variant. Armament remained unchanged from the fighter-bomber, but FuG 217J Neptun airborne intercept radar was added, the aerials being located forward of the wing (lateral beam port and vertical beam starboard). To operate the radar a second crewman was needed, and to accommodate him a cockpit was incorporated above and behind that of the pilot. Giving the Pfeil an even stranger appearance than before, the second cockpit also meant a considerable restructuring of the fuel system, with the weapons bay area given over to fuel carriage. The negative effect on performance of the extra cockpit, aerials, weight and other modifications such as flame-damping tubes over the exhaust ports was in the region of 10 per cent, but production aircraft would have offset this partially by being fitted with water-methanol boosted DB 603E engines, instead of the DB 603A units retained by the sole example. Production was scheduled to have been undertaken by

The Do 335 V1 is seen here landing at Rechlin. Fourteen prototypes (including some for the proposed Do 335B Zerstörer) were eventually completed and flown together with ten Do 335A-0s, eleven Do 335A-1s, and a pair of Do 335A-12 trainers. Fifteen more were in final assembly when US forces overran Dornier's Oberpfaffenhofen plant.

This was the seventh Do 335A-0 fighter to be built and was one of 10 evaluated by Erprobungskommando 335, which was formed in September 1944 to develop operational tactics for the type. The aircraft were armed with a 30-mm MK 103 cannon and a pair of 15-mm MG 151 machine-guns.

1 Upper rudder trim tab
2 Upper rudder
3 Upper tailfin (jettisonable by means of explosive bolts)
4 VDM airscrew of 3.30 m (10.83 ft) diameter
5 Airscrew spinner
6 Airscrew pitch mechanism
7 Starboard elevator
8 Elevator tab
9 Metal stressed-skin tailplane structure
10 Ventral rudder
11 Tail bumper
12 Tail bumper oleo shock-absorber

23 Coolant radiator
24 Fire extinguisher
25 Ventral air intake
26 FuG 25a IFF
27 FuG 125a blind landing receiver
28 Rear engine access cover latches
29 Exhaust stubs
30 Supercharger intake
31 Coolant tank
32 Engine bearer

13 Ventral tailfin (jettisonable for belly landing)
14 Coolant outlet
15 Rear navigation light
16 Explosive bolt seatings
17 Rudder and elevator tab controls
18 Hollow airscrew extension shaft
19 Rear airscrew lubricant feeds
20 Aft bulkhead
21 Coolant trunking
22 Oil cooler radiator

33 Aft Daimler-Benz DB 603E-1 12-cylinder inverted-Vee liquid-cooled engine rated at 1340 kW(1,800 hp) for take-off and 1415 kW (1,900 hp) at 1800 m (5,905 ft)
34 Supercharger
35 Aft firewall
36 FuG 25a ring antenna
37 Fuel filler cap
38 Main fuel tank (1 230-litre/270 Imp gal capacity)
39 Secondary ventral fuel tank

Heinkel in Vienna, but this plan was overtaken by events and the tooling was never assembled.

The final pair of **Do 355A** variants comprised the **Do 335A-10** and **Do 335A-12**, both featuring the second cockpit for use as conversion trainers. The former was powered by the DB 603A engine (prototype **Do 335 V11**) and the latter by the DB 603E (prototype **Do 335 V12**). With full controls in the raised cockpit for the instructor, the two prototypes were both delivered without armament, but this was rectified in the pair of Do 335A-12 production aircraft.

After development of fighter-bomber, reconnaissance, trainer and night-fighter variants, the role of heavy *Zerstörer* was next to be developed, as a direct result of the worsening war situation. During the winter of 1944/45, the **Do 335 V13** emerged from the

The nose-mounted Daimler-Benz DB 603A-2 engine was provided with an annular nose radiator, while the ventral scoop intake was for the aft powerplant. The tractor propeller was pitch-reversible.

40 Two (45-litre/9.9-Imp gal capacity) lubricant tanks (port for forward engine and starboard for rear engine)
41 Pilot's back armour
42 Rearview mirror in glazed teardrop
43 Headrest
44 Pilot's armoured ejection seat
45 Clear-vision panel
46 Jettisonable canopy (hinged to starboard)
47 Protected hydraulic fluid tank (45-litre/9.9-Imp gal capacity)

64 Ammunition box
65 Forward firewall
66 Breech of nose-mounted MK 103 cannon
67 Engine bearer
68 Forward DB 603E-1 engine
69 MG 151 cannon blast tubes
70 Gun trough
71 Hydraulically-operated cooling gills
72 Coolant radiator (upper segment)
73 Oil cooler radiator (lower segment)

91 Ejector seat compressed air bottles
92 Rudder pedals
93 Ammunition tray
94 Armour
95 Cannon fairing
96 MK 103 barrel
97 Muzzle brake
98 Ammunition feed chute
99 Starboard MK 103 wing cannon

100 Mainwheel retraction strut
101 Oleo leg
102 Starboard mainwheel
103 Mainwheel door
104 Forward face of box spar
105 Stressed wing skinning
106 Starboard navigation light
107 Wingtip structure
108 Starboard aileron
109 Aileron trim tab
110 Starboard wing fuel tank

111 Aileron control rod
112 Trim tab linkage
113 Oxygen bottles
114 Starboard flaps
115 Starter fuel tank
116 Flap hydraulic motor
117 Starboard mainwheel well
118 Boxspar
119 Compressed air bottles (emergency undercarriage actuation)
120 Mainspar/fuselage attachment points

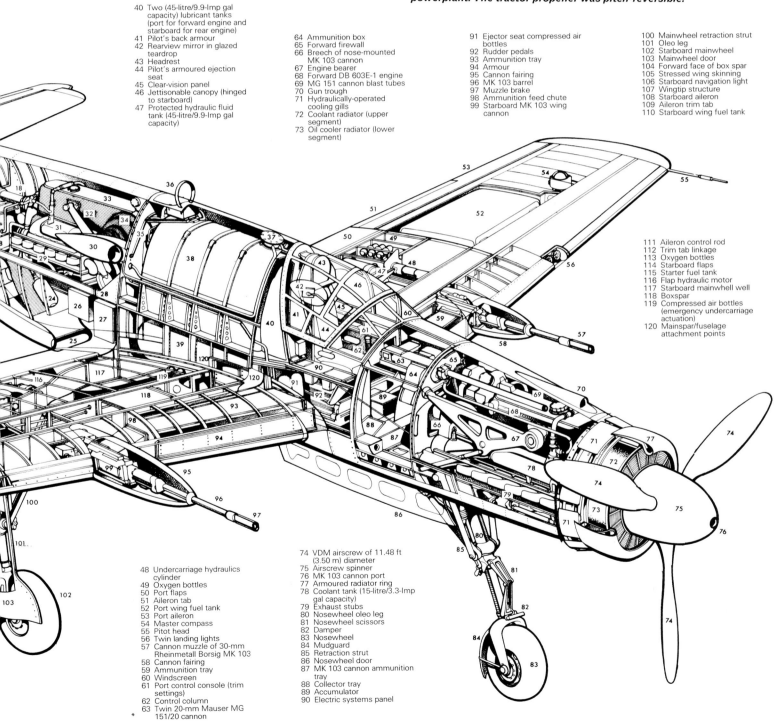

48 Undercarriage hydraulics cylinder
49 Oxygen bottles
50 Port flaps
51 Aileron tab
52 Port wing fuel tank
53 Port aileron
54 Master compass
55 Pitot head
56 Twin landing lights
57 Cannon muzzle of 30-mm Rheinmetall Borsig MK 103
58 Cannon fairing
59 Ammunition tray
60 Windscreen
61 Port control console (trim settings)
62 Control column
63 Twin 20-mm Mauser MG 151/20 cannon

74 VDM airscrew of 11.48 ft (3.50 m) diameter
75 Airscrew spinner
76 MK 103 cannon port
77 Armoured radiator ring
78 Coolant tank (15-litre/3.3-Imp gal capacity)
79 Exhaust stubs
80 Nosewheel oleo leg
81 Nosewheel scissors
82 Damper
83 Nosewheel
84 Mudguard
85 Retraction strut
86 Nosewheel door
87 MK 103 cannon ammunition tray
88 Collector tray
89 Accumulator
90 Electric systems panel

Oberpfaffenhofen factory as the **Do 335B-1**. This aircraft featured the replacement of the weapons bay by a fuel tank, and the replacement of the 15-mm cannon by 20-mm MG 151 cannon. More heavily armed was the **Do 335 V14** which, intended for service as the **Do 335B-2**, featured the same armament and an added MK 103 30-mm cannon mounted in the wings.

In the event, these were the only B-series aircraft to be completed, although others (**V15** to **V20**) were on the construction line at the termination of the project. These included more B-1 and B-2 prototypes, and a pair of **Do 335B-6** prototypes, these being night-fighters similar to the Do 335A-6 but with the heavy armament of the Do 335B-1. Other prototypes would have featured DB 603LA engines with a two-stage supercharger. One other development deserves mention, the **B-4**, **B-5** and **B-8** models which featured a 4.3-m (14-ft 10-in) increase in wing span for greater altitude performance. The development of these new outer wing panels had been undertaken by Heinkel, but they remained on the drawing board. Derivative designs included the **Do 435** night-fighter, with side-by-side seating, cabin pressurisation and long-span wooden wings, the

Do 535 mixed-powerplant fighter with the rear DB 603 replaced by a jet engine, and the **Do 635** long-range reconnaissance platform which aimed to mate two Do 335 fuselages together with a new centre-section. At the termination of production, 37 Pfeils had been completed, with about 70 others awaiting final assembly and the arrival of components.

As far as is known, the Pfeil never entered into combat, although US pilots reported seeing the strange aircraft in the sky during forays over Germany, and the Erprobungskommando was forced to send aircraft into a sky which could not be guaranteed as being free of hostile aircraft. In its single-seat version it was one of the fastest piston-engined fighters ever built, with a claimed top speed of around 765 km/h (475 mph). Despite this high performance, it was the much slower two-seat night-fighter version which would probably have proved the most effective if the war had continued. Equipped with excellent radar and powerful weapons, and blessed with good visibility, combat persistence and performance, the night-fighter would have been excellent against the RAF bomber streams.

A complicated escape

Flying the Pfeil was an experience, thanks to its high performance and unusual configuration. While the performance provided an exhilarating ride for the pilot, the configuration prompted some doubts. His main concern was the ejection seat, the Do 335 being only the second production type to feature this (after the Saab J21). Before firing the seat, explosive bolts which held the upper vertical tail surface

The Pfeil was the first production aircraft to be fitted with an ejection seat; however, the system for actually escaping was a complicated one. German pilots told of how, during the test programme, two aircraft crashed and their pilots were found still in the cockpit but with their arms missing. This was supposedly due to too firm a grip being taken on the handles, which first jettisoned the canopy before the seat could be fired out.

Left: This captured Do 335A-0 (actually the fifth of ten) is pockmarked with small calibre bullet holes, probably inflicted by a bored Allied soldier in the aftermath of victory, or perhaps a reminder of the battle to capture this anonymous airfield. The Do 335 was unable to enter frontline service before the Reich's final collapse.

Below: The ninth Do 335 prototype (Do 335 V9) which was completed to full pre-production standards and was delivered to the Erprobungsstelle at Rechlin for evaluation. Armament consisted of a single MK 103 30-mm cannon and a pair of 15-mm MG 151 machine guns, and was fitted with a Revi C 12/D reflector gun sight. This was mounted on a swivel plate and could function as either a gunsight or as a dive bombing sight.

and rear propeller were fired to clear a way for the egressing pilot. Despite the ejection seat, he had to jettison the canopy manually. As another safety feature, the lower vertical tail surface was jettisonable in case a wheels-up landing was attempted.

To conclude, the Pfeil proved to be a sound design with no major faults. If development had been allowed to continue at a steady pace, and had sufficient resources been made available, the teething problems which remained with the type could have been ironed out, and the Pfeil could have emerged as a warplane of major importance to the Luftwaffe. However, as the military situation facing Germany darkened during 1944/45, resources continued to be split between dozens of projects, and development of the Do 335 was rushed, to compensate for the dislocation wrought by allied bombing and the advance of the Allied armies. Development and production was also delayed by the state of German industry, which could not provide the necessary sub-contracted components such as propellers, engines and radios. The development effort was further diluted by unnecessary effort on unattainable advanced derivatives while the basic fighter-bomber was starved of both manpower and money.

When US forces overran Dornier's Oberpfaffenhofen factory, they found nine A-1s, four A-4s and a pair of A-12s in the final assembly stage. Several were evaluated by the USAAF. By that time, production of the Do 335A-6 night-fighter had been transferred to the Heinkel plant at Vienna, but the jigs were not reassembled before the war ended.

Dornier Do 335 Pfeil

Structure
An all-metal, cantilever monoplane, the Do 335's trapezoidal stressed skin dihedral wing had a leading edge sweep of 13°, and was built up around a single box spar. The cantilever tailplane was of similar construction, but the vertical fins had wooden leading edges. The all-metal monocoque fuselage incorporated an internal weapons bay immediately aft of the nosewheel bay.

Cockpit
The cockpit was of extremely low drag design, and this necessitated the addition of small blisters in the canopy sides, housing rear-view mirrors. On the prototypes the canopy slid aft, but on the Do 335A-0 and subsequent types, opened to starboard. In emergency, the canopy was jettisoned, and the upper fin and rear propeller were explosively separated. The pilot sat on a primitive ejection seat, in front of an armoured bulkhead which separated him from the 1230-litre (270.5-Imp gal) main fuel tank.

Dornier Do 335A-0 Erprobungskommando 335 Oberpfaffenhofen May 1945

The seventh of ten Do 335A-0 pre-production aircraft, most of which were used by Erprobungskommando 335 for service evaluation. This was as close as the revolutionary Do 335 came to Luftwaffe service. Even had the type reached frontline units it would have done little to stem the tide of the allied advance, and its unusual configuration did nothing to lessen its in-built obsolescance at the dawn of the jet age.

Tail unit
The Do 335 had a cruciform tail unit, with the conventional (dorsal) tailfin augmented by a ventral fin of similar size and shape, with a second rudder and trim tab. This lower fin could be jettisoned in the event of a belly landing. The fixed horizontal tailplane was entirely conventional, with full-span elevators and outboard trim tabs.

Dornier Do 335 Pfeil

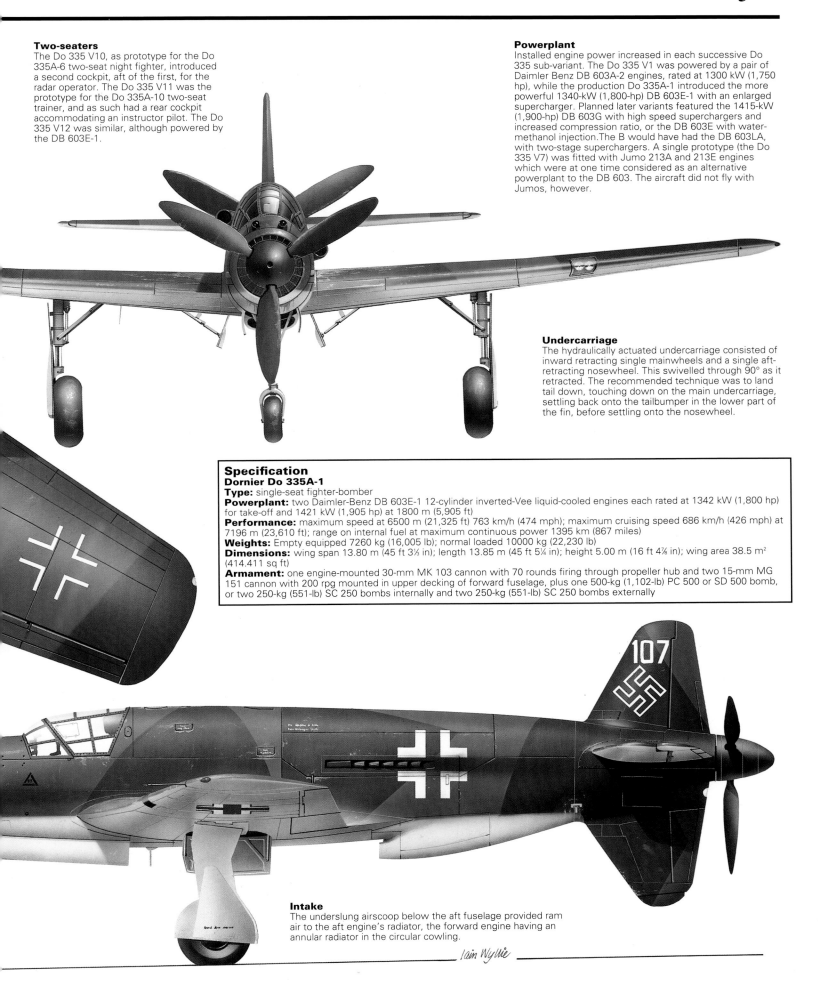

Two-seaters
The Do 335 V10, as prototype for the Do 335A-6 two-seat night fighter, introduced a second cockpit, aft of the first, for the radar operator. The Do 335 V11 was the prototype for the Do 335A-10 two-seat trainer, and as such had a rear cockpit accommodating an instructor pilot. The Do 335 V12 was similar, although powered by the DB 603E-1.

Powerplant
Installed engine power increased in each successive Do 335 sub-variant. The Do 335 V1 was powered by a pair of Daimler Benz DB 603A-2 engines, rated at 1300 kW (1,750 hp), while the production Do 335A-1 introduced the more powerful 1340-kW (1,800-hp) DB 603E-1 with an enlarged supercharger. Planned later variants featured the 1415-kW (1,900-hp) DB 603G with high speed superchargers and increased compression ratio, or the DB 603E with water-methanol injection. The B would have had the DB 603LA, with two-stage superchargers. A single prototype (the Do 335 V7) was fitted with Jumo 213A and 213E engines which were at one time considered as an alternative powerplant to the DB 603. The aircraft did not fly with Jumos, however.

Undercarriage
The hydraulically actuated undercarriage consisted of inward retracting single mainwheels and a single aft-retracting nosewheel. This swivelled through 90° as it retracted. The recommended technique was to land tail down, touching down on the main undercarriage, settling back onto the tailbumper in the lower part of the fin, before settling onto the nosewheel.

Specification
Dornier Do 335A-1
Type: single-seat fighter-bomber
Powerplant: two Daimler-Benz DB 603E-1 12-cylinder inverted-Vee liquid-cooled engines each rated at 1342 kW (1,800 hp) for take-off and 1421 kW (1,905 hp) at 1800 m (5,905 ft)
Performance: maximum speed at 6500 m (21,325 ft) 763 km/h (474 mph); maximum cruising speed 686 km/h (426 mph) at 7196 m (23,610 ft); range on internal fuel at maximum continuous power 1395 km (867 miles)
Weights: Empty equipped 7260 kg (16,005 lb); normal loaded 10000 kg (22,230 lb)
Dimensions: wing span 13.80 m (45 ft 3⅛ in); length 13.85 m (45 ft 5¼ in); height 5.00 m (16 ft 4⅞ in); wing area 38.5 m² (414.411 sq ft)
Armament: one engine-mounted 30-mm MK 103 cannon with 70 rounds firing through propeller hub and two 15-mm MG 151 cannon with 200 rpg mounted in upper decking of forward fuselage, plus one 500-kg (1,102-lb) PC 500 or SD 500 bomb, or two 250-kg (551-lb) SC 250 bombs internally and two 250-kg (551-lb) SC 250 bombs externally

Intake
The underslung airscoop below the aft fuselage provided ram air to the aft engine's radiator, the forward engine having an annular radiator in the circular cowling.

Iain Wyllie

Fieseler Fi 103

Development of the Fieseler Fi 103 flying-bomb, better known as the V-1 reprisal weapon, is well recorded in aviation history. A small, fixed-wing, pilotless aircraft, it was powered by a pulse-jet engine mounted above the rear fuselage, incorporated a simple flight control system to guide it to its target, an air log device to make it dive to the ground after travelling a preset distance and a warhead packed with high explosive The first of these weapons landed in the London area in the early hours of 13 June 1944.

Long before that, in late 1943, German officials were considering the use of piloted missiles to make precision attacks on high-priority targets, a policy that developed quite independently of the Japanese *kamikaze* attacks.

A pilot demonstrates the narrow confines of the Fi 103R-IV cockpit. The aircraft has a warhead fitted, but not the characteristic pimple for the nose-mounted impact fuse.

With a deteriorating war situation, Adolf Hitler gave the go-ahead for such a project in March 1944, and the Fi 103 was adopted for this programme, which was designated **Fi 103R** (Reichenberg). Four versions were planned initially: an unpowered **Fi 103R-I** for early flight tests; unpowered **Fi 103R-II** with a second seat where the warhead was normally attached; **Fi 103R-III** with jet fitted and ballast in place of the warhead; and the production version, the **Fi 103R-IV**, with a single cockpit just ahead of the pulse jet. It was intended that, after launch from a mother plane, the pilot would aim his R-IV at the target and then bale out, descending by parachute; in reality, his chances of escaping were slim. Piloted trials began at Lärz in September 1944, an unpowered Fi 103 being dropped from under the wing of an He 111. About 175 of these weapons were produced for intended use by 5./KG 200, the 'Leonidas' *Staffel*, but their continued development and planned use was abandoned in October 1944.

Specification
Fieseler Fi 103R-IV
Type: piloted missile
Powerplant: one 3.43-kN (772-lb) thrust Argus 109 014 pulse-jet engine
Performance: maximum speed approximately 650 km/h (404 mph)
Dimensions: span 5.72 m (18 ft 9¼ in); length 8.00 m (26 ft 3 in)

The Fi 103R-IV had simple flight instruments in the cockpit, and the canopy had guidelines for calculating the correct dive angle for attacks.

Fieseler Fi 156 Storch

All over northern Germany, one finds gigantic nests atop the chimneys of country houses. They are made by storks, which, despite their great size, have to be able to take off and land vertically. It was appropriate that when Gerhard Fieseler won the contract to supply the Luftwaffe's multi-role army co-operation aircraft he should have called it **Storch**. It was perhaps the only Luftwaffe aircraft demonstrably better than any Allied counterpart.

Fieseler was a 22-victory pilot in World War I and probably the world's greatest inter-war aerobatic pilot. With chief designer Reinhold Mewes he specialised in what today are called STOL (short take-off and landing) aircraft. In most of his company's products (notably not including the V-1 flying bomb), he could come in over the airfield at 3000 m (9,845 ft) and then descend straight downwards to make a vertical soft landing, provided there was a slight breeze to make this feat possible.

In summer 1935, Fieseler, Mewes and technical director Erich Bachem (later creator of the Ba 349 Natter VTO fighter) designed the ultimate in practical STOL aircraft, the **Fieseler Fi 156**. It was no mere exercise, and was seen as fulfilling numerous roles both in civil life and for the recently disclosed Luftwaffe. It was a three-seat, high-winged machine, powered by the excellent 179-kW (240-hp) Argus engine and with the wing liberally endowed with slats and flaps. A particular feature was the stalky landing gear arrangement, well suited to cushioning arrivals at unprecedented steep angles. The design was prepared in two versions, the **Fi 156A** with a fixed slat and the **Fi 156B** with an automatic movable slat to avoid the speed penalty of the fixed slat in cruising flight. Surprisingly, the faster Fi 156B was never built.

Instead, Fieseler manufactured three prototypes with fixed slats, the **Fi 156 V1** to **V3**. The V1 (D-IKVN) flew on or about 24 May 1936, with a metal ground-adjustable propeller. The **V2** (D-IDVS) had a wooden propeller, and the V3 (D-IGLI) had military equipment. Their performance was so impressive that the RLM (air ministry) ordered further prototypes and preparations for series production. Nevertheless, conforming with its policy of competition, the RLM wrote a specification around the Fi 156 – which by autumn 1936 was named Storch – and issued it to industry. It resulted in the Messerschmitt Bf 163, similar to the Storch but with a variable-incidence wing; the Siebel Si 201 with a fully glazed, two-seat nose cabin ahead of the pusher engine and single low-mounted tail boom; and the Focke-Wulf Fw 186 jump-start autogyro, based on Cierva technology. The autogyro was not even considered, and by the time the rivals were flying the Storch was in production.

The first production version was the **Fi 156A-1** utility and liaison machine. By mid-1937, the company had flown the ski-equipped V4,

A Fieseler Storch uses its STOL capability by taking off from a short strip of road, somewhere on the Eastern Front. The Storch has been described as the only Luftwaffe aircraft demonstrably better than any Allied counterpart, and was the best liaison and spotter aircraft. of the war.

the military V5 and 10 **Fi 156A-0** pre-production machines. One of the latter, D-IJFN, put on a dazzling show at the Zürich meeting in July at which the DB-engined Dornier Do 17 and Messerschmitt Bf 109 also swept the board, marking Germany's emergence as a superior air power. The Storch repeatedly demonstrated full-load take-offs after a ground run of never more than 45 m (148 ft), and a fully controllable speed range of 51-174 km/h (32-108 mph).

It must be admitted that the Storch was large for its job, and the US Army Piper L-4 Grasshopper, its mass-produced equivalent, did most of the same tasks on 48 instead of 179 kW (65 instead of 240 hp). On the other hand, it could be argued that the aircraft bought by the RAF for the same duties was the Westland Lysander which, despite the best efforts of Westland could not come anywhere near the German aircraft's STOL qualities even with nearly 746 kW (1,000 hp). The truest test is perhaps an aircraft's influence on history. Immediately, the Storch had emulators in at least 10 countries, US examples including the Ryan YO-51 Dragonfly, Vultee L-1 Vigilant and Bellanca O-50. As described below, a version was adopted by the USSR.

Storch configuration

There was little unconventional about the design or construction. The fuselage, which was just half as long again as that of an L-4, was of welded steel tube with fabric covering. The strongly made cabin had a glazed area all around, which was wider than the fuselage to give a clear view straight downwards. To the top of the cabin were attached the fabric-covered wooden wings, braced to the bottom fuselage longerons by steel-tube V-struts. The wings could be folded backwards. Along the entire straight leading edge were fixed aluminium slats, while the entire trailing edge was formed by wooden slotted flaps, the outer sections serving as drooping ailerons with inboard balance tabs to reduce stick forces in roll. The flaps were not of Fieseler's *Rollflugel* pattern (resembling the Fowler), but simply large slotted flaps driven by rods in the wingroot, jackscrews in the leading-edge root and, via sprockets and chains, a handwheel on the left of the cockpit. Working the flaps was little effort, and they could go to 70°. Take-off was usually with 20° or none, but 40° could be used for really 'impossible' situations. The fin was metal and fabric, but the rest of the tail was wooden, with ply skin, the tailplane having variable incidence for trim.

The inverted V-8 engine was neatly installed, and its air cooling was to be a boon on the Eastern Front during World War II. It invariably started as soon as the electric starter was selected, and the

access step projecting from the landing gear was seldom needed except to replenish oil. The standard propeller was a 2.6-m (102-in) Schwarz, with metal anti-erosion inserts in the outer leading edges. A 74-litre (16.28-Imp gal) tank was fitted in each wing, and a 205-litre (45-Imp gal) tank could be installed in place of the two passenger seats in tandem behind the pilot. The main legs and tailskid were all tall and had a long stroke, the main units having spiral springs with an oil dashpot to prevent bounce. Hydraulic brakes were hardly needed, and tyre pressure was low enough for almost any surface except fresh deep snow, although pilots soon learned to watch for ruts and large stones because the tyres were rather small. In a strong wind flaps had to be kept in on the ground or the Storch could be blown over.

Difficult target

It added up to a vehicle that could go almost anywhere and do a remarkable number of things. Tests against fighters appeared to confirm that, at around 55 km/h (34 mph), it was a very difficult target for fighters; there was almost trouble when Udet's camera-gun film showed not one picture of the elusive Storch. Another Fi 156A-0 was tested with three SC 50 (50-kg/110-lb) bombs, with aim marks painted on the Plexiglas windows, while another did successful trials against a U-boat with inert 135-kg (298-lb) depth charges. Less unexpected were supply-dropping tests and trials with smoke apparatus.

Deliveries to the rapidly growing Luftwaffe began in late 1937, some of the first Fi 156A-1s going to the Légion Condor in Spain. Fieseler had to enlarge his factory at Kassel-Bettenhausen, and then to enlarge it again. He regretted not making the retractable-slat Fi 156B, but the Luftwaffe had no requirement for a higher cruising speed and there was no spare capacity for civil production (although there was plenty of demand). So, the next version was the **Fi 156C**, which appeared in 1938 when output was about three per week. The main feature of the Fi 156C was provision for a 7.92-mm (0.312-in) MG 15 machine-gun firing through the raised rear part of the cabin. The gun was usually not installed on the **Fi 156C-1**, one or two of which were supplied to virtually every *Gruppe* in the Luftwaffe for general liaison duties. The **Fi 156C-2** did have the gun, as well as a vertical reconnaissance camera, and was crewed by a pilot and an observer/gunner, either of whom could work the radio. Optional fits included skis and attachments for a stretcher (litter).

By 1939 Fieseler was able to send a few Storchs to Finland and Switzerland. Presentation examples were given to the Italian Duce, Benito Mussolini (who had no idea how important a Storch would be later in his life) and, after a non-aggression pact in summer 1939, to

A common sight wherever German forces were operating, the Storch could perform in several valuable roles. Here an Fi 156D-1 in Tunisia illustrates the upward-hinging loading hatch on the lowered rear glazing, which permitted the carriage of one stretcher case in the rear fuselage after some arrangement of internal equipment.

Fieseler Fi 156

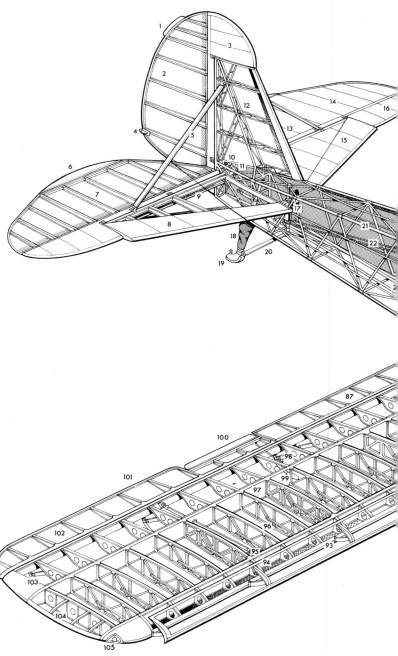

Stalin. The latter was so impressed he instructed Oleg K. Antonov to produce a copy (no licence was sought). Antonov had no experience with steel-tube fuselages, and also no As 10C engines, but he very quickly produced an excellent copy in the **OKA-38 Aist** (stork), powered by the MV-6 engine derived from the 164-kW (220-hp) Renault six-cylinder inline. The OKA-38 was adopted for production as the **ShS** (Shtabnyi samolyet, staff aircraft), but the factory was overrun by German troops before deliveries began in summer 1941.

From the start of World War II the Storch went, literally, everywhere the German army went. Despite audacious missions in full view of the enemy, it suffered amazingly few losses, the front-line life being (it was said) 10 times as long as that of the Bf 109 fighter. This is despite the fact the Wüstennotstaffeln special rescue units were officially tasked with bringing back battle casualties and downed aircrew no matter where they were, and in North Africa the long-range **Fi 156C-5** version often flew deep into trackless desert to get Luftwaffe aircrew. From late 1941, the **Fi 156D-1** was produced in parallel with the Fi 156C, the new series having most of the right side hinged to facilitate rapid loading and unloading of stretchers. Yet another version which appeared in 1941 was the **Fi 156E**, with tandem-wheel, tracked landing gears. This was not so much to reduce footprint pressure as to reduce damage and write-offs caused by taxiing over ruts and small obstructions but, although the Fi 156E appears to have performed as advertised, production was restricted to the 10 evaluation **Fi 156E-0**s.

Fieseler was increasingly required to produce Bf 109 and Focke-Wulf Fw 190 fighters, but nevertheless managed to deliver 484 Storchs in 1942. An additional 121 came from a new production line at Puteaux in France, which had previously built Morane-Saulnier M.S.406 fighters before the French capitulation.

Production transfer

Subsequently, all Storch production was transferred from the overburdened Kassel works, which delivered its last Fi 156 in October 1943. It sent the jigs and a few key workers to the Benes Mraz factory at Chocen, in what the Nazis called the Bohemia-Moravia Protectorate (Czechoslovakia). All subsequent Storch deliveries were to come from Puteaux or Chocen, and it is significant that, after the end of the war, both factories continued to build this useful aircraft even though ex-Luftwaffe machines were littering unlikely parts of the countryside. Total Luftwaffe acceptances were about 2,871, some of which were passed on to the forces of Bulgaria, Croatia, Finland, Hungary, Italy, Romania and Slovakia, all fighting on the Axis side on the Eastern Front.

So far as is known, the Storch did not fly night harassment missions with weapons on that front, as did thousands of Luftwaffe biplane trainers (many having the same As 10C engine), but the Storch nevertheless took part in many exciting actions. Certainly the most remarkable 'James Bond'-type mission of the entire war (which received little publicity because it was by the losing side) took place on 12 September 1943. Italy had reached an armistice with the Allies, and the former Fascist dictator, Mussolini, had been taken prisoner. Most of the country was at once taken over by the German army, however, and Hitler ordered SS Haupsturm-führer Otto Skorzeny to find

Mussolini and rescue him. Eventually Skorzeny located Mussolini as being held in the hotel on top of the pinnacle of the Gran Sasso in the Abruzzi mountains, reached only by cable-car. He organised a rescue using a Focke-Achgelis Fa 223 Drache helicopter, but at the last moment this was unserviceable. Undeterred, Skorzeny went in a Storch, landed on the tiny terrace at the back of the hotel, got the former dictator and, severely overloaded, took off over the sheer edge.

Fleeing Berlin

Almost equal in excitement was one of the very last missions ever flown by a Storch of the Luftwaffe. On 23 April 1945 Hitler received a communication from Reichsmarschall Hermann Goering, previously his closest aide, which made him furious. He immediately dismissed Goering as C-in-C of the Luftwaffe (Goering having got out of Berlin to safer climes), and appointed in his stead Generaloberst Ritter von

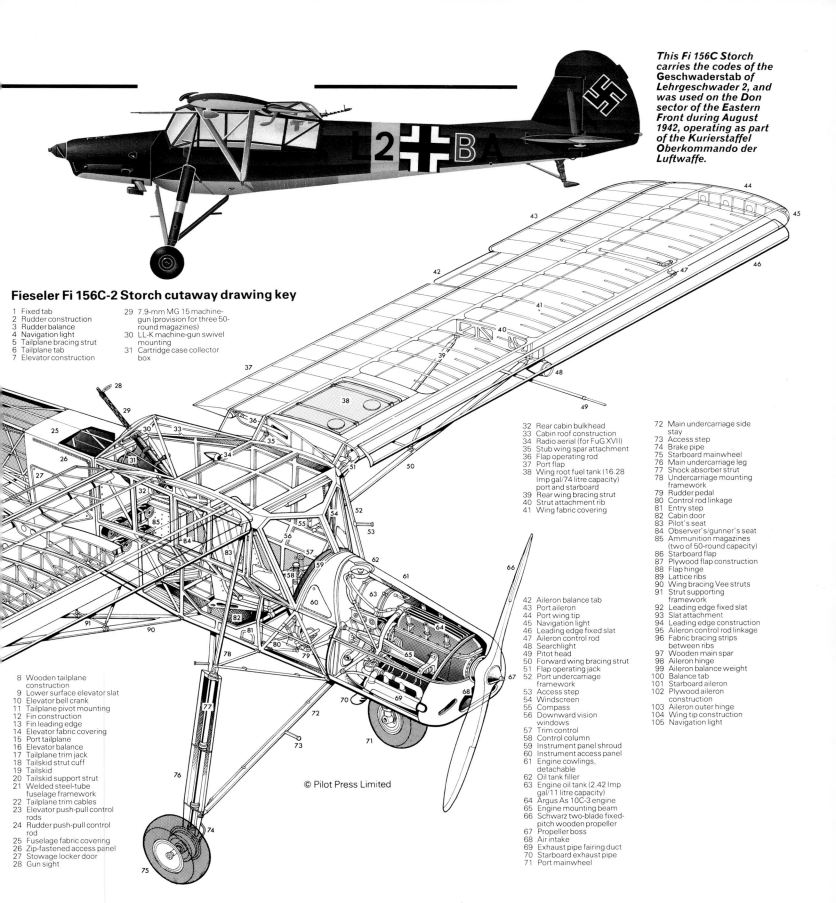

This Fi 156C Storch carries the codes of the Geschwaderstab of Lehrgeschwader 2, and was used on the Don sector of the Eastern Front during August 1942, operating as part of the Kurierstaffel Oberkommando der Luftwaffe.

Fieseler Fi 156C-2 Storch cutaway drawing key

1 Fixed tab
2 Rudder construction
3 Rudder balance
4 Navigation light
5 Tailplane bracing strut
6 Tailplane tab
7 Elevator construction
8 Wooden tailplane construction
9 Lower surface elevator slat
10 Elevator bell crank
11 Tailplane pivot mounting
12 Fin construction
13 Fin leading edge
14 Elevator fabric covering
15 Port tailplane
16 Elevator balance
17 Tailplane trim jack
18 Tailskid strut cuff
19 Tailskid
20 Tailskid support strut
21 Welded steel-tube fuselage framework
22 Tailplane trim cables
23 Elevator push-pull control rods
24 Rudder push-pull control rod
25 Fuselage fabric covering
26 Zip-fastened access panel
27 Stowage locker door
28 Gun sight

29 7.9-mm MG 15 machine-gun (provision for three 50-round magazines)
30 LL-K machine-gun swivel mounting
31 Cartridge case collector box
32 Rear cabin bulkhead
33 Cabin roof construction
34 Radio aerial (for FuG XVII)
35 Stub wing spar attachment
36 Flap operating rod
37 Port flap
38 Wing root fuel tank (16.28 Imp gal/74 litre capacity) port and starboard
39 Rear wing bracing strut
40 Strut attachment rib
41 Wing fabric covering
42 Aileron balance tab
43 Port aileron
44 Port wing tip
45 Navigation light
46 Leading edge fixed slat
47 Aileron control rod
48 Searchlight
49 Pitot head
50 Forward wing bracing strut
51 Flap operating jack
52 Port undercarriage framework
53 Access step
54 Windscreen
55 Compass
56 Downward vision windows
57 Trim control
58 Control column
59 Instrument panel shroud
60 Instrument access panel
61 Engine cowlings, detachable
62 Oil tank filler
63 Engine oil tank (2.42 Imp gal/11 litre capacity)
64 Argus As 10C-3 engine
65 Engine mounting beam
66 Schwarz two-blade fixed-pitch wooden propeller
67 Propeller boss
68 Air intake
69 Exhaust pipe fairing duct
70 Starboard exhaust pipe
71 Port mainwheel

72 Main undercarriage side stay
73 Access step
74 Brake pipe
75 Starboard mainwheel
76 Main undercarriage leg
77 Shock absorber strut
78 Undercarriage mounting framework
79 Rudder pedal
80 Control rod linkage
81 Entry step
82 Cabin door
83 Pilot's seat
84 Observer's/gunner's seat
85 Ammunition magazines (two of 50-round capacity)
86 Starboard flap
87 Plywood flap construction
88 Flap hinge
89 Lattice ribs
90 Wing bracing Vee struts
91 Strut supporting framework
92 Leading edge fixed slat
93 Slat attachment
94 Leading edge construction
95 Aileron control rod linkage
96 Fabric bracing strips between ribs
97 Wooden main spar
98 Aileron hinge
99 Aileron balance weight
100 Balance tab
101 Starboard aileron
102 Plywood aileron construction
103 Aileron outer hinge
104 Wing tip construction
105 Navigation light

© Pilot Press Limited

Greim. He sent a message from his bunker to Berlin-Gatow calling for von Greim, and Flugkapitän Hanna Reitsch brought him to the Führerbunker in a Storch, flying by night over the entire encircling Soviet armies and landing amid piles of rubble and under enemy fire. Hitler formally invested von Greim, who was then flown out again by the brilliant woman test pilot. She was the last person to get out of beleaguered Berlin, and the return trip should on any rational basis have been impossible.

During the war at least 47 Storchs, nearly all of them **Fi 156C-3/Trop** or **Fi 156C-5/Trop** versions, were taken on charge by front-line RAF squadrons in the Mediterranean theatre. In the final few months of the war, more examples came into the hands of Allied units in northern Europe. By May 1945 further undestroyed examples had been captured in Germany, and a surprisingly high proportion escaped immediate destruction. The British MAP (Ministry of Aircraft Production) carried out a formal evaluation of VX154, which numerically confirmed its outstanding qualities. Among more than 60 Storchs taken formally on RAF charge was VM472, the personal aircraft of Field Marshal Montgomery, in preference to an Allied type. Another, brought to the UK by an air marshal, was reluctantly wrest-

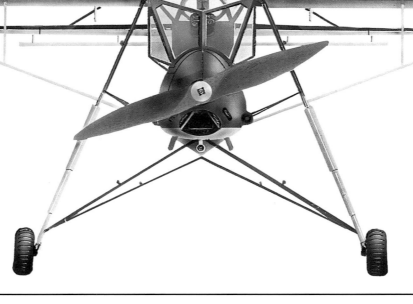

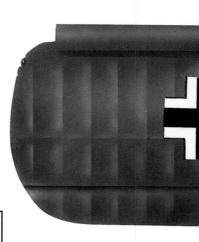

Undercarriage
The Storch's STOL capability was enhanced by its enormously strong undercarriage, whose energy-absorbing oleos could withstand the high vertical sink rates imposed by very steep approaches. With a decent wind to land into, the Storch could land within the length of its own wingspan.

Fieseler Storch variants

Fi 156 B: projected variant with movable leading-edge slats; not built
Fi 156C-0: pre-production version of an improved Fi 156A-1 with raised rear-cabin glazing to allow installation of a rear-firing 7.92-mm (0.31-in) machine-gun
Fi 156B-1: liaison and staff transport version
Fi 156C-2: reconnaissance version with one camera and two-man crew; some late examples equipped to carry one stretcher for casualty evacuation

Fi 156C-3: general-purpose version, some with improved Argus As 10P engine
Fi 156C-3/Trop: tropicalised version of the Fi 156C-3 with engine dust/sand filters
Fi 156C-5: similar to 156C-3 but with Argus As 10P engine as standard and provision to carry an underfuselage drop tank or camera installation
Fi 156C-5/Trop: tropicalised version of the above
Fi 156D-0: pre-production ambulance version with improved accommodation for one stretcher and

an enlarged loading/unloading hatch; powered by Argus As 10C engine
Fi 156D-1: production version of the above with Argus As 10P engine as standard
Fi 156E-0: designation of 10 pre-production aircraft with a form of tracked landing gear, the main units each with two wheels in tandem linked by pneumatic rubber track; no further production
Fi 256: two examples only of larger capacity (five-seat) civil version, built at Morane-Saulnier factory at Puteaux, France, during 1943-44

Powerplant
The Storch prototype was powered by an Argus As 10C eight-cylinder, air-cooled piston engine, of inverted Vee-8 configuration, with the similar As 10P adopted on the multi-role Fi 156C-3. Although a metal, variable-pitch propeller was fitted to the second Storch prototype, production aircraft had a fixed-pitch, wooden Schwarz airscrew.

Fieseler Fi 156C-3 Storch Eastern Front, 1943

Without doubt, the Fieseler Storch was the prime example of an army co-operation and observation aircraft, and certainly the design by which other types operating in these roles were judged. This anonymous Fi 156C-3, which retains four-letter factory codes instead of any unit identification, clearly illustrates the purposeful design of the undercarriage with the long compression legs incorporating long-stroke, oil-damping shock absorbers capable of coping with very high vertical descent rates. Such was the success of the Storch in its intended role that trials were conducted around supply-dropping, coastal patrol and light bombing roles, although only as secondary operations.

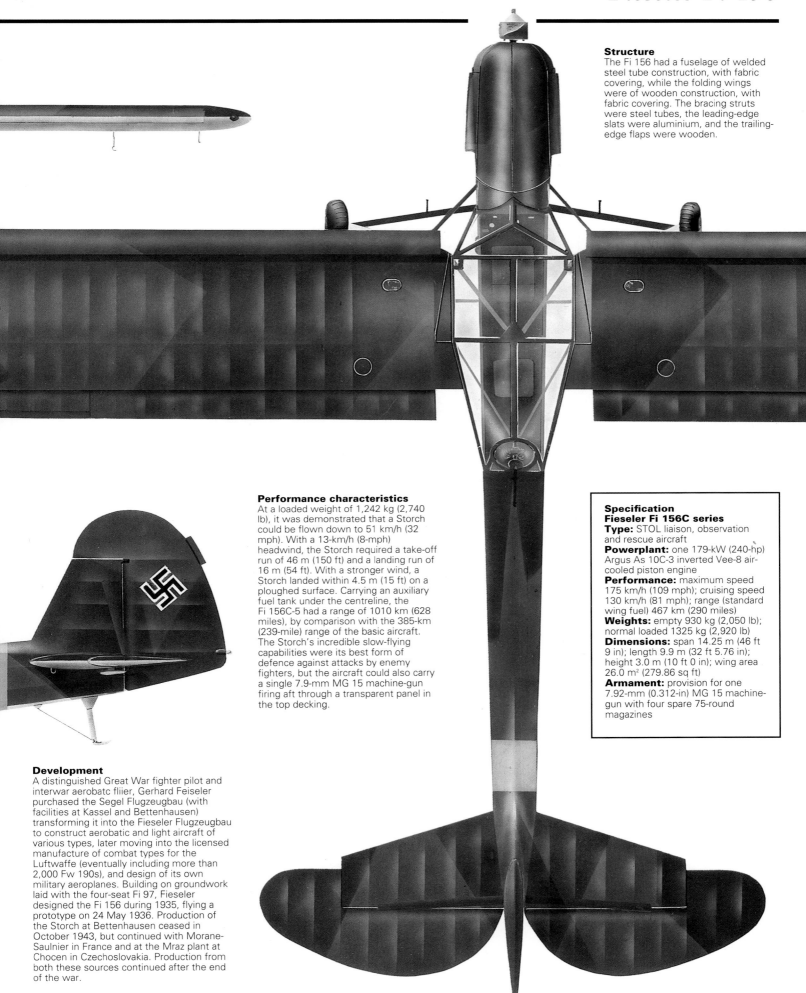

Structure

The Fi 156 had a fuselage of welded steel tube construction, with fabric covering, while the folding wings were of wooden construction, with fabric covering. The bracing struts were steel tubes, the leading-edge slats were aluminium, and the trailing-edge flaps were wooden.

Performance characteristics

At a loaded weight of 1,242 kg (2,740 lb), it was demonstrated that a Storch could be flown down to 51 km/h (32 mph). With a 13-km/h (8-mph) headwind, the Storch required a take-off run of 46 m (150 ft) and a landing run of 16 m (54 ft). With a stronger wind, a Storch landed within 4.5 m (15 ft) on a ploughed surface. Carrying an auxiliary fuel tank under the centreline, the Fi 156C-5 had a range of 1010 km (628 miles), by comparison with the 385-km (239-mile) range of the basic aircraft. The Storch's incredible slow-flying capabilities were its best form of defence against attacks by enemy fighters, but the aircraft could also carry a single 7.9-mm MG 15 machine-gun firing aft through a transparent panel in the top decking.

Development

A distinguished Great War fighter pilot and interwar aerobatc fliier, Gerhard Feiseler purchased the Segel Flugzeugbau (with facilities at Kassel and Bettenhausen) transforming it into the Fieseler Flugzeugbau to construct aerobatic and light aircraft of various types, later moving into the licensed manufacture of combat types for the Luftwaffe (eventually including more than 2,000 Fw 190s), and design of its own military aeroplanes. Building on groundwork laid by the four-seat Fi 97, Fieseler designed the Fi 156 during 1935, flying a prototype on 24 May 1936. Production of the Storch at Bettenhausen ceased in October 1943, but continued with Morane-Saulnier in France and at the Mraz plant at Chocen in Czechoslovakia. Production from both these sources continued after the end of the war.

Specification
Fieseler Fi 156C series
Type: STOL liaison, observation and rescue aircraft
Powerplant: one 179-kW (240-hp) Argus As 10C-3 inverted Vee-8 air-cooled piston engine
Performance: maximum speed 175 km/h (109 mph); cruising speed 130 km/h (81 mph); range (standard wing fuel) 467 km (290 miles)
Weights: empty 930 kg (2,050 lb); normal loaded 1325 kg (2,920 lb)
Dimensions: span 14.25 m (46 ft 9 in); length 9.9 m (32 ft 5.76 in); height 3.0 m (10 ft 0 in); wing area 26.0 m² (279.86 sq ft)
Armament: provision for one 7.92-mm (0.312-in) MG 15 machine-gun with four spare 75-round magazines

ed from him and, in 1946, in immaculate Ministry livery with serial VP546 (and British wheels), it was flown by Lieutenant Commander E. M. 'Winkle' Brown as a valued vehicle at Aero Flight, RAE Farnborough. Several others flew with the RAE's transport flight.

Many hundreds of Storchs were built after the war in both France and liberated Czechoslovakia. The Puteaux factory had in fact built two prototypes of the Fi 256, which Fieseler had designed in 1941 as a civil successor. It looked like a Storch with a wider fuselage, but in fact hardly any parts were common. The wings had automatic slats, the fuselage was more streamlined, and the cabin seated two pairs of passengers behind the pilot instead of two single seats. The engine was an As 10P of 194 kW (260 hp). There was nothing wrong with the Fi 256, but the Luftwaffe declined to order it, and there was no obvious civil market.

Chocen-built aircraft after the war were known as the **Mraz K.65 Cap**. Production was terminated soon after the Communist take-over in 1948. The Puteaux designations were **Morane-Saulnier M.S.500**, **M.S.501** and **M.S.502**: the M.S.500 resembled the standard Fieseler Fi 156C series; the M.S.501 looked like the Soviet Antonov OKA-38 in having a Renault 6Q inverted inline engine; and the most important version, made in substantial numbers, was the M.S.502 **Criquet** with a Salmson 9Abc radial. The radial seemed to suit the 'Cricket' admirably, and it had a long career with the Armée de l'Air and the Aéronavale. So, too, did the Argus-engined aircraft, and ex-French machines even served with the Vietnam forces throughout the 1950s. Another important user was the Swedish air force, whose **S14** versions from Germany were supplemented by post-war French examples. Several Storchs, from various sources, got on the British civil register, and many examples, most of them built post-war, are still flying in several countries.

An early production Fi 156C-1 lands with its massive flaps and leading-edge slats fully extended. These gave the Storch its phenomenally low stalling speed. The fully-extended oleos are also noteworthy.

Fieseler Fi 167

To meet a requirement for a ship-based two-seat torpedo bomber/reconnaissance aircraft, both Arado and Fieseler submitted proposals to the RLM. Prototypes of both aircraft were built, but testing in late 1938 soon showed that Arado's Ar 195 could not meet the requirements, whereas the Fieseler **Fi 167 V1** could not only meet but considerably exceed the specification. In configuration the Fieseler design was a two-bay foldable-wing biplane, primarily of metal construction but with some fabric covering, fixed tailwheel landing gear with tall jettisonable main units, a conventional braced tail unit and a Daimler Benz DB 601 engine. The two-man crew was

Fieseler Fi 167A-0 of Erprobungsstaffel 167, based in the Netherlands in 1942.

Despite its awkward looks, the Fi 167 displayed outstanding low-speed flying qualities. The wings folded back for stowage on a carrier, and the undercarriage could be jettisoned for emergency ditching.

accommodated in tandem, beneath a long canopy that was designed to allow for operation at the rear of a machine-gun on a pivoted mount.

As with the Fi 156, Fieseler's new aircraft had exceptional low-speed characteristics, achieved in this case by both wings incorporating ailerons and full-span automatic leading-edge slats, and the lower wing having large area trailing-edge flaps. Their effect, allied with the lift of the biplane wings, made it possible for the aircraft to sink slowly and almost vertically under complete control.

The Fi 167 was intended for service aboard the German aircraft-carrier *Graf Zeppelin*, launched on 8 December 1938, and following the completion of a second prototype (**Fi 167 V2**) a pre-production batch of 12 **Fi 167A-0** aircraft was built. These differed little from the prototypes, but incorporated some refinements considered desirable after service testing, including the addition of a two-man dinghy. When construction of the *Graf Zeppelin* was stopped, in 1940, the role for which the Fi 167 had been designed no longer existed. However, it was expected that when construction was resumed, manufacture of the Fi 167 would also go ahead; this was not to be the case for when, in 1942, orders were given for construction of the aircraft-carrier to be resumed, it was decided that a version of the Ju 87 would amply meet requirements, and no further examples of the Fi 167 were built. Erprobungsstaffel 167 was established in the summer of 1940 for a series of evaluations, based in Holland. A number of tests were undertaken, including those of various overwater camouflage schemes. The unit remained there until early 1943, when the Fi 167s were dispersed: three to an undercarriage testing unit and the rest to Romania.

Specification
Fieseler Fi 167A-0
Type: ship-based torpedo bomber/reconnaissance aircraft
Powerplant: one 820-kW (1,100-hp) Daimler Benz DB601B 12-cylinder inverted-Vee piston engine
Performance: (reconnaissance) maximum speed 325 km/h (202 mph); cruising speed 270 km/h (168 mph); service ceiling 8200 m (26,905 ft); range 1500 km (932 miles)
Weights: empty 2800 kg (6,173 lb); maximum take off 4850 kg (10,692 lb)
Dimensions: span 13.50 m (44 ft 3½ in); length 11.40 m (37 ft 4¾ in); height 4.80 m (15 ft 9 in); wing area 45.50 m² (489.77 sq ft)
Armament: one fixed forward-firing 7.92-mm (0.31-in) MG 17 machine-gun and one 7.92-mm (0.31-in) MG 15 machine-gun on pivoted mounting in aft position, plus maximum load of one 1000-kg (2,204-lb) bomb or one 765-kg (1,687-lb) torpedo

Flettner Fl 282 Kolibri

Following work with the Fl 265 single-seat helicopter, Flettner produced the improved two-seat **Fl 282 Kolibri** (hummingbird), and to speed the development of an aircraft that could prove valuable for naval use, a total of 30 prototypes and 15 pre-production examples was ordered in early 1940. Although the basic fuselage configuration was similar to that of its predecessor, the Fl 282 differed in one important respect. Its Bramo Sh 14A engine was mounted in the centre fuselage and the pilot was accommodated in the nose with enclosed, semi-enclosed and open cockpits provided in variety over the 24 prototypes that were built. Not all of these were two-seaters, but those that were accommodated an observer in a position aft of the main rotor pylon, seated so that his view was to the rear of the aircraft.

In 1942 the German navy began its trials of the Fl 282, finding the type extremely manoeuvrable, stable in poor weather conditions, and so reliable that in 1943 about 20 of the 24 prototypes were operating from warships in the Aegean and Mediterranean for convoy pro-

The Fl 282 V7 was fitted with a glazed nose surround, one of many variations.

tection duties. It was discovered that as pilots gained experience the Fl 282s could be flown in really bad weather, leading to an order for 1,000 production aircraft. These were not built, as a result of Allied bombing attacks on the BMW and Flettner works, and only three of the prototypes survived at VE-Day, the remainder being destroyed to prevent them being captured.

Specification
Flettner Fl 282 V21
Type: single-seat open-cockpit helicopter
Powerplant: one 119-kW (160-hp) Bramo Sh 14A seven-cylinder radial piston engine
Performance: maximum speed 150 km/h (93 mph) at sea level; service ceiling 3300 m (10,825 ft); range 170 km (106 miles)
Weights: empty 760 kg (1,676 lb); maximum take-off 1000 kg (2,205 lb)
Dimensions: diameter of each rotor 11.96 m (39 ft 2¾ in); length of fuselage 6 56 m (21 ft 6¼ in); height 2.20 m (7 ft 2½ in); total rotor disc area 224 69 m² (2,418.6 sq ft)

Dispatched for trials aboard German navy vessels, the Fl 282s were employed operationally on spotting duties.

Focke-Achgelis Fa 223 Drache

Using the outrigger-mounted twin-rotor layout of the Fa 61, Heinrich Focke produced a scaled-up, six-passenger version designated Focke-Achgelis Fa 266 Hornisse (hornet), developed under contract from Deutsche Luft Hansa. The prototype completed its ground running and tethered hovering programme during the summer of 1940, and the first free flight took place in August of that year. By then, the project had acquired military importance and development continued under the designation **Fa 223 Drache** (kite), 39 being ordered by the Reichsluftfahrt-ministerium for evaluation in a variety of roles, including those of training, transport, rescue and anti-submarine patrol. Equipment varied according to role

and included an MG 15 machine-gun and two 250-kg (551-lb) bombs, a rescue winch and cradle, a reconnaissance camera and a jettisonable 300-litre (66-Imp gal) auxiliary fuel tank. Ten of the 30 pre-production Fa 223s were completed at the Bremen factory before it was bombed, and another seven were built at the company's new factory at Laupheim, near Stuttgart; another plant (in Berlin) had completed just one example by the time the war ended. Only a small number of Fa 223s were actually flown, and two were acquired by US forces during May 1945 at Ainring, Austria, where they had been in service with Lufttransportstaffel 40. In September one of them, flown by its German crew, became the first helicopter

to cross the English Channel, en route to the Airborne Forces Experimental Establishment at RAF Beaulieu for evaluation; in October it was destroyed in a crash as a result of mechanical failure. After the war, two Fa 223s were built in Czechoslovakia from German-manufactured components and development was also continued in France under the designation **Sud Est SE 3000**, the first of which was flown on 23 October 1948.

Specification
Focke-Achgelis Fa 223 Drache
Type: transport/rescue/reconnaissance helicopter
Powerplant: one 746-kW (1,000-hp) BMW 301 R nine-cylinder radial engine
Performance: maximum speed 175 km/h (109 mph); cruising speed 120 km/h (75 mph); service ceiling 2010 m (6,595 ft); range with auxiliary fuel tank 700 km (435 miles)
Weights: empty 3175 kg (7,000 lb); maximum take-off 4310 kg (9,502 lb)
Dimensions: rotor diameter, each 12.00 m (39 ft 4½ in); span over rotors 24.50 m (80 ft 4¾ in); length 12.25 m (40 ft 2¼ in); height 4.35 m (14 ft 3¼ in); rotor disc area, total 226.19 m² (2,434.8 sq ft)

Although cumbersome in appearance, the Fa 223 was an effective helicopter, with a useful internal or external load-carrying ability. The type never reached service in the anti-submarine role, but was used sparingly in the transport role and for mountain rescue work. Fa 223s were extensively tested by the Allies.

Focke-Wulf Fw 56 Stösser

The first Focke-Wulf design for which Kurt Tank had responsibility from its beginning, the Focke-Wulf **Fw 56 Stösser** was evolved to meet a Reichsluftfahrtministerium specification for an advanced trainer powered by the Argus As 10C engine. Tank's design incorporated a steel-tube fuselage with metal panels forward and fabric covering aft, and a wing of wooden construction with plywood covering back to the rear spar and fabric to the trailing edge The first **Fw 56a** prototype was flown in November 1933 and, after initial testing had revealed landing gear deficiencies, the **Fw 56 V2** second machine had new main landing gear units. It also featured an all-metal wing and was without the original faired headrest behind the cockpit. The **Fw 56 V3** third aircraft, flown in February 1934, introduced further modified landing gear and had a wooden wing similar to that of the first. Three **Fw 56A-0** pre-production aircraft were built

with minor wing and engine cowling modifications; the first two carried 7.92-mm (0.31-in) MG 17 machine-guns in the upper fuselage decking and had a rack for three 10-kg (22-lb) practice bombs, while the third had a single MG 17 gun.

The Stösser was evaluated competitively at Rechlin in the summer of 1935 and was selected, in preference to the Arado Ar 76 and Heinkel He 74, for use as a Luftwaffe advanced trainer. The **Fw 56A-1** was the major production version, with provision for one or two MG 17 guns. It also played a part in the development of Ernst Udet's ideas on the techniques of dive-bombing, later used so effectively by Junkers Ju 87 Stuka units. In late 1936 Udet flew the second prototype at Berlin Johannisthal, and at his instigation it was fitted with a bomb rack beneath each wing, each carrying three 1-kg (2.2-lb) smoke bombs. Substantial production orders were placed to equip the fighter and dive-

bomber pilot schools of the Luftwaffe, the type forming the backbone of the fighter training organisation for most of the war. It was was also used as a glider tug for the DFS 230. Austria and Hungary also ordered the Stösser.

Early Fw 56 Stössers await delivery to the Luftwaffe. For most of the war, the aircraft was used by schools for both fighter and dive-bomber pilots.

Specification
Focke-Wulf Fw 56A-1
Type: single-seat advanced trainer
Powerplant: one 179-kW (240-hp) Argus As 10C eight-cylinder inverted-Vee piston engine
Performance: maximum speed 278

km/h (173 mph) at sea level; service ceiling 6200 m (20,340 ft); range 400 km (249 miles)
Weights: empty 695 kg (1,532 lb); maximum take-off 995 kg (2,194 lb)
Dimensions: span 10.50 m (34 ft 5½ in); length 7.70 m (25 ft 3 in); height 3.55 m (11 ft 7¾ in); wing area 14.00 m² (150.7 sq ft)
Armament: two 7.92-mm (0.31 in) MG 17 machine-guns

Focke-Wulf Fw 58 Weihe

Destined to see extensive service with the Luftwaffe, the Focke-Wulf **Fw 58 Weihe** (kite) was a twin-engined utility aircraft in the class of the Avro Anson. Similarly, it was assigned many different roles during World War II. Construction comprised a welded steel fuselage, mostly covered with fabric but with some metal skinning around the nose. The wing was built around metal spars and had metal covering with fabric aft of the rear spar. The wing was braced to the fuselage by a strut. The Argus As 10C engines were hung beneath the wing, with main undercar-

Many Fw 58s were assigned to important military and industrial figures as personal transports. This machine was the first Fw 58A-0, retained by the manufacturer to ferry Kurt Tank, the chief designer. In 1942 it adopted these military codes and a smart Wellenmüster camouflage.

riage units retracting into the rear of the nacelle.

The **Fw 58 V1** first prototype first flew in the summer of 1935, and was a six-seat transport, with two crew housed under separate upward-hinging canopies. The **V2** introduced gun armament in the form of two MG 15s in open positions in the nose and behind the flight deck. **Fw 58A-0** and **Fw 58A-1** aircraft were utility transports and navigation trainers. The **V6** featured a cleaned-up fuselage with a glazed nose for housing a single MG 15 gun, acting as the prototype for the **Fw 58B-1** production aircraft (preceded by a few **Fw 58B-0**s), completed as bomber-trainers with weapons carried on fuselage and wing racks. The **Fw 58B-3** was a rescue trainer. The **Fw 58C-0** was a dual-control trainer version for multi-engine training schools and liaison work, and led

to the popular **Fw 58C-1** and **Fw 58C-2**. The **Fw 58D-1** was a communications aircraft, while the **Fw 58E-1** was a weather reconnaissance platform. The **Fw 58E-2** and **Fw 58G-2** were trials aircraft, while the **Fw 58E-3** was a communications aircraft, as were most of the **Fw 58F** series.

Perhaps the best-remembered variants were the **Fw 58G-1** and **Fw 58G-3**, both completed as *Sanitätsflugzeug* (air ambulances) with accommodation for two litters, which performed sterling work, notably on the Eastern Front. They acquired the nickname *Leukoplast-bomber* (sticking-plaster bomber). The Fw 58 also enjoyed some export success (including licensed construction), most variants being designated in the **Fw 58K** series and recipients including Argentina, Austria, Brazil, Bulgaria, China, Czechoslovakia, Denmark, Hungary, the

Netherlands, Portugal, Romania, Sweden and Turkey. Production reached 1,668 for German operators and 319 for export, and the type served with distinction throughout World War II. It was additionally used for many equipment tests.

Specification
Focke-Wulf Fw 58B-1
Type: general-purpose bomber trainer
Powerplant: two 179-kW (240-hp) Argus As 10C eight-cylinder inverted-Vee piston engines
Performance: maximum speed 270 km/h (168 mph); service ceiling 5600 m (18,375 ft); range 800 km (497 miles)
Weights: empty 2400 kg (5,291 lb); maximum take-off 3600 kg (7,936 lb)
Dimensions: wing span 21.00 m (68 ft 11 in); length 14.00 m (45 ft 11 in); height 3.90 m (12 ft 9½ in); wing area 47.00 m² (505.92 sq ft)
Armament: one 7.92-mm (0.31-in) MG 15 machine-gun in rear of cabin and one in nose glazing

An Fw 58G-1 Leukoplast-bomber, complete with red cross markings. The cabin could take two stretcher cases, with a seat for one medical attendant.

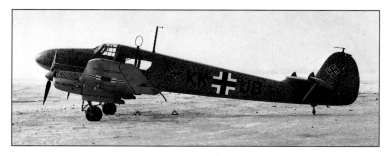

Focke-Wulf Fw 187

Kurt Tank's Focke-Wulf Fw 187 Falke (Falcon) single-seat fighter proposal was evolved originally in 1936 as a private venture, based on two Daimler Benz DB 600 engines which were then under development. The Reichsluftfahrtministerium was persuaded to sanction the manufacture of the aircraft and detail design was entrusted to Tank's assistant, Obering R. Blaser. Of all-metal construction, the Fw 187 had an exceptionally slim fuselage with a cockpit so small that some instruments had to be located on the inboard sections of the engine cowlings where they could be seen by the pilot.

The specified DB 600 engines were in short supply and RLM approval for construction had been given on condition that the Jumo 210 would be substituted. Thus powered, the **Fw 187 V1** first prototype made its maiden flight during late spring 1937, in the hands of Flugkapitän Hans Sander. The 507 kW (680 hp) provided by each of the Jumo 210Da engines was considerably below the power of the DB 600, but the aircraft nevertheless achieved a very creditable 523 km/h (325 mph), compared with the projected 560 km/h (348 mph) of the original powerplant.

Changes were made during initial tests: VDM propellers were introduced in place of the original Junkers-Hamilton variable-pitch units, and twin wheels were installed on each main gear leg; a 7.92-mm (0.31-in) MG 17 machine-gun was mounted subsequently on each side of the cockpit. The **Fw 187 V2** second prototype, flown in the summer of 1937, was similar but with Jumo 210G engines and a reduced-chord rudder.

The **Fw 187 V3** third aircraft was completed, at Udet's request, as a two-seat interdictor, necessitating fuselage redesign, longer engine bearers and revised engine nacelles. Armed with two 20-mm MG FF cannon, it was flown in the spring of 1938, followed by two similar aircraft in the summer and autumn. All three had full-span flaps. Despite the loss of the first prototype on 14 May 1938, the programme continued and a pair of 746-kW (1,000-hp) DB 600A engines was supplied to Focke-Wulf for

installation in the **Fw 187 V6**, which achieved a maximum speed of 636 km/h (395 mph). Three **Fw 187A-0** pre-production examples were built, armed with four MG 17s and two MG FFs, and these were used to defend Focke-Wulf's factory at Bremen during the summer of 1940, one of the staff claiming several (unlikely) kills. During the winter they served (unofficially) with 13. (Zerstörer) Staffel of JG 77 in Norway, while one served with the Luftschiesschule at Vaerløse in Denmark during 1942. With the Bf 110 in full production, there was little chance of the Fw 187 being produced, although it was proposed as a night-fighter in 1943. Useful work was performed by the aircraft in the weapons and equipment trials role.

With its narrow fuselage, short nose and powerful engines, the Fw 187 looked like a purposeful fighter. The prominent gun ports on the fuselage sides were for the MG 17 machine-guns; the more potent MG FF 20-mm cannon were mounted in the lower fuselage. The radio operator faced aft to watch the rear hemisphere.

Specification
Focke-Wulf Fw 187A-0
Type: two-seat heavy day fighter
Powerplant: two 522-kW (700-hp) Junkers Jumo 210Ga 12-cylinder inverted-Vee piston engines
Performance: maximum speed 529 km/h (329 mph) at 1000 m (3,280 ft); service ceiling 10000 m (32,810 ft)
Weights: empty 3700 kg (8,157 lb); maximum take-off 5000 kg (11,023 lb)
Dimensions: span 15.30 m (50 ft 2 in); length 11.10 m (36 ft 5 in); height 3.85 m (12 ft 7½ in); wing area 30.40 m² (327.23 sq ft)
Armament: four 7.92-mm (0.31 in) MG 17 machine-guns and two 20 mm MG FF cannon

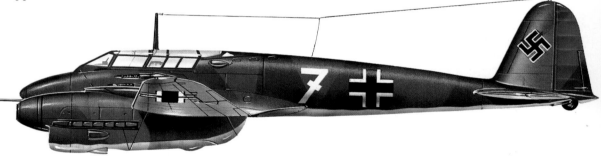

An Fw 187A-0 of the Focke-Wulf Industrie-Schutzstaffel, used to defend the Bremen factory. These aircraft were also used for propaganda.

Focke-Wulf Fw 189 Uhu

In the mid-1930s, aircraft technology was making rapid progress. The standard reconnaissance aircraft of the Luftwaffe was the He 46, a fabric-covered biplane resembling aircraft of World War I. Its replacement, first flown in autumn 1936, was the Hs 126, a stressed-skin monoplane. But even the 126 could be seen to be an interim type (although it gave good service in the early years of World War II). In February 1937 the air ministry in Berlin issued a specification for an even later aircraft with a crew of three, all-round vision and high performance.

It was a challenge, and produced one conventional response, the Arado Ar 198, and one unconventional one, the **Focke-Wulf Fw**

189. Whereas the Arado was a single-engined mid-wing monoplane, notable only for having extensive glazing on the underside of the fuselage as well as on top, the Fw 189 had an almost completely glazed central nacelle, twin engines and twin tail booms. Nor was this all: Hamburger Flugzeugbau decided to enter the contest with an even more radical aircraft, the extraordinary asymmetric BV 141, with a glazed nacelle on one side of the centreline and an unmanned 'fuselage' (with engine and tail) on the other.

The conservative officials favoured the Arado, considering both of the unconventional designs in some way inferior, if not actually faulty. Gradually they began to see the advantages of the notion of a completely glazed crew nacelle with, if necessary, an all-round field of fire for defensive guns. Moreover, Focke-Wulf's designers, led by Kurt Tank and (for the Fw 189) E. Kosel, pointed out that different kinds of nacelle could be fitted. They suggested a close-support version, a trainer and a single-seat armoured attack and anti-tank version, as well as the army co-operation and reconnaissance model (which could also fly casualty evacuation, VIP transport and light cargo missions).

Supremely versatile and universally popular, the Uhu was essentially a low-altitude aircraft, befitting its tactical reconnaissance role. The ride was extremely smooth, while the extensive glazing gave good visibility although, surprisingly, forward vision was impaired by refraction from the sloping panels.

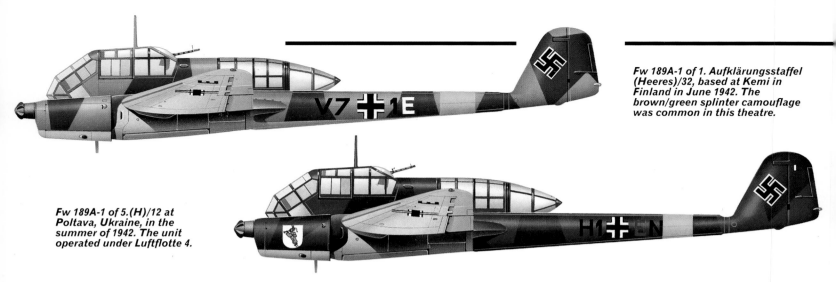

Fw 189A-1 of 1. Aufklärungsstaffel (Heeres)/32, based at Kemi in Finland in June 1942. The brown/green splinter camouflage was common in this theatre.

Fw 189A-1 of 5.(H)/12 at Poltava, Ukraine, in the summer of 1942. The unit operated under Luftflotte 4.

The odd BV 141 was destined never to go into production, although the first version flew well. Likewise, the Arado, initially the favourite of the air ministry staff, never got anywhere, but in this case it was because the prototype was a complete disappointment, on the scores of both handling and performance. In complete contrast, the Fw 189 proved to be an excellent aircraft in all respects. The **V1** (first prototype) was flown by Dipl Ing Tank in July 1938, and he was delighted with it. He called it **Eule** (Owl), although the Luftwaffe was to call the type the **Uhu** (Eagle Owl) and the official media dubbed it *das Fliegende Auge* (the Flying Eye).

Conventional structure

In fact, apart from the twin-boom configuration, which never caused any of the feared problems, the Fw 189 was quite conventional. The all-metal stressed-skin structure had a smooth flush-riveted exterior. The wing comprised a rectangular centre-section and detachable panels bolted on just outboard of the tail booms and tapered on the leading edge only. The long-span ailerons and three sections of electrically-operated split flap were all fabric-covered. Likewise, while the rest of the tail was all-metal, the elevator and rudders were fabric-covered. Each main landing gear had an H-shaped frame with twin shock absorbers in a levered suspension giving a long stroke, as in several Fw aircraft of the period. Oddly, in view of the company's predilection for all-electric actuation, the gear was raised hydraulically, swinging back under the wing into a bay in the boom closed by twin doors. Linkage also pulled up the castoring tailwheel, which retracted sideways to the left to be stowed in the tailplane. On selecting landing gear down, at speeds below 160 km/h (99 mph), the main units were hydraulically extended but the tailwheel fell under its own weight, assisted by rubber pulleys.

The chosen engine – and nobody ever regretted it – was the Argus As 410A-1, an inverted-Vee with 12 air-cooled cylinders. Very smooth at 3,100 rpm, and easy to start even in a Russian winter, this engine proved very reliable, although the 189 could be flown perfectly well on one. A single fuel tank of 110-litre (24-Imp gal) capacity was in each tail boom just behind the landing gear bay, the usual octane rating being 87. The prototype had simple fixed-pitch pro-

The first V1 prototype took to the air in July 1938, with Kurt Tank himself at the controls. The soundness of the design was such that production aircraft differed little from this machine. It was assigned the registration D-OPVN.

pellers, but from **V3** every Fw 189 had two-bladed Argus propellers with pitch controlled automatically by the prominent eight-vane cap that was free to rotate on the front of the spinner.

The central nacelle hardly changed from V1 to the last aircraft built (apart from two totally different versions described later). Basically a stressed-skin structure, almost the whole of it was covered with flat Plexiglas panels, some roof panels and those in the pointed tailcone being curved. Entry was from the wing on either side, through the huge space left by hinging up the complete side and top windows on each side. The pilot sat well forward on the left, with pedals projecting on beams ahead of the floor. Almost all necessary controls were on the left, the R/T jack socket was at the rear of the roof centreline, and the flight instruments were in a row across the front of the cockpit, slightly above eye level. The magnetic compass and rpm indicators were between the pilot's feet just ahead of the two-handed control yoke. On the right, slightly further back, was the seat for the navigator. He could face ahead and manage the floor-mounted camera(s), or take photos with a hand camera, or the GV 219d optical bombsight. Alternatively, he could swivel his seat round and aim the dorsal gun(s). At the rear of the nacelle was a quilted mattress on which the rear gunner could lie. Oddly, this third crew member was called the flight mechanic, although there was little he could do apart from keep an

The Fw 189 V4 served as a prototype for the production A-series aircraft, embodying minor changes such as revised cowlings. It later went on to various warfare trials, as seen here with Lost chemical warfare equipment under the wings for the spraying of mustard gas.

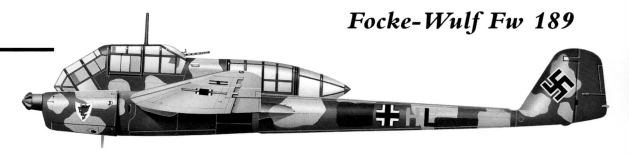

Slovakia and Hungary were supplied with the Fw 189, this being an Fw 189A-2 of the latter's Hungarian 3/1 Short-Range Reconnaissance Squadron (Ung.N.A. St). It was subordinated to Luftflotte 4 at Zamocz, eastern Poland, in March 1944.

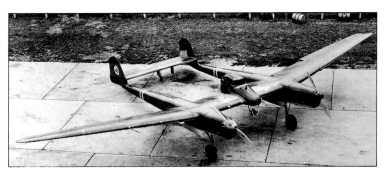

The Fw 189 V1 was rebuilt as the V1b to test the Fw 189C assault aircraft. Once again a new nacelle was fitted, this cramming a pilot and rear-facing gunner into a tiny, heavily-armoured cabin. Vision for both crew members was appalling, and the flying characteristics were altered distinctly for the worse.

der Luftwaffe expressed the view that there was no need for such an aircraft and that the Hs 126A-1 and B-1 were perfectly adequate. All the company could do was press ahead with other versions but eventually, in spring 1940, permission was given to build 10 A-0s. At about the same time, the inadequacies of the Hs 126 were becoming obvious in the campaign in the west, and Focke-Wulf was told to carry on beyond the A-0s with production **A-1**s for front-line service. This was reinforced by the excellent service evaluation by the Auflärungsstaffel and, quite suddenly, from being unwanted the Uhu became a high-priority aircraft.

Second-source production

Focke-Wulf frantically tooled up to build the A-1 in series, but became increasingly overloaded, mainly because of the Fw 190 fighter. As a second source, the Aero factory at Prague Vysocany was swiftly tooled up, and in the course of 1941 the Czech plant delivered 151 Fw 189s, compared with just 99 from the parent company at Bremen. It was obvious that the invasion of the Soviet Union, begun on 22 June 1941, was going to need all the Fw 189s that could be produced, so a major part of French industry was taken over by Focke-Wulf, and the Fw 189 production jigs were sent to France from Bremen. Breguet made outer wings at Bayonne, but most of the other parts were made by SNCASO, including the centre-section and nacelle at Bordeaux-Bacalan, booms and tail at Rochefort, and other parts at Bordeaux-Bégles. Assembly and flight test was at Bordeaux-Mérignac. This was one of the few instances of a successful production programme in German-occupied France, output working up eventually to 20 per month.

The A-1 differed only in details (such as in having twin-leg main gears) from the fourth prototype. The nose gun was omitted, and armament comprised two MG 17s and two hand-aimed MG 15s. Four SC 50 bombs were carried if necessary, and aimed either in dives or in level flight using the sight. Gas equipment was not used, but

eye out for interception from the rear. Management of the radio, which the third man might have performed, was yet one more duty for the overworked navigator.

From the outset, the mainstream Fw 189 was to be the A-series, as described. The V1 differed from production machines only in such details as the propellers, as described, and in having single-leg main gears. The **V2**, flown only a month later in August 1938, was armed with two MG 17 machine-guns in the wingroots, firing ahead and aimed via a ring/bead sight by the pilot, and three very similar MG 15s (fed by a saddle magazine instead of a belt), aimed through the nose, mid-upper position and tailcone. Four ETC 50/VIIId racks under the outer wings could carry 50-kg (110-lb) bombs or chemical containers for poison gas or smokescreens. Via additional prototypes, the pre-production **Fw 189A-0** was completely defined by the beginning of 1939, but rather to Tank's chagrin the Oberkommando

With a completely redesigned fuselage nacelle, the Fw 189B was intended as a five-seat trainer. Ten of the Fw 189B-1 production aircraft were delivered before Fw 189A production began. An Fw 189D floatplane trainer version was semi-completed.

Focke-Wulf Fw 189

Everything about the Fw 189 was slender, especially the wings and tail booms. Despite this, it was an immensely strong aircraft, able to take large amounts of battle damage. Flying low over the battlefield, this was an important attribute of the type.

S 125 smokescreen containers were a common fit. The standard camera installations in the middle of the nacelle normally housed the ubiquitous Rb 20/30, but alternatives included the 15/18, 21/18 or 50/30, and a hand-held HK 12.5 or HK 19 was almost always carried. Other equipment included FuG 25 communications radio, G4 radio direction finding, and flare cartridges.

In mid-1941 production switched to the **Fw 189A-2**, in which the single MG 15s were replaced by the neater and fast-firing MG 81Z twin installations, each firing 3,600 rpm with belt feed. The rear cone had electric rotation to assist in aiming in all rearwards directions. Small numbers were also made of the **A-3** dual-control trainer, supplemented by a few A-0 and A-1 aircraft brought up to A-3 standard. Although a few A-0s reached the 9.(H)/LG 2 training unit in 1940, the *Fliegende Auge* was hardly seen in front-line units until 1942. Then it became truly important, progressively replacing the Hs 126 in Luftwaffe and related units, and also serving with units of the Slovakian and Hungarian air forces. It proved to be a reliable, capable and very tough aircraft, on at least two occasions surviving Soviet

The cockpit of the Uhu resembled the compound eye of an insect, and even the propaganda department of the RLM called the type das Fliegende Auge. The eight vanes on each propeller spinner regulated the variable-pitch mechanism.

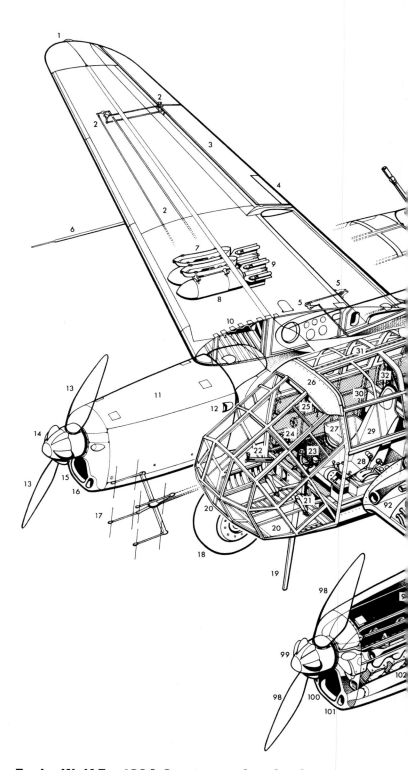

Focke-Wulf Fw 189A-2 cutaway drawing key

1 Starboard navigation light	7 ETC 50/VIIId underwing rack
2 Aileron control linkage (outer	fairings
and inner)	8 Two 50-kg (110-lb) SC 50
3 Starboard aileron	bombs
4 Aileron tab	9 Papier-maché 'screamers'
5 Starboard outer flap control	attached to bomb fins
linkage	10 Wing centre/outer section
6 Pitot tube	join

11 Starboard engine nacelle
12 Air intake
13 Argus two-bladed
controllable-pitch propeller
14 Pitch control vanes
15 Oil cooler intake
16 Engine air intake

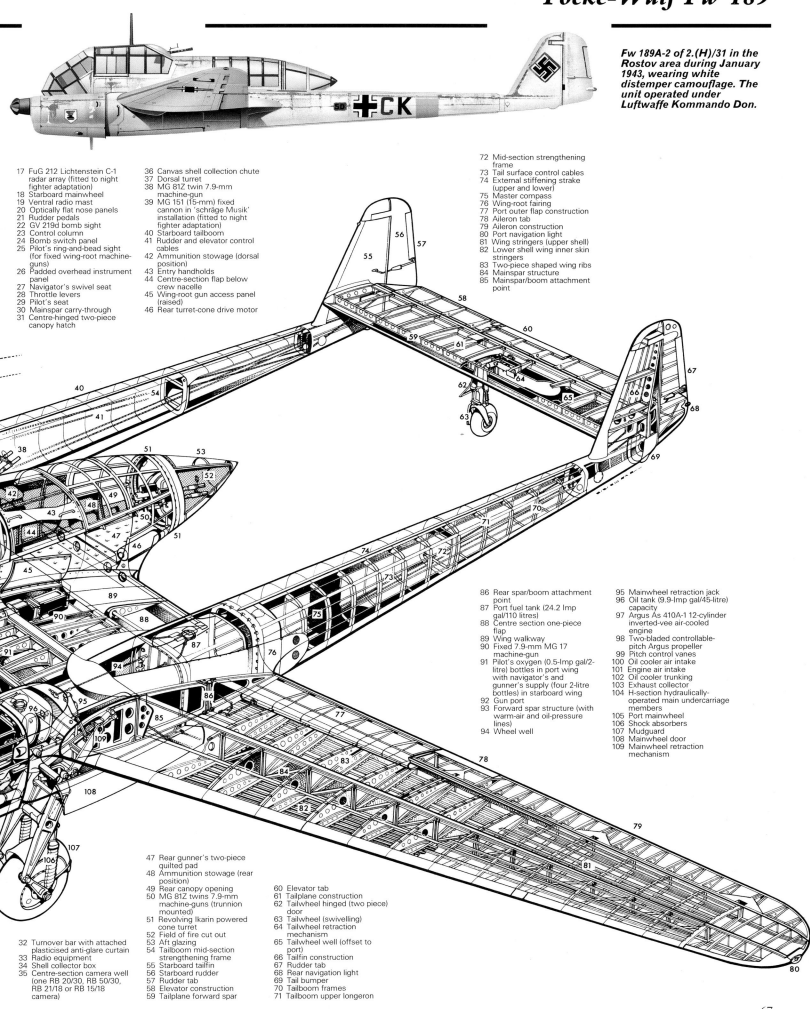

Focke-Wulf Fw 189

Fw 189A-2 of 2.(H)/31 in the Rostov area during January 1943, wearing white distemper camouflage. The unit operated under Luftwaffe Kommando Don.

17 FuG 212 Lichtenstein C-1 radar array (fitted to night fighter adaptation)
18 Starboard mainwheel
19 Ventral radio mast
20 Optically flat nose panels
21 Rudder pedals
22 GV 219d bomb sight
23 Control column
24 Bomb switch panel
25 Pilot's ring-and-bead sight (for fixed wing-root machine-guns)
26 Padded overhead instrument panel
27 Navigator's swivel seat
28 Throttle levers
29 Pilot's seat
30 Mainspar carry-through
31 Centre-hinged two-piece canopy hatch

36 Canvas shell collection chute
37 Dorsal turret
38 MG 81Z twin 7.9-mm machine-gun
39 MG 151 (15-mm) fixed cannon in 'schräge Musik' installation (fitted to night fighter adaptation)
40 Starboard tailboom
41 Rudder and elevator control cables
42 Ammunition stowage (dorsal position)
43 Entry handholds
44 Centre-section flap below crew nacelle
45 Wing-root gun access panel (raised)
46 Rear turret-cone drive motor

72 Mid-section strengthening frame
73 Tail surface control cables
74 External stiffening strake (upper and lower)
75 Master compass
76 Wing-root fairing
77 Port outer flap construction
78 Aileron tab
79 Aileron construction
80 Port navigation light
81 Wing stringers (upper shell)
82 Lower shell wing inner skin stringers
83 Two-piece shaped wing ribs
84 Mainspar structure
85 Mainspar/boom attachment point

32 Turnover bar with attached plasticised anti-glare curtain
33 Radio equipment
34 Shell collector box
35 Centre-section camera well (one RB 20/30, RB 50/30, RB 21/18 or RB 15/18 camera)

47 Rear gunner's two-piece quilted pad
48 Ammunition stowage (rear position)
49 Rear canopy opening
50 MG 81Z twins 7.9-mm machine-guns (trunnion mounted)
51 Revolving Ikarin powered cone turret
52 Field of fire cut out
53 Aft glazing
54 Tailboom mid-section strengthening frame
55 Starboard tailfin
56 Starboard rudder
57 Rudder tab
58 Elevator construction
59 Tailplane forward spar

60 Elevator tab
61 Tailplane construction
62 Tailwheel hinged (two piece) door
63 Tailwheel (swivelling)
64 Tailwheel retraction mechanism
65 Tailwheel well (offset to port)
66 Tailfin construction
67 Rudder tab
68 Rear navigation light
69 Tail bumper
70 Tailboom frames
71 Tailboom upper longeron

86 Rear spar/boom attachment point
87 Port fuel tank (24.2 Imp gal/110 litres)
88 Centre section one-piece flap
89 Wing walkway
90 Fixed 7.9-mm MG 17 machine-gun
91 Pilot's oxygen (0.5-Imp gal/2-litre) bottles in port wing with navigator's and gunner's supply (four 2-litre bottles) in starboard wing
92 Gun port
93 Forward spar structure (with warm-air and oil-pressure lines)
94 Wheel well

95 Mainwheel retraction jack
96 Oil tank (9.9-Imp gal/45-litre) capacity
97 Argus As 410A-1 12-cylinder inverted-vee air-cooled engine
98 Two-bladed controllable-pitch Argus propeller
99 Pitch control vanes
100 Oil cooler air intake
101 Engine air intake
102 Oil cooler trunking
103 Exhaust collector
104 H-section hydraulically-operated main undercarriage members
105 Port mainwheel
106 Shock absorbers
107 Mudguard
108 Mainwheel door
109 Mainwheel retraction mechanism

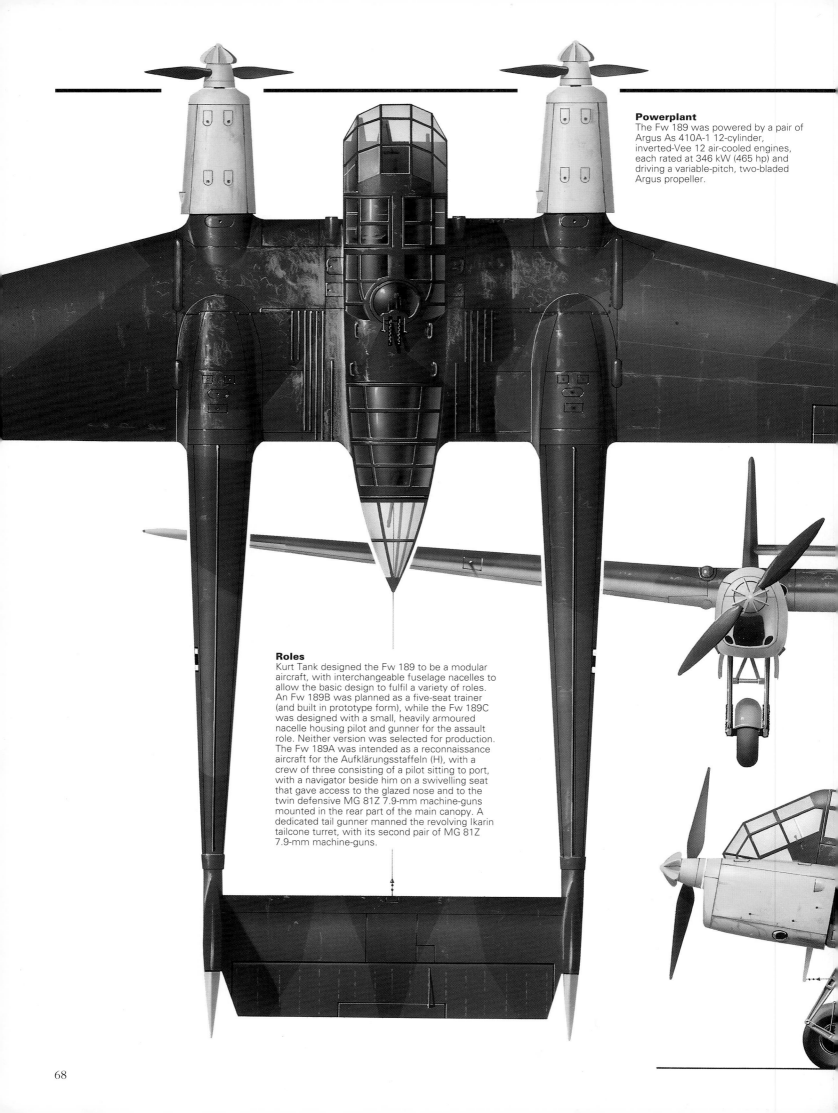

Powerplant
The Fw 189 was powered by a pair of Argus As 410A-1 12-cylinder, inverted-Vee 12 air-cooled engines, each rated at 346 kW (465 hp) and driving a variable-pitch, two-bladed Argus propeller.

Roles
Kurt Tank designed the Fw 189 to be a modular aircraft, with interchangeable fuselage nacelles to allow the basic design to fulfil a variety of roles. An Fw 189B was planned as a five-seat trainer (and built in prototype form), while the Fw 189C was designed with a small, heavily armoured nacelle housing pilot and gunner for the assault role. Neither version was selected for production. The Fw 189A was intended as a reconnaissance aircraft for the Aufklärungsstaffeln (H), with a crew of three consisting of a pilot sitting to port, with a navigator beside him on a swivelling seat that gave access to the glazed nose and to the twin defensive MG 81Z 7.9-mm machine-guns mounted in the rear part of the main canopy. A dedicated tail gunner manned the revolving Ikarin tailcone turret, with its second pair of MG 81Z 7.9-mm machine-guns.

Configuration

The Luftwaffe's Technischen Amt visualised that its requirement for a new aircraft for the Aufklärungsstaffeln, to replace the ageing Heinkel He 46, would be met by a single-engined aircraft, probably a high-winged monoplane. The competing Arado Ar 198 was just such an aircraft, but the Blohm und Voss BV 141 and the Focke-Wulf submission were more unconventional. The asymmetric BV 141 combined a glazed crew pod with a separate tailboom and single engine nacelle, while the Fw 189 featured two smaller engines, with interchangeable oval-section twin booms supporting the tail unit, and with a central crew nacelle. Of all-metal construction, the Fw 189 had three-spar stressed-skin wings, with a rectangular centre-section supporting the crew nacelles and tailboom/engine nacelles, and with tapering outer panels. The fabric-covered split trailing-edge flaps were electrically operated, while the fabric-covered, metal-framed ailerons, rudders and elevator were manually operated.

Specification
Fw 189A-2
Type: three-seat tactical reconnaissance and army co-operation aircraft
Powerplant: two Argus As 410A-1 12-cylinder inverted-Vee engines, each rated at 343.8 kW (465 hp) for take-off
Dimensions: wing span 18.40 m (60 ft 4 in); length 12.03 m (39 ft 5 in); height 3.10 m (10 ft 2 in); wing area 38.0 m² (409 sq ft)
Weights: empty 2830 kg (6,239 lb); normal loaded 3950 kg (8,708 lb); maximum loaded 4170 kg (9,193 lb)
Performance: maximum speed 350 km/h (217 mph) at 2400 m (7,875 ft); maximum cruising speed 325 km/h (202 mph) at 2400 m (7,875 ft); economical cruising speed 305 km/h (189 mph); normal range 670 km (416 miles); endurance 2 hours 10 minutes; service ceiling 7300 m (23,950 ft)
Armament: two 7.9-mm MG 17 machine-guns in wingroots; two 7.9-mm MG 81 machine-guns on flexible mounts in dorsal position; two 7.9-mm MG 81 machine-guns in revolving Ikaria powered cone turret; four ETC 50/VIIId underwing racks for 50-kg (110-lb) SC 50 bombs

Production

Production of the Fw 189 at Bremen built up rapidly, but attrition of the Hs 126A in France was such that a second production line was set up at the former Aero factory in Prague. Production at Bremen tailed off during 1941, due to the plant's commitment to Fw 190 production, and jigs were transferred to Mérignac in France, which became the sole source of Fw 189 production during early 1943. A total of 828 production Fw 189s was produced, 293 from Mérignac and 337 from Prague.

Armament

Although intended for the reconnaissance role, the Fw 189 was surprisingly well-armed. In addition to the two pairs of MG 81Z 7.9-mm machine-guns in the crew nacelle (single MG 15s in the Fw 189A-1), the aircraft had a pair of 7.9-mm MG 17 machine-guns in the wingroots and bomb racks for up to eight SC 50 (50-kg/110-lb) bombs. The final major production version, the Fw 189A-4, had increased armour protection and introduced 20-mm MG FF cannon in the wingroots.

Undercarriage

The Fw 189's tailplane retracted to port to lie within the tailplane, while the main undercarriage units retracted aft into the engine nacelle/tailboom junctions.

Focke-Wulf Fw 189A-2 Aufklärungsgruppe(H)/14 Salzburg, 1945

This Fw 189A-2 of AufklGr (H)/14 is seen with Eastern Front tactical markings in yellow, as it was when captured by US forces at Salzburg in 1945. The slender wings, matchstick booms and small Argus engines of the Fw 189 did not give rise to much optimism when viewed for the first time, yet the type achieved an enviable reputation with its pilots. Superbly agile, the Uhu could escape most fighter attacks by tight turns, while the reliable engines and smooth ride made it a comfortable aircraft in which to fly. Most served on the Eastern Front, wearing the theatre markings of yellow bands around the boom and wingtips. This is an Fw 189A-2, which introduced the MG 81Z twin machine-gun installation to both dorsal and tailcone positions.

Codes

This Fw 189 has its individual aircraft letter painted in red and outlined in white, indicating its assignment to a second *Staffel* (2., 6., 10. or 14. *Staffel*), while the last letter – K – denotes the I *Gruppe*, narrowing it down to 2.*Staffel*.

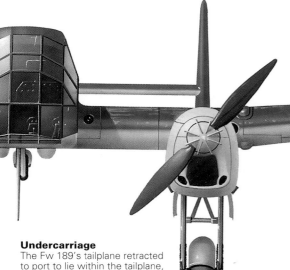

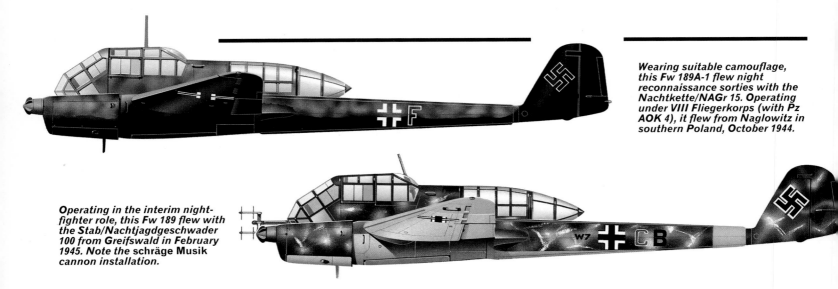

ramming attacks and frequently fighting off hostile fighters.

In late 1942 small numbers were delivered as A-4 close-support and reconnaissance aircraft, with extra armour and with the forward-firing MG 17s replaced by 20-mm MG FFs. The Bremen and Prague factories ceased production in 1943, but the French complex kept going until January 1944. Including prototypes, output comprised six in 1939, 38 in 1940, 250 in 1941, 327 in 1942, 226 in 1943 and 17 in 1944, making a grand total of 864. These numbers included a few for the North African campaign with desert survival equipment and sand filters, and two A-1s modified for use as staff transports for General-feldmarschall Kesselring and General Jeschonnek. In addition, at least 30 A-1s were modified as night-fighters, serving with I/NJG 100 and with NJG 5. Conversion involved removing reconnaissance gear and various other items, adding FuG 212 Lichtenstein C-1 interception radar, with the usual quad array of dipole aerials ahead of the nose, and replacing the mid-upper MG 81Z guns by a fixed upward-firing MG 151/15 (occasionally an MG 151//20).

There were two main branches of the family that were terminated. The **Fw 189B** was to have been a crew trainer, with accommodation for five, including dual pilot controls. The **V5** prototype was accordingly completed in early 1939 with a conventional nacelle of stressed-skin construction, with just a normal glazed cockpit and further glazing for a cockpit at the rear. Obviously far more capable and economical than existing aircraft used for crew training, the Fw 189B appealed to the Luftwaffe at a time when the 189A did not, and in 1939-40 the Bremen works delivered three pre-production **B-0**s and 10 **B-1**s. There was to have been a twin-float seaplane version, the **Fw 189D**, but this was cancelled.

The other main branch that did not go into production was the **Fw 189C**. This was to have been an armoured close-support version, the nacelle taking the form of a cramped box just big enough for the pilot and an aft-facing rear gunner, the whole thing being made of

thick armour with the exception of tiny inserts of thick armoured glass. In the winter of 1938-39, the original V1 prototype was rebuilt with the planned armoured nacelle, becoming the **V1b**, flown in spring 1939. The pilot could hardly see out and, far from being able to aim his MG 15, the gunner had hardly any vision at all. In any case, the handling of the V1b was poor and performance unimpressive. On the other hand, the rival Henschel Hs 129 was even worse.

In early 1940, Focke-Wulf flew the somewhat improved Fw 189 V6, with the revised engines and landing gear of the 189A-0, an improved armoured nacelle offering better visibility to both crew, and upgraded armament of two 20-mm MG FF plus four MG 17 firing forwards and a twin MG 81Z firing aft. In the event, although the Hs 129 was far from satisfactory, it was picked for production mainly because of its smaller size and lower cost.

Although the As 410 was an excellent engine, Focke-Wulf continued to investigate options with more power. The **Fw 189E** was to have been powered by the same French GR14M 4/5 radial of 522 kW (700 hp) as fitted to the production Hs 129B; SNCASO designed and carried out a single conversion, but this sole 189E crashed en route to evaluation in Germany in early 1943. Greater success attended the **Fw 189F**, an **A-2** powered by 447-kW (600-hp) As 411MA-1 engines as used on the Si 204D. This caused no problems, and the final 17 aircraft made at Bordeaux in 1944 were **Fw 189F-1**s. The **F-2** was to have had extra armour and electric landing gear operation, but none was built. Also unbuilt, the **Fw 189G** was to have had 708-kW (950-hp) As 402 engines and a strengthened structure.

The V6 was also completed as an Fw 189C prototype; it was essentially similar to the V1b but incorporated variable-pitch propellers and armament in the centre-section of the wing. This comprised two 20-mm MG FF cannon and four MG 17 machine-guns. A pair of MG 81s protected the rear.

Focke-Wulf Fw 190/Ta 152

Conceived in 1937 as a contemporary of the Hawker Typhoon, and for the same reason – to replace the first generation of monoplane interceptors (the Hawker Hurricane and the Messerschmitt Bf 109) – the design of the **Focke-Wulf Fw 190** was tendered with two alternative engines, the Daimler-Benz DB 601 inline and the BMW 139 radial, the latter being selected to power the prototype on account of its assumed higher power development potential. Detail design commenced under the leadership of Oberingenieur Blaser and the first prototype was flown by test pilot Hans Sander at Bremen on 1 June 1939.

The first two aircraft featured large, low-drag ducted spinners, but these were soon discarded as they were thought to cause engine overheating. After the BMW 139 had been abandoned, the **Fw 190A** entered production with the BMW 801 14-cylinder radial with fan-assisted cooling. The first nine pre-production **Fw 190A-0**s featured small wings of 15.00-m² (161.46-sq ft) area, but the definitive version had larger wings of 18.30-m² (196.99-sq ft) area.

Service trials at Rechlin went ahead in 1940 without undue problems, although Luftwaffe pilots suggested that the proposed armament of the **Fw 190A-1** (four synchronised 7.9-mm/0.31-in MG 17 machine-guns) would meet with spirited criticism in combat service. Production of the 100 Fw 190A-1s at Hamburg and Bremen was completed by the end of May 1941, and these were powered by 1194-kW (1,600-hp) BMW 801C engines which bestowed a top speed of 624 km/h (388 mph). The aircraft were flown by Erprobungsstelle Rechlin and 6./JG 26, the latter based at Le Bourget in August. The following month, the first combats were reported with RAF Supermarine Spitfire Vs, showing the German fighters to be markedly superior, albeit lacking in weapon punch.

New armament

Already, the early gun criticisms had led to the **Fw 190A-2** version with two wingroot-mounted synchronised 20-mm MG FF cannon and two MG 17 guns; with a speed of 614 km/h (382 mph), this up-

Right: Pilots walk out to their Fw 190A-4s 'somewhere in France' during 1943. Each has a belt of flare cartridges slung around his lower leg. The aircraft have received a hasty application of scribble camouflage on their flanks and fins. JG 2 and JG 26 were the main operators of the Fw 190 in the West, although the type also served with 4.(F) and 5.(F)/123 and with Nahaufklärungsgruppe 13 in the fighter reconnaissance role. Until the introduction of the Spitfire Mk IX, the Fw 190 gave the Luftwaffe fighter pilots a key advantage.

Below: Although not showing the elegance of the Spitfire, few fighters have looked more aggressively purposeful than the Fw 190. This aircraft, devoid of weapons, is an Fw 190G-3 captured by the Americans before it could be delivered to a frontline unit. The G-series Fw 190 was developed as an extended-range fighter-bomber and was externally similar to the Fw 190A-5/U-13 with ETC 501 fuselage bomb racks and no fuselage-mounted guns.

Participating in the great tank battle of Kursk in July 1943, this Fw 190A-4/U3 of the Gefechtsverband Druschel (II/SchG 1) features yellow theatre panels, fighter arm staff marks (forward black bar), Gruppe marks (aft black bar) and 4.Staffel (red) individual letter. Oberst Alfred Druschel was one of the most experienced assault pilots in the Luftwaffe, gaining the Swords and Oakleaves to the Knight's Cross. He was killed on 1 January 1945.

Temporarily painted matt black, this Fw 190A-5/U8, with centre-line bomb rack and wing drop tanks, belonged to I Gruppe, Schnellkampfgeschwader (SKG) 10 during the Jabo attacks on southern England during summer 1943. Based at Poix in France, this unit virtually obliterated all national insignia in the interests of camouflage.

'Yellow Nine' of II Gruppe Jagdgeschwader 54 'Grunherz' was an Fw 190A-5 flown by Leutnant Helmut Sturm in Estonia during June 1944. The yellow panels indicate the war theatre, and the two-tone green upper surfaces the unit's 'summer' camouflage.

gunned version still had the edge over the Spitfire V. By the end of March 1942, JG 26, commanded by Adolf Galland, was fully equipped with Fw 190A-2s. Thirty Fw 190As had accompanied the escort forces during the famous Channel break-out by the battle-cruisers *Scharnhorst* and *Gneisenau* in February, Fw 190A-2s of III/JG 26 being involved in the one-sided action against Lieutenant Commander Eugene Esmonde's Fairey Swordfish torpedo strike.

As the RAF desperately sought to introduce an answer to the Fw 190, production of the German fighter was stepped up as Focke-Wulf factories at Cottbus, Marienburg, Neubrandenburg, Schwerin, Sorau and Tutow joined the programme, as well as the Ago and Fieseler plants. The **Fw 190A-3**, with 1268-kW (1,700-hp) BMW 801DG, four 20-mm and two 7.9-mm (0.31-in) guns, joined II/JG 26 in March 1942 and shortly afterwards began to equip the only other Luftwaffe fighter *Geschwader* in the west, JG 2.

Thus, by the time the RAF was ready to introduce its new Spitfire IX and Typhoon fighters to combat over the Dieppe landings in August 1942, the Luftwaffe could field some 200 Fw 190As in opposition. Unfortunately, not only had the RAF underestimated the number of these fighters available but they were unaware that a new version, the **Fw 190A-4**, had appeared with a water-injected 1567-kW (2,100-hp) BMW 801D-2 engine and a top speed of 670 km/h (416 mph), and that a bomb-carrying variant, the **Fw 190A-3/U1**, was in service. (The suffix 'U' indicated Umrust-Bausatz, or factory conversion set.) The result was a stinging defeat for the RAF, which lost a total of 106 aircraft, including 97 to Fw 190s. As a result largely of mismanagement, neither the Spitfire IX nor the Typhoon had been able to redress the balance.

It would have been of little comfort had the RAF known that the Germans had for many months devoted all the Fw 190 resources to the Channel front, such was the esteem held for the Spitfire V. Indeed, despite the ferocious tempo of battle on the Eastern Front, which had opened in June 1941, no Fw 190A fighters fought on that front until well into 1942, when I/JG 51 received Fw 190A-4s. Fw 190A-3s and A-4s were also issued to IV/JG 5 and to JG 1 for home defence and protection of German fleet units in Norway. A reconnaissance version of the Fw 190A-3 was first flown by 9.(H)/LG 2 in March 1942 on the Russian Front. The **Fw 190A-4/U4** reconnaissance fighter joined NAufklGr 13 in France, and **Fw 190A-4/Trop** ground-attack fighter-bombers appeared in North Africa with I/SG 2 during 1942. Before the end of that year, Fw 190A-3/U1s and **Fw 190A-4/U8**s of SKG 10, each able to carry a 500-kg (1,100-lb)

The unarmed Focke-Wulf Fw 190 V1 (first prototype, D-OPZE) with fan-cooled BMW 139 and ducted spinner, is seen at the time of its first flight on 1 June 1939. Numerous other differences from subsequent production versions are evident, including small tail wheel, absence of fuselage wheel doors, and the hinged door covers on the wheel leg.

Early Focke-Wulf Fw 190A-1s undergo final assembly at Bremen in 1941. Particularly evident in this picture is the exceptionally wide-track main landing gear and the large number of hinged panels providing access to the compact BMW 801 radial engine. Just visible are the pair of nose-mounted MG 17 machine-guns.

Fw 190Gs of II Gruppe, Schlachtgeschwader 2 'Immelmann', probably in mid-1943. The unit, commanded by Major Heinz Frank, had been the first to equip with this ground-attack version in North Africa but moved to the Eastern Front (note the yellow theatre panels). Shown here are 5. Staffel aircraft (spinner tips and letters in red), several aircraft displaying the 'gun-toting Mickey Mouse' emblem of the II Gruppe.

The last of eighteen pre-production Fw 190A-0s on approach. This was the 25th Fw 190 built, and had the full-standard big wing. The first nine Fw 190A-0s had the original narrow-chord wing of the prototype, with greater taper on leading and trailing edges.

One of the few surviving Fw 190s is this two-seat Fw 190A-8/U1, now in the possession of the RAF Museum and based at RAF St. Athan, whose engine is still regularly run up. Only a handful of two-seat conversions were produced.

bomb, had embarked on a series of daylight low-level 'tip and run' attacks against cities and ports in southern England, forcing Fighter Command to deploy disproportionately heavy fighter defences to counter the threat. Some measure of the dependence now placed on the Fw 190 may be judged from the fact that more than 1,900 Fw 190A-3s and A-4s had reached the Luftwaffe in 1942 (compared with some 500 Typhoons and Spitfire IXs for the RAF).

Rocket-launchers

Early in 1943 there appeared the **Fw 190A-5** with slightly lengthened engine mountings, and with it a much increased range of *Rustsätze* (field conversion kits), including the **R6** that enabled the Fw 190A-5 (in modified form **Fw 190A-5/R6**) to carry two underwing WfrGr 21 (21-cm/8.27-in) rocket-launchers for use against the growing Boeing B-17 and Consolidated B-24 bomber fleets operated by the USAAF. The **Fw 190A-5/U2** night-bomber could carry a 500-kg (1,100-lb) bomb and two 300-litre (66-Imp gal) drop tanks; the **Fw 190A-5/U3** carried up to 1000 kg (2,205 lb) of bombs; the **Fw 190A-5/U12** was a heavily-armed fighter with six 20-mm MG 151/20 cannon and two MG 17s; while the **Fw 190A-5/U15**, of which three examples were built in November 1943, was equipped to carry a 950-kg (2,094-lb) LT 950 torpedo. A torpedo-carrying **Fw 190A-5/U14**, a lighter version of the U15 torpedo-fighter, is said to have been flown in action by Hauptmann Helmut Viedebannt of SKG 10.

The **Fw 190A-6**, in its standard form with reduced wing structure weight, was armed with four fast-firing 20-mm guns inside the wings (in addition to the two MG 17s in the nose); the **Fw 190A-6/R1** carried six 20-mm guns in underwing packs; and the **Fw 190A-6/R6** mounted four 30-mm MK 108 cannon in these packs, making it the most heavily-armed single-seater of the war. The **Fw 190A-6/R4**, with turbocharged BMW 801TS, had a top speed of 683 km/h (424 mph) at 10500 m (34,450 ft). Fighter-bomber Fw 190A-6 versions were able to carry a 1000-kg (2,205-lb) bomb under the fuselage.

The greatest single victory by Fw 190A-6s of JG 1, JG 5, JG 26, JG 51 and JG 54 was gained on 14 October 1943, when they decimated the US 8th Air Force's daylight bombers attacking Regensburg and Schweinfurt, destroying 79 and damaging 121 out of the force of 228. Had it not been for the introduction of superlative American close-escort fighters, particularly the North American P-51 Mustang, the Fw 190-equipped *Jagdflieger* would have decisively suppressed American daylight bombing attempts early in 1944.

Notwithstanding these successes, the changing fortunes of war forced the Luftwaffe to adopt a wholly defensive stance, of an increas-

Above: This Fw 190A-2 of II/JG 2 wears an unusual eye and fearsome sharkmouth on its cowling. Colourful unit markings and personal decorations were by no means rare on the Fw 190. The Fw 190A established an immediate ascendancy over the Spitfire Mk V, three Spitfires falling to Fw 190As in the first meeting, although the second resulted in the loss of an Fw 190, which the RAF believed was a captured Curtiss Hawk.

Left: Fw 190A-4/U3 Trop Jabos of Gefechtsverband Druschel (Battle Unit Druschel) taxy out, carrying underfuselage bombs and kicking up clouds of dust. This unit was a part of II/Schlachtgeschwader 1 and was heavily involved in the battles for Stalingrad and Kursk.

Right: A pair of Fw 190Fs of II Gruppe, Schlachtgeschwader 1. The aircraft carry Russian Front yellow theatre markings under the wingtips and cowling, and round the rear fuselage. Despite their assignment to the ground attack role, the Schlacht Fw 190s scored numerous kills against Soviet fighters and ground attack aircraft. During the period leading up to the evacuation of the Crimea one Schlacht pilot claimed 70 kills in only three weeks.

Below: Carrying a single SC 500 500-kg (1,102-lb) bomb on the centreline, an Fw 190F taxies out for an anti-tank mission. The schlacht Fw 190s used a wide variety of weapons against Allied tanks and other vehicles, including heavy cannon, rockets and even primitive cluster bombs.

ingly desperate nature. As the RAF night-bomber offensive increased in weight, the Luftwaffe employed Fw 190As (in particular Fw 190A-5/U2s) in the night-fighting role on moonlit nights, and the 'Wild Boar' tactics of Hajo Hermann's 30. Jagddivision, with three *Geschwader*, are reckoned to have accounted for some 200 RAF heavy bombers during the latter half of 1943.

While Fw 190A fighter-bombers were in action in the Mediterranean theatre, there appeared the **Fw 190A-7** with a pair of 20-mm cannon in the nose decking (in addition to the various wing gun combinations), and the **Fw 190A-8** with GM-1 nitrous-oxide power-boosting and all the adaptability afforded by earlier *Rustsätze* additions. The **Fw 190A-8/U1** was a two-seat version, of which three examples were produced to assist the conversion training of Junkers Ju 87 pilots to the Fw 190 for the ground-attack squadrons on the Eastern Front. The **Fw 190A-8/U3** was the upper component of the Mistel (mistletoe) composite weapon, riding the back of explosive-packed, unmanned Junkers Ju 88 aircraft. The **Fw 190A-8/U11** anti-shipping strike aircraft, with a BT 700 (700-kg/1,543-lb) torpedo-bomb, was flown in attacks against the Russian Black Sea Fleet in February 1944. The **Fw 190A-9**, with armoured wing leading edge, was powered by a 1490-kW (2,000-hp) BMW 801F (although the **Fw 190A-9/R11** had a turbocharged BMW 801TS). The **Fw 190A-10**, of which only prototypes were completed, featured provision for an increased range of bombs. Among the purely experimental versions of the Fw 190A were the **Fw 190 V74** with a seven-barrelled 30-mm SG117 Rohrblock cannon aimed by a Revi 242 gunsight, and the extraordinary **Fw 190 V75** with seven 45-cm (17.72-in) downward-firing mortars intended for low-level anti-tank use from a height of about 10 m (33 ft). Another interesting experiment was the use of large *Doppelreiter* overwing fuel tanks on the Fw 190A-8, evaluated by Erprobungskommando 25 under Major Georg Christl in July 1944.

The arrival of the Spitfire Mk IX in Fighter Command and its threat to combat domination by the Fw 190A led to the development of the **Fw 190B** series with GM-1 power-boosted BMW 801D-2 engine and pressurised cabin, but trouble with the latter led to the abandonment of this version after only a few prototypes had been pro-

duced. The **Fw 190C** series, of which five prototypes were completed with DB 603 inline engines, annular radiators, Hirth 9-2281 superchargers and four-bladed propellers, was also abandoned early in 1944.

The **Fw 190F** and **Fw 190G** series were essentially ground-attack versions of the basic Fw 190A series, the Fw 190F ('Panzer-Blitz') armoured assault aircraft appearing in the spring of 1944. Externally similar to the Fw 190A series, but with a bulged hood, this version featured gun armament reduced to two MG 17s and two 20-mm cannon, but had the ability to carry the 1000-kg (2,205-lb) bomb plus two 50-kg (110-lb) fragmentation bombs. The most important subvariant was the **Fw 190F-8**, which could carry 14 21-cm (8.27-in) rocket bombs, six 28-cm (11.02-in) rocket-launchers or 24 R4M unguided rockets; Fw 190F-8s first joined III(Pz)/KG 200 in the autumn of 1944.

The Fw 190G series actually entered operational service long before the Fw 190F, the first aircraft being sent to North Africa, joining SG 2 at Zarzoun, Tunisia, following the 'Torch' landings in November 1942. The majority, however, went to the Eastern Front where they played an active part in the great tank battle of Kursk in early July 1943. The **Fw 190G-1** version, with greatly strengthened undercarriage, could carry a 1800-kg (3,968-lb) bomb.

Having regard to the nature of the Luftwaffe's defensive operations during the last 30 months of the war, it is scarcely surprising that production assumed impressive proportions. No fewer than 20,087 Fw 190s (including 86 prototypes) were produced during the 1939-45 period, the peak daily production rate of 22 aircraft being reached early in 1944.

By the same token, many Luftwaffe pilots achieved remarkable combat feats at the controls of Fw 190s (not forgetting that of Josef Wurmheller, who shot down seven Spitfire Mk Vs in one day over the Dieppe beaches – despite concussion and a broken leg suffered in a recent accident). Pride of place must go to Oberleutnant Otto Kittel,

Hauptmann Moritz on the wing of his IV.Sturm/JG 3 Fw 190A at Schongau during the summer of 1944. Moritz was the Gruppenkommandeur, and his aircraft wears the appropriate double chevron insignia.

Focke-Wulf Fw 190/Ta 152

Pale grey Fw 190A-6/R11 of 1./NJG 10 flown by Oberleutnant Hans Krause from Werneuchen in August 1944. The pilot's insignia consisted of his nickname 'Illo' beneath the Wilde Sau emblem. Note Neptun radar arrays and two-shade grey on upper wing surface. Krause was later awarded the Knight's Cross and gained 28 night victories.

Defence of the Reich Fw 190A-8 (note red fuselage band) of I Gruppe/Jagdgeschwader 1, based at Twenthe in the Netherlands in December 1944. An aircraft with 'double chevrons' was being flown by Major Hans Ehlers, the Gruppenkommandeur, when he was shot down and killed on 27 December 1944.

the Luftwaffe's fourth-highest scoring pilot, of whose 267 air victories some 220 were gained in Fw 190A-4s and -5s. Other very high scorers in the Fw 190s included Walter Nowotny, Heinz Bär, Hermann Graf and Kurt Buhligen, all of whose scores included more than 100 victories gained with the guns of the aptly-named 'Butcher Bird'.

From radial to inline

From its first encounters with the RAF, it was clear to Focke-Wulf Flugzeugbau that the Fw 190 was a great success. Versions proliferated, among other things succeeding the Ju 87 as the chief close-support aircraft of the Luftwaffe. Its only shortcoming was that performance fell away drastically at high altitudes. Even with a massive GM-1 (nitrous oxide) boost system the performance was disappointing, and while this mattered little in the ground attack role (where the radial engines tolerance to battle damage was a major advantage), it limited the Fw 190's otherwise huge potential as an air superiority fighter, especially against Allied aircraft like the P-51D Mustang. The answer appeared to lie with a change of engine. The official view was that the Jumo 213 should be fitted, but designer Dipl Ing Kurt Tank favoured the bigger DB 603. Both were inverted-V12 liquid-cooled engines in the 1490-kW (2,000-hp) class.

From early 1942 numerous prototype and development aircraft were flown with these engines, mostly as B-series or C-series aircraft, and many having turbochargers in prominent ventral fairings. The latter looked like a coolant radiator, as on the American P-51 Mustang, but in fact all the liquid-cooled Fw 190s had an annular radiator on the nose, making them look superficially like radial-powered aircraft. Inevitably, the liquid-cooled engines increased the length of the nose, and to retain directional stability many inline-engined variants of the aircraft also had an extra section inserted into the rear fuselage. Such was the pressure on extreme-altitude performance – the RLM (Reichsluftfahrtministerium) calling for the ability to operate at 14 km

First of the 190 series to be powered by the 1238-kW (1,660-hp) BMW 801C-0 engine were the Fw 190 V5k and V5g, the former with small wing (15.0 m²/161.46 sq ft) area, illustrated here, and the latter with enlarged wing (18.3 m²/196.98 sq ft) area. The latter was chosen for production on account of its superior manoeuvrability.

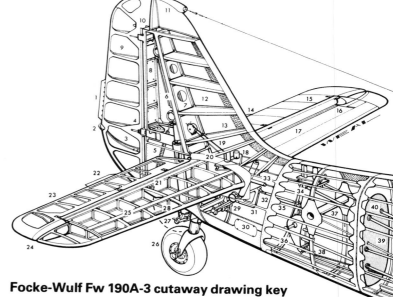

Focke-Wulf Fw 190A-3 cutaway drawing key

1 Rudder fixed tab
2 Tail navigation light
3 Leads
4 Rudder hinge/attachment
5 Tailwheel extension spring
6 Tailwheel shock-absorber leg retraction guide
7 Tailfin spar
8 Rudder post assembly
9 Rudder frame
10 Rudder upper hinge
11 Aerial attachment
12 Tailfin structure
13 Canted rib progression
14 Port elevator fixed tab
15 Port elevator
16 Mass balance
17 Port tailplane
18 Tailplane incidence motor unit
19 Tailwheel retraction pulley cables
20 Tailplane attachment
21 Starboard tailplane structure
22 Elevator fixed tab
23 Starboard elevator frame
24 Mass balance
25 Tailplane front spar
26 Semi-retracting tailwheel
27 Drag yoke
28 Tailwheel recess
29 Tailwheel locking linkage
30 Access panel
31 Actuating link
32 Push-pull rod
33 Rudder cables
34 Rudder control differential linkage
35 Fuselage/tail unit join
36 Elevator control differential
37 Fuselage lift tube
38 Elevator control cables
39 Bulkhead (No. 12) fabric panel (rear fuselage equipment dust protection)
40 Leather grommets
41 Rudder push-pull rods
42 Fuselage frame
43 Master compass
44 Flat-bottomed (equipment bay floor support) frame
45 First-aid kit

46 Optional camera (2 x Rb 12) installation (A-3/U4)
47 Control runs
48 Access hatch (port side)
49 Electrical leads
50 Distribution panel
51 Canopy channel slide cut-outs
52 Canopy solid aft fairing
53 Aerial
54 Head armour support bracket
55 Aerial attachment/take-up pulley
56 Equipment/effects stowage
57 FuG 7a/FuG 25a radio equipment bay
58 Battery
59 Cockpit aft bulkhead
60 Control runs
61 Cockpit floor/centre-section main structure
62 Wingroot fillet
63 Underfloor aft fuel tank (64 Imp gals/291 litres)
64 Underfloor forward fuel tank (51 Imp gal/232 litres)
65 Cockpit sidewall control runs
66 Seat support brackets
67 Armoured bulkhead
68 Pilot's seat
69 Canopy operating handwheel
70 14-mm armoured backplate

71 Pilot's headrest
72 Canopy
73 Windscreen frame assembly
74 Armoured-glass windscreen
75 Revi gunsight
76 Instrument panel shroud

77 Throttle
78 Port control console (trim switches/buttons)
79 Control column
80 Seat pan
81 Starboard control console (circuit breakers)
82 Underfloor linkage
83 Electrical junction box
84 Rudder pedal assembly
85 Instrument panel sections
86 Screen support frame
87 Two 7.9 mm MG 17 machine guns
88 Ammunition feed chute
89 Panel release catches
90 Fuselage armament ammunition boxes
91 Forward bulkhead
92 Inboard wing cannon ammunition boxes
93 Engine mounting lower attachment point
94 Cooling air exit louvres
95 Engine mounting upper attachment point
96 Oil pump assembly
97 Engine mounting ring

Displaying the black-white-black Defence of the Reich bands of Jagdgeschwader 4, 'White Eleven' was an Fw 190A-8 of the Geschwader's I Gruppe, based at Delmenhorst during the winter of 1944-45. Painting of the Geschwaderzeichen on the engine cowling was fairly rare at this late, hectic stage of the war.

'Blue Eight' of Schlachtgeschwader 4 during Operation Bodenplatte on 1 January 1945. This Fw 190F-8 with Spiralschnauze (spiral nose) markings was based at Köln-Wahn and featured the blue Staffel colour characteristic of bomber units.

98 Fuselage MG 17 ammunition cooling pipes
99 Machine gun front mounting brackets
100 Machine gun breech blister fairings
101 Port split flap section
102 Flap actuating electric motor
103 Port outer 20-mm MG FF cannon
104 Aileron control linkage
105 Aileron fixed tab

114 Aileron link assembly
115 Fuselage MG 17 muzzles
116 Muzzle troughs
117 Upper cowling panel
118 Fuselage MG 17 electrical synchronizing unit
119 Cowling panel ring
120 Cowling panel ring
121 BMW 801D-2 radial engine
122 Former ring
123 Upper panel release catches
124 Forward cowling support ring
125 Oil tank armour
126 Oil tank (10 Imp gal/ 45.5 litres)
127 Annular oil cooler assembly
128 Cooler armoured ring
129 Engine twelve-blade cooling fan

130 Three-blade propeller
131 Propeller boss
132 Oil cooler airflow track
133 Airflow duct fairing (to rear cylinders)
134 Lower panel release catches
135 Cowling lower panel section
136 Wingroot fairing
137 Centre-section wheel covers
138 Inboard 20-mm cannon muzzle
139 Wheel cover operating cable
140 Starboard wheel well
141 Mainwheel leg rib cut-out
142 Undercarriage retraction jack
143 Locking unit assembly
144 Inboard 20-mm cannon spent cartridge chute

145 Front spar inboard assembly
146 Ammunition feed chute
147 Fuselage/front spar attachment
148 Ammunition box bay
149 Starboard inboard 20-mm MG 151 cannon
150 Breech blister fairing
151 Fuselage/rear spar attachment
152 Rear spar
153 Starboard flap assembly
154 Inboard solid ribs
155 Rotating drive undercarriage retraction unit
156 Radius rod hinge
157 Outboard 20-mm cannon muzzle

158 Mainwheel leg strut mounting assembly
159 Undercarriage actuation drive motor
160 Starboard outboard 20-mm MG FF cannon
161 Front spar assembly
162 Ammunition drum
163 Rib cut-out
164 Aileron control linkage

165 Aileron fixed tab
166 Starboard aileron frame
167 Aileron hinge points
168 Rear spar
169 Wing lower shell outer 'floating ribs'
170 Wing undersurface inner skinning
171 Starboard detachable wingtip

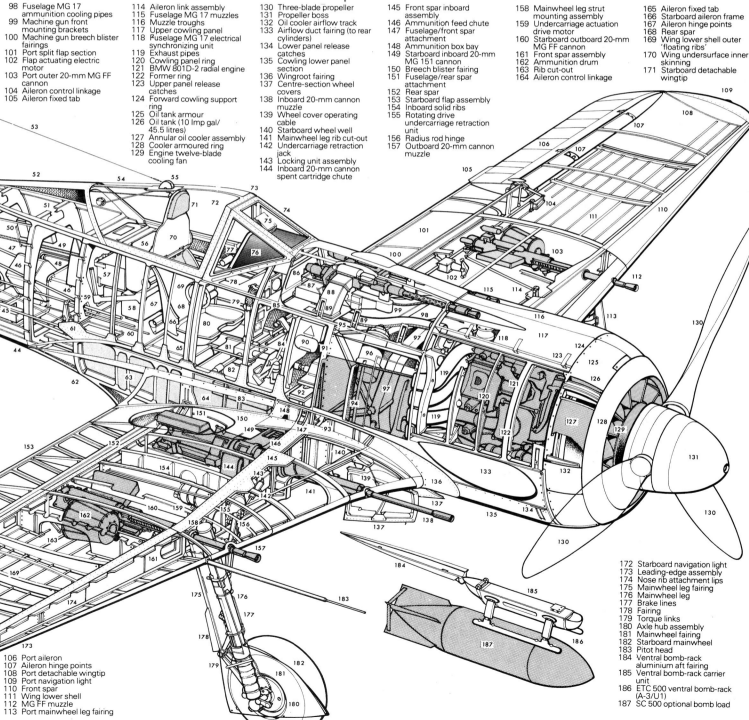

172 Starboard navigation light
173 Leading-edge assembly
174 Nose rib attachment lips
175 Mainwheel leg fairing
176 Mainwheel leg
177 Brake lines
178 Fairing
179 Torque links
180 Axle hub assembly
181 Mainwheel fairing
182 Starboard mainwheel
183 Pitot head
184 Ventral bomb-rack aluminium aft fairing
185 Ventral bomb-rack carrier unit
186 ETC 500 ventral bomb-rack (A-3/U1)
187 SC 500 optional bomb load

106 Port aileron
107 Aileron hinge points
108 Port detachable wingtip
109 Port navigation light
110 Front spar
111 Wing lower shell
112 MG FF muzzle
113 Port mainwheel leg fairing

Specification
Focke-Wulf Fw 190A-8
Type: single-seat fighter and fighter-bomber
Powerplant: one 1567-kW (2100-hp) BMW 801D-2 14-cylinder radial piston engine
Performance: maximum speed (clean) 654 km/h (408 mph); initial climb rate 720 m (2,363 ft) per minute; normal range 805 km (500 miles); service ceiling 11400 m (37,400 ft)
Weights: empty 3170 kg (7,000 lb); maximum loaded 4900 kg (10,800 lb)
Dimensions: span 10.50 m (34 ft 5½ in); length 8.84 m (29 ft 0 in); height 3.96 m (13 ft 0 in); wing area 18.3 m² (196.98 sq ft)
Armament: (A-8/R2) two 7.9-mm (0.31-in) MG 17 machine-guns, four 20-mm MG 151/20 cannon, one 500-kg (1,100-lb) and two 250-kg (550-lb) bombs, or one 300-litre (66-Imp gal) drop tank

Tail unit
The tailplane was a variable-incidence unit, driven by a motor in the base of the fin. The elevators had small internal mass balances in a small 'horn' at each end. The sturdy fin had two spars, one vertical along the rear of the structure and one angled along the leading edge. The full-height rudder had a small 'horn' at the tip and a fixed tab. The rear fuselage structure was used to house various equipment, including the master compass and cameras in some variants. At bulkhead No. 12 was a fabric panel which acted as a dust barrier for the equipment.The large tailwheel was semi-retractable. A large shock-absorber strut reached up into the fin structure.

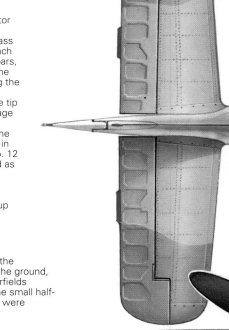

Fuselage and cockpit
The cockpit was well laid out and offered good visibility in flight. However, the broad nose and tail-down stance of the Fw 190 made ground visibility poor. The canopy, complete with fairing, slid back for ingress/egress, and could be jettisoned with explosive cartridges in emergency. Armour plate was provided behind and to the sides of the pilot. Fuel was held in two self-sealing tanks located under the pilot's seat, separated by a rear spar tie-through member. The forward tank held 193 litres (51 Imp gal), while the rear tank held 242 litres (64 Imp gal). Introduced on the Fw 190A-4, an FuG 16Z radio was installed in place of the FuG 7a equipment. A noticeable external difference was the small vertical mast for the wire aerial on the fin-tip. The aerial ran to an attaching pulley in the canopy, with a built-in take-up spring to maintain tension.

Main undercarriage
The stalky main wheel units retracted inwards to lie in the wingroots. The wide track made the aircraft stable on the ground, particularly useful when operating from the primitive airfields encountered by the Fw 190Fs on the Eastern Front. The small half-doors covering the bottom of the tyres when retracted were deleted from most bomb-carrying variants.

Focke-Wulf Fw 190A-8
5. Staffel/Jagdgeschwader 300
Löbnitz
Defence of the Reich, October 1944

One of the major production versions of the Focke-Wulf Fw 190 was the A-8 'Panzerbock', shown here in its basic configuration with the ETC 501 centre-line store rack moved forward 20 cm (7.9 in) and carrying a 300-litre (66-Imp gal) drop tank. Armed with four long-barrelled 20-mm MG 151/20 cannon in the wings and two MG 17 machine-guns in the nose, 'Red 19' was flown by Unteroffizier Ernst Schroder of 5. Staffel/Jagdgeschwader 300, in Defence of the Reich operations during October and November 1944. II (Sturm) Gruppe of JG 300 had been formed with Fw 190A-8s in July 1944 under Major Kurd Peters (awarded the Knight's Cross in October that year), and was one of the fighter units opposing the Western Allies during the invasion of Europe, adopting *Wilde Sau* night-fighting tactics during the autumn. *Staffelkapitän* of 5. Staffel was Oberleutnant Klaus Bretschneider, also a Knight's Cross holder, of whose 31 combat victories 14 were gained during *Wilde Sau* sorties, and who was shot down and killed in combat with P-51s on 24 December 1944.

Powerplant
The Fw 190A-8 was powered by the BMW 801D-2 14-cylinder two-row air-cooled radial in the lengthened engine mount of the A-5. The air-cooled engine was rated at 1268 kW (1,700 hp) for take-off and 1074 kW (1,440 hp) at 5700 m (18,700 ft). Introduced from the Fw 190A-4 onwards was provision for MW 50 water-methanol boosting. This acted as an anti-detonant, allowing higher boost pressures to be used for short periods. The extra power gained was useful, but necessitated very regular spark plug changes, and required the installation of a cylindrical 114-litre (25-Imp gal) water-methanol tank behind the pilot. A 12-bladed cooling fan was mounted in front of the engine, facilitating a build-up of air pressure in the engine compartment. This provided more than adequate cooling for the front row of cylinders. Large ducts ran either side of the engine to take cooling air to the rear row. Cooling air was dumped through louvres on either side of the engine, downstream of the flush main exhaust outlets. The oil cooler was mounted in an annular arrangement around the front of the engine. The Fw 190 smashed the theory that only sleek, inline-engined fighters could achieve good performance. At the heart of the aircraft's performance was the beautifully designed low-drag cowling around the engine, which was armoured at the front.

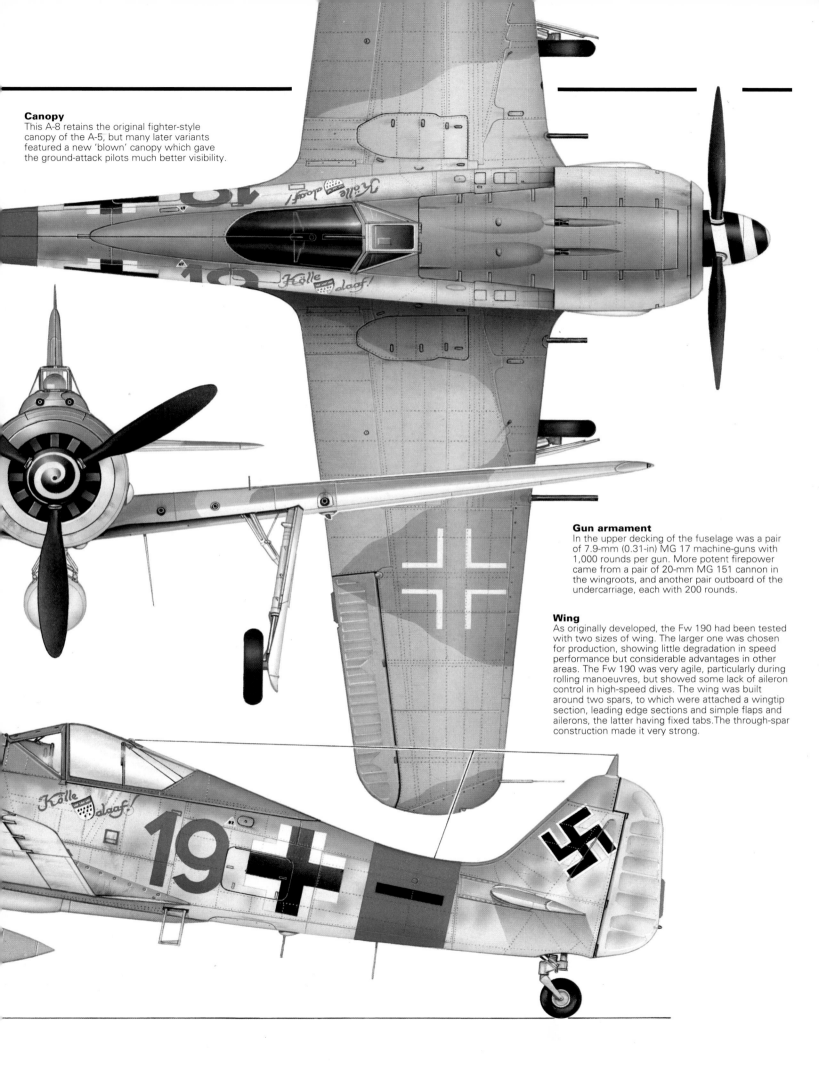

Canopy
This A-8 retains the original fighter-style canopy of the A-5, but many later variants featured a new 'blown' canopy which gave the ground-attack pilots much better visibility.

Gun armament
In the upper decking of the fuselage was a pair of 7.9-mm (0.31-in) MG 17 machine-guns with 1,000 rounds per gun. More potent firepower came from a pair of 20-mm MG 151 cannon in the wingroots, and another pair outboard of the undercarriage, each with 200 rounds.

Wing
As originally developed, the Fw 190 had been tested with two sizes of wing. The larger one was chosen for production, showing little degradation in speed performance but considerable advantages in other areas. The Fw 190 was very agile, particularly during rolling manoeuvres, but showed some lack of aileron control in high-speed dives. The wing was built around two spars, to which were attached a wingtip section, leading edge sections and simple flaps and ailerons, the latter having fixed tabs. The through-spar construction made it very strong.

Focke-Wulf Fw 190/Ta 152

The construction of the Fw 190D prototypes necessitated the conversion of six A-series airframes, which were followed by further A-7 airframes converted to serve as Fw 190D-0 pre-production aircraft with the Jumo 213A-1 engine. This aircraft is the first of them, the V53, displaying the A-7 armament of two MG 17s and four MG 151s.

(8.7 miles) – that some of the aircraft were fitted with pressurised cockpits, a turbo-supercharger and MW 50 (methanol/water) and GM-1 power boost systems.

Tank and his staff never wavered in their support for the big 445-litre (11.7-Imp gal) DB 603, and work never stopped on projects powered by it, leading to various Fw 190Cs, the Ta 152C and Ta 153. The official view continued to support the Junkers engine, and it was obvious as 1943 progressed that, as this engine would be available sooner, priority would have to be given to the **Fw 190D** series, powered by the Jumo 213A-1 rated at 1323 kW (1,776 hp) but capable of delivering 1669 kW (2,240 hp) for brief periods with MW 50 injection. It was natural, but perhaps unfortunate, that Tank should have

Above: A rare in-service view of an Fw 190D-9. About 700 Fw 190Ds were completed, but relatively few of these ever entered service. The type was involved in the futile Defence of the Reich operations against USAAF bombers, and played its part in Operation Bodenplatte, the Luftwaffe's ill-starred operation against Allied airfields in Belgium, France and the Netherlands.

The major production model was the Fw 190D-9, or 'Dora-Nine' as it was known in service. Improvements incorporated included a wider-chord fin, removal of two MG 151 cannon and the replacement of the fuselage MG 17 machine-guns by MG 131s of 13-mm calibre. Bomb racks were added and MW 50 water-methanol boosting was employed.

kept his sights consistently on the distant horizons with the DB 603 and revised airframes. This tended to make him always consider the Fw 190D as an interim aircraft, and he failed to fully exploit its potential. The problem was compounded by the fact that the Jumo 213, like the 211 before it, had been designed exclusively as an engine for bombers. The totally inaccurate rumours that filtered through to the 190 *Staffeln* were therefore to the effect that the 190D would be a lumbering, second-rate 'lash-up'.

Development of the D-series occupied two whole years, from about April 1942 until May 1944. Most of the initial flying was done with converted Fw 190A-1s, all with a fairly standard Jumo 213A in the nose (lengthening it by 0.6 m/2 ft), driving a propeller with three very broad blades, and with a 0.495-m (1.6-ft) section added to the rear fuselage immediately in front of the tail. In late 1943 some Fw 190A-7 conversions were made, most having the unchanged armament of four MG 151s in the wings and two MG 17s in the fuselage. In early 1944, however, further design changes resulted in deletion of the outboard 20-mm cannon, replacement of the 7.9-mm machine-guns by the 13-mm MG 131, and an increase in chord of the fin to improve stability in all conditions. This led to the definitive production **Fw 190D-9**, or 'Dora-Nine', in May 1944. The D-9 was fitted with three bomb racks, a low-diving sight and MW 50 injection.

Deliveries to the Luftwaffe began in August 1944, the first recipient *Gruppe* being III/JG 54 at Oldenburg. From the start it was obvious to the front-line pilots that, even though Tank himself dismissed the 'Dora-9' as "an emergency solution" when he visited them, it was actually a superb aircraft and at least a match for the P-51D or any other Allied fighter. Early in production the cockpit canopy was replaced by the bulged type previously introduced on the Fw 190F-2 to give better all-round view. Non-standard modifications included the **D-10** with an MG 151 in the left wing and an MK 108 firing through the propeller hub, and the **D-11** with a three-stage supercharger and four wing cannon, two MG 151s and two MK 108s. Many other variants appeared in the closing months of the war.

Beyond question, the 'Dora-9' was the best piston-engined fighter to see widespread service with Hitler's Luftwaffe. Despite apparent demolition by RAF bombing, and progressive capture by Allied armies, the many factories building the D-9 maintained a tremendous output, but the vast majority languished unused and undelivered because of shortages of fuel and pilots.

Acknowledging its origins

During 1942 Tank's staff concentrated on a series of more definitive offshoots of the Fw 190, designated **Fw 190Ra-1** to **Ra-6**, with the principal objective of improving high-altitude performance. Airframe modifications included a new wing centre-section, giving an increase in span to 11 m (36 ft) in short-span aircraft and to 14.8 m (48.5 ft) in others, together with a stretched fuselage with the cockpit 0.4 m (1.31 ft) further aft, and a longer rear fuselage attached to a fin of consider-

ably greater chord (much broader even than the D-9). The cockpit was pressurised and there were many minor changes, as well as a choice of several possible engines and many possible arrangements of armament. During 1943 the RLM accepted these developments in principle, to be implemented in two stages. The first, the *Sofort* programme, was to be designated **Ta 152**, the change from 'Fw' to 'Ta' showing the respect now accorded Tank personally. For the more distant future a *Fernziel* programme was to be undertaken to lead to a fighter designated **Ta 153**. Both were derived from the classic Fw 190, but the Ta 153 was to be essentially a new design.

Curiously, and in a rare bout of common sense not often repeated in Nazi Germany as it neared collapse, little effort was ever applied to the longer-term programme, priority instead being accorded to the almost achievable Ta 152. This good sense was only relative, however, since the effort expended on the Ta 152 might more usefully have been applied to improving the Fw 190D-9 and to building more of them. The Ta 153 was to have had a DB 603L with turbo-super-charger, or one of the many highly supercharged derivatives of the DB 603 such as the DB 622, 623 or 627. This was to be installed in a redesigned and enlarged fuselage containing a pressurised cockpit. The tail was to be similar to other (Ta 152) variants, with a broad fin and extended rear fuselage. The wing was also redesigned, in both short- and long-span versions, which as in the Ta 152 increased the track of the landing gear. There the matter rested, all that got off the drawing board being successive further modifications of the **Fw 190 V32** which had been built in 1942 as one of a series of Fw 190C series development aircraft with the DB 603 engine. The TK 11 turbocharger was removed, and the short-span Ta 153 wing was fitted. This aircraft resumed testing in November 1944, but nothing like a definitive Ta 153 was ever built.

Ta 152 – too late to matter

In contrast, the *Sofort* programme received massive attention, largely because by 1943 Germany could see that it was fast losing control of the sky, even in its own airspace, and superior high-altitude fighters were desperately needed. The immediate effort naturally concentrated on the Ra-1 and Ra-4 studies, because these were the long-span projects with the favoured Jumo 213 engine. Out of a profusion of projected **Ta 152A** and **Ta 152B** versions, the former with very heavy armament (such as three 30-mm and four 20-mm cannon) and the Bs

with a new fuselage, little happened beyond testing of components and armament schemes in converted Fw 190As. Many development aircraft were built in 1943-44 at Sorau, Cottbus and Hannover-Langenhagen, variously powered by the Jumo 213A (as in production for the 'Dora-9'), the 213C with provision for a cannon firing through the propeller hub, the high-altitude 213E with two-stage

The fifth pre-production Ta 152H-0 is seen on a compass-swinging platform at Cottbus, prior to delivery to the Luftwaffe. Armament of this model comprised a single 30-mm MK 108 cannon firing through the propeller spinner and two 20-mm MG 151 cannon mounted in the wing.

three-speed supercharger and intercooler, the 213F with three-stage supercharging system (with MW 50 injected before the third stage), and the 213J cleared to 3,700 rpm and with four-valve cylinders.

By mid-1944 immediate effort was being concentrated on the **Ta 152H** with the long-span wing, slightly reduced in span to 14.44 m (47 ft 4½ in)), with an area of 23.3 m² (251 sq ft) and Jumo 213E engine. The wing of the H had a full-span rear spar, the steel front spar extending only as far as the widely spaced main landing gears. The standard armament comprised a 30-mm MK 108 between the inverted-cylinder blocks firing through the propeller hub, with 90 rounds, and two 20-mm MG 151s in the inner wings each with 175 rounds, as well as a centreline rack for a 300-litre (79-Imp gal) auxiliary tank. The first two Ta 152H development prototypes were completed by July 1944, and work was speeded by many other H-series aircraft including the modified **Fw 190 V18, V29, V30, V32** and

Second unarmed prototype for the proposed high-altitude Fw 190C series was the V18, shown here in its U1 guise with DB 603A engine (which replaced the earlier DB 603G), four-bladed propeller and Hirth 9-2281 turbocharger. Inclusion of a pressurised cabin is evidenced by strengthening members on the canopy.

The Fw 190 V32 was a testbed for the Fw 190C, which was designed as a DB 603-powered pressurised high altitude fighter, and was then rebuilt as a Ta 152H-1 development aircraft with a Jumo 213 engine. It finally served as a testbed for the Ta 153, with a DB 603G, lengthened rear fuselage and short-span wings.

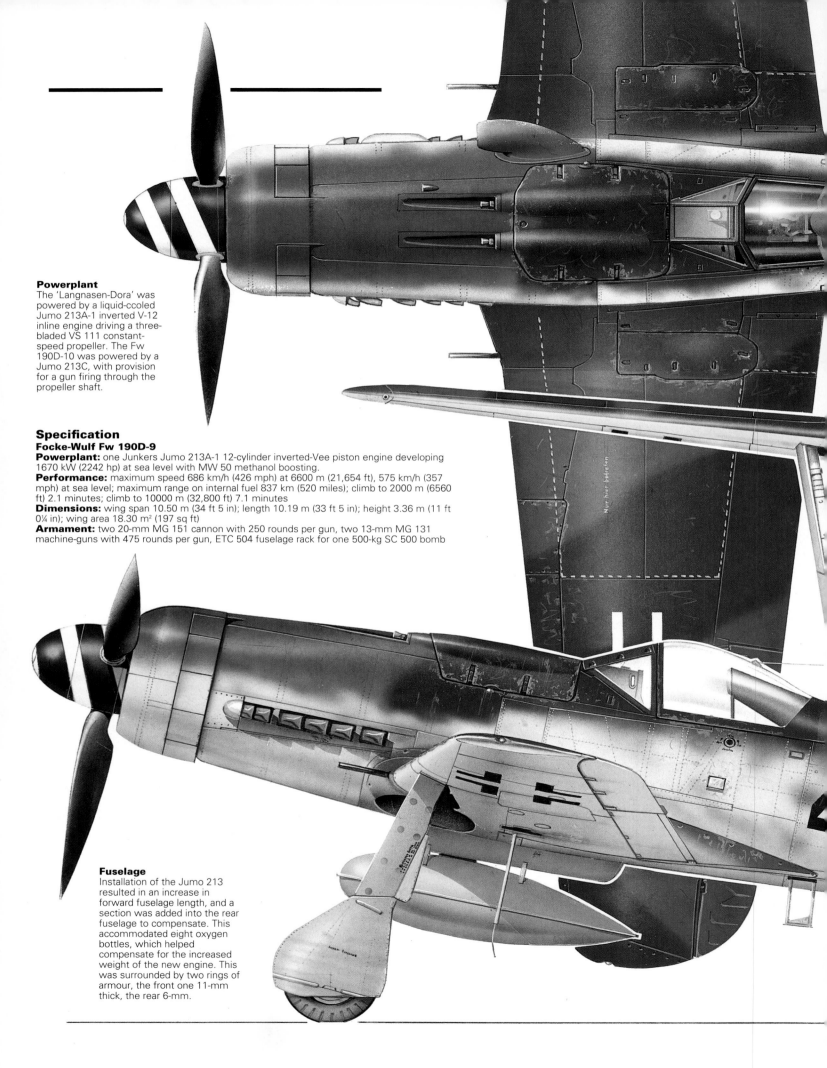

Powerplant

The 'Langnasen-Dora' was powered by a liquid-ccoled Jumo 213A-1 inverted V-12 inline engine driving a three-bladed VS 111 constant-speed propeller. The Fw 190D-10 was powered by a Jumo 213C, with provision for a gun firing through the propeller shaft.

Specification

Focke-Wulf Fw 190D-9

Powerplant: one Junkers Jumo 213A-1 12-cylinder inverted-Vee piston engine developing 1670 kW (2242 hp) at sea level with MW 50 methanol boosting.

Performance: maximum speed 686 km/h (426 mph) at 6600 m (21,654 ft), 575 km/h (357 mph) at sea level; maximum range on internal fuel 837 km (520 miles); climb to 2000 m (6560 ft) 2.1 minutes; climb to 10000 m (32,800 ft) 7.1 minutes

Dimensions: wing span 10.50 m (34 ft 5 in); length 10.19 m (33 ft 5 in); height 3.36 m (11 ft 0¼ in); wing area 18.30 m² (197 sq ft)

Armament: two 20-mm MG 151 cannon with 250 rounds per gun, two 13-mm MG 131 machine-guns with 475 rounds per gun, ETC 504 fuselage rack for one 500-kg SC 500 bomb

Fuselage

Installation of the Jumo 213 resulted in an increase in forward fuselage length, and a section was added into the rear fuselage to compensate. This accommodated eight oxygen bottles, which helped compensate for the increased weight of the new engine. This was surrounded by two rings of armour, the front one 11-mm thick, the rear 6-mm.

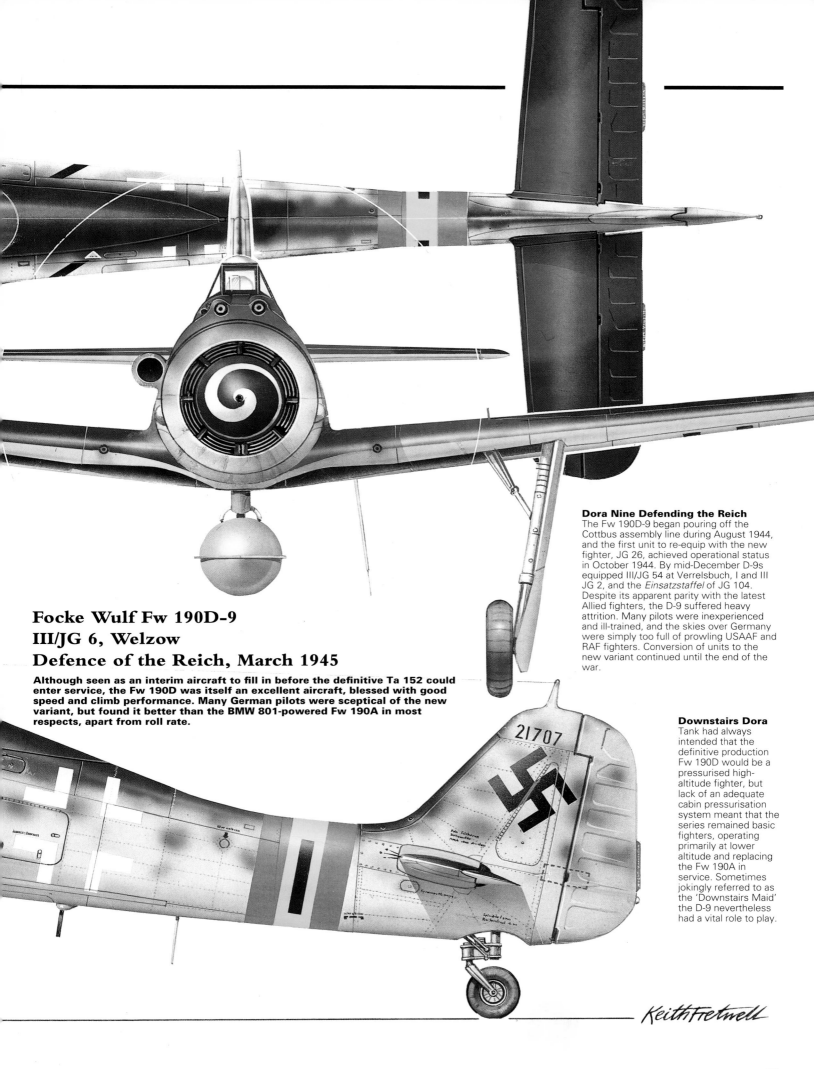

Focke Wulf Fw 190D-9
III/JG 6, Welzow
Defence of the Reich, March 1945

Although seen as an interim aircraft to fill in before the definitive Ta 152 could enter service, the Fw 190D was itself an excellent aircraft, blessed with good speed and climb performance. Many German pilots were sceptical of the new variant, but found it better than the BMW 801-powered Fw 190A in most respects, apart from roll rate.

Dora Nine Defending the Reich
The Fw 190D-9 began pouring off the Cottbus assembly line during August 1944, and the first unit to re-equip with the new fighter, JG 26, achieved operational status in October 1944. By mid-December D-9s equipped III/JG 54 at Verrelsbuch, I and III JG 2, and the *Einsatzstaffel* of JG 104. Despite its apparent parity with the latest Allied fighters, the D-9 suffered heavy attrition. Many pilots were inexperienced and ill-trained, and the skies over Germany were simply too full of prowling USAAF and RAF fighters. Conversion of units to the new variant continued until the end of the war.

Downstairs Dora
Tank had always intended that the definitive production Fw 190D would be a pressurised high-altitude fighter, but lack of an adequate cabin pressurisation system meant that the series remained basic fighters, operating primarily at lower altitude and replacing the Fw 190A in service. Sometimes jokingly referred to as the 'Downstairs Maid' the D-9 nevertheless had a vital role to play.

21707

Keith Fretwell

V33. By October 1944 the Luftwaffe Erprobungskommando Ta 152 had been formed at the test establishment at Rechlin, with the initial 20 **Ta 152H–0** aircraft from Cottbus. These lacked the crucial MW 50 and GM-1 power boost systems, as well as additional wing tankage bringing capacity up to 1618 litres (355 Imp gal) exclusive of the external tank and the power-boost fluids. The MW 50 and GM-1 had been tested on the V33 prototype and all deficiencies were rectified in the Ta 152H-1 series of November 1944.

Covering the jets

The extra fuel and power-boost systems more than countered the relatively light armament and made the 152H a heavy aircraft at 5217 kg (11,501 lb). The **H-1/R31** had even greater fuel capacity and weighed 5505 kg (12,136 lb). There were predictably numerous sub-types of Ta 152H, including versions for reconnaissance and as the upper (piloted) component of Mistel composite aircraft, but most were delivered purely as fighters. At least 150 were delivered from Cottbus before the factory had to be evacuated, small numbers serving with JG 301, chiefly to fly over Me 262 bases when the jets were taking off and landing, and were therefore at their most vulnerable. This kind of low altitude air defence task was one which could have been fulfilled by earlier Fw 190 variants, and it is hard to regard the Ta 152 as anything but a waste of time and resources and another distraction from the Luftwaffe's main aim of trying to stem the allied advance.

In August 1944 the RLM at last sanctioned fitting the DB 603, and there was an immediately frantic effort to fit this bigger engine to a variant designated **Ta 152C**. **Fw 190 V21** was converted with the

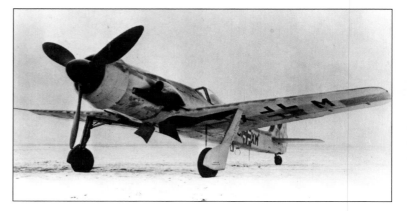

Intended primarily as a Zerstörer, the Ta 152C series featured short-span wings and the Daimler-Benz DB 603 engine, a big improvement in terms of power over the Jumo 213. This aircraft is the V7 prototype, otherwise known as the Ta 152C-0/R11 and featuring **Rüstsatz** *bad-weather equipment and an MW 50-boosted DB 603EM engine.*

DB 603E in November 1944, and a mass of other 190s and 152s followed with the 603L and 603EM engines rated with MW 50 at up to 1676 kW (2,250 hp). All C-series aircraft had the 11-m (36-ft) wing and various heavy armament, such as four MG 151 and one MK 108. Many versions were planned, including a torpedo carrier, but no Ta 152C reached the production stage.

Focke-Wulf Fw 190 and Ta 152 variants

Fw 190 V1 to **V80** (plus six others): prototypes and progressive development aircraft, 1939-44; served as prototypes for Fw 190A to G series and some Ta 152s
Fw 190A-0: nine aircraft with small wings, remaining 11 with large wings; BMW 801C-1; four 7.9-mm (0.31-in) guns
Fw 190A-1: four 7.9-mm (0.31-in) guns
Fw 190A-2: two 20-mm and two 7.9-mm (0.31-in) guns; BMW 801C-2
Fw 190A-3: four 20-mm and two 7.9-mm (0.31-in) guns, BMW 801D-2, also **U1** fighter-bomber, **U3** ground-attack fighter, **U4** reconnaissance fighter and **U7** fighter-bomber; 'Trop' sub-variants
Fw 190A-4: FuG 16Z radio, BMW 801D-2 with MW 50 injection; **U1** and **U8** fighter-bombers, **U4** ground-attack fighter, **R6** bomber-destroyer; 'Trop' sub-variants, introduced first *Rüstsätze*
Fw 190A-5: slightly lengthened mounting for BMW 801D-2; **U2** night ground-attack aircraft, **U3** similar with increased bomb load, **U4** reconnaissance aircraft, **U6** and **U8** fighter-bombers, **U11** bomber-destroyer, **U13** ground-attack fighter, **U14** and **U15** torpedo fighters, **U16** bomber-destroyer; **U17** was prototype for Fw 190F-3; 'Trop' sub variants
Fw 190A-6: FuG 16Ze and FuG 25 radio, lighter wing structure; **R1** to **R4** bomber-destroyer, R4 with BMW 801TS, **R6** bomber-destroyer with underwing rockets; 'Trop' sub-variants
Fw 190A-7: two 20-mm and two 13-mm (0.51-in) guns; *Rüstsätze* conversions as for Fw 190A-6
Fw 190A-8: FuG 16ZY radio GM-1 powerboosting; *Rüstsätze* conversions **R1** to **R6** as for Fw

190A-6; **R7** had armoured cockpit; **R11** all-weather fighter had PKS 12 and FuG 125 radio similar but with two 30-mm guns; **U1** two-seat trainer; **U3** upper component of Mistel weapon; **U11** fighter/torpedo bomber
Fw 190A-9: BMW 801F; *Rüstsätze* conversions similar to Fw 190A-6, but **R11** had BMW 801TS, and **R12** similar but two 30-mm guns
Fw 190A-10: numerous prototypes only; BMW 801TS/TH; three bomb or drop tank stations; four 20-mm and two 13-mm (0.51-in) guns
Fw 190B-0: three prototypes modified from Fw 190A-1s; various wing planforms; failure of pressure cabin caused discontinuation; one
Fw 190B-1 not completed
Fw 190C-0: six prototypes, including one modified Fw 190A-1; various engines with Hirth supercharger; development abandoned
Fw 190D-0: 10 aircraft converted from Fw 190A-7s; Junkers Jumo 213A engines with annular radiators; first 'long-nose' Fw 190s
Fw 190D-9: Jumo 213A; two 20-mm and two 13-mm (0.51-in) guns; most aircraft had bulged hoods; **R11** all-weather fighter with FuG 125 radio
Fw 190D-10: two prototypes converted from Fw 190D-0s; single 30-mm hub gun replaced guns in nose decking
Fw 190D-11: seven prototypes only; two 20-mm and two 30-mm guns; **R20** with PKS 12 radio; **R21** with FuG 125 radio
Fw 190D-12: one 30-mm and two 20-mm guns; armoured Jumo 213F; **R5** ground-attack fighter; **R11** all-weather fighter; **R21** with MW 50 injection; **R25** with Jumo 213EB
Fw 190D-13: Jumo 213EB; three 20-mm guns; **R5, R11, R21** and **R25** as for Fw 190D-12
Fw 190D-14: DB 603A; two

prototypes converted from Fw 190D-9 and Fw 190D-12
Fw 190D-15: DB 603EB; not built; intended as conversions from Fw 190A-8s and Fw 190F-8s
Fw 190E: reconnaissance fighter project, not built
Fw 190F-1: armoured fighter-bomber; one ETC 501 and two ETC 50 bomb racks; bulged canopy
Fw 190F-2: similar to Fw 190F-1 but additional ER4 adaptor bomb rack
Fw 190F-3: provision for underwing drop tanks; **R3** with two underwing 30-mm guns
Fw 190F-8: provision for variety of rockets and anti-personnel weapons; **U1** was proposed two-seat trainer; **U2** and **U3** had provision to carry various torpedo-bombs; **U14** was torpedo-fighter; **R1, R2, R3, R5, R8, R11, R14 R15** and **R16** all provided for various armament combinations
Fw 190F-9: armoured version of Fw 190A-9 and production in parallel; BMW 801TS
Fw 190F-10 to F-14: unbuilt projects
Fw 190F-15: one prototype, Fw 190F-8, BMW 801TS/TH
Fw 190F-16: one prototype, increased armour; BMW 801TS/TH
Fw 190G-0: two 20-mm guns; maximum bomb load 1000 kg (2,205 lb)
Fw 190G-1: strengthened undercarriage, one 1800-kg (3,968-lb) bomb; Junkers bomb rack
Fw 190G-2: as above but Messerschmitt bomb rack
Fw 190G-3: as above but Focke-Wulf bomb rack; **R5** could carry four fragmentation bombs under the wings
Fw 190G-4: three ETC 503 bomb racks
Fw 190G-7: intended to carry single 900-litre (198-Imp gal) drop tank
Fw 190G-8: BMW 801D-2, otherwise similar to Fw 190A-8; **R4**

had GM 1 power boost
Fw 190H-1: proposed high-altitude fighter with DB 603G, but not built
Ta 152A-1: unbuilt project similar to Fw 190D-9 with FuG 24 radio
Ta 152A-2: unbuilt project as above but with four 20-mm guns
Ta 152B-1: unbuilt project with hub-firing 30-mm gun
Ta 152B-2: unbuilt project with GM 1 power boost
Ta 152B-3: armoured ground-attack fighter project
Ta 152B-4: heavy fighter project; **R1** with two 13-mm and two 20-mm guns; **R2** with three 30-mm and two 20-mm guns
Ta 152B-5: one prototype built (**Fw 190 V53**); three 20-mm guns; **R11**, three prototypes built (**Ta 152 V19, V20** and **V21**)
Ta 152C: three prototypes built, DB 603L; all-weather fighter
Ta 152C-0 and **C-1:** three prototypes completed; DB 603L; many gun combinations proposed
Ta 152E-1: photo-reconnaissance aircraft; two prototypes completed
Ta 152E-2: high-altitude version of Ta 152E-1; one prototype (**Ta 152 V26**) completed
Ta 152H: high-altitude fighter; Jumo 213E; three modified Fw 190 prototypes (**Fw 190 V29, V30** and **V32**) completed
Ta 152H-0: 20 pre-production aircraft built at Cottbus in 1944; Jumo 213EB, **R11, R21** and **R31** variants with engine boost and radio variations
Ta 152H-1: one prototype (**Ta 152 V26**) modified from Ta 152E-2 and about a dozen production completed; **Ta 152H-10** was fighter reconnaissance version not completed at the end of the war
Ta 153: one prototype (**Fw 190 V32**) modified from Ta 152H prototype to include very high aspect ratio wing

Focke-Wulf Fw 200 Condor

In contrast with the belief that the Germans are painstakingly methodical, it must be remembered that the Nazis planned carefully for World War II as a *Blitzkrieg* (lightning war) without considering the possibility that it might last for years. A deliberate absentee from the Luftwaffe's ranks was a large long-range bomber and ocean reconnaissance aircraft. To some degree this stemmed from the death in 1936 of General Wever and his replacement as Luftwaffe chief of staff by Kesselring, but it was basic policy to concentrate on twin-engined tactical bombers (among other things, Goering could boast to Hitler of the hundreds built). So the Luftwaffe showed only cursory interest when the **Focke-Wulf Fw 200 V1** (first prototype) flew on 27 July 1937.

In fact, the Fw 200 was the best long-range airliner in Europe, if not in the world. It resulted from discussions held by Dipl Ing Kurt Tank, technical director of Focke-Wulf Flugzeugbau of Bremen, and the board of DLH (Deutsche Lufthansa), the state airline, in the spring of 1936. For some time Tank had wished to design a modern long-range airliner to beat the Douglas DC-3 and replace the Junkers Ju 52/3m as the chief DLH equipment on trunk routes. What Tank finally decided to build was a four-engined aircraft with unprecedented range, able to fly the North Atlantic non-stop. This had been far beyond the capability of any previous payload-carrying aircraft, and Tank's objective was primarily for propaganda purposes.

The basic requirement was the carriage of a crew of four and 26 passengers. Over 'European' ranges this could have been done by an aircraft of DC-3 size, but the Fw 200 was made much larger and

Above: This is the sole Fw 200B-1, which was taken over by KGzbV 105 for transport work.

Right: The Fw 200 V3 Immelmann III was flown by the Luftwaffe as Hitler's personal transport.

Designed as a long-range airliner, the Fw 200 was improvised into a long-range maritime reconnaissance aircraft to meet a Japanese navy requirement, and was pressed into Luftwaffe service because the Heinkel He 177 was unavailable, still being engaged in prototype trials.

powered by four engines, initially imported Pratt & Whitney Hornets of 652.5 kW (875 hp), each driving two-bladed VDM-Hamilton propellers. Aerodynamically, the aircraft was outstanding, with no excrescences and a cantilever wing with an aspect ratio of 9.15 for high range efficiency. The wing was built as a horizontal centre-section including the engines, with dihedralled and tapered outer panels. Structure was stressed-skin throughout, with flush riveting, except for the fabric-covered wing aft of the rear spar and fabric-covered control surfaces. The latter were simple manual surfaces but with

Focke-Wulf Fw 200 Condor

Posed in front of 'their' Condor, which already has its engines turning, this KG 40 crew reviews their map details before leaving Bordeaux-Mérignac on another long mission.

geared tabs and electrically-driven trim tabs. The split flaps were hydraulic. Tank made a special point of retracting all three units of the landing gear forwards, so that they would free-fall and be locked by air drag. The main wheels were distinctively carried ahead of the legs on swing-links with diagonal shock struts. Split flaps were used, with skinning of Elektron (magnesium alloy).

Tank himself made the very successful maiden flight. The Fw 200 V1 had nine wide Plexiglas windows along each side of the cabin, but was initially unfurnished and unpainted. Later it was registered D-AERE in DLH livery, with the name 'Saarland' (which Hitler had lately reoccupied). Right at the start of the programme Tank had secured his board's agreement to three prototypes and nine **Fw 200A-0** production aircraft, and these followed at rapid intervals. Few changes were needed apart from adding slight sweepback to the outer wings, revising the tail surfaces and switching to the licensed Hornet engine, the BMW 132 (in 132G-1 form of 536.9 kW/720 hp). The **Fw 200 V2** was delivered to DLH, while the **Fw 200 V3** had a long career as D-2600 *Immelmann III*, Hitler's personal aircraft. Of the nine **Fw 200A** series, two were sold to DDL of Denmark and two to Syndicato Condor Ltda of Rio de Janeiro.

Long-range flights

In early 1938 the Fw 200 V1 was fitted with extra tankage and re-painted as D-ACON *Brandenburg*. Tank had specially secured the RLM (air ministry) number 200 for propaganda purposes, and the V1 now became the **Fw 200S** (special). On 10 August 1938 it took off from Berlin-Tempelhof in the hands of Flugkapitäne Henke and von Moreau. It made a remarkable non-stop flight against headwinds to Floyd Bennett airport, New York, covering the estimated 6558 km (4,075 miles) in 24 hours 55 minutes. The return was flown in 19

This is believed to have been the first photograph taken of a Condor in the air. It shows the Fw 200 V1 climbing out of Bremen on its first flight on 27 July 1937; at this time it had not been painted. Note the single-wheel main landing gear, common to all Condors prior to the ocean-attack C-series.

hours 47 minutes, the average of 330 km/h (205 mph) being just double the speed of the typical landplanes of Imperial Airways. On 28 November 1938 the same aircraft and pilots left to fly via Basra, Karachi and Hanoi to Tokyo, in a total elapsed time of only 46 hours 18 minutes. On the return, in a way never publicly explained, D-ACON ran out of fuel on the first leg and ditched near Manila.

While in Japan, the Fw 200 created intense interest. By this time the Bremen factory was in production with what was envisaged as the standard version, the **Fw 200B**, with BMW 132Dc or 132H engines of 633.8 or 618.9 kW (850 or 830 hp), and with appreciably increased weights. No orders appeared forthcoming, however, because the Condor was too big and costly for the predominantly short-haul DLH network. Export sales were thus eagerly sought, five being ordered by Dai Nippon KK of Japan. This was soon followed by an order for two by Aero O/Y of Finland. In the event World War II prevented delivery of these aircraft, and the Fw 200Bs served in ones and twos with DLH and with the Luftwaffe KGrzbV 105. Attrition was high, only one aircraft, **Fw 200B-2** *Pommern*, surviving the war. The penultimate DLH Condor, Fw 200B-2 *Hessen*, crashed on high ground while overloaded with the last Nazi leaders to escape from Berlin on 21 April 1945.

Condor over the Far East

There was a secret additional contract from Japan which called for a long-range reconnaissance version for the Imperial navy. Tank was eager to build this, because he was convinced such a machine could be useful to the Luftwaffe. He therefore picked the **Fw 200 V10**, the **B-series** prototype, for conversion. This was fitted with 60 per cent more fuel in fuselage cabin tanks, provision for over 2000 kg (4,409 lb) of cameras, flares, markers, dinghies and other mission equipment, and also with three 7.9-mm (0.31-in) MG 15 machine-guns, one in a small dorsal turret above the trailing edge and the others firing to front and rear from a ventral gondola offset to the right. There was no bomb bay.

In spring 1939 it suddenly looked as if Hitler's gambles might not win for ever, and that a war was a near-term prospect. Luftwaffe Chief of Staff Jeschonnek ordered Oberstleutnant Edgar Petersen, a very experienced pilot, to form a squadron which could sink ships out in the Atlantic, on which the obvious enemies, France and especially the UK, would depend during a war. The problem was that there was no suitable aircraft. The intended machine, the Heinkel He 177, was years from combat duty. The only answer seemed to be the 'Japanese' Fw 200 V10.

As in the case of the Ju 52/3m, Dornier Do 17 and several other types, the RLM was faced with botching up a combat aircraft from a commercial transport, which is ironic, because British observers thought at the time the Luftwaffe was busily developing bombers in the false guise of civil aircraft. The Fw 200 was fundamentally unsuited to its new role because it had been designed to operate at lighter weights and at civil load factors. The airframe would henceforth have to operate from rough front-line airstrips with heavy loads of fuel and weapons, and in combat would certainly have to 'pull g' in tight turns or dive pull-outs, and all at low level in dense air. The Bremen stressmen did what they could to beef up the structure, but this consisted

CE+IB, seen here with the yellow theatre band of the Eastern Front, was one of two transport Condors – Fw 200C-4/U1 (illustrated) and U2 – built in 1942. These had all regular C-4 improvements but only had four 7.9-mm (0.31-in) MG 15 guns, two in small dorsal turrets and two in a short gondola. There were 11 passenger seats.

Focke-Wulf Fw 200 Condor

The Focke-Wulf Fw 200C-3/U2 was readily identified by the bulge in the gondola for the Lofte 7D bombsight. Fitting this accurate device necessitated a reorganisation of the ventral armament.

which was planned as the definitive version although it still had a weak structure, very vulnerable fuel system (especially from below), no armour except behind the captain's seat and many inconvenient features. The main addition to the Fw 200C-1 was a ventral gondola, offset as in the Japanese Fw 200 V10 but longer in order to provide room for a weapon bay (which was normally used to carry a cement bomb with 250-kg/551-lb ballistics dropped as a check on bombsight settings). At the front of the gondola was a 20-mm MG FF aimed with a ring-and-bead sight mainly to deter any AA gunners aboard the enemy ships. At the rear was an MG 15 replacing the previous ventral gun. The only other change was to replace the forward turret by a raised cockpit canopy with a hand-aimed MG 15 firing ahead.

Operational experience

The normal crew numbered five: pilot, co-pilot and three gunners, one of the last being the engineer and another the overworked radio-operator/navigator. There was plenty of room inside the airframe, and all crew stations had provision for heating and electric light, but from the start the crews of Petersen's new maritime unit, Kampfgeschwader (KG) 40, were unhappy with the Condor's structural integrity and lack of armament. There is no evidence any Condors were delivered to any prior combat unit, as sometimes stated, but only to the transport *Gruppe* already mentioned. KG 40 was henceforth to be virtually the sole Fw 200C operating unit. There were never to be enough Condors to go round. Focke-Wulf was well aware of the demand, and organised dispersed manufacture at five plants with final assembly at Bremen and Cottbus, and also by Blohm und Voss at Finkenwerder. It is thus a reflection on the frustrations of the programme, which did not enjoy top priority, that by the termination in February 1944 only 252 Fw 200C Condors had been built. Moreover, because of high attrition, KG 40 never had full wing strength and seldom had more than 12 aircraft available. Indeed, more than half the aircraft delivered in the first year suffered major structural failure, at least eight breaking their backs on the airfield.

The first missions by 1./KG 40 were flown from Danish bases from 8 April 1940 against British ships. In late June, the *Geschwader* was transferred to Bordeaux-Mérignac, which was to be the main base until it had to be evacuated in autumn 1944. Initially, from July 1940, the Condors simply added their small offensive weight to the Luftwaffe's assault on the UK, usually flying a wide sweep west of Cornwall and normally west of Ireland, dropping four bombs and heading for Norway, making the return trip a day or two later. At least two were shot down, although a pilot of No. 87 Sqn, who unusually caught a Condor on the direct run to Plymouth, ran out of ammunition so continued to intercept on camera-gun film only. From August the Condors got on with their real task and within two months had been credited with 90,000 tonnes of British shipping. On 26 October they made headlines for the first time when Oberleutnant Bernhard Jope and crew found the 38418-tonne (42,348-ton) *Empress of Britain* south-west of Donegal. Their bombs crippled the liner, which was then torpedoed by a U-boat. By 9 February 1941 1./KG

of a few local reinforcements which added just 29 kg (63.9 lb) to the airframe weight. Ideally they should have started again, but the proposed **Fw 200C-series** was almost immediately accepted when it was offered in August 1939. A pre-production batch of 10 **Fw 200C-0** aircraft was ordered just after the start of the war, and by agreement as many as possible were modified from B-series transports already on the line. The first four had to be delivered as Fw 200C-0 transports. Their only modifications were to introduce twin-wheel main gears, long-chord cowlings with gills and various internal equipment items. All four were delivered just in time for the invasion of Norway in April 1940.

Definitive sub-variant

The remaining six Fw 200C-0s were given the locally reinforced structure and simple armament comprising three MG 15s, one in a small (almost hemispherical) turret behind the flight deck, one in a rear dorsal cockpit with a fold-over hood and the third fired from a rear ventral hatch. An offensive load of four 250-kg (551-lb) bombs could be carried, two hung under the enlarged outer nacelles and the others on racks immediately outboard under the roots of the outer wings. Production continued immediately with the **Fw 200C-1**,

The initial production reconnaissance model of the Condor for Luftwaffe service was the Fw 200C-1. This picture clearly shows the ventral gondola and forward dorsal blister toting MG 15 machine-guns, and similar armament in the rear dorsal position. Bombs could be hung beneath the enlarged outer nacelles.

This Condor, F8+GH, was photographed serving with I/KG 40 in Greece in 1942. It does not carry the white Mediterranean theatre band and was probably on temporary detachment. It is an Fw 200C-3, for it has large wing stores attachments, an MG 151/20 in the front of the gondola and Fw 19 turret.

Focke-Wulf Fw 200 Condor

Left: This Fw 200C-1 wears the codes and insignia of 1.Staffel KG 40, the first Luftwaffe Condor unit. Operating first from Danish bases with Fw 200C-0s, the unit transferred to Bordeaux-Mérignac in June 1940, where it began operations with the C-1, flying missions around the West of Ireland to land in Norway, attacking targets of oportunity.

Right: This Fw 200C-6 of 9./KG 40 is fitted with nose-mounted antennas for the FuG 200 Hohentwiel radar, (used mainly for blind bombing) and carries a pair of Henschel Hs 293A missiles underwing. The C-6 was produced by conversion of C-3/U1 and C-3/U2 airframes, the new-build missile launcher being the Fw 200C-8.

40's claim had reached 363,000 tonnes. By this time it had been joined by two further *Staffeln*, totalling a nominal 36 aircraft.

In the winter of 1940-41, Cottbus delivered a few interim **Fw 200C-2** Condors, whose main improvement was scalloped outer nacelle racks and low-drag wing racks, the former also being plumbed for small (300-litre/66-Imp gal) external tanks. The big advance came with the **Fw 200C-3**, first flown in February 1941. This was a major redesign with a real attempt to cure the structural problems despite even higher weights; the attempt did not quite succeed. Engines were BMW-Bramo Fafnir 323R-2s, with water-injection rating of 894.8 kW (1,200 hp). The bomb load was increased by clearing the nacelles to 500 kg (1,102 lb) each and adding 12 SC 50 bombs (50 kg/110 lb) in the gondola. The forward dorsal blister was replaced by an Fw 19 turret (one MG 15) and two more MG 15s were aimed through sliding panels in each side of the rear fuselage, the crew rising to six. The **Fw 200C-3/U1** at last gave real defensive firepower with an MG 151/15 in an HDL 151 forward turret, and the MG FF was replaced by an MG 151/20, but the big turret reduced top speed at sea level from some 305 km/h (190 mph) to little over 275 km/h (171 mph).

In 1941 only 58 Condors were built, these including the **Fw 200C-3/U2** with the complex but extremely accurate Lofte 7D bombsight, which caused a prominent bulge under the front of the gondola and necessitated replacement of the cannon by a 13-mm (0.51-in) MG 131. Most Fw 200C-3/U2s also reverted to the small Fw 19 turret. Next came the **Fw 200C-3/U3** whose dorsal armament comprised two MG 131s, one in an EDL 131 forward turret and the other in the manually aimed rear position. The **Fw 200C-3/U4** had increased internal fuel, bringing maximum weight to 22700 kg (50,045 lb), which the reinforced airframe could just manage. The beam guns were changed for MG 131s, giving much greater firepower, but the forward turret went back to the Fw 19.

Standard and special versions

If any Condor sub-type can be considered 'standard' it was the **Fw 200C-4**, from February 1942, which added search radar, initially the pre-production Rostock and then the standard FuG 200 Hohentwiel, the latter giving blind-bombing capability. Oddly, the Fw 200C-4 went back to the HDL 151 turret and MG 15s elsewhere except for the front of the gondola, which had the MG 131 or MG 151/20 depending on whether or not the Lofte 7D was fitted. Two 'special' variants in 1942 included the **Fw 200C-4/U1** and **Fw 200C-4/U2** transports, with VIP interiors and just four MG 15s. The former, flown in 1945 at Farnborough, was Himmler's personal transport, the Gestapo chief having a vast leather chair with heavy armour and a personal escape hatch.

In early 1943 some Fw 200C-3s were modified to launch and guide the Hs 293A anti-ship missile, which was hung under the outer nacelles. The associated Kehl/Strassburg radio guidance installation was in the nose and front of the gondola. These missile carriers were designated **Fw 200C-6**, and the last few Condors to be built, in the winter of 1943-44, were **Fw 200C-8**s specially designed to carry the Hs 293 and with deeper outboard nacelles and a longer forward section to the gondola.

Focke-Wulf Fw 200C-4/U3 cutaway drawing key

1 Starboard navigation light
2 Wing skinning
3 Starboard aileron
4 Aileron trim tabs
5 Outboard mainspar
6 Aileron control run
7 Wing ribs (centre section)
8 Wing ribs (forward section)
9 Wing dihedral break point
10 Starboard flap (outer section)
11 Starboard flap (centre section)
12 Starboard flap (inner section)
13 Wing fuel tank covers
14 Inboard mainspar structure
15 Starboard outer oil tank
16 Multiple exhaust stubs
17 Cooling gills
18 Starboard outer nacelle (angled)
19 Three-blade VDM controllable-pitch metal-bladed propeller
20 Propeller boss
21 Carburettor air intake
22 Auxiliary fuel tank (66 Imp gal/300 litre capacity)
23 Starboard inner nacelle
24 FuG 200 Hohentwiel search radar array (port antenna omitted for clarity)
25 Nose D/F loop
26 Nose bulkhead
27 Rudder pedals
28 Hand-held 13-mm 131 machine-gun (D-Stand)
29 Lotfe 7D bomb sight fairing
30 Ventral gondola side windows (gondola offset to starboard)
31 Rear dorsal gunner's take-off seat
32 Pilot's circular vision port
33 First pilot's seat
34 Sliding windscreen panel
35 Co-pilot's seat (co-pilot also served as bomb-aimer)
36 Flight deck entry
37 Arc-of-fire interrupter gate
38 Cabin air inlet (starboard side only)
39 Hydraulically-operated Fw 19 turret mounting single 7.9-mm MG 15 machine-gun (A-Stand)
40 Gunner's seat

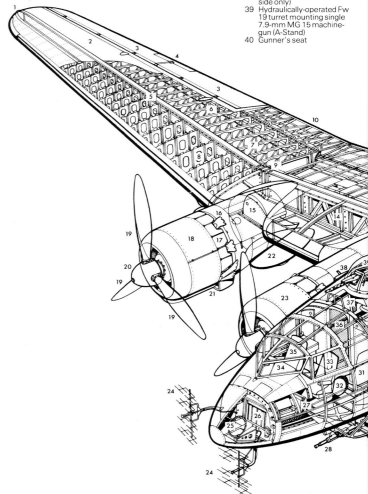

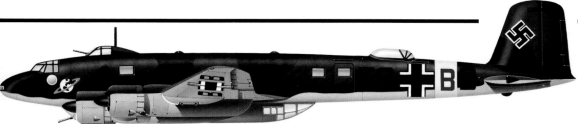

F8+BB was one of the first Fw 200C-1 Condors with ventral gondola and full maritime patrol and bombing equipment. Assigned to Stab I/KG 40, it was painted with the unit badge just in time to ferry troops and equipment to Oslo/Gardermoen airport at the start of the invasion of Norway on 9 April 1940.

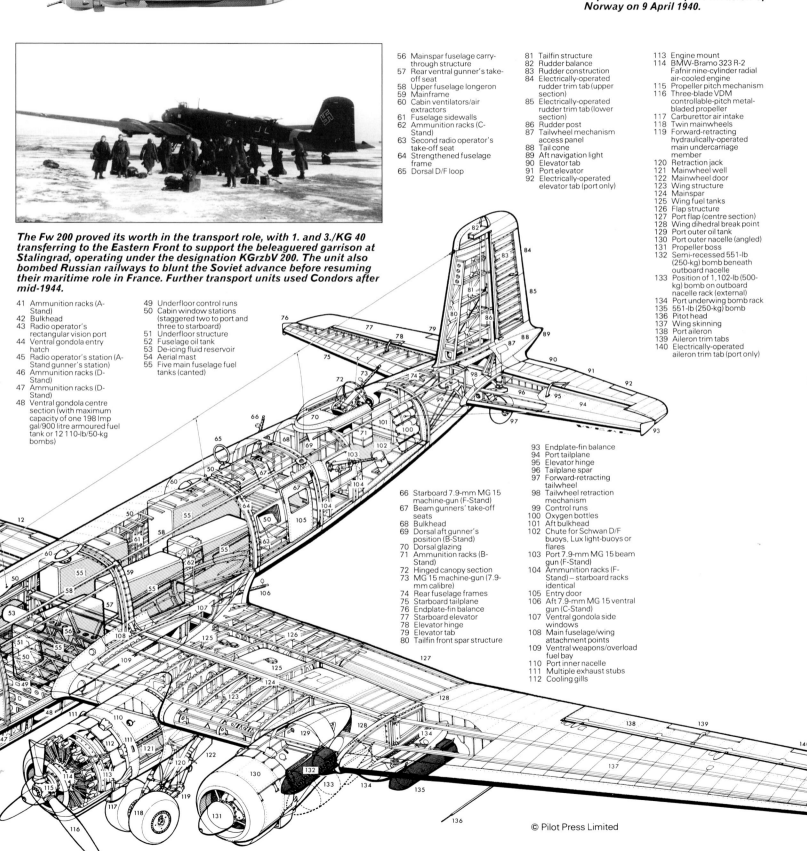

The Fw 200 proved its worth in the transport role, with 1. and 3./KG 40 transferring to the Eastern Front to support the beleaguered garrison at Stalingrad, operating under the designation KGrzbV 200. The unit also bombed Russian railways to blunt the Soviet advance before resuming their maritime role in France. Further transport units used Condors after mid-1944.

41 Ammunition racks (A-Stand)
42 Bulkhead
43 Radio operator's rectangular vision port
44 Ventral gondola entry hatch
45 Radio operator's station (A-Stand gunner's station)
46 Ammunition racks (D-Stand)
47 Ammunition racks (D-Stand)
48 Ventral gondola centre section (with maximum capacity of one 198 Imp gal/900 litre armoured fuel tank or 12 110-lb/50-kg bombs)
49 Underfloor control runs
50 Cabin window stations (staggered two to port and three to starboard)
51 Underfloor structure
52 Fuselage oil tank
53 De-icing fluid reservoir
54 Aerial mast
55 Five main fuselage fuel tanks (canted)

56 Mainspar fuselage carry-through structure
57 Rear ventral gunner's take-off seat
58 Upper fuselage longeron
59 Mainframe
60 Cabin ventilators/air extractors
61 Fuselage sidewalls
62 Ammunition racks (C-Stand)
63 Second radio operator's take-off seat
64 Strengthened fuselage frame
65 Dorsal D/F loop

66 Starboard 7.9-mm MG 15 machine-gun (F-Stand)
67 Beam gunners' take-off seats
68 Bulkhead
69 Dorsal aft gunner's position (B-Stand)
70 Dorsal glazing
71 Ammunition racks (B-Stand)
72 Hinged canopy section
73 MG 15 machine-gun (7.9-mm calibre)
74 Rear fuselage frames
75 Starboard tailplane
76 Endplate-fin balance
77 Starboard elevator
78 Elevator hinge
79 Elevator tab
80 Tailfin front spar structure

81 Tailfin structure
82 Rudder balance
83 Rudder construction
84 Electrically-operated rudder trim tab (upper section)
85 Electrically-operated rudder trim tab (lower section)
86 Rudder post
87 Tailwheel mechanism access panel
88 Tail cone
89 Aft navigation light
90 Elevator tab
91 Port elevator
92 Electrically-operated elevator tab (port only)
93 Endplate-fin balance
94 Port tailplane
95 Elevator hinge
96 Tailplane spar
97 Forward-retracting tailwheel
98 Tailwheel retraction mechanism
99 Control runs
100 Oxygen bottles
101 Aft bulkhead
102 Chute for Schwan D/F buoys, Lux light-buoys or flares
103 Port 7.9-mm MG 15 beam gun (F-Stand)
104 Ammunition racks (F-Stand) – starboard racks identical
105 Entry door
106 Aft 7.9-mm MG 15 ventral gun (C-Stand)
107 Ventral gondola side windows
108 Main fuselage/wing attachment points
109 Ventral weapons/overload fuel bay
110 Port inner nacelle
111 Multiple exhaust stubs
112 Cooling gills

113 Engine mount
114 BMW-Bramo 323 R-2 Fafnir nine-cylinder radial air-cooled engine
115 Propeller pitch mechanism
116 Three-blade VDM controllable-pitch metal-bladed propeller
117 Carburettor air intake
118 Twin mainwheels
119 Forward-retracting hydraulically-operated main undercarriage member
120 Retraction jack
121 Mainwheel well
122 Mainwheel door
123 Wing structure
124 Mainspar
125 Wing fuel tanks
126 Flap structure
127 Port flap (centre section)
128 Wing dihedral break point
129 Port outer oil tank
130 Port outer nacelle (angled)
131 Propeller boss
132 Semi-recessed 551-lb (250-kg) bomb beneath outboard nacelle
133 Position of 1,102-lb (500-kg) bomb on outboard nacelle rack (external)
134 Port underwing bomb rack
135 551-lb (250-kg) bomb
136 Pitot head
137 Wing skinning
138 Port aileron
139 Aileron trim tabs
140 Electrically-operated aileron trim tab (port only)

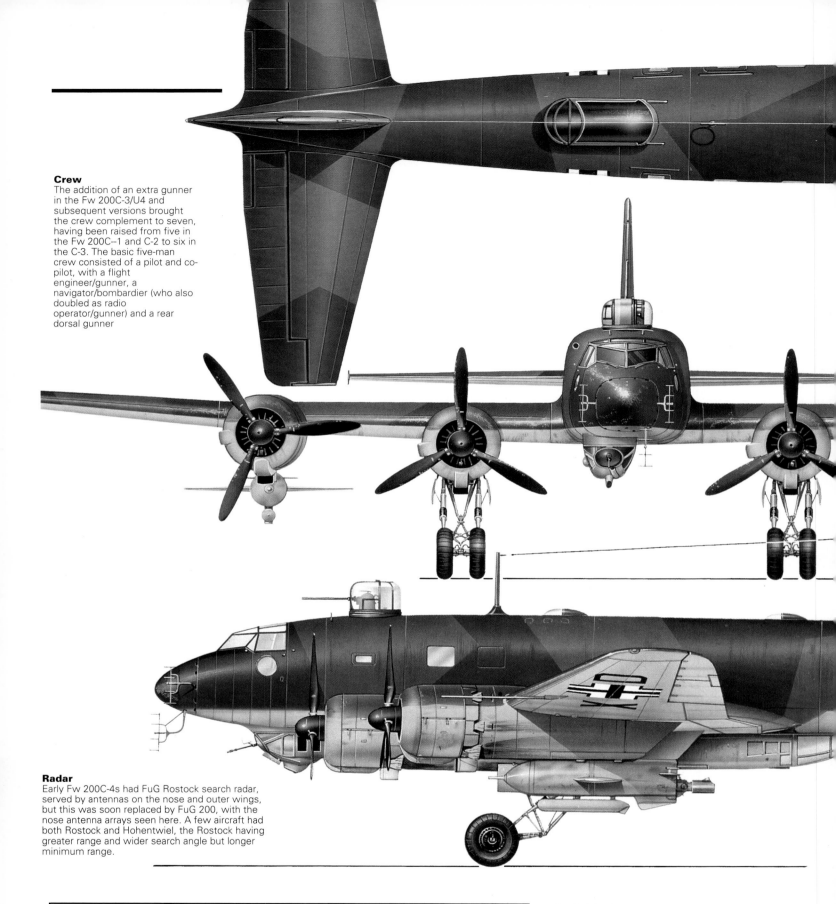

Crew
The addition of an extra gunner in the Fw 200C-3/U4 and subsequent versions brought the crew complement to seven, having been raised from five in the Fw 200C–1 and C-2 to six in the C-3. The basic five-man crew consisted of a pilot and co-pilot, with a flight engineer/gunner, a navigator/bombardier (who also doubled as radio operator/gunner) and a rear dorsal gunner

Radar
Early Fw 200C-4s had FuG Rostock search radar, served by antennas on the nose and outer wings, but this was soon replaced by FuG 200, with the nose antenna arrays seen here. A few aircraft had both Rostock and Hohentwiel, the Rostock having greater range and wider search angle but longer minimum range.

Specification
Focke-Wulf Fw 200C-3/U-4 Condor
Type: long-range reconnaissance bomber
Powerplant: four 895-kW (1,200-hp) BMW-Bramo 323R-2 Fafnir nine-cylinder radial piston engines
Performance: maximum speed 360 km/h (224 mph); cruising speed 335 km/h (208 mph); service ceiling 6000 m (19,685 ft); range 3560 km (2,212 miles); endurance 14 hours
Weights: empty 17005 kg (37,490 lb); maximum take-off 24520 kg (50,057 lb)
Dimensions: span 32.85 m (107 ft 9 in); length 23.45 m (76 ft 11 in); height 6.30 m (20 ft 8 in); wing area 119.85 m² (1,290.10 sq ft)
Armament: four 13-mm (0.51-in) MG 131 machine-guns in dorsal and beam positions, and one MG 131 or one 20-mm MG 151 cannon in forward ventral gondola; maximum bomb load of 2100 kg (4,630 lb) comprising two 500-kg (1,102-lb), two 250-kg (551-lb) and 12 50-kg (110-lb) bombs

Anti-shipping operations
By late 1943, the main role of the Condor was to interdict Allied convoys from Gibraltar, whose departure was usually reported by German agents in Spain. The aircraft would usually take off in fours, flying out to an initial point at sea level and in close formation. They would then split up, fan out and fly parallel tracks some 40 km (25 miles) apart, periodically climbing to 300 metres (1,000 ft) and making a broad circuit while they searched for shipping with Hohentwiel radar. When contact was made the aircraft would contact the others and all would climb to make their attacks, which were made from a minimum altitude of 2,700 m (9,000 ft).

Powerplants

The Fw 200C was powered by the same 620-kW (830-hp) BMW 132H air-cooled, nine-cylinder piston engines as its airline progenitor, the Fw 200B-2, although the nacelles were lengthened and the aircraft received long-chord cowlings. The Fw 200C-3 and subsequent versions were powered by the BMW-Bramo 323R-2 Fafnir, rated at 745 kW (1,000 hp) for take off, or 894 kW (1,200 hp) with water-methanol injection. The Fw 200C-2 introduced low drag, cut-down outboard engine nacelles, although C-6 and C-8 missile carriers had deeper outboard nacelles.

Defensive armament

The first four basic Fw 200C-0s were unarmed transports, but the next six had defensive armament and bomb racks for the maritime reconnaissance role. The defensive armament consisted of a single 7.9-mm MG 15 machine-gun in the vestigial turret above and behind the flight deck, with two similar weapons firing from a downward hatch and from the glazed fairing above the rear fuselage. The C-1 replaced the ventral MG 15 with an offset gondola, in the nose of which was a 20-mm MG FF on a flexible mounting, and with an MG 15 in its tail. The turret above the fuselage was replaced by a fixed cupola with an MG 15 on a flexible mounting. The C-3 replaced the cupola with a powered turret, and introduced two MG 15s behind sliding beam panels, while the C-3/U1 introduced an HDL 151 turret with a 15-mm MG 151 cannon. The gondola's MG FF was replaced by another MG 151. The C-3/U2 and U4 reintroduced the Fw 19 forward upper turret, while the C-3/U3 had an EDL 131 turret with a 13-mm MG 131, and with another MG 131 in the aft dorsal position. The C-4, C-6 and C-8 reintroduced the high drag HDL 151 turret and had MG 131s in the aft dorsal and beam positions.

Focke-Wulf Fw 200C-8/U-10 Condor Kampfgeschwader 40 France, 1944

The last of the Condor sub-variants, the Fw 200C-8/U10 was a dedicated missile-carrier, with pylons under the outboard engine nacelles for a pair of Henschel Hs 293A anti-ship missiles. This example, one of a the final handful delivered in January-February 1944, is shown still in four-letter factory codes, which would usually be replaced by a Luftwaffe letter/number code some time after allocation to KG 40. The obvious features of this late version include the big HDL 151 forward turret, the enlarged ventral gondola, and FuG 200 Hohentwiel search radar. By 1944, the Fw 200 was far from being the 'Scourge of the Atlantic' described by Winston Churchill, but was a lumbering, vulnerable leviathan, vulnerable to patrolling fighters or even to Allied maritime reconnaissance aircraft. When KG 40 mounted its first operation with the new Hs 293A missile, it was cut short when the missile-carrying Condor was forced down by an RAF Sunderland. When the invasion of France closed its bases, KG 40 got rid of most of its aircraft, one *Staffel* surviving and transferring to Norway and another withdrawing to Germany. Most of the unit's surviving Condors were simply passed to transport units, where attrition proved astonishingly rapid.

Focke-Wulf Fw 200 Condor

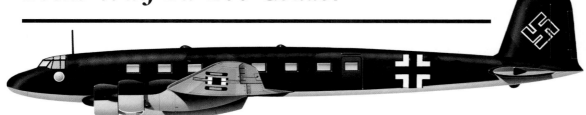

Differing from the Fw 200 V1 in having BMW engines (although basically a licensed Hornet) and enlarged vertical tail, the Fw 200 V3 was taken on Luftwaffe strength as D2600, the Führermaschine, for the use of Hitler and other top Nazis. The aircraft went through three changes of livery before receiving wartime camouflage. It was based at Berlin-Tempelhof.

In 1940 the Bremen factory delivered four Fw 200C-0 transports. These were not only the first batch of Condors for the Luftwaffe but also the first with long-chord cowls, three-bladed propellers and twin-wheel main gear. X8+BH is shown on Stalingrad supply duties from Zaporozhye with KGrzbV 200 in January 1943.

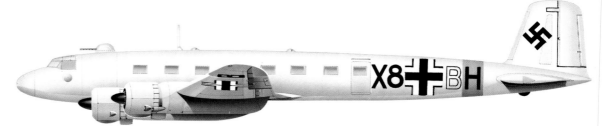

Left: An Fw200C-3/U2 showing to advantage the early-style Fw 19 dorsal turret, accommodating a single 7.9-mm machine-gun and initial type of ventral gondola. This had a 13-mm MG 131 machine-gun in place of the usual 20-mm MG 151, because the larger calibre weapon's breach interfered with the Lofte 7D bombsight. The Condor's unusual main undercarriage is clearly visible.

Below: The nose of the Fw 200C-8 was festooned with antenna arrays for the FuG 200 Hohentwiel radar. This sub-variant was specifically designed for carrying the Henschel Hs 293A missile. The missile-carrying Condors had a short life, most surviving examples of the type transferring to the transport role after the loss of its bases on the coast of the Bay of Biscay, leaving a handful of maritime aircraft in Norway.

Had such aircraft been available in 1940, the 'Scourge of the Atlantic' would have been much more deadly even than it was. Fortunately, while the weak early Condors were almost unopposed, the improved models had a very hard time, from ship AA guns, from Grumman Martlets (Wildcats) based on escort carriers and, not least, from the CAM (catapult-armed merchantman) Hawker Hurricanes, which scored their first kill on 3 August 1941. Even a Short Sutherland could catch a Condor and shoot it down, and from 1942 Condors tried never to come within the radius of Coastal Command Bristol Beaufighters and de Havilland Mosquitoes. In addition, their effectiveness was hampered not only by poor serviceability, but also by repeated urgent calls to undertake transport duties in various the-atres, including Stalingrad. KG 40 was disbanded in autumn 1944, its Biscay bases having been captured, and the few surviving Condors finished the war as rarely used transports.

Focke-Wulf Fw 200 variants

Fw 200 V1: prototype, Hornet S1E-G engines; later modified as **Fw 200S-1**
Fw 200 V2 and **V3:** prototypes with BMW 132G-1; V3 completed as Hitler's *Führermaschine*
Fw 200A-0: pre-production fourth to ninth prototypes, most for DLH, plus OY-DAM and -DEM for DDL and PP-CBI/CBJ for SCL Brazil
Fw 200B: production transports with (**Fw 200B-1**) 633.8-kW (850-hp) BMW 132Dc and (**Fw 200B-2**) 618.9-kW (830-hp) 132H; Japanese and Finnish aircraft completed for DLH/Luftwaffe as Fw-200B-2s
Fw 200 V10: single aircraft for Japanese navy for armed reconnaissance; retained in Germany

Fw 200C-0: pre-production C-series, locally strengthened airframe, twin main wheels, long-chord cowlings, three-bladed constant-speed propellers; four unarmed transports, six with four bomb racks and three MG 15 guns
Fw 200C-1: added ventral gondola with 20-mm MG FF and relocated near ventral gun
Fw 200C-2: reduced-drag wing and nacelle bomb racks
Fw 200C-3: strengthened structure, 894.8-kW (1,200-hp) Bramo 323R-1 engines, increased bomb load, Fw 19 turret plus two MG 15 beam guns
Fw 200C-3/U1: HDL 151 turret and MG 151/20 replacing MG FF
Fw 200C-3/U2: Lofte 7D sight, Fw 19 turret, MG 131 instead of MG 151/20

Fw 200C-3/U3: dorsal guns both 13-mm (0.51-in) MG 131, forward gun in EDL 131 turret
Fw 200C-3/U4: greater fuel capacity, two MG 131 beam guns but turret reverted to Fw 19
Fw 200C-4: fitted with radar, initially Rostock, later Hohentwiel, HDL 151 turret
Fw 200C-4/U1 and **U2:** two VIP transport conversions with short gondola, four MG 15, no provision for radar or bombs
Fw 200C-4/U3: fitted with Hohentwiel radar, turret changed to Fw 19
Fw 200C-6: conversions of C-3/U1 and C-4 to carry Hs 293A missiles
Fw 200C-8 and C-8/U10: final series designed for Hs 293A, plus Hohentwiel

Focke-Wulf Ta 154 Moskito

In order to combat the RAF's nightly bombing raids against German urban and industrial centres, the Reichsluftfahrtministerium ordered the development of a specialised two-seat night-fighter, outlined in a specification issued in August 1942. The resulting contenders were the all-metal Heinkel He 219 and Tank's **Focke-Wulf Ta 154**, the latter a twin-engined shoulder-wing monoplane of wooden construction throughout in order to utilise the skills of trained woodworkers. Powered by two 1119-kW (1,500 hp) Jumo 211N engines, the **Ta 154 V1** first prototype was flown by Kurt Tank at Hannover/Langenhagen on 1 July 1943, joined soon after by the similarly powered **Ta 154 V2** second prototype (fitted with FuG 212 Lichtenstein C-1 radar and *Matratzen* antenna array) in handling and performance trials. The **Ta 154 V3** third prototype (**Ta 154A-03/U1**), flown on 25 November 1943 and powered by Jumo 211R engines, was armed with single forward-firing 20-mm MG 151/20 and 30-mm MK 108 cannons on each side of

the fuselage below the cockpit. Four additional prototypes were flown at Langenhagen between January and March 1944, some featuring *Hirschgeweih* antennas for FuG 220 Lichtenstein SN-2 radar. The remaining eight aircraft of the original RLM order were assembled at Erfurt under the designation **Ta 154A-0**.

Two production **Ta 154A-1**s took to the air in June 1944, but the second example crashed when the wing disintegrated in flight. The prototype and pre-production aircraft had used Tego-Film adhesive but, when the factory which produced it at Wuppertal was bombed, the alternative cold glue adhesive which was substituted brought disastrous results by eating into the wooden structure.

Eight Ta 154A-1s were built at a new production facility at Poznan (Posen) in Poland, but the programme was terminated on 14 August 1944, following two further crashes of production aircraft. Variants on the drawing board were the **Ta 154C** with Jumo 213A engines, sliding teardrop canopy and twin 30-mm MK 108 cannon in a *schräge Musik* installation, the **Ta 254A** high-altitude fighter with larger wings and Jumo 213 power, and the similar **Ta 254B** with DB 603 engines.

A few Ta 154A-1s did see operational service with I/NJG 3 from Stade during January 1945,

Left and right: Two views show the Ta 154 V7, last of the prototypes and completed for high-speed trials.

equipped with FuG 218 Neptun radar, while the type was considered for three bizarre anti-bomber weapon systems. All utilised Ta 154s packed with explosives which would be detonated within streams of Allied bombers. One system involved an Fw 190 attached to the top of the Ta 154 in a *Hückepack* arrangement, the Fw 190 pilot releasing the Ta 154 as it neared the bombers. Another scheme was to tow a Ta 154 'bomb' behind another into the bomber stream before release and explosion. Finally, a *Pulk-Zerstörer* scheme would have used an explosive-filled Ta 154 flown from a rudimentary cockpit in the rear fuselage into the bomber stream, whereupon the pilot escaped via a downward-firing ejection seat prior to detonation. Six unfinished Ta 154A-1s were completed in this configuration

The Ta 154A-0 V15 was the last pre-production aircraft, and featured Hirschgeweih antennas for Lichtenstein SN-2 radar.

(as **Ta 154A-2/U3**s) at Poznan but not flown.

Specification
Focke-Wulf Ta 154A-1
Type: two-seat night-fighter
Powerplant: two 1119-kW (1,500-hp) Jumo 211R 12-cylinder inverted Vee piston engines
Performance: maximum speed 650 km/h (404 mph); climb to 8000 m (26,250 ft) in 14 minutes 30 seconds; service ceiling 10900 m (35,760 ft); range 1365 km (848 miles)
Weights: empty 6405 kg (14,121 lb); maximum take-off 8930 kg (19,687 lb)
Dimensions: span 16.00 m (52 ft 6 in); length 12.10 m (39 ft 8½ in); height 3.50 m (11 ft 5¾ in), wing area 32.40 m² (348.76 sq ft)
Armament: two nose-mounted 20-mm MG 151/20 and two 30-mm MK 108 cannon, and one Mk 108 in the rear fuselage firing upward and forward at an angle of 45°

Gotha Go 145

The Gotha company, having been closed down in 1919 under the terms of the Versailles Treaty, was reformed on 2 October 1933. Its first product was the Gotha **Go 145** trainer, a single-bay biplane of wooden construction with fabric covering, powered by an Argus As 10C engine. The prototype was first flown in February 1934 and the type entered service with the Luftwaffe in the following year. Principal variants were the **Go 145A** dual-control trainer, **Go 145B** with enclosed cockpit and wheel-spats, and the **Go 145C** gunnery trainer with one 7.92-mm (0.31-in) MG 15 machine-gun on a pivoted mounting in the rear cockpit. Although used

originally as a pilot training aircraft, the Go 145 served also with the Störkampfstaffeln that were set up in December 1942, when the Luftwaffe decided to emulate the Russians' use of the Polikarpov Po-2 as a 'nuisance raider' during the hours of darkness. In October 1943 these units were redesignated Nachtschlachtgruppen, and remained operational on the Eastern Front until the end of the war. Go 145s equipped six Nachtschlachtgruppen and the Ost-Flieger Gruppe, operating with light bombs, guns, rockets and loudspeakers. Fewer than 10,000 Go 145s were built by Gotha, Ago, BFW and Focke Wulf in Germany; the type was licence-

built in Spain as the **CASA 1145-L**, and also in Turkey.

Specification
Type: two-seat basic/gunnery trainer
Powerplant: one 179-kW (240-hp) Argus As 10C inverted-Vee piston engine
Performance: maximum speed 212 km/h (132 mph) at sea level; cruising speed 180 km/h (112 mph); service ceiling 3700 m (12,140 ft); range 630 km (391 miles)

Weights: empty 880 kg (1,940 b); maximum take off 1380 kg (3,043 lb)
Dimensions: span 9.00 m (29 ft 6¼ in); length 8.70 m (28 ft 6½ in); height 2.90 m (9 ft 6 in); wing area 21.75 m² (234.12 sq ft)

The Go 145A was used in large numbers by the Luftwaffe's training schools, but its main combat use came on the Eastern Front where it was employed as a nocturnal nuisance raider.

Gotha Go 229 (Horten Ho IX)

Almost unknown today, the all-wing twin-jet **Go 229** was probably the most startling and unconventional warplane built during World War II. It stemmed from the belief of the brothers Walter and Reimar Horten that a flying wing was the most efficient form of heavier-than-air flying machine. They set out to prove this with a series of gliders, beginning with the Horten I of 1931. From 1936 the brothers were officers in the Luftwaffe, but continued their work, which led in 1942 to studies for a flying-wing jet fighter.

The first major step was to build a trainer to familiarise Luftwaffe pilots; this, the **Ho VII**, flew in 1943. It had tandem dual controls and two 179-kW (240-hp) As 10C pusher engines. The brothers kept quiet about their intentions, and the Ho VII

(20 of which were ordered, but 18 cancelled) was described as for aerodynamic research and communications. Meanwhile, the brothers' Sonderkommando 9 at Göttingen had already begun construction of the definitive twin-jet fighter, the **Ho IX**. None of this had any official sanction by the Reichsluftfahrt-ministerium, but the brothers had good political connections. Once Reichsmarschall Goering had seen the drawings, he insisted that this futuristic machine should fly as soon as possible.

Accordingly, work was hastened on two prototypes, which was all the small team could contemplate. The **Ho IX V1** was to fly as a glider, subsequently being modified to install two BMW 003A turbojets. Gliding trials at Oranienburg began in about May 1944, and from the start the han-

dling characteristics were outstandingly good. The Ho IX comprised a centre-section and outer panels. The centre-section was thick enough to house the pilot, engines, guns, tricycle landing gear and nearly all the fuel. It was made of welded steel tube with plywood skin, except near the engines where it was aluminium or steel. The slender, sweptback outer wings were all wood, some of it being *Formholz* composite made of wood shavings bonded with resin adhesive and moulded to shape under high pressure. The structure was stressed to 7*g*, strong enough to out-turn virtually any other aircraft.

Tests with the fully instrumented V1 glider suggested that a production Ho IX would do just this, but the V1 was wrecked later in 1944 when the pilot forgot to retract a long incidence pole before landing. By May 1944 the outstanding potential of the aircraft had led to full RLM blessing, with control passed to the Gothaer Waggonfabrik, the new designation being Go 229. In addition to V1 and V2, seven more prototypes were ordered, plus 20 production fighters. These were to have a span of

16.75 m (54 ft 11½ in), two Jumo 004B engines and armament of four 30-mm guns (MK 103 or 108). The pilot was to have had a simple ejection seat. The **Go 229 V2** began its flight test programme at Oranienburg in January 1945. Take-off required less than 450 m (1,475 ft) and handling was superb. By early March the landing gear was being retracted and speeds had reached 800 km/h (497 mph), when the aircraft crashed on approach because of sudden failure of one of the engines.

The programme advanced no further. The Gotha factory at Friedrichsroda had virtually completed the production prototype V3, and had many other Go 229s in an advanced state of assembly.

Specification
Gotha Go 229A-0 (estimated)
Type: single-seat fighter-bomber
Powerplant: two Junkers Jumo 004B turbojets, each rated at 8.73 kN (1,962 lb) thrust
Performance: maximum speed 977 km/h (607 mph) at 12000 m (39,370 ft); initial climb rate 1320 m (4,330 ft) per minute; service ceiling 16000 m (52,493 ft); range (internal fuel) 1900 km (1,180 miles), (with drop tanks) 3170 km (1,970 miles)
Weights: empty equipped 4600 kg (10,141 lb); maximum overload 9000 kg (19,841 lb)
Dimensions: wing span 16.76 m (54 ft 11¾ in); length 7.47 m (24 ft 6 in); height 2.80 m (9 ft 2 in) wing area 52.50 m² (565 sq ft)
Armament: four 30-mm MK 103 or MK 108 cannon and two 1000-kg (2,250-lb) bombs

Following aerodynamic trials with the glider Ho IX V1, the V2 introduced power in the shape of two Jumo 004Bs buried in the centre-section either side of the cockpit.

Gotha Go 242/Go 244

The work of Dipl Ing Albert Kalkert, the Gotha **Go 242** assault glider was developed with the approval of the Reichsluft-fahrtministerium since it offered almost three times the troop-carrying capacity of the DFS 230 then in use. The fuselage pod was of steel tubular construction with fabric covering, and carried

jettisonable landing gear and two retractable skids; the wings were made of wood with fabric and plywood covering. The aircraft could carry 21 fully-equipped troops, or equivalent weight in military loads, such as a *Kubelwagen* utility vehicle, loaded through the hinged rear fuselage. Two prototypes were flown in

early 1941, and pre-production **Go 242A-0**s and production **Go 242A-1**s followed without delay, permitting entry into service in 1942. The Go 242A-1 featured deeper tail booms and a braking plough on the nose skid, and provision for up to four MG 15 machine-guns in the tail, sides and cockpit roof. Several were tested with 'snow-shoe' undercarriage, the first such examples being used operationally in early 1942 on the Eastern Front. The A-1 was essentially a cargo transport, but the similar **Go 242A-2** was used for carrying troops, with extra doors in the rear section. Heinkel He 111 tugs were usually employed and rocket-

assisted take-off equipment could be fitted, the variety of propulsion units including four 4.9-kN (1,102-lb) Rheinmetall-Borsig Rl 502 solid fuel rockets.

The **Go 242B** was introduced in 1942, with jettisonable nose-wheel landing gear. The two initial versions were the **Go 242B-1** and **Go 242B-2**, which differed principally in the design of the main landing gear; troop carrying equivalents were the **Go 242B-3** and **Go 242B-4**, both with double rear doors. The **Go 242B-5** incorporated dual controls for pilot training. Under the designation **Go 242C-1**, a variant was specially developed for attacks on marine targets, in particular for a raid on the British fleet anchorage at Scapa Flow. This version, with planing hull and underwing stabilising floats, was to have carried a small assault boat with an explosive charge. It was not used operationally, although a number were delivered to 6./KG 200.

A trio of Go 242A-1s is seen during a resupply mission in 1942 on the southern sector of the Eastern Front. The aircraft display very different schemes.

Gotha Go 244B-1 of 4./KGzbV 106 on the Eastern Front in early 1943.

During Go 242 development, consideration had been given to motorising the glider, including the addition of a single engine on the nose to maintain altitude after a towed launch. After the fall of France, the French Gnome-Rhône 14M radial engine became available to the Germans in large numbers, and the Go 242 was modified to serve as the **Go 244** twin-engined transport, each of the twin booms being extended forward of the leading edge of the wing to mount one of these engines; at the same time, fixed tricycle landing gear was installed. A total of 133 conversions was made from the five Go 242B variants, and these were designated correspondingly **Go 244B-1** to **B-5**.

First deliveries were made in March 1942 to the Greece-based KGrzbV 104 and to KGrzbV 106 in Crete, but they proved to be underpowered and relatively easy targets for Allied fighter aircraft, and had been withdrawn by November 1942 and distributed

This Go 244B-1 shows how the rear fuselage hinged upward to allow the loading of bulky items and small vehicles.

to paratroop training schools. Some Go 244s had 492-kW (660-hp) BMW 132Z, or captured Russian Shvetsov M-25As each of 559 kW (750 hp).

Specification
Gotha Go 244B-2
Type: assault/troop transport
Powerplant: two 522-kW (700-hp) Gnome-Rhône 14M 14-cylinder radial piston engines

The operational career of the Go 244 was very brief, as the aircraft was decidedly underpowered. One engine could barely keep the aircraft aloft, even when empty. This is a standard Go 244B-1 cargo transport.

Performance: maximum speed 290 km/h (180 mph); service ceiling 7500 m (24,605 ft); range 600 km (373 miles)
Weights: empty 5100 kg (11,243 lb); maximum take-off 7800 kg (17,196 lb)

Dimensions: span 24.50 m (80 ft 4½ in); length 15.80 m (51 ft 10 in); height 4.70 m (15 ft 5 in); wing area 64.40 m² (693.22 sq ft)
Armament: four 7.92-mm (0.31-in) MG 15 machine-guns (optional)

Heinkel He 46

The emerging Luftwaffe's need for an army co-operation and reconnaissance aircraft was met in 1931 by the Heinkel He 46, flown originally in **He 46a** prototype form as an unequal-span single-bay biplane. Small as the lower wing was, it reduced the field of view available to the observer and so it was soon removed, necessitating an increase of 2.50 m (8 ft 2½ in) in the span of the upper parasol wing. Power was supplied by a licence-built 336-kW (450-hp) Bristol Jupiter engine, also fitted originally to the **He 46b** second prototype, which flew in 1932. The second aircraft was later re-engined with the Siemens SAM 22B radial, which was adopted as powerplant for the production versions, beginning with the **He 46c**. A total of 478 aircraft of all versions was built by Heinkel at Warnemunde (200), and by Fieseler (12), Gotha (24), MIAG at Leipzig (83) and by Siebel (159), all of them built between 1933 and 1936.

The initial production He 46c (later redesignated **He 46C-1**) could carry a camera, or up to 20

10-kg (22-lb) bombs stored vertically beneath the rear cockpit; 20 of this version were sent to Spain in September 1938 for use by the Nationalist forces, and generally-similar aircraft were built for Bulgaria, these differing by introducing NACA-type engine cowlings. Minor improvements were incorporated in six **He 46d** (**He 46D-0**) pre-production aircraft, and the addition of NACA cowlings resulted in the production **He 46e** (**He 46E-1**), but because of engine serviceability problems these aircraft were often flown without the cowlings; a small number were supplied to Hungary. The designation **He 46f** was allocated to an experimental aircraft which combined an He 46C airframe with a 418-kW (560-hp) Armstrong Siddeley Panther engine complete with cowling. Successful testing of this aircraft resulted in the production of 14 similarly-powered **He 46F-1** and **He 46F-2** unarmed observer training aircraft.

The Luftwaffe's reconnaissance squadrons had been equipped with the He 46 by 1936 and,

although replaced progressively by the Henschel Hs 126 from 1938, the He 46 remained in service with five squadrons on the outbreak of war, 4.(H)/31 seeing service in the Polish campaign. By the time of the assault on the Low Countries in May 1940, the He 46 had been relegated to second-line duties, apart from eight aircraft with the Aufklärungs-staffel Oberost. Hungarian He 46s served during the early months of the war on the Eastern Front, and from spring 1943 the type was used by the Luftwaffe's Störkampfstaffeln (later Nacht-schlachtgruppen) for night nuisance attacks. In this role the He 46 remained, until the disbandment of the night attack units.

Specification
Heinkel He 46C-1
Type: two-seat reconnaissance/army co-operation aircraft
Powerplant: one 485-kW (650-hp) Siemens (Bramo) SAM 22B nine-cylinder radial piston engine
Performance: maximum speed 250 km/h (155 mph); cruising speed 210 km/h (130 mph); service ceiling 6000 m (19,685 ft); range 1000 km (621 miles)
Weights: empty 1765 kg (3,892 lb); maximum take-off 2300 kg (5,071 lb)
Dimensions: span 14.00 m (45 ft 11 in); length 9.50 m (31 ft 2 in); height 3.45 m (11 ft 4 in); wing area 32.20 m² (346.61 sq ft)
Armament: one 7.92-mm (0.31-in) MG 15 machine-gun and 20 10-kg (22-lb) bombs carried internally

This He 46C was employed on night nuisance raids over the Eastern Front with Nachtschlachtgruppe 7.

Heinkel He 50

In 1931 Heinkel flew its **He 50aW**, a sturdy twin-float seaplane. It was followed by the **He 50aL** landplane, powered by a Bristol Jupiter VI radial. This was tested by the Luftwaffe as a dive-bomber, leading to procurement of the type for this role as the **He 50L** (later **He 50A**). The He 50A in the dive-bombing role had the rear seat faired over and a forward-firing MG 17 fitted, although it could operate as a two-seat reconnaissance aircraft with the rear seat open for an observer and a flexible mount added for an MG 15. The **He 50b** (also designated **He 66**) was an export model for Japan, and the **He 66aCh** and **He 66bCh** versions were sold to China.

He 50As were delivered to the Luftwaffe from 1933, initially for training. They formed the Luftwaffe's first dive-bomber unit (Fliegergruppe Schwerin, later I/StG 162) in 1935, and later partially equipped nine squadrons. These were progressively retired to training units as Hs 123s and Ju 87s became available.

In the spring of 1943, the surviving He 50s were rounded up from the schools and delivered to the Eastern Front for use by 1. and 2. Staffel, Nachtschlachtgruppe 11 on night harassment duties on the Eastern Front until September 1944, when the aircraft were finally grounded through lack of spares.

Specification
Heinkel He 50A
Type: two-seat light bomber and reconnaissance aircraft
Powerplant: one Bramo 322B nine-cylinder radial piston engine rated at 485 kW (650 hp)
Performance: maximum speed 235 km/h (146 mph); service ceiling 6400 m (21,000 ft); range 600 km (373 miles)
Weights: empty 1600 kg (3,527 lb); loaded 2620 kg (5,776 lb)
Dimensions: wing span 11.50 m (37 ft 8¾ in); length 9.60 m (31 ft 6 in); height 4.40 m (14 ft 5¼ in); wing area 34.80 m² (374.59 sq ft)
Armament: one 7.9-mm (0.31-in) MG 15 machine-gun in observer's cockpit plus 250-kg (551-lb) bomb load

With hastily applied snow camouflage, these He 50As were flown by NSGr 11 on the northern sector of the Eastern Front. The unit was largely manned by Estonians.

Heinkel He 51

Heinkel He 51B serving with A/B schule 123 at Agram (Zagreb) in 1942.

When the Heinkel **He 49a** single-seat biplane made its first flight in November 1932, it was ostensibly a civilian advanced trainer. However, its BMW VI engine gave it a top speed of almost 320 km/h (199 mph), which was in keeping with its true role as the forerunner of the first fighter to serve with the Luftwaffe upon its official formation in April 1935. Two more prototypes were built, the **He 49b** flown in February 1933 with a fuselage lengthened by 0.40 m (1 ft 3¾ in), and the **He 49c** with faired landing gear. The type was ordered as the **He 51**, the initial **He 51A-0** pre-production example being flown for the first time in May 1933. Of all-metal construction, with fabric covering, the He 51 was a single-bay biplane, armed with two 7.92-mm (0.31-in) MG 17 machine-guns mounted above the engine. Deliveries of the initial **He 51A-1** production version began in July 1934, and in April 1935 some of them equipped the Luftwaffe's first fighter unit, the Jagdgeschwader 'Richthofen'. In January 1936 the **He 51B** was introduced on the production line; it was a structurally strengthened version of which 12 pre-production aircraft were built under the designation **He 51B-0**, then followed by 12 generally similar **He 51B-1** aircraft. An He 51A-1 converted to have float landing gear was the forerunner of 38 **He 51B-2** floatplane fighters. The final major version was the **He 51C-1**, intended primarily for export. A total of 79 was shipped to Spain, 51 being used by the Nationalist air force and the balance going to the Légion Condor. Subsequently, a small number of **He 51C-2**s, which differed by having improved radio equipment, was supplied to the Luftwaffe. Some He 51s remained in first-line service with the Luftwaffe until 1938, then being relegated to the training role, in which capacity they were used for much of World War II.

Specification
Heinkel He 51B-1
Type: single-seat fighter
Powerplant: one 559-kW (750-hp) BMW VI 7,3Z 12-cylinder inverted-Vee piston engine
Performance: maximum speed 330 km/h (205 mph) at sea level; cruising speed 280 km/h (174 mph) at sea level; service ceiling 7700 m (25,260 ft); range 570 km (354 miles)
Weights: empty 1460 kg (3,219 lb); maximum take-off 1895 kg (4,178 lb)
Dimensions: span 11.00 m (36 ft 1 in); length 8.40 m (27 ft 6¾ in); height 3.20 m (10 ft 6 in); wing area 27.20 m² (292.79 sq ft)
Armament: two 7.92-mm (0.31-in) MG 17 machine-guns

Heinkel He 59

Designed by Reinhold Mewes in 1930 as a reconnaissance bomber, the Heinkel He 59 twin-engined biplane was first flown in September 1931, the aircraft involved being the **He 59b** second prototype which was fitted with wheeled landing gear. The first prototype, the **He 59a**, flown in January 1932, had twin single-step floats, and all subsequent aircraft were completed in marine configuration. In early 1932 a small batch of **He 59A** evaluation aircraft was built, followed by a run of 16 **He 59B-1** aircraft which featured a 7.92-mm (0.31-in) MG 15 machinegun in the nose.

Heinkel and Arado then initiated production of the He 59B-2, which introduced an all-metal nose with glazed panels for the bomb-aimer, plus a glazed ventral position housing an MG 15 gun to supplement those in nose and dorsal positions. It was followed by the reconnaissance He 59B-3 with fuselage fuel tanks to supplement those contained in the floats. By 1938 the He 59Bs were approaching obsolescence for operational use, and the Walter Bachmann Flugzeugbau at Ribnitz began a series of more specialised conversions. They resulted in the **He 59C-1** – a stripped-down version for training, the **He 59C-2** – equipped to carry six inflatable dinghies, medical supplies and an external

folding ladder for use in air-sea rescue, and the **He 59D-1**, which combined the roles of both He 59C variants. A torpedo bombing trainer was then developed under the designation **He 59E-1**, while the **He 59E-2** reconnaissance trainer carried three cameras. Final variant was the **He 59N** navigation trainer, produced as conversions of the He 59D-1.

With the outbreak of World War II, the majority of He 59s were deployed as trainers, but some of the reconnaissance versions continued in use during the early months of the war. KGzbv 108 See used the type for transport during the Norwegian campaign, while 12 aircraft were used to land troops along a Dutch canal to seize a bridge with complete surprise. During the battle of Britain, He 59C-2s and He 59D-1s, operating in all-white schemes and carrying red crosses and civil registrations, flew rescue missions in the Channel. The

British alleged they were also used to lay mines across the Thames estuary and to land German agents. Several were later shot down, and the aircraft reverted to military colours. The type served widely in the rescue role, but was progressively replaced by Do 18s and Do 24s until it retired to training duties in 1943.

Specification
Heinkel He 59B-2
Type: coastal reconnaissance floatplane

Heinkel He 59D-1 of Seenotzentrale Ägaisches Meer, used for air-sea rescue duties in the Aegean Sea during 1941.

Powerplant: two 492-kW (660-hp) BMW VI 6,0 ZU 12-cylinder Vee piston engines
Performance: maximum speed 220 km/h (137 mph) at sea level; cruising speed 215 km/h (133 mph); ceiling 3500 m (11,480 ft); range 1750 km (1,087 miles)
Weights: empty 6215 kg (13,702 lb); maximum take-off 9000 kg (19,482 lb)
Dimensions: span 23.70 m (77 ft 9 in); length 17.40 m (57 ft 1 in); height 7.10 m (23 ft 3½ in); wing area 153.30 m² (1,650.16 sq ft)
Armament: three 7.92-mm (0.31-in) MG 15 machine-guns in nose, dorsal and ventral positions, plus a bomb load of 1000 kg (2,205 lb), or one torpedo

The He 59D-1 was produced for the navigation training and air-sea rescue roles, seeing service mainly in the latter.

Heinkel He 60

Like the He 59, the Heinkel He 60 was designed by Reinhold Mewes and was a twin-float single-bay biplane of mixed construction, developed for catapult operations from the larger German warships. The **He 60a** prototype was flown in early 1933; its powerplant was a 492-kW (660-hp) BMW VI engine which provided insufficient power and which was replaced in the **He 60b** second machine by a 559-kW (750-hp) version of the same engine. This installation provided only marginally improved performance and was not adopted for subsequent aircraft. The **He 60c** third prototype was the first to be equipped for catapult launching, and was used for shipboard trials which established the type's suitability for its intended role. Fourteen pre-production **He 60A** unarmed trainers were built, and these

entered service with Kriegsmarine training units during the summer of 1933, followed by a pre-production batch of **He 60Bs**. The first true production variant was the **He 60C**, with only minor changes. The **He 60D** added a forward-firing MG 17 and had better radio equipment. Six of these aircraft were dispatched to Spain under the designation **He 60E**.

In Luftwaffe service the He 60 proved to have excellent water-handling, and was serving with several Küstenfliegergruppen at the outbreak of war. It was considered to be very vulnerable, and had been withdrawn from front-line units by early 1940. In 1941, however, it reappeared with the Seeaufklärungsgruppen on coastal patrol work, serving with 1./SAGr 125 and all three *Staffeln* of SAGr 127 in the Baltic, and with 1./SAGr 126 in the

Mediterranean. The type retired in October 1943, 3./SAGr 127 being the last operator.

Specification
Heinkel He 60B
Type: shipboard reconnaissance aircraft/trainer
Powerplant: one 492-kW (660-hp) BMW VI 12-cylinder Vee piston engine
Performance: maximum speed 240 km/h (149 mph) at sea level; cruising speed 215 km/h (134 mph); service ceiling 5000 m (16,405 ft); range 950 km (590 miles)

Weights: empty 2725 kg (6,009 lb); maximum take-off 3425 kg (7,552 lb)
Dimensions: span 13.50 m (44 ft 3½ in); length 12.50 m (37 ft 8¾ in); height 5.30 m (17 ft 4½ in); wing area 56.20 m² (604.95 sq ft)
Armament: one 7.9-mm (0.31-in) MG 15 machine-gun on trainable mount in rear cockpit

Despite the addition of a machine-gun to the He 60D-1 (illustrated), the type was very vulnerable, owing to its sedate performance. In its favour, water-handling was considered excellent.

Heinkel He 100

Although Messerschmitt's Bf 109 had been adopted as the Luftwaffe's standard monoplane fighter in preference to Heinkel's He 112 submission, Heinrich Hertel and Siegfried Gunter designed a new high-speed fighter with a design maximum speed of 700 km/h (435 mph). It was also engineered for ease of production with few curves and the minimum number of parts and components. The resulting Heinkel **He 100a** prototype made its first flight on 22 January 1938, powered by a Daimler-Benz DB 601 engine with a special pressurised evaporative cooling system. A second prototype, with a DB 601M engine, captured the 100-km (62-mile) closed-circuit landplane record on 6 June 1938, piloted by Ernst Udet. The aircraft was referred to officially as an **He 112U**, to boost the reputation of the He 112B sold to Japan and Spain. The third prototype, built for an attempt on the world absolute speed record had reduced wing span, a more streamlined cockpit canopy and a boosted DB 601 engine, but it crashed in September and was replaced by the similar eighth prototype. In this aircraft Hans Dieterle raised the record to 746.61 km/h (463.92 mph) at Oranienburg on 30 March 1939. The fourth and fifth aircraft were designated **He 100B**. Prototypes

six, seven and nine were completed to **He 100C** standard; the third of these was the first He 100 to be armed, carrying two 20-mm MG FF cannon and four 7.9-mm (0.31-in) MG 17 machine-guns.

Handling deficiencies revealed during service evaluation at Erprobungsstelle Rechlin resulted in the introduction of the **He 100D** with enlarged tail surfaces and with a conventional, semi-retractable ventral radiator in place of the earlier enclosed system. It was armed with a 20-mm MG FF cannon in the nose and two 7.9-mm (0.31-in) MG 17 machine-guns in the wings. Fifteen He 100Ds were built, comprising three **He 100D-0** pre-production examples and 12 **He 100D-1** production aircraft. As DB 601 engines had been earmarked for Bf 109 production, the He 100 was not adopted for Luftwaffe use and the company was authorised to offer it for foreign

Two illustrations depicting He 100D-1s in spurious unit markings for propaganda purposes. The nearest the angular fighter got to action was defending Heinkel's Rostock factory.

licence-manufacture. In October 1939 Japanese and Soviet teams visited Marienehe and, as a result, three He 100D-0 aircraft were sold to Japan and three He 100D-1s to the USSR. Proposed Japanese, Soviet and Hungarian production did not materialise. The He 100D-1s fulfilled an unusual purpose in the spring of 1940, being used for a series of propaganda photographs showing line-ups of the fighters in various scenarios with many different unit badges. Dubbed the '**He 113**', the aircraft was depicted as being in widespread Luftwaffe service, but in fact there were only nine, and these were

retained at Rostock for factory defence duties, although no shots were ever fired in anger.

Specification
Heinkel He 100D-1
Type: single-seat fighter
Powerplant: one 876-kW (1,175-hp) Daimler-Benz DB 601M 12-cylinder Vee piston engine
Performance: maximum speed 670 km/h (416 mph); service ceiling 9890 m (32,450 ft); range 1005 km (625 miles)
Weights: empty 2070 kg (4,563 lb); maximum take-off 2500 kg (5,512 lb)
Dimensions: span 9.42 m (30 ft 10¼ in); length 8.19 m (26 ft 10¼ in); height 2.50 m (8 ft 2½ in); wing area 14.50 m² (156.08 sq ft)
Armament: one 20-mm MG FF cannon and two 7.9-mm (0 31-in) MG 17 machine-guns

Heinkel He 111

Designed under the leadership of Siegfried and Walter Gunter in response to demands at the time of the Luftwaffe's secret birth for a fast airliner capable of minimum adaptation for the bombing role, the **He 111** was in effect a twin-engined, scaled-up version of the He 70 Blitz that had entered Luft Hansa service in 1934, retaining its elliptical wing and tail surfaces. Powered by 448-kW (600-hp) B.M.W. VI 6,0Z engines, the first prototype was flown at Marienehe by Gerhard Nitschke on 25 February 1935, being followed by the second less than three weeks later. The third prototype, forerunner of the **He 111A** series bomber version, showed itself to possess a performance better than many then-current fighters.

As six 10-seat **He 111C-0**s entered service with Lufthansa during 1936, the first of 10 military **He 111A-0**s were being evaluated at Rechlin but, owing to inadequate engine power when carrying a warload, were summarily rejected, all 10 aircraft being sold to China.

Anticipating the problem of power shortage, Heinkel produced the **He 111B**, of which the pre-production **He 111B-0** series was powered by 746-kW (1,000-hp) Daimler-Benz DB 600A engines. Despite a considerable weight increase, this version returned a top speed of 360 km/h (224 mph). By the end of 1936 the first production **He 111B-1**s with 656-kW (880-hp) DB 600C engines appeared and, following successful trials, joined 1./KG 154 (later renamed KG 157), KG 152, KG 155, KG 253, KG 257 and KG 355. Thirty He 111B-1s were also shipped to Spain to provide the bomber force of K/88 of the Légion Condor fighting in the Civil War. The **He 111B-2** was produced in 1937 with 709-kW (950-hp) DB 603CG engines.

Few examples of the **He 111D-0** and **D-1**, with 709-kW (950-hp) DB 600Ga engines, were built as a result of a shortage of this engine, and in 1938 production switched to the **He 111E** with 746-kW (1,000-hp) Junkers Jumo 211A-1s. Some 200 of these aircraft were produced, and they proved capable of lifting a 2000-kg (4,409-lb) bomb load – roughly similar to that of the RAF's much slower Armstrong Whitworth Whitley III heavy bomber.

Meanwhile efforts had been made to simplify the He 111's wing structure for ease of production, and a new planform with straight leading and trailing edges had appeared on the seventh prototype.

First prototype of the He 111 was the He 111a (later styled the He 111 V1) flown by Gerhard Nitschke at Marienehe on 24 February 1934 and powered by 492-kW (660-hp) BMW VI 6,0Z engines. Although built as a bomber, British intelligence authorities persisted in believing it to be a high-speed commercial aircraft.

Serving with the Légion Condor's bomber element, Kampfgruppe 88, during the Spanish Civil War in 1937, this He 111B-1 carried a variety of individual markings, including the name 'Holzauge' (literally 'Wooden Eye') and a black scottie-dog on the fin.

A Jumo-powered He 111E-1 whose maximum bomb load (carried internally) had been increased to 2000 kg (4,410 lb); this version eventually equipped all four bomber Staffeln of Kampfgruppe 88 of the Legion Condor in Spain during 1938.

This wing was introduced into production with the **He 111F**, which emerged from the shops of Heinkel's new showpiece factory at Oranienburg in 1938; powered by 821-kW (1,100-hp) Jumo 211A-3s, 24 **He 111F-1**s were sold to Turkey, while the Luftwaffe's version was the **F-4**. The **He 111G** series comprised nine examples, of which five (powered variously by BMW 132Dc and BMW 132H-1 radials and DB 600G inlines) were delivered to Lufthansa and the remainder went to Turkey as **He 111G-5**s. Produced simultaneously with the **He 111G** series, the **He 111J** series was developed as a torpedo-carrying version, of which about 90 were produced, but in fact served as a normal bomber with the Kriegsmarine-allocated KGr 806 in 1939.

Hitherto all He 111s had featured a conventional 'stepped' windscreen profile but, following the appearance of the eighth prototype in

Armourers handling an SC 500 (500-kg/1,102-lb) bomb on an airfield at the Eastern Front during the summer of 1941, with a Heinkel He 111H-6 of Kampfgeschwader 55 in the background. The He 111 provided the Luftwaffe's main heavy bomber strength for much of World War II.

January 1938, the **He 111P** adopted the smooth nose profile with extensive glazing that so characterised the aircraft thereafter. This design incorporated a nose gun mounted offset to port, and a small hinge-up windscreen to improve the pilot's view during landing. The He 111P series entered production before the end of 1938, the type joining KG 157 in the following April. Although this series was intended as an interim version pending arrival of the **He 111H**, it survived in Luftwaffe service long after the outbreak of war in 1939.

By September that year the He 111H was well established with operational units, the Luftwaffe deploying 400 such aircraft compared with 349 He 111P series, 38 He 111E series and 21 He 111J series aircraft. Of this total of 808 aircraft, 705 were serviceable on the eve of Germany's attack on Poland. In that fateful campaign the Heinkels of KG 1, KG 4, KG 26, KG 27, and II/LG1 were in constant action, starting with raids far beyond the front line, but as the Poles fell back towards Warsaw, were launching devastating bombing raids on the Polish capital.

Heinkel He 111

Displaying three white bars on the rudder for fighter escort identification during the Battle of Britain, this He 111H-2 of the Geschwaderstab, KG 53 'Legion Condor' with additional nose and ventral MG 15 guns, was based at Lille-Nord, Belgium, in 1940.

Thirty He 111H-3s and H-5s were converted to H-8 standard, with a large and drag-inducing rig for cutting barrage balloon cables. The aircraft were not particularly successful in operations over Britain, and the survivors were modified as He 111H-8/R2 glider tugs.

Owing to the lack of suitable airfields, only three He 111-equipped units (KG 4, KG 26 and KGr 100) operated in the Norwegian campaign, the other Geschwader deploying in readiness for the German attack in the West, which opened on 10 May 1940. Four days later 100 Heinkels of KG 54 attacked Rotterdam – now known to have occurred owing to the fact that a recall message was not received by many of the bombers, whose radio operators were already manning their guns; as it was 57 aircraft dropped 97 tons of bombs in the centre of the city, killing 814 Dutch civilians.

Battle of Britain

By the beginning of the Battle of Britain the He 111H had almost entirely replaced the He 111P series (although most staff crews still flew the older aircraft, and it was in an He 111P that Oberst Alois Stoeckl, commanding KG 55, was shot down and killed near Middle

Large bombs were carried externally, this being a 1000-kg (2,204-lb) weapon. The aircraft is operating on the Eastern Front in January 1943, and has a soluble white distemper applied over the standard camouflage for winter operations.

Wallop on 14 August 1940). From the outset the He 111H, with its 435-km/h (270-mph) top speed, proved a difficult aircraft to shoot down (compared with the Dornier Do 17), and showed itself capable of weathering heavy battle damage. The 17 *Gruppen* flying the He 111H during the battle operated an average strength of about 500 (compared with He 111P series aircraft, of which some 40 served in the reconnaissance role with the *Aufklärungsgruppen*), losing some 246 of their number in air combat in the course of the four-month battle. Among the outstanding attacks by He 111s were those by KG 55 on the Bristol aircraft factory on 25 September, and the same unit's devastating raid on Supermarine's factory at Southampton the following day.

The majority of the He 111Hs employed during the Battle of Britain were **He 111H-1**s, **-2**s, **-3**s, and **-4**s, the latter two initially powered by 821-kW (1,100-hp) Jumo 211D engines. Perhaps the

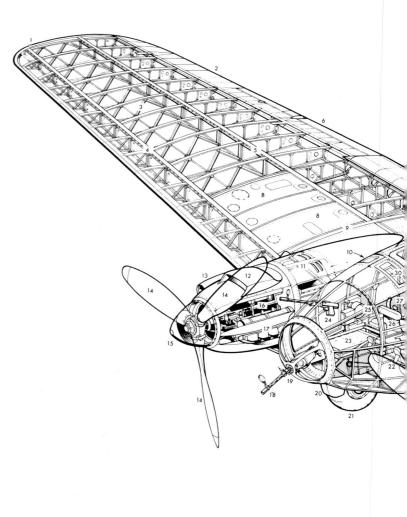

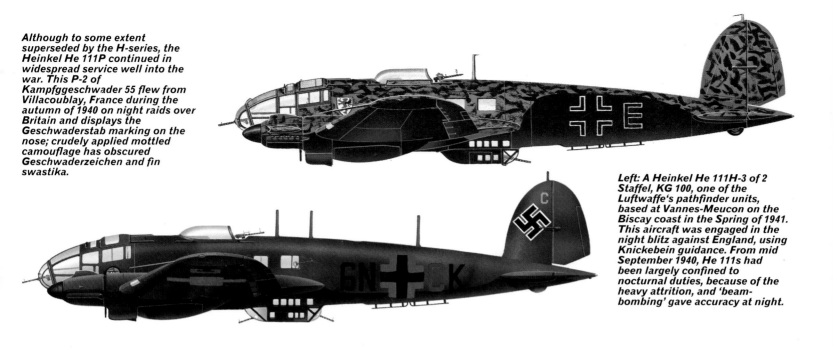

Although to some extent superseded by the H-series, the Heinkel He 111P continued in widespread service well into the war. This P-2 of Kampfggeschwader 55 flew from Villacoublay, France during the autumn of 1940 on night raids over Britain and displays the Geschwaderstab marking on the nose; crudely applied mottled camouflage has obscured Geschwaderzeichen and fin swastika.

Left: A Heinkel He 111H-3 of 2 Staffel, KG 100, one of the Luftwaffe's pathfinder units, based at Vannes-Meucon on the Biscay coast in the Spring of 1941. This aircraft was engaged in the night blitz against England, using Knickebein guidance. From mid September 1940, He 111s had been largely confined to nocturnal duties, because of the heavy attrition, and 'beam-bombing' gave accuracy at night.

Heinkel He 111H-3 cutaway drawing key

1 Starboard navigation light
2 Starboard aileron
3 Wing ribs
4 Forward spar
5 Rear spar
6 Aileron tab
7 Starboard flap
8 Fuel tank access panel
9 Wing centre section/outer panel break line
10 Inboard fuel tank (154 Imp gal/700 litre capacity) position between nacelle and fuselage
11 Oil tank cooling louvres
12 Oil cooler air intake
13 Supercharger air intake
14 Three-blade VDM airscrew
15 Airscrew pitch-change mechanism
16 Junkers Jumo 211 D-1 12-cylinder inverted-vee liquid-cooled engine
17 Exhaust manifold
18 Nose-mounted 7.9-mm MG 15 machine gun
19 Ikaria ball-and-socket gun mounting (offset to starboard)
20 Bomb sight housing (offset to starboard)
21 Starboard mainwheel
22 Rudder pedals
23 Bomb aimer's horizontal pad
24 Additional 7.9-mm MG-15 machine-gun (fitted by forward maintenance units)

25 Repeater compass
26 Bomb aimer's folding seat
27 Control column
28 Throttles
29 Pilot's seat
30 Retractable auxiliary windscreen (for use when pilot's seat in elevated position)
31 Sliding entry panel
32 Forward fuselage bulkhead
33 Double-frame station
34 Port ESAC bomb bay (vertical stowage)
35 Fuselage windows (blanked)
36 Central gangway between bomb bays
37 Double-frame station
38 Direction finder
39 Dorsal gunner's (forward) sliding canopy
40 Dorsal 7.9-mm MG 15 machine gun
41 Dorsal gunner's cradle seat
42 FuG 10 radio equipment
43 Fuselage window
44 Armoured bulkhead (8-mm)
45 Aerial mast
46 Bomb flares

47 Unarmoured bulkhead
48 Rear fuselage access cut-out
49 Port 7.9-mm beam MG 15 machine gun
50 Dinghy stowage
51 Fuselage frames
52 Stringers
53 Starboard tailplane
54 Aerial
55 Starboard elevator
56 Tailfin forward spar
57 Tailfin structure
58 Rudder balance
59 Tailfin rear spar/rudder post
60 Rudder construction
61 Rudder tab
62 Tab actuator (starboard surface)

63 Remotely-controlled 7.9-mm MG 17 machine gun in tail cone (fitted to some aircraft only)
64 Rear navigation light
65 Elevator tab
66 Elevator structure
67 Elevator hinge line
68 Tailplane front spar
69 Semi-retractable tailwheel
70 Tailwheel shock-absorber
71 Tail surface control linkage
72 Fuselage/tailfin frame
73 Control pulley

74 Push-pull control rods
75 Master compass
76 Observation window fairing
77 Glazed observation window in floor
78 Ventral aft-firing 7.9-mm MG 15 machine gun in tail of 'Sterbebett' ('Death-bed') bath

79 Ventral bath entry hatch
80 Ventral gunner's horizontal pad
81 Forward-firing 20-mm (Oerlikon) MG FF cannon (for anti-shipping operations)
82 Rear spar carry-through
83 Forward spar carry-through
84 Oil cooler
85 Anti-vibration engine mount
86 Oil tank
87 Engine bearer
88 Exhaust flame-damper shroud
89 Radiator air intake
90 Radiator bath
91 Port mainwheel
92 Mainwheel leg
93 Retraction mechanism
94 Mainwheel door (outer)
95 Multi-screw wing attachment
96 Trailing-aerial tube (to starboard of ventral bath)
97 Rear spar attachment
98 Port outboard fuel tank (220 Imp gal/1000 litre capacity)
99 Flap control rod

100 Landing light
101 Pitot head
102 Pitot head heater/wing leading-edge de-icer
103 Flap and aileron coupling
104 Flap structure
105 Aileron tab
106 Tab actuator
107 Rear spar
108 Forward spar
109 Port aileron
110 Port navigation light

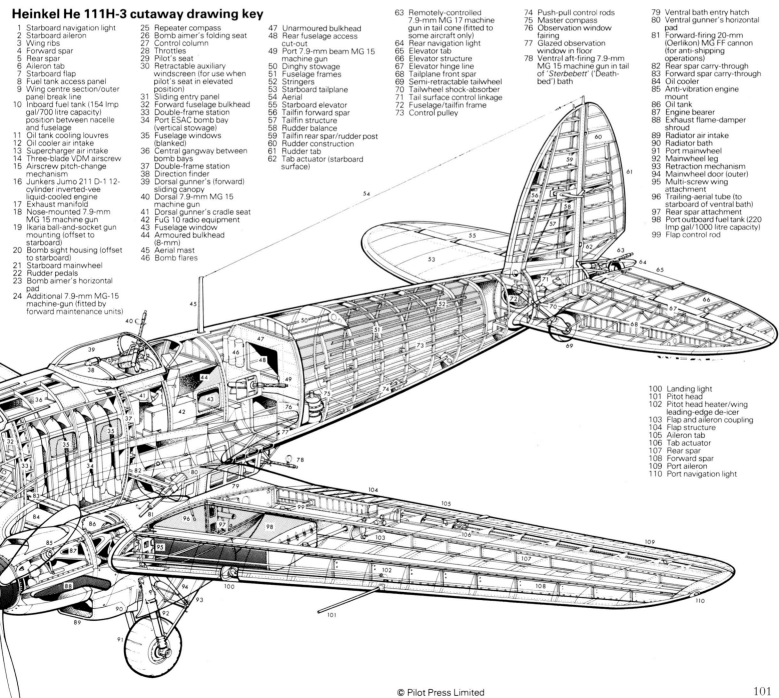

Heinkel He 111H-2
9. Staffel
Kampfgeschwader 53
Lille-Nord, France, 1940

The aircraft depicted here, Wkr Nr 3340, 'Yellow B' of 9./KG 53 'Legion Condor' is shown with the wing bars carried (for fighter identification and station-keeping) during the big Luftwaffe daylight raids on London during Sunday 15 September 1940 – the climax of the Battle of Britain. The three white panels have always been said to indicate the III Gruppe of a *Geschwader*, although so many anomalies exist as to throw doubt on this assumption. This aircraft was in fact damaged in action on that day and force landed at Armentiers with two wounded crew members; recent computerised research suggests that it was probably attacked by Spitfires of No. 66 (Fighter) Sqn.

Crew accommodation

The standard crew of the He 111H was five. The pilot sat back in the glazed section, offset to port. The navigator/bombardier sat alongside him for take-off on a folding seat, but for operations he moved forwards to a pad in the extreme nose from where he could aim the bombs and fire the nose gun. In the rear crew compartment was the radio operator, who fired the dorsal gun, this position having a sliding glazed cover. Two further gunners were carried, to operate the weapons in the beam positions and ventral gondola, which was known to the crew as the '*Stertebett*' (death-bed).

Unit history

KG 53 began the war with all three *Gruppen* and the *Stab* equipped with the He 111H, subordinated to Luftflotte 3. The unit did not take part in the Polish or Norwegian campaigns, but did contribute aircraft to the assault on the Low Countries. After the fall of France, KG 53 moved to the north of the country to be in the thick of the bombing raids on England during the Battle of Britain. From 13 August to mid-September the *Geschwader* flew on daylight attacks, suffering considerable losses to fighters and flak, before switching to night operations, which continued through the winter. In early 1941 KG 53 moved east, and joined KG 27 and KG 55 in the opening attack against the Soviet Union on 22 June. The unit remained in this theatre until September 1944, although it was not used for transport duties on the Stalingrad airlift. However, in June 1944 it took part in the hugely successful raid on US 'shuttle bombers' at Poltava in which 43 B-17s and 15 P-51s were destroyed. Back in the West, KG 53 became the main Fi 103 missile-launching unit, having absorbed III/KG 3 (at Venlo) as the new I/KG 53. II/KG 53 began missile attacks from bases in the Bremen/Oldenburg area, while the surviving aircraft of the disbanding KG 27 equipped III/KG 53. Missile launches continued until 14 January 1945.

Specification
Heinkel He 111H-16
Type: five-seat medium night-bomber/pathfinder and glider tug
Powerplant: two 1006-kW (1,350-hp) Junkers Jumo 211F-2 inline piston engines
Performance: maximum speed 435 km/h (270 mph) at 6000 m (19,685 ft); service ceiling 8500 m (27,890 ft); normal range 1950 km (1,212 miles)
Weights: empty 8680 kg (19,136 lb); maximum take-off 14000 kg (30,864 lb)
Dimensions: span 22.60 m (74 ft 1 in); length 16.40 m (53 ft 9 in); height 4.00 m (13 ft 1 in); wing area 86.50 m² (931.1 sq ft)
Armament: one 20-mm MG FF cannon, one 13-mm (0.51-in) MG 131 and up to seven 7.9-mm (0.31-in) MG 15 and MG 81 machine-guns, plus one 2000-kg (4,409-lb) bomb carried externally and one 500-kg (1,102-lb) bomb internally, or eight 250-kg (551-kg) bombs all internally

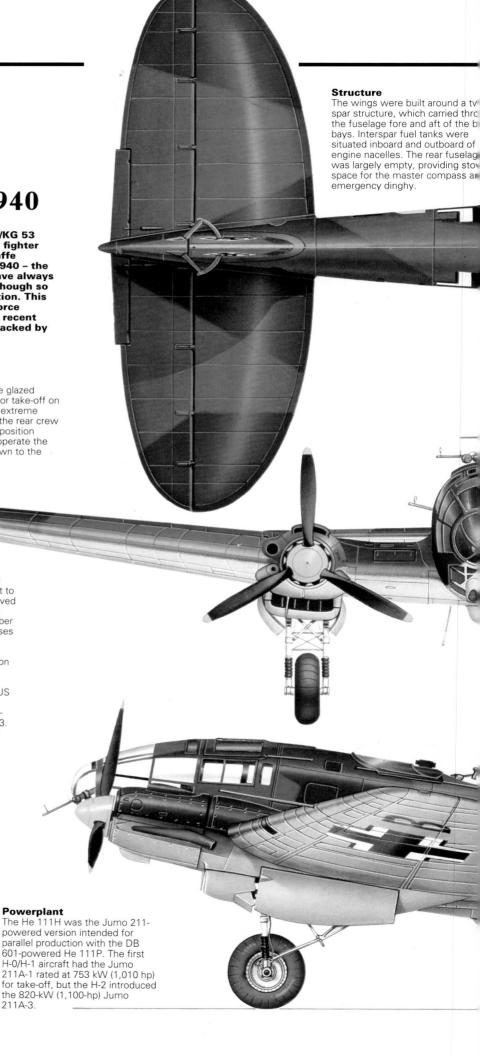

Structure
The wings were built around a tv... spar structure, which carried thr... the fuselage fore and aft of the b... bays. Interspar fuel tanks were situated inboard and outboard of engine nacelles. The rear fuselag... was largely empty, providing sto... space for the master compass a... emergency dinghy.

Powerplant
The He 111H was the Jumo 211-powered version intended for parallel production with the DB 601-powered He 111P. The first H-0/H-1 aircraft had the Jumo 211A-1 rated at 753 kW (1,010 hp) for take-off, but the H-2 introduced the 820-kW (1,100-hp) Jumo 211A-3.

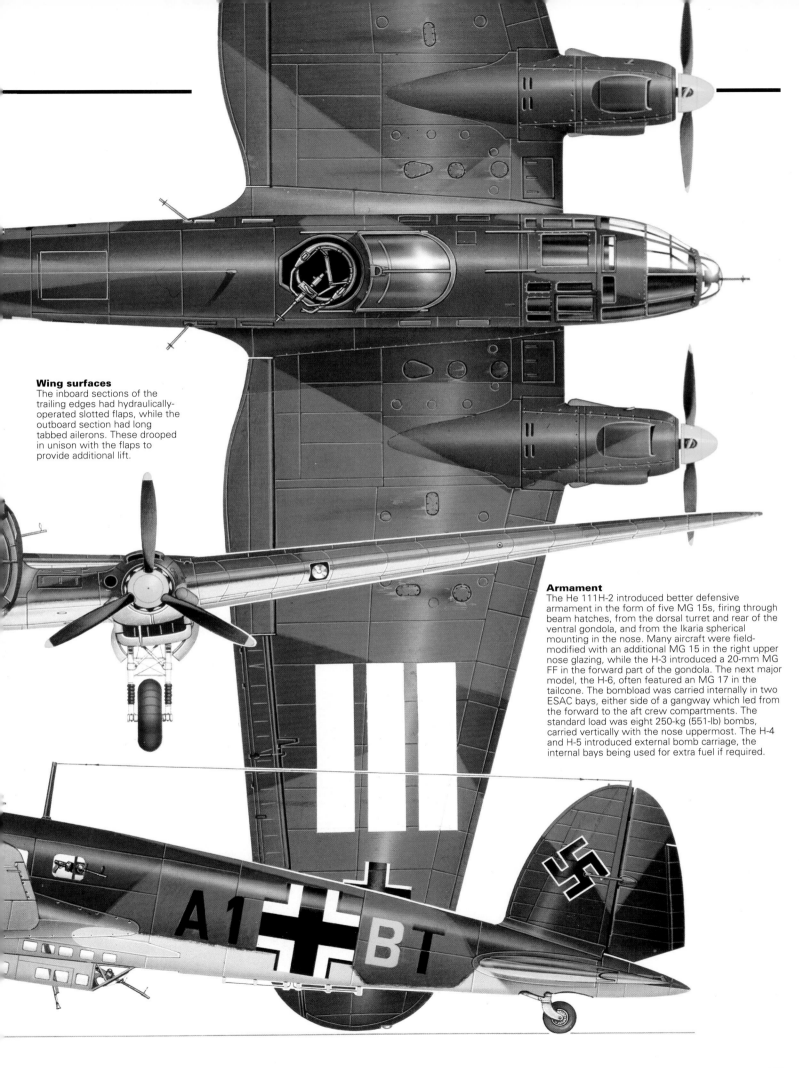

Wing surfaces
The inboard sections of the trailing edges had hydraulically-operated slotted flaps, while the outboard section had long tabbed ailerons. These drooped in unison with the flaps to provide additional lift.

Armament
The He 111H-2 introduced better defensive armament in the form of five MG 15s, firing through beam hatches, from the dorsal turret and rear of the ventral gondola, and from the Ikaria spherical mounting in the nose. Many aircraft were field-modified with an additional MG 15 in the right upper nose glazing, while the H-3 introduced a 20-mm MG FF in the forward part of the gondola. The next major model, the H-6, often featured an MG 17 in the tailcone. The bombload was carried internally in two ESAC bays, either side of a gangway which led from the forward to the aft crew compartments. The standard load was eight 250-kg (551-lb) bombs, carried vertically with the nose uppermost. The H-4 and H-5 introduced external bomb carriage, the internal bays being used for extra fuel if required.

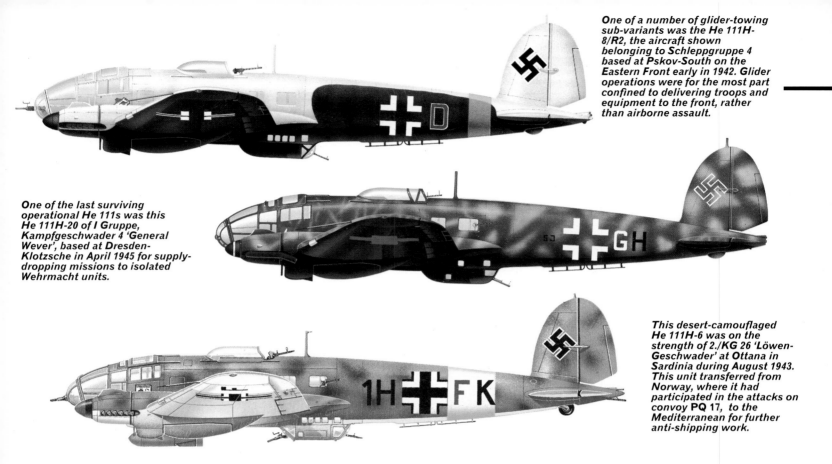

One of a number of glider-towing sub-variants was the He 111H-8/R2, the aircraft shown belonging to Schleppgruppe 4 based at Pskov-South on the Eastern Front early in 1942. Glider operations were for the most part confined to delivering troops and equipment to the front, rather than airborne assault.

One of the last surviving operational He 111s was this He 111H-20 of I Gruppe, Kampfgeschwader 4 'General Wever', based at Dresden-Klotzsche in April 1945 for supply-dropping missions to isolated Wehrmacht units.

This desert-camouflaged He 111H-6 was on the strength of 2./KG 26 'Löwen-Geschwader' at Ottana in Sardinia during August 1943. This unit transferred from Norway, where it had participated in the attacks on convoy PQ 17, to the Mediterranean for further anti-shipping work.

main significance of their losses lay in their five-man crews, whereas the other bombers, the Ju 88 and Do 17, were crewed by only four.

Heavy He 111H-5

The next variant to join the Kampfgeschwader was the **He 111H-5**, which incorporated additional fuel tanks in place of the wing bomb cells, and featured two external racks each capable of lifting a 1000-kg (2,205-lb) bomb; its maximum all-up weight was increased to 14055 kg (30,985 lb). He 111H-5s were widely used during the winter Blitz of 1940-41, these aircraft carrying the majority of the heavy bombs and parachute mines to fall on British cities in that campaign. The He 111H-5 could also carry a single 1800-kg (3,968-lb) bomb externally.

The **He 111H-6** came to be the most widely-used of all He 111s, entering production at the end of 1940. With provision to carry a pair of 765-kg (1,687-lb) LT F5b torpedoes, this version was armed with six 7.9-mm (0.31-in) MG 15 machine-guns and a forward-firing 20-mm cannon, and some aircraft featured an MG 17 or remotely-operated grenade launcher in the extreme tail. Despite its torpedo-carrying ability, most He 111H-6s were used as ordinary bombers, the first unit to fly torpedo-equipped He 111H-6s being I/KG 26, flying these aircraft from Bardufoss and Banak in northern Norway against the North

Cape convoys from June 1942 onwards and participating in the virtual annihilation of the convoy PQ 17.

The **He 111H-7** and **He 111H-9** designations covered minor equipment alterations in the He 111H-6, while the **He 111H-8** featured an outsize balloon fender designed to deflect barrage balloon cables to cutters in the wing tips; these were found to be of little use so surviving He 111H-8s were later converted to glider tugs, as **He 111H-8/R2**s. The **He 111H-10** was similar to the He 111H-6 but included a 20-mm MG FF cannon in the ventral gondola and *Kuto-Nase* cable cutters in the wings.

Varied roles

Following the successful use of He 111Hs as pathfinders by KGr 100, this role featured prominently in subsequent development of the aircraft, the **He 111H-14**, **He 111H-16/R3** and **He 111H-18** being specially fitted with FuG Samos, Peil-GV, APZ 5 and FuG Korfu radio equipment for the task; **He 111H-14**s were flown on operations by Sonderkommando Rastedter of KG 40 in 1944.

As the He 111 was joined by such later bombers as the Heinkel He 177 Greif, Dornier Do 217 and others, it underwent parallel development as a transport; the **He 111H-20/R1** was fitted out to accommodate

The Heinkel He 111H-6 was the most widely-used version of the aircraft and is pictured here carrying a pair of practice torpedoes on fuselage PVC racks. Among the operational units to employ torpedo-carrying He 111s was KG 26, based in Norway for attacks on the Allied Murmansk-bound convoys.

The Heinkel He 111H-11 with 13-mm (0.51-in) MG 131 heavy machine-gun in the extreme nose and five 250-kg (550-lb) bombs on a special rack-plate under the fuselage; this version also featured considerably increased armour protection, some of which could be jettisoned in the interests of speed in an emergency.

The He 111 bore the brunt of the Luftwaffe's bombing efforts during the opening attacks in the West. It subsequently became an important type on the Eastern Front, and on the major anti-shipping effort.

The He 111H-14 was a specialist pathfinder model with FuG Samos, Peil-GV, APZ 5 and FuG 351 Korfu equipment. These served with KG 100 and the Sonderkommando Rastedter/KG 40.

16 paratroops and the **He 111H-20/R2** was equipped as a freight-carrying glider tug. Nevertheless, bomber versions continued to serve, particularly on the Eastern Front where the **He 111H-20/R3** with a 2000-kg (4,410-lb) bomb load and the **He 111H-20/R4**, carrying 20 50-kg (110-lb) fragmentation bombs, operated by night.

Perhaps the most outstanding, albeit forlorn, of all operations by the He 111H bombers and transports was that in support of the Wehrmacht's attempt to relieve the German 6th Army at Stalingrad between November 1942 and February 1943. As the entire available force of Junkers Ju 52/3m transports was inadequate for the supply task, He 111 bombers of KG 27, KG 55 and I/KG 100 joined

KGrzbV 5 and KGrzbV 20 (flying an assortment of He 111D, F, P and H transports) and embarked on the job of flying in food and ammunition to the beleaguered army. Although the bombers were occasionally able to attack the Russian armour as it tightened its grip on the city, bad weather severely hampered the supply operations, and by the end of the Stalingrad campaign the Luftwaffe had lost 165 He 111s, a sacrifice from which the Kampfgeschwader never fully recovered.

The He 111 also underwent two of what were unquestionably the most bizarre of all the Luftwaffe's wartime operational experiments. The first involved the carriage of a Fieseler Fe 103 flying-bomb (the

---

He 111 variants

He 111a (He 111 V1): first prototype; two 448-kW (600-hp) BMW VI6, OZ with two-bladed propellers

He 111 V2: second prototype (D-ALIX); reduced trailing-edge curvature

He 111 V3: third prototype (D-ALES); span reduced to 22.61 m (74 ft 1 in)

He 111 V4: fourth prototype (D-AHAO); 10-passenger airliner; three-bladed propellers

He 111C-0: six aircraft (D-ABYE, -AMES, -AQUY, -AQYF, -ATYL, -AXAV); two delivered to Kommando Rowehl for clandestine reconnaissance

He 111A-1: 10 aircraft based on V3; rejected by Luftwaffe and sold to China

He 111 V5: DB 600A; all-up weight 8600 kg (18,959 lb)

He 111B-0: pre-production version accepted by Luftwaffe; one aircraft with Jumo 210Ga

He 111B-1: production bombers; early aircraft with DB 600Aa, later DB 600C; all-up weight 9323 kg (20,536 lb); maximum bomb load 1500 kg (3,307 lb)

He 111B-2: supercharged DB 600CG engines; all-up weight 10000 kg (22,046 lb)

He 111 V7: prototype with straight tapered wing

He 111G-01: also termed **He 111 V12** (D-AEQU); BMW VI 6,OZu; passed to DLH

He 111G-02: also termed **He 111 V13** (D-AYKI); passed to DLH

He 111G-3: two aircraft, **V14** (D-ACBS) with BMW 132Dc and **V15** (D-ADCF) with BMW 132H-1; both passed to DLH and restyled **He 111L**

He 111G-4: also termed **He 111 V16** (D-ASAR); DB 600G; used by

Milch as personal transport

He 111G-5: four aircraft with DB 600Ga engines; sold to Turkey

He 111 V9: modified from B-2 airframe with DB 600Ga; became He 111D prototype with wing radiators

He 111D-0: pre-production batch with DB 600Ga and radiators moved to engine nacelles

He 111D-1: small number of production aircraft; abandoned due to shortage of DB engines

He 111 V6: prototype (D-AXOH) from modified B-0 with Jumo 610Ga

He 111 V10: prototype He 111E (D-ALEQ) from modified D-0 with Jumo 211A-1

He 111E-0: pre-production aircraft, 1700-kg (3,748-lb) bomb load; all-up weight 10315 kg (22,740 lb)

He 111E-1: production bombers, 2000-kg (4,409-lb) bomb load; all-up weight 10775 kg (23,754 lb)

He 111E-3: minor internal alterations; internal bomb load only

He 111E-4: half bomb load carried externally

He 111E-5: as E-4 but introduced extra internal fuel tanks

He 111 V11: prototype He 111F with straight-tapered wing; Jumo 211A-3

He 111F-0: pre-production aircraft; all-up weight 11000 kg (24,250 lb)

He 111F-1: 24 aircraft sold to Turkey in 1938

He 111F-4: 40 aircraft for Luftwaffe with E-4 bomb load arrangement

He 111J-0: pre-production aircraft; DB 600CG; external bomb load only

He 111J-1: 90 production aircraft intended as torpedo-bombers but several served as bombers only

He 111 V8: modified B-0 (D-AQUO) with stepped cockpit profile

He 111P-0: pre-production batch similar to V8, following J-1 in factory

He 111P-1: production; DB 601A-1; maximum speed 398 km/h (247 mph)

He 111P-2: as P-1 but with FuG 10 radio

He 111P-3: P-1s and P-2s modified as dual-control trainers

He 111P-4: provision for additional defensive armament; extra internal fuel; external bomb load

He 111P-6: introduced DB 601N engines; reverted to internal bomb load; **P-6/R2** was later conversion to glider tug; others transferred to Hungary

He 111 V19: prototype (D-AUKY); Jumo 211 engines

He 111H-0: pre-production batch similar to P-2 (FuG 10) but with Jumo 211

He 111H-1: production version of H-0

He 111H-2: as H-1 but with Jumo 211A-3 engines

He 111H-3: introduced anti-shipping role with forward-firing 20-mm gun in gondola; Jumo 211D-1 engines

He 111H-4: early aircraft had Jumo 211D-1, but later 211F-1 engines

He 111H-5: provision for 2500-kg (5,511-lb) bomb loads; all-up weight increased to 14055 kg (30,982 lb)

He 111H-6: included all previous modifications and provision for two 765-kg (1,686-lb) LT 5b torpedoes and increased defensive armament; Jumo 211F-1; **He 111H-7** and **H-9** were similar but with minor equipment changes

He 111H-8: H-3 and H-5 airframes with balloon cable-fender and cutters; **H-8/R2** had fenders removed and was modified as glider tug

He 111H-10: H-6 development with 20-mm gun removed from gondola to nose; *Kuto-Nase* balloon cable-cutters; Jumo 211F-2

He 111H-11: fully enclosed dorsal gun position with increased

armament and armour; **H-11/R1** had twin MG 81 guns in beam positions; **H-11/R2** was glider tug

He 111H-12: ventral gondola omitted to allow carriage of Hs 293A missiles; FuG 230b and FuG 203b radio equipment

He 111H-14: pathfinder development of H-10; 20 **H-14/R2**s were glider tugs

He 111H-16: 'standard' bomber; **H-16/R1** had electric dorsal turret; **H-16/R2** was glider tug with rigid boom; **H-16/R3** was pathfinder with reduced bomb load

He 111H-18: pathfinder similar to He 111H-16/R3 with special flame-damped exhausts

He 111H-20: built as glider tug/transport; **H-20/R1** was paratrooper with jump hatch; **H-20/R2** was freighter/tug with 30-mm gun in electric dorsal turret; **H-20/R3** modified as bomber; **H-20/R4** modified as bomber with external load of 20 50-kg (110-lb) bombs

He 111H-21: introduced Jumo 213; maximum speed 480 km/h (298 mph); bomb load 3000 kg (6,614 lb); all-up weight increased to 16000 kg (35,275 lb); Rustsatze for He 111H-20

He 111H-23: similar to H-20/R1 with Jumo 213 engines

He 111 V32: single H-6 modified with turbocharged DB 601U engines as prototype for proposed **He 111R** high-altitude bomber; **He 111R-1** and R-2 were proposed but not built

He 111Z-1: two He 111 composited with fifth engine added; glider tug; all-up weight 28500 kg (62,831 lb)

He 111Z-2: long-range bomber project similar to Z-1 intended to carry four Hs283A missiles

He 111Z-3: proposed version of Z-1 for long-range reconnaissance

Heinkel He 111

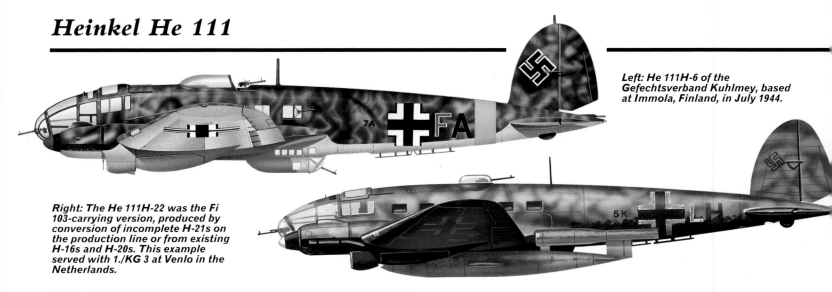

Left: He 111H-6 of the Gefechtsverband Kuhlmey, based at Immola, Finland, in July 1944.

Right: The He 111H-22 was the Fi 103-carrying version, produced by conversion of incomplete H-21s on the production line or from existing H-16s and H-20s. This example served with 1./KG 3 at Venlo in the Netherlands.

Left: Under Operation Rumpelkammer He 111H-22s were used in a concerted campaign against Britain, air-launching the Fi 103 (FZG 76) against city targets.

V-1) under one wing. Following trials at Peenemunde in 1943, about 20 He 111H-6s, He 111H-16s and He 111H-21s (all re-designaed **He 111H-22**s) were modified and delivered to III/KG 3 in July 1944. Within six weeks this unit, based in the Netherlands, had launched 300 Fi 103s against London, 90 against Southampton and 20 against Gloucester, the tactics being to approach the shoreline at low level to escape radar detection before the aircraft climbed to about 450 m (1,475 ft), release the weapon and then dive to make good their escape.

Geschwader assault

Believing this campaign to have achieved worthwhile results, the Luftwaffe equipped all three *Gruppen* of KG 53 with about 100 He 111H-22s and, based in western Germany, these joined the assault on the UK in December, one raid being launched against far-distant Manchester on Christmas Eve. In the seven months of operations the three *Gruppen* launched 1,200 flying-bombs but lost 77 aircraft; moreover, not more than 20 per cent of the bombs reached their target cities.

The other experiment involving the He 111 resulted in the extraordinary five-engined **He 111Z** (Z denoting Zwilling, or twin), achieved by joining together two He 111s by means of a new wing centre-section carrying a fifth engine. The resulting aircraft, with a span of 35.20 m (115 ft 6 in), was intended to tow the huge Messerschmitt Me 321 Gigant glider or three Gotha Go 242 gliders at 225 km/h (140 mph) at 4000 m (13,125 ft). Trials proved successful, and the He 111Z-1 served with Grossraumlastenseglerkommando 2 based at Obertraubling in 1943 for supply missions on the Eastern Front. The **He 111Z-2**, which is not thought to have been flown operationally, was equipped to carry four Henschel Hs 293A rocket bombs over long distances, and the projected **He 111Z-3** was to have been a long-range reconnaissance version. The He 111Z had a crew of seven, of which four members (including the pilot) were located in the port fuselage, the others in the starboard fuselage.

Above: Displaying the soluble white distemper applied for winter operations over the standard camouflage, this He 111H-10 served with 5./KG 4 on the Eastern Front.

Left: After service in the Battle of Britain, KG 27 took its He 111s to the Eastern Front in June 1941. These bomb-carrying aircraft from 2. Staffel are H-16s, used as makeshift transports during 1942-43 on the Stalingrad resupply effort. KG 27 disbanded in September 1944, its swansong being the successful attack on US aircraft at Poltava on 22 June.

Outstanding among the final operations by He 111 bombers was the attack on Poltava airfield in the Soviet Union on the night of 21-22 June 1944. The previous day 114 USAAF Boeing B-17s and their escorting North American P-51s had flown to the USSR after bombing Berlin. Heinkel He 111s of KG 4, KG 27, KG 53 and KG 55 caught the Americans unawares and, by the light of flares, the bombers destroyed 43 B-17s and 15 P-51s on the ground.

He 111 transports equipped Transportgruppe 30 at the end of 1944,

An example of the remarkable He 111Z-1 is seen on the Eastern Front in January 1943. These oddities, together with their Me 321 gliders, arrived too late to help the Stalingrad airlift. The aircraft were operated by the Grossraum-Lastenserglergruppe Me 321.

these aircraft dropping paratroops behind the American lines at the beginning of the Ardennes campaign. By the end of the war the aircraft was being used solely in the transport role, flown by KG 4, TGr 30 and Schleppgruppe 1 in the last days of the Third Reich.

Heinkel He 114

Heinkel began development of a more advanced successor to the He 60 twin floatplane in the summer of 1935. The **He 114** emerged as an unusual aircraft, of biplane configuration but with the lower wing of a very short span and elliptical leading-edge planform. N-struts joined the top wing to the fuselage and angled Y-struts formed the interplane bracing. Two single-step floats were braced to the fuselage, and the cockpit had accommodation for the pilot and a rear-facing gunner/observer. Power was intended to be the BMW 132 radial, but owing to a shortage of such engines, the **He 114 V1** flew for the first time in 1936 with a DB 600A inline, and the **V2** was powered by a Jumo 210Ea.

Further prototypes were produced with BMW 132 engines, but all showed poor water and flying characteristics, necessitating a series of changes to float and wing design. None of the remedies was satisfactory, and the type never enjoyed anything like the handling of its predecessor, the He 60, or the Ar 196 which filled the breach.

In addition to coastal patrol,

The principal combat employment of the He 114 came in 1941, when aircraft diverted from a Romanian order were used for coastal patrol in support of the onslaught on the Soviet Union. This is one of these He 114C-1s, which flew with 1./SAGr 125.

the He 114 had been intended for catapult launch from German warships, but after trials aboard the *Gneisenau* with the V2, the type was deemed unsuitable for this task. Five prototypes were followed by 10 **He 114A-0** pre-production machines and 33 **He 114A-1s**, which differed by having broader tail surfaces to improve stability. The **He 114A-2** had a strengthened rear fuselage, and reintroduced catapult attachment points, although these were never used by the Luftwaffe. Most A-2s were powered by the BMW 132K and had fuel tankage in the floats.

Due to the unsatisfactory nature of the He 114, the type was not considered as strategical-ly important, and was consequently cleared for export. To help sales the aircraft was issued to one Luftwaffe unit, 1./Küstenfliegergruppe 506, in 1938, but in 1939 the unit was glad to return to its old He 60s. In export form the He 114A-2 was known as the **He 114B**, and 12 **He 114B-1s** were sold to Sweden. Denmark also ordered the type but the occupation in 1940 put an end to the sale. Romania purchased 12 **He 114B-2s** with an option for a further 12 **He 114C-1s** with two fixed forward-firing MG 17 machine-guns. In the event, these aircraft were issued to 1./SAGr 125 of the Luftwaffe in 1941 to fly coastal patrols, supporting the push through the Baltic states to the Gulf of Finland. At the end of the year

they were delivered to Romania, which flew the type in action in the Black Sea until late 1943. A few aircraft were delivered to Spain for service on catapult-equipped vessels.

Specification
Heinkel He 114A-2
Type: two-seat patrol floatplane
Powerplant: one 716-kW (960-hp) BMW 132K nine-cylinder radial engine
Performance: maximum speed 335 km/h (208 mph) at 1000 m (3,280 ft); service ceiling 4900 m (16,075 ft); climb to 1000 m in 4⅓ minutes; range 920 km (572 miles)
Weights: empty 2300 kg (5,070 lb); maximum loaded 3670 kg (8,091 lb)
Dimensions: wing span 13.60 m (44ft 7½ in); length 11.65 m (38 ft 2½ in); height 5.23 m (17 ft 2 in); wing area 42.27 m² (455 sq ft)
Armament: one 7.9-mm MG 15 machine-gun on flexible mount in rear cockpit, with 600 drum-held rounds; optional external racks for two SC 50 50-kg (110-lb) bombs

Heinkel He 115

Wor ld War II was the last conflict in which twin-float seaplanes played a significant part. Of dozens of types used, the biggest and most powerful seaplane used in quantity was the **Heinkel He 115**. What makes its story even more fascinating is that it saw service not only with Germany but also with Norway, Sweden, Finland and the British RAF.

This is despite the fact that the He 115 was, like many contemporaries, obsolescent from the start. Though designed as a warplane to fly not only patrol but also torpedo and bombing missions, the 115 was always too slow and ill-defended to have any chance against fighters. This was far from obvious when the requirement for a new See-Mehrzweckeflugzeug was issued in July 1935. In early 1938 prototypes of the He 115 proved superior to the rival Ha 140, and Heinkel was awarded the first of several production contracts. These were ultimately to total 138 aircraft, of which 76 were built by Flugzeugbau 'Weser'.

The **He 115 V1** made its first flight in August 1937. A conventional all-metal stressed-skin machine, it had a slim fuselage, mid-mounted wing with a rectangular centre-section and sharply tapered outer panels, braced tailplane, twin BMW 132K engines (derived from the Pratt & Whitney Hornet) each rated at 715 kW (960 hp), and single-step floats each attached by tandem struts and multiple bracing wires. The wings had simple slotted flaps, the tailplane was fixed and there were large trim tabs on all control surfaces. The fuselage was arranged to accommodate a crew of three. The pilot's cockpit was above the wing leading edge, covered by a sliding canopy. In the glazed nose was a seat for the observer who also had a bombsight and, in an upper cupola, an MG 15 machine-gun. Above the trailing edge was the cockpit for the radio operator, who also had an MG 15 for upper rear defence. The fuselage beneath the wing was designed as an internal weapons bay, able to accommodate an 800-kg (1,763lb) torpedo or three SC 250 1250-kg (550-lb) bombs.

Altogether the He 115 showed itself to be extremely strong, to handle well and to have no significant shortcomings. In March 1938, by which time the 115 had been picked for the Luftwaffe Seeflieger, the prototype was modified with streamlined fairings over the nose and dorsal cockpits and given greater fuel capacity, and used to gain

A close-up of an He 115B shows the extensive glazing in the nose area. The bombardier had flat-pane windows in the bottom of the nose for accurate aiming, and it was his duty to fire the nose-mounted MG 15.

world records for speed with load, covering closed circuits of up to 2000 km (1,242 miles) with payloads up to 2000 kg (4,410 lb) at an average speed of 328 km/h (203 mph). By this time two further prototypes had flown, the **V3** being almost representative of the production aircraft. The outer wings had more taper on the leading edge and less on the trailing edge, the nose was lengthened and made more streamlined with a gun cupola on the nose, and the pilot's cockpit was joined to that of the radio operator by a continuous 'greenhouse'. The radio operator was provided with simple controls with which it was hoped he could bring the aircraft back should the pilot be incapacitated.

Displaying the distinctive wing shape of the earlier Heinkel He 70, a Heinkel He 115B taxis in Norwegian waters. Despite a certain amount of obsolescence, the type proved to be particularly tough, especially in rough seas, and was also able to sustain a great deal of combat damage. Water and flight handling were excellent, as was its speed.

Right: A sturdy seaplane, the He 115 was vulnerable to fighter attack, and was largely relegated to the Norwegian theatre, where opposition was less intense.

Below: Seen during an operational evaluation, this He 115B-1 is having a practice torpedo hoisted into its internal weapons bay.

In 1938 two export orders were received: six He 115s for Norway and 12 for Sweden. These were built almost to the same standard as the **He 115A-1** which went into production for the Luftwaffe in January 1939. The A-1 closely resembled the V3 prototype, with the addition of underwing racks for two further SC 250 bombs. Delivery to the first Küstenfliegerstaffel, l/KüFlGr 106, began with the outbreak of war, but Heinkel's Marienehe plant terminated production at the 62nd aircraft at the start of 1940. This total comprised 10 pre-production **A-0**s, 18 export aircraft (called **A-2**s and differing in radio, guns and other equipment) and 34 A-1 and A-3 seaplanes for the Luftwaffe. The A-3s had improved radio and weapon-release equipment.

All subsequent production was handled by 'Weser' at Einswarden, starting with 10 **B-0**s with increased fuel capacity. By 1940 the **B-1** was in production, with various *Rustsätze* (conversion kits) for bombing, minelaying (for example), carrying two 500-kg (1,100-lb) bombs, LMA III mines or a single monster LMB III of 920-kg (2,028 lb) or photo-reconnaissance. The last 18 B-series were completed as **B-2**s with reinforced floats fitted with steel skate-like runners for operation from ice or compacted snow. This was often to prove a considerable operational advantage, though pilots had to devise a mild rocking technique, by opening and closing the throttles, to unstick the floats if they were frozen in.

Last of the line

Production by 'Weser' was completed with various sub-types of **He 115C**. This basically resembled the B-series but introduced heavier armament. It had been apparent for some time that two MG 15s was not adequate defensive firepower for a large aircraft with a cruising speed of about 270 km/h (167 mph). In early 1940 the **V5** prototype was tested with a 20-mm MG FF cannon aimed by hand from the nose, and one might have thought this, plus a similar cannon aimed by the radio operator, could have provided the answer. What actually happened was that the **He 115C-1** went into production with an MG 151/15 fixed under the nose to fire ahead, and two MG 17 machine-guns were added in the engine nacelles firing directly to the rear. The forward-firing gun was a high-velocity weapon with excellent ballistics, but to be effective the big floatplane had to be flown like a fighter. It was virtually useless for defence. As for the aft-firing guns,

In late 1939, Heinkel stopped production of the He 115, all the tooling being moved to Einswarden for the 'Weser' Fleugzeugbau factory. The new production model ws the He 115B, incorporating a greater structural strength and more fuel. This is an He 115B-1 on pre-delivery trials in early 1940.

these could not be aimed at all, and (assuming an attacking fighter knew of their presence) were relatively easy to evade. The **C-2** had the ice/snow skids, the **C-3** was a specialised minelayer, and the **C-4** was an Arctic-equipped torpedo carrier with no forward-firing armament.

During their active careers, in 1942, surviving He 115s of all kinds were almost all fitted with the MG 81Z twin machine-gun package in place of the MG 15 in the radio operator's cockpit. This was a neater and very much faster-firing installation which did go some way to improving defensive firepower. Some aircraft, and possibly most, were retrofitted with a powerful MG 151/20 under the nose, in a prominent box which also housed the ammunition. The gun was carried on the left side and caused a noticeable nose-down pull to the left when fired. The original nose MG 15 was retained.

The V1's record-breaking flight led to the first export order from Norway, which purchased six for the Marinens Flyvevaben. Three of these He 115A-2s were successful in escaping to Britain affer the invasion, together with one captured German aircraff. They were converted for clandestine operations for the RAF.

Additional power

There was one attempt to increase flight performance, which had progressively deteriorated as a result of the increased weight of fuel, weapons and equipment of successive versions. In 1939 Heinkel had proposed an improved He 115 fitted with much more powerful engines, and this materialised in 1940 when an ex-Luftwaffe aircraft was returned to Marienehe and considerably modified. The structure was locally strengthened to accept bigger engines and increased gross weights, and two 1194-kW (1,600-hp) BMW 801A 14-cylinder radial engines were installed in installations generally similar to those of the early Do 217E. The fuselage was rearranged for a crew of four, with a 20-mm MG 151 under the left side of the nose, an MG 81 in the nose cupola and MG 81Z twin machine-guns in both the rear dorsal and ventral positions. Maximum speed was increased from about 295 to 380 km h (183 to 236 mph), despite the increase in weight to 12640 kg (27,865 Ib), but only the one aircraft was ever converted. Known as the **He 115D-0**, it later served with the Küstenfliegerstaffel.

From the start the He 115 had a good reputation for strength, reliability and all-round capability. They were intensively used by both the Luftwaffe and Norwegian naval air service during the invasion of

Heinkel He 115

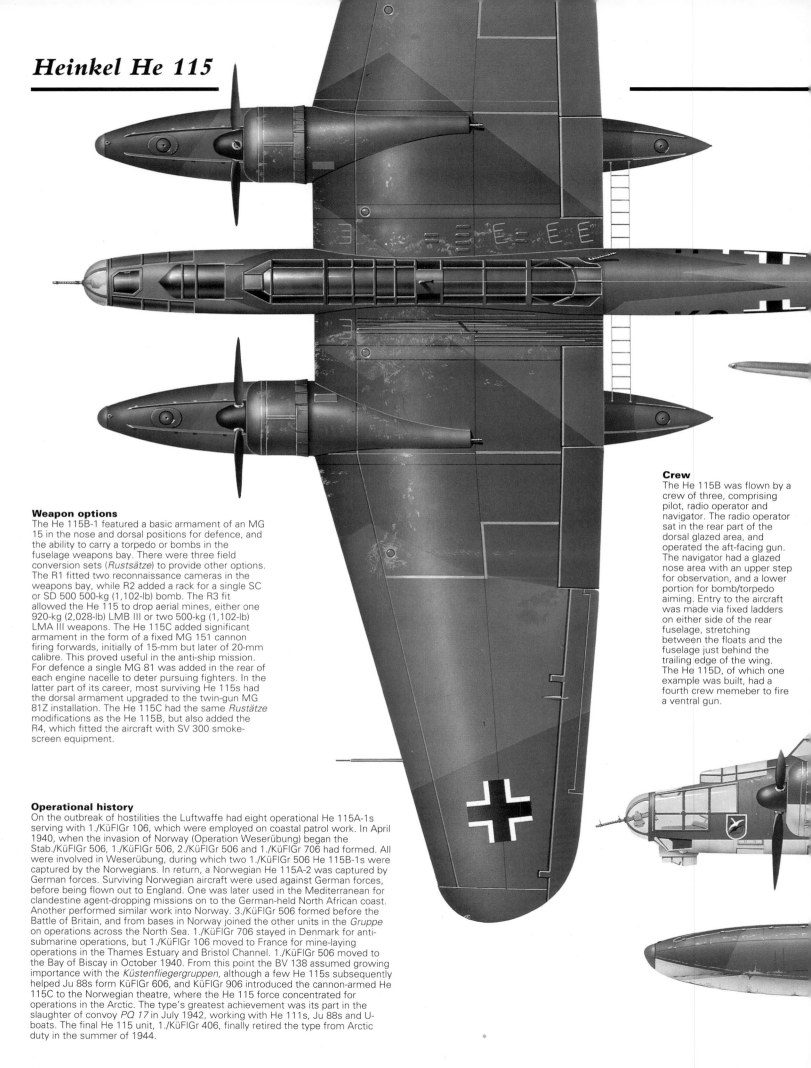

Weapon options

The He 115B-1 featured a basic armament of an MG 15 in the nose and dorsal positions for defence, and the ability to carry a torpedo or bombs in the fuselage weapons bay. There were three field conversion sets (*Rustsätze*) to provide other options. The R1 fitted two reconnaissance cameras in the weapons bay, while R2 added a rack for a single SC or SD 500 500-kg (1,102-lb) bomb. The R3 fit allowed the He 115 to drop aerial mines, either one 920-kg (2,028-lb) LMB III or two 500-kg (1,102-lb) LMA III weapons. The He 115C added significant armament in the form of a fixed MG 151 cannon firing forwards, initially of 15-mm but later of 20-mm calibre. This proved useful in the anti-ship mission. For defence a single MG 81 was added in the rear of each engine nacelle to deter pursuing fighters. In the latter part of its career, most surviving He 115s had the dorsal armament upgraded to the twin-gun MG 81Z installation. The He 115C had the same *Rustätze* modifications as the He 115B, but also added the R4, which fitted the aircraft with SV 300 smoke-screen equipment.

Crew

The He 115B was flown by a crew of three, comprising pilot, radio operator and navigator. The radio operator sat in the rear part of the dorsal glazed area, and operated the aft-facing gun. The navigator had a glazed nose area with an upper step for observation, and a lower portion for bomb/torpedo aiming. Entry to the aircraft was made via fixed ladders on either side of the rear fuselage, stretching between the floats and the fuselage just behind the trailing edge of the wing. The He 115D, of which one example was built, had a fourth crew memeber to fire a ventral gun.

Operational history

On the outbreak of hostilities the Luftwaffe had eight operational He 115A-1s serving with 1./KüFlGr 106, which were employed on coastal patrol work. In April 1940, when the invasion of Norway (Operation Weserübung) began the Stab./KüFlGr 506, 1./KüFlGr 506, 2./KüFlGr 506 and 1./KüFlGr 706 had formed. All were involved in Weserübung, during which two 1./KüFlGr 506 He 115B-1s were captured by the Norwegians. In return, a Norwegian He 115A-2 was captured by German forces. Surviving Norwegian aircraft were used against German forces, before being flown out to England. One was later used in the Mediterranean for clandestine agent-dropping missions on to the German-held North African coast. Another performed similar work into Norway. 3./KüFlGr 506 formed before the Battle of Britain, and from bases in Norway joined the other units in the *Gruppe* on operations across the North Sea. 1./KüFlGr 706 stayed in Denmark for anti-submarine operations, but 1./KüFlGr 106 moved to France for mine-laying operations in the Thames Estuary and Bristol Channel. 1./KüFlGr 506 moved to the Bay of Biscay in October 1940. From this point the BV 138 assumed growing importance with the *Küstenfliegergruppen*, although a few He 115s subsequently helped Ju 88s form KüFlGr 606, and KüFlGr 906 introduced the cannon-armed He 115C to the Norwegian theatre, where the He 115 force concentrated for operations in the Arctic. The type's greatest achievement was its part in the slaughter of convoy *PQ 17* in July 1942, working with He 111s, Ju 88s and U-boats. The final He 115 unit, 1./KüFlGr 406, finally retired the type from Arctic duty in the summer of 1944.

Heinkel He 115B-1
1./Küstenfliegergruppe 406
Sørreisa, Tromsø, 1942

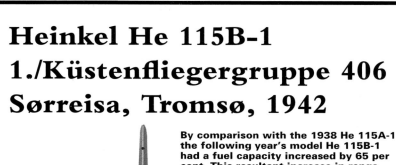

By comparison with the 1938 He 115A-1 the following year's model He 115B-1 had a fuel capacity increased by 65 per cent. This resultant increase in range could, in turn, be traded for a larger bomb load, and soon after the outbreak of war He 115s found themselves dropping magnetic mines in British waters, these being the first German aircraft adapted to carry this weapon.

Markings
Most He 115s wore a standard splinter pattern, although often a pale shade of grey was used for Arctic operations. The aircraft wears standard tactical codes 'K6' (for KüFlGr 406), 'L' (individual aircraft) in white (for first *Staffel* in the *Gruppe*) and H for the 1. Staffel. Yellow theatre bands are worn, as the war in Norway was loosely regarded as the Eastern front. This aircraft wears kill markings on the tail.

Specification
Heinkel He 115B-1
Type: coastal reconnaissance and torpedo bomber floatplane
Powerplant: two 645-kW (856-hp) BMW 132N 9-cylinder radial piston engines
Performance: maximum speed 355 km/h (220 mph) at 3400 m (11,155 ft); cruising speed 295 km/h (183 mph); service ceiling 5500 m (18,045 ft); maximum range 3350 km (2,082 miles)
Weights: empty 5300 kg (11,684 lb); maximum take-off weight 10400 kg (22,928 lb)
Dimensions: span 22.00 m (72 ft 2 in); length 17.30 m (56 ft 9 in); height 6.60 m (21 ft 8 in)
Armament: one fixed forward-firing and one rear-firing 7.9-mm (0.31-in) MG 15 machine-gun, plus a maximum bomb load of 1250 kg (2,756 lb)

Heinkel He 115

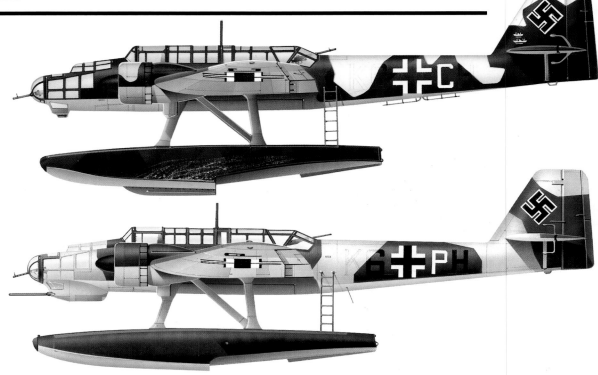

An He 115B-2 of 1./KüFlGr 406 operating in Norway. During winter a white distemper was applied to the normal splinter scheme to camouflage the aircraft in snow conditions. Note the ship kill marks on the fin and the steel skids under the floats for operations from ice.

'K6+PH' was an He 115C-1 serving with 1./KüFlGr 406 during 1942, when the unit was involved in attacking convoys taking equipment from Britain to the Soviet Union via the North Cape route.

This He 115C-1 of 3./KüFlGr 106 (code M2) shows the original 15-mm MG 151 cannon installation in the nose. Night minelaying operations were undertaken by the He 115 in British waters, and for this reason they were hastily applied with black paint to mask the light grey undersides, national insignia and white code letter.

Norway in April/May 1940. At the end of this conflict one Norwegian aircraft was flown to Finland, where it was repaired and put into service with the Ilmavoimat, where in 1943 it was joined by two He 115Cs supplied from Germany. Three Norwegian He 115A-2s and a captured B-1 were flown to Scotland, where they received RAF serial numbers BV184-187. All continued flying until they were destroyed or the spares ran out. All were modified, the most obvious changes being replacement of the long 'glasshouse' by metal panels and fitting of British armament. Aircraft 185 and 187 were modified for clandestine operations, one startling change being the addition of four Browning machine-guns firing ahead from the leading edge of the wings, plus four more firing to the rear. In October 1941 BV185 was flown round via Gibraltar to Malta, where it enjoyed a charmed life in Luftwaffe markings, making numerous missions to North Africa by night and by day inserting and picking up Allied agents. On one occasion it landed in Tripoli harbour in broad daylight, took on board two agents and returned to Malta. Eventually it was destroyed at Malta by bombing. Meanwhile 187, the former Luftwaffe B-1, flew several long missions between Woodhaven, on the Firth of Tay, and points in Norway. Eventually it was decided that these missions posed too great a risk, mainly from destruction by RAF fighters.

Twilight misions

Luftwaffe He 115s had carried out minelaying operations from the the start of the war, and from 1942 surviving examples were all grouped in northern Norway for operations against Allied convoys. The most important and most successful missions were against the ill-fated convoy PQ 17 in July 1942. Eight He 115C-1s of the KüFlGr 406 made torpedo attacks on 2 July, the Staffelkapitän being shot down but rescued, with his crew, by another 115 which alighted on the stormy sea. On 4 July aircraft of KüFlGr 906 disabled one ship, and subsequently aircraft of both units played a part in hunting down and sinking 23 of the 36 vessels that had comprised the convoy. A few 115s lingered on into mid-1944, but they saw little action.

The He 115C-1 replaced the B on the production line during 1940, this adding a fixed 15-mm cannon under the nose and rearward firing MG 17 machine-guns in the rear of the engine nacelle. During 1942-43, the 15-mm cannon was replaced by a 20-mm MG 151 in a bathtub fairing, as seen here on this 1./KüFlGr 906 aircraft.

Heinkel He 162 Salamander

Today it is quite normal for the various pre-feasibility study and countless other phases of a new aircraft project to take more than 10 years. We seem to have forgotten that a totally new jet fighter can move from being a mere idea to a flying prototype in 90 days, with at least 300 completed and nearly 1,000 more on the assembly lines after a further 90 days.

In autumn 1944, Hitler's Germany was beset by powerful foes to the west, south and east, and Allied air power was reducing the whole country to rubble. Desperate measures were needed, and strong Nazi bosses took over the reins and began making desperate decisions. Under the overall control of Albert Speer's armaments ministry, Party Leader Karl-Otto Saur schemed a *Volksjäger* (people's fighter). This was to be small (not over 2000 kg/4,410 lb, loaded), simple, jet-propelled and thus able to fly rings round the hordes of Allied fighters, carry one or two 30-mm guns, be easy to look after and make absolutely minimum demands on skilled labour and scarce materials.

This requirement was issued on 8 September 1944, and was immediately studied by all the leading aircraft firms. Some, such as Messerschmitt and Dipl Ing Tank of Focke-Wulf, together with the outspoken General der Jagdflieger, Adolf Galland, said the whole idea was unrealistic. To go into colossal mass production with such a crude and untried aircraft, expect it to be flown by totally inexperienced Hitler Youth (it was said they could complete their training by flying the *Volksjäger* in combat) and adopt the policy that maintenance did

not matter, as unserviceable or damaged fighters could at once be replaced by a dozen fresh ones, was, they judged, an unsound policy that might actually detract from the war effort. Instead, they argued for all effort to go into Me 262 production.

Their protests fell on deaf ears. Eventually, by 15 September, the proposals had been whittled down to just two, the Blohm und Voss P.211 and **Heinkel P.1073**. On every count the P.211 – which looked like a cross between the F-86 and MiG-15 but on a smaller scale – was judged superior. Heinkel, however, had done a great deal of work on just such a project, and by sheer frantic work, day and night, they simply steamrolled the opposition, so that on 24 September they got the go-ahead from not only Saur but also from Goering. There was no offficial final choice, and every comparative document showed the P.211 to be the better aircraft.

Programme go-ahead

After stormy meetings the final go-ahead was granted on 30 September, with a planned initial output of 1,000 aircraft per month. The programme (not the aircraft itself) was given the name **Salamander**. Heinkel called the P.1073 the **Spatz** (sparrow). At first it was proposed to allocate the designation **He 500**, but to confuse Allied intelligence the number of the stillborn Messerschmitt 'Jaguar' of 1937 was repeated, the *Volksjäger* becoming the **He 162**. Construction of the **He 162 V1** prototype, its design, the testing of

Right: Pilots of JG 1 at Leck stand in front of a well-shrouded He 162A-1. Intended as a mount for novice Hitlerjugend pilots with a little gliding experience, the He 162 was possessed of such tricky handling characteristics that even experienced fighter pilots with thousands of hours on Bf 109s or Fw 190s found it unforgiving, incapable of hard manoeuvring, and something of a handful. He 162 pilots avoided combat assiduously, under orders to do so until the aircraft had been fully tested. I/JG 1 was the first operator of the He 162, and in May 1945 absorbed the various other He 162 users, including II/JG 1, JV 44, and III/KG 30.

Below: Considerable numbers of Heinkel He 162s were captured in various degrees of repair by the Allies, and some still exist in museums. This aircraft was flown on 26 flights by the British RAE at Farnborough. It was restored for display at RAF St Athan.

Heinkel He 162 Salamander

A Heinkel He 162A-1 at speed shows clearly the turned-down wingtips first introduced on the V3 to overcome excessive dihedral problems. The A-1s were manufactured in parallel with prototypes, which themselves were regarded as A-0 pre-production airframes.

Production aircraft did not differ greatly from this, the V1 first prototype, except for turned-down wingtips, enlarged ailerons and compound taper on the trailing edge near the wingroot. The V1 had only been flying for four days when it broke up in mid-air.

parts and the establishment of a huge sub-contracting and assembly programme all went ahead more or less simultaneously.

The design could hardly have been simpler. The beautifully streamlined fuselage was a light-alloy semi-monocoque structure of circular section, with a moulded plywood nose. Next came the cockpit, the first to look like a fighter of today, with an upward-hinged clear canopy and cartridge-actuated ejection seat. Fuel was housed in a 695-litre (153-Imp gal) tank amidships, but a further 181 litres (40 Imp gal) could be added in the inter-spar space in the wing centre-section. All three units of the tricycle landing gear retracted into the fuselage, actuation being hydraulic, with extension assisted by springs. Wheels and brakes were of Bf 109G type. At the rear was the unusual twin-finned tail, incidence of which could be adjusted by a screwjack in the fuselage tailcone. The relatively small wing was built almost wholly of wood, but the hydraulically-powered flaps were light alloy. All flight

JG 1 was supposed to prove the He 162 to be a practical warplane in Luftwaffe hands before its deployment with Volksjäger units. The first such formation was the Geschwader's own 1.(Volkssturm) Staffel.

controls were balanced surfaces driven directly by pilot forces. The chosen engine, the BMW 003 turbojet, was attached directly above the high-mounted wing by three bolts, covered by fixed front and rear cowls and quickly-opened central panels. A Riedel two-stroke piston engine was used for starting, as on the Jumo 004B engines of the Me 262. The guns were to be mounted low on the sides of the forward fuselage.

Austrian production

The Salamander programme was centred on Heinkel's factory at Vienna-Schwechat, which was also one of the hubs of the He 219 night-fighter programme. Schwechat was initially ordered to produce 10 prototypes, He 162 V1 to **V10**, which were also considered as the **He 162A-0** pre-production batch. The planned **He 162A-1** production fighter was then to be mass-produced by a growing number of factories and sub-contract plants. The biggest groups were Heinkel-Nord at Rostock Marienehe, to build 1,000 per month; Junkers at Bernburg (also 1,000 per month); and the gigantic underground Mittelwerke (middle works) in the Harz mountains, run by brutally expendable slave labour and already the chief production centre for the V-1 and V-2 weapons, which was to build 2,000 per month. The Vienna complex was itself added to the programme, with assembly in a former chalk mine at Hinterbrühl, also to work up to 1,000 per month. No fewer than 140 main, and hundreds of subsidiary factories, were to make major and minor airframe parts, while the basic production of the BMW 003 turbojet was set at 6,000 per month, starting at BMW Zühlsdorf and progressively moving to a salt mine at Urseburg and (2,000 per month) to the vast Mittelwerke.

The entire Salamander programme was managed by a special organisation, Baugruppe Schlempp, headed by Heinrich Lübke. The schedule called for the V1 prototype to fly before the end of December 1944, for the first 1,000 fighters to be completed by the end of April, and for production to reach 2,000 per month by the end of May 1945.

In the event, the first prototype made its first take-off, in the hands of Flugkapitän Peter, from Schwechat airport on 6 December 1944. In view of the urgency of the project, Peter opened up to full power for a maximum-speed run on this very first flight, and having attained 840 km/h (522 mph) at 600 m (19,685 ft) trouble reared its head. The aircraft made a normal landing, after having been in the air 20 minutes, when it was discovered that one of the doors covering the

Wearing the red arrow of JG 1, this He 162A-2 also displays the badge of 3. Staffel. Ex Ju-188 pilots from III/KG 30 were assigned to the squadron, but many never completed conversion.

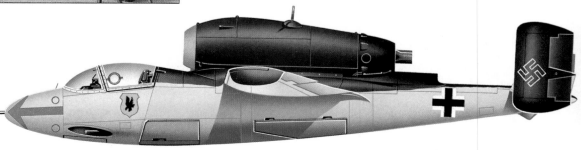

The He 162A-2 standardised on the BMW 003E-1 turbojet in place of the BMW 003A0-1 used earlier. Later, two development aircraft were fitted with Jumo 004Ds for intended production as the He 162A-8. This was to overcome any shortages of the BMW powerplant.

This He 162A-2 was allocated to 3./JG 1 at its Leck base, in May 1945. By this time the 50 aircraft at Leck were reorganised into one single Gruppe, Einsatz-Gruppe I/JG 1; many pilots from other fragmented units at Leck were absorbed by this new Gruppe.

retracted main landing gears had failed structurally, most of it breaking away. The doors were of adhesively bonded wood, as were many other parts including the wings and fins. On 28 June 1944, a Focke-Wulf Ta 154 had crashed following structural failure at high speed. This aircraft had an airframe made mainly of wood designed to be bonded by the Tego-Film process by the Goldmann factory at Wuppertal. After the RAF destroyed the Goldmann works a substitute adhesive was used containing acid, which progressively destroyed the wood. Careful examination showed that the same insufficiently neutralised acid was eating into the wood of the He 162s.

Official debut

The problem had stopped the Ta 154 in its tracks, but the He 162 was a desperate programme, not to be delayed in the slightest. While substitute adhesives were sought, and eventually found in the phenol-based FZ-film, testing of the first aircraft pressed ahead. Peter seemed reasonably happy with the inevitably tricky little jet, but mentioned a tendency to longitudinal instability. On 10 December, bearing in

mind that to a considerable degree the future of Nazi Germany rested on it, the prototype was demonstrated before a large audience composed of Luftwaffe, RLM (air ministry) and Nazi party officials. Flugkapitän Peter included a low-level pass at full power, and when over the Schwechat airfield the entire right wing leading edge came off the wing. In the ensuing violent roll and yaw the right aileron and wingtip also separated before the aircraft crashed.

To show confidence, the first flight of the **V2** prototype was made on 22 December by the Schwechat technical director, Dipl Ing Franke. He boldly explored the limits of the flight envelope, discovering unacceptable lateral and directional instabilities, especially in tight left-hand turns. As a result, the tail was slightly enlarged and the wingtips were tilted downwards at an anhedral angle of 55°. It had also been discovered that the centre of gravity without guns fitted was approximately over the main gears. The aircraft tended to tip on to its tail, so a metal weight was bolted into the extreme nose.

Armament options

From the outset there had been arguments over the armament. The requirement was for one or two 30-mm guns, which were naturally taken to mean the small MK 108s (the huge MK 103 being far too powerful). The design team under Karl Schwarzler found that it was impossible to accommodate more than 50 rounds per gun, whereas if the high-velocity 20-mm MG 151 was substituted each gun could have 120 rounds. The V1 prototype was therefore designed for the 20-mm guns, but the RLM insisted on the V2 having two MK 108s, and in early January firing trials were carried out with these weapons.

This He 162A-2 is seen in the colours of 3./JG 1, based at Leck in May 1945. No encounters with Allied aircraft have been confirmed, although it is likely that He 162 pilots saw some action. They were still awaiting official approval for combat when the war ended.

Heinkel He 162 Salamander

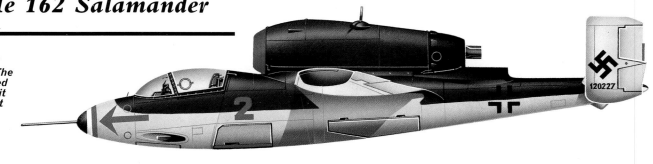

A Heinkel He 162A-2 of II/Jagdgeschwader 1. The day after the unit arrived at Leck for operations, it was reorganised as part of the large Einsatz-Gruppe I/JG 1.

Symbolic of the last days of the Reich's aviation industry are these Heinkel He 162As under construction in a former salt mine at Tarthun, near Magdeburg, safe for a time from Allied bombing. Some 170 He 162s were delivered to the Luftwaffe, and at the end of the war 100 or more were complete awaiting flight test, and 800 more were almost complete.

It was judged that the resulting vibration was unacceptable and although MK 108s were also fitted to the **V6** aircraft, the Heinkel engineers' opinion was eventually vindicated and the production **He 162A-2** was standardised with the MG 151, each with 120 rounds. The RLM never abandoned its preference for the heavier weapons, and Heinkel restressed the forward fuselage for a proposed **He 162A-3** model with MK 108s, but this never got into production. So far as is known the only other aircraft fitted with MK 108s were **V25** to **V28** inclusive, planned as development aircraft for a proposed **He 162A-6** version with the stronger fuselage extended from 9.04 m (29 ft 8 in) to 9.17 m (30 ft 1 in).

Austrian production

By February 1945 approximately 100 aircraft had been completed, including over 30 prototype and development machines completed at Hinterbrühl, most of them planned to lead to future production versions. They included two aircraft powered by the somewhat larger Junkers Jumo 004D-4 turbojet, and two more completed as prototypes of the **He 162S** tandem-seat training glider, which could dive at 418 km/h (260 mph) despite having fixed landing gears. The Jumo-engined aircraft was expected to lead to the production **A-8** version

This He 162A-2 had been hit in a strafing attack by Allied fighters, but the shattered windscreen suggests that it had already been immobilised and abandoned by retreating forces.

with greater endurance from increased fuel capacity, and maximum speed at medium heights increased from 840 to 887 km/h (522 to 551 mph).

The early prototypes had been fitted with the BMW 003A-1 rated at 7.8 kN (1,764 lb). The standard production engine in the A-2 was the 003E-1 or E-2, with a throttle capable, in emergency, of being moved to an override position that gave a thrust of 9.02 kN (2,028 lb) for up to 30 seconds. The German engines inevitably had an extremely short life and poor reliability, and using the emergency thrust resulted in scrapping the engine (it could have been overhauled, but there was never time). This increased maximum speed to 904 km/h (562 mph) at 6000 m (19,685 ft).

Pilot shortage

By early 1945 the gigantic production programme for the He 162A-2 was getting into its stride, yet there was no parallel gigantic programme to train pilots. The year 1944 had seen the Luftwaffe's once mighty fighter force decimated by Allied fighters and bombers, and hardly any skilled pilots (so-called *Experten*) were left. One of the greatest was Oblt Heinz Bär (220 victories), who at the end of January 1945 was posted from the command of JG 3 to activate the vital Erprobungskommando 162, or special test unit 162, at the Luftwaffe's central test establishment at Rechlin. No matter how great the urgency, fantasy had not quite taken over and the Luftwaffe insisted on checking that the He 162A-2 could serve as a fighter. A few days later, on 6 February, I/JG 1, the first *Gruppe* of the Luftwaffe's premier (at least numerically) fighter wing handed its Fw 190s to II Gruppe and began converting to the He 162 at Parchim.

Subsequently, II/JG 1 also converted but, in the dying weeks of the Third Reich, chaos and fuel shortage were just two factors pre-

Heinkel He 162A-2 cutaway key

1 Pitot tube
2 Moulded plywood nose cap
3 Nosewheel retraction mechanism
4 Spring-loaded nosewheel extension assembly
5 Shock absorber moulded scissor
6 Nosewheel
7 Nosewheel fork
8 Nosewheel leg
9 Nosewheel door
10 Gun trough
11 Nosewheel well
12 Rudder pedal
13 Window panel (visual nosewheel retraction check)
14 Wooden instrument panel
15 One-piece moulded windscreen
16 Revi 16G gunsight (interchangeable with the Revi 16B)
17 Jettisonable hinged clear-vision canopy
18 Ventilation disc
19 Heinkel cartridge-operated ejection seat
20 Ejection seat handle grip
21 Throttle control quadrant
22 Retractable entry step
23 Gun barrel shroud in cockpit wall
24 Port 20-mm MG 151 cannon
25 Ammunition chute
26 Main oxygen supply bottle (3.5-pint/2-litre capacity)
27 Explosive charge ejector rail
28 Pilot's headrest
29 Canopy hinge

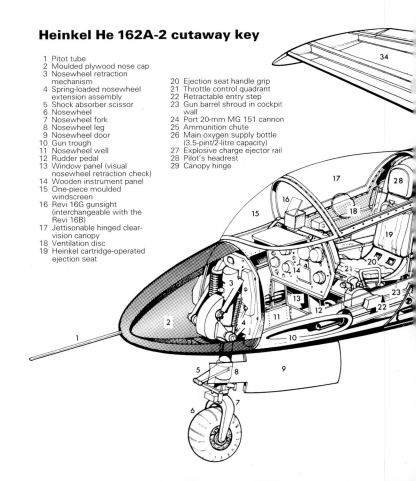

venting effective operations. Hitler appointed SS Obergruppenführer Kammler to be in charge of all jet aircraft, whereupon piqued Goering appointed Gen Kammhuber as the Luftwaffe's head of 'all jet and rocket aircraft'. Plans went ahead for an entire year's intake of Hitler Youth, irrespective of flying aptitude, to carry out brief training on gliders and then go straight to the He 162. At the same time, Heinkel was scheming at least 26 variations on the He 162, including versions with bigger turbojets, single or twin Argus-Rohr 109-014 pulse-jets, and swept-back or forward-swept wings. And while all these things were happening the Allied armies and air forces were closing in across Germany until, on 26 April 1945, they met.

One of the Salamanders transported to Britain was this aircraft (120072), which made four evaluation flights after the war from Farnborough. On the last of these, the aircraft broke up in a roll, killing the pilot, Flight Lieutenant R. A. Marks.

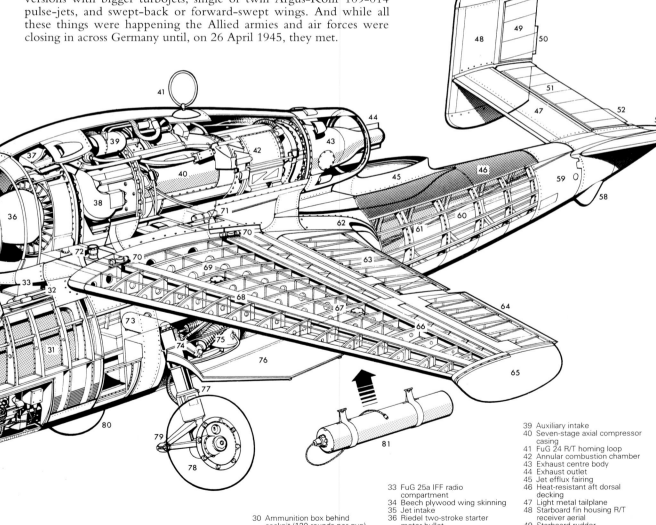

30 Ammunition box behind cockpit (120 rounds per gun)
31 Flexible main tank (153-Imp gal/695 litre capacity)
32 Fuel lines
33 FuG 25a IFF radio compartment
34 Beech plywood wing skinning
35 Jet intake
36 Riedel two-stroke starter motor bullet
37 Oil tank
38 BMW 003E-1 Sturm axial-flow turbojet
39 Auxiliary intake
40 Seven-stage axial compressor casing
41 FuG 24 R/T homing loop
42 Annular combustion chamber
43 Exhaust centre body
44 Exhaust outlet
45 Jet efflux fairing
46 Heat-resistant aft dorsal decking
47 Light metal tailplane
48 Starboard fin housing R/T receiver aerial
49 Starboard rudder
50 Rudder tab
51 Elevator
52 Elevator tab
53 Tailcone (movable through +3° to −2°)
54 Port tailfin structure
55 Rudder structure
56 Tailplane/tailfin attachment
57 Port tailfin upper and lower plates (housing R/T transmitter and IFF aerials)
58 Tailskid
59 Dural fuselage skinning
60 Monocoque fuselage construction
61 Control cables
62 Downswept wingroot fillet
63 Hydraulically-operated flaps
64 Port aileron
65 Detachable downswept aluminium wingtip
66 Wooden T-section rear spar
67 Wooden wing structure
68 Wooden T-section forward mainspar
69 Impregnated integral wing tank (36.9-Imp gal/180-litre capacity)
70 Vertical wing/fuselage attachment bolts (four stations)
71 Single rear horizontal engine mounting/attachment bolt
72 Two forward vertical engine mounting/attachment bolts
73 Port mainwheel well
74 Mainwheel hydraulic retraction jack
75 Mainwheel extension spring
76 Wooden mainwheel door
77 Mainwheel leg
78 Mainwheel tyre (660 mm × 190 mm)
79 Shock absorber scissor
80 Narrow-track main undercarriage assembly

Heinkel He 162A-2 3./Jagdgeschwader 1 Leck, May 1945

The Heinkel He 162 was a rushed attempt to provide a mass-produced fighter that would stem the Allied bomber tide, but its hasty development produced many problems – structural, aerodynamic and in production. This He 162A-1 was assigned to 3. Staffel, Einsatzgruppe I/JG 1 and was the personal aircraft of Staffelkapitän Oberleutnant Erich Demuth. It carried his 16 victory marks on the tail, but these had been gained on other aircraft types. The machine was captured by the British at Leck.

Service
Erprobungskommando 162 (also known as the Volksjäger Erprobungskommando) formed under Heinz Bär at the end of January 1945 at Rechlin, soon moving to München-Riem. The first operational unit, I/JG 1 moved to Parchim to begin conversion on 6 February 1945, reducing to three *Staffeln* before it moved to Ludwigslust on 8 April, and then on to Husum and Leck, where it arrived in late April. II/JG 1 moved to Marienehe on 8 April to begin conversion, but had to flee to Leck in the face of the Russian advance, arriving on 3 May. On 4 May all surviving He 162s were formed into a three-*Staffel Einsatzgruppe* (I/JG 1) with 50 aircraft on strength. Pilots came from far and wide, including some from III/KG 30, whose Me 262 conversion had been cancelled. In April 1945 Galland's elite JV 44 had taken over the aircraft and pilots of the Erprobungskommando, but destroyed its aircraft on 3 May to prevent them falling into Allied hands.

Configuration
The experts predicted that the He 162's unusual top-mounted engine would suffer airflow problems, (which did not occur to a great extent) but did not foresee the pitch instability which made the aircraft so tricky to fly or fight in.

Powerplant

The He 162A-2 was powered by a single BMW 003E-1 or E-2 axial-flow turbojet, rated at 7.8 kN (1,764 lb st) with a 9.02-kN (2,028-lb st) emergency rating available for periods of up to 30 seconds. The pre-production aircraft had been powered by the BMW 003A-1, while some prototypes flew with the BMW 003R, combining the 7.8-kN (1,764-lb st) BMW 003A turbojet with a 12-kN (2,700-lb st) BMW 718 liquid-fuel rocket. Shortages of BMW 003s led to the investigation of the Jumo 004D as a possible alternative, and this engine was installed in two prototypes. Future versions were designed with the Heinkel Hirth 011A turbojet or with two Argus-Rohr As 014 pulse jets, and with forward swept or conventional swept wings, but none of these projects came to fruition.

Volksjäger

The He 162 was developed to meet an 8 September 1944 requirement for a simple, lightweight jet fighter, drawing on the Spatz project and ordered into mass production on 30 September, five days after Hitler's decree calling for the establishment of a *Volkssturm*, which inspired Reichsmarshall Goering to envisage *Volksjäger* units as their airborne equivalent. In their world of fantasy, the Nazi leaders were quite happy to believe that half-trained schoolboys could go straight from gliders to the He 162, acquiring combat skills on actual operations.

Specification

Heinkel He 162A-2 Salamander

Powerplant: one BMW 003E-1 axial-flow turbojet rated at 7.8 kN (1,763 lb) for take-off and 9.02 kN (2,028 lb) for maximum bursts of up to 30 seconds

Performance: maximum speed at normal thrust 790 km/h (490 mph) at sea level or 838 km/h (520 mph) at 6000 m (19,685 ft); maximum speed using short burst extra thrust 890 km/h (553 mph) at sea level or 905 km/h (562 mph) at 6000 m (19,685 ft); range at full throttle 620 km (385 miles) and at 6000 m (19,685 ft); range with six 30-second bursts 595 km (369 miles) at 6000 m (19,685 ft); initial climb rate 1152 m (3,780 ft) per minute (normal power) or 1406 m (4,613 ft) per minute (short burst); service ceiling 12010 m (39,400 ft)

Weights: empty 1663 kg (3,666 lb); empty equipped 1758 kg (3,876 lb); loaded 2805 kg (6,184 lb)

Dimensions: wing span 7.20 m (23.6 ft); length 9.05 m (29 ft 8 in); height 2.60 m (8 ft 6 in); wing area 11.20 m² (120 sq ft)

Armament: two 20-mm MG 151 cannon in forward fuselage, each with 120 rounds

The industrial programme

The establishment of production lines was carried out in parallel with prototype construction, leading to a very rapid build up in production. Final assembly planst were instituted at Marienehe, Bernburg and Nordhausen, which were expected to eventually reach a production total of 4,000 aircraft per month, fed with components from a wide range of contractors. Two groups of woodworking/furniture manufacturing companies were established in Erfurt and Stuttgart, while metal fuselages were to be produced at Aschersleben, Barth, Bernburg, Halberstadt, Leopoldshall, Oranienburg, Pütnitz, Schönbeck, and Stassfurt, and in former saltmines at Egeln and Tarthun. Engines were to be produced in a saltmine in Urseburg, to which the Berlin-Spandau and Basdorf-Zülsdorf engine plants had transferred. Pre-production aircraft were produced at Schwechat, which phased into the mass production effort using a former chalkmine at Hinterbrühl.

Iain Wyllie

Heinkel He 177 Greif

In the final three years of World War II, Hitler's Germany was steadily reduced to rubble by the greatest fleets of heavy bombers the world will ever see. In reply, the mighty Luftwaffe fielded just one type of heavy bomber, which achieved very little except to frighten its crews to death (often literally). Not to put too fine a point on it, it suffered from problems.

To be frank, while the RAF and US Army Air Force was deeply imbued with the urge to deploy strategic air power, the Luftwaffe was primarily a tactical force dedicated to support the Wehrmacht in its land battles. Moreover, when in 1936 Goering was asked to back the launch of a heavy bomber, he explained the Führer was only interested in how many bombers there were, not how big they were. At that time, the Berlin air ministry was supporting the development of a 'Ural-bomber' programme with two rival types, the Do 19 and Ju 89. Had these continued, they would have been obsolescent by World War II. This programme was cancelled in 1937, and replaced by a requirement called 'Bomber A' which it was hoped would lead to a better aircraft. This requirement demanded a maximum speed of 540 km/h (335 mph) and the ability to carry a 2000-kg (4,410-lb) bomb load over a radius of 1600 km (995 miles) at a cruising speed of 500 km/h (310 mph) – challenging figures. To make matters much more difficult it also required the capability of making medium-angle diving attacks.

Heinkel's heavy bomber

Ernst Heinkel AG was given the job, without competition, and **Projekt 1041** was actually started in late 1936. Under Technical Director Hertel, the gifted Gunter twin brothers planned a bomber incorporating many radical new features, intended to give it the highest possible performance. Later designated **He 177**, the new bomber was marvellously clean aerodynamically. The fuselage was like a tube, with a glazed nose and a gun position in the glazed tailcone. The mid-mounted wing had high aspect ratio, for maximum efficiency, and under it was room for a large bomb bay. Clearly, power had to come from four engines of about 895 kW (1,200 hp) or two of 1790 kW (2,400 hp), but there were no 1790-kW (2,400-hp) engines. Boldly, in partnership with Daimler-Benz, Heinkel had designed a dive bomber, the He 119, powered by a DB 606 double engine comprising two DB 601 inverted-V12 engines side-by-side joined through a common gearbox to a single propeller. Two of these were to power the new heavy bomber, clearly offering lower drag and better manoeuvrability than four separate engines. To reduce drag further it was planned to augment the engine cooling by using surface condensation of steam in sandwich panels forming part of the wing skin. There were to be four main landing gears, one retracting inwards and another outwards under each engine to lie in the wing ahead of the main spar. Defensive guns were to be in remotely controlled turrets above the forward fuselage, in the front and rear of a ventral gondola, as well as

Shortly before the Geschwader ceased operations, a group of six He 177s from KG 40 prepares for a mission from the bomb-damaged airfield at Bordeaux-Mérignac in June 1944.

in the manned tail position. Altogether the He 177 promised to have lower drag than any previous aircraft (even an unarmed civil one) of its size.

Things began to go wrong from the outset. By early 1939, when the **V1** first prototype was taking shape, it was reluctantly concluded that steam cooling was impractical. Much larger radiators had to be used (they were made circular, round the front of each double engine). In turn this meant greater drag, which demanded extra fuel which meant increased weight, in a vicious circle. The ministry officials then decreed that this big bomber had to be able to make steep 60° dive attacks, which resulted in a considerable increase in structural weight, further reducing performance and also requiring the addition of large dive brakes under the wings. To slow the landing of the over-weight aircraft full-span Fowler flaps were adopted, the outer portions coming out from under the ailerons. Again there were problems because the wing had not been stressed for the large lift and drag loads of the flaps.

First flight

The V1 made its maiden flight on 19 November 1939. Despite being unarmed it failed to come anywhere near the Bomber A requirement, maximum speed being 460 km/h (285 mph) and range being inadequate. On the other hand, it handled reasonably well, and the few snags recorded gave no indication of the years of toil and disaster that were to follow.

The He 177 had a checkered career in Luftwaffe service, its advantages negated by a plague of troubles mostly concerning the propulsion system. Worst of these problems was a tendency for the engines to catch fire without warning, leading to the uncomplimentary nickname 'Luftwaffenfeuerzeug' (flying lighter).

The He 177 V1 first flew on 19 November 1939, but was only aloft for 12 minutes before engine temperatures soared, heralding a long saga of such problems. Another problem to surface was the inadequacy of the tail surfaces, which were increased on the second prototype, and again on production machines.

Aside from the engine problems, the He 177 exhibited a nasty swing on take-off, resulting in several accidents. The A-1 version introduced larger tail surfaces and stronger damping on the tailwheel. This is the A-03 pre-production aircraft, showing the unique mainwheel arrangement.

Seven further prototypes followed, each heavier than its predecessor. Vertical tail area was increased, triple bomb bays were incorporated, various types of defensive armament fitted (low-drag remotely controlled guns were replaced by conventional turrets or hand-aimed guns) and ceaseless efforts made to try to eliminate the most serious problem, which was the frequency of engine fires. **V2** suffered flutter and disintegrated, **V4** crashed into the sea and **V5**'s engines caught fire at low level, the aircraft flying into the ground and exploding.

Pre-production aircraft

In 1939 a total of 30 **He 177A-0** pre-production aircraft was ordered, plus five from Arado. These had many changes, including a redesigned nose for a crew of five, armament comprising a 7.9-mm MG 81 in the multi-pane hemispherical nose, a 20-mm MG FF in the front of the gondola, a twin MG 81Z at the rear of the gondola, a 13-mm MG 131 in the roof turret and a hand-aimed MG 131 in the tail. In the course of production the dive brakes were removed, partly because the He 177 was structurally unable to meet the requirement and partly because the dive bomber had shown itself to be vulnerable. There were many other changes, but the most urgently needed concerned the powerplants.

Below: This aircraft is an He 177A-3/R1, which flew with KG 40 while the unit was at Châteaudun. Of note is the dorsal barbette housing a single MG 131, and the undernose MG FF cannon.

Right: This He 177A-3/R2 was on the strength of FFS (B) 16 for training. The R2 introduced the MG 151 cannon in place of the nose MG FF. Note the rear-view mirror above the pilot's position.

Heinkel He 177 Greif

When one studies the detailed reports on some of the many hundreds of serious He 177 engine fires one marvels that the usually impressive Germanic design efficiency could have been so often forgotten. Many features of the DB 606 installation might almost have been deliberately arranged to give trouble. The oil scavenge pumps were oversized, and at heights over 6000 m (19,685 ft) the oil tended to aerate and foam, leading to breakdown in lubrication and to seizures, con-rods breaking through the crankcase, and fires. Almost always the oil dripped on to the white-hot exhaust manifold serving the two inner banks of cylinders, and radiant heat from this frequently ignited oil and fuel that collected in the bottom of the cowling. Many other fires resulted from fuel leaks from the high-pressure injection pumps and rigid piping, and the whole engine was installed so tight up to the main spar that there was no room for a firewall. The piping, electric cables and other services were jammed in so tightly that, especially when soaked in leaking fuel and oil, the fire risk was awesome. There were even problems caused by the handing (opposite rotation) of the big 4.52-m (14-ft 8-in) four-bladed propellers. Seen from behind, the left propeller rotated anti-clockwise and the right propeller clockwise, and the engines with inserted idler wheels to reverse output rotation often suffered from torsional vibration causing crankshaft failure. At least seven A-0 aircraft were badly damaged in take-off accidents caused by uncontrollable swing to left or right, despite enlargement of the fin and rudder, and it became standard practice on take-off to keep the tailwheel on the ground as long as possible.

Production system

Over 25 of the 35 A-0s were destroyed from various causes, and the rest were used for crew training at Ludwigslust. Whereas at the start Heinkel had predicted the He 177 would be in service in 1940, by the end of that year production had not even begun. Indeed, for various reasons, Heinkel's Oranienburg factory never built the initial production model at all, partly because, despite increasing pressure for the He 177 to get into action, the A-1 version was still seen to be imperfect to the point of being dangerous. All 130 examples of the **He 177A-1** were made by Arado, between March 1942 and June 1943, with the tails and parts of the fuselage being supplied from a factory at Mielec in Poland. The A-1 retained 2014-kW (2,700-hp) DB 606 engines, and incorporated only a few of the dozens of planned improvements, but it could carry very heavy bomb loads weighing up to 6000 kg (13,230 lb). It could not, however, carry the FX 1400 or Hs 293 guided bombs, although Field Marshal Milch thought it could. Hitler urged the aircraft be brought into service, to range far beyond the Eastern Front at night and to escort U-boats and blockade runners in the North Atlantic.

Operational training was undertaken by the Flugzeugführerschule (B) 16 at Burg near Magdeburg, initially with ex-KG 40 He 177A-1s but later with improved models such as this He 177A-3/R2. The A-3 had a lengthened fuselage and redesigned engine mountings.

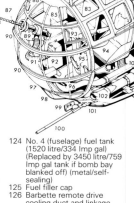

1 Starboard navigation light
2 Detachable wingtip
3 FuG 101 radio altimeter (FM)
4 Aileron control runs
5 Starboard aileron
6 Aileron trim tab
7 Spring-loaded geared tab
8 Aileron counter-balance
9 FuG 102 radio altimeter (pulsed)
10 Tab mechanism
11 Fowler flap outboard track
12 Fowler flap position (extended)
13 Aileron tab control linkage
14 Flap actuating cylinder (hydraulic)
15 Control cables
16 Main spar (outboard section)
17 Wing ribs
18 Auxiliary front spar
19 Heated leading edge
20 Oil radiator intake
21 Starboard Hs 293 radio-controlled glide-bomb
22 Starboard outer mainwheel door (open position)
23 Starboard outer mainwheel well
24 Balloon cable-cutter in leading edge
25 Starboard ETC weapons rack
26 Twin oil radiators (starboard engines)
27 Radiator outlet flap
28 Hot-air ducting
29 Mainwheel door actuating cylinder
30 No. 8 (starboard outer) fuel tank of 1,120 litre/246.5 Imp gal capacity (flexible bag)
31 Fuel filler cap
32 Fowler flap outer section
33 auxiliary rear spar
34 Wing dihedral break point
35 Fowler flap track
36 Starboard fuel starting tank (9 litre/2 gal capacity)
37 Starboard oil tanks
38 Main hydraulic tank (starboard only) (32 litre/7 gal capacity)
39 Fuel filler cap
40 No. 3 (starboard inner) fuel tank of 621 litre/136.5 Imp gal capacity (metal/self sealing)
41 Fowler flap inner section
42 Main spar (inboard section)
43 Starboard inner mainwheel well
44 Engine supercharger
45 Nacelle fairing
46 Wing spar attachment point and fairing
47 Engine accessories
48 Daimler-Benz DB 610A-1 24-cylinder liquid-cooled engine
49 Anti-vibration side-mounting pad
50 Supercharger and wing de-icing intakes
51 Nacelle former
52 Coolant vents
53 Engine forward mounting
54 Cooling gills
55 Double-gear crank casing
56 Single propeller shaft
57 Propeller de-icing saddle tank
58 Nacelle cooling profile
59 Propeller variable-pitch mechanism
60 Propeller boss
61 Blade cuffs
62 VDM four-bladed propeller (right-handed)
63 Chin intake
64 Flame damper exhaust
65 Starboard outer mainwheel leg
66 Starboard inner mainwheel leg
67 Starboard outer mainwheel
68 D/F loop in dorsal blister
69 Emergency hydraulic cylinder (25 litre/5.5 Imp gal)
70 No. 7 fuselage frame
71 C-Stand ammunition tank (1,000 rounds)
72 Dorsal barbette remote drive motor
73 Revi gunsight with slotted 10-mm armour protection
74 Remote control sighting cupola
75 Barbette traverse control handle
76 Barbette elevation control handle
77 Main radio panel (FuG 10P; general-purpose set) (FuG17Z: VHF communication and homing) (FuG BL 2F: Blind-approach)
78 First-aid pack
79 Navigator's take-off/landing station
80 Window
81 Gunner's seat
82 Emergency jettison panels (port and starboard)
83 Bomb aimer's seat (raised)
84 External rear-view mirror
85 Engine control panel (starboard)
86 Internal rear-view mirror
87 Offset ring-and-bead gunsight
88 MG 81 7.9-mm machine-gun (A1-Stand)
89 Circular gun mounting
90 Balloon cable-cutters in nose horizontal frames
91 Ammunition feed

92 A1-Stand ammunition tank (1,000 rounds)
93 Hinged window panel (port and starboard)
94 Pilot's seat (armour plate; 9-mm back, 6-mm seat)
95 Rudder pedals
96 Cockpit hot-air
97 Lower glazed section often overpainted/armoured
98 Lotfe 7D bombsight fairing
99 'Boxed' gunsight
100 MG 151 20-mm cannon (A2-Stand)
101 Bullet-proof glass in nose of 'bola'
102 De-icing intake
103 Ventral crew entry hatch
104 Telescopic ladder
105 Actuating arm
106 MG 151 20-mm cannon ammunition feed
107 De-icing air heater/blower
108 A2-Stand ammunition tank (300 rounds)
109 Toilet installation
110 C-Stand ammunition feed
111 Thermos flasks
112 Circular vision port
113 MG 131 13-mm machine gun (C-Stand) at rear of 'bola'
114 'Fritz X' (Kramer X-1) radio-controlled bomb
115 Cruciform main fins
116 SAP warhead
117 Tail fin structure
118 Air-brake attachment
119 Ventral bomb rack (only fitted if forward bomb bay blanked off)
120 Forward-bomb bay (often blanked off)
121 Fuel tank retaining strap lugs
122 Internal bomb shackle
123 Bomb bay central partition
124 No. 4 (fuselage) fuel tank (1520 litre/334 Imp gal) (Replaced by 3450 litre/759 Imp gal tank if bomb bay blanked off) (metal/self-sealing)
125 Fuel filler cap
126 Barbette remote drive cooling duct and linkage
127 Remote control dorsal barbette (B1-Stand)
128 Twin 13-mm MG 131 guns
129 No. 13 fuselage frame
130 Barbette structure
131 B1-Stand double ammunition tank (1,000 rounds per gun)
132 Central bomb bay (often blanked off)
133 Bomb bay door (outer section)
134 Port inner mainwheel well
135 No. 5 (fuselage) fuel tank (1520 litre/334 Imp gal) (Replacd by 3450 litre/759 Imp gal tank if bomb bay blanked off) (metal/self sealing)
136 Fuel filler cap
137 No. 19 fuselage frame
138 Main spar carry-through
139 Main spar/fuselage attachment points
140 Aft bomb bay
141 Auxiliary rear spar/fuselage attachment points
142 No. 1 (Fuselage) main fuel tank (1140 litre/330 Imp gal) (metal/self sealing)

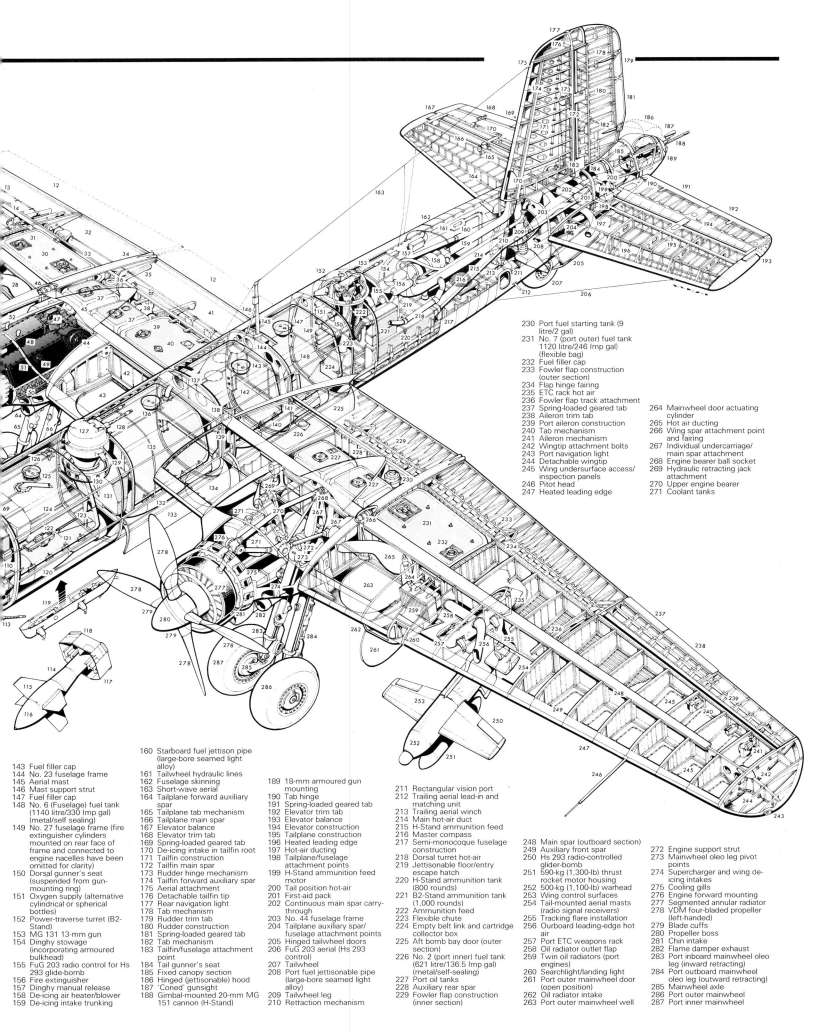

230 Port fuel starting tank (9 litre/2 gal)
231 No. 7 (port outer) fuel tank 1120 litre/246 Imp gal) (flexible bag)
232 Fuel filler cap
233 Fowler flap construction (outer section)
234 Flap hinge fairing
235 ETC rack hot air
236 Fowler flap track attachment
237 Spring-loaded geared tab
238 Aileron trim tab
239 Port aileron construction
240 Tab mechanism
241 Aileron mechanism
242 Wingtip attachment bolts
243 Port navigation light
244 Detachable wingtip
245 Wing undersurface access/ inspection panels
246 Pitot head
247 Heated leading edge

264 Mainwheel door actuating cylinder
265 Hot air ducting
266 Wing spar attachment point and fairing
267 Individual undercarriage/ main spar attachment
268 Engine bearer ball socket
269 Hydraulic retracting jack attachment
270 Upper engine bearer
271 Coolant tanks

143 Fuel filler cap
144 No. 23 fuselage frame
145 Aerial mast
146 Mast support strut
147 Fuel filler cap
148 No. 6 (Fuselage) fuel tank (1140 litre/330 Imp gal) (metal/self sealing)
149 No. 27 fuselage frame (fire extinguisher cylinders mounted on rear face of frame and connected to engine nacelles have been omitted for clarity)
150 Dorsal gunner's seat (suspended from gun-mounting ring)
151 Oxygen supply (alternative cylindrical or spherical bottles)
152 Power-traverse turret (B2-Stand)
153 MG 131 13-mm gun
154 Dinghy stowage (incorporating armoured bulkhead)
155 FuG 203 radio control for Hs 293 glide-bomb
156 Fire extinguisher
157 Dinghy manual release
158 De-icing air heater/blower
159 De-icing intake trunking

160 Starboard fuel jettison pipe (large-bore seamed light alloy)
161 Tailwheel hydraulic lines
162 Fuselage skinning
163 Short-wave aerial
164 Tailplane forward auxiliary spar
165 Tailplane tab mechanism
166 Tailplane main spar
167 Elevator balance
168 Elevator trim tab
169 Spring-loaded geared tab
170 De-icing intake in tailfin root
171 Tailfin construction
172 Tailfin main spar
173 Rudder hinge mechanism
174 Tailfin forward auxiliary spar
175 Aerial attachment
176 Detachable tailfin tip
177 Rear navigation light
178 Tab mechanism
179 Rudder trim tab
180 Rudder construction
181 Spring-loaded geared tab
182 Tab mechanism
183 Tailfin/fuselage attachment point
184 Tail gunner's seat
185 Fixed canopy section
186 Hinged (jettisonable) hood
187 'Coned' gunsight
188 Gimbal-mounted 20-mm MG 151 cannon (H-Stand)

189 18-mm armoured gun mounting
190 Tab hinge
191 Spring-loaded geared tab
192 Elevator trim tab
193 Elevator balance
194 Elevator construction
195 Tailplane construction
196 Heated leading edge
197 Hot-air ducting
198 Tailplane/fuselage attachment points
199 H-Stand ammunition feed
200 Tail position hot-air
201 First-aid pack
202 Continuous main spar carry-through
203 No. 44 fuselage frame
204 Tailplane auxiliary spar/ fuselage attachment points
205 Hinged tailwheel doors
206 FuG 203 aerial (Hs 293 control)
207 Tailwheel
208 Port fuel jettisonable pipe (large-bore seamed light alloy)
209 Tailwheel leg
210 Retraction mechanism

211 Rectangular vision port
212 Trailing aerial lead-in and matching unit
213 Trailing aerial winch
214 Main hot-air duct
215 H-Stand ammunition feed
216 Master compass
217 Semi-monocoque fuselage construction
218 Dorsal turret hot-air
219 Jettisonable floor/entry escape hatch
220 H-Stand ammunition tank (800 rounds)
221 B2-Stand ammunition tank (1,000 rounds)
222 Ammunition feed
223 Flexible chute
224 Empty belt link and cartridge collector box
225 Aft bomb bay door (outer section)
226 No. 2 (port inner) fuel tank (621 litre/136.5 Imp gal) (metal/self-sealing)
227 Port oil tanks
228 Auxiliary rear spar
229 Fowler flap construction (inner section)

248 Main spar (outboard section)
249 Auxiliary front spar
250 Hs 293 radio-controlled glider-bomb
251 590-kg (1,300-lb) thrust rocket motor housing
252 500-kg (1,100-lb) warhead
253 Wing control surfaces
254 Tail-mounted aerial masts (radio signal receivers)
255 Tracking flare installation
256 Outboard leading-edge hot air
257 Port ETC weapons rack
258 Oil radiator outlet flap
259 Twin oil radiators (port engines)
260 Searchlight/landing light
261 Port outer mainwheel door (open position)
262 Oil radiator intake
263 Port outer mainwheel well

272 Engine support strut
273 Mainwheel oleo leg pivot points
274 Supercharger and wing de-icing intakes
275 Cooling gills
276 Engine forward mounting
277 Segmented annular radiator
278 VDM four-bladed propeller (left-handed)
279 Blade cuffs
280 Propeller boss
281 Chin intake
282 Flame damper exhaust
283 Port inboard mainwheel oleo leg (inward retracting)
284 Port outboard mainwheel oleo leg (outward retracting)
285 Mainwheel axle
286 Port outer mainwheel
287 Port inner mainwheel

Below: An He 177A-5 of KG 100 rests between missions. Of note is the enormous diameter of the four-bladed propeller, necessary to transmit the power from the coupled engine, and the unique double mainwheel units which retracted outwards and inwards either side of the engine nacelle.

Above: Early A-5 series aircraft retained the three bomb bays of the A-3, with the forward unit blanked off. However, the A-5/R6 dispensed with two of the weapons bays for the maritime attack role. These aircraft of II./KG 40 are seen at Mérignac after the adoption of the Atlantic reconnaissance role in spring 1944.

which in the final year of war was the chief operational version. The main advantage of the A-5 was that it introduced the more powerful DB 610 engine, and as the weights were only fractionally heavier than those of the first versions the performance was improved, especially in ceiling which went up from a poor 7000 m (22,965 ft) to just over 8000 m (26,245 ft). Standard features of the A-5 included a strengthened airframe, shorter main-gear legs, normal ailerons without Fowler flaps extending to the wingtips, and racks under the forward fuselage and outer wings for three Hs 293s, or two Hs 294s or two FX 1400 bombs. Like the A-3/R7 the A-5 could also release the LT 50 glider torpedo, which was fitted with a small glider airframe enabling it to be released from a height of 250 m (820 ft) several kilometres from a target.

At last, in October 1942, Heinkel began delivering the improved **He 177A-3**, but far from a tempo of 70 per month the huge Oranienburg plant found it hard to get beyond five per month. The A-3 did its best to eradicate the faults. The engine remained the 606, although it had been hoped to fit the 2312.4-kW (3,100-hp) DB 610 (made up of a pair of DB 603s). However, the engines were mounted 20 cm (7 in) further forward, the exhaust system was redesigned and many other dangerous features were altered. To balance the engines the rear fuselage was extended by 1.6 m (5 ft 2 in) and a second dorsal turret added. Like the A-1, the A-3 was produced with different *Rüstsätze* giving different armament, almost all sub-types having an MG 151/20 in the front of the gondola and a second of these hard-hitting cannon in the tail, aimed by a gunner who did not lie but sat comfortably under a Plexiglas bulge under the rudder. Other weapons carried included the Hs 293 radio-controlled attack missile and, in the **A-3/R7** and all A-5 versions, a range of anti-ship torpedoes.

He 177A-5, the prime version

Heinkel made 170 A-3s, following which, from February to December 1943, Heinkel and Arado delivered 261 **He 177A-5**s,

Bombing London

Until manufacture of all aircraft other than fighters was virtually abandoned in October 1944, Heinkel and Arado together delivered no fewer than 565 He 177A-5s, and their operational record was much better than that of earlier versions. By far the most important Luftwaffe units to use the He 177 were KG 40 and KG 100, the former being concerned chiefly with the Battle of the Atlantic with the Hs 293 and both taking part in Operation Steinbock, the revenge attacks on London in the early weeks of 1944. In Steinbock experienced crews found they could climb to almost 9000 m (29,527 ft) before nearing England. Then, at full power and in a shallow dive, they stood a chance of avoiding interception by keeping speed at about 700 km/h (435 mph). On the other hand, the effectiveness of these missions was extremely low. On 13 February 1944 Goering was at Rheine to watch 2. and 3./KG 100 set off for England; 14 taxied out, 13 took off, eight soon returned with overheated or burning engines, four reached London but only three came back.

There were many sub-variants made in small numbers. Front-line armourers near Stalingrad – which was resupplied at great cost by a handful of He 177s used as transports – fitted 50-mm BK 5 anti-tank guns under the nose. Later the **He 177A-3/R5** was fitted with the 75-mm gun, but this strained the structure and was altogether too powerful and only five were built. Several were flown with an electrically powered tail turret with two MG 151/20 guns, and the planned **He 177A-6** was to have either this turret or one with four MG 81s. The A-6, of which six were built, had a pressurised cabin, as did the **A-5/R8**, the latter being a single aircraft with remotely controlled barbettes in the chin and tail locations. One of the last of the numerous development prototypes, the **V38** (basically an A-5), was stripped down at the Letov factory at Prague and (it was said) prepared to carry 'the German atomic bomb'. This may have been a mere rumour, but unlike several of the later variants which deleted the front and middle

6. Staffel of Kampfgeschwader 100 was based at Toulouse-Blagnac during May 1944, using its He 177A-5s on bombing missions. This He 177A-5/R2 still has factory codes applied prior to delivery. Note the underwing and ventral racks for Hs 293 missiles and Fritz X guided bombs.

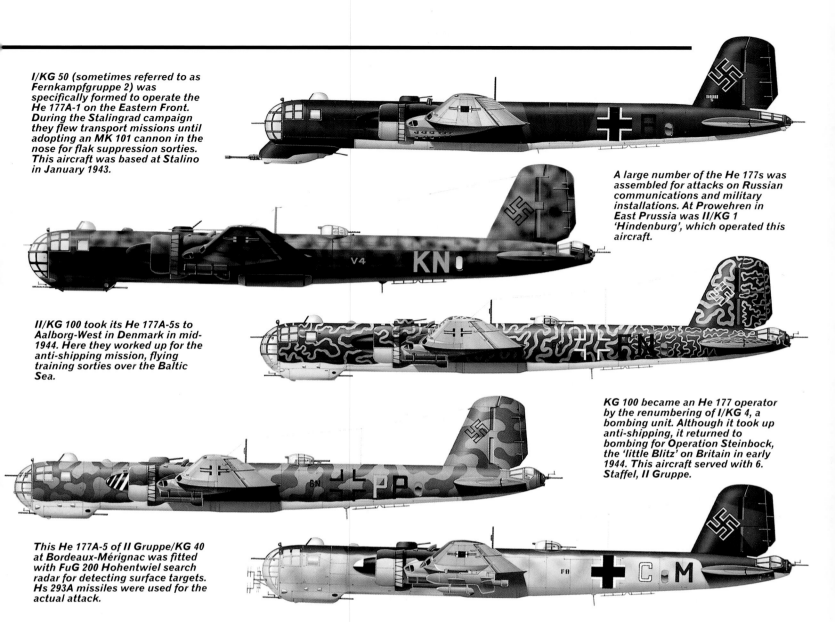

I/KG 50 (sometimes referred to as Fernkampfgruppe 2) was specifically formed to operate the He 177A-1 on the Eastern Front. During the Stalingrad campaign they flew transport missions until adopting an MK 101 cannon in the nose for flak suppression sorties. This aircraft was based at Stalino in January 1943.

A large number of the He 177s was assembled for attacks on Russian communications and military installations. At Prowehren in East Prussia was II/KG 1 'Hindenburg', which operated this aircraft.

II/KG 100 took its He 177A-5s to Aalborg-West in Denmark in mid-1944. Here they worked up for the anti-shipping mission, flying training sorties over the Baltic Sea.

KG 100 became an He 177 operator by the renumbering of I/KG 4, a bombing unit. Although it took up anti-shipping, it returned to bombing for Operation Steinbock, the 'little Blitz' on Britain in early 1944. This aircraft served with 6. Staffel, II Gruppe.

This He 177A-5 of II Gruppe/KG 40 at Bordeaux-Mérignac was fitted with FuG 200 Hohentwiel search radar for detecting surface targets. Hs 293A missiles were used for the actual attack.

Right: The He 177A-5/R2 was primarily intended as a carrier for torpedoes, Hs 293 missiles or the FX 1400 Fritz X. The three bomb bays were retained, but the forward bay was blanked off and a ventral weapons hardpoint added. Seen here on the carrier is a Fritz X.

bomb bays, the V38 was to have had a single gigantic bomb bay. Another unusual version was intended for destroying formations of heavy bombers. The **He 177 Zerstörer**, three of which were produced in 1944 by conversion of bombers (believed to be A-3s), were fitted with a battery of 33 large rocket launch tubes aimed upwards, slightly ahead and slightly to the right. The idea was that the He 177 should formate below, behind and to the left of the bombers, but Allied fighters made the idea impractical.

Last version to get into limited production, and then only in an interim form, the A-7 had a wing extended in span from 31.46 m (103 ft 2 in) to 36.6 m (120 ft). It was intended to have 2685.6-kW (3,600-hp) DB 613 engines, but these were not ready. It carried extra fuel, and intensely interested the Japanese who considered building it under licence. They planned to fit four separate engines, but Heinkel's own **He 277** with four separate engines never had official approval and only a string of prototypes were built mainly with DB 603A engines.

The weapon most associated with the Heinkel He 177 in the anti-shipping role is the Henschel Hs 293A missile. These could be carried under the wings or, as here, on a special pylon fitted to the blanked-off forward bomb bay. Releases were usually made between 10 and 14 km (6.2 and 8.7 miles) from the target.

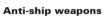

Camouflage
The He 177s of KG 40 and KG 100 wore a variety of overwater camouflage, this example being standard for most of KG 100's aircraft. For participation in Operation Steinbock, the undersides were painted black for night bombing.

Markings
This aircraft wears standard tactical codes, the '6N' standing for KG 100. The white 'H' was the individual aircraft letter, painted white to signify the first *Staffel* within the *Gruppe*, while the 'M' signified 4. Staffel/II Gruppe. KG 100's aircraft usually wore a two-digit black code on the ventral gondola.

Anti-ship weapons
The He 177A-5 was produced primarily as a launch platform for anti-ship weapons, which were poetically known as '*grosse Lachse*' (large salmon). It could carry weapons on three external racks: two under the wings outboard of the oil radiator intakes and one under the blanked-off forward bomb bay. In addition to the Henschel Hs 293 and FX 1400 Fritz X missiles, the He 177 could also carry torpedoes. Initially, the Italian L5 was used, two being carried under the fuselage and one on each wing rack. Subsequently, the new LT 50 was used, this electrically-driven torpedo being dropped from about 250 m (820 ft) some considerable distance from the target, the weapon descending by parachute.

A-5 variants
The He 177A-5 was a major production version, the A-5/R2 being the standard model with three bomb bays, although the forward bay was blanked off. Other sub-variants were the single R5 with a ventral gun barbette aft of the bomb bays, the R6 which had the two forward bomb bays deleted, the R7 with a pressurised cabin for high-altitude flight and the R8, which had remotely-controlled gun barbettes in the chin and tail positions. Only one R8 was completed.

Missile guidance
For controlling the Hs 293 and FX 1400 anti-ship missiles, the He 177 was fitted with an FuG 203 Kehl transmitter. Using a *Knüppel* joystick in the gondola, the bombardier guided the missile visually, using flares on the rear of the weapon to help him follow its course. The weapon had the FuG 230 Strassburg equipment, which received control inputs from the Kehl. Operating in daylight proved dangerous to the He 177s, so nocturnal tactics were evolved, using a group of aircraft dropping flares on one side of the shipping convoy, while missile-carriers approached from the other. The ships were therefore silhouetted against the illuminated sky behind them, allowing the missiles to be launched from about 10-15 km (6-9 miles) while the He 177 flew towards them, greatly easing aiming and guidance.

Specification
Heinkel He 177A-5/R2
Powerplant: Daimler-Benz DB 610A-1 (port) and B-1 (starboard) 24-cylinder liquid-cooled engines, each rated at 2200 kW (2,950 hp) for take-off
Performance: maximum speed 488 km/h (303 mph) at 6100 m (20,000 ft); maximum range 5500 km (3,417 miles) with two Hs 293A; service ceiling 8000 m (26,246 ft); time to 3050 m (10,000 ft) 10 minutes
Weights: empty equipped 16800 kg (37,037 lb); maximum take-off 31000 kg (68,342 lb)
Dimensions: wing span 31.44 m (103 ft 1 in); length 22.00 m (72 ft 1 in); height 6.39 m (21 ft); wing area 102 m² (1,098 sq ft)
Armament: one 7.9-mm MG 81J machine-gun in glazed nose; one 20-mm MG 151 in front ventral gondola; two 7.9-mm MG 81 in rear ventral gondola; two 13-mm MG 131 in dorsal barbette; one 13-mm MG 131 in dorsal turret; one 20-mm MG 151 in tail; internal weapons bay for 16 SC 50 bombs or four SC 250 or two SC 500; external pylons for two LMA III parachute sea mines, LT 50 torpedoes, Henschel Hs 293A or FX 1400 Fritz X missiles

Heinkel He 177A-5/R2 Greif
4. Staffel, II Gruppe
Kampfgeschwader 100
Bordeaux-Mérignac, France, 1944

The basic design of the Heinkel He 177 was sound, the type receiving favourable reports from most pilots in terms of handling and performance. The long wings and sleek fuselage were of good aerodynamic form, giving a healthy range of 5500 km (3,417 miles) with two Hs 293A missiles. However, the DB 610 engines were always a source of problems, and these overshadowed the potential success of the type. Initial deliveries went to KG 40 for maritime attack and reconnaissance work, followed by aircraft for bomber units (KG 4 and KG 50) on the Eastern Front. KG 4 renumbered as KG 100 and joined KG 40 in the West, although KG 50 used the type in Russia. Here its success was limited, being hastily impressed into the transport role during the Stalingrad airlift. During this period, a few KG 50 aircraft were fitted with a massive anti-tank gun for close support work. Subsequently KG 50 renumbered as part of KG 40, concentrating the He 177 force on the French coast for anti-convoy work. Nevertheless, the aircraft did see further action in its original intended role during January-March 1944, when Hitler launched the bombing campaign known as Operation Steinbock. In the face of an increasingly aggressive Allied campaign against German cities, Steinbock was merely a reprisal against London, which proved rather ineffective. It also robbed front-line bomber units in other theatres of their desperately needed aircraft. While their bombs had little effect, the 35 He 177s which took part did prove their ability to operate in a hostile night-fighter environment, but only by attacking in dives which allowed them to outrun any interception attempts. Only four He 177s were lost to flak or fighters during the campaign, but a large number of sorties were lost through the inevitable engine fires and other operational problems. Anti-shipping operations from France came to an end in the summer of 1944 and the He 177's usefulness declined sharply. However, a few aircraft were still on hand in the early months of 1945, used as Hs 293 missile carriers by the Versuchskommando/Kampfgeschwader 200.

Powerplant
The He 177A-5 standardised on the DB 610 engine (coupled DB 603s) as opposed to the DB 606 (coupled DB 601s) of the earlier variants. Despite tests with one aircraft which had identified and fixed 56 potential causes for engine fires, these problems continued. It was felt that to incorporate the modifications would have severely disrupted the production lines.

Defensive weapons
The He 177A-5/R2 mounted a heavy defence against enemy fighters. The tail H-Stand turret had a 20-mm MG 151, fed from an ammunition tank (300 rounds) in the rear fuselage. The rear dorsal turret (B2-Stand) had a single MG 131 with 750 rounds, while the forward dorsal barbette (B1-Stand) had two MG 131s each with 750 rounds. This was aimed remotely from the glazed dome above the flight deck. The A1-Stand was the MG 81J machine-gun in the forward glazing (with 2,000 rounds), the A2-Stand was the MG 151/20 position in the front of the ventral gondola (300 rounds), while C-Stand was the rear gondola position, which mounted two MG 81s with 2,000 rounds each.

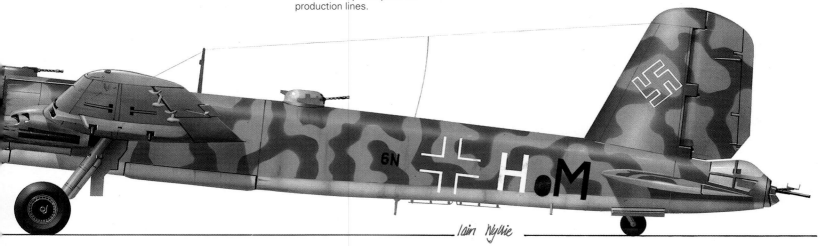

Iain Wyllie

Heinkel He 219 Uhu

Britain's Sir Sydney Camm used to say "Follow the official specification and you are dead!" There have been countless occasions when superior combat aircraft have been created because the engineering team was able to get on with the job and do it in the best and most efficient way. Obvious examples are the de Havilland Mosquito and General Dynamics F-16; another was the **Heinkel He 219**. Designed as a versatile multi-role aircraft, it was finally developed purely for night-fighting and then criticised because it was so specialised.

Ernst Heinkel AG was one of the largest aircraft firms in Hitler's Germany, and it was certainly the most experienced in producing combat aircraft. In mid-1940 the Rostock-Marienehe head office had surplus design capacity, and this was put to use in creating a number of projects, one of which was **Projekt 1064**. This was a *Kampf-Zerstörer*, literally a war-destroyer but meaning a multi-role fighter, attack, reconnaissance and even torpedo aircraft. It incorporated many new features, including a tandem-seat pressurised cockpit in a rather serpent-like nose, a shoulder-high wing, giant underslung engine nacelles housing twin-wheel main units of a tricycle landing gear, twin tail fins and remotely-controlled defensive gun barbettes.

The design was just what the Luftwaffe really needed, but long-term planning at the Ob.d.L. (Luftwaffe high command) was conspicuously absent. Instead, Projekt 1064 was looked at unfavourably because it used so many radical innovations. The 'American' idea of nosewheel gear was scorned, and Heinkel even had the temerity to pick the Daimler-Benz DB 603 engine, a big and powerful unit that, like the Heinkel project, had never been requested officially, and thus was itself under a cloud. Projekt 1064 was filed away and forgotten.

Fighting a lone battle to build up the Luftwaffe's vital night-fighter force was the harassed General der Nachtjägd, Josef Kammhuber. He consistently failed in his efforts to get a truly advanced night-fighter designed for the job, but eventually he managed to gain an interview with Hitler. He left the room with 'special powers' enabling him to overrule his opponents, and as a result in October 1941 Projekt 1064 became the He 219, with a development contract. Kammhuber had

been impressed by the potential of this design on a visit to Rostock, and considered it could be the night-fighter he was seeking. (At the same time, Focke-Wulf received a contract for a night-fighter which became the Ta 154, dubbed 'Moskito' because of its wooden construction; it never entered widespread service.)

Few changes were made to the Heinkel design, which retained its twin MG 131 barbettes above and below the rear fuselage and also the 2000-kg (4,409-lb) bomb load. Forward-firing armament was to comprise two MG 151/15 cannon in the wingroots and a ventral installation of two MG 151/20s or a large 30-mm MK 103. The basic aircraft was a clean and efficient stressed-skin design, with powerful slotted flaps (often described incorrectly as Fowler-type). The engines had circular radiators giving the appearance of radials, and a retractable ladder was provided for access to the lofty cockpit, where pilot and radar observer sat back-to-back with an excellent all-round view. A 13-mm (0.51-in) MG 131 was provided for rear defence. In the centre fuselage were three tanks housing 2600 litres (572 Imp gal).

First flight

The **He 219 V1** (first prototype) made its maiden flight on 15 November 1942, and demonstrated outstanding handling and performance. The only real problem was poor yaw/roll stability, rectified in the third aircraft by enlarging the tail and extending the rear fuselage. There then began a process of development and tinkering with the armament and equipment that became so complex that today it is impossible to unravel. Even during the war, the RLM (air ministry) asked whether the profusion of types and designations could be simplified. The prototypes flew with a recorded 29 different variations of armament, while the plans for a manufacturing programme were thrown into disarray by repeated air raids on Rostock in March and

Illustrated in this view of the pre-production He 219 V5 are several characteristic features including the stalky nosewheel member, this turning through 90° and retracting to lie flat beneath the cockpit. Also visible are the wingroot and belly-tray apertures for the six MG 151/15 guns, and radar aerial sockets.

G9+FB was an early He 219A-0 model operated by I/NJG 1 from Venlo in Holland in June 1943. On 11/12 June, flown by Major Werner Streib, the aircraft destroyed five Lancasters – and this on the He 219's first operational sortie. Ironically, the aircraft crashed due to inoperative flaps when returning to base.

April 1942, which twice destroyed virtually all the He 219 drawings. These attacks prompted Heinkel to plan for production at Vienna-Schwechat, fuselages being supplied from Mielec in Poland; continued bitter opposition, led by Generalfeldmarschall Erhard Milch, repeatedly delayed any production of what any impartial observer must have concluded was an outstanding aircraft.

Competition and contracts

Back in August 1942, Kammhuber had urged Heinkel to think in terms of a complete operational *Gruppe* (wing) by 1 April 1943, but at that date the sum total of He 219s was five prototypes. In the first week of 1943 the third prototype He 219 was flown in mock combat against a Junkers Ju 188 (a type favoured as a night-fighter by Milch), leading to a highly biased RLM report which put in all the He 219's faults and omitted the enthusiastic comments of test pilots. It even suggested the Messerschmitt Bf 110 as an alternative to the new fighter. Nevertheless, later in that month Heinkel did receive the first production contract, for 127 aircraft.

On 25 March 1943 came a more detailed fly-off between an He 219 (probably the V4, with FuG 212 Lichtenstein C-1 radar), flown by the *Gruppenkommandeur* of I/NJG 1, Major Werner Streib, and a Ju 88S and a Dornier Do 217N. The Dornier soon withdrew, but the Junkers was flown by a pilot as famous as Streib, Oberst Wiktor von Lossberg of the technical staff. Brilliant as von Lossberg was, he had to concede defeat to the He 219, which by this time was becoming known as the **Uhu** (owl). The initial pre-series **He 219A-0** was delivered from late May 1943 in **He 219A-0/R1** and **R2** sub-types, respectively with the belly tray housing four MK 108s or four MK 103s. Both guns were of 30-mm calibre, but the MK 108 was a compact low-velocity weapon weighing 59 kg (130 lb), while the MK 103 was a massive gun weighing 145 kg (320 lb) and having tremendous power. Wing guns usually remained MG 151/20s. The pilot had a two-pronged control column, partly to ease the choice of either hand and partly to carry more switches and triggers. Guns were fired by the right hand, the top button firing the fuselage guns and the front trigger those in the wings. A further addition in at least one He 219A-0 was a compressed-air ejection seat for both occupants, the first in service in the world. There was an MF radio wire from the

cockpit mast to each fin, but these were no real problem in emergency escape, and Heinkel was in fact looking ahead to the time when the He 219 would be jet-propelled. This also explained his original choice of nosewheel-type landing gear.

Initial deliveries went to I/NJG 1 at Venlo, on the Dutch frontier, where Streib determined to show what the type could do. It had C-1 radar, the intermediate set that followed FuG 202, and used the same group of small dipole aerials tuned to the 490 MHz frequency, but with two displays showing a direct view and a plan. The first combat mission was flown by Streib himself with backseater Fischer on the night of 11/12 June 1943 in He 219A-0 G9+FB. The mission was an epic, for the Uhu shot down five RAF heavy bombers. On returning, however, Streib totally misjudged the approach because of a misted windscreen. Seeing the dim runway lights at the last moment he selected full flap at too high a speed; the circuits shorted and the flaps blew back under the air load. The aircraft hit the ground so hard it broke up, but both men walked away without a scratch.

Mosquito kills

On hearing this, Milch said, "Yes, but perhaps Streib would have shot down just as many had he been flying another type of aircraft." But over the next 10 days these immature machines, in just six more sorties, destroyed another 20 RAF bombers, including six Mosquitoes. No Mosquito had ever before been intercepted at night, and not even Milch could ignore this achievement. The main trouble was that, despite having an assembly line at Schwechat, another about to start deliveries at Marienehe and a third being set up at the vast plant at Oranienburg (on tapering off of He 111 production), Heinkel's huge

Above: The He 219 V1 made its maiden flight on 15 November 1942. The first three prototypes had a distinctive step in the upper fuselage to allow for the installation of remotely controlled dorsal and ventral barbettes, each with a pair of 13-mm MG 131 machine-guns. These proved difficult to aim, having too little hydraulic power to counter airflow effects and thus pointing in a different direction to the separate periscopic sights which were slaved to them.

Left: This early prototype is something of a mystery ship. It has the lengthened sharp nacelle tails associated with the production He 219, as well as production-standard enlarged tail surfaces. It has an unstepped fuselage, but appears to lack armament, and is not fitted with radar or operational equipment. It may be the He 219 V11.

Heinkel He 219 Uhu

Photographed during evaluation in Britain after the war, this He 219A-5/R2 shows the aft cockpit canopy redesigned to eliminate the provision for an aft-firing MG 131 machine-gun – a feature discarded earlier by most He 219s in operational use.

network of plants simply could not deliver He 219s. This was partly because of the fantastic profusion of sub-variants, many of them launched to meet official criticisms. It was also because of shortages of critical parts, notably engines. Whereas the basic plan was for 100 aircraft to be delivered monthly, actual acceptances hardly ever exceeded 12 per month.

Deadly jazz

Subsequent He 219 sub-types are listed separately. Few of these attained production status, although features that did become standard included longer nacelles housing extra fuel, removal of the rear gun (except on the three-seat **He 219A-5/R4**), installation of the powerful FuG 220 Lichtenstein SN-2 radar with huge *Hirschgeweih* (stag's antlers) dipole aerial array, FuG 220 tail-warning radar, the ejection seat and, not least, the *schräge Musik* (literally 'slanting music', or jazz) armament. This scheme dated from 1941, having been proposed by armament engineers at Tarnewitz and tested by an NJG *Experte*, Oberleutnant Rudolf Schoenert. The idea was that oblique upward-firing guns could be brought to bear accurately in a no-deflection shot by formating below and slightly behind the enemy bomber, using a special upward-looking sight. The scheme was made possible by the amazing fact that British heavy bombers not only had not one gun firing downwards but also not one window from which a formating night-fighter could be seen. The usual *schräge Musik* installation in the He 219 comprised two MK 108s each with 100 rounds, fixed aft of the fuselage tanks at an angle of 65°.

By mid-1944, the RLM officials who had time to think about the matter realised that the campaign against the Uhu had been misguided. Milch himself had gone, production being henceforth a series of massive dictates by civilian Albert Speer. One of these, the *Notprogramm* (emergency programme) of 1 November 1944, virtually halted all aircraft manufacture except that of jets and single-engined fighters. Thus, the He 219 never did become the massive programme that should have been possible. The He 219 never equipped any unit except I/NJG 1 (ones and twos reached II/NJG 1, NJGr 10, Erg./JG 2 and NJSt 'Finnland' and 'Norwegen', but the numbers were trivial). By June 1944, I/NJG 1 had 20 Uhus, almost all of the current production **He 219A-2** and **He 219A-5** types. By this time RAF Mosquitoes were making themselves felt not only as pathfinders and bombers but also as intruders, and the number of He 219s that failed to return from night sorties climbed significantly. Previous attrition had been very low, although I/NJG 1 lost three *Kommandeure* in succession in 1944, two of them having been killed in mid-air collisions.

Heinkel He 219A-5 cutaway drawing key

1. FuG 212 Lichtenstein C-1 antenna
2. FuG 220 Lichtenstein SN-2 antenna
3. Armoured nose
4. Curved one-piece windscreen
5. Windscreen washer/wiper
6. Handhold
7. Inner armourglass windscreen
8. Revi 16B gunsight
9. Armoured visor (deleted on late production models)
10. Control column
11. Revi 16A-N overhead gunsight (*schräge Musik*)
12. Folding headrest
13. Pilot's compressed-air ejection seat
14. Port instrument console
15. Footholds
16. Crew entry ladder (hinged rearwards)
17. Nosewheel leg
18. Nosewheel doors
19. Compressed air bottles
20. Nosewheel retraction gear
21. Ejection seat mounting
22. Radar operator's ejection seat
23. Flare pistol port
24. Hinged headrest
25. Aerial mast
26. FuG 212 radar screen
27. FuG 220 radar screen
28. Fuselage frame (No. 9)
29. Port wing root cannon port
30. Forward fuel tank (244 Imp gal/1100 litres)
31. Fuel filler cap
32. Suppressed D/F aerial
33. Main spar connection joint
34. Flame damper tube
35. Liquid coolant tank
36. Airscrew shaft
37. Airscrew boss
38. VDM constant-speed airscrew
39. Daimler-Benz DB 603E engine
40. Supercharger
41. Oil tank
42. Airscrew de-icing tank
43. Main wing spar
44. Starboard wing heating unit
45. Intake
46. FuG 101 radio altimeter
47. Starboard navigation light
48. Starboard aileron
49. Wing construction
50. Aileron tab
51. Flap construction
52. Flap actuator
53. Underwing inspection panels
54. Nacelle fuel tank (86 Imp gal/390 litres)
55. Main undercarriage well
56. Inboard flap section
57. Mainwheel doors
58. Undercarriage pivot point
59. Firewall
60. Starter fuel tank
61. Centre fuel tank (110 Imp gal/500 litres)
62. Fuel filler cap
63. Fuselage frame (no. 17)
64. Wing/fuselage aft attachment point
65. Port 20-mm MG 151 cannon
66. Wing/fuselage main attachment point
67. Ammunition troughs (300 rpg; wing root and ventral port rear cannon)
68. Ammunition trough (300 rpg; ventral port forward cannon)
69. Airscrew de-icing tank
70. Oil tank
71. Engine accessories
72. Engine bearer
73. Daimler-Benz DB 603E engine

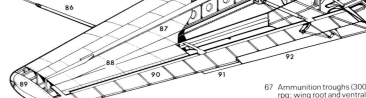

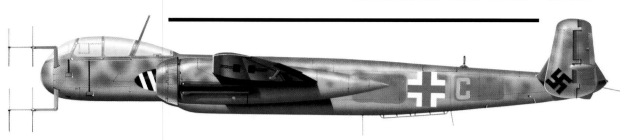

Operating from Finsterwalde in December 1944, this He 219A-5 shows signs of the four-letter fuselage callsign having been overpainted, and the addition of fighter-type spirals to the propeller spinners. Produced at Schwechat and Marienehe, the first A-5 production example was handed over in March 1944.

74 Liquid coolant tank
75 Controllable radiator gills
76 Airscrew boss
77 VDM constant-speed airscrew
78 Armoured-front annular radiator
79 Flame damper tube
80 Supercharger intake trunking
81 Port wing heating unit
82 Flap actuating jack
83 Aileron control quadrant
84 Landing light
85 Aileron tab control linkage
86 Pitot tube
87 Main wing spar
88 Wing skinning
89 Port navigation light
90 Port aileron
91 Fixed trim tab (port side only)
92 Auxiliary aileron tab
93 Twin mainwheel undercarriage
94 Mainwheel doors
95 Mainwheel leg
96 Starter fuel tank
97 Undercarriage retraction jack

106 Twin oblique-mounted 30-mm MK 108 cannon (schräge Musik)
107 Electrical supply cables (starboard fuselage wall)
108 Compressed air cylinders
109 Maintenance platform
110 Ventral antenna
111 FuG 25A (IFF) aerial
112 Service entry hatch
113 Walkway
114 Main electrical compartment
115 Crew escape dinghy
116 D/F loop (homing approach)
117 BLO 30/U fuselage heating and tailplane de-icing unit
118 Heating ducts
119 Fuselage frame (no. 31)
120 Tail unit control linkage
121 Intake
122 Tailplane construction
123 Aerials
124 Tailfin construction
125 Starboard rudder
126 Rudder tab
127 Rudder control hinge
128 Elevator construction
129 Elevator trim tab
130 Flettner auxiliary tab
131 FuG 220 tail-warning antenna
132 Trailing-aerial tube
133 Tail navigation light
134 Perspex tail cone

135 Tail bumper
136 Fuselage frame (no. 33)/ tailplane attachment
137 Port elevator
138 Rudder tab hinge fairing
139 Port rudder
140 Built-in aerial (port tailfin leading-edge)
141 Tailfin skinning
142 Ventral weapons tray
143 Fuselage frame (no. 20)
144 Ventral maintenance hatch
145 Main junction boxes
146 Weapons access hatches
147 Ammunition feed chutes
148 Rear (inboard) 20-mm MG 151 cannon
149 Forward (outboard) 20-mm MG 151 cannon
150 Blast tubes
151 Gun sighting/correction hatch
152 Cannon ports

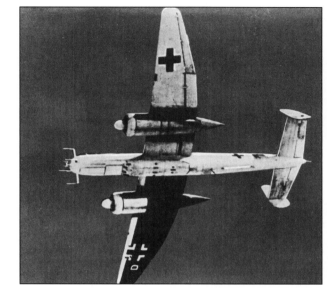

This underside view of an He 219A-0, with an unusual single black wing, shows to advantage the type's ventral cannon tray. This tray accomodated four 30-mm Mk 108 cannon in the V1, four 20-mm MG 151 cannon in the V2, V3 and V4 and six 15-mm MG 151s in the V5. Pre-production aircraft had either four 30-mm Mk 108s (He 219A-0/R1) or four Mk 103s (He 219A-0/R2).

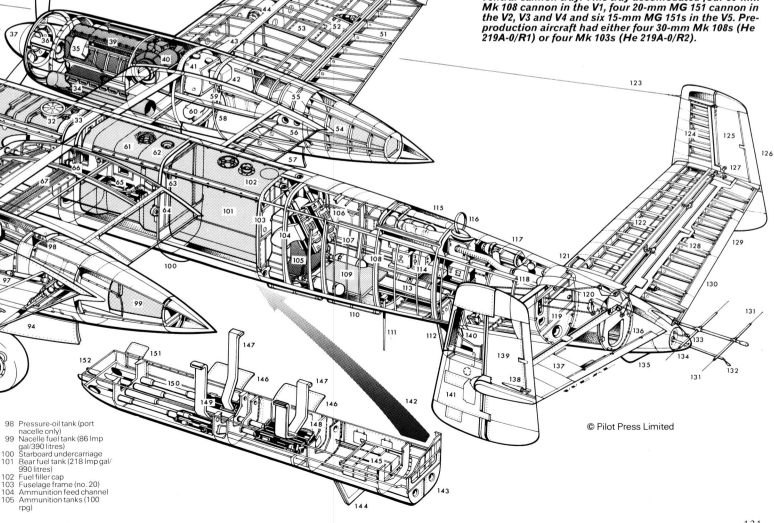

98 Pressure-oil tank (port nacelle only)
99 Nacelle fuel tank (86 Imp gal/390 litres)
100 Starboard undercarriage
101 Rear fuel tank (218 Imp gal/ 990 litres)
102 Fuel filler cap
103 Fuselage frame (no. 20)
104 Ammunition feed channel
105 Ammunition tanks (100 rpg)

Heinkel He 219 Uhu

Service
The first He 219A-2/R1s were accepted by I/NJG 1 in October 1943. I/NJG 1 remained the sole operator of the type, crippled by the slowness of deliveries. By January 1945, I/NJG 1 had 64 on charge, with 20 more with the Stabschwarm.

Radar
The first production aircraft, (the first 12 He 219A-2/R1s) were fitted simply with FuG 212 Lichtenstein C-1 with four small antenna arrays on the nose. On subsequent A-2s aircraft had a single antenna for the C-1, with four large *Hirschgeweih* antennas for the new FuG 220 Lichtenstein SN-2. Some A-5s omitted C-1 radar, and often had the SN-2 antennas canted to reduce interference. The A-7 added the newer FuG 218 Neptun radar to Litchenstein SN-2.

Undercarriage
The He 219's tricycle undercarriage was an extremely novel feature on a Luftwaffe aircraft, the RLM calling it 'this unnecessary American innovation'. In fact the combination of single nosewheel (which rotated as it retracted aft) and twin pairs of mainwheels gave superb take-off and landing characteristics.

Alternative roles
One of the reasons for Milch's hostility to the He 219 was that he saw it as being unable to perform any other role. Heinkel accordingly designed the He 219A-3 three-seat fighter-bomber and the He 219A-4 long-span high-altitude recce aircraft. Production would have been at the expense of the night fighter (already too slow) and was not authorised, but a point had been made.

Heinkel He 219A-7/R2
Stab I/NJG 1
Münster
June 1944

Illustrating one of the range of camouflage schemes worn by the Heinkel He 219 is an aircraft from Stab I/NJG 1, as flown by Hauptmann Paul Forster during June 1944. The sole *Nachtjagdgruppe* to be equipped with the Uhu in its various production configurations, I/NJG 1 suffered from aircraft being in constantly short supply, but nevertheless achieved good results against the RAF's night-bombers until meeting its match in the form of the night-fighting Mosquito. Expensive and time-consuming to produce, the He 219 nevertheless justified the faith shown in it by General der Nachtjagd Kammhuber, in the face of considerable opposition from Milch, who was influenced by a desire to minimise the number of aircraft types in production, and by personal animosity he felt to Kammhuber and Ernst Heinkel.

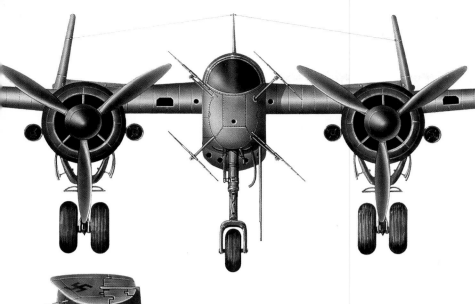

Powerplant

The He 219 prototypes, and the pre-production He 219A-0 and production He 219A-2, were powered by the 1303-kW (1,750-hp) liquid-cooled, inverted V-12 DB 603A. It had been intended to replace this in production aircraft with the 1415-kW (1,900-hp) DB 603G (with increased compression ratio and a higher speed supercharger), but unavailability led to proposals to fit the DB 603E (which had a large supercharger and GM-1 nitrous oxide injection) as a stop-gap. This was no more available than the DB 603G and the production He 219A-2 had to revert to the DB 603A. The DB 603G was finally incorporated in the He 219A-7, which proved the most widely produced variant, while the stripped-down anti-Mosquito He 219A-6 used the 1565-kW (2,100-hp) DB 6703L which was essentially a DB 603E with both MW-50 and GM-1 and a two-stage supercharger.

Heinkel He 219 variants

He 219 V1: first prototype, 1305-kW (1,750-hp) DB 603As; originally unarmed, later two MG 151/20 and pivoted MG 131; provision for two rear barbettes
He 219 V3: first with longer fuselage and larger tail; **V5** with C-1 radar; **V6** with six MG 151/15s and barbettes eliminated
He 219A-0: pre-production series, most with DB 603A, 14 armament schemes, at least one with ejection seats
He 219A-1: planned production with 1342.3-kW (1,800-hp) DB 603E; one only
He 219A-2: first production version, two-seater with DB 603As; basic armament two MK 108 and four MG 151/20, but following *Rustsätze* kits offered variations: **R1** six MG 151/20; **R2** four MK 103 and two MG 151/20; **R3** four MK 108 and two MG 151/20; **R4** four MG 151/20 and two MK 108 oblique
He 219A-3: fighter-bomber with three crew and 1416.8-kW (1,900-hp) DB 603Gs; not built
He 219A-4: long-span reconnaissance-bomber with Jumo 222s; not built
He 219A-5: major production version, initially DB 603As, most 1342.3-kW (1,800-hp) DB 603Es; usual armament six MG 151/20 and two MK 108 oblique but many R-kits and other variations; **R4** adding third cockpit with raised canopy and pivoted MG 131
He 219A-6: lightweight 'anti-Mosquito' version, 11950 kg (26,345 lb) loaded, DB 603L two-stage engines with

MW 50 and GM-1 boost; 650 km/h (404 mph) at up to 12000 m (39,370 ft)
He 219A-7: final production version 1416.8-kW (1,900-hp) DB 603Gs, all with two MK 108 oblique plus; **R1** two MK 108 wings and two MK 103 ventral; **R2** four or six forward-firing MK 108; **R3** two MG 151/20 wings and two MG 151/20 plus two MK 108 ventral; **R4** two MG 151/20 wings and two more ventral
He 219B: series of developed long-span machines with extended fuselage; most DB 603As though planned for Jumo 222
He 219C: long-span wing of He 219B combined with totally new longer fuselage with four-seat pressure cabin at front and gunner in HDL 131V tail turret (four MG 131); **He 219C-1** night-fighter with two MK 108 under cockpit, two oblique behind cockpit and two MG 151/20 wings; **He 219C-2** fighter-bomber with two forward MK 103 and three SC 500 (500-kg/1,102-lb) bombs under fuselage
He 319: unbuilt multi-role derivative
He 419: various derived projects culminating in **He 419B-1/R1**, six of which were flown; He 319 tail, very long-span wing of 59 m² (635 sq ft), two MG 151/20 wings and four MK 108 ventral; 679 km/h (422 mph) to 13600 m (44,619 ft)
Hü 211: high-altitude reconnaissance aircraft designed by Dr Ing Hütter with the He 219 fuselage and tail married to 24.54-m (80-ft 6-in) wooden wing; tremendous range, speed and height but destroyed before completion

M. Hasegawa

Armament

The He 219A-2 abandoned the rearward facing MG 131, which was not fitted again, except to the He 219A-5/R4 which had a stretched forward fuselage and a new three-man cockpit. All He 219s had a pair of 20-mm MG 151 cannon in the wingroots, and provision for two 30-mm MK 108s in an upward-firing *schräge Musik* installation. Contents of the ventral tray varied, with two MG 151s, two Mk 103s or two Mk 108s in the A-2, two Mk 108s in the A-5 and a choice in the He 219A-7 – two Mk 103s and two MG 151s (A-7/R1), two Mk 103s and two Mk 108s (A-7/R2), two Mk 108s and two MG 151s (A-7/R3) or two MG 151s (A-7/R4).

Specification
Heinkel He 219A-7/R2
Type: two-seat night-fighter
Powerplant: two 1342-kW (1,800-hp) Daimler-Benz DB 603E 12-cylinder engines
Performance: maximum speed 460 km/h (286 mph) at sea level, 585 km/h (363 mph) at 6000 m (19,685 ft); range at maximum cruise 1850 km (1,150 miles); service ceiling 9800 m (32,150 ft)
Weights: empty 8345 kg (18,398 lb); maximum loaded 15100 kg (33,289 lb)
Dimensions: span 18.50 m (60 ft 8.3 in); length (including antennas) 16.34 m (53 ft 7¼ in); height 4.10 m (13 ft 5.4 in); wing area 44.50 m² (478.99 sq ft)
Armament: two 20-mm MG 151 cannon with 500 rpg in ventral tray, two 20-mm MG 151 cannon with 400 rpg in wingroots and two 30-mm MK 108 cannon with 100 rpg mounted at an angle of 65° in *schräge Musik* installation

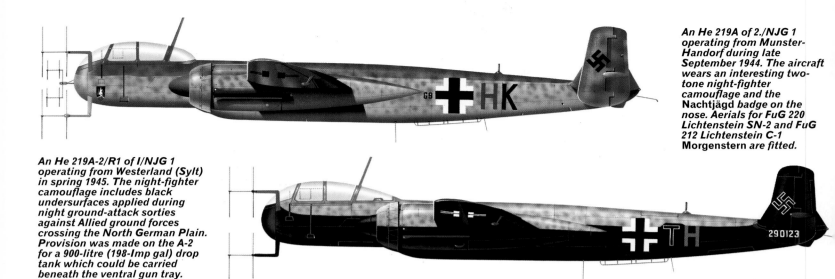

An He 219A of 2./NJG 1 operating from Munster-Handorf during late September 1944. The aircraft wears an interesting two-tone night-fighter camouflage and the Nachtjägd badge on the nose. Aerials for FuG 220 Lichtenstein SN-2 and FuG 212 Lichtenstein C-1 Morgenstern are fitted.

An He 219A-2/R1 of I/NJG 1 operating from Westerland (Sylt) in spring 1945. The night-fighter camouflage includes black undersurfaces applied during night ground-attack sorties against Allied ground forces crossing the North German Plain. Provision was made on the A-2 for a 900-litre (198-Imp gal) drop tank which could be carried beneath the ventral gun tray.

In January 1945, I/NJG 1's establishment was up to 64 aircraft, and total deliveries of all versions reached 268, plus about 20 development aircraft modified to acceptable operational standard by field units and a further six (not on any official documents) which were assembled and put into action by I/NJG 1 from replacement components and spares.

So, how does one assess this controversial aircraft? There is no doubt it was a 1940 design of exceptional merit which could in a more ordered society have been developed for many roles with telling effect, as was the UK's Mosquito. The mass of sub-types merely diluted the main production effort, and the consistent failure of Daimler-Benz and Junkers to deliver the hoped-for engines killed the advanced versions that would have kept the He 219 in front. As for the aircraft itself, opinions are divided.

Photographed at Farnborough in 1945, the He 219A-7 with G-series engines could be identified by its oblique 'sharkmouth' engine air inlets in the leading edge. The Roman VI indicated fitment of FuG 220d with Streuwelle (dispersal waveband) no. VI. Only this one aircraft (Nr 310 189) reached I/NJG 1 for evaluation.

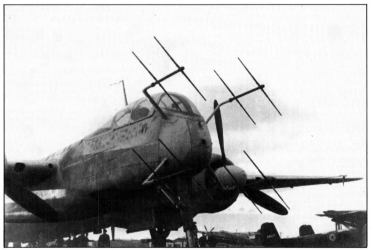

According to Gebhard Aders (author of *Geschichte der deutschen Nachtjägd*), the He 219 "never achieved the values given in its manual. With almost full tanks and full armament, the He 219 could not get above 8000 m (26,247 ft). With Lichtenstein and flame dampers, the maximum fell to about 500 km/h (311 mph) at this height." On the other hand, he states "The 219 was the only German night-fighter that could still climb on one engine, and even go round again for another landing attempt," a belief echoed by many former Uhu pilots. Yet that greatest of test pilots, Captain E. M. 'Winkle' Brown, who flew several captured He 219s, wrote in *Air International* that the type was "somewhat overrated... It suffered from what is perhaps the nastiest characteristic that any twin-engined aircraft can have: it was underpowered. This defect makes take-off a critical manoeuvre in the event of an engine failing, and a landing with one engine out can be equally critical. There certainly could be no overshooting with the He 219 in that condition."

This marginal performance is the more remarkable when it is remembered that the DB 603 was the largest of the inverted V-12 engines used by the Luftwaffe, with a cubic capacity 65 per cent greater than that of the Merlin. The problem lay squarely in the growth of systems and equipment with which the Uhu was packed, so that a typical **He 219A-7** version weighed more empty than any Ju 88 night-fighter, and more than a fully-loaded Mosquito.

Above: With a BMW 003 in a ventral housing, the He 219 V14 acted as a testbed for the He 162 programme. There was never any proposal to produce a jet-assisted He 219, performance being adequate for the night fighting role until the arrival of the Mosquito night fighters.

Left: The final A-series He 219 was the A-7, the most important model to reach operational status. Utilising the improved DB 603G powerplant, this heavily-armoured high-altitude night-fighter provided ejection seats for both crew members, improved avionics and increased armament. One reached I/NJG 1.

Heinkel He 274/277

Developed to substitute for the planned He 177A-4 high-altitude bomber, the **Heinkel He 274** was the detail design responsibility of Société Anonyme des Usines Farman's Suresnes factory in occupied France. Fitted with a pressurised cabin, the aircraft was powered by four 1305-kW (1,750-hp) Daimler-Benz DB 603A-2 engines and featured a lengthened version of the He 177A-3 fuselage, with a new high aspect-ratio wing and twin fins and rudders. Two prototypes were ordered in May 1943, together with four **He 274A-0** pre-production examples, which were to have 1417-kW (1,900-hp) DB 603G engines. Despite an unsuccessful German attempt to destroy the almost-complete first prototype when they retreated from Paris in July 1944, the aircraft was completed by the French after the liberation and flown from Orléans-Bricy in December 1945 as the **AAS 01A**. It was used later to test-fly models of such aircraft as the Aerocentre NC 270 and the Sud-Ouest SO 4000, until broken up in 1953.

In an effort to overcome the problems being experienced with the coupled DB 606 engines of the He 177, Heinkel suggested in 1940 that four separate DB 603s should be substituted. Although the Reichsluftfahrtsinisterium rejected the plan, work continued unofficially under the designation **He 177B** and the design was resurrected in response to Hitler's May 1943 demand for a heavy bomber to facilitate effective strikes on London. Converted from an He 177A-3/R2

airframe, with four DB 603A engines, the first Heinkel **He 277** prototype (designated **He 177B-0**) flew at Vienna-Schwechat in the closing months of 1943, followed by the second aircraft on 28 February 1944. Directional instability resulted in the fitting of a twin fin and rudder tail unit to the **V3** third prototype. Eight 1305-kW (1,750 hp) DB 603A-powered **He 277B-5/R2** production models were completed before the priority given to fighter production in July 1944 brought the programme to an end. Variants on the drawing board included the **He 277B-6** with increased wing

span and the **He 277B-7** long-range reconnaissance aircraft, the latter being completed but unflown when Soviet troops arrived.

Specification
Heinkel He 277B-5/R2
Type: heavy bomber
Powerplant: four Daimler-Benz DB 603A 12-cylinder engines each rated at 1380 kW (1,850 hp)
Performance: maximum speed 570 km/h (354 mph); ceiling 15000 m (49,210 ft); range 6000 km (3,728 miles)
Weights: empty equipped 21800 kg (48,060 lb); maximum loaded 44500 kg (98,105 lb)
Dimensions: wing span 31.44 m (103 ft 1¾ in); length 22.15 m (72 ft 8 in); height 6.67 m (21 ft 10½ in); 100 m²

Wearing French markings, the He 274 V1 is seen after completion by Ateliers Aéronautiques de Suresnes as the AAS 01A.

(1076.4 sq ft)
Armament: one 7.9-mm MG 81J or 15-mm MG 151/15 or 20-mm MG 151/20 cannon in nose glazing, four 7.9-mm MG 81 machine-guns in FDL 81V chin turret, two 13-mm MG 131 machine-guns in remotely-controlled forward FDL 131E/F2 barbette, one 13-mm MG 131J in EDL 131A-2 dorsal turret and four 7.9-mm MG 81 in HDL 81V tail turret; internal bomb load of 500-kg (1,102-lb) bombs plus FX 1400 Fritz X, Hs 293, Hs 294 or 2500-kg (5,512-lb) bombs externally

The He 277 V1 (alias He 177B-0) flew in 1943 from Vienna-Schwechat, and was basically a four-engined He 177A-2/R2.

Heinkel He 280

When work on the He 178 was discontinued in the autumn of 1939, effort was concentrated on a more advanced twin-engined design that was to be powered by pairs of two new Heinkel turbojets, the HeS 8 and HeS 30. Neither engine was ready for flight when the **Heinkel He 280** prototype airframe was itself complete, and first trial flights, which began on 22 September 1940, were unpowered, the aircraft being towed to release height behind a Heinkel He 111. A pair of the HeS 8 engines was installed in March 1941 and Fritz Schafer made the first powered flight on 2 April. The engines

were producing little more than 4.9 kN (1,102 lb) thrust, however, and although available thrust had risen to some 5.89 kN (1,323 lb) by early 1943 when the second and third prototypes were flown, in April of that year BMW 109 003 engines were adopted. Six additional prototypes were built, the eighth featuring a V-tail, but the rival Messerschmitt Me 262 was selected for production and the He 280s were regarded only as useful research aids.

Specification
Heinkel He 280 V6
Type: single-seat interceptor
Powerplant: two Junkers Jumo

004A Orkan turbojets rated at 8.24 kN (1,852 lb) thrust each
Performance: maximum speed 817 km/h (508 mph); service ceiling 11400 m (37,400 ft); range 615 km (382 miles)
Weight: loaded 5205 kg (11,475 lb)
Dimensions: wing span 12.00 m (39 ft 4½ in); length 10.20 m (33 ft 5½ in); height 3.20 m (10 ft 5¾ in); wing area

21.50 m² (231.5 sq ft)
Armament: three 20-mm MG 151 cannon in nose

On 2 April 1941, the He 280 V1 flew at Marienehe under its own power, albeit with the HeS 8A centrifugal turbojets left uncowled. Previously, it had undertaken 41 gliding flights.

Henschel Hs 123

In 1934 the Luftwaffe issued a two-stage requirement for a dive-bomber. While the second phase would be filled by a new technology design, the first phase highlighted immediacy as the main goal. Henschel and Fieseler were asked to develop the first-phase aircraft, both teams choosing the BMW 132A-3 radial engine for their designs. Both designs flew in early 1935, the **Hs 123 V1** showing a marked superiority over the Fi 98 from the outset of flight trials.

The Hs 123 V1 was an ungainly biplane, featuring a wide-chord NACA-style cowling, unequal-span wings and virtually no interplane bracing, most of the loads being borne by two large outward-canted struts. The **V2** prototype introduced a shorter-chord, narrower cowl with 18 fairings to house the valves. The **V3** was similar except for substituting a two-bladed, variable-pitch propeller for the three-bladed adjustable-pitch unit of the preceding aircraft. All three went to Rechlin for trials, where two were lost within three weeks. Both had shed the upper wing, and so hasty strengthening of the centre-section struts was introduced from the **V4** prototype onwards. With this modification the V4 demonstrated adequate performance, including pulling out of dives at near-vertical angles.

First deliveries of production **Hs 123A-1**s were made in the summer of 1936, the initial unit being Stukagruppe I/162 'Immelmann'. Power came from a BMW 132Dc and armament consisted of two MG 17 machine-guns in the upper fuselage decking. A 250-kg (551-lb) bomb was carried on a crutch which swung forward from between the main wheels, and four 50-kg (110-lb) bombs could be carried on wing racks.

Five Hs 123A-1s were dispatched to Spain for combat evaluation, but from their debut in early 1937 they were mainly used in a ground attack role. In this they proved remarkably successful, flying close support over the battlefield despite the lack of any communications with ground forces. Spain acquired all five aircraft, and ordered another 11.

Close support debate

Back in Germany, the Ju 87 had started to replace the Hs 123 with the Stukagruppen in 1937, and the Hs 123 was diverted to the close support units, equipping two of the five to form. Debate was raging in the Luftwaffe over the respective merits of the dedicated dive-bomber and the close support aircraft. The dive-bomber protagonists won, and the Ju 87 was also given a close support role, signalling the end of production for the Hs 123. Two variants built in prototype form were the **Hs 123B** with a BMW 132K engine under a long-chord cowling, and the **Hs 123C** which had additional machine-guns under the wings and an armoured headrest with a sliding hood. The latter feature was adopted by service Hs 123As.

In late 1938, after the Sudeten crisis had passed, the close support units were officially disbanded. Nevertheless, one (Schlachtfliegergruppe 10) survived the axe and was incorporated into Lehrgeschwader 2 as II (Schlacht)/LG 2. In September 1939 it was the only front-line Hs 123 unit, all other aircraft having been passed to training units.

II (Schlacht)/LG 2 was in the lead air assault against Poland on 1 September 1939 that opened World War II. Armed with 50-kg bombs on the wing racks and the MG 17 guns, the Hs 123s flew just feet above the heads of the Polish cavalry brigades for 10 days. More effective than the armament was the terrifying noise of the BMW radial, which was every bit as effective at dispersing mounted columns

The first prototype Hs 123 featured a smooth NACA-style cowling. It flew in early 1935 and demonstrated excellent performance.

as explosives. So effective was the Hs 123 in the lightning Polish campaign that plans to re-equip II (Schlacht)/LG 2 were immediately reversed.

For the unit, the next target was Belgium, supporting the 6th Army as it smashed through from 10 May 1940. The first action was to ward off Belgian sappers attempting to destroy brdige crossings over the Albert Canal. Sweeping through Luxembourg and the Ardennes, Hs 123s were soon in France, and by 21 May were the most forward-based Luftwaffe unit when they reached Cambrai. With victory in France achieved, II (Schlacht)/LG 2 was withdrawn to Germany for re-equipment with the Bf 109E, but the Hs 123 had by now built a legendary reputation for its ability to absorb battle damage, and the *Gruppe* only partially equipped with the Messerschmitt fighter.

Eastern Front

After a spell in the Balkans from April 1941, the unit joined the fight against the Soviet Union, operating on the southern front. It was incorporated into the newly-formed Schlachtgeschwader 1 and again proved the considerable capability of the Hs 123 in the close support role. Armed with either four SC 50 bombs, twin 20-mm MG FF cannon or containers each bearing 92 SC 2 anti-personnel bombs under the wings, and with a fuel tank on the centreline, the Hs 123 proved so effective and dependable that there were calls even as late as 1943 for its reinstatement into production. When conditions were so

Above: Undertaking the first ground support missions of World War II were the Hs 123A-1s of II (Schlacht)/LG 2, which flew from Alt-Rosenberg on 1 September 1939 as the Wehrmacht crashed into Poland.

Left: An Hs 123A-1 assigned to a Flugzeugführerschule training unit in 1941. Many aircraft were returned to front-line status to meet the demands of the operational close support units serving on the Eastern Front.

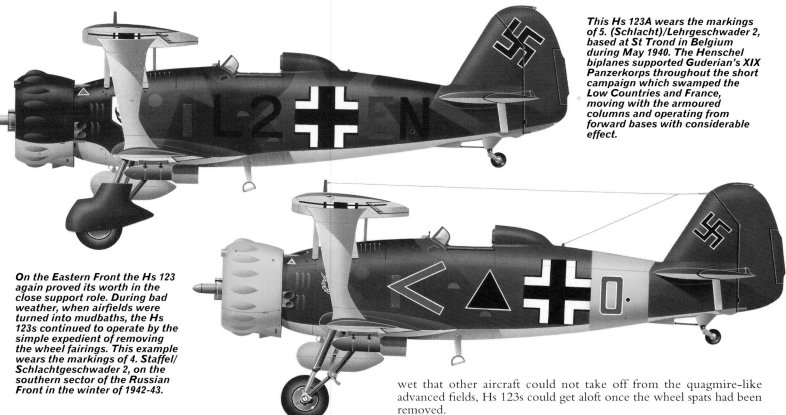

This Hs 123A wears the markings of 5. (Schlacht)/Lehrgeschwader 2, based at St Trond in Belgium during May 1940. The Henschel biplanes supported Guderian's XIX Panzerkorps throughout the short campaign which swamped the Low Countries and France, moving with the armoured columns and operating from forward bases with considerable effect.

On the Eastern Front the Hs 123 again proved its worth in the close support role. During bad weather, when airfields were turned into mudbaths, the Hs 123s continued to operate by the simple expedient of removing the wheel fairings. This example wears the markings of 4. Staffel/Schlachtgeschwader 2, on the southern sector of the Russian Front in the winter of 1942-43.

wet that other aircraft could not take off from the quagmire-like advanced fields, Hs 123s could get aloft once the wheel spats had been removed.

Without new production aircraft to swell the ranks, attrition slowly took its toll on the Hs 123, which ended its days in mid-1944, the remaining aircraft having been grouped in II/Schlachtgeschwader 2.

Specification
Henschel Hs 123A-1
Type: single-seat dive-bomber and close support aircraft
Powerplant: one BMW 132Dc nine-cylinder radial engine rated at 656 kW (880 hp) for take-off and 649 kW (870 hp) at 2500 m (8,200 ft)
Performance: maximum speed 341 km/h (212 mph) at 1200 m (3,940 ft) and 333 km/h (207 mph) at sea level; cruising speed 317 km/h (197 mph) at 2000 m (6,560 ft); initial climb rate 900 m (2,950 ft) per minute; service ceiling 9000 m (29,525 ft); range 860 km (534 miles)
Weights: empty 1505 kg (3,318 lb); normal loaded 2217 kg (4,888 lb)
Dimensions: wing span (upper) 10.50 m (34 ft 5⅓ in), (lower) 8.00 m (26 ft 3 in); length 8.33 m (27 ft 4 in); height 3.22 m (10 ft 6¾ in); wing area 24.85 m² (267.5 sq ft)
Armament: two 7.9-mm (0.31-in) MG 17 machine-guns in upper fuselage decking; underwing racks for four 50-kg (110-lb) bombs, two containers with 92 2-kg (4.4-lb) anti-personnel bombs or two 20-mm MG FF cannon pods

Above: With its large cowling and tail-dragging configuration, the Hs 123 did not offer the pilot much forward vision on the ground. Ground crew often rode on the wing to give directions to the pilot, especially over the rough ground typical of Eastern Front airfields.

Right: An Hs 123A of Schlachtgeschwader 1 displays the badge of the close support units – the Infanterie-Sturmabzeichen. The aircraft carries the standard weapon load of four SC 50 bombs under the wing racks. For the original dive-bomber role, the HS 123 was fitted with a crutch under the fuselage for a single SC 250 bomb, but in reality this was usually used for an auxiliary fuel tank.

Henschel Hs 126

In 1933 the Luftwaffe issued a request for an advanced battlefield observation aircraft which would improve on the Heinkel He 46 (which had not then entered service). Henschel responded with the **Hs 122**, a neat parasol monoplane which offered an outstanding all-round view and excellent low-speed and short-field characteristics. The prototype flew in early 1935 powered by a Rolls-Royce Kestrel, although the Siemens Sh 22B radial was the intended powerplant. Flight tests showed the design to be sound, but the Luftwaffe was disappointed with the maximum speed, which was little better than the He 46. Accordingly, Henschel was asked to develop the type with the Bramo 323 Fafnir radial, this design becoming the **Hs 126**.

Henschel took the opportunity to revise the design, with a longer fuselage, more angular wing planform and cantilever undercarriage. The fourth pre-production **Hs 122B-0** was modified to become the **Hs 126 V1**, powered by a Jumo 210 pending the availability of the Fafnir. Two more prototypes followed, with radial engines and refinements to the vertical tail.

Flight trials revealed excellent short-field capability and docile handling. A pre-production batch of 10 **Hs 126A-0**s was completed, some of which were issued to reconnaissance squadrons for evaluation. The first production aircraft were delivered in early 1938, these **Hs 126A-1**s switching to the BMW 132Dc engine to overcome the non-availability of the Fafnir. The cockpit accommodated the pilot and a gunner/observer, both provided with a sliding canopy. The back-seater operated a Zeiss Rb topographic camera in a bay behind him, a hand-held camera and the 7.9-mm MG 15 machine-gun (with 975 drum-held rounds). The pilot aimed the fixed MG 17 machine-gun (with 500 rounds) mounted in the upper starboard fuselage, and for light attack missions the aircraft could carry five 10-kg (22-lb) bombs in the camera bay and a single 50-kg (110-lb) bomb on a port-side strut which was braced to the wing and the fuselage.

Combat evaluation

Six Hs 126A-1s were sent to Spain in 1938 for combat evaluation with A/88 of the Légion Condor, where they proved very successful in both the light bombing and reconnaissance roles. The five survivors remained in Spain after the end of the Civil War, and a further 16 were exported to Greece. By September 1939, Hs 126 production was in full swing, and the type had virtually replaced the elderly He 45 and He 46 biplanes with the Aufklärungsstaffeln (H). The **Hs 126B-1** was now available, powered by the originally intended Fafnir 323 radial, offering better performance. Radio equipment was also

The Hs 126 V1 first prototype was originally the fourth pre-production Hs 122B-0. It was powered by a Jumo 210 and did not have the sliding canopy of production aircraft. First flight was in 1936.

upgraded, with the FuG 17 VHF set as standard. Thirteen reconnaissance squadrons of Hs 126s took part in the Polish campaign in September 1939. In addition to their traditional roles of army co-operation, battlefield reconnaissance and artillery spotting, they also strafed and bombed Polish positions. In the absence of effective air defence, the Hs 126 could operate with relative impunity.

Hs 126s were next in action over France, performing reconnaissance missions along the Maginot Line in late 1939. However, by the time the Luftwaffe turned on France in earnest, in May 1940, the Hs 126 was beginning to prove easy meat for fighters. Production of the aircraft slowed dramatically with the decision to procure the Fw 189 for the battlefield reconnaissance role, and the last aircraft was delivered in January 1941.

While the Aufklärungsstaffel (H) waited for the Fw 189, there was still plenty of fighting to be done. 2.(H)/14 flew the Hs 126 in North Africa, but all remaining units were sent to the Russian front. Here

Above: Production Hs 126A-1s line up at Henschel's Schönefeld factory field in 1938 prior to acceptance by the Luftwaffe. Later in the year six were sent to Spain for service with the Légion Condor's A/88 reconnaissance element. The type was originally intended to feature the Bramo Fafnir 323 engine, but the demands on this powerplant were such that the Hs 126A-1 featured the BMW 132.

Hs 126s served widely in the east on army co-operation duties. Their service in Greece was notable, the aircraft at right being seen over Athens. Shown above is an Hs 126B-1 of 2.(H)/31, as seen during the Greek campaign in April 1941. The yellow theatre bands were worn as the campaign was in mainland Europe. Aircraft on operations outside Europe (principally North Africa) wore white bands.

Henschel Hs 126

Left: This Hs 126B-1 served with 3.(H)/21 on the Don front in January 1943. The winter camouflage was usually applied over the normal green, with codes and theatre bands reapplied.

Right: Following their service with the army reconnaissance units, several Hs 126B-1s were used from the spring of 1943 on night harassment sorties. This aircraft was still operating with 2./NSGr 12 from Graz in April 1945.

2.(H)/14 took the Hs 126 to war in the Polish campaign, and then to North Africa, being the only Hs 126 unit in that theatre. Wheel spats were often removed when operating from difficult terrain.

Right: An important task for the Hs 126 after its front-line days had ended was as a glider tug for the DFS 230. Aircraft served with II and III Gruppen of Luftland-geschwader 1 from 1942.

they progressively re-equipped with newer types from the spring of 1942, the displaced Hs 126s being relegated to second-line duties. Among these was the towing of DFS 230 gliders, flying with II/ and III/Luftlandgeschwader 1. From the autumn of 1942, a handful were used as night harassment aircraft by the Nachtschlachtgruppen. Two such units operated in the Balkans, operating a few examples of the aircraft right until the last days of the war.

Specification
Henschel Hs 126B-1
Type: two-seat reconnaissance and army co-operation aircraft
Powerplant: one BMW-Bramo Fafnir 323A-1 or Q-1 nine-cylinder radial engine rated at 634 kW (850 hp) for take-off and 619 kW (830 hp) at 4000 m (13,120 ft)
Performance: maximum speed 310 km/h (193 mph) at sea level, 349 km/h (217 mph) at 4000 m (13,120 ft); climb to 4000 m (13,120 ft) in 7.2 minutes; service ceiling 8230 m (27,000 ft); range 580 km (360 miles) at sea level, 720 km (447 miles) at 4200 m (13,780 ft); endurance 2 hours 15 minutes
Weights: empty 2032 kg (4,480 lb); maximum loaded 3270 kg (7,209 lb)
Dimensions: wing span 14.50 m (47 ft 6¾ in); length 10.85 m (35 ft 7 in); height 3.75 m (12 ft 3½ in); wing area 31.60 m² (340.15 sq ft)
Armament: one fixed forward-firing 7.9-mm (0.31-in) MG 17 machine-gun in upper forward fuselage with 500 rounds, one flexibly-mounted 7.9-mm (0.31-in) MG 15 machine-gun in rear cockpit with 975 rounds; 10 10-kg (22-lb) bombs or camera in rear fuselage bay and one 50-kg (110-lb) bomb on optional fuselage side rack

Above: Providing extra striking power for the Hs 126 was this optional fuselage side rack, able to carry a single SC 50 bomb in addition to the four smaller bombs under the wings.

Right: An Hs 126 operating on the Eastern Front. The type's outstanding short- and rough-field capability allowed it to operate from virtually anywhere.

Henschel Hs 129

The **Henschel Hs 129** was the only aircraft of World War II – and, apart from today's A-10, virtually the only aircraft in all history – to be designed explicitly for destroying hostile armour. Apart from the Soviet *Sturmovik*, which was a more versatile armoured attacker, the Allies had no aircraft in this class. All the RAF had were a few Hurricanes fitted with 40-mm guns; which by comparison were totally inadequate. Yet Hitler's Germany completely failed to foresee how crucially important the Hs 129 would become, and there were nothing like sufficient numbers to make much impact on the tide of Soviet armour in 1944-45.

When the infant Luftwaffe was laying its plans for the future in 1935, it was generally believed that aircraft could do little to influence a land battle. Aircraft in close proximity to hostile armies were clearly highly vulnerable. If they were heavily armoured, they would be slow and sluggish, and their weapon load would be severely restricted. The effect of a few bullets or bombs seemed likely to be minimal, but in the Spanish Civil War of 1936-39 aircraft were seen to be not only effective but sometimes decisive (although against troops in unprepared positions). In April 1937 the Technische Amt issued a specification for a close support aircraft, to carry at least two 20-mm cannon and to have two low-powered engines and the smallest possible size, with armour and 75-mm glazing around the crew.

The finalists in the competition were Henschel, which proposed a neat single-seater, and Focke-Wulf, which scored because it suggested using a modified version of the Fw 189, which was already being built. The Fw 189 version was very much a compromise, but so was

Above: The Hs 129 operated effectively in the mud and cold of the Eastern front, despite its many shortcomings.

the rival Hs 129, the first prototype of which was flown in February or March 1939. Comparative testing was hampered by the fact that both aircraft were disastrous. They were sluggish in the extreme, and the Hs 129 had such a cramped cockpit that the engine instruments had to be mounted on the inner sides of the engine nacelles, and the control column was so short that great force was needed for even modest manoeuvres.

Opting for the Hs 129

In the end, what tipped the scales in favour of the Hs 129 was that it was smaller and cost only about two-thirds as much as the Focke-Wulf rival. The decision was taken to go ahead with eight pre-production **Hs 129A-0** aircraft, and these were all delivered by the time the Blitzkrieg was unleashed in Western Europe on 10 May 1940. They were put through prolonged trials and evaluation programmes and some later equipped the Schlachtflieger training *Staffel* at Paris-Orly.

Basically, the Hs 129 was a completely conventional aircraft with a simple, stressed-skin structure. The wing, with all the taper on the trailing edge, carried hydraulically driven slotted flaps, and was built as a centre-section integral with the fuselage and two bolted outer panels. The 343.8-kW (465-hp) Argus As 410A-1 air-cooled inverted Vee-12 engines driving Argus automatic controllable-pitch propellers were almost identical to the installations used in the Fw 189, which was already in production. Fuel was housed in a single cell in the fuselage and a tank in each wing inboard of the nacelles. The single-wheel main landing gears retracted backwards hydraulically, part of each wheel remaining exposed to avoid damage in a wheels-up landing.

Where the Hs 129 was unusual was that the fuselage was remarkably slim, with a triangular section (narrow at the top, broad at the bottom), with the front end in the form of a cramped cockpit surrounded by welded armour of 6-mm or 12-mm thickness, and with small panes of glass 75 mm thick. Total weight of the nose armour was 1080 kg (2,380 lb). As already noted, the great wish to minimise overall dimensions severely hampered the pilot's ability to fly a practical ground-attack mission, and for a large pilot made it almost impossible. On the other hand, the aircraft did carry the required armament, there being one 20-mm MG FF cannon in each side of the fuselage (with a prominent blister fairing over the ammunition drum) superimposed over a 7.92-mm MG 17 machine-gun in the lower flank of each forward fuselage with the breech ahead of the wing spar.

It was obvious to Chief Engineer Dipl Ing Fr. Nicolaus that a much

Below: Ground crew rearm and refuel an Hs 129B-2/R2 of IV(Pz)/SG 9 at Czernovitz in March 1944. On the Eastern Front in winter, aircraft were often daubed with white distemper over their regular camouflage for operations. This was soluble and easily washed off.

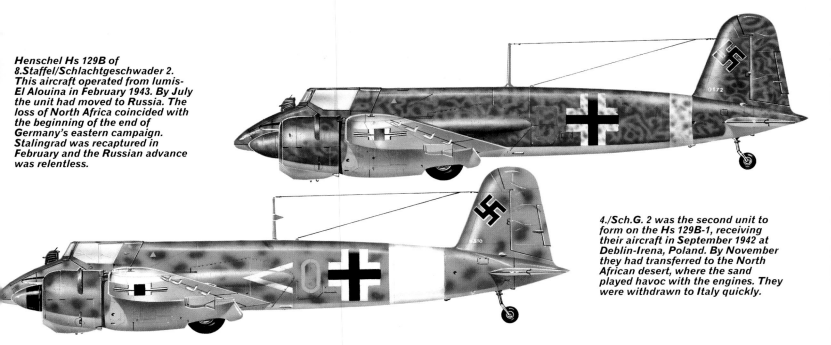

Henschel Hs 129B of 8.Staffel/Schlachtgeschwader 2. This aircraft operated from Iumis-El Alouina in February 1943. By July the unit had moved to Russia. The loss of North Africa coincided with the beginning of the end of Germany's eastern campaign. Stalingrad was recaptured in February and the Russian advance was relentless.

4./Sch.G. 2 was the second unit to form on the Hs 129B-1, receiving their aircraft in September 1942 at Deblin-Irena, Poland. By November they had transferred to the North African desert, where the sand played havoc with the engines. They were withdrawn to Italy quickly.

This is the second Hs 129B-0, the pre-production aircraft being distinguished by having the gun blast troughs faired over.

An Hs 129B-1/R2 is towed along a Libyan road near Tripoli in December 1942. 8./Sch.G. 2 was the fifth Staffel to get the Hs 129, formed from former JG 27 and JG 53 staff. Following a move to the Eastern Front, the unit was redesignated 13.(Pz)/Sch.G. 9 in October 1943.

better aircraft could be built, using more powerful engines. His team accordingly prepared drawings for the P.76, a slightly larger aircraft to be powered by two 522-kW (700-hp) Gnome-Rhône 14M radials, large numbers of which had become available following the defeat of France. It was decided, however, that too much time would be lost in tooling up for a bigger aircraft, and so the final compromise was merely to modify the existing **Hs 129A** to take the bigger and more powerful French radial engines. Remarkably few modifications were needed, but in one respect the resulting **Hs 129B** did incorporate a

The Hs 129A-0 pre-production aircraft were powered by the Argus As 410-A-1 inline engine, which proved woefully underpowered. After disastrous service trials with 5./LG 2, the Hs 129As were relegated to a Schlachtflieger training unit, 4./SG 101 at Paris-Orly.

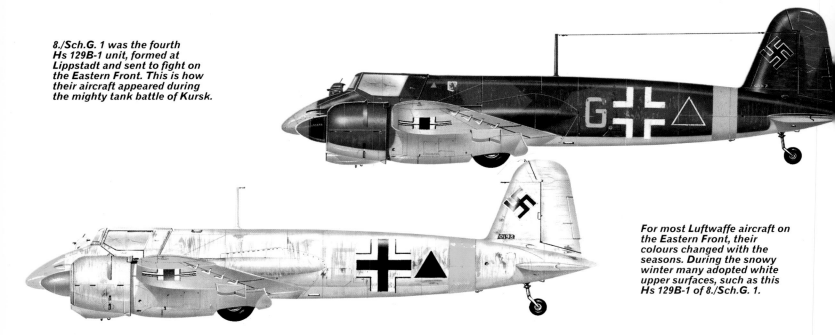

8./Sch.G. 1 was the fourth Hs 129B-1 unit, formed at Lippstadt and sent to fight on the Eastern Front. This is how their aircraft appeared during the mighty tank battle of Kursk.

For most Luftwaffe aircraft on the Eastern Front, their colours changed with the seasons. During the snowy winter many adopted white upper surfaces, such as this Hs 129B-1 of 8./Sch.G. 1.

major improvement. The cockpit was modified with large slabs of armour glass to give much better vision, although possibly at the expense of slight increase in vulnerability. The French engines were installed very much in the way used in existing French aircraft, driving three-bladed Ratier electrically-controlled, constant-speed propellers.

Overall, the Hs 129B was a great improvement, although it was still a poor performer. It was slower than the Ju 87D, had a much shorter range and was nowhere near as agile or pleasant to fly, despite continual tinkering with the flight controls which resulted in the addition of fast-acting electric trim tabs.

Operation Barbarossa

After the invasion of the Soviet Union in June 1941, it became evident that the Hs 129 was in principle an aircraft of great importance. In Poland and France the little Hs 123, despite the fact that it was an obsolescent biplane of very limited capability, had demonstrated what the General Staff had previously been reluctant to believe: that aircraft could play a valuable, and even crucial, role in land battles. So the Hs 129B was put into immediate production with high priority. A late change was to replace the MG FF cannon by the much harder-hitting MG 151, occasionally in the high-velocity 15-mm form but usually in 20-mm calibre, with 125 rounds each (the bulges on each side of the fuselage were retained). Provision was also made for the addition of various field modification kits to add specialised weapons or equipment, normally hung either beneath the fuselage or under each outer wing.

The first pre-production **Hs 129B-0** was delivered at the end of 1941, but Henschel suffered many severe problems and delays which

seriously held back the build-up of the planned *Schlachtgeschwader* force. Modifications were continually having to be introduced to rectify faults, equipment and parts were late on delivery, and the planned output of 40 per month was not attained until mid-1943. By far the biggest single problem was the engine, which showed itself to be severely intolerant of either dust on the Eastern Front or, worse, sand in North Africa. Its reliability was extremely poor, and despite the most urgent investigations it took six months to find any sort of real cure. The first *Staffel*, 4./Sch.G. 1, had a very depressing experience in the push for the Caucasus in mid-1942, while at the end of the year the next unit, 4./Sch.G. 2, suffered a series of disasters in North Africa and was eventually evacuated with no aircraft.

During 1943 the tempo of Hs 129B effort increased greatly, but difficulties in production and high attrition made the actual build-up of Sch.G. units a frustrating process. On the other hand, the combat effectiveness of the aircraft increased considerably with the fitting of the modification kits, most notably the addition of a huge 30-mm MK 101 gun under the fuselage, with 30 shells. This had a lethal effect against all armoured vehicles except main battle tanks, and even these were sometimes vulnerable when attacked from the rear. Other add-on loads included an internal camera, a battery of four MG 17 machine-guns or various loads of small bombs, especially boxes of 4-kg

The trailing-edge taper of the Hs 129 was a characteristic feature. Rustsätze conversions for the B-1 included the R2 (one 30-mm MK 101 cannon in a ventral pack), R3 (four uncowled 7.9-mm MG 17 machine-guns under the fuselage), R4 (bomb racks) and R5 (internal reconnaissance camera).

This Hs 129B-1 is seen in RAF colours after capture. On either side of the nose were mounted MG 17 7.9-mm (0.31-in) machine-gun (lower) and a MG 151 20-mm cannon (upper). The machine-gun had 500 rounds per gun in the fuselage, while the cannon had only 125.

(8.8-lb) SD4 hollow-charge bomblets which had considerable armour-penetration capabilities.

A flying gun

Production gave way to the **Hs 129B-2/Wa** (Waffentrager), the suffix meaning that the very powerful MK 103 gun was fitted not as a field modification but at the factory. The MK 103 had greater anti-tank effectiveness. As an alternative, some aircraft were fitted with a BK 3,7, as used on the very effective Ju 87G. This gun necessitated removal of the MG 17 machine-guns in order to accommodate its ammunition. (Of course, whereas the Ju 87G had carried two of the 37-mm guns, the **Hs 129B-2** carried only one.)

The massive build-up in Soviet strength with thick-skinned tanks contrasted with the faltering strength of the Sch.G. units, which continued to be afflicted by poor engine reliability despite the addition of properly designed air filters. The overriding need was for more powerful anti-armour weapons, and on 10 January 1944 a special unit, Erprobungskommando 26, was formed at Udetfeld out of previous Sch.G. units to centralise the desperate effort to devise new weapons

and tactics. Its Hs 129s soon appeared with various new armament, some of which were too much for what was, after all, a small aircraft.

Radical new weapons

The outstanding example of the new weapons was the radically different Forstersonde SG 113A. This comprised a giant tube resembling a ship's funnel in the centre fuselage just behind the fuselage tank. Inside this were fitted six smooth-bore tubes, each 1.6 m (5 ft 3 in) long and of 77-mm calibre. The tubes were arranged to fire down and slightly to the rear, and were triggered as a single group by a photocell sensitive to the passage of a tank close beneath. Inside each tube was a combined device consisting of a 45-mm armour-piercing shell (with a small high-explosive charge) pointing downwards and a heavy steel cylinder of full calibre pointing upwards. Between the two was the propellant charge, with a weak tie-link down the centre to joint the parts together. When the SG 113A was fired, the shells were driven down by their driving sabots at high velocity, while the steel slugs were fired out of the top of each tube to cancel the recoil. Unfortunately, trials at Tarnewitz Waffenprufplatz showed that the photocell system often failed to pick out correct targets.

Another impressive weapon was the huge PaK 40 anti-tank gun of 75-mm calibre. This gun weighed 1500 kg (3,306 lb) in its original ground-based form, and fired a 3.2-kg (7-lb) tungsten-carbide cored

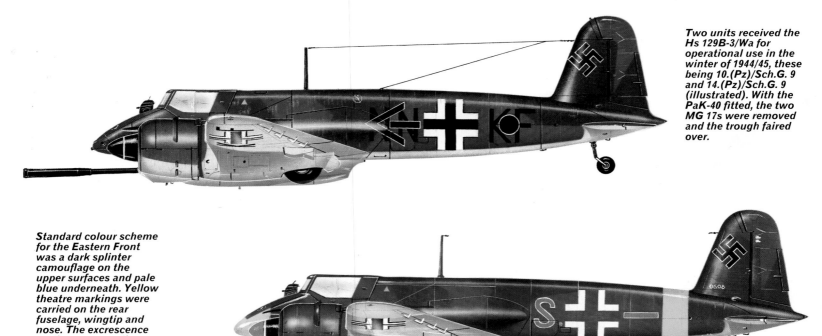

Two units received the Hs 129B-3/Wa for operational use in the winter of 1944/45, these being 10.(Pz)/Sch.G. 9 and 14.(Pz)/Sch.G. 9 (illustrated). With the PaK-40 fitted, the two MG 17s were removed and the trough faired over.

Standard colour scheme for the Eastern Front was a dark splinter camouflage on the upper surfaces and pale blue underneath. Yellow theatre markings were carried on the rear fuselage, wingtip and nose. The excrescence on the nose was the Revi C 12/C gunset, offset to starboard.

Specification
Henschel Hs 129B-2
Type: single-seat close support aircraft
Powerplant: two Gnome-Rhône 14M 4/5 radial engines developing
522 kW (700 hp) for take-off
Dimensions: wing span 14.2 m (46 ft 5 in); length 9.75 m (31 ft 9 in); height 3.25 m (10 ft 6 in);
wing area 29 m² (312 sq ft)
Weights: empty 3810 kg (8,400 lb); maximum loaded 5250 kg (11,574 lb)
Performance: maximum speed 407 km/h (253 mph); range 688 km
(427 miles); initial climb rate 486 m/min (1,600 ft/min); service ceiling
9000 m (29,530 ft)
Armament: two 7.9-mm MG 17 machine-guns and two 20-mm MG 151 cannon in nose; either one
30-mm MK 101 cannon in ventral pod, four
MG 17 machine-guns, four 50-kg (110-lb) bombs, 92 2-kg (4.4-lb)
anti-personnel bombs or one 250-kg bomb beneath fuselage; two 50-kg
(110-lb) bombs or 48 2-kg (4.4-lb) anti-personnel bombs on wing racks

Powerplant
A ready supply of captured Gnome-Rhône 14M radials
allowed Henschel to introduce the better-performing Hs 129B
series. However, the engine required a series of urgent
'fixes' to overcome serious reliability problems. The engine
nacelle was given armour plate to prevent damage from
groundfire.

Henschel Hs 129B-2/R2
Eastern Front

The Henschel Hs 129 is best
remembered in its Hs 129B-3/Wa
form, carrying the PaK-40 75-
mm anti-tank cannon. However,
most of its work was performed
with weapons of a much smaller
calibre. This is a typical Eastern
Front aircraft, a B-2 with the
centreline 30-mm MK 101
cannon fairing, in addition to the
internal MG 17 machine-guns
and MG 151 cannon. Small racks
on the wings could carry small
bombs for use against personnel
or vehicles. After an
inauspicious start to its life,
dogged by reliability problems
with the engines, the Hs 129 did
achieve some success in the
later months of the war.

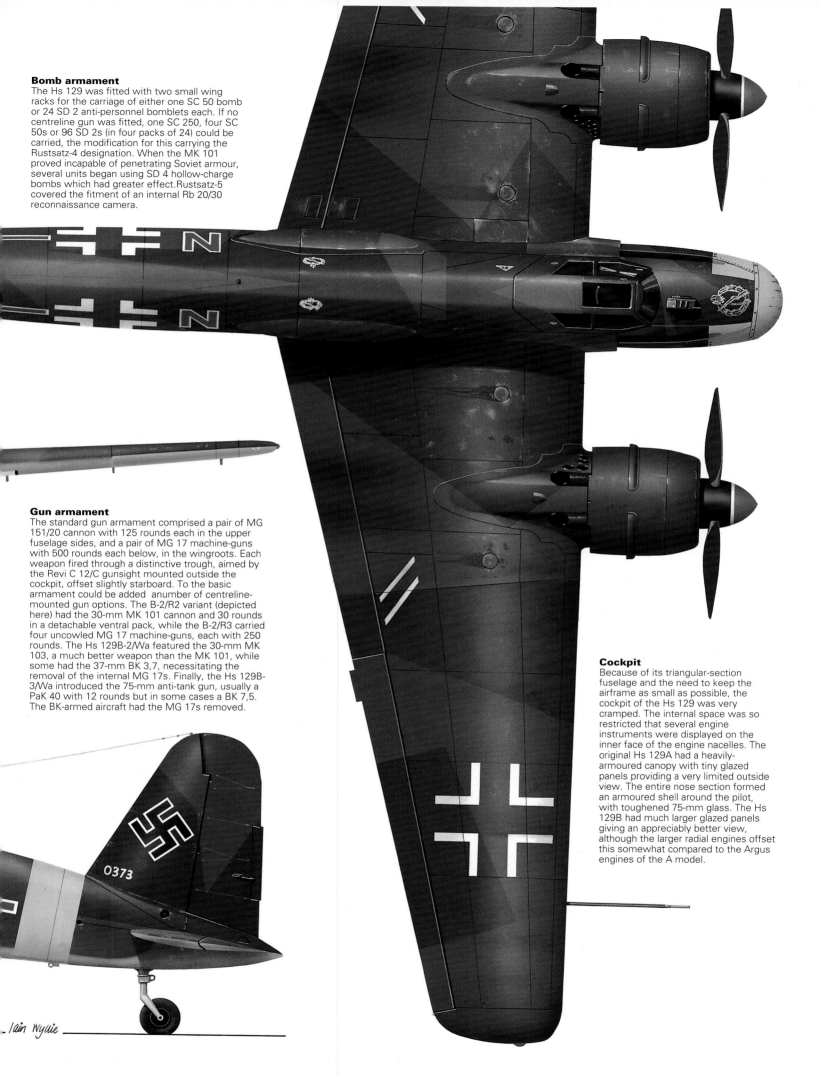

Bomb armament

The Hs 129 was fitted with two small wing racks for the carriage of either one SC 50 bomb or 24 SD 2 anti-personnel bomblets each. If no centreline gun was fitted, one SC 250, four SC 50s or 96 SD 2s (in four packs of 24) could be carried, the modification for this carrying the Rustsatz-4 designation. When the MK 101 proved incapable of penetrating Soviet armour, several units began using SD 4 hollow-charge bombs which had greater effect.Rustsatz-5 covered the fitment of an internal Rb 20/30 reconnaissance camera.

Gun armament

The standard gun armament comprised a pair of MG 151/20 cannon with 125 rounds each in the upper fuselage sides, and a pair of MG 17 machine-guns with 500 rounds each below, in the wingroots. Each weapon fired through a distinctive trough, aimed by the Revi C 12/C gunsight mounted outside the cockpit, offset slightly starboard. To the basic armament could be added a number of centreline-mounted gun options. The B-2/R2 variant (depicted here) had the 30-mm MK 101 cannon and 30 rounds in a detachable ventral pack, while the B-2/R3 carried four uncowled MG 17 machine-guns, each with 250 rounds. The Hs 129B-2/Wa featured the 30-mm MK 103, a much better weapon than the MK 101, while some had the 37-mm BK 3,7, necessitating the removal of the internal MG 17s. Finally, the Hs 129B-3/Wa introduced the 75-mm anti-tank gun, usually a PaK 40 with 12 rounds but in some cases a BK 7,5. The BK-armed aircraft had the MG 17s removed.

Cockpit

Because of its triangular-section fuselage and the need to keep the airframe as small as possible, the cockpit of the Hs 129 was very cramped. The internal space was so restricted that several engine instruments were displayed on the inner face of the engine nacelles. The original Hs 129A had a heavily-armoured canopy with tiny glazed panels providing a very limited outside view. The entire nose section formed an armoured shell around the pilot, with toughened 75-mm glass. The Hs 129B had much larger glazed panels giving an appreciably better view, although the larger radial engines offset this somewhat compared to the Argus engines of the A model.

0373

Iain Wyllie

Henschel Hs 129

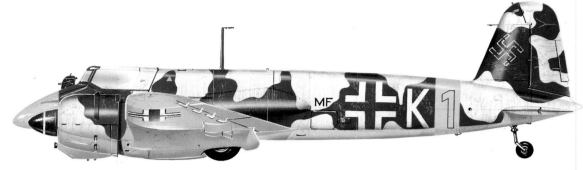

Hs 129B-2/R2 of IV(Pz)/Sch.G. 9 in temporary winter markings. The B-2 incorporated various improvements over the B-1, mostly as a result of combat experience. As the Soviet tank armies grew larger, so the R2 30-mm cannon became standard factory fit.

This close-up shows just how cramped the cockpit was, particularly at head-height. Note the infantry-attack badge of the Schlacht units.

In order to provide a hard-hitting weapon against Soviet tanks, the Hs 129B-3/Wa was evolved, with a 75-mm Panzerabwehrkanone 40 in a large ventral fairing. Performance and agility were drastically reduced, although one shot could knock out the biggest Soviet tank.

projectile at 933 m/sec (3,060 ft/sec). Even at a range of 1000 m (3,280 ft), the shell could penetrate 133 mm (5¼ in)of armour if it hit square-on. Modified as the PaK 40L, the gun had a much bigger muzzle brake to reduce recoil and electro-pneumatic operation to feed successive shells automatically. Installed in the **Hs 129B-3/Wa**, the giant gun was provided with 26 rounds which could be fired at the cyclic rate of 40 rounds per minute, so that three or four could be fired on a single pass. Almost always, a single good hit would destroy a tank, even from head-on. The main problem was that the PaK 40L was too powerful a gun for the aircraft. Quite apart from the severe

muzzle blast and recoil, the sheer weight of the gun made the Hs 129B-3/Wa almost unmanageable, and in emergency the pilot could sever the gun's attachments and let it drop.

Limited production

In late September 1944, the entire manufacturing programme was abandoned, along with virtually all other German aircraft except for the 'emergency fighter programme'. Total production had amounted to only 870, including prototypes. Because of attrition and other problems, the Hs 129 was never able to equip the giant anti-tank force that could be seen to be needed as early as winter 1941-42, and its overall effect on the war was not great. Towards the end, in autumn 1944, operations began to be further restricted by shortage of high-octane petrol, and by the final collapse only a handful of these aircraft remained.

Below: The angular yet sturdy lines of the Hs 129B are illustrated here by this aircraft captured in North Africa. It was shipped to the United States for evaluation, wearing the 'Foreign Equipment' registration 'FE-4600'. The white fuselage band denoted the Mediterranean theatre.

This aircraft is an Hs 129B-2/R2 of 4. Staffel/Schlachtgeschwader 1, operating on the Eastern Front during the summer of 1943. The aircraft has the ventral 30-mm MK 101 cannon fitted, but does not have the usual fairing over it. In October the unit redesignated as 10. (Panzer) Staffel/SG 9.

The Hs 129B equipped the three *Staffeln* of the 8th Assault Wing of the Royal Romanian Air Corps. On 23 August 1944 there was a coup in Romania, as a result of which the country changed from being an ally of Germany to being an enemy. These Hs 129Bs, accordingly, were used against the German armies, finally being combined into a unit equipped with the Ju 87D.

There were plans for a supposedly improved **Hs 129C**. It would have been powered by 626.8-kW (840-hp) Isotta-Fraschini Delta IV inverted Vee-12s, giving better performance, and would normally have carried twin MK 103 guns mounted in a kind of turret beneath the fuselage, with a small amount of traverse under pilot control. This version was abandoned because of non-availability of the Italian engines.

Henschel Hs 130

German fascination with high-altitude flight resulted in some unusual aircraft, not least of which was the **Hs 130**. Development began with the **Hs 128**, two prototypes of which first flew in 1939. These were dedicated research vehicles for testing pressure cabins and engine superchargers, and featured cantilever wings of 26.00-m (85-ft 4½-in) span. The **V1** was powered by DB 601s and the **V2** by Jumo 210s; both had fixed undercarriage. Trials with a variety of superchargers were not particularly successful, but the theoretical high altitude potential caught the attention of Theodor Rowehl, commander of the AufklGr Ob.d.L., the Luftwaffe High Command's special reconnaissance unit. Rowehl's idea of using the aircraft for reconnaissance missions led to the RLM issuing instructions to Henschel to adapt the Hs 128 to this role under the designation **Hs 130A**.

Three prototypes were built, the first flying before the end of 1940. It had a wing span reduced to 22.01 m (72 ft 6 in), DB 601R engines with single-stage superchargers and retractable undercarriage. A bay in the rear fuselage could house two remotely-controlled Rb 75/30 cameras.

Five **Hs 130A-0** pre-production aircraft followed, with wing span increased to 25.50 m (83 ft 8 in). These were delivered in early 1941 and underwent intensive testing and much modification, the trials revealing serious powerplant problems and performance deficiencies. The ultimate

A model was the **Hs 130A-0/ U6**, modified with even longer wings of 29.00 m (95 ft 1¾ in) and with two DB 605B engines with Hirth superchargers and GM 1 nitrous oxide boosting. This variant also had underwing drop tanks for extra fuel. None of the Hs 130A configurations proved satisfactory, and it never entered service.

Bomber developments were the unbuilt **Hs 130B**, which was a minimum-change variant of the Hs 130A with bombs held in the camera bay, and the **Hs 130C**. The latter was almost a different aircraft, tailored to the abortive 'Bomber B' competition. It had wings of only 24.70-m (81-ft 0½-in) span and a (still pressurised) extensively glazed crew compartment. The **V1** and **V2** flew with BMW 801 radials, but the **V3** had DB 603A engines and was fitted with defensive armament. These were the only three C models to be completed.

Further reconnaissance development led to the **Hs 130D**, which would have featured DB 605 engines with complex two-stage superchargers if these could have been made to work, and the **Hs 130E**, a reworking of the Hs 130A with the HZ (Höhen Zentrale)-Anlage system. This circumvented some of the problems of engine superchargers by providing blown air from a third engine mounted within the fuselage. Two wing-mounted DB 603Bs were augmented by a central DB 605T, which had an array of air scoops under the fuselage. Although the three-man

pressurised cabin of the Hs 130A remained largely unchanged, the rest of the aircraft differed significantly. The nose was extended considerably to offset the extra weight of the HZ-Anlage engine, and to provide more fuel capacity, while the wings were extrapolated from those of the Hs 130C to an enmormous span. The C's undercarriage was adapted. Drop tanks could be carried, and the mission equipment bay could house three cameras. First flying in September 1942, the **Hs 130E V1** did not use the Höhen Zentrale system for the first few flights, and neither did the **V2** when it joined the programme in November. However, when the system was employed, altitudes of 12500 m (41,000 ft) could be attained. The V2 was lost after an inflight engine fire, and was replaced by the **V3**.

A batch of seven **Hs 130E-0s** followed, the first flying in May 1943. A production order for the **Hs 130E-1**, with defensive armament and provisions for wing-mounted 1800-kg (3,968-lb) bombs in place of the drop tanks, was cancelled after the test

fleet suffered continuous failures of the unusual propulsion system. A variant with heavy cannon armament remained unbuilt, as did the **Hs 130F**, a version of the E which would have attempted to overcome the problems of the HZ-Anlage by using four supercharged BMW 801s.

Specification
Henschel Hs 130E-0
Type: high-altitude reconnaissance platform
Powerplant: two Daimler Benz DB 603B 12-cylinder engines, supercharged by a DB 605T, each rated at 1305.5 kW (1,750 hp) for take-off and 1074 kW (1,440 hp) at 13700 m (45,000 ft)
Performance: maximum speed 610 km/h (379 mph); maximum cruising speed 515 km/h (320 mph) at 12000 m (39,370 ft); service ceiling 15090 m (49,500 ft); range with drop tanks 2995 km (1,860 miles)
Weights: normal loaded 16650 kg (36,700 lb); maximum loaded 18100 kg (39,900 lb)
Dimensions: wing span 33.00 m (108 ft 3¼ in); length 22.00 m (72 ft 2 in); height 5.60 m (18 ft 4½ in); wing area 85.00 m² (914 sq ft)

An Hs 130E-0 displays the unusual HZ-Anlage arrangement, the large airscoops under the fuselage aspirating a DB 605 engine mounted in the central fuselage.

Junkers Ju 52

Fairly widely recognised as the world's most efficient national airline at the end of the 1920s (while others struggled to survive the great depression), Deutsche Lufthansa flew highly competitive services throughout Europe using a heterogeneous fleet of aircraft largely comprising designs progressively developed from Professor Hugo Junkers' original J 1 all-metal monoplane of 1915. The great majority of these early aircraft (the J 10, F 13, A 20, F 24, W 33, W 34, Ju 46 and Ju 52) were single-engined, low-wing monoplanes, but in 1924 there appeared a three-engined airliner, the G 23, powered by a 145-kW (195-hp) Junkers L 2 and two 75-kW (100-hp) Mercedes engines. It is thought that, as a result of Versailles Treaty restrictions imposed on German aircraft manufacture, this prototype was produced at Junkers' Fili factory near Moscow; production of about nine aircraft (as well as that of the much more numerous G 24) was subsequently undertaken in Sweden. The G 24, usually powered by three 209/231-kW (280/310-hp) Junkers L 5 inline engines, served in numerous configurations and with a number of airlines, including Lufthansa, which retained them in service until 1933/34.

1926 was a busy year for the Junkers concern, with two new designs (the G 31 tri-motor transport and the W 33/34) being the most important to fly. The former was a beefier version of the successful G 24, and the latter an excellent single-engined transport which was built in large numbers. Almost at once, the Junkers designers embarked on a new but considerably enlarged single-engined transport, the Ju 52, which embodied the cumulative experience of earlier designs and was primarily intended for freight carrying. Like its predecessors, it was of standard Junkers all-metal construction with corrugated, load-sustaining duralumin skinning, and featured the patented Junkers full-span double wing. Five aircraft were built, of which four under-

went development with various powerplants in Germany and one (CF-ARM) went to Canada. The first aircraft flew on 13 October 1930. Despite its single engine (usually of around 582-615 kW/780-825 hp), the Ju 52 was able to carry 15-17 passengers when required. However, the following year the Junkers design team, under Dipl Ing Ernst Zindel, undertook work to adapt the Ju 52 to feature three 392-kW (525-hp) Pratt & Whitney Hornet nine-cylinder radials, and the prototype of this version, the **Ju 52/3m** (Dreimotoren, or three-motor), made its maiden flight in April 1932. Subsequent deliveries were made to Finland, Sweden and Brazil, as well as to Deutsche Lufthansa. Ultimately, Ju 52/3ms flew with airlines in Argentina, Austria, Australia, Belgium, Bolivia, China, Colombia, Czechoslovakia, Denmark, Ecuador, Estonia, France, Great Britain, Greece, Hungary, Italy, Lebanon, Mozambique, Norway, Peru, Poland, Portugal, Romania, South Africa, Spain, Switzerland, Turkey and Uruguay. Powerplants included Hispano-Suiza, BMW, Junkers Jumo, Bristol Pegasus, Pratt & Whitney Hornet and Wasp engines. Commercial Ju 52/3ms delivered to Bolivia were employed as military transports towards the end of the Gran Chaco war of 1932-35.

From late in 1932, Ju 52/3ms were delivered to Lufthansa, with D-2201 'Boelcke' and D-2202 'Richthofen' inaugurating the airline's Berlin-London and Berlin-Rome services before the end of that year. In due course, no fewer than 230 Ju 52/3ms were registered with Deutsche Lufthansa, continuing to fly commercial services to Spain, Portugal, Sweden, Switzerland and Turkey almost to the end of

The Ju 52/3m was the unsung hero of the Blitzkrieg, dropping paratroops in Norway, Greece and the Low Countries, towing gliders, and keeping the armies resupplied as they scythed through Europe. Later, the Ju 52/3m was the backbone of the massive assault on Crete.

Operating in the ice and snow of Norway or Russia, or the sand and heat of North Africa, the Ju 52 attended to the German army wherever it went. Although it was rugged and reliable, and an uncomplaining load-carrier, the aircraft was highly vulnerable to enemy air power. Here Ju 52s and Bf 110s are seen at a make-shift North African landing strip.

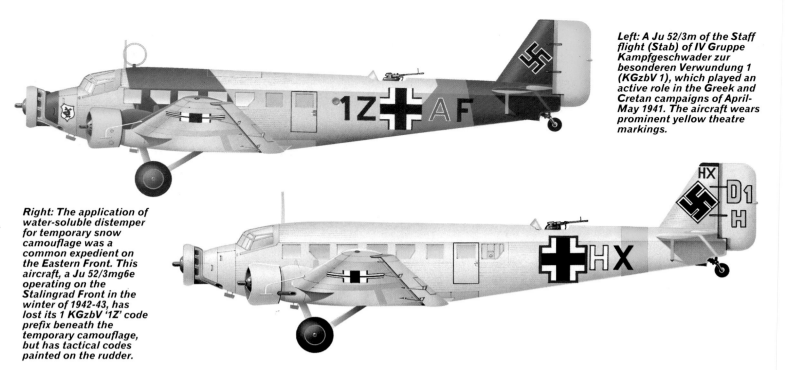

Left: A Ju 52/3m of the Staff flight (Stab) of IV Gruppe Kampfgeschwader zur besonderen Verwundung 1 (KGzbV 1), which played an active role in the Greek and Cretan campaigns of April-May 1941. The aircraft wears prominent yellow theatre markings.

Right: The application of water-soluble distemper for temporary snow camouflage was a common expedient on the Eastern Front. This aircraft, a Ju 52/3mg6e operating on the Stalingrad Front in the winter of 1942-43, has lost its 1 KGzbV '1Z' code prefix beneath the temporary camouflage, but has tactical codes painted on the rudder.

The German Fallschirmjäger (paratroops) were Luftwaffe soldiers who were air mobile in the widest sense, arriving by parachute, glider or aircraft, as demanded. Here a section watches as a Ju 52/3m takes off from the Norwegian airfield to which it has been delivered.

World War II. Despite the stringencies of treaty restrictions imposed on Germany since 1919, clandestine adventures had continued by which potential military personnel had undergone training in foreign lands, particularly the USSR. When, after its walk-out from the disarmament talks in 1932, Germany set about the covert establishment of a military air force, it fell to such aircraft as the Ju 52/3m to provide the basis of its flying equipment, and in 1934 the first military version, the **Ju 52/3mg3e**, appeared.

The Ju 52/3mg3e was an attempt to produce a bomber version quickly and without unduly interrupting the highly profitable commercial production line. Powered by three 392-kW (525-hp) BMW 132A-3 radials, this version normally carried a bomb load of 600 kg (1,321 lb), comprising six 100-kg (220-lb) bombs and featured a dorsal gun position and a ventral 'dustbin', each mounting a single 7.92-mm (0.31-in) MG 15 machine-gun. Deliveries of the Ju 52/3mg3e to the new Luftwaffe totalled 450 in 1934-5, the first unit thus equipped being Kampfgeschwader 152 'Hindenburg'. In 1937 this Geschwader's IV Gruppe was redesignated KGrzbV 1; this designation (Kampfgruppe zur besonderen Verwendung, or bomber group for special operations) was roughly comparable to the RAF's 'bomber transport' category, and was intended to reflect a dual role of bombing and military transport duties. It thereby perpetuated the originally intended function of the Ju 52/3m. In the event, Ju 52/3m-equipped KGrzbV seldom, if ever, engaged in bombing operations during World War II. When, on 18 July 1936, the Spanish Civil War broke out and Germany quickly aligned herself with the right-wing Nationalists, 20 Ju 52/3ms and six Heinkel He 51s were sent to Spain, being absorbed into the Légion Condor under General Hugo Sperrle during the following November. It was as transports that the Junkers were initially employed, bringing 10,000 Moorish troops to Spain from Morocco. Thereafter, they were deployed in three bomber Staffeln of Kampfgruppe 88, and were flown in raids on the Republican-held Mediterranean ports and in support of the land battle for Madrid. By mid-1937, they were deemed to be poor bombers and were largely replaced by such aircraft as the Dornier Do 17 and Heinkel He 111. Nevertheless, the Ju 52/3mg3e continued to serve as both a bomber and a transport with German and Spanish Nationalist forces until the end of the Civil War.

Operations from Germany's poorly-surfaced military airfields had resulted, in 1935, in the introduction of the **Ju 52/3mg4e** with tailwheel in place of tailskid, and by 1938 this version was being standardised among the KGrzbV. In March that year, at the time of the Austrian Anschluss, German troops were carried forward by KGrzbV 1 and 2 in a massive show of strength – the former based at Furstenwalde with 54 aircraft, and the latter at Brandenburg-Briest. By the time Germany was ready to crush Poland, the Luftwaffe's Transportverband possessed an inventory of 552 aircraft, of which 547 were Ju 52/3mg3e and Ju 52/3mg4e aircraft (the balance being two obsolete He 111 transports, a Junkers G 38, a Ju 90 and a Focke-Wulf Fw 200). Losses in the month-long campaign in September amounted to 59 Junkers Ju 52/3ms, all but two to ground fire or flying accidents. In the course of 2,460 flights, the aircraft carried 19,700 troops and 1451 tonnes (1,600 tons) of supplies.

In the relatively swift and clinically organised invasion of Norway in 1939, the number of Ju 52/3ms available had risen to 573, equipping all four Gruppen of KGzbV 1, and KGrzbV 101, 102, 103, 104, 105, 106 and 107 – an average of 52 aircraft in each Gruppe. A small number of twin float-equipped **Ju 52/3m Wasser** aircraft were also employed in the Norwegian campaign, alighting in the fjords to disembark troops, engineers and supplies. A new version, the **Ju 52/3mg5e** with provision for alternative wheel, float or ski landing gear, had been introduced, powered by three 619-kW (830-hp) BMW 132T-2 engines. Among the operations undertaken by Junkers in Norway were the capture by airborne forces of Stavanger-Sola airport and the Vordingborg bridge. A total of 29,000 men, 1180000 litres (259,300 Imp gal) of aviation fuel and 2155 tonnes (2,376 tons) of supplies were airlifted during the campaign, for the significant loss of 150 aircraft.

Prior to the conclusion of the Norwegian campaign, the majority of

A Ju 52/3m of an unidentified transport unit is seen at a forward airfield on the Eastern Front during the harsh winter of 1943. The Ju 52/3m had as vital a role to play during the difficult closing stages of the war as it had performed during the easy, early victories. On the Eastern Front it was the Ju 52/3m that supplied (and often evacuated) Wehrmacht troops wherever they found themselves surrounded, at Stalingrad, in the Demyansk pocket, and from Tunisia, the transport pilots often struggling on in the face of horrifying losses as their lumbering and vulnerable trimotors fell victim to Allied fighters or flak.

Ju 52/3ms were being withdrawn back to Germany in preparation for Operation Yellow, the great assault in the West. As a result of losses in Norway, the number of Junkers available was only 475, to which was now added 45 DFS 230 assault gliders, the whole transport force being commanded by General Putzier. Because of the need to conserve the Ju 52/3ms for a likely air assault on the UK, the Luftwaffe's transports were largely confined to airborne attacks in the initial stage, and it was against the Netherlands and Belgium that most of these were launched, in particular on the Moerdijk bridges and on Rotterdam's Waalhaven airport. Large numbers of Ju 52/3ms were employed in each attack and losses, mainly from anti-aircraft gunfire, were extremely heavy; in the five days that it took the Wehrmacht to crush the Netherlands, no fewer than 167 Junkers were totally destroyed, and a similar number badly damaged. By the end of 1940 a total of 1,275 Ju 52/3ms had been delivered to the Luftwaffe, of which some 700 aircraft had already been struck off charge.

After the collapse of France, no further major operations involving the use of Ju 52/3ms were launched until the advance by German forces through the Balkans in April 1941. By then, a number of new versions had appeared, namely the **Ju 52/3mg6e**, which was similar to the Ju 52/3mg5e but equipped with improved radio, and the **Ju 52/3mg7e** with automatic pilot, accommodation for up to 18 troops and wider cabin doors; it also featured provision for two 7.92-mm (0.31-in) machine-guns to fire through the cabin windows. Operations in the Balkans and Aegean also saw the first operations by the Minensuchgruppe (minesweeping group), equipped with the Ju 52/3mg6e fitted with large dural hoops energised by an auxiliary motor to explode Allied mines sown in abandoned harbours. Despite its ultimate capture, Crete proved a disaster for the Transportverband. Assigned to the task of an airborne invasion of the island, the 493 Ju 52/3ms and about 80 DFS 230 gliders were intended to attack in three waves. However, as a result of confusion on the ground caused

by dense clouds of dust, there were numerous collisions and delays, so that what had been planned as an attack concentrated in time and area degenerated into widespread confusion and dissipated effort. German casualties were more than 7,000 men (of whom about 2,000 were paratroopers) and 174 Ju 52/3ms, representing more than a third of the Luftwaffe's available transport force. It has often been said that the Balkan campaign was a lost cause for the Allies, yet the heavy losses inflicted on this vital enemy assault arm proved of immense importance when Germany launched Operation Barbarossa less than two months later, and henceforth (apart from isolated instances of commando-type operations) the use of air transport was confined within the Luftwaffe to logistic supply and evacuation. On the opening day of Barbarossa, the Luftwaffe could field no more than 238 serviceable Ju 52/3ms, a far cry from the numbers available in 1939 and 1940.

The nature of warfare on the Eastern Front quickly determined the role to be played by the Ju 52/3m, with 'scorched earth' tactics employed by the retreating Russians demanding considerable dependence by the Wehrmacht on air supplies. Production of the Ju 52/3m increased to 502 in 1941, 503 in 1942 and 887 in 1943. New versions continued to appear: the **Ju 52/3mg8e** dispensed with the wheel spats (found to be a hindrance in the quagmire conditions on the Eastern Front), but included a 13-mm (0.51-in) MG 131 gun in the dorsal position, while some aircraft had 634-kW (850-hp) BMW 132Z engines; the **Ju 52/3mg9e**, which appeared in 1942, featured strengthened landing gear to permit a take-off weight of 11500 kg (25,353 lb) and was equipped to tow the Gotha Go 242 glider; the **Ju 52/3mg10e** was a naval version with provision for floats; and the **Ju 52/3mg12e** had 597-kW (800-hp) BMW 132L engines. Only one other version reached the Luftwaffe (late in 1943), namely the **Ju 52/3mg14e** with an MG 15 machine-gun mounted in a streamlined position over the pilot's cabin. It may be said of the Ju 52/3m that its star shone brightest in adversity from 1942. In February of that

A Ju 52/3mg6e of 2.Staffel, KGzbV 102, in Italy during 1942. The aircraft has an unusual gun turret above the flight deck. The fuselage Balkenkreuze is applied in white outline form only, and the aircraft has white Mediterranean theatre markings on the wingtips and encircling the rear fuselage.

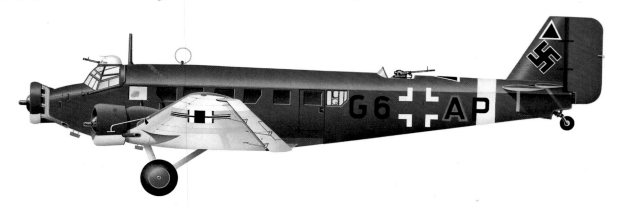

The 18-seat Ju 52/3mg7e, shown here, was a major production variant and featured automatic pilot and wide cabin doors. Subsequent versions had the wheel fairings removed, as sand and mud tended to clog the wheels.

Three Junkers Ju 52/3mg6e mine-clearance aircraft of the Minensuchgruppe, probably over the Mediterranean. The rudder markings are said to have denoted the number of minesweeping sorties flown – a somewhat hazardous task.

year, when six German divisions were trapped at Demyansk, the Luftwaffe performed the prodigious task of sustaining 100,000 troops, and in three months delivered 22045 tonnes (24,300 tons) of materiel, airlifted 15,446 men into the pocket and evacuated 20,093 casualties; the cost of this effort was a loss of 385 flying personnel (including Major Walter Hammer, commanding KGrzbV 172) and 262 aircraft. Far greater disasters befell the German armies at Stalingrad and in North Africa, and in a single raid on Sverevo in the dreadful winter of 1942-43, 52 Junkers were destroyed by Russian bombers. In the final attempts to assist (and eventually to evacuate) the Axis armies in Tunisia in April 1943, the Luftwaffe lost 432 transport aircraft, almost all of them Ju 52/3ms, in less than three weeks.

The story of 'Tante Ju' did not end on VE-Day, when fewer than 50 such aircraft remained airworthy of the 4,835 said to have been built in Germany. The principal post-war operator of the aircraft was France, where Ateliers Aéronautiques de Colombes produced more than 400 examples of a version known as the **AAC 1 Toucan**; apart from 85 which flew post-war services for Air France, others were operated by Aero-Cargo, Air Atlas, Aigle Azur, Air Nolis, Air Ocean, TAI and many other airlines. The Toucan served with the Armée de l'Air and Aéronavale, and was used in fairly large numbers in the Algerian and Indo-China wars. In Spain, CASA produced 170 aircraft, known as the **C-352-L**, with licence-built BMW 132 radials. Ten aircraft were reconditioned by Short Bros and Harland at Belfast, and entered service on 18 November 1946 with British European Airways as G-AHOC to G-AHOL on the Croydon-Liverpool-Belfast service. In Switzerland, three Ju 52/3mg4e transports that were originally delivered to the Swiss Fliegertruppe on 4 October 1939 were still flying with the air force until the early 1980s.

In common with most of Germany's successful wartime aircraft, the Ju 52/3m underwent extensive development, resulting in the appearance of the Ju 252 and Ju 352 (see separate entries). The former, whose prototype first flew in October 1941, was a larger aircraft than the Ju 52/3m, powered by three 1000-kW (1,340-hp) Junkers Jumo 211F liquid-cooled engines in annular cowlings, and had accommodation for 21 passengers in a pressurised cabin; the corrugated skinning was dispensed with. Originally it was intended to produce 25 aircraft for Lufthansa but, in view of the deteriorating war situation, the order was reduced to 15, and all were delivered to the Luftwaffe. Some Ju 252As served with Lufttransportstaffel 290 (later redesignated Transportstaffel 5). The marginally larger Junkers Ju 352 Herkules was first flown on 1 October 1943 and featured mixed wood and steel construction. Two prototypes and 10 pre-production aircraft were built, powered by three 746-kW (1,000-hp) Bramo 323R-2 radials. Armed with a dorsal 20-mm and two beam 13-mm (0.51-in) guns, the Ju 352 was intended as a military transport from the outset, but in the event only one specially formed unit (commanded by Major Gunther Mauss) used the aircraft in any numbers, almost exclusively on the Eastern Front. A total of 33 production Ju 352As was delivered between April and September 1944.

1 Starboard navigation light
2 Drooping aileron section of Junkers 'double wing'
3 Aileron hinge fairings
4 Control linkage
5 Underwing inspection panels
6 Corrugated wing skin
7 Aerial mast
8 Wing strut diagonal bracing
9 Starboard oil filler cap
10 House-flag mast
11 Starboard engine cowling (NACA cowling)
12 Junkers metal two-blade propeller
13 Centre BMW 132A radial engine (in Townend ring)
14 Exhaust
15 Filter intakes
16 Engine bearers
17 Bulkhead
18 Centre oil tank
19 Oil filler cap
20 Flat windscreen panels
21 Co-pilot's seat
22 Radio-operator's jump-seat
23 Pilot's seat
24 Control column
25 Rudder pedals
26 Raised cockpit floor level
27 Control linkage
28 Control lines
29 Port BMW 132A radial engine (in NACA cowling)

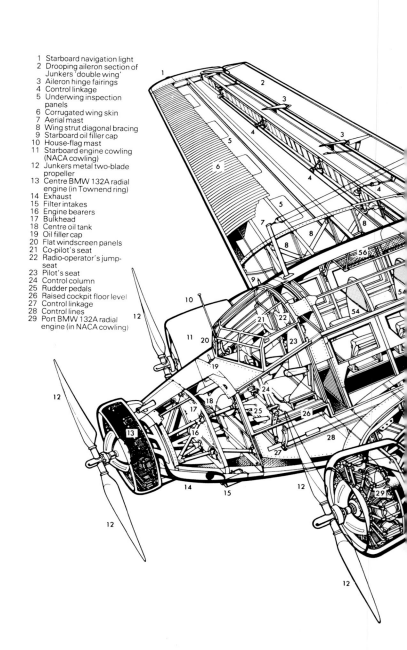

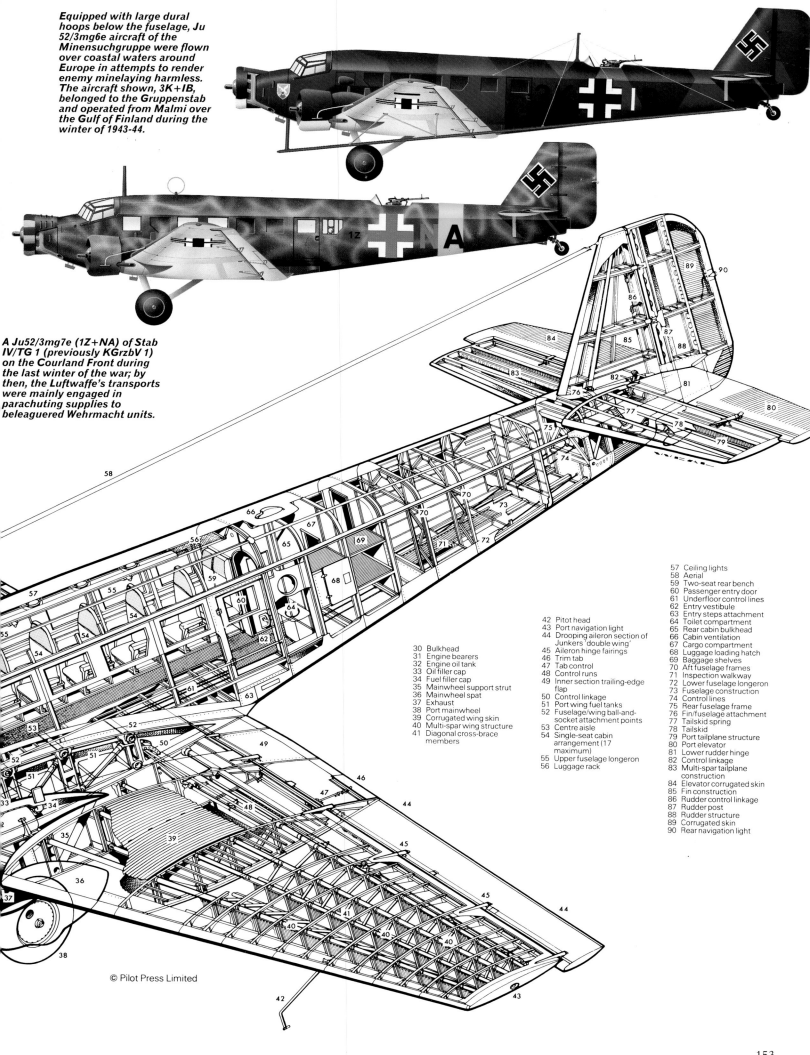

Equipped with large dural hoops below the fuselage, Ju 52/3mg6e aircraft of the Minensuchgruppe were flown over coastal waters around Europe in attempts to render enemy minelaying harmless. The aircraft shown, 3K+IB, belonged to the Gruppenstab and operated from Malmi over the Gulf of Finland during the winter of 1943-44.

A Ju52/3mg7e (1Z+NA) of Stab IV/TG 1 (previously KGrzbV 1) on the Courland Front during the last winter of the war; by then, the Luftwaffe's transports were mainly engaged in parachuting supplies to beleaguered Wehrmacht units.

© Pilot Press Limited

30 Bulkhead
31 Engine bearers
32 Engine oil tank
33 Oil filler cap
34 Fuel filler cap
35 Mainwheel support strut
36 Mainwheel spat
37 Exhaust
38 Port mainwheel
39 Corrugated wing skin
40 Multi-spar wing structure
41 Diagonal cross-brace members
42 Pitot head
43 Port navigation light
44 Drooping aileron section of Junkers 'double wing'
45 Aileron hinge fairings
46 Trim tab
47 Tab control
48 Control runs
49 Inner section trailing-edge flap
50 Control linkage
51 Port wing fuel tanks
52 Fuselage/wing ball-and-socket attachment points
53 Centre aisle
54 Single-seat cabin arrangement (17 maximum)
55 Upper fuselage longeron
56 Luggage rack
57 Ceiling lights
58 Aerial
59 Two-seat rear bench
60 Passenger entry door
61 Underfloor control lines
62 Entry vestibule
63 Entry steps attachment
64 Toilet compartment
65 Rear cabin bulkhead
66 Cabin ventilation
67 Cargo compartment
68 Luggage loading hatch
69 Baggage shelves
70 Aft fuselage frames
71 Inspection walkway
72 Lower fuselage longeron
73 Fuselage construction
74 Control lines
75 Rear fuselage frame
76 Fin/fuselage attachment
77 Tailskid spring
78 Tailskid
79 Port tailplane structure
80 Port elevator
81 Lower rudder hinge
82 Control linkage
83 Multi-spar tailplane construction
84 Elevator corrugated skin
85 Fin construction
86 Rudder control linkage
87 Rudder post
88 Rudder structure
89 Corrugated skin
90 Rear navigation light

Specification

Junkers Ju 52/3mg7e

Type: 18-seat military transport
Powerplant: three 619-kW (830-hp) BMW 132T-2 nine-cylinder air-cooled radial engines
Performance: maximum speed, at sea level 295 km/h (183 mph); initial rate of climb 208 m (680 ft) per minute; service ceiling 5500 m (18,045 m); range 1290 km (802 miles)
Weights: empty 6560 kg (14,462 lb); maximum take-off 10515 kg (23,180 lb)
Dimensions: span 29.25 m (95 ft 11½ in); length 18.80 m (62 ft); height 4.50 m (14 ft 9 in); wing area 110.50 m² (1,189.45 sq ft)
Armament: (typical) one 7.92-mm (0.31-in) MG 15 machine gun in dorsal position and two 7.92-mm (0.31-in) machine-guns mounted to fire abeam through the side windows

Defensive armament

A single 7.92-mm MG 15 machine-gun was fired from a dorsal hatch, the gun facing rearwards when not in use. To protect the gunner from the airstream, a transparent fairing was placed upstream of the hatch. Some aircraft had provision for beam guns, while the 3mg14e model introduced a gun above the cockpit.

Tail unit

Both tail and tailplane were built, like the wing, on a multi-spar structure. The elevators (and ailerons) featured distinctive balancing horns to lighten control forces.

Wing

A feature of Junkers designs of the period was the detached flap/aileron assembly positioned below and behind the main wing structure. The ailerons drooped at low speed to act as partial flaps which, together with the normal slotted inboard flaps, gave the type tremendous STOL capability. The entire wing could be detached from the fuselage and was attached by eight ball-and-socket joints.

Undercarriage

The Ju 52/3m had a fixed undercarriage of immense strength, although its narrow track made it prone to bouncing from side to side. The 3mg5e version had provisions for wheel, ski or even float undercarriage to match the operational environment in which it found itself. Early Ju 52/3ms had a tailskid but, due to the poor nature of Germany's military airfields, a tailwheel was introduced from the 3mg4e onwards. This greatly improved manoeuvrability on the ground. The Ju 52/3m was factory-fitted with large spats to streamline the mainwheels, but in the operational environment most of these were removed, as they rapidly clogged with sand or mud.

Operational use

Obsolete in its intended bomber role by the time World War II began, and anachronistic even as a transport, the Ju 52/3m's reliability, ruggedness and easy handling nevertheless inspired tremendous affection among its crews and the troops who so often depended on it for the safe delivery of supplies and mail. After the war, many were taken over and used by the victorious Allies.

Cabin

When fitted with seats, the Ju 52/3m could carry up to 18 passengers, with two rows of single seats separated by a single aisle. By removing the seats, the cabin could hold a surprising amount of cargo. Entry to the cabin was made through a door on the port side. This could be opened in flight to permit para-dropping of either supplies or troops. On the starboard side was a large cargo loading door, with upward- and downward-hinging flaps. The space behind the cabin door was often used for cargo storage or provided the stand for the gunner. Behind the gunner, an inspection tunnel with reinforced floor-way provided access to the control linkages under the tail. The Ju 52 was originally envisaged as a bomber/transport, carrying weapons in two internal bays. As such, it was used during the Spanish Civil War, while transport Ju 52/3ms were later used as bombers by the French in Indo-China. World War II Luftwaffe use was largely restricted to the transport role, but until 1943 the Ju 52 units retained their KGrzbV appellation, this standing for Kampfgruppe zur besonderen Verwendung, or 'bomber wing for special purposes'. The large aerial above the cockpit was a mast for the single wire aerial which ran to the tail. Behind it, a loop aerial served the direction-finding equipment.

Corrugations

The Ju 52/3m was an all-metal aircraft, covered mainly with corrugated duralumin skinning. The skin was load-bearing, and the corrugations gave it immense strength for little weight penalty. Corrugation was a feature of many early Junkers designs.

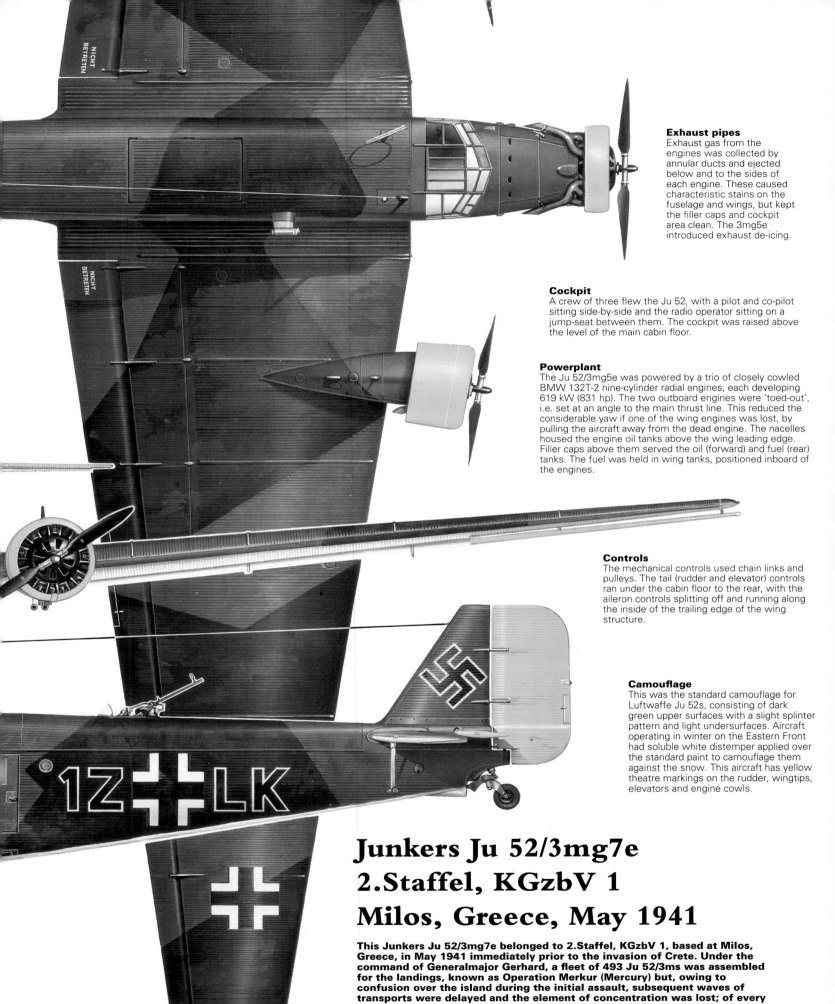

Exhaust pipes
Exhaust gas from the engines was collected by annular ducts and ejected below and to the sides of each engine. These caused characteristic stains on the fuselage and wings, but kept the filler caps and cockpit area clean. The 3mg5e introduced exhaust de-icing.

Cockpit
A crew of three flew the Ju 52, with a pilot and co-pilot sitting side-by-side and the radio operator sitting on a jump-seat between them. The cockpit was raised above the level of the main cabin floor.

Powerplant
The Ju 52/3mg5e was powered by a trio of closely cowled BMW 132T-2 nine-cylinder radial engines, each developing 619 kW (831 hp). The two outboard engines were 'toed-out', i.e. set at an angle to the main thrust line. This reduced the considerable yaw if one of the wing engines was lost, by pulling the aircraft away from the dead engine. The nacelles housed the engine oil tanks above the wing leading edge. Filler caps above them served the oil (forward) and fuel (rear) tanks. The fuel was held in wing tanks, positioned inboard of the engines.

Controls
The mechanical controls used chain links and pulleys. The tail (rudder and elevator) controls ran under the cabin floor to the rear, with the aileron controls splitting off and running along the inside of the trailing edge of the wing structure.

Camouflage
This was the standard camouflage for Luftwaffe Ju 52s, consisting of dark green upper surfaces with a slight splinter pattern and light undersurfaces. Aircraft operating in winter on the Eastern Front had soluble white distemper applied over the standard paint to camouflage them against the snow. This aircraft has yellow theatre markings on the rudder, wingtips, elevators and engine cowls.

Junkers Ju 52/3mg7e
2.Staffel, KGzbV 1
Milos, Greece, May 1941

This Junkers Ju 52/3mg7e belonged to 2.Staffel, KGzbV 1, based at Milos, Greece, in May 1941 immediately prior to the invasion of Crete. Under the command of Generalmajor Gerhard, a fleet of 493 Ju 52/3ms was assembled for the landings, known as Operation Merkur (Mercury) but, owing to confusion over the island during the initial assault, subsequent waves of transports were delayed and the element of concentration was lost; of every four paratroopers dropped or landed by glider or Ju 52, one was killed or wounded. By the end of the operation, more than 170 Ju 52/3ms had been lost or seriously damaged. The Fallschirmjäger captured Crete, but it was a somewhat Pyrrhic victory, since the German paratroops were never again able to mount a major airborne operation, so heavy were their losses.

Junkers Ju 86

Right: The Ju 86 V5 was the production prototype for the Ju 86A bomber.

In 1934 a specification was issued to both Heinkel and Junkers to produce an aircraft that would fill the roles of high-speed airliner for Luft Hansa, and medium bomber for the still-secret Luftwaffe. Heinkel produced the He 111, while Junkers designed the **Ju 86**. Discarding previous Junkers construction techniques, the Ju 86 was a sleek monoplane with oval-section fuselage, although it still bore the hallmark 'double-wing' flap and aileron configuration.

First flying on 4 November 1934 at Dessau, the **Ju 86ab1** prototype was powered by two Siemens SAM 22 radials, and was in bomber configuration. A dorsal open gun position was added, as was a ventral 'dustbin' for lower hemisphere defence. It was followed by the **Ju 86cb**, which introduced glazed panels for the bombardier and a nose gun turret. It was re-engined in March 1935 with the intended Jumo 205C diesel engine. The third aircraft was a Jumo 205-powered airliner prototype, the **Ju 86ba1**, which led to the **Ju 86B** and **Ju 86C** airliners.

Bomber development continued with the **Ju 86 V5** with a modified wing to cure some of the early prototypes' undesirable handling characteristics, and this was considered the production forerunner for the **Ju 86A** bomber. Thirteen **Ju 86A-0** aircraft were delivered to the Luftwaffe for evaluation from February 1936, closely followed by the **Ju 86A-1**, which formed the initial equipment of KG 152 (later KG 1) 'Hindenburg'. The bomber carried a crew of four and had a warload of eight SC 100 bombs. It was supplanted on the Dessau production line by the **Ju 86D-1**, which cured a directional stability problem by replacing the short tailcone of the A-1 with a wedge-shaped extension that projected beyond the tailplane trailing edge.

Many nations purchased Ju 86 bombers, but most specified radial engines. Sweden bought **Ju 86K**s with Pratt & Whitney Hornet or Bristol Pegasus radials, while Portugal and Chile opted for the US engine for their Ju 86Ks. Hungary's aircraft were powered by the Gnome-Rhône, and went on to serve as bombers in World War II until 1942. The civil version was exported as the **Ju 86Z**, one recipient being South Africa, which modified its **Ju 86Z-7** aircraft as reconnaissance bombers and used them on maritime patrols and bombing sorties, including action against German ships.

In Luftwaffe service, the Ju 86A and D were proving somewhat unreliable, and also inferior in most respects to the rival He 111B. Junkers was ordered to modify the aircraft to take the BMW 132F radial, the resulting aircraft being designated **Ju 86E-1**. These were delivered from the summer of 1937, and were a considerable improvement over the diesel-powered aircraft. The **Ju 86E-2** introduced the more powerful BMW 132N.

One further criticism of the bomber was the appalling view offered to the pilot during taxiing and take-off until the tailwheel left the ground. Accordingly, Junkers designed a completely new front end, with the cockpit moved forward and the nose glazing given a rounded profile, to rectify the problem. This was the **Ju 86G-1**, and was delivered during 1938. Total production of all variants reached 390.

During the course of 1939, the Ju 86 was completely phased out of front-line service. Only IV/KG 1 (and possibly III(K)/LG 1) remained with the type at the beginning of the Polish campaign, and these had re-equipped before the dust settled. The diesel-engined Ju 86As and Ds were retired, while the BMW-engined Ju 86Es and Gs were issued to bomber training schools. With these units they performed sterling work, but many were lost at the hands of inexperienced young pilots and numbers dwindled.

Although the Ju 86 had largely disappeared from front-line Luftwaffe service at the outbreak of World War II, the type was destined to play a part in the conflict as a high-altitude bomber and

A Kette of Ju 86A-1s shortly after delivery to the Luftwaffe in 1936. The Jumo-powered A and D series had a short service life, mostly being retired by 1939.

reconnaissance platform. Junkers had continued development of the diesel engine after it had been discarded as a bomber powerplant, and had derived the Jumo 207 high-altitude engine, with two centrifugal superchargers working in series. The company had also been testing cabin pressurisation systems. In September 1939 it suggested to the RLM that a high-altitude version of the Ju 86 be produced, and three prototypes were ordered immediately.

High-altitude developments

Initially designated **Ju 86H**, the variant emerged as the **Ju 86P**. Using a Ju 86D fuselage, Junkers added a new two-man pressurised cabin, which could maintain a cabin pressure equivalent to that at 3000 m (9,840 ft). The system was driven by tapping the port engine supercharger, and the cabin utilised Plexiglas dry-air sandwich panes. Access for the crew was through a circular hatch in the lower starboard underside. The prototype **Ju 86P V1** flew in February 1940, the **V2** following in March, and both proved capable of reaching over 10000 m (32,800 ft) on the power of the Jumo 207A-1 diesel engines. The **V3** introduced increased-span outer wing panels to gain yet more altitude, this aircraft being able to hold altitude above 11000 m (36,000 ft) for over 2½ hours.

Forty conversions were immediately ordered, consisting of two variants. The **Ju 86P-1** was a bomber, with two vertical bomb cells in the fuselage and small bay doors in the centre-section, while the **Ju 86P-2** was a reconnaissance platform, with cameras in place of the bomb bays. In the summer of 1940 one of the prototypes was delivered to the Aufklärungsgruppe Oberbefehlshaber der Luftwaffe, and immediately performed a reconnaissance mission over Britain during which it attained 12500 m (41,000 ft) and remained undetected.

Left: The Ju 86G-1 was the only version left operational at the start of World War II.

Above: The Ju 86P V1 was the first high-altitude aircraft, but retained the original wing span.

BMW 132-powered Ju 86E-2s served the bomber training schools from 1939 to late 1942, when the survivors were rounded up and sent to provide emergency transport cover on the Eastern Front during the airlift into Stalingrad. Fifty-eight aircraft were deployed: 42 were lost in two months.

Additional missions were undertaken by 2./AufklGr.Ob.d.L., including flights over the Home Fleet anchorage at Scapa Flow. In January 1941, 4./AufklGr.Ob.d.L. (also known as the Versuchsstelle für Höhenfluge - high-altitude test centre) received the type, and undertook sporadic bombing missions over the UK from August 1941. In January 1942 the Ju 86 unit had been redesignated 1./Versuchsverband Ob.d.L., and a handful of Ju 86P-2s were deployed to Crete for operations by 2.(F)/AufklGr 123.

Often seen by patrolling fighters, the Ju 86s proved immune to interception until 24 August 1942, when a specially-stripped Spitfire Mk V clawed its way up from its Aboukir (Egypt) base to shoot down a Ju 86P at 12800 m (42,000 ft) to the north of Cairo. 'Respect' armament in the form of a single aft-firing MG 17 was immediately fitted, but two more Ju 86Ps were shot down by Aboukir Spitfires, and 2.(F)/AufklGr 123 ended its Ju 86 days in August 1943. Back over England, the Ju 86P raids, often dropping just single bombs on a variety of targets, were a considerable thorn in the side of Fighter Command and much effort was expended to stop them. The hastily-modified Spitfire Mk VI, with a pressurised cabin and extended-span wings, waited to intercept the raiders, but despite several attempts none was caught, a Spitfire on one occasion stalling when it tried to fire its guns at the raider still above it. One Ju 86P dived from 12200 m (40,000 ft) to just 150 m (500 ft) to escape the attentions of a Spitfire. The last of 12 bombing missions over Britain was flown on 9 September 1942.

In early 1942 Junkers had realised that the Allies would soon develop an interceptor which could easily reach the Ju 86P, and flew the first **Ju 86R** in mid-1942. This variant was converted from the Ju 86P and had more powerful Jumo 207B-3 engines (with nitrous oxide boosting) and wing span increased to an incredible 32.00 m (104 ft 11¾ in). This gave a ceiling of 14400 m (47,250 ft), and extra fuel provided an endurance of over seven hours. Conversions from Ju 86Ps confusingly reversed the suffix digit, producing the **Ju 86R-1** reconnaissance aircraft and the **Ju 86R-2** bomber. A few Ju 86R-1s were delivered to 1./Versuchsverband Ob.d.L., which flew a number of missions until mid-1944. Three Ju 86R-2s were delivered to 14./KG 6 in the Netherlands in September 1942, but the unit was disbanded in October. Planned variants were the **Ju 86R-3**, to have been powered by the Jumo 208 for even greater altitude, and the **Ju 186** research aircraft which would have featured four engines.

The service career of the elderly Junkers bomber did not end with the high-altitude flights, for 58 Ju 86Es and Gs were hauled out of the bomber schools to form two emergency transport units, Kampfgruppe zur besondere Verwendungen 21 and 22. These were hurriedly thrown into the airlift to supply the cut-off troops of the Fourth Panzer and Sixth Armies at Stalingrad. In less than two months, 42 of the aircraft had been lost and the units were disbanded. The 16 survivors returned to training bomber crews, but in early 1944 a few were used operationally once again to attack partisans in the Balkans.

Above: Close-up detail reveals the bomb bay doors of the Ju 86P-1. Up to 16 bombs could be carried vertically.

Above: The Ju 86P-2 was the reconnaissance model, and had flat-pane windows for cameras in the lower fuselage.

One of the Ju 86P-1 raiders used by 4./Aufkl.Ob.d.L. over Britain; little success was achieved, but Fighter Command resources were diverted.

Specification
Junkers Ju 86P-1
Type: two-seat high-altitude bomber
Powerplant: two Junkers Jumo 207A-1 six-cylinder diesel engines, each rated at 712 kW (950 hp) for take-off and 510 kW (680 hp) at 9753 m (32,000 ft)
Performance: maximum speed 360 m (224 mph) at 6000 m (19,685 ft), 300 km/h (186 mph) at 12000 m (39,370 ft); long-range cruising speed 260 km/h (161 mph) at 11000 m (36,090 ft); service ceiling 12000 m (39,370 ft); range 1040 km (645 miles)
Weights: empty 7000 kg (15,432 lb); maximum loaded 10156 kg (22,390 lb)
Dimensions: wing span 25.6 m (83 ft 11¾ in); length 16.5 m (54 ft 0 in); height 4.1 m (13 ft 4½ in)
Armament: one remotely-controlled aft-firing 7.9-mm (0.31-in) MG 17 in rear fuselage; four 250-kg (551-lb) bombs or 16 50-kg (110-lb) bombs in centre-section vertically-stacked bomb bays

The Ju 86R-1 featured an even greater wing span, enabling it to add another 2200 m (7,200 ft) to the already impressive ceiling of the Ju 86P. A few R-1s were used on reconnaissance missions by the Versuchsverband Ob.d.L., but little is known of their service or ultimate fate. It appears that the Ju 86R-2 bomber conversion was not used during the conflict.

'Trumpets of Jericho' sirens were fitted to the Ju 87's landing gear spats to generate the Stuka's terrifying scream as it dived down towards the target. Here a single SC 250 (250-kg/551-lb) bomb and four smaller 50-kg (110-lb) SC 50s drop away as the aircraft begins its 6 g pullout. Entry into the dive and the pullout were completely automatic, leaving the pilot with the task of steering the aircraft in the dive to put his bombsight reticule over the target.

Junkers Ju 87

Few aircraft have ever caused such terror, to seasoned troops and helpless civilians alike, as the ugly **Junkers Ju 87** dive-bomber. Widely known as the 'Stuka', from the German word for a dive-bomber (Sturzkampfflugzeug), the Ju 87 also sank more ships than any other type of aircraft in history, and possibly destroyed more tanks than any other aircraft except the Soviet Ilyushin Il-2. Its stock-in-trade was the accurate placement of heavy bombs on point targets, and this it could do supremely well – provided it was not molested by fighters.

Thus, in the first year of World War II, it acquired a reputation that was almost legendary. In the Battle of Britain its bubble of invincibility was burst for ever, and for the rest of the war it went steadily downhill until it was reduced to skulking just above the ground on dark nights, with the conspicuous exception of one *Gruppe* led by a man who personally flew 2,530 combat missions and continued to fly on the Eastern Front in daylight until the final German collapse.

The technique of dive-bombing was familiar in World War I, but no aircraft designed for the job existed until the 1920s. One of the first was the Junkers K 47, of which two were flown in 1928 with Jupiter engines, and 12 with Pratt & Whitney Hornet engines were sold to China. These did extensive research, and demonstrated that a 90° dive is the most accurate. In turn, this demands a strong aircraft and a resolute pilot, as well as an indicator of dive angle (60° feels like almost 90°). Many who later were to head Hitler's Luftwaffe became convinced that the dive-bomber had to be a central weapon in an air force dedicated to close support of ground forces. When plans could be made for new combat aircraft for the Luftwaffe, in 1933, the immediate need was ultimately met by a trim biplane, the Henschel Hs 123, while Junkers worked on the definitive Stuka. The design staff under Hermann Pohlmann adopted the same configuration as that of the K 47: a single-engined low-wing monoplane with prominent fixed landing gear and twin fins and rudders. The Ju 87 differed in having an all-metal stressed-skin structure, without the corrugated skin previously used on Junkers all-metal aircraft, and a cranked wing of so-called inverted-gull form. Like that of the K 47, the entire trailing

Armourers load a Ju 87B-1 for cameramen from the propaganda magazine Signal. *This colourfully decorated Stuka almost certainly received its garish decoration specifically for the photographers' benefit, and the unit involved remains unidentified. Ju 87B-1s of 3./StG1 opened the attacks on Poland on 1 September 1939. Nine* Gruppen *(wings) were committed to the attack on Poland, with 336 aircraft. Thirty-one Stukas were lost in the campaign, reflecting the absence of fighter opposition. Stukas most often operated in* Ketten *of three aircraft.*

Below: A gaggle of more than a dozen Ju-87B-2s (some of them from 7./StG 77) returns to base after a successful dive-bombing mission against British ships during the long, bloody battle for the island of Crete. The battles of France and Britain had shown the Ju 87 to be exceptionally vulnerable to fighter opposition, but the type continued to perform useful service in the Mediterranean and on the Eastern Front.

Use of the Ju 87 by the Italian Regia Aeronautica gave rise to the incorrect belief it was made in Italy as the Breda 201. This Ju 87B-2 was based at Gars el Arid in September 1941 with the 209ª Squadriglia, 101° Gruppo Autonomo (independent group). This unit painted its emblem on the wheel spats.

Seen in temporary white finish for the winter of 1941-42, this Ju 87B-2 also wears the yellow theatre band which by that time was becoming standard on the Eastern Front. It flew with Stab II/StG 1 (originally III/StG 51), whose unit emblem was painted on the cowling. The projection from the main leg is the siren.

edge was occupied by patented double-wing flaps and ailerons, and the crew of two sat back-to-back under a large glazed canopy. The prototype flew in the spring of 1935 with a 477-kW (640-hp) Rolls-Royce Kestrel engine. Dive-brakes were then added under the outer wings, but on one of the first pullouts the tail collapsed and the air-craft crashed.

Full-scale production

After much further development (in the course of which the engine was changed to the intended German unit, the 447-kW (640-hp) Junkers Jumo 210Ca driving a three-bladed variable-pitch pro-peller), a new single-fin tail was adopted, and the **Ju 87A-1** entered full-scale production in early 1937. About 200 of the **A-0**, **A-1** and **A-2** series were built, all with large trouser fairings over the landing gears, and the A-2 with the 507-kW (680-hp) Jumo 210Da and an improved VDM propeller. They equipped four *Gruppen*, of which StG 163 sent three aircraft to see action with the Légion Condor in Spain, where the type proved outstandingly effective.

In 1939 all A-series aircraft were transferred to training units, and the swelling ranks of Stukageschwader (dive-bomber wings) were equipped with the much more capable **Ju 87B**. Visually this differed in having neater spats over the main wheels, but the chief difference was that it had double the power, in the form of the new Jumo 211A, driving a broad-bladed constant-speed propeller. The full production sub-type, the **Ju 87B-1**, had the 895-kW (1,200-hp) Jumo 211Da with a direct-injection fuel system giving immunity from icing, or engine-cuts in inverted flight, or negative-*g* manoeuvres (the Ju 87 could perform all normal aerobatics). Another important feature was an automatic dive-control, set by the pilot to a chosen pullout height

Seen over the central sector of the Eastern Front in the summer of 1942, this Ju 87D-1 served with the Gruppenstab, II Gruppe, Stukageschwader 2 'Immelmann'. Most of this unit's aircraft wore nose art. Note the fuselage leg-mounted siren.

1 Spinner
2 Pitch-change mechanism housing
3 Blade hub
4 Junkers VS 11 constant-speed airscrew
5 Anti-vibration engine mounting attachments
6 Oil filler point and marker
7 Auxiliary oil tank (5.9 Imp gal/26.8 litre capacity)
8 Junkers Jumo 211J-1 12-cylinder inverted-vee liquid cooled engine
9 Magnesium alloy forged engine mount
10 Coolant (Glysantin-water) header tank
11 Ejector exhaust stubs
12 Fuel injection unit housing
13 Induction air cooler
14 Armoured radiator
15 Inertia starter cranking point
16 Ball joint bulkhead fixing (lower)
17 Tubular steel mount support strut
18 Ventral armour (8 mm)
19 Main oil tank (9.9 Imp gal/45 litre capacity)
20 Oil filling point
21 Transverse support frame
22 Rudder pedals
23 Control column
24 Heating point
25 Auxiliary air intake
26 Ball joint bulkhead fixing (upper)
27 Bulkhead
28 Oil tank (6.8 Imp gal/31 litre capacity)
29 Oil filler point and marker (Intava 100)
30 Fuel filler cap
31 Self-sealing starboard outer fuel tank (33 Imp gal/150 litre capacity)
32 Underwing bombs with *Dienartstab* percussion rods
33 Pitot head
34 Spherical oxygen bottles
35 Wing skinning
36 Starboard navigation light
37 Aileron mass balance
38 'Double wing' aileron and flap (starboard outer)
39 Aileron hinge
40 Corrugated wing rib station
41 Reinforced armoured windscreen
42 Reflector sight
43 Padded crash bar

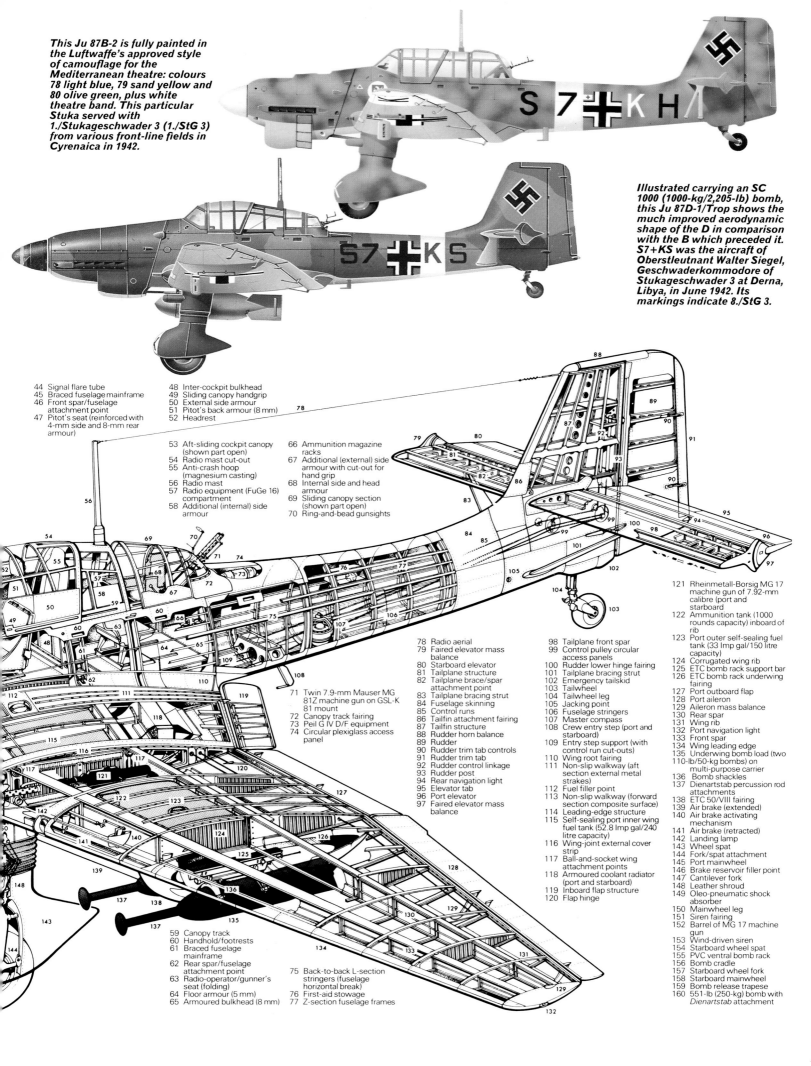

This Ju 87B-2 is fully painted in the Luftwaffe's approved style of camouflage for the Mediterranean theatre: colours 78 light blue, 79 sand yellow and 80 olive green, plus white theatre band. This particular Stuka served with 1./Stukageschwader 3 (1./StG 3) from various front-line fields in Cyrenaica in 1942.

Illustrated carrying an SC 1000 (1000-kg/2,205-lb) bomb, this Ju 87D-1/Trop shows the much improved aerodynamic shape of the D in comparison with the B which preceded it. S7+KS was the aircraft of Oberstleutnant Walter Siegel, Geschwaderkommodore of Stukageschwader 3 at Derna, Libya, in June 1942. Its markings indicate 8./StG 3.

44 Signal flare tube
45 Braced fuselage mainframe
46 Front spar/fuselage attachment point
47 Pilot's seat (reinforced with 4-mm side and 8-mm rear armour)
48 Inter-cockpit bulkhead
49 Sliding canopy handgrip
50 External side armour
51 Pilot's back armour (8 mm)
52 Headrest
53 Aft-sliding cockpit canopy (shown part open)
54 Radio mast cut-out
55 Anti-crash hoop (magnesium casting)
56 Radio mast
57 Radio equipment (FuGe 16) compartment
58 Additional (internal) side armour
59 Canopy track
60 Handhold/footrests
61 Braced fuselage mainframe
62 Rear spar/fuselage attachment point
63 Radio-operator/gunner's seat (folding)
64 Floor armour (5 mm)
65 Armoured bulkhead (8 mm)
66 Ammunition magazine racks
67 Additional (external) side armour with cut-out for hand grip
68 Internal side and head armour
69 Sliding canopy section (shown part open)
70 Ring-and-bead gunsights
71 Twin 7.9-mm Mauser MG 81Z machine gun on GSL-K 81 mount
72 Canopy track fairing
73 Peil G IV D/F equipment
74 Circular plexiglass access panel
75 Back-to-back L-section stringers (fuselage horizontal break)
76 First-aid stowage
77 Z-section fuselage frames
78 Radio aerial
79 Faired elevator mass balance
80 Starboard elevator
81 Tailplane structure
82 Tailplane brace/spar attachment point
83 Tailplane bracing strut
84 Fuselage skinning
85 Control runs
86 Tailfin attachment fairing
87 Tailfin structure
88 Rudder horn balance
89 Rudder
90 Rudder trim tab controls
91 Rudder trim tab
92 Rudder control linkage
93 Rudder post
94 Rear navigation light
95 Elevator tab
96 Port elevator
97 Faired elevator mass balance
98 Tailplane front spar
99 Control pulley circular access panels
100 Rudder lower hinge fairing
101 Tailplane bracing strut
102 Emergency tailskid
103 Tailwheel
104 Tailwheel leg
105 Jacking point
106 Fuselage stringers
107 Master compass
108 Crew entry step (port and starboard)
109 Entry step support (with control run cut-offs)
110 Wing root fairing
111 Non-slip walkway (aft section external metal strakes)
112 Fuel filler point
113 Non-slip walkway (forward section composite surface)
114 Leading-edge structure
115 Self-sealing port inner wing fuel tank (52.8 Imp gal/240 litre capacity)
116 Wing-joint external cover strip
117 Ball-and-socket wing attachment points
118 Armoured coolant radiator (port and starboard)
119 Inboard flap structure
120 Flap hinge
121 Rheinmetall-Borsig MG 17 machine gun of 7.92-mm calibre (port and starboard)
122 Ammunition tank (1000 rounds capacity) inboard of rib
123 Port outer self-sealing fuel tank (33 Imp gal/150 litre capacity)
124 Corrugated wing rib
125 ETC bomb rack support bar
126 ETC bomb rack underwing fairing
127 Port outboard flap
128 Port aileron
129 Aileron mass balance
130 Rear spar
131 Wing rib
132 Port navigation light
133 Front spar
134 Wing leading edge
135 Underwing bomb load (two 110-lb/50-kg bombs) on multi-purpose carrier
136 Bomb shackles
137 Dienartstab percussion rod attachments
138 ETC 50/VIII fairing
139 Air brake (extended)
140 Air brake activating mechanism
141 Air brake (retracted)
142 Landing lamp
143 Wheel spat
144 Fork/spat attachment
145 Port mainwheel
146 Brake reservoir filler point
147 Cantilever fork
148 Leather shroud
149 Oleo-pneumatic shock absorber
150 Mainwheel leg
151 Siren fairing
152 Barrel of MG 17 machine gun
153 Wind-driven siren
154 Starboard wheel spat
155 PVC ventral bomb rack
156 Bomb cradle
157 Starboard wheel fork
158 Starboard mainwheel
159 Bomb release trapese
160 551-lb (250-kg) bomb with Dienartstab attachment

Weather-beaten Ju 87B-2s of II/StG 1 on the Eastern Front, probably in autumn 1941. Nine more Ju 87s are in the distance at lower level. These aircraft are probably returning from a combat mission, with bomb racks empty. Spats were still in use at this time, and opposition to the Stuka was still generally feeble.

The Ju 87D-5 introduced a wing of greater span to allow the heavy weapon loads to be carried with a better margin of safety. This D-5 was photographed on final landing approach, with full flap, on return from a mission with 8./StG 2 in the Kursk area in the summer of 1943. Its code was T6+AS, T6 being that of StG 2 itself.

on a contact altimeter. Having gone through a list of 10 vital actions, the pilot opened the underwing dive-brakes, which automatically set up the dive, the pilot adjusting the angle manually by lining up the visual horizon with red lines painted at various angles on the canopy. The pilot then aimed at the target manually as in a fighter, using aileron alone to achieve the correct bomb line. Often the angle was 90°, the dive being entered in a wing-over from directly above the target.

Curiously, the Ju 87 was the one aircraft in which 90° did not feel like an over-the-vertical bunt; indeed, it seemed more at home in its

rock-steady dive than in normal cruising flight, when its vulnerability (accentuated by the transparent canopy down to elbow-level) was all too evident. When a signal light on the contact altimeter came on, the pilot pressed a knob on top of the control column for the pullout at 6 *g* to happen by itself, with usual terrain clearance of 450 m (1,476 ft). If it did not, the pilot had to haul back with all his strength, assisted by very careful use of elevator trimmer.

The usual load on the Ju 87B series was an SC 500 (500-kg/1,102-lb) bomb on crutches that swung out from the belly to let go of the

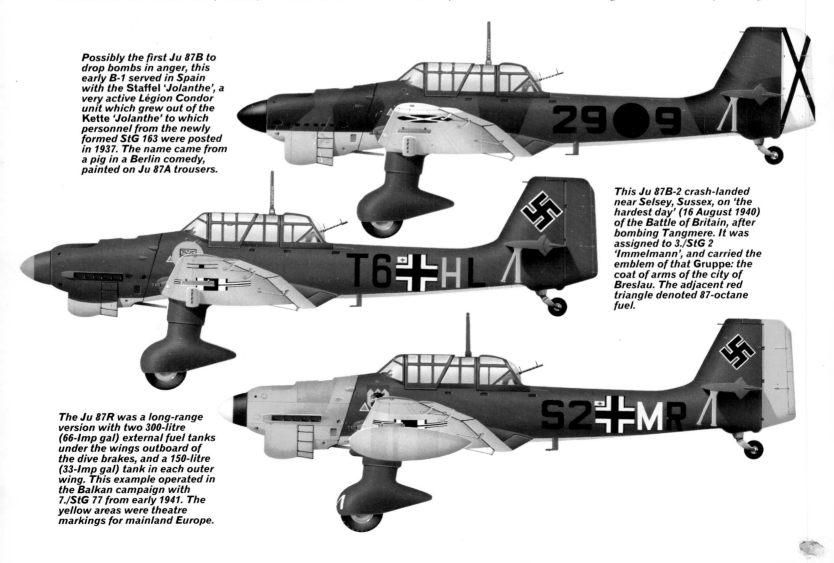

Possibly the first Ju 87B to drop bombs in anger, this early B-1 served in Spain with the Staffel 'Jolanthe', a very active Légion Condor unit which grew out of the Kette 'Jolanthe' to which personnel from the newly formed StG 163 were posted in 1937. The name came from a pig in a Berlin comedy, painted on Ju 87A trousers.

This Ju 87B-2 crash-landed near Selsey, Sussex, on 'the hardest day' (16 August 1940) of the Battle of Britain, after bombing Tangmere. It was assigned to 3./StG 2 'Immelmann', and carried the emblem of that Gruppe: the coat of arms of the city of Breslau. The adjacent red triangle denoted 87-octane fuel.

The Ju 87R was a long-range version with two 300-litre (66-Imp gal) external fuel tanks under the wings outboard of the dive brakes, and a 150-litre (33-Imp gal) tank in each outer wing. This example operated in the Balkan campaign with 7./StG 77 from early 1941. The yellow areas were theatre markings for mainland Europe.

Even more cumbersome and vulnerable than previous variants, the anti-tank Ju 87G-1 nevertheless proved extremely effective in the hands of an expert. This early example is seen in the markings of the Versuchskommando fur Panzerbekampfung (test commando for anti-armour warfare) in April 1943; note the Kommando tank emblem.

bomb well away from the propeller. Speed built up to about 550 km/h (342 mph), and it became common practice to fit sirens – called 'Trumpets of Jericho' – to the landing gears to strike extra terror into people near the target. Over short ranges, four SC 50 (50-kg/110-lb) bombs could also be hung under the wings. The pilot could fire two 7.92-mm (0.31-in) MG 17 guns mounted in the wings outboard of the kink, while the radio operator had an MG 15 of the same calibre to give protection above and behind. Production was transferred from Dessau to Weser Flugzeugbau in the great oval building at Berlin-Tempelhof airport, where it built up to 60 a month by mid-1939. Three B-1s made the first combat mission of World War II when they took off from Elbing at 04.26 on 1 September 1939 and devastated the approaches to the Dirschau bridge over the Vistula at 04.34, some 11 minutes before the Nazis declared war on Poland. Subsequently, the Ju 87B-1 played a tremendous part in the Polish campaign, destroying all but two of the Polish surface warships, heavily bombing Polish troops (on many occasions within 100 m/330 ft of advancing German forces), and on one ghastly occasion virtually wiping out an entire Polish infantry division at Piotrkow railway station.

Carrierborne variant

Alongside the improved **Ju 87B-2** variants, which as single-seaters could carry an SC 1000 (1000-kg/2,205-lb) bomb, Weser built a batch of **Ju 87C-0**s with folding wings, hooks and many other changes to suit them for use aboard the carrier *Graf Zeppelin*, which was never completed. Another derived model was the extended-range **Ju 87R** series, with extra tanks in the outer wings and provision for under-wing drop tanks. They entered service in time for the Norwegian campaign – where one put a radio station off the air by ramming the aerials – and then proved useful in the Balkans, Greece and Mediterranean theatres. One Ju 87R tested a large container, hung on the main bomb crutch, intended to carry spares and other cargo.

The Ju 87B and derivatives wrought havoc throughout Europe in the first two years of World War II, meeting only one serious setback. Over England its losses were unacceptably heavy, 41 being shot down in the period 13-18 August 1940, so that from 19 August Stukas were withdrawn from attacks against UK targets. The type had already shown that, with German air supremacy, it could knock out the vital British coastal radars; however, it was those same radars that enabled

the defending fighters unfailingly to intercept, and the vulnerability of the Ju 87 was suddenly apparent. The aircraft had been designed on the basis of good fighter protection, and in such conditions it had demonstrated such devastating effectiveness that many in the UK – foot-soldiers, journalists and politicians alike – cried, "Where are our dive-bombers?" In fact, the country had dive-bombers, such as the Blackburn Skua and Hawker Henley, but they played little part in the war, and the whole concept of the dive-bomber became a subject of violent argument.

A continuous record

Even at the outbreak of war, the Ju 87 was recognised as a some-what dated design, but this was masked by its fantastic successes. As with so many other old Luftwaffe types, lack of a replacement resulted in planned termination of production being countermanded and, like that of the Messerschmitt Bf 110 and He 111, Ju 87 output increased from 1941 to 1944. The standard basic type throughout this period was the **Ju 87D**, designed in 1940, first flown in early 1941 and in action on the Eastern and North African Fronts by the end of 1941. The D was powered by the 1044-kW (1,400-hp) Jumo 211J-1 driving a VS 11 propeller with very broad blades, making a major difference to flight performance; this was put to use in carrying much heavier loads. Maximum bomb load rose to 1800 kg (3,968 lb), the main crutch being able to take the PC 1400 (3,086-lb) armour-piercing bomb and the wing racks the SC 500 (1,102-lb) or a wide range of other stores including gun pods each housing either twin 20-mm cannon or six 7.92-mm (0.31-in) MG 81 machine-guns. Defensive armament at the rear was replaced by a pair of MG 81s, exceptionally light but fast-firing weapons with belt feed instead of 75-round magazines. Additionally, the entire aircraft was refined to reduce drag, the most noticeable improvement being to the cowling and canopy. The landing gear was cleaned up, but from 1942 the spats and leg fairings were increasingly discarded.

The most numerous variant was the **Ju 87D-3**, which embodied better protection for the crew and vital parts of the aircraft, reflecting the Ju 87's increasing use as a *Schlachtflugzeug* (close-support aircraft). From 1942 all versions were often called upon to fly missions other than dive-bombing, such as glider-towing, anti-partisan attacks and general utility transport with a diversity of loads. A few **Ju 87D-4**s

A winter-camouflaged Ju 87D-3 of the Gruppenstab of I/StG 2 'Immelmann' during the autumn or early winter of 1942. Commanded by Major Dr Ernst Küpfer, the Geschwader fought in the southern sector of the Eastern Front, operating under Fliegerkorps IV and going into action over the Caucasus and Stalingrad. The Ju 87D was powered by the Jumo 211J-1 driving a VS-11 propeller.

Tailplane
The strong tailplane was a two-spar structure. On the Ju 87B it was externally braced by two struts; in the refined Ju 87D these struts were formed into one aerodynamic strut. The elevators were not large, but provided enough authority to pull the aircraft easily out of a 90° dive.

Junkers Ju 87G-1 10 (Pz). Staffel, II/Schlachtgeschwader 3 Jakobstadt, Latvia, 1944

The Ju 87G-1 anti-tank aircraft was the last variant of the Ju 87 to become operational, apart from the Ju 87H trainer. The G-1 was not a new-build variant, but was converted from Ju 87D-5 airframes. The basic Ju 87D-5 was adapted to carry a pair of massive Flak 18 (BK 3,7) 37-mm cannon pods under its outer wing panels. It could carry bombs instead of guns, but had no dive-brakes. The removal of dive-bombing equipment made the G-1 most unrepresentative among Stuka variants. The concept was the brainchild of the extraordinary Hans-Ulrich Rudel who, despite being shot down 30 times, flew no fewer than 2,530 combat sorties and destroyed 519 Russian tanks. 10 (Pz.)/SG3 formed in March 1944 through the redesignation of 4./StG2, and was based at Jakobstadt in Latvia as part of Luftflotte I between April and July 1944. The unit helped cover the retreat westwards, becoming incorporated in I/SG 9 as 2. Staffel on 7 January 1945, and ending the war in the Courland pocket.

Cockpit
The Ju 87 featured a crew of two, although Bs were often flown as single-seaters. Both pilot and radio operator/gunner sat under separate sliding canopies, the latter facing to the rear. Armour was provided where possible.

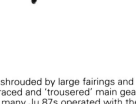

Undercarriage
The immensely sturdy main undercarriage was shrouded by large fairings and spats around the wheels, these replacing the braced and 'trousered' main gear of the Ju 87A. On the Eastern Front in the winter, many Ju 87s operated with the spats removed, as the mud quickly clogged the wheels.

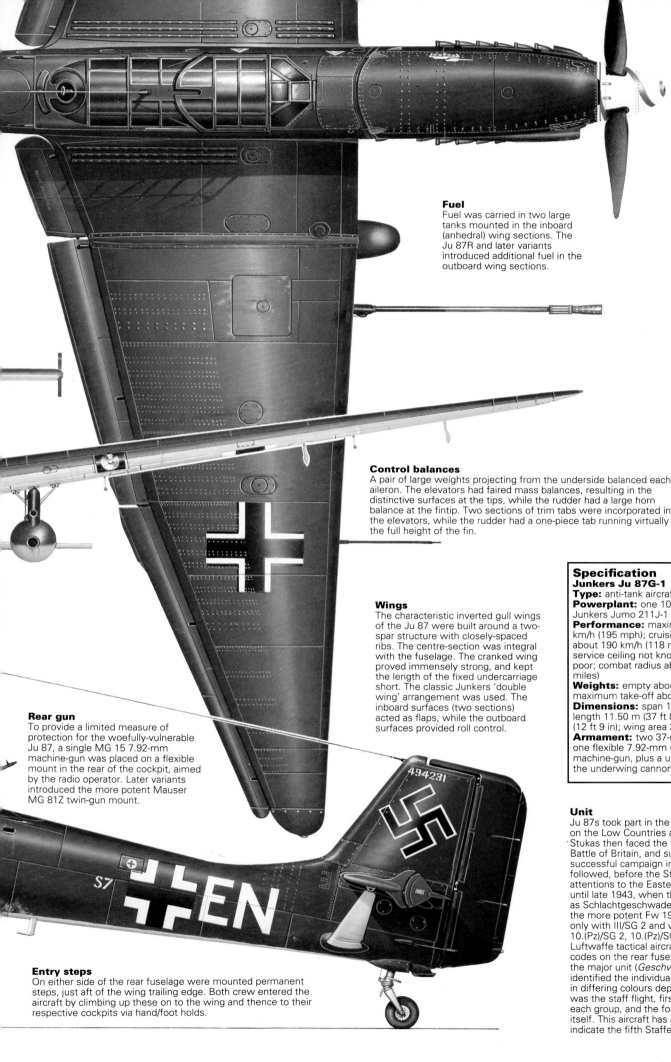

Fuel
Fuel was carried in two large tanks mounted in the inboard (anhedral) wing sections. The Ju 87R and later variants introduced additional fuel in the outboard wing sections.

Powerplant
The Ju 87B was powered by a Junkers Jumo 211Da 12-cylinder liquid-cooled engine. This unit was rated at 900 kW (1,200) hp for take-off (2,400 rpm) and 825 kW (1,100 hp) at 1500 m (4,920 ft). The increase in power offered by this engine over the earlier Jumo 210 of the A-series enabled a greater bomb load to be carried. The radiator was housed in an armoured 'bath' beneath the engine. Hydraulically-operated cooling gills immediately behind increased airflow through the engine at low speeds. The Ju 87B-1 model featured simple port exhausts, but the B-2 introduced ejector-type stubs behind an aerodynamic fairing. Angled back, these provided a small but useful amount of thrust. The Ju 87D offered more power, with a Jumo 211J-1 rated at up to 1050 kW (1,410 hp) with an induction air cooler and a strengthened crankshaft.

Control balances
A pair of large weights projecting from the underside balanced each aileron. The elevators had faired mass balances, resulting in the distinctive surfaces at the tips, while the rudder had a large horn balance at the fintip. Two sections of trim tabs were incorporated in the elevators, while the rudder had a one-piece tab running virtually the full height of the fin.

Wings
The characteristic inverted gull wings of the Ju 87 were built around a two-spar structure with closely-spaced ribs. The centre-section was integral with the fuselage. The cranked wing proved immensely strong, and kept the length of the fixed undercarriage short. The classic Junkers 'double wing' arrangement was used. The inboard surfaces (two sections) acted as flaps, while the outboard surfaces provided roll control.

Rear gun
To provide a limited measure of protection for the woefully-vulnerable Ju 87, a single MG 15 7.92-mm machine-gun was placed on a flexible mount in the rear of the cockpit, aimed by the radio operator. Later variants introduced the more potent Mauser MG 81Z twin-gun mount.

Entry steps
On either side of the rear fuselage were mounted permanent steps, just aft of the wing trailing edge. Both crew entered the aircraft by climbing up these on to the wing and thence to their respective cockpits via hand/foot holds.

Specification
Junkers Ju 87G-1
Type: anti-tank aircraft
Powerplant: one 1044-kW (1,400-hp) Junkers Jumo 211J-1 inline piston engine
Performance: maximum speed about 314 km/h (195 mph); cruising speed normally about 190 km/h (118 mph); rate of climb and service ceiling not known, but extremely poor; combat radius about 320 km (199 miles)
Weights: empty about 4400 kg (9,700 lb); maximum take-off about 6600 kg (14,550 lb)
Dimensions: span 15.00 m (49 ft 2 in); length 11.50 m (37 ft 8 in); height 3.90 m (12 ft 9 in); wing area 33.69 m² (362.6 sq ft)
Armament: two 37-mm BK 3,7 cannon and one flexible 7.92-mm (0.331-in) MG 81 machine-gun, plus a useful bomb load when the underwing cannon were not being carried

Unit
Ju 87s took part in the Polish campaign, the attacks on the Low Countries and the Battle of France. The Stukas then faced the fighters of the RAF in the Battle of Britain, and suffered accordingly. Another successful campaign in Greece and the Balkans followed, before the Stukegeschwader turned their attentions to the Eastern Front, where they fought until late 1943, when the units were redesignated as Schlachtgeschwader, most later transitioning to the more potent Fw 190. The Ju 87G-1s served only with III/SG 2 and with 10.(Pz)/SG 1, 10.(Pz)/SG 2, 10.(Pz)/SG 3, and 10 (Pz)/SG 77. Luftwaffe tactical aircraft carried four-digit/letter codes on the rear fuselage. The first pair denoted the major unit (Geschwader or Gruppe), the third identified the individual aircraft and was presented in differing colours depending on whether the unit was the staff flight, first, second or third Staffel of each group, and the fourth identified the Staffel itself. This aircraft has an 'N' which would usually indicate the fifth Staffel, yet belonged to the tenth!

Left: This Ju 87B-1 wears the markings of the Gruppenstab of IV (Stuka) Gruppe of Lehrgeschwader 1 commanded by Hauptmann von Brauchitsch. This operational training, evaluation and demonstration unit saw extensive use as a conventional combat formation, notably in Poland.

Right: A Ju-87B-1 of 7./StG 51 (which became 4./StG 1) as it appeared during the Battle of France in May-June 1940. The unit's charging bison badge was carried in a bold yellow shooting star along the fuselage side. Unusually, the individual aircraft letter (J) was repeated above and below the wingtips. When it met fighter opposition, the Stuka was a sitting duck, and the French campaign provided a foretaste of the 'Turkey shoot' suffered over England.

were equipped as torpedo-bombers, but the next main variant was the **Ju 87D-5** with extended wingtips to help counter the considerably increased weight of Ju 87D versions. Reflecting the increasing peril of day operations, the **Ju 87D-7** was a night variant with the more powerful Jumo 211P engine and long exhaust pipes extending back across the wing. Together with the day-flying **Ju 87D-8**, it replaced the wing guns with the far more powerful 20-mm MG 151, and dive-brakes were at last omitted. The Ju 87D-8 was the last version in production, the total number built by late September 1944 – when almost all aircraft production other than fighters was terminated – being generally accepted as 5,709.

Anti-armour

There were several schemes for successors, including the **Ju 87F** and **Ju 187**, but the only other Stuka variants were built by conver-

A line-up of Ju 87B-2s of Stukageschwader 2 at a Greek airfield during preparations for the invasion of Crete. During Operation Merkur, the Stukas attacked ground targets in support of the paratroops and mountain troops on the ground, and attacked Royal Navy warships.

sions of the ubiquitous D models. The most important sub-type was the **Ju 87G** series, of which only the **Ju 87G-1** became operational. The Ju 87G was a specialised anti-armour version, fitted with two BK 3,7 (Flak 18) guns hung under the wings just outboard of the landing gears. This 37-mm gun was a formidable weapon weighing over 363 kg (800 lb) and in wide service as ground-based Flak (anti-aircraft artillery) equipment. In 1942 a trial installation was tested in a converted Ju 87D-5 and found more effective than the many other Luftwaffe anti-tank aircraft such as the Henschel Hs 129 and Junkers Ju 88P. Fed by clips of six rounds, the BK 3,7 had a muzzle velocity with armour-piercing ammunition exceeding 850 m (2,790 ft) per second, and the greatest exponent of the Ju 87G-1, Hans-Ulrich Rudel, was ultimately credited with the personal destruction of 519 Russian armoured vehicles. It was he who flew 2,530 combat missions and continued to lead Stuka formations in daylight long after the other *Stukagruppen* had replaced their vulnerable aircraft with the Focke-Wulf Fw 190.

Another variant produced by converting aircraft of the Ju 87D series was the **Ju 87H** dual-control trainer. No trainer had been considered necessary in the early days of Ju 87 service, but by 1943 the art

Right: The water-soluble white distemper used as snow camouflage by Luftwaffe aircraft in Russia weathered rapidly, washing off aircraft spines and becoming heavily stained by exhaust gases. Here Ju 87Ds from an unidentified Geschwader turn in for an attack against Soviet armour. At least 16 Ju 87s are visible in the original print.

Below right: A Kette of three Ju 87Bs in ecehelon port. More than 5,700 Stukas had been built by the time construction ended in 1944. The overall drab upper surfaces seen here were soon replaced by a disruptive two-tone splinter camouflage, with various special schemes for desert theatres and for the Eastern Front.

of surviving in the type had become so specialised and important on the Eastern Front that even experienced bomber and fighter pilots had to go out with a Ju 87 instructor before taking up their places in the decimated ranks of the *Stukagruppen*. Almost all versions of Ju 87D were converted into H models, retaining the same suffix numbers. Outwardly the differences included removal of armament and the addition of bulged side panels in the rear cockpit to give the instructor a measure of forward vision.

All versions could fly with tropical equipment and sand/dust filters, and many aircraft on the Eastern Front operated on skis in winter. There were several experimental variants, mainly concerned with tests of weapons intended for later aircraft. One of the most striking test programmes concerned one Ju 87D-3 fitted with large streamlined overwing passenger cabins. The idea was that the Ju 87, an aircraft well used to front-line operations, should become a vehicle for putting down agents behind enemy front lines. The trials programme got under way in early 1944 at the Graf Zeppelin Research Institute at Ruit, and the final design of cabin seated two men in tandem, both facing forward, with ample side windows which gave the pilot some lateral vision. In a shallow dive, the two pods were to be pulled off the wing by streaming large parachutes, but there is no record of this actually being done, although the pods were flown with passengers.

The Ju 87 was widely used by all the Axis air forces, including those of Italy, Hungary, Slovakia, Romania and Bulgaria. When Ju 87s were discovered in Italian markings, the totally fictitious belief arose among the British that the type was being made in Italy; even the invented type-designation of Breda 201 Picchiatelli was widely published. In fact, from 1939 every Ju 87 was made by Weser in the same Tempelhof building.

Above: A Ju 87D-3 with experimental personnel transport pods overwing. These seated two passengers in tandem, and were designed to be released in a shallow dive, descending to the ground on the end of a massive parachute.

Junkers Ju 88

With the exception of close dogfighting, it is difficult to think of any military duty of the World War II era for which the **Ju 88** was not adapted. The original missions were level- and dive-bombing, but to these were added long-range escort, night-fighting, intruding, tank-busting, anti-ship attack, destruction of Allied maritime aircraft, anti-submarine warfare, supply dropping, towing, training, transport, reconnaissance, torpedo dropping, close support, pathfinding and pilotless (missile) attack. Direct developments were the Ju 188 and Ju 388 (the Ju 288 was a completely new design). Today's industry may wistfully note that the number of Ju 88 prototypes and development aircraft exceeded 100, which is about 10 times the total production run of some modern aircraft.

Versatility was the last thing considered at the start of the programme. Indeed, in 1935 the RLM (German air ministry) doubted the practicality of a *Kampfzerstörer* (war destroyer) able to fly bomber, bomber-destroyer and reconnaissance missions. It issued a replacement requirement for a simple *Schnellbomber* (fast bomber) to fly at 500 km/h (311 mph) and carry a bomb load of up to 800 kg (1,765 lb). Junkers went flat-out to win, even hiring two designers who had pioneered advanced stressed-skin structures in the USA, despite the fact that the company had already moved on from corrugated skin and produced numerous smooth-skinned prototypes. In the first three months of 1936 two proposals were submitted, in the form of the **Ju 85** with a twin-finned tail and the Ju 88 with a single rudder well aft of the elevators. Competition came from the Henschel Hs 127 and Messerschmitt Bf 162 (the latter being falsely publicised in 1940 as a major Luftwaffe type, the 'Jaguar'), which were eliminated by late 1937 for various reasons.

Secret flight

The **Ju 88 V1** (prototype 1) was flown by chief test pilot Kindermann on 21 December 1936 with registration D-AQEN. Flying was based at Dessau, but no announcement was made and the type remained unknown to British intelligence, as did the Focke-Wulf Fw 190 in 1939. The Ju 88 V1 crashed at the start of its high-speed testing, but not before it had shown the design to be thoroughly sound with promising performance. The **Ju 88 V2** retained DB 600Aa engines with distinctive annular cooling radiators, but the **Ju 88 V3** switched to Junkers' own Jumo 211A and had full military equipment with a raised cabin roof, dorsal machine-gun, fixed gun firing

A Ju 88A-5 of III/KG 30. The A-5 was basically a Ju 88A-1 with the long-span wings developed for the up-engined Ju 88A-4, which was delayed by engine problems. It entered service in time for the Battle of Britain.

ahead and internal bomb load of 500 kg (1,102 lb) aimed by a sight in a chin blister. The **Ju 88 V4** introduced the familiar four-seat crew compartment with a large 'insect-eye' nose glazed with 20 flat panes and a ventral gondola with an aft-firing MG 15. Last of the pure prototypes was the **Ju 88 V5** (D-ATYU), shaped for minimum drag and flown in April 1938. On 9 March 1939 it set a startling world 1000-km (621-mile) circuit record with 2000-kg (4,409-lb) load at 517 km/h (321.25 mph). The Ju 88 was thereby revealed to the world and, incidentally, credit for its design was heaped entirely upon chief designer Ernst Zindel; the Americans were not mentioned.

The **Ju 88 V6**, flown in June 1938, introduced one of the type's distinctive features. Previous prototypes had featured American-style twin-oleo main gear units with electric retraction, but the Ju 88 V6 intro-

One of the most numerous versions, and the basis for many others, the Ju 88A-4 four-seat bomber introduced the long-span wing and also an induction cooling-duct fairing under the engines; these Ju 88A-4s are pictured with III/LG 1 in mid-1942. Lehrgeschwader 1 (instructional group 1) was based in the Mediterranean.

Stooks of corn in the field below are hard to explain in this picture of the Ju 88 V1 (first prototype), because its flying career extended only from December 1936 until the following spring. Note the swivelling ciné camera in the position reserved for the upper rear gun, and the separate oil coolers under the DB 600s.

Swinging the compass of what is believed to have been the first Ju 88A-1 produced at Bernburg; the date was probably June 1939. Note the tall single-leg main gears with large tyres, three-bladed VDM propellers and short-span wings with ailerons extending to the tips. Colours were black-green and very pale blue.

duced a bold gear with tall single legs in which shocks were absorbed by a *Ringfeder* (ring spring) assembly of high-tensile steel rings with tapered profiles which expanded radially under compressive loads, bounce being prevented by the friction as the rings pushed their way apart. Retraction was hydraulic, the wheels rotating 90° to lie flat in the rear of the nacelles. Thus, although the wheels were made much larger, with low-pressure tyres able to operate from mud and sand at weights double that of the Ju 88 V1, the nacelle became slimmer and drag was reduced. The landing gear later needed patient refinement, but by 1940 was an outstanding piece of engineering.

Later pre-war prototypes introduced large slatted dive brakes under the outer wings and four bomb-carriers under the inner wings, each stressed for an SC 500 (500-kg/1,102-lb) bomb but normally limited to SC 100 (100-kg/220-lb) weapons when the enlarged pair of inter-

A Ju 88A-4 of III/LG 1 (known as the 'Helbig fliers' after their Kommodore) over the Greek Coast during 1942. LG 1 spent most of the war in the Mediterranean, although detached elements saw service on most fronts.

nal bays was loaded to its limit of 28 SC 50 (50-kg/110-lb) bombs. This total load of 1800 kg (3,968 lb) was impressive enough, but testing at Dessau and Tarnewitz cleared the pre-production **Ju 88A-0** for overload missions with four external SC 500s, increasing total load to 2400 kg (5,291 lb). At the same time, the Ju 88's capabilities were leading to problems which included wing-spar failure, main-leg failure and other faults caused by overloading. All were cured, but the service-test Erprobungskommando 88 crews had many 'hairy' incidents in the spring of 1939 with the Ju 88A-0 batch flying under operational conditions, and even production **Ju 88A-1**s which reached the Luftwaffe in August 1939 had to be flown carefully, with aerobatics prohibited.

Powerplants

The engine of the Ju 88A-1 was the 895-kW (1,200-hp) Jumo 211B-1, one of the classic Junkers series of inverted-Vee 12-cylinder units with direct fuel injection. In several early prototypes and Ju 88A-0s, it drove a four-bladed propeller, but the production standard propellers on almost all subsequent versions had three blades of high

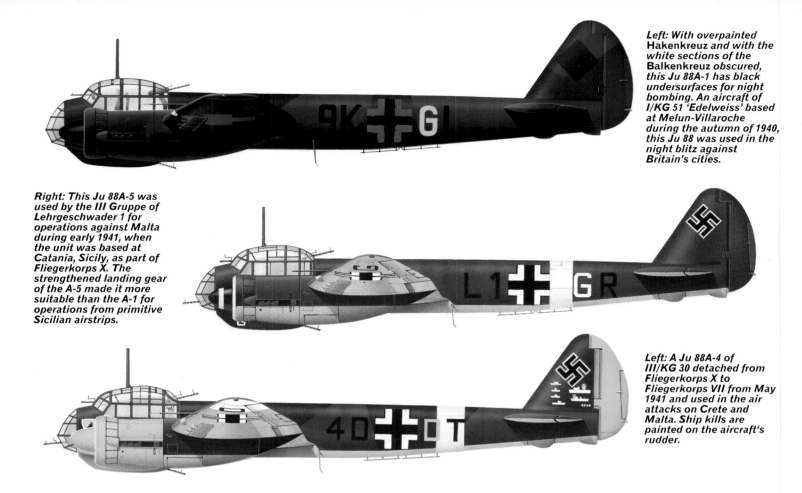

Left: With overpainted Hakenkreuz *and with the white sections of the* Balkenkreuz *obscured, this Ju 88A-1 has black undersurfaces for night bombing. An aircraft of I/KG 51 'Edelweiss' based at Melun-Villaroche during the autumn of 1940, this Ju 88 was used in the night blitz against Britain's cities.*

Right: This Ju 88A-5 was used by the III Gruppe of Lehrgeschwader 1 for operations against Malta during early 1941, when the unit was based at Catania, Sicily, as part of Fliegerkorps X. The strengthened landing gear of the A-5 made it more suitable than the A-1 for operations from primitive Sicilian airstrips.

Left: A Ju 88A-4 of III/KG 30 detached from Fliegerkorps X to Fliegerkorps VII from May 1941 and used in the air attacks on Crete and Malta. Ship kills are painted on the aircraft's rudder.

solidity (large chord) which increased further with the introduction of the more powerful Jumo 213 and BMW 801s. Blades were fully feathering and fitted with alcohol de-icing, and the annular radiators used on all liquid-cooled Ju 88s were particularly neat. Usually the top centre matrix was the oil cooler, and airflow was controlled by annular gills. As in many period German aircraft, the engines were hung on two giant *Elektron* (magnesium alloy) forging beams with lower compression braces, all picking up on four rubber-damped mounts on the firewall at the leading edge. The nacelles were thus unusually long, the Ju 88 becoming universally known as *die Dreifinger* (the three-finger).

Like almost all Luftwaffe aircraft, the Ju 88 was designed for use in tactical warfare where ranges were moderate. Normal fuel capacity was thus only 1677 litres (369 Imp gal) in tanks between the spars inboard and outboard of the engines, although the capacious bomb bays were plumbed in many versions, including most bombers, for

extra tanks bringing the total up to 3575 litres (786.4 Imp gal). The wings had considerable dihedral from the roots and the entire trailing edge was formed by patented 'double-wing' slotted surfaces drooped as flaps for landing. The outer sections also served as ailerons, and like the other control surfaces were fabric-covered. The wing had hot-air de-icing, while in most versions the forward-mounted tailplane had pulsating pneumatic de-icers.

Crew conditions

The crew compartment was typically Germanic, and while British propaganda claimed the four men were grouped together to bolster their morale, in fact the arrangement was in many ways cramped and inefficient. The pilot sat high on the left with a stick having a two-pronged aileron wheel, and in dive-bombing he did the sighting through a sight swung down from the roof, the usual angle being 60°.

The Totenkopf *(death's head) emblem of this Ju 88A-5 identifies it as an aircraft of I/KG 54. The I and II Gruppen of KG 54 converted to the Ju 88 from the Heinkel He 111 in time to participate in the Battle of Britain. Although able to evade even a Spitfire by diving, the Ju 88 suffered heavy losses at the hands of RAF fighters (albeit significantly lower than the attrition suffered by other German bombers committed to the operation) and armour protection and defensive armament were increased. Ju 88s were used against Royal Navy ships during 1939 and early 1940, and KG 30 and LG 1 participated in the closing stages of the Battle of France. The Battle of Britain, however, marked the first major action in which the aircraft participated fully. By Adlertag (1 August), KG 30 and KG 51 had three Ju 88 Gruppen each, LG 1 and KG 54 had two, and KG 1, KG 4 and KG 40 had one Gruppe each. The Ju 88s made several unescorted attacks against British aerodromes during the battle.*

Right: A Ju 88 (probably a Ju 88A-1 or perhaps a Ju 88A-5) of KG 30, the first operational unit, which initially operated primarily in the anti-shipping role from its succession of bases in Germany, Denmark, the Netherlands and Norway. The aircraft carries a pair of bombs under the inner wings. The offset bomb-aimer's gondola can be clearly seen.

Below: Lt Johannes Geismann of I/KG 77 inspects the impressive kill tally on the rudder of his Ju 88. KG 77 transferred from the Russian Front to Sicily in the early summer of 1942, from where it was primarily engaged in attacks against allied merchantmen supplying Malta and North Africa.

Level bombing was carried out with a sight in the nose by the bomb-aimer low on the right, who in some versions sat higher and doubled as second pilot. Behind on the left was the engineer who manned the upper rear armament, while alongside him on the right was the radio (later also radar) operator who looked after the lower rear gun. The pilot, engineer and lower rear gun position were armoured.

Success story

It was clear as early as 1938 that the Ju 88 was potentially a great aircraft, far in advance of the Dornier Do 17 or Heinkel He 111, and plans for production were widespread. Dessau, the HQ, played little part in production, fuselages being assigned to Aschersleben, wings to Halberstadt, tails to Leopoldshall and assembly and test to Bernburg. Other giant plants brought into the programme included Arado at Brandenburg-Neuendorf, Dornier at Wismar, Heinkel at Oranienburg, Henschel at Berlin-Schonefeld and Volkswagen at Wolfsburg. By 1944 many other plants were contributing parts or complete aircraft, including ATG at Leipzig-Mockau, Siebel at Halle and factories in Czechoslovakia and France.

Right: A Ju 88A-10 of II/LG 1 operating from Crete for anti-shipping strikes against the Royal Navy during October 1942. Desert camouflage is a hangover from an earlier period of duty in North Africa, supporting Rommel's Afrika Korps. Lehrgeschwader 1 performed the majority of Ju 88 operations in the Mediterranean.

Left: Another Ju 88A-4, this time belonging to I/KG 54 and used for attacks against the invasion forces at Salerno and Sicily. The aircraft has light grey Wellenmüster camouflage sprayed over the standard two-tone Mediterranean camouflage.

Right: The skeletal hand insignia on the nose of this Ju 88A-14 indicates that the aircraft was attached to the Gruppenstab of II/ZG 1 at Mamaia, Romania, during the spring of 1944.

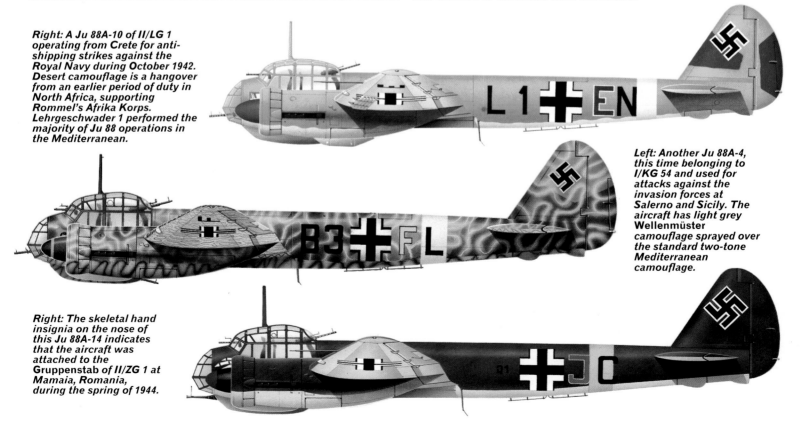

In 1939, however, production was slow to build up even to one Ju 88 a week, and I/KG 25 had a mix of Ju 88A-1 and Ju 88A-0 bombers when the war began. On 22 September 1939 the *Gruppe* was redesignated I/KG 30, and for the rest of the war KG 30 was a famed exponent of Ju 88 bombers. Its first major mission came four days later against the British Home Fleet, which escaped major damage largely because SC 500 bombs failed to detonate. On 9 October the first two Ju 88A-1s were shot down, one of them being the aircraft of the *Gruppenkommandeur*. This was the first of numerous losses to RAF fighters, which by September 1940 had led to the inefficient lash-up of no fewer than four separate MG 15s in the upper rear position, all aimed individually by hand through separate ball/socket mountings, and all with 75-round magazines changed after three seconds' firing. There were at least 40 different armament schemes for Ju 88s, but most later bombers (except the **Ju 88S**) used the light and fast-firing 7.92-mm (0.31-in) MG 81, often in pairs, combined with 13-mm (0.51-in) MG 131s.

A plethora of variants

Sub-types of A-series bombers are listed in the variants, but all from mid-1940 were based on the long-span **Ju 88A-4** which had better handling, no structural limitations and more powerful Jumo 211J engines. The new wing had inset ailerons which were metal-skinned. More than half the total production of Ju 88s was made up of A-series

Above: A Ju 88G-1, which was the first production night-fighter version of the Ju 88 with radial engines, all previous service versions having had inline engines with annular radiators. The new version also adopted the enlarged, angular tail surfaces of the Ju 188.

variants, which were later used for every conceivable kind of duty including training, glider towing, freight and passenger transport (including bulky items attached to the Dobbas welded-tube interface carried between the inboard wing racks) and conversion into various Mistel (mistletoe) pilotless missiles.

Further fighter developments

The **Ju 88B** series featured a more capacious and seemingly more streamlined crew compartment. The proposal began in 1936 but was held back by various factors, including delays with engines, and ultimately led to the Ju 188 with long-span, pointed wings, a dorsal turret and enlarged tail. The **Ju 88C** was another early proposal, this time for a *Zerstörer* (heavy fighter). This too was delayed, but at about the time war began the Ju 88 V7 prototype was crudely modified with a 20-mm MG FF and three MG 17s firing ahead through the nose, as the **Ju 88C-1**. Although there was no official requirement, Junkers was allowed to convert a few Ju 88A-1s into **Ju 88C-2**s in 1940 with unglazed noses with the same guns, plus 10 SC 50s in the rear bomb bay (the forward bay being occupied by a fuel tank). Subsequent RAF raids led to a sudden need by mid-1940 for night-fighters, and eventually

Left: The Ju 88C was conceived as a Zerstörer and Nachtjager, with fixed forward-firing armament in a solid nose. This Ju 88C-6 of 4./KG 76 at Taganrog was used primarily for train-busting and had its nose painted to simulate a glazed bomber nose to deceive enemy fighter pilots.

Right: Some night fighters were also painted to resemble earlier, less-capable Ju 88 variants. This Ju 88G-7a of IV/NJG 6 at Schwabisch Hall has its fin painted to resemble the outline of a Ju 88C tail, for example.

over 3,200 C-series aircraft were delivered almost exclusively for this role. The chief versions were the **Ju 88C-6b** and **Ju 88C-6c**, which had Jumo engines and from late 1942 had Lichtenstein BC or Lichtenstein C-1 radar, or (early 1944) Lichtenstein SN-2 radar, plus many other sensors such as FuG 227 Flensburg which homed in on RAF Monica tail-warning radars (installed to protect the heavy bombers) and FuG 350 Naxos Z which homed-in on the H₂S radars. From 1943 the *schräge Musik* (Jazz) upward-firing armament was being used against RAF heavies by night, with devastating results. By late 1941 the MG 151 had largely replaced the old MG FF in the 20-mm calibre, and there were many armament schemes, the usual *schräge Musik* installation comprising two MG 151s at an inclination of 70°.

Heavy and night-fighter variants

The **Ju 88D** was a family of standard long-range reconnaissance aircraft, in some versions fitted with wing bomb racks, and which like other glazed-nose Ju 88s served with several satellite air forces including those of Romania and Hungary. In letter sequence the next family is the **Ju 88G**, although chronologically this did not emerge until mid-

An early Ju 88A runs up its engines on a grass strip. As a bomber, the type could carry a useful load at good speed. This example has large bombs suspended from pylons under the inner wings.

1943. By this time the overburdened C-series night-fighters were suffering heavy casualties caused by deterioration in low-speed handling, and a **Ju 88R-2** (described separately) was modified with the large tail of the Ju 188, becoming the **Ju 88 V58**. The completely revised armament comprised six MG 151s, two staggered at 3° nose-down angle in the right-hand side of the nose and the other four angled down at 5° in a box under the left-hand side of the belly. A single MG 131 was provided for upper rear defence.

In the production G-series, the two right-hand side guns were removed, as they blinded the pilot, and most used the ventral tray plus two upward-firing MG 151s. The long endurance, tremendous performance and wealth of electronic devices made the G-series extremely formidable aircraft which wrought terrible havoc on RAF heavies and would have posed a very serious threat had they appeared earlier in the war. As it was, they were available in numbers only from mid-1944, by

Beautifully restored at RAF St Athan, this Ju 88R-1 is one of only three known Ju 88s in existence. It owes its survival to the remarkable fact that its crew from NJG 3 agreed to defect, and on 9 May 1943 flew to Dyce (Aberdeen). This photograph was taken a day or two later at Farnborough, the radar having been removed.

The prototype Mistel pilotless missile project comprised this manned Ju 88A-4 linked to a Bf 109F-4. The principle of all Mistels was that the fighter was supported at its centre of gravity, the light tail strut falling back on a rear-fuselage crutch at the moment of release. Later, all struts were thicker.

which time output was falling, and only about 800 could be completed by the time of the final collapse. Ultimate versions had liquid-cooled engines and advanced centimetric radars.

The Ju 88H family was initially ultra-long-range reconnaissance aircraft with the fuselage stretched to 17.647 m (57 ft 3 in). The **Ju 88H-1** had Hohentwiel radar, while the **Ju 88H-2** had a devastating battery of six MG 151s for use against aircraft or ships far out in the Atlantic. The **Ju 88H-4** was further stretched to 20.38 m (66 ft 10 in) but found use only as the radar-equipped lower component of the *Führungsmachine* (guiding machine) long-range pathfinder which had an extra main gear and a *Doppelreiter* (overwing-tanked) Fw 190A-8 riding on top as escort.

Only a few dozen were delivered of the various P-series Ju 88s with anti-tank or anti-bomber guns. Related to these was a test aircraft, the **Ju 88N** or **Ju 88Nbwe**, with Professor Dornberger's six-barrelled launcher of 21/28-cm (8.27/11.02-in) rocket shells.

The **Ju 88R-1** was a Ju 88C-6b night-fighter powered by BMW 801MA engines, while the **Ju 88R-2** had BMW 801Ds. This series was produced in parallel with the C-series from early 1943 until about a year later, when it was replaced by the G-series.

The S-series stemmed from Ju 88 prototype **V93** of late 1942, which resulted from the urgent need to make the basic bomber faster, to restore a good chance of returning from a daylight mission. The **Ju 88 V93** was powered by BMW 801D engines and given a smooth glazed nose for minimum drag, the underwing carriers being removed. Most production versions had engines giving even greater power at high altitude, and the ventral gondola and most armour was removed to increase performance further. Speed reached about 612 km/h (380 mph) with either the BMW or Jumo engines, still slower than the

A severely weathered Ju 88A-4 flies over the Eastern Front. It appears to have lost all vestiges of its temporary winter camouflage, except above the starboard wing.

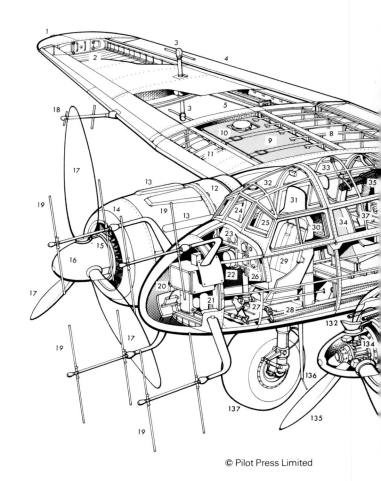

© Pilot Press Limited

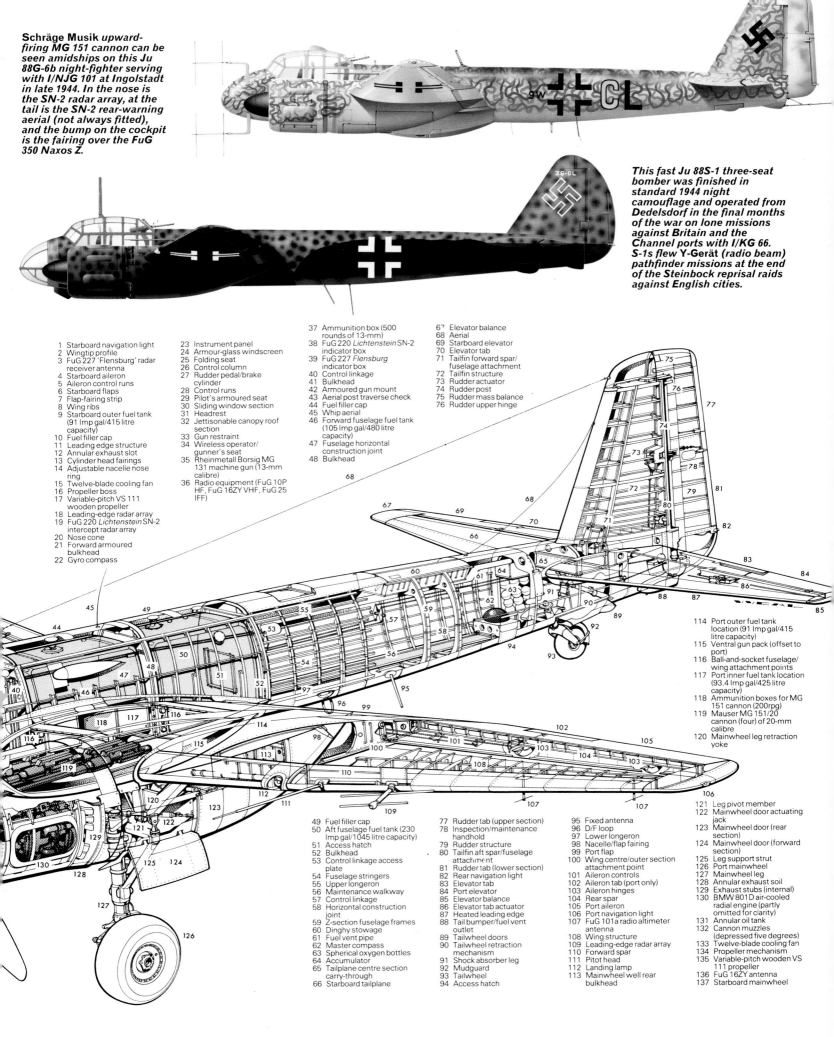

Schräge Musik *upward-firing MG 151 cannon can be seen amidships on this Ju 88G-6b night-fighter serving with I/NJG 101 at Ingolstadt in late 1944. In the nose is the SN-2 radar array, at the tail is the SN-2 rear-warning aerial (not always fitted), and the bump on the cockpit is the fairing over the FuG 350 Naxos Z.*

This fast Ju 88S-1 three-seat bomber was finished in standard 1944 night camouflage and operated from Dedelsdorf in the final months of the war on lone missions against Britain and the Channel ports with I/KG 66. S-1s flew Y-Gerät (radio beam) pathfinder missions at the end of the Steinbock reprisal raids against English cities.

1 Starboard navigation light
2 Wingtip profile
3 FuG 227 'Flensburg' radar receiver antenna
4 Starboard aileron
5 Aileron control runs
6 Starboard flaps
7 Flap-fairing strip
8 Wing ribs
9 Starboard outer fuel tank (91 Imp gal/415 litre capacity)
10 Fuel filler cap
11 Leading edge structure
12 Annular exhaust slot
13 Cylinder head fairings
14 Adjustable nacelle nose ring
15 Twelve-blade cooling fan
16 Propeller boss
17 Variable-pitch VS 111 wooden propeller
18 Leading-edge radar array
19 FuG 220 *Lichtenstein* SN-2 intercept radar array
20 Nose cone
21 Forward armoured bulkhead
22 Gyro compass

23 Instrument panel
24 Armour-glass windscreen
25 Folding seat
26 Control column
27 Rudder pedal/brake cylinder
28 Control runs
29 Pilot's armoured seat
30 Sliding window section
31 Headrest
32 Jettisonable canopy roof section
33 Gun restraint
34 Wireless operator/gunner's seat
35 Rheinmetall Borsig MG 131 machine gun (13-mm calibre)
36 Radio equipment (FuG 10P HF, FuG 16ZY VHF, FuG 25 IFF)

37 Ammunition box (500 rounds of 13-mm)
38 FuG 220 *Lichtenstein* SN-2 indicator box
39 FuG 227 *Flensburg* indicator box
40 Control linkage
41 Bulkhead
42 Armoured gun mount
43 Aerial post traverse check
44 Fuel filler cap
45 Whip aerial
46 Forward fuselage fuel tank (105 Imp gal/480 litre capacity)
47 Fuselage horizontal construction joint
48 Bulkhead

67 Elevator balance
68 Aerial
69 Starboard elevator
70 Elevator tab
71 Tailfin forward spar/fuselage attachment
72 Tailfin structure
73 Rudder actuator
74 Rudder post
75 Rudder mass balance
76 Rudder upper hinge

49 Fuel filler cap
50 Aft fuselage fuel tank (230 Imp gal/1045 litre capacity)
51 Access hatch
52 Bulkhead
53 Control linkage access plate
54 Fuselage stringers
55 Upper longeron
56 Maintenance walkway
57 Control linkage
58 Horizontal construction joint
59 Z-section fuselage frames
60 Dinghy stowage
61 Fuel vent pipe
62 Master compass
63 Spherical oxygen bottles
64 Accumulator
65 Tailplane centre section carry-through
66 Starboard tailplane

77 Rudder tab (upper section)
78 Inspection/maintenance handhold
79 Rudder structure
80 Tailfin aft spar/fuselage attachment
81 Rudder tab (lower section)
82 Rear navigation light
83 Elevator tab
84 Port elevator
85 Elevator balance
86 Elevator tab actuator
87 Heated leading edge
88 Tail bumper/fuel vent outlet
89 Tailwheel doors
90 Tailwheel retraction mechanism
91 Shock absorber leg
92 Mudguard
93 Tailwheel
94 Access hatch

95 Fixed antenna
96 D/F loop
97 Lower longeron
98 Nacelle/flap fairing
99 Port flap
100 Wing centre/outer section attachment point
101 Aileron controls
102 Aileron tab (port only)
103 Aileron hinges
104 Rear spar
105 Port aileron
106 Port navigation light
107 FuG 101a radio altimeter antenna
108 Wing structure
109 Leading-edge radar array
110 Forward spar
111 Pitot head
112 Landing lamp
113 Mainwheel well rear bulkhead

114 Port outer fuel tank location (91 Imp gal/415 litre capacity)
115 Ventral gun pack (offset to port)
116 Ball-and-socket fuselage/wing attachment points
117 Port inner fuel tank location (93.4 Imp gal/425 litre capacity)
118 Ammunition boxes for MG 151 cannon (200rpg)
119 Mauser MG 151/20 cannon (four) of 20-mm calibre
120 Mainwheel leg retraction yoke

121 Leg pivot member
122 Mainwheel door actuating jack
123 Mainwheel door (rear section)
124 Mainwheel door (forward section)
125 Leg support strut
126 Port mainwheel
127 Mainwheel leg
128 Annular exhaust soil
129 Exhaust stubs (internal)
130 BMW 801D air-cooled radial engine (partly omitted for clarity)
131 Annular oil tank
132 Cannon muzzles (depressed five degrees)
133 Twelve-blade cooling fan
134 Propeller mechanism
135 Variable-pitch wooden VS 111 propeller
136 FuG 16ZY antenna
137 Starboard mainwheel

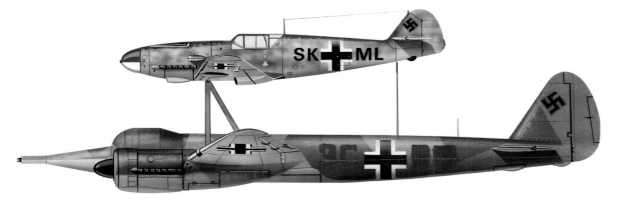

At the end of the war, the Ju 88 was a favourite aircraft for conversion to unmanned flying bomb configuration to serve as the lower half of a Mistel composite. Some retained their noses for training, while others had a massive warhead attached, as seen here.

This Ju 88A-5 served as a testbed for the BMW 003 jet engine, powerplant for the Me 262 and Arado 234 jets. As the war progressed, such second-line duties became the lot of early Ju 88 variants.

later G-series night-fighters. Parallel reconnaissance aircraft were of the T-series, not built in quantity.

Not included in the variants list, the Mistel missiles were (usually war-weary) Ju 88s rebuilt as pilotless missiles, with the nose replaced by an extremely large warhead, usually a 3800-kg (8,380-lb) hollow-charge device with a long stand-off fuse.

In May 1916 a Bristol Scout was carried to a height of 305 m (1,000 ft) on the centre-section of a Porte Baby flying-boat, to test the feasibility of carrying a fighter to within firing range of the German Zeppelins which were carrying out raids on England. In 1943 the wheel turned full circle, with the possibility of pick-a-back aircraft for military purposes revived in Germany following experiments with light aircraft mounted above gliders. The proposal was that time-expired Junkers Ju 88 airframes be converted to pilotless missiles by the installation of a warhead packed with explosives. One of these would then be flown to within range of a target, controlled by the pilot of a single-engined fighter which was mounted on struts above the bomber's centre-section. The fighter would release the Ju 88 and then guide it to the target.

Initial conversions

The first conversion combined a Ju 88A-4 and a Messerschmitt Bf 109F, and this proved sufficiently successful for Junkers to be contracted to convert 15 Ju 88As to Mistel (mistletoe) configuration, as it was called, presumably to imply its parasitic connection; the programme was codenamed 'Beethoven'. An initial batch of trainers was converted, using Bf 109F-4s as the upper component. The lower component was stripped of non-essential equipment but retained a two-crew layout for training. The nose section could be removed by quick-release bolts and a 3800-kg (8,378-lb) warhead attached.

Operational flying began in mid-1944 when four Allied ships were attacked at night, all being hit but not sunk. Encouraged by these

---

Junkers Ju 88 variants

Ju 88A series (four-seat bombers):
Ju 88A-1 had a span of 18.37 m (60 ft 3 in), two 895-kW (1,200-hp) Jumo 211B-1 engines; **Ju 88A-2** had 211G-1 engines, RATO units; **Ju 88A-3** was a dual conversion trainer; **Ju 88A-4** had a span of 20 m (65 ft 7 in), 1000-kW (1,340-hp) Jumo 211J-1 or J-2; **Ju 88A-5** was as A-4 but with earlier B or G engines; **Ju 88A-6** was as the Ju 88A-5 with large balloon fender and cable cutter; **Ju 88A-6/U** modified without fender but three seats, Hohentwiel radar, 211J engines and drop tanks; **Ju 88A-7** was as the Ju 88A-5 with 211H engines and dual pilot controls; **Ju 88A-8** was a three-seater with 211F engines and cable cutters; **Ju 88A-9** was a tropical Ju 88A-1 with sand filters, survival gear, sunblinds, etc.; **Ju 88A-10** was a tropical Ju 88A-5; **Ju 88A-11** was a tropical Ju 88A-4; **Ju 88A-12** was a Ju 88A-4 trainer conversion without armament, gondola or dive brakes; **Ju 88A-13** was a close-support Ju 88A-4 with extra armour, 16 forward-firing guns and fragmentation bombs; **Ju 88A-14** was an improved Ju 88A-4 with many small changes, often 20-mm cannon firing against ships from front of gondola; **Ju 88A-15** had three seats, wooden bomb bay extension, total 3000-kg (6,614-lb) internal bomb load; **Ju 88A-16** was a dual unarmed Ju 88A-14; **Ju 88A-17** was a Ju 88A-4 torpedo conversion with two LT F5b

torpedoes and equipment fairing beside nose

Ju 88B series:
four-seat bombers with enlarged streamlined crew compartment, various BMW-engined prototypes leading to Ju 188; 10 **Ju 88B-0** used as operational reconnaissance aircraft

Ju 88C series (three-seat heavy or night-fighters):
Ju 88C-1 based on Ju 88A-1 with 20-mm MG FF and three 7.92-mm (0.31-in) MG 17; **Ju 88C-2** was the same but had a new unglazed nose; **Ju 88C-3** had BMW 801 engines but engines reserved for Fw 190s; **Ju 88C-4** was a new-build night-fighter based on Ju 88A-4 with two extra MG FF in offset gondola and provision for 12 MG 81 in pods; **Ju 88C-5** had 1268-kW (1,700-hp) BMW 801D-2 engines; **Ju-88C-6** was the major variant with 211J engines, various guns; **Ju 88C-6b** had radar and new HF radio; **Ju 88C-6c**, SN-2 radar and other sensors later, some with 211TK turbocharged engines; later *schräge Musik* guns; **Ju 88C-7a** had forward bomb bay with two MG FF instead of bombs; **Ju 88C-7b** was as Ju 88C-7a but with external bomb racks; **Ju 88C-7c** had BMW engines, MG 151 nose gun(s)

Ju 88D-series (four-seat reconnaissance aircraft):
Ju 88D-0 had Jumo 211B-1, large camera installations, no external bomb

racks; **Ju 88D-1** not built; **Ju 88D-2** had 211B, 211G or 211H, external bombs or drop tanks; **Ju 88D-3** was a tropical Ju 88D-1; **Ju 88D-4** was a tropical Ju 88D-2; **Ju 88D-5** standardised on triple fan of cameras

Ju 88G series (night-fighters):
Ju 88G-1 was based on Ju 88C-6c but tail of Ju 188, BMW 801D engines, four ventral MG 151, SN-2 radar and other sensors (see large three-view drawing, p. 179) which increased crew workload, later demanding a fourth man; **Ju 88G-2/3/5** not built; **Ju 88G-4** had small changes; **Ju 88G-6a** had BMW 801G engines, usually rear-warning SN-2 aerial and (like many Ju 88G-1 and Ju 88G-4) *schräge Musik*; **Ju 88G-6b** had FuG 350 Naxos Z in cockpit roof; **Ju 88G-6c** had 1306-kW (1,750-hp) Jumo 213A engines, *schräge Musik* moved to immediately behind cockpit; **Ju 88G-7** had high-blown 213E engines with very broad propeller blades; **Ju 88G-7a** had canted SN-2 array; **Ju 88G-7b** had SN-3 or FuG 218 Neptun radar; **Ju 88G-7c** had FuG 240 Berlin centimetric radar and speed of 674 km/h (402 mph)

Ju 88H series (long-fuselage long-range versions):
Ju 88H-1 was a three-seat reconnaissance machine; **Ju 88H-2** was a three-seat *Zerstörer* with six forward-firing MG 151; **Ju 88H-3** was a further stretch with 1671-kW (2,240-hp)

Jumo 213A-12 engines for ultra-long-range reconnaissance; **Ju 88H-4** was as Ju 88H-3 plus large surveillance nose radar and two drop tanks

Ju 88P series (anti-tank aircraft):
Ju 88P-1 was a two- or three-seater, based on Ju 88A-4, with 7.5-cm PaK 40 gun (prototype had KwK 39) aimed by pilot using MG 81 for sighting, with hand-loading for two shots on each firing pass; **Ju 88P-2** had twin BK 3,7 in large gondola; **Ju 88P-3** was as Ju 88P-2 but more armour; **Ju 88P-4** had a single BK 5

Ju 88S series
high-speed three-seat bomber, based on Ju 88A-4 but with gondola deleted, smooth nose and more power; **Ju 88S-0** had BMW 801D engines, single 13-mm (0.51-in) dorsal gun, bomb load only 14 SD 65 (65-kg/143-lb) bombs in forward bay; **Ju 88S-1** had BMW 801Gs, GM-1 boost system, could carry two SD 1000 externally; **Ju 88S-2** had turbocharged BMW 801TJ engines, giant wooden bomb bay as on Ju 88A-15; **Ju 88S-3** had 1671-kW (2,240-hp) Jumo 213A engines with GM-1

Ju 88T series:
three-seat reconnaissance variant of Ju 88S; **Ju 88T-1** based on Ju 88S-1 with both bomb bays occupied by fuel or GM-1 tanks; **Ju 88T-3** based on Ju 88S-3, and capable of 660 km/h (410 mph) without drop tanks

Right: Ju 88As of an unidentified unit somewhere on the Eastern Front. One of the aircraft in the background has what appears to be a V3, V6, V8 or V9 unit identifier, which does not tie up with the known Ju 88 operators on the Eastern Front, who included III/KG 1 with a V4 identity prefix.

Below: Ground crew dig snow from the wheels of a Ju 88 (perhaps a Ju 88A-5 reconnaissance aircraft) on the Eastern Front, while one of the aircrew watches from his perch above the starboard engine. The aircraft has long-range fuel tanks below the inner wings.

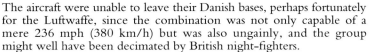

The aircraft were unable to leave their Danish bases, perhaps fortunately for the Luftwaffe, since the combination was not only capable of a mere 236 mph (380 km/h) but was also ungainly, and the group might well have been decimated by British night-fighters.

Mistel action

The next assault was to be against Soviet arms factories, with a planned date during March 1945. A total of 125 Mistels was then on order, of which 100 were required for this operation, which had to be cancelled when advancing Soviet troops occupied the airfields which were to have been used.

Sporadic attacks were made against bridges on the Eastern and Western Fronts, but heavy losses were suffered by the Mistels. Development continued, however, including the use of new Ju 88G-10 and Ju 88H-4 airframes on the production line. The Ju-88G-10s were twinned with Fw 190A-8s with overwing long-range tanks as Mistel 3C aircraft, while the Ju 88H-4/Fw 190A-8 composite became the Mistel 3B. A different role was served by a modified Mistel 3B where the lower component with a crew of three became an ultra-long-range pathfinder, carrying its own Fw 190A-8 escort as the upper component, for launch only in emergency.

One of the last Mistel combinations tested consisted of a Ta 152H/Ju 88G-7 which flew in the last few weeks of the war. Total Mistel production has been estimated at around 250. By 1945, Ju 88G-10s and Ju 88H-4s were being turned into Mistel aircraft on the assembly line, never flying as ordinary aircraft. Including them in the 355 'fighters' built in 1945, the total Ju 88 production is usually calculated to be 14,780, including 104 prototypes.

results, the Luftwaffe ordered a further 75 Ju 88G-1 fighters to be converted, this time with Focke-Wulf Fw 190A-6 or Fw 190F-8 fighters as the upper components of what became the Mistel 2 composite. Unfortunately, the combination of the Ju 88G with full fuel load and warhead, plus the Fw 190, meant that the lower component was considerably overloaded and burst tyres caused a number of disastrous take-off accidents.

Plans for a night attack on the British Fleet in Scapa Flow by 60 Mistel combinations, in December 1944, were thwarted by bad weather.

First of the radar-equipped night-fighter versions, the Ju 88C-6b was powered by 999-kW (1,340-hp) Jumo 211J engines and fitted with FuG 202 Lichtenstein BC radar. The radar receiver aerials were on the wings, and this Ju 88C-6b also has wing dipoles further back for FuG 227 Flensburg which homed-in on RAF tail-warning radars.

The Ju 88P series was uniformly clumsy, sluggish and vulnerable, although the aircraft were well protected against ground fire. This example was a Ju 88P-3, with two BK 3,7 (Flak 38) high-velocity guns of 37-mm calibre housed in a large ventral box, with the guns offset to the left. Similar aircraft were used against bombers.

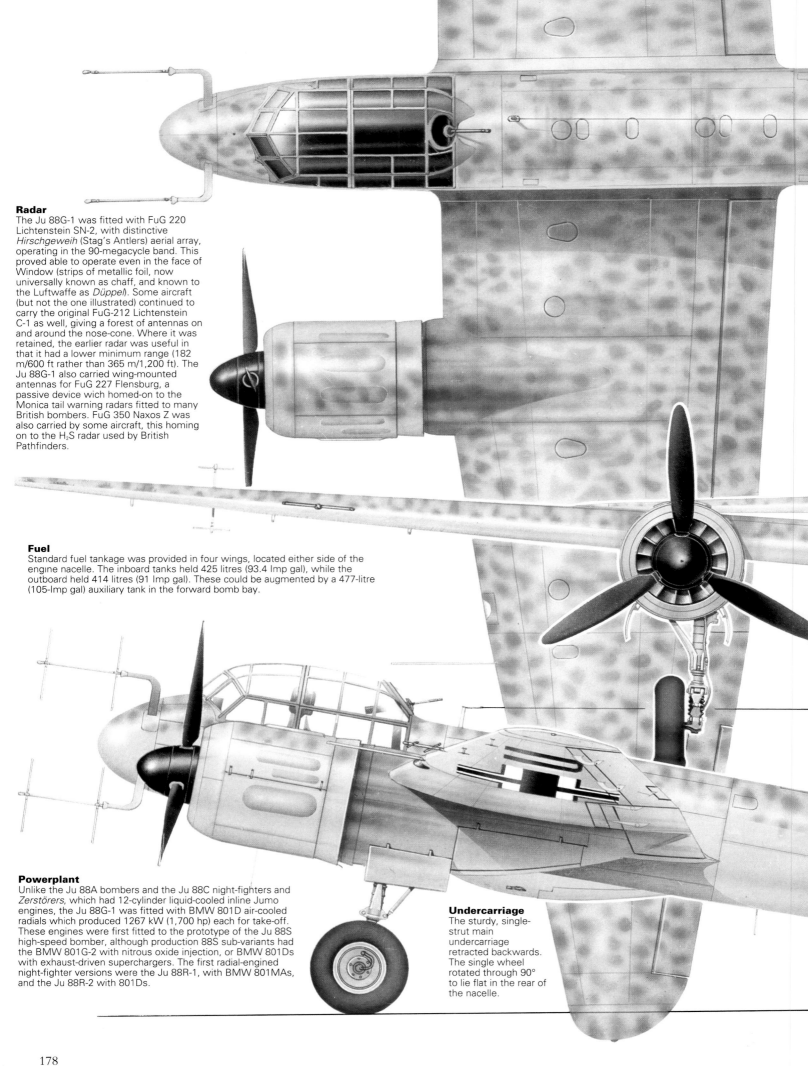

Radar
The Ju 88G-1 was fitted with FuG 220 Lichtenstein SN-2, with distinctive *Hirschgeweih* (Stag's Antlers) aerial array, operating in the 90-megacycle band. This proved able to operate even in the face of Window (strips of metallic foil, now universally known as chaff, and known to the Luftwaffe as *Düppel*). Some aircraft (but not the one illustrated) continued to carry the original FuG-212 Lichtenstein C-1 as well, giving a forest of antennas on and around the nose-cone. Where it was retained, the earlier radar was useful in that it had a lower minimum range (182 m/600 ft rather than 365 m/1,200 ft). The Ju 88G-1 also carried wing-mounted antennas for FuG 227 Flensburg, a passive device wich homed-on to the Monica tail warning radars fitted to many British bombers. FuG 350 Naxos Z was also carried by some aircraft, this homing on to the H₂S radar used by British Pathfinders.

Fuel
Standard fuel tankage was provided in four wings, located either side of the engine nacelle. The inboard tanks held 425 litres (93.4 Imp gal), while the outboard held 414 litres (91 Imp gal). These could be augmented by a 477-litre (105-Imp gal) auxiliary tank in the forward bomb bay.

Powerplant
Unlike the Ju 88A bombers and the Ju 88C night-fighters and *Zerstörers*, which had 12-cylinder liquid-cooled inline Jumo engines, the Ju 88G-1 was fitted with BMW 801D air-cooled radials which produced 1267 kW (1,700 hp) each for take-off. These engines were first fitted to the prototype of the Ju 88S high-speed bomber, although production 88S sub-variants had the BMW 801G-2 with nitrous oxide injection, or BMW 801Ds with exhaust-driven superchargers. The first radial-engined night-fighter versions were the Ju 88R-1, with BMW 801MAs, and the Ju 88R-2 with 801Ds.

Undercarriage
The sturdy, single-strut main undercarriage retracted backwards. The single wheel rotated through 90° to lie flat in the rear of the nacelle.

Tail unit
The Ju 88G-1 was essentially similar to the Ju 88C-6c, but with revised armament, more powerful radial engines and more angular, increased-area tail surfaces (taken from the Ju 188) to restore longitudnal stability and improve pitch control.

Junkers Ju 88G-1 7./NJG 2 Gilze-Rijen July 1944

Crew
The crew of the Ju 88 night-fighter was reduced to three, by elimination of the bombardier/second pilot. The pilot sat in the front of the upper cockpit, offset to port, while in the rear of the upper cabin sat the flight engineer, and the radio operator, who operated the rearward-facing 13-mm MG 131 machine-gun. A fourth crewmember was added later, to cope with the increased number of detection devices. The ventral gondola inherited from the bomber was finally deleted, and replaced by a gun pack (offset to port) containing four MG 151 20-mm cannon.

In the spring of 1944, RAF heavy bombers were being hacked down in droves. Concentrations of Flak (AAA) were blamed, and the bombers continued to cruise through the German sky like lighthouses, emitting up to three sets of radar signals, while so blind underneath that there was not so much as a porthole, let alone a gun. The fact that most of the losses were due to night-fighters emerged gradually, and it was near the end of the war before it was belatedly realised that many of these formated under the bomber and fired upwards in a perfect no-deflection shot. The most formidable night-fighter was almost unknown until, by a fantastic piece of luck, the crew of 4R+UR, a Ju 88G-1 of 7./NJG 2, became hopelessly lost on the night of 12/13 July 1944. Obergefreiter (equivalent to an RAF LAC) Mäckle had been looking for minelaying Stirlings and suffered compass failure. Eventually he homed on a radio beacon which seemed in the right direction, found an airfield and landed. He had brought the vital SN-2 radar and FuG 227 Flensburg to RAF Woodbridge, Suffolk. The *Hirschgeweih* (Stag's Antlers) aerials of the SN-2 are on the nose (a very few expert pilots had them on the rear fuselage). Wing dipole aerials received emissions from RAF Monica tail-warning radars and fed them to the Flensburg direction finder.

Keith Fretwell.

Junkers Ju 188

By the start of World War II, it was obvious to the German Reichsluftfahrtministerium that the Ju 88 was an aircraft of outstanding merit. Indeed, its very excellence was to some extent a drawback to Junkers, in that any major development was considered unnecessary. Right at the start of the programme in January 1936, the company had sketched a Ju 85B and Ju 88B with a revised crew compartment forming a fully glazed forward fuselage of smooth aerodynamic shape, with no separate windscreen, and developments of these designs were projected with new and more powerful engines such as the BMW 139 and Jumo 213.

Junkers was at last allowed to try out this new crew compartment in a single Ju 88B, and began its flight test programme in early 1940. Apart from having 1194-kW (1,600-hp) BMW 801 radial engines, the rest of the 88B was virtually the same as an 88A, although a bomb rack was added under each outer wing, outboard of the dive brakes. In 1940 Junkers also built 10 pre-production Ju 88B-0 aircraft, but although these proved efficient and popular it was considered that there was no point in disrupting Ju 88A production. The B-0s were adapted as reconnaissance aircraft, with bomb racks removed and extra fuel in the bomb bay. One was modified with a different version of the BMW 801 engine and a dorsal turret mounting an MG 131 gun, and this machine, the Ju 88E-0, was used during 1941 for various tests.

For the future, all hopes rested on the next generation, the so-called Bomber B. The contenders for this programme were eventually whittled down to three: the Do 317, Fw 191 and Ju 288. By the autumn of 1942, it was increasingly clear that none of these programmes was likely to produce anything that the Luftwaffe could use for a long time to come. This threw increased emphasis on the possibility of major improvements to the existing aircraft, and none seemed a better candidate than the Ju 88. Junkers had never completely halted such developments, and had managed to make major changes to the airframe which improved handling at high gross weights.

Changing face of the Ju 88

The Ju 88 V27, flown in September 1941, had an airframe resembling the Ju 88E-0 but with extended outer wings, the new pointed tips having a span increased from 20 to 22 m (65.6 to 72.2 ft). The Ju 88 V44, flown in the spring of 1942, continued the improvements with an enlarged tail, the span of the horizontal tail being increased and the fin and rudder being enlarged into an almost rectangular shape (this tail was later adopted for the Ju 88G night-fighter, and the new wing on the 88G-7).

In October 1942 the critical decision was made to transfer some staff from the Ju 288 and put full development resources into a development of the Ju 88 designated Ju 188. The basis was to be the Ju 88 V44, which thereupon became the **Ju 188 V1**. By January 1943, a second prototype was in the air at the Bernburg plant, which had been selected as the Ju 188 assembly centre (Dessau remaining the main design centre). The RLM decreed that the initial production **Ju 188A-0** should be a bomber, capable of both level and dive bombing, and fitted with the same slatted dive-brakes and automatic pull-out gear as the Ju 88A. The ministry further stipulated that, to avoid delays due to engine

Left: A line-up of Ju 188D-2s of 1.(F)/FAGr 124 at Kirkenes, Norway. The Ju 188D-2 was intended primarily for the maritime strike and reconnaissance role, and most had FuG 200 Hohentwiel radar.

Below: The Ju 88 V44 was the second of the Ju 188 development vehicles, and introduced the enlarged tail surfaces. As such, it was redesignated as the Ju 188 V1 during mid-1942, joined on the flight test programme by another aircraft to hasten development.

shortages, the 188 should be able to be powered by either the BMW 801 or Jumo 213, each in the form of a 'bolt on' power egg requiring the minimum of aircraft modification.

The first production aircraft to leave the assembly line were actually **Ju 188E-0**s and **E-1**s, because they had BMW engines (the A-series was powered by the Jumo 213). The E-0 and E-1 entered service with Ekdo d.Lw 188 and KG 6 in May 1943, the first operational *Gruppe* being I/KG 6, which began missions in the Pathfinder role on 20 October 1943. By the end of that year production of the Ju 188, so long ignored, was in full swing. Bernburg had delivered 283 aircraft, and assembly lines were in action at ATG (Leipzig) and Siebel (Halle).

The first operational unit to receive the Ju 188 was I/KG 6, and it used its aircraft for pathfinder duties. The wing was heavily involved in the spring 1944 'Little Blitz' over England, during which time this Ju 188A-2 is seen being loaded for a mission.

In fact ,there were differences apart from the engines between the two initial production versions. Both the Ju 188A-1 and E-1 were four-seat medium bombers with the same airframe, from which the dive-brakes and pull-out gear had been eliminated (dive bombing no longer being a requirement). The dorsal turrets were the main difference, the A-series having the EDL 151 with an MG 151/20 cannon and the E-series having the originally proposed EDL 131 with the MG 131 of 13-mm calibre. In general, the A-series had slightly higher performance, especially when using the MW50 power boosting system. The **A-3** version was a torpedo bomber, able to carry two LT 1B or F5b torpedoes under the inner wings, and with a long bulge along the right side of the forward fuselage to accommodate the torpedo aiming and steering gear. The equivalent BMW-engined version was the **E-2**, and this frequently had the dorsal turret not fitted. Both the A-3 and E-2 often carried FuG 200 Hohentwiel anti-ship radar.

At the start of the programme, Junkers had proposed fitting the FA15 type of remotely sighted and power-controlled tail barbette, housing an MG 131Z (twin 13-mm guns). This complex and weighty installation was flown in the **Ju 188C-0**, a converted A-0. It was concluded that poor aiming accuracy and reliability, coupled with the other penalties, made the scheme not worthwhile. On the other hand,

Above: Most Ju 188s had a rearward-firing 13-mm MG 131 and one MG 151 turret-mounted 7.62-mm. The Ju 188 was derived from the Ju 88B, and featured the same deeper, more heavily glazed forward fuselage.

Right: The BMW 801-powered Ju 188E series was delivered to the Luftwaffe slightly ahead of the Jumo 213-powered Ju 188A. This pre-production Ju 188E-0 was modified to serve as a fast staff transport for General-Luftzeugmeister Erhard Milch.

Junkers Ju 188

Torpedo-bomber versions were produced of both A- and E-series, this aircraft being a Ju 188E-2. Racks under the wingroots could carry an 800-kg (1,763-lb) LT 1B or 765-kg (1,686-lb) LT F5b torpedo each, while guidance equipment was contained in a fairing on the side of the nose. FuG 200 Hohentwiel radar was fitted.

the urgent need of the Luftwaffe for a high-performance reconnaissance aircraft led to many Ju 188As being completed as **Ju 188D-1** or **D-2** aircraft. These had no forward-firing MG 151 cannon, only three crew, increased fuel capacity and gross weight increased to 15200 kg (33,510 lb). These versions carried various arrangements of Rb 50/30, 70/30, NRb 40/25 or 50/25 cameras, and the D-2 invariably was fitted with FuG 200 radar for maritime operations.

The equivalent BMW-engined versions were the **Ju 188F-1** and **F-2**, the latter being the radar-equipped maritime aircraft. Engines were BMW 801D-2 or G-2, rated at 1268 kW (1,700 hp). Further developments of the BMW aircraft were aimed at overcoming the blind spot in the defensive system directly behind the tail. Having reluctantly rejected the FA15 barbette, Junkers considered fitting a manned tail gun. One possibility was a gunner lying prone and aiming a single pivoted MG 151, this requiring only minor structural alterations. The idea was rejected in favour of a manned version of the FA15, with superimposed MG 131 guns manned by a small gunner who could just squeeze into it (and could never have got out in a hurry). The resulting aircraft, the **Ju 188G-0**, looked very like the C-0, but the limits of the arc of fire of the turret were very poor. In the end, this answer was rejected by the Luftwaffe, and Junkers pressed for renewed effort on the FA15 barbette. This was intended for the production **Ju 188G-2** bomber and the **H-1** reconnaissance aircraft. In the event, these projects were overtaken by developments of the generally superior Junkers Ju 388.

Combat experience

Junkers never did succeed in providing the Ju 188 with an adequate all-round defence system. From the summer of 1940, the start of the Battle of Britain, it had been obvious that the kind of fast bomber envisaged by the Luftwaffe in the mid-1930s, and built in enormous numbers, could not survive in the face of interception by modern fighters. Both hasty lash-ups and considered improvements (such as the EDL cannon turrets) were tested, but to the end of the war aircraft in this class had a perilous career in any part of the sky infested with Allied fighters.

This is the first production Ju 188E-1, which beat the Ju 188A into service because of the readier supply of BMW 801 engines which powered it. The aircraft had a 13-mm machine-gun in the dorsal turret, instead of a 20-mm cannon.

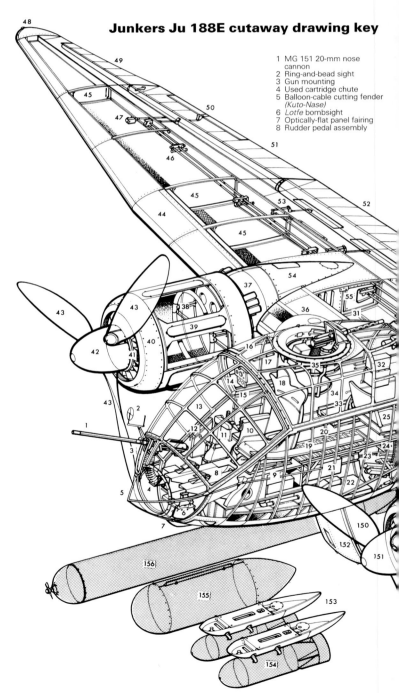

Junkers Ju 188E cutaway drawing key

1 MG 151 20-mm nose cannon
2 Ring-and-bead sight
3 Gun mounting
4 Used cartridge chute
5 Balloon-cable cutting fender (*Kuto-Nase*)
6 *Lotfe* bombsight
7 Optically-flat panel fairing
8 Rudder pedal assembly

This aircraft at Bordeaux-Mérignac is a Ju 188E-2 with its Hohentwiel radar removed. The EDL 131 turret which normally sat atop the canopy has been removed in favour of a radio aerial.

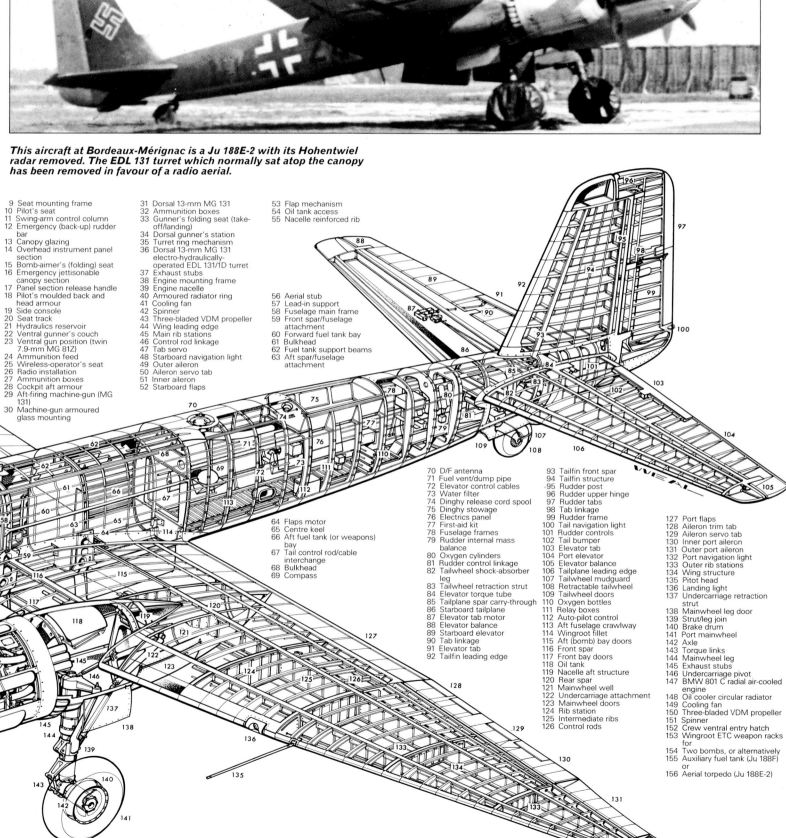

9 Seat mounting frame
10 Pilot's seat
11 Swing-arm control column
12 Emergency (back-up) rudder bar
13 Canopy glazing
14 Overhead instrument panel section
15 Bomb-aimer's (folding) seat
16 Emergency jettisonable canopy section
17 Panel section release handle
18 Pilot's moulded back and head armour
19 Side console
20 Seat track
21 Hydraulics reservoir
22 Ventral gunner's couch
23 Ventral gun position (twin 7.9-mm MG 81Z)
24 Ammunition feed
25 Wireless-operator's seat
26 Radio installation
27 Ammunition boxes
28 Cockpit aft armour
29 Aft-firing machine-gun (MG 131)
30 Machine-gun armoured glass mounting

31 Dorsal 13-mm MG 131
32 Ammunition boxes
33 Gunner's folding seat (take-off/landing)
34 Dorsal gunner's station
35 Turret ring mechanism
36 Dorsal 13-mm MG 131 electro-hydraulically-operated EDL 131/1D turret
37 Exhaust stubs
38 Engine mounting frame
39 Engine nacelle
40 Armoured radiator ring
41 Cooling fan
42 Spinner
43 Three-bladed VDM propeller
44 Wing leading edge
45 Main rib stations
46 Control rod linkage
47 Tab servo
48 Starboard navigation light
49 Outer aileron
50 Aileron servo tab
51 Inner aileron
52 Starboard flaps

53 Flap mechanism
54 Oil tank access
55 Nacelle reinforced rib

56 Aerial stub
57 Lead-in support
58 Fuselage main frame
59 Front spar/fuselage attachment
60 Forward fuel tank bay
61 Bulkhead
62 Fuel tank support beams
63 Aft spar/fuselage attachment

64 Flaps motor
65 Centre keel
66 Aft fuel tank (or weapons) bay
67 Tail control rod/cable interchange
68 Bulkhead
69 Compass

70 D/F antenna
71 Fuel vent/dump pipe
72 Elevator control cables
73 Water filter
74 Dinghy release cord spool
75 Dinghy stowage
76 Electrics panel
77 First-aid kit
78 Fuselage frames
79 Rudder internal mass balance
80 Oxygen cylinders
81 Rudder control linkage
82 Tailwheel shock-absorber leg
83 Tailwheel retraction strut
84 Elevator torque tube
85 Tailplane spar carry-through
86 Starboard tailplane
87 Elevator tab motor
88 Elevator balance
89 Starboard elevator
90 Tab linkage
91 Elevator tab
92 Tailfin leading edge

93 Tailfin front spar
94 Tailfin structure
95 Rudder post
96 Rudder upper hinge
97 Rudder tabs
98 Tab linkage
99 Rudder frame
100 Tail navigation light
101 Rudder controls
102 Tail bumper
103 Elevator tab
104 Port elevator
105 Elevator balance
106 Tailplane leading edge
107 Tailwheel mudguard
108 Retractable tailwheel
109 Tailwheel doors
110 Oxygen bottles
111 Relay boxes
112 Auto-pilot control
113 Aft fuselage crawlway
114 Wingroot fillet
115 Aft (bomb) bay doors
116 Front spar
117 Front bay doors
118 Oil tank
119 Nacelle aft structure
120 Rear spar
121 Mainwheel well
122 Undercarriage attachment
123 Mainwheel doors
124 Rib station
125 Intermediate ribs
126 Control rods

127 Port flaps
128 Aileron trim tab
129 Aileron servo tab
130 Inner port aileron
131 Outer port aileron
132 Port navigation light
133 Outer rib stations
134 Wing structure
135 Pitot head
136 Landing light
137 Undercarriage retraction strut
138 Mainwheel leg door
139 Strut/leg join
140 Brake drum
141 Port mainwheel
142 Axle
143 Torque links
144 Mainwheel leg
145 Exhaust stubs
146 Undercarriage pivot
147 BMW 801 C radial air-cooled engine
148 Oil cooler circular radiator
149 Cooling fan
150 Three-bladed VDM propeller
151 Spinner
152 Crew ventral entry hatch
153 Wingroot ETC weapon racks for
154 Two bombs, or alternatively
155 Auxiliary fuel tank (Ju 188F) or
156 Aerial torpedo (Ju 188E-2)

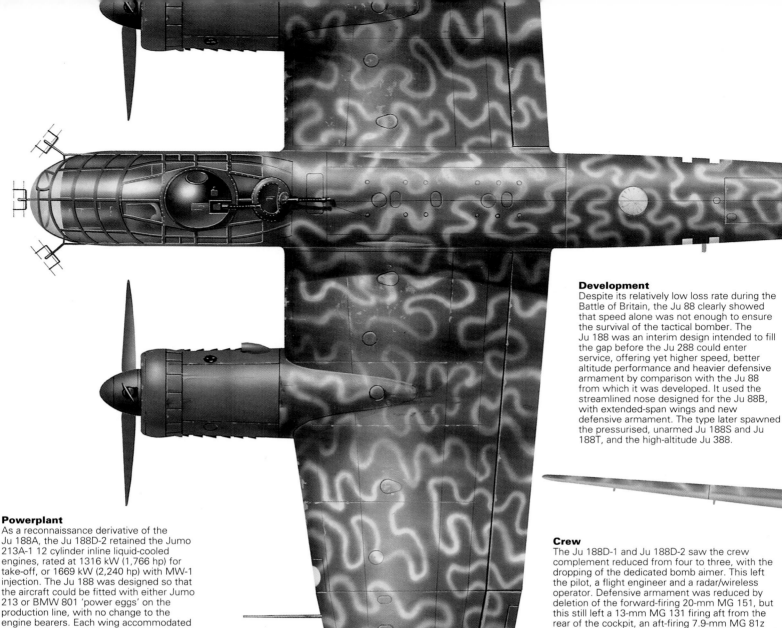

Development

Despite its relatively low loss rate during the Battle of Britain, the Ju 88 clearly showed that speed alone was not enough to ensure the survival of the tactical bomber. The Ju 188 was an interim design intended to fill the gap before the Ju 288 could enter service, offering yet higher speed, better altitude performance and heavier defensive armament by comparison with the Ju 88 from which it was developed. It used the streamlined nose designed for the Ju 88B, with extended-span wings and new defensive armament. The type later spawned the pressurised, unarmed Ju 188S and Ju 188T, and the high-altitude Ju 388.

Powerplant

As a reconnaissance derivative of the Ju 188A, the Ju 188D-2 retained the Jumo 213A-1 12 cylinder inline liquid-cooled engines, rated at 1316 kW (1,766 hp) for take-off, or 1669 kW (2,240 hp) with MW-1 injection. The Ju 188 was designed so that the aircraft could be fitted with either Jumo 213 or BMW 801 'power eggs' on the production line, with no change to the engine bearers. Each wing accommodated a 150-litre (33-Imp gal) methanol-water tank and an 832- and an 850- litre (183- and 187-Imp gall) fuel tank. These were augmented by a 1682-litre (370-Imp.gal) tank in the fuselage and an optional 500-litre (110-Imp gal) auxiliary tank in the bomb bay.

Camouflage

This Ju 188 has pale blue-grey *Wellenmüster* sprayed over its standard green camouflage scheme. *Balkenkreuz* and *Hakenkreuz* are applied in outline form only.

Crew

The Ju 188D-1 and Ju 188D-2 saw the crew complement reduced from four to three, with the dropping of the dedicated bomb aimer. This left the pilot, a flight engineer and a radar/wireless operator. Defensive armament was reduced by deletion of the forward-firing 20-mm MG 151, but this still left a 13-mm MG 131 firing aft from the rear of the cockpit, an aft-firing 7.9-mm MG 81z twin machine-gun below the forward fuselage and a turret-mounted MG 151 20-mm cannon in a power-operated turret above the cockpit.

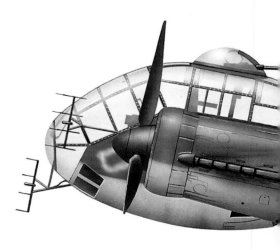

Wing

By comparison with the Ju 88B the Ju 188 had a wing of extended span, with both wingtips and ailerons being extended outboard to give a distinctive pointed outline in plan view. The slotted dive-brakes of the basic Ju 88 were omitted from production versions.

Specification
Junkers Ju 188D-2
Powerplant: two Junkers Jumo 213A-1 12-cylinder liquid-cooled piston engines, each rated at 1268 kW (1,776 hp) for take-off and 1194 kW (1,600 hp) at 5500 m (18,045 ft) (unboosted), or 1671 kW (2,240 hp) for take-off and 1402 kW (1,880 hp) at 4725 m (15,590 ft) (with MW 50 injection)
Dimensions: span 22.0 m (72 ft 2 in); length 14.95 m (49 ft 0½ in); height 4.44 m (14 ft 6 in); wing area 56.0 m² (602 sq ft)
Weights: empty 9900 kg (21,825 lb); maximum loaded 15195 kg (33,500 lb)
Performance: maximum speed 539 km/h (335 mph) at 6200 m (20,340 ft); economical cruising speed 480 km/h (298 mph); service ceiling 10000 m (32,800 ft); range with drop tanks 3395 km (2,200 miles) at 6000 m (19,685 ft)
Armament: one 20-mm MG 151 cannon firing from a streamlined dorsal turret; one 13-mm MG 131 machine-gun firing aft above fuselage; one 7.9-mm MG-81Z twin machine-gun installation firing aft below fuselage; various camera combinations including twin Rb 50/30 or 75/30 for day missions and twin NRb 40/25 or 50/25 for night work

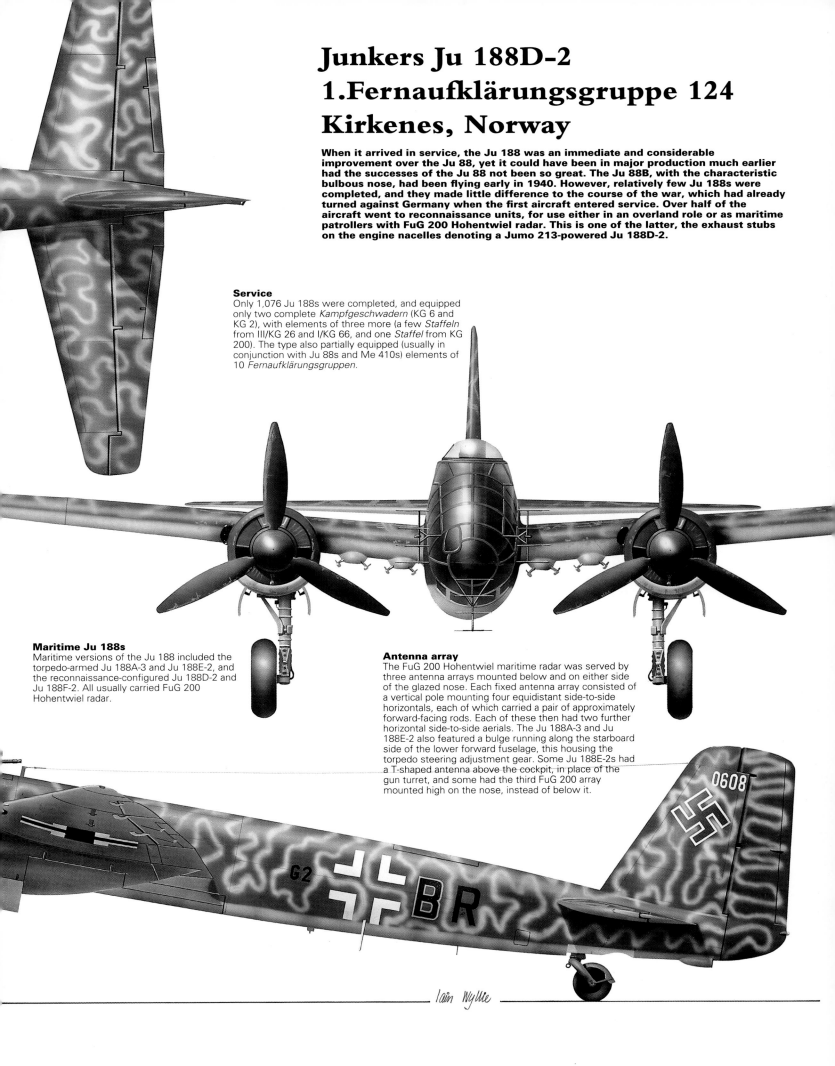

Junkers Ju 188D-2
1.Fernaufklärungsgruppe 124
Kirkenes, Norway

When it arrived in service, the Ju 188 was an immediate and considerable improvement over the Ju 88, yet it could have been in major production much earlier had the successes of the Ju 88 not been so great. The Ju 88B, with the characteristic bulbous nose, had been flying early in 1940. However, relatively few Ju 188s were completed, and they made little difference to the course of the war, which had already turned against Germany when the first aircraft entered service. Over half of the aircraft went to reconnaissance units, for use either in an overland role or as maritime patrollers with FuG 200 Hohentwiel radar. This is one of the latter, the exhaust stubs on the engine nacelles denoting a Jumo 213-powered Ju 188D-2.

Service
Only 1,076 Ju 188s were completed, and equipped only two complete *Kampfgeschwadern* (KG 6 and KG 2), with elements of three more (a few *Staffeln* from III/KG 26 and I/KG 66, and one *Staffel* from KG 200). The type also partially equipped (usually in conjunction with Ju 88s and Me 410s) elements of 10 *Fernaufklärungsgruppen*.

Maritime Ju 188s
Maritime versions of the Ju 188 included the torpedo-armed Ju 188A-3 and Ju 188E-2, and the reconnaissance-configured Ju 188D-2 and Ju 188F-2. All usually carried FuG 200 Hohentwiel radar.

Antenna array
The FuG 200 Hohentwiel maritime radar was served by three antenna arrays mounted below and on either side of the glazed nose. Each fixed antenna array consisted of a vertical pole mounting four equidistant side-to-side horizontals, each of which carried a pair of approximately forward-facing rods. Each of these then had two further horizontal side-to-side aerials. The Ju 188A-3 and Ju 188E-2 also featured a bulge running along the starboard side of the lower forward fuselage, this housing the torpedo steering adjustment gear. Some Ju 188E-2s had a T-shaped antenna above the cockpit, in place of the gun turret, and some had the third FuG 200 array mounted high on the nose, instead of below it.

This aircraft is the Ju 188 V2 after modification to serve as the prototype for the Ju 188G series. Just visible is the deepened rear fuselage, which housed a manned gun turret containing twin MG 131s. Traverse of the guns was poor and the turret very cramped.

Left: Reducing the crew to three, removing cannon and replacing bombs with drop tanks made the Ju 188 a capable reconnaissance platform. Jumo-powered aircraft were Ju 188Ds, while BMW-powered aircraft were Ju 188Fs. This is an F-1 for overland reconnaissance.

Below: This Ju 188D-2 was captured intact by the Allies and extensively tested at RAE Farnborough, where it is seen with Hohentwiel radar and dorsal gun removed. Test pilots were impressed with its good handling and performance.

FuG 200 Hohentwiel-equipped Ju 188D-2 of 1.(F)/122 at Kirkenes, Norway in 1944.

Above: This damaged Ju 188, formerly operated by KG 6 and captured at Melsbroek in 1944, wears temporary black undersurfaces, and was used for night pathfinder missions over the British Isles.

In the autumn of 1943, the project staff at Dessau had rushed into a major effort on high-altitude Ju 188s, with a pressurised crew compartment. Proposals were made for the **Ju 188J** *Zerstörer*, the **188K** bomber and the **188L** reconnaissance aircraft. These obviously made sense, and in September 1943 Junkers was ordered to hasten these under a new 8-series RLM type number of 388 (thus, these became the 388J, K and L). At the same time, Junkers was requested to use the same pressurised forward fuselage in the **Ju 188S** high-altitude intruder and **188T** reconnaissance aircraft.

The S and T were to be devoid of defensive armament, relying on their height and speed to evade interception. Thus, both had an almost perfectly streamlined forward fuselage, the engines being Jumo 213E-1s fitted with GM-1 nitrous oxide power boosting to give 1260 kW (1,690 hp) at 9570 m (31,400 ft). The **S-1** could carry 800 kg (1,763 lb) of bombs internally, and with full bomb load could reach 685 km/h (426 mph) at 11500 m (37,730 ft). The lighter **T-1**, with two large Rb cameras, could reach 700 km/h (435 mph) at the same height, posing a major interception problem. Both versions went into limited production, and deliveries of the S-1 from the ATG factory began in about May 1944. Neither reached the Luftwaffe in quantity, however, and this was partly due to a change in priority. By late 1944, most of the S-1 aircraft, both those completed and on the assembly line, had cabin pressurisation removed, together with the GM-1 system, and equipment added to fit them for low-level ground attack. A 50-mm BK 5 gun was mounted under the fuselage, streamlined by a large blister fairing, and armour was added around the engines and crew compartment. The new designation was **Ju 188S-1/U**. Some did go into action, usually with a crew of two.

Small numbers (between 10 and 80) of S-1 and T-1 aircraft were transferred to the Merseburg plant, where they are reported to have been converted into Ju 388L-0 reconnaissance aircraft. Some Junkers records even suggest that other Ju 388s began life as Ju 188S or T aircraft, but the evidence was lost in the chaos at the end of the war.

From the outset, the Ju 188 had a reputation in the Luftwaffe which, if anything, was even greater than that of the great Ju 88. It handled better, especially at high weights, and it was able to make full use of the power of the BMW 801 and Jumo 213 engines (which the Ju 88 could not do). Nevertheless, partly because of the lost two years

during which Bomber B held centre stage, the Ju 188 was unable to be made in anything resembling adequate numbers. Whereas production of the Ju 88 exceeded 15,000, total acceptances of all versions of the Ju 188 by the Luftwaffe amounted to only 1,076 − 283 in 1943 and 793 in 1944. (Output of the Ju 388, of course, never got into its stride at all.) Of this modest total, something like 570 were Ju 188D and 188F reconnaissance aircraft.

Even the reconnaissance aircraft accomplished little. No photographs were brought back of the huge and prolonged build-up of forces in England prior to D-Day, and reconnaissance flights over the British Isles were almost non-existent until the advent at the end of 1944 of the Arado Ar 234B. The same held true on the Italian front, where the Arado jet ended a long period in which Field Marshal Kesselring had been virtually devoid of any reconnaissance information.

Of the bomber versions, most were fitted with FuG 200 and operated in the anti-shipping role from Denmark and Norway. These aircraft would have been extremely valuable in the era of the desperate convoys to the northern ports of the Soviet Union in 1942, but in late 1944 there was little for them to do but wait for the order from Admiral Doenitz to surrender. They had no anti-submarine capability.

At the end of the war, the excellent qualities of the Ju 188 were recognised by France's resurgent Aéronavale, which adopted the type for front-line use as its chief land-based bomber. It put at least 30 captured Ju 188Es and Fs into use, each being fully overhauled and given various different items of equipment and instruments. At least 12 new Ju 188Es were delivered by SNCASE (later Sud-Est Aviation) at Toulouse, these making use of various German components as well as many made in French factories. The Aéronavale Ju 188s (which shared the same powerplant as the Nord 1402 Noroit amphibian) had a relatively short active life with the squadrons, but nine were subsequently used for valuable test programmes. These programmes included the development of piston engines, turbojets and guided missiles.

A Ju 188, two Bf 109s and an Fw 190 await destruction by Allied hands. Sabotaged before capture, they were not selected for evaluation and have been parked together for burning, bales of petrol-soaked hay waiting for the match.

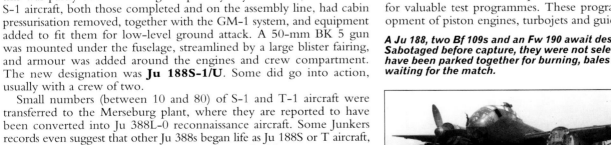

Junkers Ju 252

Construction of three Ju 252 prototypes began in July 1940, the design being a result of various studies to provide a Ju 52/3m follow-on for Deutsche Luft Hansa. When it emerged, the **Ju 252 V1** bore little resemblence to its illustrious forebear other than the trimotor layout. The *Trapoklappe* hydraulic rear loading ramp was an important feature, enabling the carriage of light vehicles and the dropping of para-retarded loads in flight. Power came from a trio of Jumo 211Fs and the cabin was pressurised.

The Ju 252 V1 (D-ADCC) first flew in October 1941, followed by the **V2** and **V3** in the winter months. Despite an order from DLH for 25 aircraft, the needs of the Luftwaffe were by now far greater than the airline, and Junkers was ordered to develop the aircraft for military needs. Consequently the first production prototype, the **Ju 252 V4** (DF+BP), featured defensive armament.

The V4 underwent acceptance trials at Rechlin, before being used for special transport tasks, these including the delivery of DB 606 engines to KG 40 for its He 177s. Junkers proposed that the Ju 252 should replace the Ju 52/3m with transport units, but the transport situation was so desperate that it was felt imprudent to upset the production lines. Furthermore, the Ju 252 would place a greater strain on the supply of strategic materials.

Major assemblies for 11 further aircraft had been completed when work on the Ju 252 was called to a halt, although Junkers was allowed to complete them. Assigned prototype numbers **V5** to **V15**, they were officially designated **Ju 252A-1** and were delivered during the latter part of 1942. The *Trapoklappe* installation, good range and high internal capacity made them naturals for covert missions. One was delivered to the viermotorigen Transportstaffel (later LTS 290) to fly alongside the Ju 290, while others joined the Gruppe Gartenfeldt, which used them for special missions such as agent drops in North Africa on behalf of the Reichssicherheitshauptamt. By the time this unit was redesignated I/KG 200 in February 1944, two Ju 252s were still on charge.

Specification
Junkers Ju 252A-1
Type: general purpose transport
Powerplant: three Junkers Jumo 211F inverted-Vee 12-cylinder engines, each rated at 1000 kW (1,340 hp) for take-off
Performance: maximum speed 438 km/h (272 mph); maximum cruising speed 390 km/h (242 mph); service ceiling 6300 m (20,670 ft); range with maximum payload 3980 km (2,473 miles); range with 2000-kg (4,410-lb) load 6600 km (4,100 miles)
Weights: empty 13100 kg (28,880 lb); normal loaded 22480 kg (49,560 lb); maximum overload 24000 kg (52,910 lb)
Dimensions: wing span 34.09 m (111 ft 10 in); length 25.10 m (82 ft 4 in); height 5.75 m (18 ft 10¼ in); wing area 122.6 m² (1,320 sq ft)
Armament: one 13-mm MG 131 machine-gun in EDL 131 dorsal turret, two 7.9-mm MG 15 machine-guns in beam positions

The **Trapoklappe** *allowed for easy loading and offloading of bulky items. Here a DB 606 engine is delivered to KG 40 at Bordeaux-Mérignac by the Ju 252 V4.*

Junkers Ju 287

One of the most remarkable aircraft of World War II stemmed from work began in early 1943 by Dipl.-Ing Hans Wocke to produce a heavy bomber with speed higher than those of contemporary fighters. Jet engines and swept-wing technology provided the basic answers, but the low-speed handling of normal swept wings proved a problem. Wocke suggested a forward-swept wing, which would alleviate these problems, although causing structural aeroelasticity problems of its own. So radical was the programme that it was decided to fly a full-scale testbed, the **Ju 287 V1**. This consisted of the new forward-swept wings mated to a He 177 fuselage, Ju 388 tail, fixed Ju 352 mainwheels (with large spats) and a nosewheel from a captured B-24 Liberator. Two jet engines were huing in pods under the wing trailing edge, while another two were mounted either side of the forward fuselage. For take-off a pair of Walter 501 rocket packs were carried under the engine

nacelles, being jettisoned after take-off.

This contraption flew for the first time on 16 August 1944, and completed 17 fairly uneventful flights, proving the basic soundness of the concept. Work proceeded on the 'true' prototype, the **V2**, which had a new fuselage, retractable undercarriage and six BMW 003A-1 turbojets in clusters of three under the leading edges of each wing. The **V3** would have featured a pressure cabin, weapon bay and the full operational equipment intended for the **Ju 287A-1** bomber. The **Ju 287B-1** was to have had four 12.75-kN (2,866-lb) thrust Heinkel-Hirth 011A-1 jets, while the **Ju 287B-2** would have had two 34.26-kN (7,700-lb) thrust BMW 018 engines.

The V2 was virtually complete when Soviet forces overran the factory. The aircraft, and the development team (including Wocke), were ferried back to Russia, where the aircraft was flown for the first time in 1947 after completion at Podberezhye.

Specification
Junkers Ju 287 V1
Type: aerodynamic test-bed
Powerplant: four Junkers Jumo 004B-1 Orkan turbojets each rated at 8.83 kN (1,984 lb) thrust
Performance: maximum speed 558 km/h (347 mph) at 6000 m (19,685 ft)
Weights: empty 12500 kg (27,557 lb); maximum loaded 20000 kg (44,092 lb)
Dimensions: wing span 20.11 m (65 ft 11¾ in); length 18.30 m (60 ft 0½ in); wing area 61.00 m² (656.6 sq ft)

Flight tests revealed no serious flaws in the Ju 287 wing, although high-speed aeroelasticity problems did surface (as expected). In July 1944 work on all German bomber programmes was terminated, although work on the Ju 287 started again in early 1945. The operational Ju 287A-1 would have been able to carry a bomb-load of about 4000 kg (8,800 lb) at a speed of 793 km/h (493 mph) over a range of 1585 km (985 miles).

Junkers Ju 290

When the 'Ural Bomber' programme was cancelled at the end of 1936, Junkers was left with two examples of the Ju 89 heavy bomber, and components for a third. With a view to providing a long-range transport and to salvage something from the design effort expended on the Ju 89, Junkers obtained permission to mate the wings and tail assembly, complete with undercarriage and engines of the unbuilt Ju 89 V3 with a new fuselage optimised for transport. The only stipulation was that, apart from the prototype, the aircraft could not use the strategically important Jumo 211 or DB 600 engines.

Nevertheless, the **Ju 90 V1** (D-AALU – 'der grosse Dessauer') made its first flight on 28 August 1937, this to be followed by three prototypes and 10 production aircraft. As these early aircraft would have to be powered by the BMW 132 radial of insufficient power output, design work was already under way of a new version to complement the BMW engine better – the **Ju 90S**.

Meanwhile, the three prototypes and 10 **Ju 90B-1** production airliners were under construction. The **V2** (D-AIVI) and **V3** (D-AURE) flew during early 1938, following the crash of V1 in February. The V3's career was also short, ending during route-proving trials for Deutsche Luft Hansa in December. Despite this inauspicious start, DLH confirmed their order for eight of the airliners, the other two being purchased by South African Airways, which specified Pratt & Whitney Twin Wasp engines. In the event, these two **Ju 90Z-2s** were never to be delivered to SAA, but those of DLH went into service from late 1938 onwards, with deliveries completed by the summer of 1939.

Ju 90S influence

These aircraft were completed to the original design, with the Ju 89 wing featuring the Junkers 'double wing' flap arrangement. However, in early 1939, the **V4** was rebuilt to reflect the Ju 90S studies, this incorporating a new wing with an untapered centre-section, sturdier twin-wheel undercarriage and enlarged and more elegant vertical fins. In the rear fuselage was fitted a *Trapoklappe*, a hydraulically-operated ramp which raised the cabin to the level position, while providing a ramp for vehicles to drive straight up into the cabin. The ramp could also be lowered in flight for paradropping.

In late 1939, Junkers spread its Ju 90 programme over three offices, Dessau retaining prototype construction and flight trials while Letnany in Czechoslovakia took on design, mock-up and static test work and

Bernburg assumed production duties. In early 1940 the DLH aircraft were impressed into service with the Luftwaffe in the transport role, although later two were returned to the airline, while others went back to Junkers for participation in the Ju 90S (now called **Ju 290**) programme.

Developments in this direction had seen the V4 re-engined with the more powerful BMW 801 radial and the **Ju 90 V7** fitted with an extended fuselage which not only gave the aircraft greater carriage potential, but also helped nagging yaw and centre of gravity problems. The **Ju 90 V8** then introduced defensive armament in the shape of a dorsal turret, waist guns, tail gun and undernose gondola (one forward- and one rearward-firing gun), for by now the type was being considered for the long-range maritime surveillance role. Finally the **Ju 90 V11** introduced angular fins, redesigned windows and wing. Although unarmed, it was now felt that the Ju 90S programme had been developed to the point that the aircraft could assume the designation **Ju 290 V1**.

Maiden flight

First flight of the aircraft occurred in August 1942, and immediate production began at Bernburg. Two **Ju 290A-0** pre-production aircraft were first, followed by five **Ju 290A-1s**. Possessing similar armament to the Ju 90 V8, these aircraft were completed as transports and swiftly delivered to the Luftwaffe. So great was the need for transport aircraft, that even the Ju 290 V1 was impressed, this and one of the A-0s dispatched quickly to help the relief of Stalingrad, where the V1 was lost and the A-0 badly damaged. At the same time, in January 1943, LTS 290 was established to operate the aircraft, plus survivors of the Ju 90 fleet. It flew from Germany until March, when it moved to the Mediterranean theatre. By the end of April it had lost its two Ju 290A-1s, and the unit was redesignated Transportfliegerstaffel 5.

Meanwhile, the need for a long-range maritime patroller was also great, and the **Ju 290A-2** answered the call. Little was changed except for the addition of an aft dorsal turret, changes to navigation equipment and the addition of FuG 200 Hohentwiel search radar. Flying by the summer of 1943, the first example went to Rechlin for tests while two further machines were delivered to the newly-established Fernauflärungsgruppe 5. Five **Ju 290A-3s** followed, these having low-drag Focke-Wulf gun turrets. 1./FAGr 5 began operations from Mont-de-Marsan on 15 October 1943, followed a month later by 2./FAGr 5. Covering a large area of the Atlantic, the Ju 290s provided

Two or three Ju 90B-1s were used to ferry Luftwaffe personnel and equipment to Iraq. The aircraft sported hastily applied Iraqi insignia.

The first production aircraft were 10 Ju 90B-1 airliners for Deutsche Luft Hansa, able to carry up to 40 passengers. Two were sold to South Africa Airways as Ju 90Z-2s, but were never delivered.

target information for U-boats, but also flew general reconnaissance missions for the hard-worked KG 40 at nearby Mérignac.

Five **Ju 290A-4**s were the next aircraft from the line, these introducing the Focke-Wulf turret in the forward dorsal position also. Armament for these comprised a single 20-mm MG 151 cannon. With A-2s, A-3s and A-4s in regular service, several operational shortcomings were noted, and these were rectified largely by the **Ju 290A-5** version. Chief among these was the introduction of protection for the fuel tanks and heavy armour around the flight crew. The waist gun positions were improved and fitted with MG 151s in place of the MG 131 machine-guns used in earlier models. The crew complement went from seven to nine to provide more dedicated gunners.

Operations across Europe

The A-5 was the most numerous version with 11 examples, entering service in the spring of 1944 to general acclaim by its crews. 4./FAGr 5 formed around this time, but throughout its career the Gruppe rarely had even 20 aircraft on strength, totally inadequate for its taskings. This situation was further worsened by the withdrawal of three aircraft for special transport duties. They were stripped of armour and armament at Finsterwalde and fitted with additional fuel tanks. So configured they left Odessa and Mielec for a non-stop flight to Manchuria with special cargo for the Japanese, before returning to Mielec with strategic materials that were in short supply in Germany.

With the Normandy landings in June 1944, the Mont-de-Marsan base became threatened by Allied invasion, and FAGr 5 left for Germany in August 1944. Throughout its operational career the Ju 290A had been well-liked by its crews, and although several were lost to Allied attack, none were lost to any other causes. Most of the Ju 290s, deprived of their true operational environment, were relegated to transport tasks. Perhaps with foresight, the patrollers had retained their *Trapoklappe* for emergency transport tasks, and this was used widely during the last year of the war. The clandestine unit I/KG 200 was a major user, employing the type for long-range agent drops, the aircraft being hastily fitted with a trap-door in the lower fuselage.

Maritime missile carrier

Work had progressed on the maritime versions, the next development being the **Ju 290A-7**. This would have been a major type, with 25 aircraft laid down. It featured a bulbous glazed nose turret, which introduced another MG 151 cannon, raising total armament to one MG 131 and seven MG 151s. With Hohentwiel radar mounted above the glazed section, the Ju 290A-7 also introduced an offensive capability in the shape of pylons for Henschel Hs 293, Hs 294 or FX 1400 Fritz X anti-ship missiles. Production began shortly before FAGr 5's move from France, but only a few were completed before the Bernburg plant ceased operations. One was captured intact by US forces, and subsequently flown to America for evaluation.

Three **Ju 290A-9**s were also built – extended range patrollers with extra internal tankage and reduced armament to push the range to 8300 km (5,157 miles). Another aircraft built at this time was the sole **Ju 290A-6**, a pressurised personal transport for Hitler. Pressurisation was abandoned at an early stage, the aircraft being completed as a 50-seat transport. Flying with I/KG 200 at Finsterwalde, it made a well-known flight to Barcelona in the last week of April 1945.

Flying the aircraft was Hauptmann Braun, the original commander of LTS 290. After serving with FAGr 5 he had followed the Ju 290s to KG 200. Whether the Ju 290A-6 was carrying escaping leaders on its flight to Spain is unknown, but conjecture is rife. However, the aircraft remained in Spain until purchased by the Spanish government in May 1950 from an Allied Commission. After overhaul it was used as a personnel transport by the Escuela Superior de Vuelo at Salamanca until a minor accident forced its retirement in the mid-1950s.

One last A-variant deserves mention, this being the **A-8** developed alongside the A-7. This differed principally in adding two further dorsal gun positions (four in all) and a twin-MG 151 tail turret. Ten machines were laid down, but only two or three were completed before the Czech plant at Ruzyne was overrun by Soviet forces.

Further refinements to wing, fin and fuselage were tested on one of the Ju 90B-1s, this becoming the Ju 290 V1. First flying in August 1942, the aircraft lacked armament, but was fitted with the nose gondola that would characterise the type.

Above: From the V4, the Ju 90s had a completely redesigned wing and fins, and from the V7 (illustrated) had a fuselage plug aft of the wing. The Trapoklappe rear loading ramp was fitted, this raising the tail to maintain a level cabin floor and allowing vehicles to drive in.

Above: Anticipating its full military role, the Ju 90 V8 introduced defensive armament, this comprising 20-mm MG 151 cannon in the dorsal turret and tail position, and a forward-firing MG 151 and aft-firing 13-mm MG 131 in an undernose gondola. Two MG 131 could be fitted to waist positions.

However, the second pre-production aircraft was discovered mostly complete. Transported to the Letov factory, it was reassembled using other components from war spoils (including Fw 190 propellers) and flown in August 1946. Designated the **L 290 Orel**, it was offered to the Czech airline, which showed no interest. Although an Israeli buyer attempted to purchase the aircraft, it did not leave Czechoslovakia, and was finally scrapped in 1956 at Letnany.

Above: One of the Ju 90B-1s in Luftwaffe service is shown under attack from RAF fighters. The original Ju 89 wing with the characteristic Junkers 'double wing' is obvious, as are the large horn balances on the rudders.

Other versions of the Ju 290 were planned from late 1943 onwards, the most important being the **Ju 290B**. Intended as a bomber, the B-1 carried all its warload externally and featured four-gun nose and tail turrets, two dorsal turrets and a remotely-controlled ventral barbette. Flying in the summer of 1944, the first **Ju 290B-1** featured wooden mock-up turrets and without the cabin pressurisation intended for the bomber. It undertook flight trials in Czechoslovakia until March 1945.

The first Ju 290s (including the V1) were hurriedly taken on by the Luftwaffe as transports, and at least two were soon involved in the Stalingrad airlift in January 1943. During these operations the V1 was lost on take-off and one Ju 290A attacked by LaGG-3 fighters, forcing it to return to base.

During the last year of the war, KG 200 operated the surviving Ju 290s on agent-dropping and other clandestine transport tasks. The Ju 290A-6 had been specially produced as Hitler's personal transport, but in the event was used by KG 200. It made an April 1945 flight to Barcelona with escaping leaders.

Due to the increasing vulnerability of the Fw 200, production of the Ju 290 turned to the role of maritime reconnaissance, various versions serving with Fernaufklärungsgruppe 5 at Mont-de-Marsan. This is a Ju 290A-5, the most numerous version with 11 built.

Junkers Ju 290A-5
Fernaufklärungsgruppe 5
Mont-de-Marsan, France, 1944

October 1943 saw the first use of the Ju 290 with FAGr 5 in the long-range maritime reconnaissance role. Initially A-2s and A-3s were used, subsequently joined by A-4s and then the much-improved A-5 (illustrated) in the spring of 1944. Most of the missions were aimed at providing target information for U-boats, using the FuG 200 Hohentwiel radar to detect convoys at ranges approaching 100 km (62 miles). At any stage, only about 20 aircraft were on the strength of the *Gruppe*, totally inadequate for their taskings. FAGr 5 ranged over a huge area of the Atlantic, the boundaries of which stretched from Gibraltar and the northwest coast of Africa, out to the 30°W line of longitude and up to 55°N latitude, then back to the west coast of Ireland but also including the Hebrides.

Operational history

The Ju 290A saw its first service in the role of an emergency transport, the first Ju 290A-0 and the V1 prototype taking part in the Stalingrad airlift. Subsequently the Ju 290A-1 went into transport duty with LTS 290, initially operating from Berlin, and then from Grosseto in Italy. Maritime reconnaissance aircraft of 1./FAGr 5 began operations on the type on 15 October 1943, joined in November by 2. Staffel. In addition to taskings from its own unit, the Ju 290A force also flew occasional reconnaissance missions on behalf of KG 40. The Ju 290A-5 joined the fleet from early spring 1944, and a third *Staffel* (4./FAGr 5) was formed. Shortly after, three aircraft were ordered back to Finsterwalde, where they were stripped of armament and given auxiliary fuel tanks. Staging from Mielec in Poland and Odessa, the aircraft flew non-stop to Manchuria, returning with special cargoes. FAGr 5 was forced to withdraw from France in August 1944, and the surviving Ju 290As were switched to transport tasks. Several joined 3. Staffel/Kampfgeschwader 200, the Luftwaffe's special operations unit, flying agent-dropping missions with a hatch cut into the cabin floor. This unit also flew the sole Ju 290A-6, originally developed as a pressurised personal transport for Hitler, and in April 1945 used the type for a one-way flight to Madrid. The aircraft was later used by the Spanish air force. One Ju 290A-7, a variant which did not enter service, was ferried to the USA for trials.

Defences

The Ju 290A-5 was the first version to offer realistic protection. Fuel could be rapidly dumped in an emergency, and the fuel tanks were given protection. Heavy armour was incorporated around the pilot and co-pilot, giving protection against rounds of up to 20-mm calibre. Defensive armament was improved, consisting of two Focke-Wulf low-drag dorsal turrets each with a 20-mm MG 151, similar weapons firing from two streamlined lateral positions and one more in the tail. The ventral gondola mounted an MG 151 in the front, and a 13-mm MG 131 in the rear.

Iain

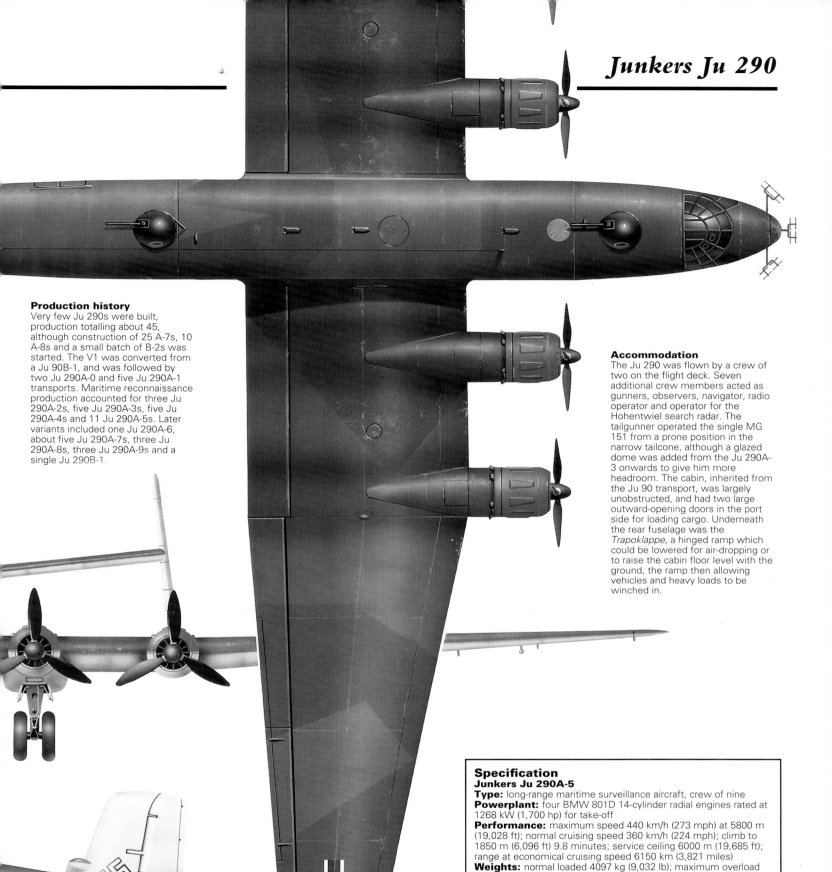

Production history

Very few Ju 290s were built, production totalling about 45, although construction of 25 A-7s, 10 A-8s and a small batch of B-2s was started. The V1 was converted from a Ju 90B-1, and was followed by two Ju 290A-0 and five Ju 290A-1 transports. Maritime reconnaissance production accounted for three Ju 290A-2s, five Ju 290A-3s, five Ju 290A-4s and 11 Ju 290A-5s. Later variants included one Ju 290A-6, about five Ju 290A-7s, three Ju 290A-8s, three Ju 290A-9s and a single Ju 290B-1.

Accommodation

The Ju 290 was flown by a crew of two on the flight deck. Seven additional crew members acted as gunners, observers, navigator, radio operator and operator for the Hohentwiel search radar. The tailgunner operated the single MG 151 from a prone position in the narrow tailcone, although a glazed dome was added from the Ju 290A-3 onwards to give him more headroom. The cabin, inherited from the Ju 90 transport, was largely unobstructed, and had two large outward-opening doors in the port side for loading cargo. Underneath the rear fuselage was the *Trapoklappe*, a hinged ramp which could be lowered for air-dropping or to raise the cabin floor level with the ground, the ramp then allowing vehicles and heavy loads to be winched in.

Specification
Junkers Ju 290A-5

Type: long-range maritime surveillance aircraft, crew of nine
Powerplant: four BMW 801D 14-cylinder radial engines rated at 1268 kW (1,700 hp) for take-off
Performance: maximum speed 440 km/h (273 mph) at 5800 m (19,028 ft); normal cruising speed 360 km/h (224 mph); climb to 1850 m (6,096 ft) 9.8 minutes; service ceiling 6000 m (19,685 ft); range at economical cruising speed 6150 km (3,821 miles)
Weights: normal loaded 4097 kg (9,032 lb); maximum overload 4497 kg (9,914 lb)
Dimensions: wing span 42.00 m (137 ft 9 in); length 28.64 m (93 ft 11 in); height 6.83 m (22 ft 5 in); wing area 203.6 m² (2,192 sq ft)
Armament: one 20-mm MG 151 in each of two dorsal turrets; one MG 151 in extreme tail; two MG 151s firing from aft waist positions; one MG 151 in front of ventral gondola and one 13-mm MG 131 machine-gun in rear of ventral gondola

Junkers Ju 290A-5 of FAGr 5 at Mont-de-Marsan. This variant was much better protected against attack with armour, fuel-dumping and heavier armament.

Before the Ju 290B-1 could enter production, the programme had switched to the **B-2**, which dispensed with the troublesome turrets and pressurisation. In fact similar to the A-8, no examples were completed before Ju 290 production was halted due to the lack of important materials. Left unbuilt were the **Ju 290B MS** with degaussing loop for mine-clearing, **Ju 290C** transport/reconnaissance aircraft with redesigned loading ramp incorporating twin MG 151 cannon, **Ju 290D** bomber with Hs 293 control equipment and **Ju 290E** with internal bomb bays.

Junkers giant

However, one major Ju 290 development had been flying for some time, the **Ju 390**. The leader of the Ju 290 team, Dipl Ing Kraft, had realised that the Ju 290 could be easily scaled up by adding extra wing and fuselage sections, so early in 1942 work began on a six-engined enlarged version that could perform the transport, maritime reconnaissance or bomber role. Three prototypes were ordered to represent the three tasks and work began immediately, the **V1** built at Dessau and the **V2** at Bernburg. First flying in August 1943, the V1 was powered by six BMW 801D engines, and had a wing span of 50.30 m (165 ft) and a length of 31.1 m (102 ft). The Ju 390 made extensive use of Ju 290A components, but added an extra set of main undercarriage units under the middle engines. These were used only to support the higher weights.

The V1 was the transport prototype, and performed well, carrying a 10000-kg (22,045-lb) load over a distance of 8000 km (4,971 miles) at 330 km/h (205 mph). During 1944 it was sent to Prague-Ruzyne for flight refuelling trials, where it was to be used as a tanker for Ju 290As to extend their on-station time.

Meanwhile the V2 flew for the first time in October 1943, this having an even longer fuselage (33.6 m/110 ft 2 in). Equipped as a

maritime patroller, it had Hohentwiel radar and defensive armament (two dorsal turrets with MG 151, one MG 151 firing forward from the ventral gondola, one MG 151 in the tail, one MG 131 firing aft from the gondola and two MG 131s firing from lateral positions). As such it was delivered to FAGr 5 for evaluation in January 1944. After some short hops, its 32-hour endurance was put to the full during an Atlantic flight that took it from Mont-de-Marsan to within 20 km (12 miles) of the US coast near New York.

Bomber development centred on the **Ju 390 V3**, but this was a low priority due to Ju 290 production. Nevertheless, work continued on the **Ju 390A** bomber, powered by BMW 801E engines and featuring uprated armament including a four-gun turret in the nose and tail. Carrying its offensive load externally, the **Ju 390A-1** was the subject of Japanese interest, the nation acquiring a manufacturing licence, but this proceeded no further. Similarly, a high-altitude reconnaissance model with 55.36-m (181-ft 7-in) wing span was not built, and in the event the Ju 390 V1 and V2 remained the only examples constructed. Apart from the V2's remarkable flight, the Ju 390 is best-remembered as the largest conventional aircraft ever built in Germany. The design had come a long way from the Ju 89 bomber of 1936.

Right: Extensive use was made of Ju 290 components for the giant Ju 390. The two completed prototypes flew in August and October 1943 respectively, the V2 completed as a reconnaissance aircraft with FuG 200 radar. So equipped it was evaluated by FAGr 5, which flew it to within 20 km (12 miles) of the US coast from Mont-de-Marsan.

Below: Supplanting the A-5 on the line was the A-7, which featured an enlarged nose with a trainable MG 151 and radar (not fitted here). Underwing pylons could carry guided missiles or bombs. Few were completed before the US overran the factory, this example being evaluated in the US after the war.

Junkers Ju 352 Herkules

The tremendous success of the pre-war Ju 52/3m airliner naturally led Junkers to look for a successor, and after several designs settled on the Ju 252. However, the Ju 252 was a metal aircraft and the raw materials were in short supply for transport aircraft, as were the Jumo 211 engines. In order to redress this, Junkers began design of a wooden version powered by BMW-Bramo 323R-2 engines in the spring of 1942. The resultant **Ju 352** superficially resembled the Ju 252, but the wooden wing was mounted further back on the fuselage, which itself was a composite structure. Incorporated in the rear was a *Trapoklappe*, a hydraulically-powered loading ramp which allowed the rapid loading of bulky items, although vehicles were usually winched up the ramp rather than driven. A detachable tailcone could be replaced by a towing hook for gliders. Defensive armament consisted of a single MG 151 20-mm

cannon in a turret behind the cockpit.

Dubbed the 'Herkules' by the manufacturer, the **Ju 352 V1** made its first flight on 1 October 1943, from the satellite plant at Fritzlar. The **V2** second prototype flew soon after, and an order for 10 pre-production **Ju 352A-0s** came quickly. Production **Ju 352A-1s** were delivered to the Luftwaffe from February 1944, but by the summer the worsening war situation led to the cancellation of transport aircraft production. A total of two prototypes, 10 Ju 352A-0s and 33 Ju 352A-ls was completed.

In service, the type showed itself a worthy successor to the Ju 52/3m, proving rugged and reliable. The wooden propellers featured reverse pitch, which was appreciated greatly by crews, considerably reducing the landing run.

The aircraft were assigned to various transport units for special missions, among them the infa-

The Ju 352 was distinguishable from the Ju 252 by having radial engines and a more angular fin. This is a Ju 352A-1 production aircraft.

mous I/KG 200. Most ended up with the Grossraum-Transportgruppe at Tutow, although only a few supply missions were flown towards the end of the war. On 25 April 1945, 23 were still on strength but most were destroyed as the Allies neared the airfield.

At least two escaped the destruction, one being ferried to Britain for evaluation. The other surfaced after the war in Czechoslovakia, where it was restored and presented as a personal gift from the Czech government to Josef Stalin. Developments were planned, including the **Ju 352B** with 1343-kW (1,800-hp) BMW 801

radial engines, although none left the drawing board.

Specification
Junkers Ju 352A-1
Type: medium transport
Powerplant: three BMW-Bramo 323R-2 nine-cylinder radials, 895 kW (1,200 hp) each
Performance: maximum speed 370 km/h (230 mph); service ceiling 6000 m (19,685 ft); range 2995 km (1,860 miles)
Weights: empty 12769 kg (28,150 lb); maximum take-off 19595 kg (43,200 lb)
Dimensions: wing span 34.21 m (112 ft 2¾ in); length 24.60 m (80 ft 8½ in); height 5.75 m (18 ft 10½ in); wing area 128.19 m² (1,379.93 sq ft)
Armament: one 20-mm MG 151 cannon in HD 151/2 power-operated turret

Junkers Ju 388

The failure of the Junkers Ju 288, brought about primarily by technical problems and continual requests by the RLM for design changes, left a gap in the programme for a high-speed long-range bomber. Fortunately, Junkers had initiated development of high-altitude versions of the Ju 188 and three of these, designated Ju 188J, Ju 188K and Ju 188L became respectively the **Ju 388J** all-weather fighter, **Ju 388K** bomber and **Ju 388L** photo-reconnaissance aircraft.

High-altitude reconnaissance had the highest priority, and the first prototype was a **Ju 388L-0** converted from a Ju 188T. The pre-production batch which followed was converted from Ju 88S airframes, the first of them being handed over to the Luftwaffe in August 1944 and all featuring a teardrop ventral fair-

A few Ju 388L-1s entered service on reconnaissance duties. The ventral pannier (seen here with the doors open) held the mission cameras and additional fuel.

ing housing two aft-firing MG 81 machine-guns. The **Ju 388L-1** followed, with the gun fairing replaced by a ventral pannier for cameras and fuel, and an FA 15 remotely-controlled tail barbette and FuG 217 Neptun tail-warning radar. A handful were delivered to 3. Staffel des Versuchsverband Ob.d.L., which undertook some operational reconnaissance missions. Teething troubles with the tail barbette led to a field modification which added an MG 131 gun in the rear of the cockpit glazing, such aircraft being designated **Ju 388L-1/b**. One or two **Ju 388L-3s** were completed, these being powered by the Jumo 213E-1 engine.

The other variants were not so fortunate. The **Ju 388 V2** was completed as a night-fighter with FuG 220 Lichtenstein SN-2 radar and two 20-mm MG 151 and two 30-mm MK 108 cannon in a ventral tray. The **V4** and **V5** were also **Ju 388J-0** night-fighters, but featuring FuG 218 Neptun radar with *Morgenstern* (morning star) aerials in place of the *Hirschgeweih* (antlers) of the FuG 220. These were the only Ju 388Js completed, plans for aircraft with tail barbettes (**Ju 388J-2**), Jumo 213 engines (**Ju 388J-3**) and twin 50-mm MK 114 cannon armament (**Ju 388J-4**) being cancelled.

Acting as prototype for the Ju 388K bomber series, the **V3** featured a ventral pannier for carrying larger numbers of bombs over short distances, and was fol-

lowed by 10 **Ju 388K-0** pre-production aircraft and five **Ju 388K-1s** with tail barbette fitted. Further planned variants were the **Ju 388K-2** and **K-3** with Jumo 213 and Jumo 222 power respectively, and the **Ju 388M** winged torpedo carrier.

Specification
Junkers Ju 388L-1
Type: three-seat high-altitude photo-reconnaissance aircraft
Powerplant: two 1409-kW (1,890 hp) BMW 801TJ radial piston engines
Performance: maximum speed 615 km/h (382 mph) at 12285 m (40,305 ft), or 655 km/h (407 mph) at 9080 m (29,790 ft) with MW 50 water/methanol boost; service ceiling 13440 m (44,095 ft); maximum range with auxiliary fuel 3475 km (2,159 miles)
Weights: empty 10252 kg (22,601 lb); maximum take off 14675 kg (32,353 lb)
Dimensions: span 22.00 m (72 ft 2 in); length 15.20 m (49 ft 10½ in); height 4.35 m (14 ft 3¼ in); wing area 56.00 m² (602.80 sq ft)
Armament: one remotely controlled tail barbette with two 13-mm (0.51-in) MG 131 machine-guns

The Ju 388 V2 was the prototype for the Ju 388J night-fighter. Later prototypes had schräge Musik upward-firing guns installed.

Messerschmitt Bf 109

Three Bf 109G-6s of 7./JG 27 flying over the Mediterranean during late 1943. The two aircraft in the background are so-called 'Kanonen Booten', Bf 109G-6/R6s with MG 151 cannon in underwing gondolas. White 9 is the aircraft of Emil Clade, one of III./JG 27's aces.

Willy Messerschmitt's Bf 109 was the Luftwaffe's benchmark fighter throughout World War II. It was the mount of the vast majority of the German aces and scored more kills than any other Axis aircraft. Few fighters of the period bettered the Bf 109's longevity, either. The aircraft entered service in time to be blooded in Spain, and it remained the backbone of the Luftwaffe fighter arm until the end of the war. Even after 1945 it continued to serve with several air forces and briefly went back to war in Israeli hands. The aircraft rapidly gained something of a reputation, which was carefully nurtured by Nazi Germany's expert propagandists, and this lived on even after the aircraft had begun to show its age, and while newer fighters on both sides were clearly its betters. For its achievements up to 1940 alone, the Bf 109 deserves to go down in history as one of the World's great fighter aircraft, and if the same level of superiority over all opposition eluded the Bf 109 from the Battle of Britain onwards, this should not tarnish the fighter's reputation. Indeed, in the face of a constantly changing air war, the Bf 109 proved adaptable enough to accept new powerplants and weapons with a minimum of modification, allowing the family of variants and

sub-variants to grow rapidly, with scarcely a break in production. This versatility was probably the key to the aircraft's colossal success, and was due to straightforward sensible design practise.

The birth of the Bf 109 was the outcome of political feuding between Erhard Milch and Willy Messerschmitt, which threatened extinction of the private Bayerische Flugzeugwerke. The company's M-20 monoplane airliner failed spectacularly, the prototype and two production aircraft crashing and Deutsche Luft Hansa cancelling all orders. This led the company to the brink of financial ruin, but recovery was made possible when Luft Hansa were forced to take delivery of the aircraft they had ordered. As head of Luft Hansa Milch had accused Messerschmitt of building unsafe aircraft and as Reich Commissioner for aviation his hostility ensured that the company would only receive small orders to license build aircraft designed by others, and would not be asked to design its own aircraft for the rear-

The Bf 109 V4 in flight. This was the first Bf 109B-0, and was powered by a Jumo 210 engine, with an engine-mounted MG 17 machine-gun firing through the spinner and two similar weapons in the top decking. The Bf 109 proved superior to the competing He 112, except in its ground handling, where the wide-track Heinkel enjoyed some advantages.

To speed production by an as-yet small industry, the Bf 109 was licensed in 1937 to Fieseler and in 1938 to Focke-Wulf and Erla. This photograph was taken at Bremen in August 1938 and shows the first 10 Bf 109C-2s completed by Focke-Wulf. The C-2 was the final Jumo-engined version, with five MG 17s.

The Bf 109 V10 flown by Ernst Udet in July 1937 at the Zürich International Flying Meeting. Despite demonstrating an excellent performance, Udet crashed the aircraft during the Circuit of the Alps race after failure of the DB 600 engine.

Wearing the insignia of the Gruppenkommandeur, I. Gruppe, of a Jagdgeschwader in 1939, the Bf 109D was powered by the DB 600A and was, in effect, the production version developed from the V10 prototype. Its performance was in most respects better than a Spitfire Mk I.

mament of the Luftwaffe. This situation finally changed after the company negotiated to supply a Romanian cartel with a new transport aircraft in 1933. Infuriated by Messerschmitt's touting for overseas business, officials at the Reichsluftfahrtministerium (RLM, or State Ministry of Aviation) drew from Messerschmitt the retort that he had been obliged to seek business elsewhere because of the lack of support from Berlin itself. Stung by this accusation, the RLM awarded a contract which resulted in the highly successful Bf 108 Taifun, and soon afterwards awarded fighter development contracts to Arado, BFW, Focke-Wulf and Heinkel, it being confidently expected that Messerschmitt's lack of experience in high-speed aircraft design would mean that his contender would stand little chance of success.

Rolls-Royce Kestrel

Employing features of his excellent Bf 108 Taifun four-seat tourer, Messerschmitt's design emerged as a small angular low-wing cantilever monoplane with retractable landing gear, leading-edge slats and enclosed cockpit. These features, together with its all-metal, flush-riveted monocoque fuselage, made it the most modern of the contenders, since the Heinkel had an open cockpit and no slats, the Arado an open cockpit and fixed landing gear, and the Focke-Wulf a braced, unslatted high wing. Such modernity was striking, and rather controversial, drawing from Ernst Udet the comment that the aircraft would 'never make a fighter'. It had been intended to use the new Junkers Jumo 210A engine, but this was not available for the **Bf 109 V1** prototype so an imported Rolls-Royce Kestrel VI of 518 kW (695 hp) was used, the aircraft being rolled out and flown in September 1935. Though no-one was to know it at the time, this choice of powerplant would be echoed years later, when the last Bf 109 variant, the Spanish Buchon, used another Rolls-Royce engine, this time the Merlin.

When flown in competition with the Ar 80 V1, Fw 159 V1 and He 112 V1, at the Travemunde trials, the Bf 109 V1 performed well

despite minor problems and, amid general surprise, was rewarded by a contract for 10 prototype development aircraft (although it was not in fact declared the outright winner, 10 Heinkel aircraft also being ordered). One problem experienced by the Bf 109 was the collapse of its narrow track landing gear on arrival at the Rechlin test centre. At the time, most put it down to bad luck, but the incident foreshadowed what was to be one of the aircraft's greatest weaknesses throughout its life, unforgiving ground handling characteristics that were to cause the loss or damage of hundreds of production aircraft. Definitive evaluation trials were held at Travemunde in November 1935, and these resulted in final victory over the Heinkel He 112. Superior performance, a spectacular display by Dr Ing Herman Wurster and a lower manufacturing cost settled the issue and the Bf 109 was selected for production.

Three further prototypes (the **Bf 109 V2** registered D-IUDE, **Bf 109 V3** D-IHNY and **Bf 109 V4** D-IOQY) were flown in 1936, powered by Jumo 210A engines and with provision for two synchronised MG 17 machine-guns in the nose decking. However, rumours abounded that the British Hawker Hurricane and Supermarine Spitfire were to be armed with four guns, so that by the time the **Bf 109 V4** prototype flew a third MG 17 was planned to fire through the propeller hub.

Off to sunny Spain

The proposed two-gun **Bf 109A** production version did not therefore materialise, and the first pre-production **Bf 109B-0** examples were flown early in 1937, at the same time as the **Bf 109 V5**, **Bf 109 V6** and **Bf 109 V7** prototypes. Considerable operational experience was gained during the Spanish Civil War by three Staffeln of Jagdgruppe 88, fighter component of the 'volunteer' Légion Condor, which received the V3, V4 and V5 for combat evaluation, and which was equipped with production examples of the **Bf 109B-1**, **Bf 109B-2** and **Bf 109C-1** versions as soon as they became available, having complained that its initial equipment of Heinkel He 51s simply

J-310 was the first Bf 109 to serve with Switzerland's Fliegertruppe, delivered on 17 December 1938. Powered by a 507-kW (680-hp) Jumo 210Da engine (like the German Bf 109B), it had an armament of four MG 17 machine-guns (as fitted to the Bf 109C). The Swiss used Bf 109s until the end of 1949, some being assembled locally.

Called 'tripala' by the Spanish (the earlier models had a two-bladed propeller), the Bf 109E-1 was by far the best fighter in Spain in early 1939, when this picture was taken at a Légion Condor base. Armament was two cannon and two MG 17 machine-guns. The Légion transferred 40 Bf 109s to Spain, which built other models post-war.

Messerschmitt Bf 109

A Bf 109E-3 of III/JG 2 'Richthofen' during the Battle of France in June 1940. The sides of many aircraft were hastily overpainted during the French campaign to give a lower camouflage demarcation line. The thumb and top hat insignia is the emblem of 7. Staffel, JG 2, while the 'R' on the shield is the Geschwader badge.

This Bf 109E-3 was the aircraft of Hauptmann Henschel, the Gruppenkommandeur of II/JG 77 while it was based at Aalborg, Denmark in July 1940. The aircraft clearly shows the basic 1940 Bf 109 colour scheme, with the Hellblau undersurfaces extending up over the fuselage sides, leaving only the upper surfaces camouflaged on the ground.

could not cope against the Republicans' Polikarpov I-16s. This experience assisted in the development of the aircraft itself and in the development of air combat tactics in general; for it was largely through men such as Werner Molders and Adolf Galland who fought in Spain with the Bf 109, that basic air fighting tactics were evolved which were to last well into the jet age.

By the beginning of World War II in September 1939, the Luftwaffe had standardised its fighter Geschwader on the Bf 109. The **Bf 109D** series, although produced in fairly large numbers and still in service, was already giving place to the **Bf 109E** (widely known as the 'Emil'). Ten pre-production **Bf 109E-0s** appeared late in 1938 with two nose-mounted MG 17 machine-guns and two in the wings, and powered by the 821-kW (1,100-hp) DB 601A engine, which promised to solve the reliability and other problems of the DB 600 which was to have been used by the 'Dora'.

The mighty Emil

Production **Bf 109E-1s** started leaving the Augsburg factory at the beginning of 1939 with alternative provision for two 20-mm MG FF cannon in place of the wing machine-guns, although late delivery of the new engine meant that the first few Es to come off the line were put into storage to await their engines. Maximum speed was 570 km/h (354 mph) at 3750 m (12,305 ft) and service ceiling 11000 m (36,090 ft), performance figures which helped the Bf 109E to eclipse all of its opponents in the first eight months of the war. A sub-variant, the **Bf 109E-1/B**, introduced soon after, was a fighter-bomber capable of carrying a 250-kg (551-lb) bomb under the fuselage.

Production of the Emil was shifted from Augsburg to Regensburg in 1939 (to make way for the Bf 110 twin-engined fighter) as a massive subcontract programme was undertaken by Ago, Arado, Erla and WNF, 1,540 aircraft being delivered that year. Despite deliveries of 10 Jumo-engined Bf 109Cs, and thirty Bf 109Es to Switzerland, Bf 109E deliveries were almost too fast for the aircraft to be absorbed by the

newly forming Jagdgruppen. Nevertheless, on the eve of the invasion of Poland the Jagdverband comprised 12 Gruppen flying 850 **Bf 109E-1s** and **Bf 109E-1/Bs** and one with Ar 68s. Some 235 **Bf 109D-1s** were still serving with the Zerstörergeschwader. A handful of Bf 109Bs were on charge with II/ZG 1, while I/JG 21 had a few Bf 109Cs on charge. Five Bf 109 Gruppen actually participated in the invasion of Poalnd, with just over 200 aircraft. 67 Bf 109s were lost, most, but by no means all, to ground fire. The first occasion on which Bf 109s fought the RAF was during the daylight raid by 24 unescorted Vickers Wellingtons on Wilhelmshaven on 18 December 1939, 12 of the bombers being destroyed for the loss of two Bf 109Es of JG 77.

In 1940 production of the Emil increased to 1,868 aircraft, the D-

Above: By comparison with the Bf 109B, the Bf 109C had vestigial exhaust pipes projecting from the exhaust ports, and had a deeper, reshaped radiator bath. Most Bf 109Cs had been relegated to training duties by the beginning of the war. This line up of Bf 109C wears the markings of the Légion Condor.

Bf 109B-2s of the Jagdfliegerschule of Luftreiskommando II during early 1939. The B-2 featured a two-bladed Hamilton metal airscrew (manufactured under license by VDM) in place of the original wooden Schwarz fixed pitch propeller.

A Bf 109E-1 of 2./JG 20 (later redesignated 8./JG 51) wearing the original Bf 109 colour scheme of dark green topsides and light blue grey undersides, with a low demarcation line. Two tones of dark green were used, though this is seldom apparent in photographs.

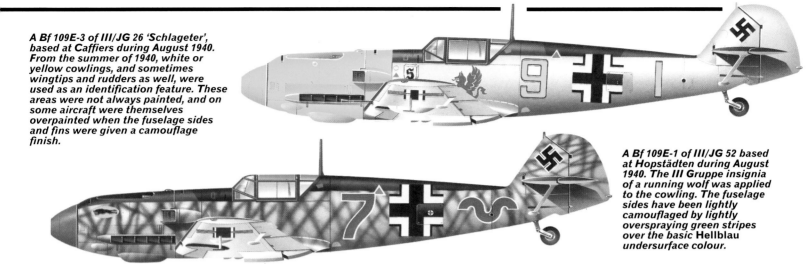

A Bf 109E-3 of III/JG 26 'Schlageter', based at Caffiers during August 1940. From the summer of 1940, white or yellow cowlings, and sometimes wingtips and rudders as well, were used as an identification feature. These areas were not always painted, and on some aircraft were themselves overpainted when the fuselage sides and fins were given a camouflage finish.

A Bf 109E-1 of III/JG 52 based at Hopstädten during August 1940. The III Gruppe insignia of a running wolf was applied to the cowling. The fuselage sides have been lightly camouflaged by lightly overspraying green stripes over the basic Hellblau undersurface colour.

series being almost entirely discarded from front-line use. Principal sub-variants produced that year were the **Bf 109E-2**, **Bf 109E-3** (with two MG 17s in the nose and two in the wings, plus an MG FF/M firing through the propeller shaft) and the **Bf 109E-4** (with two nose MG 17s and two wing MG FF cannon). All these versions saw widespread action during the *Blitzkrieg* against France and the Low Countries (with sixteen *Gruppen*), and in the great daylight battles over southern England during the Battle of Britain. When employed in the 'free chase' tactic they proved deadly, the combination of experienced pilots and fast Bf 109 proving generally superior to the mostly novice RAF pilots in their Hurricanes. The Bf 109s initially bettered even the Spitfire, except in what became, in the Battle of Britain at least, the all-important arena of turn performance. The Bf 109E, though suffering heavy attrition, wreaked havoc on the RAF's fighters, but simple arithmetic was against it. The Bf 109 had insuffi-

cient fuel to stay and fight for more than a few minutes, and damaged aircraft inevitably failed to make it home, while downed pilots became POWs. Similarly damaged RAF aircraft and downed RAF pilots were usually airborne again within hours. Moreover, as is now well known, the capabilities of the Bf 109E were frequently squandered when the aircraft were too often tied to close escort of bomber formations, a role in which the Bf 109Es were deprived of their greatest assets, speed and manoeuvrability. At the same time, the enemy was not slow to learn from his mistakes, and RAF fighter pilots rapidly ditched the cumbersome pre-war tactics which had led to so many losses. Unfortunately for the RAF, it was less easy to switch from the

Below: A Bf 109E-1B (foreground) and a Bf 109E-4B of II (Schlacht)/LG 2 at Calais Marck at the height of the Battle of Britain, when these aircraft were making frequent hit-and-run raids over the British Isles. Schlacht Bf 109s enjoyed some success, proving hard to intercept.

Above: A heavily camouflaged Bf 109F-1 of JG 2 'Richthofen' taking off from an advanced airfield in France during the Battle of Britain. The Bf 109E proved able to outrun, outclimb and outdive the Hurricane and Spitfire, but could not out-turn the British fighters. A further, fatal, weakness was the aircraft's limited fuel capacity which reduced its endurance over England to a matter of minutes.

Right: Two Bf 109E-4 Trops of JG 27 patrolling over the Western Desert. White codes identify the aircraft as belonging to the first Gruppe. The Bf 109E enjoyed great success in North Africa, although it was rapidly replaced by later versions, on which the African aces built up their scores, primarily against obsolescant Kittyhawks and Hurricanes.

Messerschmitt Bf 109

small-calibre light machine-gun armament used on most RAF fighters, and which proved ineffective against most targets, unless the pilot could get close enough to score multiple hits. Nevertheless, by the end of the Battle, the Luftwaffe had lost 610 Bf 109s (of an overall total of 1,792 aircraft destroyed on operations) while the RAF's 1,172 losses included 403 Spitfires, 631 Hurricanes, 115 Blenheims and 23 Defiants. These figures obscure the fact that RAF losses were falling, while Bf 109 attrition was reaching worrying levels. Later in the Battle of Britain the Bf 109E was also employed as a fighter-bomber (the **Bf 109E-4/B**), proving particularly difficult to intercept. *Jabo* versions of the Emil were later used with great success in other theatres, one such aircraft successfully sinking the British cruiser HMS *Fiji* during the invasion of Crete in 1941. Other variants, which appeared soon after the Battle of Britain, included the **Bf 109E-5** and **Bf 109E-6** reconnaissance fighters, the latter with DB 601N engine, the **Bf 109E-7** with provision for belly drop tank, and the **Bf 109E-7/Z** with GM-1 nitrous oxide engine boost.

Tropicalising the Emil

Early in 1941 the Emil was beginning to appear in the Mediterranean theatre, with tropicalised versions of the above subvariants serving with JG 27 in North Africa. Here the combination of experienced pilots with Bf 109Es were able to repeat their success against the RAF, though scoring mainly against ageing Hurricanes and Kittyhawks. By the time Germany opened its great attack on the Soviet Union in June 1941, the Bf 109F series was beginning to join the front-line fighter squadrons, although the Emil provided one third of the fighter strength for the initial assault and continued to serve for

Pictured at Schipol, Netherlands, in the summer of 1940, these Bf 109E-1s equipped 7./JG 52 and were one of the expertly flown units that established total air superiority in the race to the Channel in May of that year. Note KLM Fokker and Lockheed transports in the background. JG 52 gained 10,000 air victories by September 1944.

Pilots of III/JG 54 brief in front of their Messerschmitt Bf 109E-3s. These aircraft wear the standard 1940 colour scheme, with no over-painting of the fuselage sides and tailfin. The aircraft also lack coloured rudders and engine cowlings, dating the picture as being taken during the early summer.

a long time yet, especially in the ground attack role.

Powered by the 895-kW (1,200-hp) DB 601E, the **Bf 109F** was generally regarded as the most attractive of the entire Bf 109 family, and its design represented almost a textbook exercise in drag-reduction. It introduced extended and rounded wingtips and an enlarged spinner, while Frise ailerons and plain flaps replaced the Emil's slotted flaps. A fully retractable tailwheel superseded the earlier fixed type, and a cantilever tailplane, without bracing struts, was introduced. In the matter of gun armament, however, the Bf 109F was widely criticised, for it deleted the wing-mounted MG FF cannon in favour of a higher-velocity MG 151 firing through the propeller hub with two MG 17s above the nose. While this tended to satisfy the German *Experten* (aces) as benefitting the aircraft's performance, it was pointed

Messerschmitt Bf 109G-14/U4 cutaway drawing key

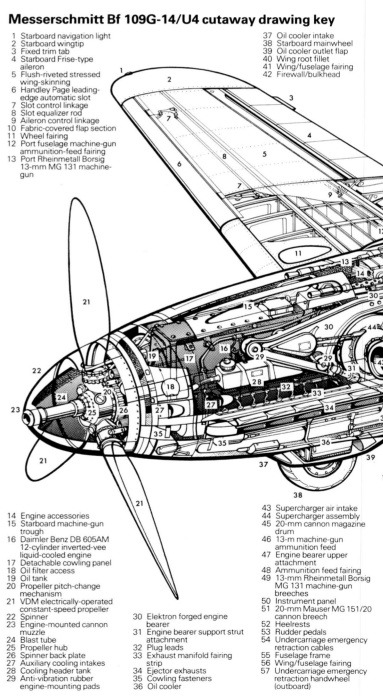

1 Starboard navigation light
2 Starboard wingtip
3 Fixed trim tab
4 Starboard Frise-type aileron
5 Flush-riveted stressed wing-skinning
6 Handley Page leading-edge automatic slot
7 Slot control linkage
8 Slot equalizer rod
9 Aileron control linkage
10 Fabric-covered flap section
11 Wheel fairing
12 Port fuselage machine-gun ammunition-feed fairing
13 Port Rheinmetall Borsig 13-mm MG 131 machine-gun

14 Engine accessories
15 Starboard machine-gun trough
16 Daimler Benz DB 605AM 12-cylinder inverted-vee liquid-cooled engine
17 Detachable cowling panel
18 Oil filter access
19 Oil tank
20 Propeller pitch-change mechanism
21 VDM electrically-operated constant-speed propeller
22 Spinner
23 Engine-mounted cannon muzzle
24 Blast tube
25 Propeller hub
26 Spinner back plate
27 Auxiliary cooling intakes
28 Cooling header tank
29 Anti-vibration rubber engine-mounting pads

30 Elektron forged engine bearer
31 Engine bearer support strut attachment
32 Plug leads
33 Exhaust manifold fairing strip
34 Ejector exhausts
35 Cowling fasteners
36 Oil cooler

37 Oil cooler intake
38 Starboard mainwheel
39 Oil cooler outlet flap
40 Wing root fillet
41 Wing/fuselage fairing
42 Firewall/bulkhead

43 Supercharger air intake
44 Supercharger assembly
45 20-mm cannon magazine drum
46 13-m machine-gun ammunition feed
47 Engine bearer upper attachment
48 Ammunition feed fairing
49 13-mm Rheinmetall Borsig MG 131 machine-gun breeches
50 Instrument panel
51 20-mm Mauser MG 151/20 cannon breech
52 Heelrests
53 Rudder pedals
54 Undercarriage emergency retraction cables
55 Fuselage frame
56 Wing/fuselage fairing
57 Undercarriage emergency retraction handwheel (outboard)

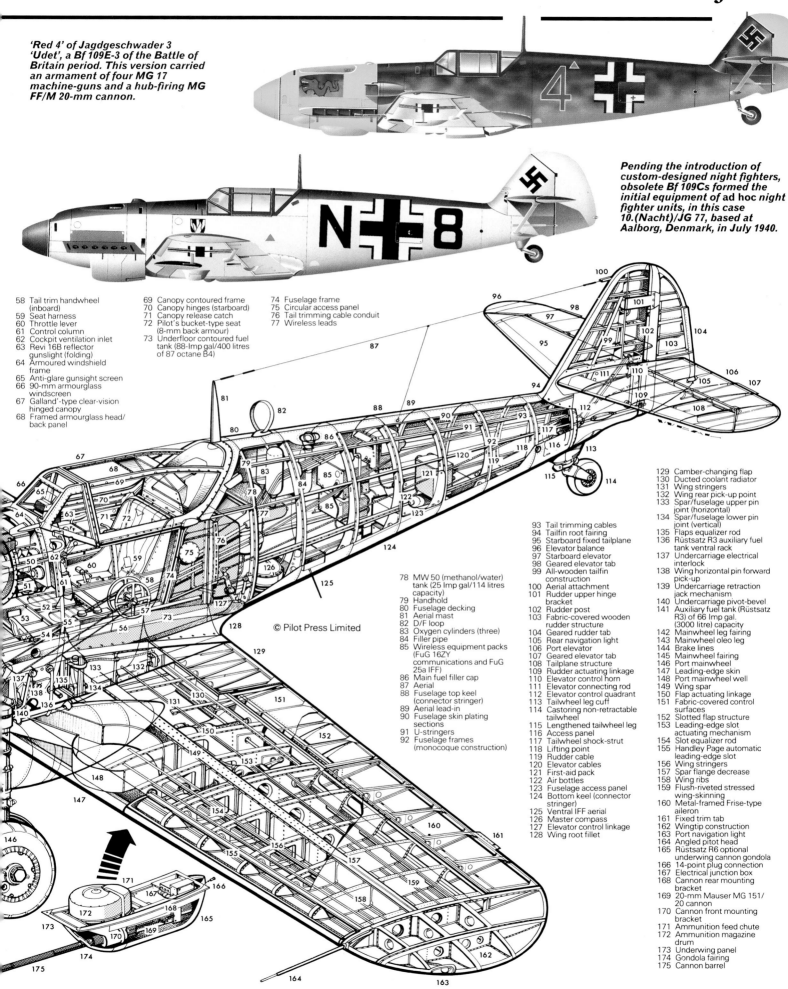

'Red 4' of Jagdgeschwader 3 'Udet', a Bf 109E-3 of the Battle of Britain period. This version carried an armament of four MG 17 machine-guns and a hub-firing MG FF/M 20-mm cannon.

Pending the introduction of custom-designed night fighters, obsolete Bf 109Cs formed the initial equipment of ad hoc night fighter units, in this case 10.(Nacht)/JG 77, based at Aalborg, Denmark, in July 1940.

58 Tail trim handwheel (inboard)
59 Seat harness
60 Throttle lever
61 Control column
62 Cockpit ventilation inlet
63 Revi 16B reflector gunsight (folding)
64 Armoured windshield frame
65 Anti-glare gunsight screen
66 90-mm armourglass windscreen
67 Galland'-type clear-vision hinged canopy
68 Framed armourglass head/back panel

69 Canopy contoured frame
70 Canopy hinges (starboard)
71 Canopy release catch
72 Pilot's bucket-type seat (8-mm back armour)
73 Underfloor contoured fuel tank (88-Imp gal/400 litres of 87 octane B4)

74 Fuselage frame
75 Circular access panel
76 Tail trimming cable conduit
77 Wireless leads

78 MW 50 (methanol/water) tank (25 Imp gal/114 litres capacity)
79 Handhold
80 Fuselage decking
81 Aerial mast
82 D/F loop
83 Oxygen cylinders (three)
84 Filler pipe
85 Wireless equipment packs (FuG 16ZY communications and FuG 25a IFF)
86 Main fuel filler cap
87 Aerial
88 Fuselage top keel (connector stringer)
89 Aerial lead-in
90 Fuselage skin plating sections
91 U-stringers
92 Fuselage frames (monocoque construction)

93 Tail trimming cables
94 Tailfin root fairing
95 Starboard fixed tailplane
96 Elevator balance
97 Starboard elevator
98 Geared elevator tab
99 All-wooden tailfin construction
100 Aerial attachment
101 Rudder upper hinge bracket
102 Rudder post
103 Fabric-covered wooden rudder structure
104 Geared rudder tab
105 Rear navigation light
106 Port elevator
107 Geared elevator tab
108 Tailplane structure
109 Rudder actuating linkage
110 Elevator control horn
111 Elevator connecting rod
112 Elevator control quadrant
113 Tailwheel leg cuff
114 Castoring non-retractable tailwheel
115 Lengthened tailwheel leg
116 Access panel
117 Tailwheel shock-strut
118 Lifting point
119 Rudder cable
120 Elevator cables
121 First-aid pack
122 Air bottles
123 Fuselage access panel
124 Bottom keel (connector stringer)
125 Ventral IFF aerial
126 Master compass
127 Elevator control linkage
128 Wing root fillet

129 Camber-changing flap
130 Ducted coolant radiator
131 Wing stringers
132 Wing rear pick-up point
133 Spar/fuselage upper pin joint (horizontal)
134 Spar/fuselage lower pin joint (vertical)
135 Flaps equalizer rod
136 Rüstsatz R3 auxiliary fuel tank ventral rack
137 Undercarriage electrical interlock
138 Wing horizontal pin forward pick-up
139 Undercarriage retraction jack mechanism
140 Undercarriage pivot-bevel
141 Auxiliary fuel tank (Rüstsatz R3) of 66 Imp gal. (3000 litre) capacity
142 Mainwheel leg fairing
143 Mainwheel oleo leg
144 Brake lines
145 Mainwheel fairing
146 Port mainwheel
147 Leading-edge skin
148 Port mainwheel well
149 Wing spar
150 Flap actuating linkage
151 Fabric-covered control surfaces
152 Slotted flap structure
153 Leading-edge slot actuating mechanism
154 Slot equalizer rod
155 Handley Page automatic leading-edge slot
156 Wing stringers
157 Spar flange decrease
158 Wing ribs
159 Flush-riveted stressed wing-skinning
160 Metal-framed Frise-type aileron
161 Fixed trim tab
162 Wingtip construction
163 Port navigation light
164 Angled pitot head
165 Rüstsatz R6 optional underwing cannon gondola
166 14-point plug connection
167 Electrical junction box
168 Cannon rear mounting bracket
169 20-mm Mauser MG 151/20 cannon
170 Cannon front mounting bracket
171 Ammunition feed chute
172 Ammunition magazine drum
173 Underwing panel
174 Gondola fairing
175 Cannon barrel

© Pilot Press Limited

Messerschmitt Bf 109

Equipped with dust filter on the nose intake, this Bf 109E-7/Trop fighter-bomber was among the first German fighters to operate in the Mediterranean, equipping 7./JG 26 'Schlageter' at Gela in March 1941 for attacks on Malta.

Displaying the wasp markings of the famous 'Wespen-Geschwader' (Zerstörergeschwader 1), the Bf 109E-4/B fighter-bomber supplemented the Bf 110 in the ground-attack role and provided top cover after dropping its bomb.

out that the majority of Luftwaffe fighter pilots needed a heavier armament with which to achieve a 'kill'.

Pre-production **Bf 109F-0**s were evaluated by the Luftwaffe during the second half of 1940, and **Bf 109F-1**s were delivered early the following year. Both initial variants had an engine-mounted MG FF due to shortages of the MG 151. A number of accidents indicated that removal of the tailplane struts left the entire tail unit vulnerable to sympathetic vibration at certain oscillating frequencies of the engine, and strengthening modifications were quickly put in hand. With these in place the Bf 109F proved superior in performance and agility to the Emil, and many pilots preferred its handling characteristics. Thereafter, the increasing weight and engine power which accompanied the essential stream of modifications steadily degraded the Bf 109's handling characteristics. After the **Bf 109F-2** (with 15-mm MG 151 finally replacing the 20-mm MG FF) came the principal version, the **Bf 109F-3**, early in 1942 with a top speed of 628 km/h (390 mph) at 6700 m (21,980 ft).

Bf 109Fs had joined the Geschwaderstab and III Gruppe of Adolf Galland's JG 26 'Schlageter' early in 1941 on the Channel coast, and during the early stages of Operation Barbarossa in the East this version equipped Major Gunther Lutzow's JG 3 'Udet', Werner Molders' JG 51, Major Gunther von Maltzahn's JG 53 'Pik As' and Major Johannes Trautloft's JG 54. The superiority of the new fighter (even over the Spitfire Mk V in the West) quickly became apparent as the German fighter pilots' victory tallies soared.

The 'Friedrick' underwent progressive improvement and development: the **Bf 109F-4** had an MG 151 rebarrelled to 20-mm, while also introducing morale-boosting windscreen and cockpit armour, and the larger F2Z supercharger, the **Bf 109F-4/R1** could be fitted with a *Rustsatz* (field conversion kit) comprising two 20-mm MG 151 guns in underwing packs for the bomber-destroyer role, the **Bf 109F-4/B** fighter-bomber was capable of carrying up to 500 kg (1,102 lb) of

bombs, and the **Bf 109F-5** and **Bf 109F-6** reconnaissance fighters were introduced later in 1942. It was principally in the tropicalised Bf 109F-4 that the 22-year-old Oberleutnant Hans-Joachim Marseille became the highest-scoring Luftwaffe fighter pilot in the West with 158 air victories, although he died bailing out from a Bf 109G-2 on 30 September 1942 in North Africa.

Gustav, the universal soldier

The **Bf 109G** (dubbed the 'Gustav' by German pilots) was introduced into service in the late summer of 1942 and came to be built in larger numbers than any other version, serving with more units, although its characteristics were such that it rapidly came to be regarded as Germany's second fighter, the Focke-Wulf Fw 190 equipping the most important units. The emergence of the Spitfire Mk IX and P-51D had finally shown the Bf 109 to be on the verge of obsolescence, and to counter this, Messerschmiit finally sacrificed handling and manoeuvrability for outright performance. The Gustav was thus powered by the much heavier 1100-kW (1,475-hp) DB 605A, although pre-production **Bf 109G-0**s retained the DB 601E. Basic armament remained two nose-mounted MG 17s and hub-firing 20-mm MG 151/20 cannon. The **Bf 109G-1**, with pressure cabin, was powered by the DB 605A-1 with GM-1 power boosting, and the tropical version, the Bf 109G-1/Trop, carried 13-mm (0.51-in) MG 131s in place of the MG 17s, necessitating larger breech blocks and giving rise to the nickname 'Beule' (bump) on account of the raised fairings forward of the windscreen. The **Bf 109G-2** dispensed with the pressure cabin and the **Bf 109G-2/R1** was a fighter-bomber; the **Bf 109G-3** was similar to the **Bf 109G-1** but with FuG 16Z radio, and the **Bf 109G-4** was an unpressurised version of the Bf 109G-3. The **Bf 109G-5** introduced the DB 605D engine with MW-50 water-methanol power-boosting (making possible a maximum power of 1343 kW/1,800 hp for combat bursts), while the **Bf 109G-5/R2**

Aircraft VK+AB was Bf 109 V24 (prototype no. 24), works number 5604. It was built in 1940 alongside V23 (CE+BP) as the third and fourth development aircraft for the Bf 109F, with round wingtips, a better-streamlined engine installation and other changes. The Bf 109F was the nicest of all 109s to fly.

A Bf 109F-2 of JG 2 pictured at an airfield on the channel coast. The arrival of the Bf 109F prevented the Spitfire Mk V from gaining the ascendancy it would have enjoyed over the Emil. The Bf 109F's improved armament and better handling was accompanied by a deterioration in handling qualities

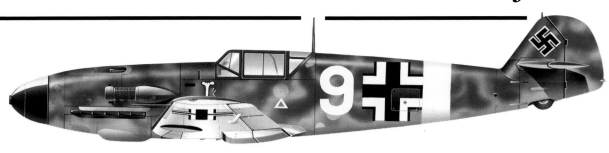

This Bf 109F-2Trop wears the emblem of I/LG 2 although it actually belonged to II/JG 27 at Sanyet in September 1942. I/LG 2 was redesignated as I/JG 77 during early 1942, explaining this apparent discrepancy. The white band around the rear fuselage, and the white wingtip undersurfaces are Mediterranean theatre markings.

A Bf 109F-2 of III/JG 54 'Grünherz', during the fighting for Leningrad in early 1942. A disruptive winter camouflage has been produced by overpainting large areas with white distemper. The devil's head badge is the insignia of 9. Staffel, and the red shield and back cross is that of the III Gruppe.

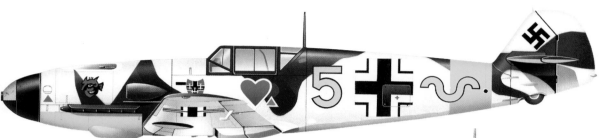

This sand camouflaged Bf 109F-2 Trop has a green overspray and served with III/JG 27 at Qasaba during the Autumn of 1942. The Bf 109s of JG 27 scored heavily against Desert Air Force P-40s and Hurricanes, though the tables were turned, to some extent, by the arrival of Spitfires.

This Bf 109G-2 of II/JG 54 'Grünherz' based at Siverskaya in the Northern part of the Eastern Front during the Autumn of 1942 wears a most unusual camouflage scheme. The shield in front of the windscreen is the emblem of the II Gruppe and is the badge of Vienna-Aspern.

Below: The Bf 109F-4B of the Staffelkapitän of 10.(Jabo) Staffel, JG 2, Oberleutnant Liesendahl, whose rudder displays a tally of enemy ships.

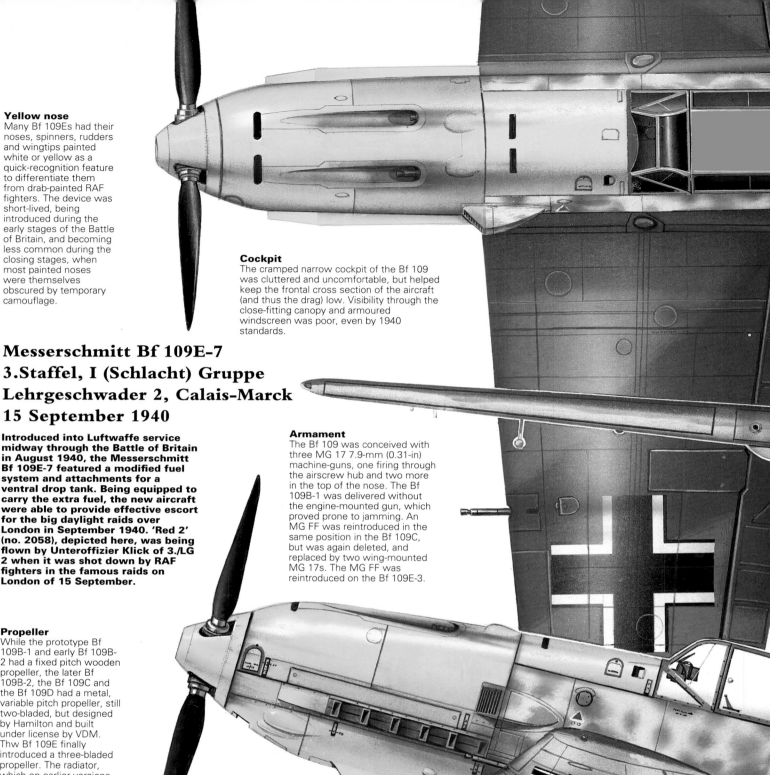

Yellow nose
Many Bf 109Es had their noses, spinners, rudders and wingtips painted white or yellow as a quick-recognition feature to differentiate them from drab-painted RAF fighters. The device was short-lived, being introduced during the early stages of the Battle of Britain, and becoming less common during the closing stages, when most painted noses were themselves obscured by temporary camouflage.

Cockpit
The cramped narrow cockpit of the Bf 109 was cluttered and uncomfortable, but helped keep the frontal cross section of the aircraft (and thus the drag) low. Visibility through the close-fitting canopy and armoured windscreen was poor, even by 1940 standards.

Messerschmitt Bf 109E-7
3.Staffel, I (Schlacht) Gruppe
Lehrgeschwader 2, Calais-Marck
15 September 1940

Introduced into Luftwaffe service midway through the Battle of Britain in August 1940, the Messerschmitt Bf 109E-7 featured a modified fuel system and attachments for a ventral drop tank. Being equipped to carry the extra fuel, the new aircraft were able to provide effective escort for the big daylight raids over London in September 1940. 'Red 2' (no. 2058), depicted here, was being flown by Unteroffizier Klick of 3./LG 2 when it was shot down by RAF fighters in the famous raids on London of 15 September.

Armament
The Bf 109 was conceived with three MG 17 7.9-mm (0.31-in) machine-guns, one firing through the airscrew hub and two more in the top of the nose. The Bf 109B-1 was delivered without the engine-mounted gun, which proved prone to jamming. An MG FF was reintroduced in the same position in the Bf 109C, but was again deleted, and replaced by two wing-mounted MG 17s. The MG FF was reintroduced on the Bf 109E-3.

Propeller
While the prototype Bf 109B-1 and early Bf 109B-2 had a fixed pitch wooden propeller, the later Bf 109B-2, the Bf 109C and the Bf 109D had a metal, variable pitch propeller, still two-bladed, but designed by Hamilton and built under license by VDM. Thw Bf 109E finally introduced a three-bladed propeller. The radiator, which on earlier versions had been 'chin-mounted' below the nose, was deleted and twin glycol radiators were added below the wing.

Powerplant
While the prototype was powered by a 518-kW (695 hp) Rolls-Royce Kestrel, and the Bf 109B and Bf 109C by the Jumo 210 engine, the Bf 109D was to have introduced the DB 600, but in fact powered by the 522-kW (700-hp) Jumo 210Da. It was left to the Emil to introduce the 783-kW (1,050-hp) Daimler Benz DB 601A-1. Subsequent versions all used derivatives of this basic Daimler Benz inline liquid-cooled V-12 engine, which could claim to be the German Merlin – widely used and with enormous potential for development and improvement.

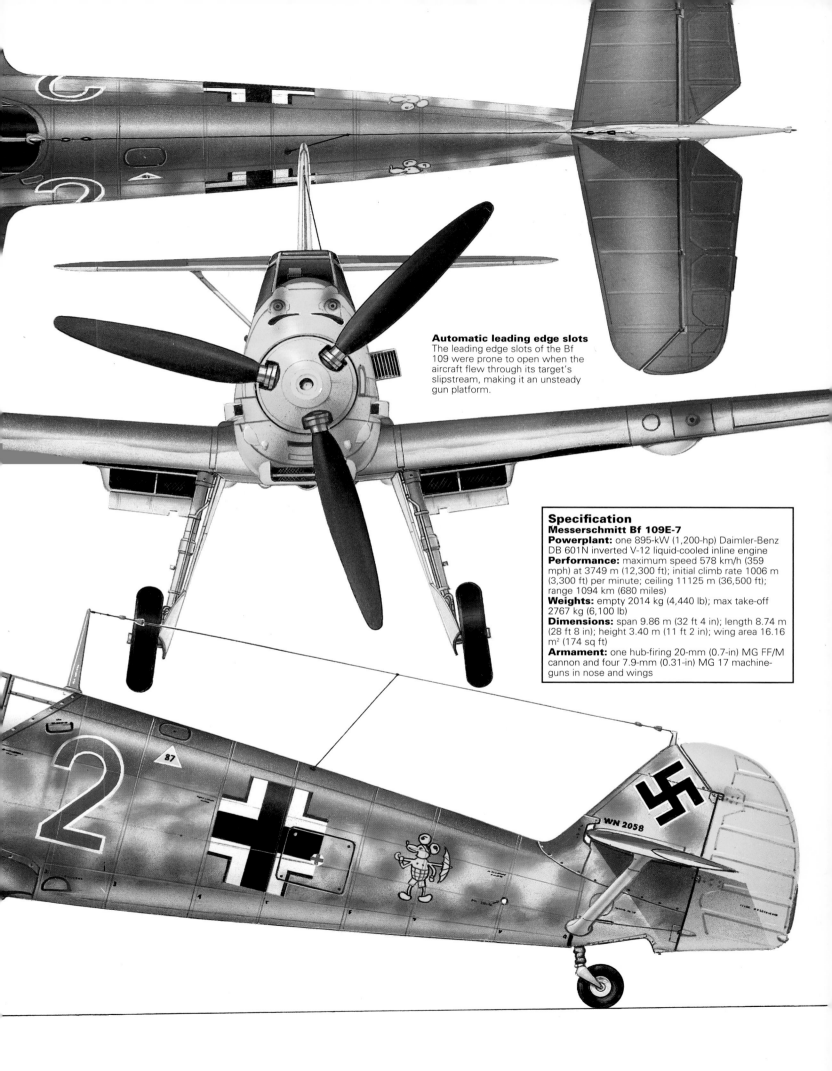

Automatic leading edge slots
The leading edge slots of the Bf 109 were prone to open when the aircraft flew through its target's slipstream, making it an unsteady gun platform.

Specification
Messerschmitt Bf 109E-7
Powerplant: one 895-kW (1,200-hp) Daimler-Benz DB 601N inverted V-12 liquid-cooled inline engine
Performance: maximum speed 578 km/h (359 mph) at 3749 m (12,300 ft); initial climb rate 1006 m (3,300 ft) per minute; ceiling 11125 m (36,500 ft); range 1094 km (680 miles)
Weights: empty 2014 kg (4,440 lb); max take-off 2767 kg (6,100 lb)
Dimensions: span 9.86 m (32 ft 4 in); length 8.74 m (28 ft 8 in); height 3.40 m (11 ft 2 in); wing area 16.16 m² (174 sq ft)
Armament: one hub-firing 20-mm (0.7-in) MG FF/M cannon and four 7.9-mm (0.31-in) MG 17 machine-guns in nose and wings

Messerschmitt Bf 109

The Bf 109E-4/B remained in service in the fighter bomber role long after fighter squadrons had re-equipped with the F-model or the Gustav. This III/SKG 210 E-4/B was based at El Daba during October 1942, and carries a 250 kg bomb under the centreline.

Left: This Bf 109E-7B of II/Schlachtgeschwader 1 was used during the battle for Stalingrad during the Winter of 1942. The rifle and laurel leaves insignia is the badge of the Infanterie-Sturmabzeichen, and was often carried by Schlacht aircraft.

A Bf 109G-6 of I/JG 3 'Udet' during June 1943. This version was the most important Gustav model, and was available with a wide array of armament options, many intended for destroying bombers.

featured a taller rudder and lengthened tailwheel leg in an effort to counter the aircraft's swing on take-off. Ever since the introduction of the Bf 109F had removed wing-mounted guns from the 109, a controversy had raged over how a fighter should be armed. In the hands of an expert the Bf 109F's three guns were adequate against fighter targets, but the quality of Luftwaffe gunnery training had steadily declined (young pilots being expected to learn most of their skills on the job) and the Bf 109's most important targets had become heavily armoured Russian Shturmoviks and large American bombers, making three relatively slow-firing guns clearly inadequate. Therefore the Bf 109G-5 introduced a basic armament of a single hub-firing 30-mm MK 108 cannon, and two nose-mounted MG 131s, whose larger breech blocks were covered by the distinctive 'beulen'.

Most important of all the 'Gustavs' was the **Bf 109G-6** which, in various sub-variants, was powered by AM, AS, ASB, ASD or ASM versions of the DB 605 engine; with provision for two underwing 20-mm MG 151/20 guns. Numerous *Rustsätze* kits were produced to

increase armament, including those to produce the **Bf 109G-6/R1** fighter-bomber with a bomb load of up to 500 kg (1,102 lb). Most aimed at improving the Bf 109's capability as a bomber-destroyer however, as the Defence of the Reich role steadily assumed greater importance. The **Bf 109G-6/R2** bomber-destroyer had two 21-cm (8.27-in) WGr 210 'Dodel' rockets replacing the underwing cannon, while the **Bf 109G-6/U4** (with an *Umrust-Bausatz* or factory conversion set) was armed with two 30-mm MK 108 underwing cannon, and the **Bf 109G-6/U4N** night-fighter carried radar. Tropicalised versions of most of these were also produced. The **Bf 109G-7** was not built, but the **Bf 109G-8** reconnaissance fighter formed part of the equipment of Nahaufklärungsgruppe 13 late in 1943 on the Channel coast. Fastest of all 'Gustavs' was the **Bf 109G-10** with the DB 605D with MW-50 and bulged cockpit canopy (known as the 'Galland hood'), and a top speed of 690 km/h (429 mph) at 7400 m (24,280 ft); the **Bf 109G-10/R2** and **R6** possessed the revised tail and tailwheel assembly of the Bf 109G-5/R2 and were equipped with

Leutnant Steindl poses his Bf 109E-4B for a wingman's camera during a bombing mission to Stalingrad in the Spring of 1942. The aircraft is in the standard 1940 colour scheme, albeit with heavily camouflaged fin and fuselage sides, and with cowling, rudder and wingtips in yellow. Steindl was the Geschwader adjutant of JG 54.

A Bf 109G-6/R1 of JG 3 'Udet', armed with a centreline 250-kg bomb. Massive bulges at the rear of the cowling covered the larger breeches of the 13-mm MG 131 guns adopted on the Bf 109G-5 and subsequent versions. Bf 109G-6s were delivered with the original short tail, and the taller wooden tail unit.

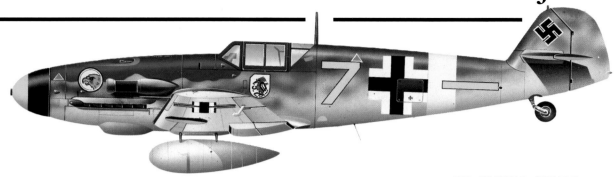

A Bf 109G-2/Trop of II/JG 51 'Molders' based at Casa Zeppera, Sardinia, during the summer of 1943. The eagle's head badge of JG 51 is carried on the engine cowling with the badge of II Gruppe below the cockpit. The umbrella carrying bird in this badge refers to former British Prime Minister Neville Chamberlain.

This Bf 109G-6 of IV/JG 5 wears a most unusual winter camouflage. It was based at Petsamo during the winter of 1943. The G-6 was the first 109 model intended from the outset to accept various Rustsätze (Field Conversion Sets) and was perhaps the most widely used version of the fighter during the latter part of the war.

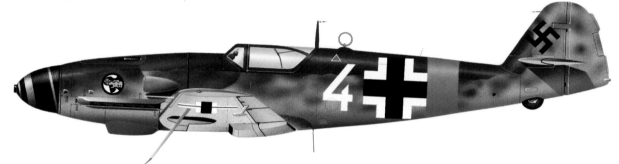

A wooden-tailed Bf 109K-4 of I/JG 27, based at Rheine during December 1944. The aircraft has a green Defence of the Reich band around its rear fuselage. These coloured identification markings were used at the turn of the year, but then gradually fell into disuse as the Reich slid towards final collapse.

FuG 25a IFF equipment; the **Bf 109G-10/U4** had provision for a belly gun pack containing two MK 108 30-mm guns, but this could be replaced by a non-jettisonable fuel tank known as the *Irmer Behalter*. The **Bf 109G-12** was a two-seat trainer, field-modified from the Bf 109G-1 to provide conversion training on the *Schulejagdgeschwader*, notably JG 101, 102, 104, 106, 107 and 108 in 1944. Last operational version was the 'universal' **Bf 109G-14** with lightened fixed armament but with provision for external guns, WfrGr 210 rockets or bombs. The **Bf 109G-16** heavily armoured ground-attack fighter-bomber entered production before Germany's surrender but did not see operational service. The Gustav formed the backbone of the Luftwaffe's last mass operation, the ill-fated Operation Bodenplatte, a

mass attack against allied airfields in France, Belgium and Holland aimed at destroying troublesome USAAF and RAF fighter bombers on the ground. Unfortunately, the Luftwaffe fighters suffered heavy losses while inflicting little damage, while destroying General der Jagdflieger Adolf Galland's preferred plan ('Big Blow') which was conceived as a mass operation (with 1500-2000 fighters) to destroy 500+ US bombers, whose crews would be irreplaceable. Galland believed that allied fighter bombers would be quickly replaced, and

These lightly-armed Bf 109F-5s wear the markings of 1.(F)/122, a tactical reconnaissance unit based on Sardinia during February 1943. Makeshift sun shades over the cockpits prevent cockpit temperatures from building up too much.

Messerschmitt Bf 109

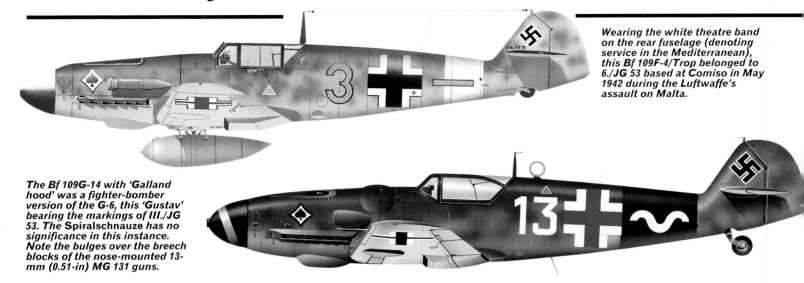

Wearing the white theatre band on the rear fuselage (denoting service in the Mediterranean), this Bf 109F-4/Trop belonged to 6./JG 53 based at Comiso in May 1942 during the Luftwaffe's assault on Malta.

The Bf 109G-14 with 'Galland hood' was a fighter-bomber version of the G-6, this 'Gustav' bearing the markings of III./JG 53. The Spiralschnauze has no significance in this instance. Note the bulges over the breech blocks of the nose-mounted 13-mm (0.51-in) MG 131 guns.

that while pilots in Bodenplatte would inevitably fall into Allied hands, many pilots shot down in 'Big Blow' would parachute safely into German territory.

Development of the **Bf 109H** high-altitude fighter started in 1943, being a progression from the F-series with increased wing span and the GM-1 boosted DB 601E. Maximum speed was 750 km/h (466 mph) at 10100 m (33,135 ft). Pre-production aircraft were evaluated operationally in France and a few sorties were flown by production **Bf 109H-1s**, but wing flutter problems caused the H-series to be abandoned, although projects included the **Bf 109H-2** with Jumo 213E, and the **Bf 109H-5** with DB 605 engines.

Last main operational version of the Bf 109 was the K-series, developed directly from the Gustav; indeed the **Bf 109K-0** pre-production aircraft were converted G-series airframes. The **Bf 109K-2** and **Bf 109K-4** (pressurised) were powered by MW-50 boosted 1492-kW (2,000-hp) DB 605 ASCM/DCM engines and armed with one 30-mm MK 103 or MK 108 cannon and two 15-mm (0.59-in) MG 151 heavy machine-guns, and the **Bf 109K-6** had provision for two underwing 30-mm MK 103s. Only two **Bf 109K-14**s (DB 605L with MW-50 and a top speed of 725 km/h; 450 mph) saw action before the end of the war, being delivered to Major Wilhelm Batz's Gruppenstab, II./JG 52, in April 1945.

Trials and experiments

With the Focke-Wulf Fw 190 reaching full operational status only after two years of war, the Bf 109 provided the backbone of the Luftwaffe's fighter arm throughout World War II: with more than 30,000 examples produced (because of confusion caused by bombing of factories, an accurate production total could not be arrived at, but only the Russian Ilyushin Il-2 had a higher figure, with 36,163 models built), it was natural that experiments and projects abounded.

For example, among the more bizarre trials were those conducted

Despite the absence of unit markings it is known that this Bf 109 was serving in autumn 1943 with II./JG 26, one of the crack fighter units in northern France. It is a G-6/R6, the R6 modification adding the pair of 20-mm MG 151 cannon and ammunition in underwing gondolas. The slats are clearly visible here.

on Bf 109Es to carry a parachutist in an over-wing 'paracapsule'. Another (in the *Starr-Schlepp* programme) involved the mounting of a Bf 109E on a DFS 230 troop-carrying glider as a means of delivering airborne forces; this experiment was followed later in the war by the well-known *Beethoven-Gerät* composite weapon system involving the use of Bf 109s and Fw 190s mounted atop unmanned Junkers Ju 88s loaded with explosives. A number of radical operational tactics were pioneered by Bf 109 units, including the aerial bombing of American bomber formations with 250-kg (551-lb) bombs dropped from Bf 109Gs (pioneered by JG 1 in 1943), and the use by JG 300 of day fighters for freelance night combat against night-bombers, known as *Wilde Sau* tactics.

A development of the Emil was the **Bf 109T** carrierborne fighter, intended for deployment aboard the German carrier *Graf Zeppelin*. Featuring folding long-span wings, arrester hook and catapult spools,

Above: This Bf 109G-12 trainer was converted from a Bf 109G-6 airframe, others being based on randomly selected Bf 109G-2s and Bf 109G-4s. Less than 100 two-seaters were built, of a planned total of over 900 trainer variants.

Below: Taken in 1944, when many Bf 109s were being used in the anti-bomber role with heavy rocket mortars, this photograph shows a pair of G-6/R2s with the most common of these weapons, the WfrGr 21 which lobbed 21-cm rockets from the tubes under the wings. They were called Pulk Zerstörer (formation destroyer)

A Bf 109G-6/R3 taxies out for a mission. The later Bf 109s featured the less heavily framed Erla Haube canopy seen here. Some late G-6s also had the taller wooden tail unit of the G-14 and subsequent variants.

10 pre-production **Bf 109T-0**s and 60 **Bf 109T-1**s were produced between 1939 and 1941, but when the carrier's construction was finally abandoned most of these aircraft were delivered to the Luftwaffe for land-based operation.

Perhaps the most ambitious of all projects was the **Bf 109Z** Zwilling, involving the union of two Bf 109F airframes and outer wing panels by means of new wing and tail sections; the pilot was to have been accommodated in the port fuselage and two versions were proposed, a *Zerstörer* with five 30-mm guns and a fighter-bomber with a 1000-kg (2,205-lb) bomb load. A prototype was built but this was never flown.

Bf 109s were supplied to numerous foreign air forces from 1939 onwards, and considerable licence-production of the 'Gustav' was undertaken by Avia at Prague and IAR at Brasov in Romania. The most successful of the foreign air arms with Bf 109s was the Finnish air force, its highest-scoring pilot, Lentomestari Eino Juutilainen, achiev-

ing 94 victories, of which 59 were scored in 'Gustavs'; he was the highest-scoring non-German/Austrian fighter pilot of all time and his aircraft were never once hit in combat.

Spain undertook licence-assembly of the Bf 109 during and after World War II using the Hispano-Suiza 12-Z-89 and 12-Z-17 engines in German-supplied airframes, and later the Rolls-Royce Merlin; these aircraft, termed Hispano **HAS 1109-J1L**, **HA 1110-K1L** (two-seater) and **HA 1112-K1L**, remained in service until the 1960s. Other post-war use of the Bf 109 included a number of **C-199** 'Mezec' (Czech-built Jumo 211F-powered 'Gustavs') flown by Israel against the Egyptian air force in 1948. The Bf 109 was widely supplied to German satellite states in World War II, and was also used by neutral countries such as Spain and Switzerland.

Messerschmitt Bf 109 variants

Bf 109a (later Bf109 V1): D-IABI, first prototype; 518-kW (695-hp) Rolls-Royce Kestrel V engine; first flight in September 1935
Bf 109 V2, V3 and V4: three prototypes (D-IUDE, D-IHNY and D-IOQY); Jumo 210A engines
Bf 109B: pre-production **Bf 109B-0** with Jumo 210B; **Bf 109B-1** with Jumo 210D; **Bf 109B-2** with Jumo 210E and later, 210G engines
Bf 109 V10 and V13: two prototypes (D-ISLU and D-IPKY); Daimler-Benz DB 600 engines
Bf 109C: developed from Bf 109 V8 prototype; **Bf 109C-0** and **Bf 109C-1** with four MG 17 guns; **Bf 109C-2** with five MG 17
Bf 109 V13: modified with boosted DB 601 engine; world speed record of 610.54 km/h (379.38 mph) on 11 November 1937
Bf 109D: developed from Bf 109 V10 and V13 prototypes; **Bf 109D-0** with DB 600Aa and armament of one 20-mm and two 7.9-mm (0.31-in) guns; **Bf 109D-1** similar; **Bf 109D-2** with two wing MG 17s; **Bf 109D-3** with two MG FFs in wings
Bf 109 V14: prototype (D-IRTT); fuel injection DB 601A engine; two 20-mm and two 7.9-mm (0.31-in) guns; Bf 109 V15 (D-IPHR) similar but one 20-mm gun
Bf 109E: Bf109E-0 with four 7.9-mm (0.31-in) guns; **Bf 109E-1** (and

Bf 109E-1/B bomber) similar; **Bf 109E-2** with two 20-mm and two 7.9-mm (0.31-in) guns; **Bf 109E-3** with one hub 20-mm and four 7.9-mm (0.31-in) guns; **Bf 109E-4** (also **Bf 109E-4/B** and **Bf 109E-4/Trop**) similar to **Bf 109E-3** but no hub gun; **Bf 109E-4/N** with DB 601N engine; **Bf 109E-5** and **Bf 109E-6** reconnaissance fighters with two 7.9-mm (0.31-in) guns; **Bf 109E-7** similar to **Bf 109E-4/N** with provision for belly tank (**Bf 109E-7/U2** ground attack sub-variant); **Bf 109E-7/Z** with GM-1 boost; **Bf 109E-8** with DB 601E engine; **Bf 109E-9** reconnaissance fighter
Bf 109F: Bf 109F-0 from E-airframes with DB 601N engine; **Bf 109F-1** with one 20-mm and two 7.9-mm (0.31-in) guns; **Bf 109F-2** with one 15-mm and two 7.9-mm (0.31-in) guns (Bf 109F-2/Z with GM-1); **Bf 109F-3** with DB 601E engine; **Bf 109F-4** (and **Bf 109F-4/B**) with one 20-mm and two 7.9-mm (0.31-in) guns and DB 601E; **Bf 109F-5** and **Bf 109F-6** reconnaissance fighters with two 7.9-mm (0.31-in) guns; trials aircraft included one with BMW 801 radial, one with Jumo 213, one with butterfly tail and one with wing fences
Bf 109G: Bf 109G-0 with DB 601E engine; **Bf 109G-1** with DB 605A-1 and GM-1; **Bf 109G-1/Trop** with

one 20-mm and two 15-mm guns (*Beule*); **Bf 109G-2** was unpressurised version of **Bf 109G-1** (also **Bf 109G-2/R1** fighter-bomber); **Bf 109G-3** with FuG 16Z radio; **Bf 109G-4** unpressurised version of **Bf 109G-3**; **Bf 109G-5** with enlarged rudder had DB 605D with MW-50; **Bf 109G-6** with variations of DB 605 (see text) and two 13-mm (0.51-in), one 30-mm and two underwing 20-mm guns (also R and U sub-variants, see text); **Bf 109G-8** reconnaissance fighter; **Bf 109G-10** with DB 605G and MW-50; **Bf 109G-12** was two-seat trainer; **Bf 109G-14** with one 20-mm and two 15-mm guns plus provision for underwing guns or rockets; **Bf 109G-16** ground-attack fighter
Bf 109H: high-altitude fighter developed from F-series; **Bf 109H-0** pre-production; **Bf 109H-1** with DB 601E; **Bf 109H-2** and **Bf 109H-3** with Jumo 213; **Bf 109H-5** with DB 605L
Bf 109J: proposed Spanish licence-built version; not proceeded with
Bf 109K: development from **Bf 109G-10; Bf 109K-0** with DB 605D and GM-1; **Bf 109K-2** and **Bf 109K-4** (pressurised) with DB 605ASCM/DCM and MW-50, and one 30-mm and two 15-mm guns; **Bf 109K-6** with three 30-mm and two 15-mm guns; **Bf 109K-14** with DB 605L and MW-50
Bf 109L: proposed version with

Jumo 213E engine; maximum estimated speed 763 km/h (474 mph); not built
Bf 109S: proposed version with blown flaps; not built
Bf 109T: carrierborne version of **Bf 109E** for carrier *Graf Zeppelin*; 10 **Bf 109T-0** converted by Fieseler; 60 **Bf 109T-1** with DB 601N engine; **Bf 109T-2** was conversion of T-1 with deck gear removed
Bf 109TL: project based on near-standard Bf 109 with two underwing Jumo 109-004B turbojets; abandoned in 1943
Bf 109Z Zwilling: twin Bf 109F airframes with single pilot and five 30-mm guns (**Bf 109Z-1**); **Bf 109Z-2** with two 30-mm guns and 1000-kg (2,205-lb) bomb load; **Bf 109Z-3** and **Bf 109Z-4** conversion of **Bf 109Z-1** and **Bf109Z-2** respectively with Jumo 213 engines; one prototype built but not flown; led to Me 609 project
Me 209 V1, V2, V3 and V4: D-INJR, D-IWAH, D-IVFP and D-IRND; high-speed prototypes developed for speed records
Me 309 V1, V2, V3 and V4: GE-CU, GE-CV, GE-CW and GE-CX; high-speed, high-altitude fighter prototypes intended to replace Bf 109F
Me 609: projected development of **Bf 109Z Zwilling** twin Bf 109; abandoned

Messerschmitt Bf 110

Speed, acceleration and tight manoeuvrability in the cut and thrust of a dogfight were the objectives laid before the fighter designers of all nations following the end of the war in Europe in 1918, and accordingly it was the single-seat biplane, of high power:weight ratio and relatively low wing-loading, that held the position of pre-eminence in the world's air forces. Then came the monoplane revolution of the 1930s, with monocoque fuselages, retractable landing gear, cantilever tail units, and stressed single- or double-spar wings; the configuration of the fighter remained essentially the same, with armament and fuel tankage carefully restricted so as not to detract from speed and manoeuvrability. However, combat operations over the Western Front during 1917-18 had accentuated the need for fighters with extended range and endurance, and in particular for those with a combat radius of action that could enable them to accompany bombers on missions deep into enemy airspace, either as escort fighters or in order to gain air supremacy in an appointed area.

To design such an aircraft was considered to be well nigh impossible but, in 1934, the idea was resurrected. Whether the long-range strategic fighter concept was to be committed to offensive or defensive tasks is still a matter for argument. For the Luftwaffe at least, the requirement for this type, termed the *Zerstörer* (destroyer), was the pursuit and destruction of enemy bombers operating over the Reich, plus the additional ability to harass over a lengthy period on the withdrawal.

Attending to the RLM specifications for the development of a heavy strategic fighter, the team at the Bayerische Flugzeugwerke AG (later Messerschmitt AG) started work on the project in the summer of 1935 with their wayward brilliance, ignoring much of the specification data and concentrating their efforts on the design of a lean, all-metal, twin-engined monoplane. The prototype **Messerschmitt Bf 110 V1** first flew from Augsburg-Haunstetten on 12 May 1936, with Rudolf Opitz at the controls. Powered by two Daimler Benz DB 600A engines, the Bf 110 V1 achieved maximum speed of 505 km/h (314 mph) at 3175 m (10,415 ft), considerably in excess of that reached by the single-engined Messerschmitt Bf 109B-2 fighter. Of course, acceleration and manoeuvrability, as noted by the test pilots and later by those at the Erprobungsstelle (service trials detachment) on this and subsequent prototypes, in no way compared with those of lighter fighters. But Hermann Goering ignored the misgivings of the Luftwaffe regarding the Messerschmitt Bf 110's potentialities, and ordered that production should proceed. The first pre-production model, the **Bf 110B-01** powered by two Junkers Jumo 210Ga engines, first flew on 19 April 1938 in the wake of a major reorganisation of the Luftwaffe's units.

Engine trouble

The shortage of Daimler Benz powerplants and the retention of the Jumo 210Ga engines conferred only a mediocre capability on the **Bf 110B-1** series that emanated from the Augsburg production lines in the summer. Armed with two 20-mm Oerlikon MG FF cannon and four 7.92-mm (0.31-in) MG 17 machine-guns, the Bf 110B-1

Left: A pair of Bf 110D-3s of 9./Zerstörergeschwader 26 flies over the Mediterranean during 1941, carrying a pair of 900-litre (198-Imp gal) fuel tanks for extended endurance in the convoy protection role. The Bf 110D-3 was specifically tailored for the convoy protection role, and carried an underfuselage auxiliary oil tank, with provision for 300- or 900-litre (66- or 198-Imp gal) auxiliary fuel tanks under the outer wings. The tailcone was extended to house a dinghy.

Below: While waiting for the supply of new engines to become less erratic, Messerschmitt redesigned the aircraft and produced the higher-performance Bf 110C, the main variant involved in the Battle of Britain.

A Messerschmitt Bf 110C-4 operated by Zerstörergeschwader 52 flies over the French coastline in late 1940. Such units were to receive a severe mauling in the aerial offensive over Britain.

had a maximum speed of 455 km/h (283 mph) at its rated altitude of 4000 m (13,125 ft); the service ceiling was 8000 m (26,245 ft). This version was the first to enter service, equipping a number of *Schweren Jagdgruppen* (heavy fighter wings) in the autumn of 1938.

Polish campaign

Early in 1939, the Messerschmitt **Bf 110C-0** pre-production fighters were issued to the newly-formed *Zerstörergruppen* (ex-*Schweren Jagdgruppen*); these featured the modified airframe that was to endure throughout the aircraft's lifetime, and were powered by the 12-cylinder, inverted-Vee direct-injection Daimler Benz DB 601A-1 engines rated at 820 kW (1,100 hp) at 3700 m (12,140 ft). The production **Bf 110C-1**s were highly effective long-range fighters, and the crews of I(Zerst)/Lehrgeschwader Nr 1, I/Zerstörergeschwader Nr 1 and I/ZG 76, who manned the new type, represented the cream of the Luftwaffe's fighter arm. Just before the outbreak of war, in September 1939, each *Gruppe* had two *Staffeln* with Bf 110C-1s and a conversion

This Messerschmitt Bf 110C-2 fighter reveals the type's slim fuselage and graceful lines. The aircraft was hard put to stay the pace with single-seat Allied fighters, although many German aces claimed high scores. The type's vulnerability has been overemphasised, and it was the mainstay of Germany's night-fighter force from 1940 to 1945.

unit with **Bf 110B-3** trainers. The crews used their heavy aircraft well during the short campaign in Poland during September, flying top cover to the Heinkels and Dorniers and conducting sweeps at 6000 m (19,685 ft) and above; they quickly recognised the stupidity of entering turning matches with the nimble Polish PZL P.11c fighters, and adopted climb-and dive tactics while maintaining good airspeed at all times. Oberst Walter Grabmann's I(Z)/LG 1 (led by Hauptmann Schleif) downed five PZL P.11s over Warsaw on the evening of 1 September while covering the Heinkel He 111Ps of II/KG 1. The centralised armament, aimed by a Revi C.12/C reflector sight, was found to be devastating: one burst of 1-2 seconds was sufficient to blow off a wing of an opposing fighter. But was this enough?

Already it was apparent that the *Zerstörergruppen* had eschewed what was probably the originally intended role, and were being employed

Ground crew prepare to load an Rb 50/30 camera on to a Bf 110C-5. Operating from Greece prior to the German airborne invasion of Crete, such photo missions failed to reveal the island's hostile terrain.

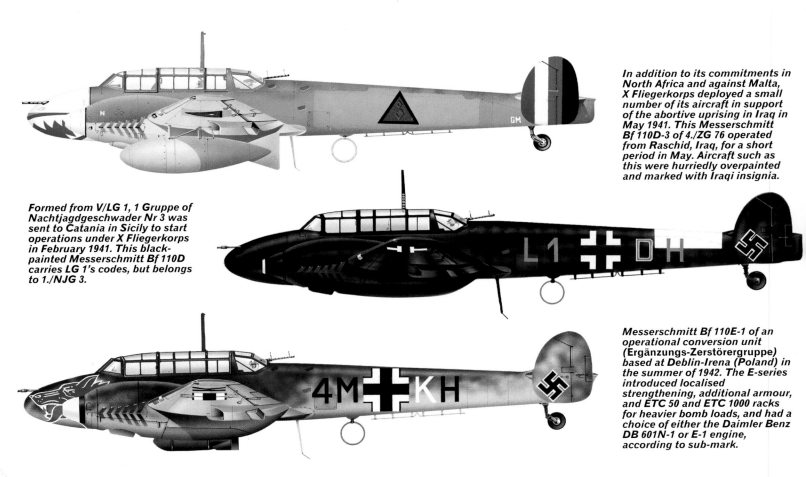

In addition to its commitments in North Africa and against Malta, X Fliegerkorps deployed a small number of its aircraft in support of the abortive uprising in Iraq in May 1941. This Messerschmitt Bf 110D-3 of 4./ZG 76 operated from Raschid, Iraq, for a short period in May. Aircraft such as this were hurriedly overpainted and marked with Iraqi insignia.

Formed from V/LG 1, 1 Gruppe of Nachtjagdgeschwader Nr 3 was sent to Catania in Sicily to start operations under X Fliegerkorps in February 1941. This black-painted Messerschmitt Bf 110D carries LG 1's codes, but belongs to 1./NJG 3.

Messerschmitt Bf 110E-1 of an operational conversion unit (Ergänzungs-Zerstörergruppe) based at Deblin-Irena (Poland) in the summer of 1942. The E-series introduced localised strengthening, additional armour, and ETC 50 and ETC 1000 racks for heavier bomb loads, and had a choice of either the Daimler Benz DB 601N-1 or E-1 engine, according to sub-mark.

*Above: II Gruppe of ZG 26 was known as the **Haifischgruppe** (shark wing) and decorated its aircraft with a gaudy sharkmouth. This aircraft, a Bf 110C, was photographed during the Battle of France in 1940.*

*Below: Reformed from SKG 210, Zerstörergeschwader Nr 1 operated in the USSR in 1942, seeing action in the Caucasus and Stalingrad theatres under VIII Fliegerkorps. When the North African crisis developed in October 1942, Gruppen of ZG 1 were posted to Sicily under Luftflotte 2; pictured here is a **Staffel** of the group's Bf 110G-2s.*

on escort and superiority sorties against enemy single-engined fighters. In theory there was little wrong in the performance parameters of the Bf 110C-1: for its size and configuration, it was the finest heavy fighter extant. With a combat weight of 5900 kg (13,007 lb) it attained 540 km/h (336 mph) at a rated altitude of 6050 m (19,850 ft), faster than most Allied contemporary fighters, and only 32-43 km/h (20-30 mph) slower than its next opponents, the French Dewoitine D.520 and the British Supermarine Spitfire Mk I. But, in fighter-versus-fighter combat, snappy rates of roll and swift acceleration win the day, with maximum-rate turns being a factor of power, wing-loading and pilot strength.

Battle of Britain

Few problems were encountered by the *Zerstörer* pilots over Poland and Scandinavia, and their undoubted ability was awarded with the accolade that suggested to all that the Bf 110C-1 was an outstanding combat aircraft. Staunch fighter opposition over France and southern England in 1940 was to destroy much of that myth. On *freie Jagd*

A Messerschmitt Bf 110G-2/R3 day fighter of 7./ZG 26 serving under Luftwaffenbefehlshaber Mitte in the defence of the Reich in 1943. Liberally equipped with 20-mm and 30-mm cannon and Wfr Gr 21 rocket-mortars, the aircraft was a killer. The Luftwaffe failed to foresee the introduction of US escort fighters.

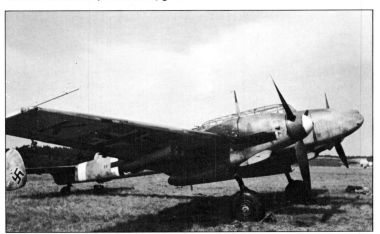

Right: A Bf 110C-2 of I/ZG 52, operating from Charleville during June 1940, as the Battle of France reached its zenith. Whereas in the Polish and Norwegian campaigns the Bf 110 had been up against largely obsolete single-seat fighters, in France (and later in the Battle of Britain) it faced more modern fighter opposition, and attrition rose alarmingly in both campaigns.

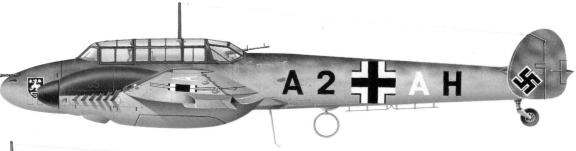

Left: The Bf 110C-4s of ZG 1 (the so-called Wespe (wasp) Geschwader) wore an intricate wasp insignia on their noses. This aircraft served with the unit's fifth Staffel in the Caucasus during October 1942. The upper surfaces of this aircraft's wings had an unusual combination of splinter and dapple camouflage.

Right: II/ZG 76 reformed in the air defence role from a variety of Zerstörer schools and night-fighter units during August 1943. This is one of the Gruppe's Bf 110F-2s, and carries a yellow Reich Defence band (a standard marking for all Zerstörer Gruppen operating in defence of Germany), which could be confused with the Russian Front theatre band. The unit was based at Wertheim in the winter of 1943.

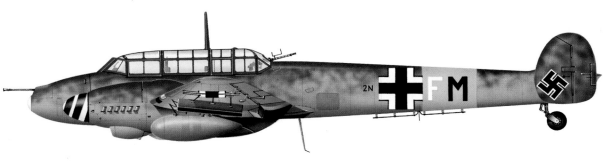

Right: A Kette of Bf 110E-1s of II/SKG 210, which operated alongside II Gruppe of ZG 26 (from which its nucleus had been drawn) during the opening stages of Operation Barbarossa. II/SKG 210 later redesignated to become II/ZG 1. The Bf 110E introduced ETC 50 bomb racks under the outer wing panels.

Below: In this pair of Bf 110Ds, the nearest wears the codes of 8./ZG 26 'Horst Wessel', and the other retains its factory codes. During early 1942, III/JG 26 (less its seventh Staffel in North Africa) was based at Trapani under II Fliegerkorps for the assault on Malta.

sweeps over Sussex and Kent at heights above 6700 m (21,980 ft), the Bf 110C-1s and **Bf 110C-4**s were virtually immune throughout the Battle of Britain, with RAF tacticians acknowledging the fact that it out-performed the Hurricane Mk I in all regimes, and that it could out-climb the Spitfire Mk I; the dive-and-climb tactics of the Bf 110s were effective, and the armament had to be watched with care. The horrendous casualties sustained by I/ZG 76 and Zerstörergeschwader Nrn 2 and 26 during the battle occurred almost without exception during medium-level bomber escort missions. Throttled back and at slow speed, the Bf 110Cs were cut to pieces, being wholly unable to out-turn the lighter Spitfires and Hurricanes. The pilots of the Messerschmitt Bf 109E-4s suffered similar disadvantage, but to an extent that was not as disastrous.

During the Battle of Britain, the extended-range Messerschmitt **Bf 110D-1/R1** saw service with I/ZG 76 at Stavanger, while the fighter-bomber **Bf 110C-4/B**s of Erprobungskommando 210 flew several audacious, and often costly, missions on precision targets in southern England. In the winter of 1940-41, the III/ZG 26 took its **Bf 110D-3**s to Sicily and thence to North Africa; other *Gruppen* of

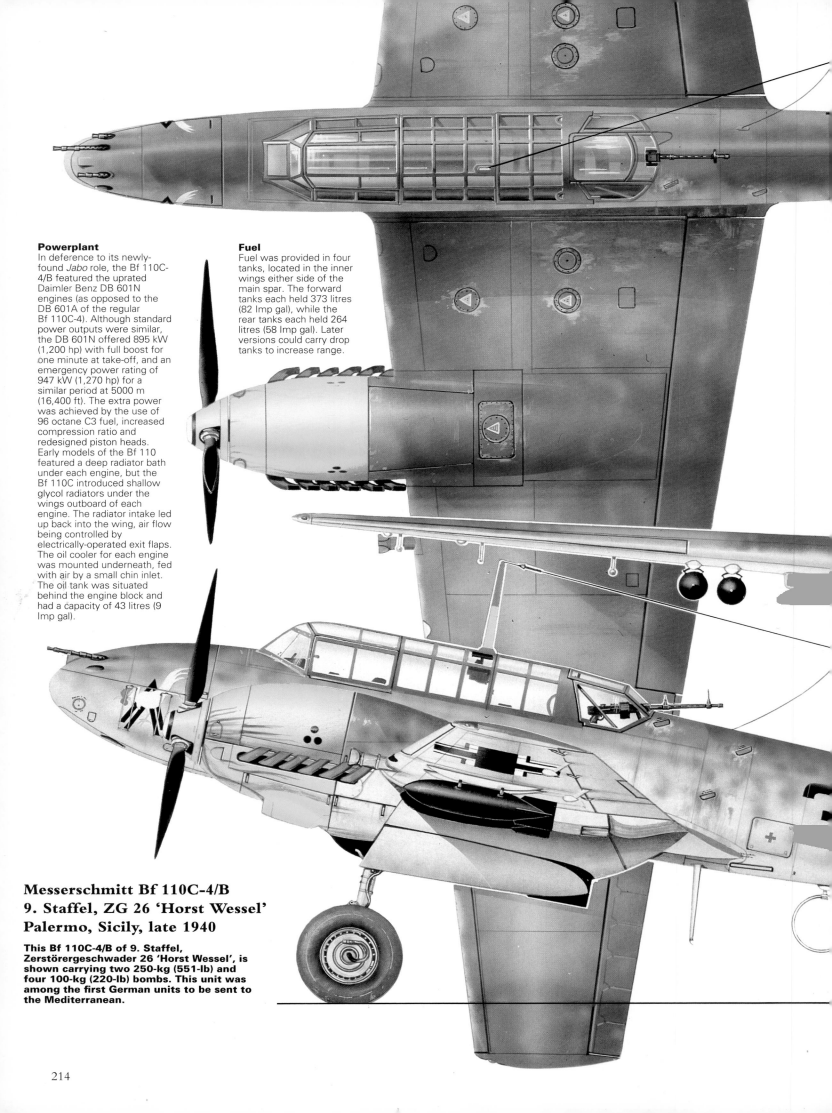

Powerplant

In deference to its newly-found *Jabo* role, the Bf 110C-4/B featured the uprated Daimler Benz DB 601N engines (as opposed to the DB 601A of the regular Bf 110C-4). Although standard power outputs were similar, the DB 601N offered 895 kW (1,200 hp) with full boost for one minute at take-off, and an emergency power rating of 947 kW (1,270 hp) for a similar period at 5000 m (16,400 ft). The extra power was achieved by the use of 96 octane C3 fuel, increased compression ratio and redesigned piston heads. Early models of the Bf 110 featured a deep radiator bath under each engine, but the Bf 110C introduced shallow glycol radiators under the wings outboard of each engine. The radiator intake led up back into the wing, air flow being controlled by electrically-operated exit flaps. The oil cooler for each engine was mounted underneath, fed with air by a small chin inlet. The oil tank was situated behind the engine block and had a capacity of 43 litres (9 Imp gal).

Fuel

Fuel was provided in four tanks, located in the inner wings either side of the main spar. The forward tanks each held 373 litres (82 Imp gal), while the rear tanks each held 264 litres (58 Imp gal). Later versions could carry drop tanks to increase range.

Messerschmitt Bf 110C-4/B
9. Staffel, ZG 26 'Horst Wessel'
Palermo, Sicily, late 1940

This Bf 110C-4/B of 9. Staffel, Zerstörergeschwader 26 'Horst Wessel', is shown carrying two 250-kg (551-lb) and four 100-kg (220-lb) bombs. This unit was among the first German units to be sent to the Mediterranean.

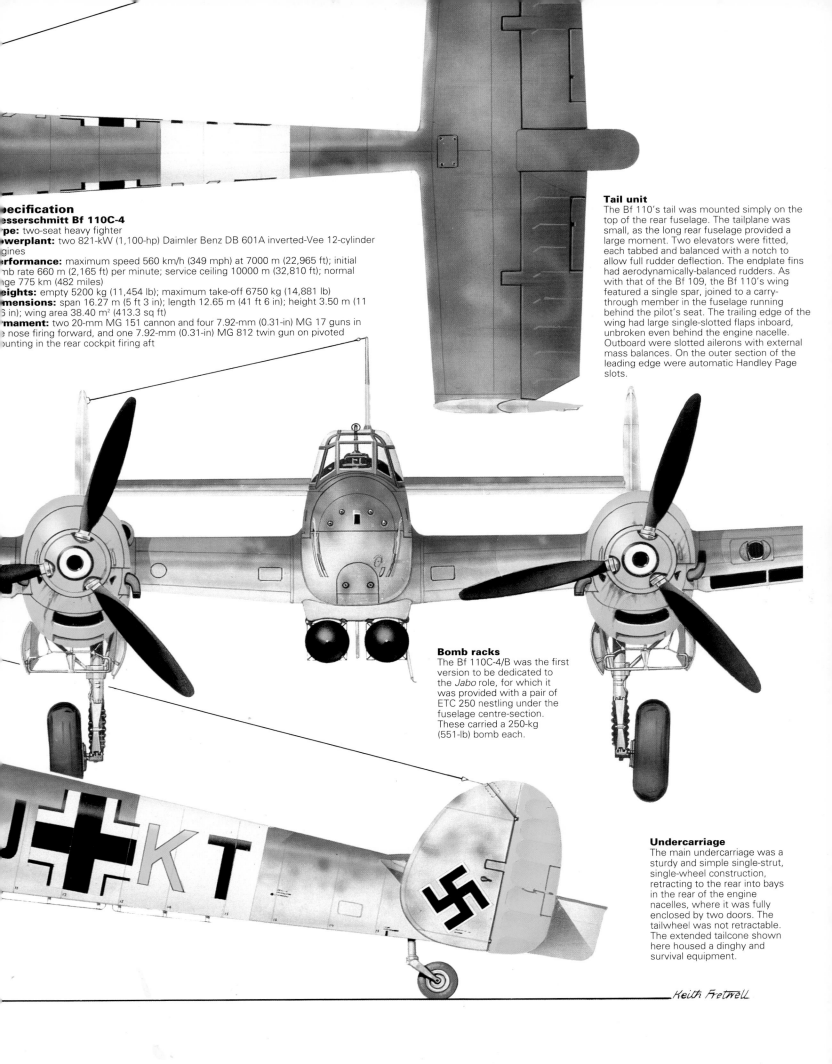

Specification

Messerschmitt Bf 110C-4

Type: two-seat heavy fighter

Powerplant: two 821-kW (1,100-hp) Daimler Benz DB 601A inverted-Vee 12-cylinder engines

Performance: maximum speed 560 km/h (349 mph) at 7000 m (22,965 ft); initial climb rate 660 m (2,165 ft) per minute; service ceiling 10000 m (32,810 ft); normal range 775 km (482 miles)

Weights: empty 5200 kg (11,454 lb); maximum take-off 6750 kg (14,881 lb)

Dimensions: span 16.27 m (5 ft 3 in); length 12.65 m (41 ft 6 in); height 3.50 m (11 ft 6 in); wing area 38.40 m² (413.3 sq ft)

Armament: two 20-mm MG 151 cannon and four 7.92-mm (0.31-in) MG 17 guns in the nose firing forward, and one 7.92-mm (0.31-in) MG 812 twin gun on pivoted mounting in the rear cockpit firing aft

Tail unit

The Bf 110's tail was mounted simply on the top of the rear fuselage. The tailplane was small, as the long rear fuselage provided a large moment. Two elevators were fitted, each tabbed and balanced with a notch to allow full rudder deflection. The endplate fins had aerodynamically-balanced rudders. As with that of the Bf 109, the Bf 110's wing featured a single spar, joined to a carry-through member in the fuselage running behind the pilot's seat. The trailing edge of the wing had large single-slotted flaps inboard, unbroken even behind the engine nacelle. Outboard were slotted ailerons with external mass balances. On the outer section of the leading edge were automatic Handley Page slots.

Bomb racks

The Bf 110C-4/B was the first version to be dedicated to the *Jabo* role, for which it was provided with a pair of ETC 250 nestling under the fuselage centre-section. These carried a 250-kg (551-lb) bomb each.

Undercarriage

The main undercarriage was a sturdy and simple single-strut, single-wheel construction, retracting to the rear into bays in the rear of the engine nacelles, where it was fully enclosed by two doors. The tailwheel was not retractable. The extended tailcone shown here housed a dinghy and survival equipment.

Keith Fretwell

Opposite page, right: The Bf 110G-4 was produced by essentially adding FuG 202 Lichtenstein B/C radar to the Bf 110G-2 Zerstörer, and it was to become the basis for virtually all the night-fighter variants. All aircraft with this radar retained the small G-2-type fins.

the parent *Geschwader* operated over the Balkans, Greece and Crete during the spring. For the invasion of the Soviet Union on 22 June 1941 (Operation Barbarossa), the II Fliegerkorps controlled the Bf 110C-4s of Major Karl-Heinz Stricker's Schnellkampfgeschwader Nr 210 (I and II Gruppen), and the VIII Fliegerkorps controlled the Bf 110C-4s of Oberst Johannes Schalk's Zerstörergeschwader Nr 26 (I and II Gruppen); remaining units equipped with the day-fighting Bf 110s were I and II/ZG 6, based at Kirkenes in northern Norway, and at Jever and Nordholz in Germany. Production of the big Messerschmitt had been reduced in favour of its replacement, the Messerschmitt Me 210A-1, while many Zerstörergruppen had been reformed as night-fighter units. Upgunned and with increased power, the **Bf 110E**, **Bf 110F** and **Bf 110G** series continued to operate in small numbers throughout the campaigns in the USSR and North Africa.

In August 1943 the decimated elements were withdrawn from the USSR and Italy to form I-III/ZG 26 at Wunstorf and I-III/ZG 76 at Ansbach for the daylight defence of the Reich with Messerschmitt **Bf 110G-2**s: these carried a variety of weapons, including 20-mm MG 151/20 and 30-mm MK 108A-3 cannon, 37-mm Flak 18 guns, and 21-cm Werfergranate (WfrGr 21) rocket mortars. Against unescorted formations of B-17 Flying Fortressess and B-24 Liberators, this new breed of fighter wrought mayhem in its role of *Pulk-Zerstörer* (forma-

Left: A Bf 110C-4b after capture by the Desert Rats of General Montgomery's Eighth Army. The Bf 110 played an important role in the Western Desert, providing Zerstörer support for Rommel's Afrika Korps.

Below: A pair of late-model Bf 110G-4/R-3 night-fighters waits for night to fall. Severely outclassed in the day fighter role, the design was well-suited to attacking bombers at night. The type featured good endurance, a capacity to carry radar and other electronic equipment, and was heavily armed.

tion destroyer) until the appearance of P-47D Thunderbolts with 410-litre (90-Imp gal) auxiliary tanks. Their slaughter was on a scale that dwarfed the losses sustained in 1940, and by April 1944 the Messerschmitt Bf 110G-2, with the exception of those with II/ZG 76 at Wien-Seying in Austria, was finally withdrawn from service. In other theatres, however, especially where there was no danger from marauding Allied fighters, Bf 110s continued to be used effectively. In Norway, for example, Bf 110s accounted for significant numbers of RAF Coastal Command long-range ASW aircraft.

Without doubt, the Messerschmitt Bf 110's most successful service record was performed as a night-fighter in the defence of the Reich, a duty that it performed with lethal efficiency for nearly five years. On 20 July 1940, Goering ordered Oberst Josef Kammhuber to form a night-fighter force: the I/Nachtjagdgeschwader Nr 1 (I/NJG 1) was formed from I/ZG 1 and IV/JG 2 with Bf 110C-2s at Venlo in the Netherlands towards the end of the month, to create the nucleus of a full *Geschwader*. The crews of I/ZG 1 had already taken up night-fighter training, transferring to Dusseldorf after the end of the campaign in France. On the evening before its official formation, I NJG 1 scored its first kill: Hauptmann Werner Streib of 2./NJG 2, flying

Messerschmitt Bf 110 variants

Messerschmitt Bf 110 V1: first prototype powered with two Daimler Benz DB 600A engines; first flight on 12 May 1936

Messerschmitt Bf 110 V2: second prototype featuring some refinements; to E-Stelle Rechlin for service evaluation on 14 January 1937

Messerschmitt Bf 110 V3: armament test prototype with initial flight on 24 December 1936; four 7.92-mm (0.31-in) MG 17 machine-guns fitted in nose

Messerschmitt Bf 110A-0: production models intended for DB 600Aa engines, but considered underpowered and phased out; some with Junkers Jumo 210Da engines

Messerschmitt Bf 110B-1: production version following the redesigned Bf 110B-01, with modified nose for an armament of four 7.92-mm (0.31-in) MG 17 and two 20-mm Oerlikon MG FF cannon; rear gunner had one 7.92-mm (0.31-in) MG 15; powerplant of two Junkers 210Gas

Messerschmitt Bf 110B-2: reconnaissance version with camera installed in place of MG FF cannon

Messerschmitt Bf 110B-3: conversion trainer with armament removed, and improved radio and instruments

Messerschmitt Bf 110C-0: pre-production aircraft with two Daimler Benz DB 601A-1 engines each rated at 820 kW (1,100 hp)

Messerschmitt Bf 110C-1: armament and engines standardised in this major military version at four MG 17s, two MG FFs and DB 601A-1s

Messerschmitt Bf 110C-2: improved H/F Lorenz FuG 10 radio in place of FuG IIIa

Messerschmitt Bf 110C-3: improved Oerlikon MG FF/M cannon

Messerschmitt Bf 110C-4: additional 9-mm armour for pilot

Messerschmitt Bf 110C-4/B: fighter-bomber version with two ETC 250 racks under fuselage and two Daimler-Benz DB 601N-1 engines each rated at 895 kW (1,200 hp)

Messerschmitt Bf 110C-5: reconnaissance version with reduced armament, and with single Rb 50/30 camera; Bf 110C-5/N with DB 601N-1s

Messerschmitt Bf 110C-6: twin 20-mm MG FFs replaced by single 30-mm MK 101 cannon

Messerschmitt Bf 110C-7: basic Bf 110C-4/B with stronger landing gear and two ETC 500 belly racks for increased load

Messerschmitt Bf 110D-0: pre-production long-range fighter

Messerschmitt Bf 110D-1/R1: similar to Bf 110C series but with 1200-litre (264-Imp gal) external belly tank for extended range missions

Messerschmitt Bf 110D-1/R2: similar to Bf 110C with two 900-litre (198-Imp gal) wing-mounted drop tanks

Messerschmitt Bf 110D-2: long-range fighter-bomber with two ETC 500 racks, and provision for two 300-litre (66-Imp gal) drop tanks

Messerschmitt Bf 110D-3: long-range shipping patrol version with either two 300-litre (66-Imp gal) or two 900-litre (198-Imp gal) drop tanks, a supplementary oil tank, and stowage in tailcone for two-man liferaft

Messerschmitt Bf 110E-1: definitive fighter-bomber series with additional four ETC 50 racks under wing surfaces, and increased load to 1200 kg (2,645 lb); initially with two DB 601A-1s then two DB 601N-1 engines; updated ancillary equipment, improved armour

Messerschmitt Bf 110E-1/U1: modified to night-fighter work, with infra-red Spanner Anlage sighting device

Messerschmitt Bf 110E-1/U2: night-fighter with extra crew member

Messerschmitt Bf 110E-2 and Bf 110E-3: fighter-bomber and reconnaissance versions of standard Bf 110E-1 with updated ancillary equipment

Messerschmitt Bf 110F-1: introduced two 1005-kW (1,350-hp) Daimler Benz DB 601F-1 engines; close-support aircraft with standard gunnery, some with ETC 500 and four ETC 50 racks, and 57-mm armour-glass windshield plus additional armour

Messerschmitt Bf 110F-2: heavy fighter with deletion of ETC racks

Messerschmitt Bf 110F-3: reconnaissance version

Messerschmitt Bf 110F-4: definitive night-fighter version, with improved UV instrument lighting and radio equipment; optional two 30-mm MK 108 cannon in place of MG-FF/Ms in ventral tray; some later with twin 30-mm *schräge Musik* oblique-firing cannon in aft cockpit area (Bf 110F-4/U1)

Messerschmitt Bf 110F-4a: radar-equipped night-fighter with Telefunken FuG 202 Lichtenstein BC; 20-mm MG FF/Ms replaced by twin 20-mm MG 151/20 guns

Messerschmitt Bf 110G-1: introduced two DB 605B-1 engines rated at 1100 kW (1,475 hp); heavy day fighter with four MG 17s and twin 20-mm MG 151/20 cannon

Messerschmitt Bf 110G-2: revised vertical tail, strengthened landing gear, and twin 7.92-mm (0.31-in) MG 81Z for rear gunner; fighter or close-support version with ETC 250 and ETC 50/VIII or 300-litre (66-Imp gal) drop tanks

Messerschmitt Bf 110G-2/R1: bomber destroyer with single 37-mm BK 3, 7 (Flak 18) cannon in belly tray, with deletion of MG 17; the Bf 110G-2/R2 was similar but with provision of GM-1 power-boosting

Messerschmitt Bf 110G-2/R3: heavy fighter version with twin 30-mm MK 108 cannon in place of the quadruple 7.92-mm (0.31-in) MG 17s, but retaining the MG 151s

Messerschmitt Bf 110G-3: reconnaissance fighter

Messerschmitt Bf 110G-4: definitive radar-equipped night-fighter, with return to four 7.92-mm (0.31-in) MG 17s and twin MG 151 cannon

Messerschmitt Bf 110G-4a: night-fighter with twin FuG 212 Lichtenstein C-1 radar; field modification (*Rustsätze*) Bf 110G-4a/R1 with one 37-mm BK 3,7 cannon, Bf 110G-4a/R2 with GM 1 boosting, and Bf 110G-4a/R3 with twin 30-mm MK 108s in place of MG 17s

Messerschmitt Bf 110G-4b: night-fighter with new FuG 220 Lichtenstein SN-2 radar, but with retention of earlier FuG 212 for close-in work

Messerschmitt Bf 110G-4c: night-fighter with improved FuG 220b Lichtenstein SN-2 radar to overcome short-range AI limitations; various *Rustsätze* for weaponry, fuel tanks and GM-1 equipment

Messerschmitt Bf 110H: manufactured in small numbers in parallel with the Bf 110G series, differing in use of engines, in this case DB 605Es, Bf 110H-2, Bf 110H-3 and Bf 110H-4 delivered

Messerschmitt Bf 110

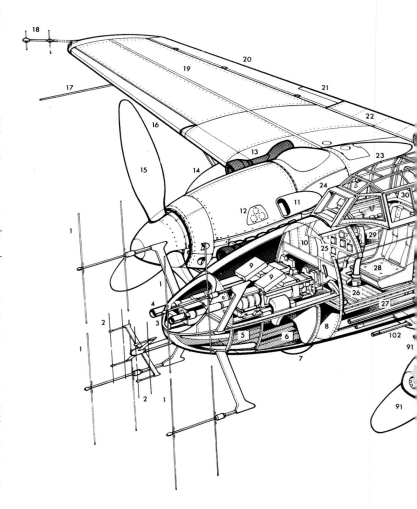

Bf 110G-2s of III/ZG 26 'Horst Wessel' escort a formation of Ju 52s low over the Mediterranean. By 1943, most Bf 110s were serving as night-fighters, and only elements of three **Zerstörergeschwader** remained Bf 110-equipped.

from Gütersloh, claimed a Whitley as the first official night kill of the new *Nachtjagdtruppe*. In the attempt to increase the chances of visual identification a number of aids were used, mostly without success: an infra-red sighting device (the AEG Spanner Anlage I) which detected the exhaust heat of enemy aircraft, registering on a Q-tube in the cockpit was soon fitted, despite its very limited range, and resulted in the **Bf 110D-1/U1**. The Spanner Anlage I, and the subsequent Spanner II, III and IV, were passive devices, and were rendered virtually ineffective when the RAF started fitting flame dampers to the exhausts of its night-bombers. For the most part, crews relied on radar-assisted searchlights to illuminate their prey over strictly demarked territorial zones. In addition, use of ground radar, the AN-Freya (FuMG 80), enabled interception to be made over the sea.

Night-fighting techniques with the Messerschmitt Bf 110C-2s were enhanced with the introduction of high-frequency Wurzburg FuMG 62 ground radars: one plotted the approaching enemy bomber following early warning from a longer-ranged Freya, while a second kept track of the German fighter. Using a map display, the controller gave R/T instructions to the fighter which, hopefully, closed to visual range. The system, known as *Himmelbett* (four-poster bed), was more cumbersome than the British GCI radar system, but nevertheless it worked. By 1942 the system of box-like *Himmelbett* GCI areas stretched from the northern tip of Denmark to the Swiss border, to give early warning and fighter control to counter the depredations of RAF Bomber Command.

Airborne radar was deemed essential, and during 1941 a *Staffel* of I/NJG 1 based at Venlo with **Bf 110E-1/U1**s experimented with the Telefunken FuG 202 (Lichtenstein BC) pre-production AI (Air Interception) radar, which worked on 490 MHz; maximum range was 3.5 km (2.2 miles) with a minimum of 200 m (655 ft). It was not until July 1942, following the series of massed raids on Bremen and Cologne, that AI radar, in the form of FuG 212 Lichtenstein, arrived in the front-line units. By now the standard night-fighter was the Messerschmitt **Bf 110F-4** (two Daimler Benz DB 601F-1 engines), which carried four 7.92-mm (0.31-in) MG 17 machine-guns and two Mauser MG 151/20 cannon; the radar-equipped Bf 110F-4a usually carried two 300-litre (66-Imp gal) drop tanks, flame-dampers, and night-glimmer HE ammunition. The increase in weight to 9275 kg (20,448 lb) and the additional drag of the *Maikäferfüler* radar antennas reduced speed to 510 km/h (317 mph) at 5600 m (18,375 ft). Despite the RAF's recently adopted tactics of streaming in order to swamp a particular *Himmelbett* area, pilots such as Lent, Falk, Strieb, Meurer, Schnaufer and Becker achieved many successes with the

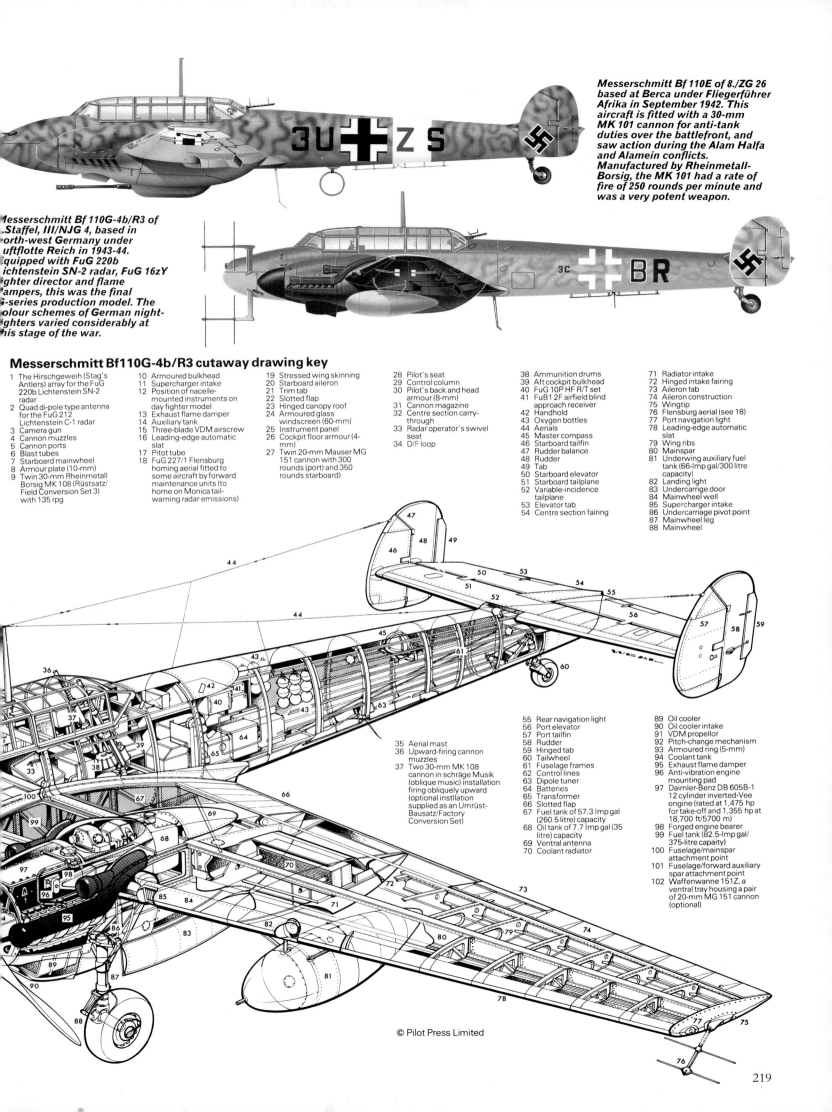

Messerschmitt Bf 110E of 8./ZG 26 based at Berca under Fliegerführer Afrika in September 1942. This aircraft is fitted with a 30-mm MK 101 cannon for anti-tank duties over the battlefront, and saw action during the Alam Halfa and Alamein conflicts. Manufactured by Rheinmetall-Borsig, the MK 101 had a rate of fire of 250 rounds per minute and was a very potent weapon.

Messerschmitt Bf 110G-4b/R3 of Staffel, III/NJG 4, based in north-west Germany under Luftflotte Reich in 1943-44. Equipped with FuG 220b Lichtenstein SN-2 radar, FuG 16zY fighter director and flame dampers, this was the final G-series production model. The colour schemes of German night-fighters varied considerably at this stage of the war.

Messerschmitt Bf110G-4b/R3 cutaway drawing key

1 The Hirschgeweih (Stag's Antlers) array for the FuG 220b Lichtenstein SN-2 radar
2 Quad di-pole type antenna for the FuG 212 Lichtenstein C-1 radar
3 Camera gun
4 Cannon muzzles
5 Cannon ports
6 Blast tubes
7 Starboard mainwheel
8 Armour plate (10-mm)
9 Twin 30-mm Rheinmetall Borsig MK 108 (Rüstsatz/Field Conversion Set 3) with 135 rpg
10 Armoured bulkhead
11 Supercharger intake
12 Position of nacelle-mounted instruments on day fighter model
13 Exhaust flame damper
14 Auxiliary tank
15 Three-blade VDM airscrew
16 Leading-edge automatic slat
17 Pitot tube
18 FuG 227/1 Flensburg homing aerial fitted to some aircraft by forward maintenance units (to home on Monica tail-warning radar emissions)
19 Stressed wing skinning
20 Starboard aileron
21 Trim tab
22 Slotted flap
23 Hinged canopy roof
24 Armoured glass windscreen (60-mm)
25 Instrument panel
26 Cockpit floor armour (4-mm)
27 Twin 20-mm Mauser MG 151 cannon with 300 rounds (port) and 350 rounds starboard)
28 Pilot's seat
29 Control column
30 Pilot's back and head armour (8-mm)
31 Cannon magazine
32 Centre section carry-through
33 Radar operator's swivel seat
34 D/F loop
35 Aerial mast
36 Upward-firing cannon muzzles
37 Two 30-mm MK 108 cannon in schräge Musik (oblique music) installation firing obliquely upward (optional instllation supplied as an Umrüst-Bausatz/Factory Conversion Set)
38 Ammunition drums
39 Aft cockpit bulkhead
40 FuG 10P HF R/T set
41 FuB1 2F airfield blind approach receiver
42 Handhold
43 Oxygen bottles
44 Aerials
45 Master compass
46 Starboard tailfin
47 Rudder balance
48 Rudder
49 Tab
50 Starboard elevator
51 Starboard tailplane
52 Variable-incidence tailplane
53 Elevator tab
54 Centre section fairing
55 Rear navigation light
56 Port elevator
57 Port tailfin
58 Rudder
59 Hinged tab
60 Tailwheel
61 Fuselage frames
62 Control lines
63 Dipole tuner
64 Batteries
65 Transformer
66 Slotted flap
67 Fuel tank of 57.3 Imp gal (260.5 litre) capacity
68 Oil tank of 7.7 Imp gal (35 litre) capacity
69 Ventral antenna
70 Coolant radiator
71 Radiator intake
72 Hinged intake fairing
73 Aileron tab
74 Aileron construction
75 Wingtip
76 Flensburg aerial (see 18)
77 Port navigation light
78 Leading-edge automatic slat
79 Wing ribs
80 Mainspar
81 Underwing auxiliary fuel tank (66-Imp gal/300 litre capacity)
82 Landing light
83 Undercarriage door
84 Mainwheel well
85 Supercharger intake
86 Undercarriage pivot point
87 Mainwheel leg
88 Mainwheel
89 Oil cooler
90 Oil cooler intake
91 VDM propellor
92 Pitch-change mechanism
93 Armoured ring (5-mm)
94 Coolant tank
95 Exhaust flame damper
96 Anti-vibration engine mounting pad
97 Daimler-Benz DB 605B-1 12 cylinder inverted-Vee engine (rated at 1,475 hp for take-off and 1,355 hp at 18,700 ft/5700 m)
98 Forged engine bearer
99 Fuel tank (82.5-Imp gal/375-litre capaity)
100 Fuselage/mainspar attachment point
101 Fuselage/forward auxiliary spar attachment point
102 Waffenwanne 151Z, a ventral tray housing a pair of 20-mm MG 151 cannon (optional)

© Pilot Press Limited

The first night-fighter unit was I/NJG 1, formed in July 1940 by renumbering I/ZG 1 although the 'G9' code was retained. Early equipment included Bf 110Cs. When I/ZG 76 was retrained and renumbered as II/NJG 1, in September, it began to operate Bf 110D-1/U1 aircraft with Spanner-Anlage infra-red sensors.

Left: The hunter hunted: a Lichtenstein SN-2-equipped Bf 110 is fatally trapped in front of an RAF fighter over Germany. Luftwaffe crews most feared the Mosquito, which could outmanoeuvre and outperform the German aircraft in night combat.

Above: By the summer of 1943, 7./ZG 26 was operating Bf 110G-2/R3s in the home defence role, often armed with underwing Wfr.Gr.21 mortars.

Messerschmitt Bf 110F-4 during 1942-43: the aircraft was sufficiently fast, had excellent visibility and retained its gentle flight characteristics. On achieving visual contact, the pilot usually throttled back and eased his aircraft some 76 m (250 ft) into a position directly below his quarry, before pulling up into a 50° pitch-up and opening fire into the bomber's belly and fuel tanks with 20-mm or 30-mm HE/I and armour-piercing/incendiary. The type's single biggest drawback was its limited range and endurance, which meant that it had to be airborne, in approximately the right area, to stand any reasonable chance of affecting an intercept.

With the failure of the Messerschmitt Me 210 series, and a shortage of Ju 88 airframes, the Luftwaffe was forced to retain the Bf 110 in front-line service primarily as a night-fighter, and in 1942 the Daimler Benz DB 605B-1 engine was installed to produce the **Bf 110G** series. The definitive Messerschmitt **Bf 110G-4**, equipped first with FuG 212 and, after the introduction of ECM chaff ('Window'), with Lichtenstein SN-2 (FuG 220) radar, bore the brunt of Luftflotte Reich's night-fighter commitment in late 1943. During 1943, upward-firing cannon were introduced to the night-fighting Bf 110s so that the night-fighter merely had to keep station below the target and open fire. Influenced by the success of his CO's special Do 217J (which had upward-firing cannon), an armourer from II/NJG 5, Oberfedwebel Mahle, mounted two redundant MG FFs in a Bf 110 in a home-made upward-firing mounting. A kill was achieved using the new guns within days, and an official version of the modification, with twin 30-mm MK 108 cannon, was installed in the aft cockpit to fire at an angle of 60-70° from the horizontal. The modification was known as *schräge Musik* (slanting music, or jazz) and proved highly effective, aircraft so equipped being designated **Bf 110G-4/U1**.

For a year after its introduction, the Bf 110G-4 was plagued by problems, mostly engine related, which led to many losses and disas-

Left: This Bf 110D-0 carries a semi-conformal 1200-litre (264-Imp gal) Dackelbauch (Dachshund belly) fabric-covered plywood auxiliary fuel tank under the belly.

Below: During the day, the night-fighter Messerschmitts hid from Allied bombers under elaborate camouflages involving nets and foliage. This aircraft has the Rustsatz-3 applied, which replaced four forward-firing MG 17 guns with two Mk 108 30-mm cannon.

This front view of a Lichtenstein C-1 Bf 110 shows Wfr.Gr.21 mortars under the wing racks. This weapon was an attempt to hit bombers with a far larger explosive charge than possible with cannon, ensuring the destruction of any target.

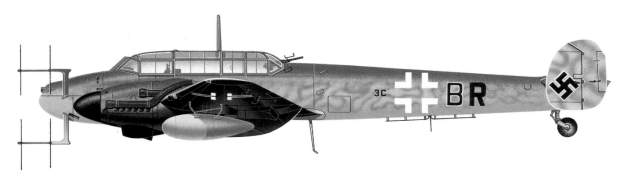

This Messerschmitt Bf 110G-4b/R3 flew with 7 Staffel of III/Nachtjagdgeschwader 4, which defended the skies of northern Germany during 1944. The mottled grey camouflage on the upper surfaces was common, with either black or grey undersides.

The tail of this Bf 110G-4b/R3 shows RAF bomber kills. Flown by Wilhelm Johnen, one of the top-scoring night aces, it was landed by accident in Switzerland, where it was interned. His unit at the time was Nachtjagdgeschwader 5.

Improvements to the Bf 110 continued apace, with the introduction of the FuG 227 Flensburg which homed on RAF bomber's tail warning radar emissions, and, on a handful of aircraft, even the highly effective FuG 218 Neptun radar. No one was more successful as an exponent of the Messerschmitt Bf 110G-4 than Major Heinz-Wolfgang Schnaufer, the last *Kommodore* of NJG 4 and a recipient of the Diamonds to the Knight's Cross, who claimed no less than 121 nocturnal kills in the war. The numbers of aircraft declined steadily, not least because many were used (and lost) in suicidal day operations against the heavily escorted American bomber formations, while the night sky became increasingly dangerous as marauding Mosquito and Beaufighter night-fighters roamed over Germany.

One of the best

There was no doubt that despite its detractors, and the fact that only 6,170 were produced, the Messerschmitt Bf 110 should go down in the annals of World War II as a highly efficient, effective and versatile, all-purpose, twin-engined combat aircraft, for few twins could stand the test against well-flown single-engined fighters by day; not the Bristol Beaufighter, the Kawasaki Ki-45 Toryu, nor even the excellent Lockheed P-38 Lightning or the the de Havilland Mosquito.

Late Bf 110G-4c aircraft had the antennas of the Lichtenstein SN-2 canted to improve detection capability. This close-up shows the cannon ports for the MG 151 and MK 108 weapons, of 20-mm calibre (lower nose) and 30-mm calibre (upper nose), respectively.

trous inflight fires. Increased equipment weight and high-drag radar antennas had also necessitated the incorporation of GM-1 nitrous oxide injection, giving a boost in maximum power on the **Bf 110G-4/U-7**. By June 1944, the Bf 110G-4 equipped the majority of *Gruppen* (14 of 22) within Nachtjagdgeschwader 1, 3, 4, 5 and 6, stationed from Aalborg in Denmark to Reims in France, and from Schleissheim to the Romanian border. They thus formed the backbone of the Luftwaffe's night-fighter arm. The longer-ranging, higher-endurance Junkers Ju 88C-6b and Ju 88G-1 night-fighters, with their spacious cockpits, autopilots, provision for fourth crew members and heavier armament, became preponderant in the course of the last year of the war, and the Messerschmitt became less numerous, although many *Experten* (aces) preferred this type to the heavy Junkers.

Messerschmitt Me 163

In three-quarters of a century of air warfare there have been only very few occasions when a nation has gone into battle with an aircraft so advanced in concept that its enemies did not at first know how to tackle it. The **Me 163** was very small, agile and nearly twice as fast as most of its opponents. With relief, the Allies found that it tended to appear only in very small numbers, it clearly had a brief flight endurance, and its effectiveness was not impressive. Two were actually shot down before the type had scored a single combat success.

The story started in 1926 when Dr Alexander Lippisch built his first tailless glider. Over the next decade Lippisch built many tailless aircraft and also became involved with rocket propulsion, so it was no great surprise when, in 1937, he was asked by the research section of the RLM (German air ministry) to design an aircraft to test a new rocket motor intended for manned aeroplanes, the Walter I-203, rated at 3.92 kN (882 lb) thrust. This operated on a mixture of two liquids which reacted violently if allowed to meet: *T-stoff*, consisting mainly of concentrated hydrogen peroxide, and *Z-stoff*, a solution of calcium permanganate in water. With such reactive propellants it was decided to design the fuselage in metal and, as the DFS (the German glider research institute) where Lippisch worked was not equipped for the task, the fuselage construction was sub-contracted to Heinkel.

In the event, Heinkel never built the metal fuselage, but did build the rocket-propelled He 176, whose abysmal showing in June 1939 almost caused loss of interest in any rocket aircraft. It was a very frustrated Lippisch who, early in 1939, left the DFS and teamed up with Messerschmitt. At Augsburg, Willy Messerschmitt showed frosty disinterest, but Lippisch was allowed to carry on with his own team, in strict security, and in late 1939 decided that his preliminary research aircraft, the all-wood **DFS 194**, could in fact be flown by the rocket and not by the intended small piston engine. The machine was taken in early 1940 to Karlshagen, the test airfield at Peenemunde, where the I-203 rocket was installed. On 3 June 1940 famed glider pilot Heini Dittmar made a successful first flight, reporting superb handling. Later this flimsy machine, designed for 300 km/h (186 mph), reached 547 km/h (340 mph) in level flight, and also demonstrated fantastic steep climbs.

Suddenly, it was all systems go. The Walter company had by this time developed the II-203b motor rated at 7.36 kN (1,653 lb) to assist heavy aircraft to take off, and was working on a still more powerful unit. Lippisch was instructed to design a fast-climbing interceptor to use the latter motor, the short flight endurance being no problem to a target-defence aircraft which could stay on the ground until enemy bombers were almost overhead. The designation **Me 163B** was allocated, the **Me 163A** being a series of six prototypes to be powered by the II-203b modified as a permanently installed main engine.

Carefree flight

The first Me 163, with factory letters KE+SW, was completed except for its motor at Lechfeld in March 1941, and was at once put through a programme of trials as a glider, towed off by a Messerschmitt Bf 110. Dittmar again was enraptured at the handling, but the aircraft was such a good glider it consistently refused to land, and invariably almost went off the far side of the field. On one occasion Dittmar had to sideslip between two hangars and even then floated between all the airfield buildings while trying to land. The maiden

An interesting study shows one of the Me 163A-0 prototypes in company with an early production Me 163B. The larger size of the fuselage and the nose-mounted generator turbine of the Me 163B are noteworthy.

flight under power took place at Karlshagen on 13 August 1941 and, although he did not intend to reach high speed, Dittmar was informed that the level speed as measured by ground instruments was over 800 km/h (497 mph). Soon speeds were exceeding 885 km/h (550 mph). On 2 October 1941, Dittmar was towed to over 4000 m (13,125 ft) by a Bf 110; he then cast off and started the motor. He accelerated, but suddenly lost control as the nose dropped violently. It was possibly the first occasion on which a human had approached the speed of sound, compressibility trouble being experienced at about Mach 0.84. The speed of 1004 km/h (624 mph) was 250 km/h (155 mph) above the official world speed record.

The problem getting airborne

Subsequent research led to a modified wing with large fixed slots over the outer leading edge, which rendered the aircraft spin-proof, although the stall remained severe. Basically, the Me 163A could hardly have been simpler, but one feature was to endure into the production Me 163B and cause endless problems and catastrophic accidents. The Lippisch glider background made it seem normal to take off from a wheeled dolly, jettisoned once airborne, and to land on a sprung skid. In fact, the piloting difficulties were immense. If the aircraft was not dead into wind it would slew around and possibly overturn, the rudder being useless at low speeds. Any bump in the surface caused premature take-off or a bounce on landing; this combined with the totally unsprung dolly to cause spinal damage to any pilot and, by shaking up the propellants, the occasional devastating explosion.

So tricky were the liquids that for the big R II-211 motor, which was made fully controllable, the *Z-stoff* was replaced by *C-stoff* (hydrazine hydrate solution in methyl alcohol). Although testing of the motors was twice punctuated by explosions which destroyed the entire building, work went ahead on the six Me 163A prototypes, 10

Captured by Allied forces during the latter stages of World War II, this Messerschmitt Me 163B-1a was preserved at RAF St Athan. Note the large dolly undercarriage unit, which was attached to the rear of the skid.

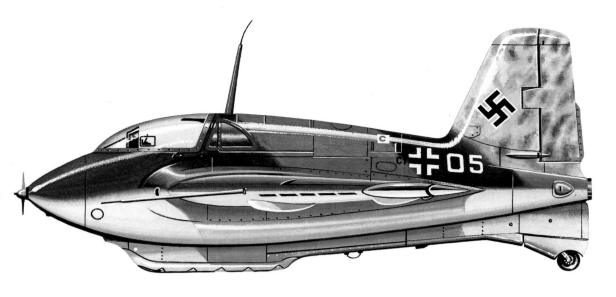

This Me 163B-1a was one of the first to become operational with the Luftwaffe in the summer of 1944. It was assigned to Erprobungskommando 16, at Bad Zwischenahn, where scorch marks on the hardstandings gave RAF photo interpreters their first clue of the existence of the Komet. The small propeller drove the generator.

Me 163A-0 pre-production aircraft and 70 pre-production versions of the Me 163B interceptor, which was given the name **Komet**. During 1941, procurement chief Ernst Udet had become an enthusiastic supporter of the project. His suicide in November 1941 did not help matters, because the little rocket interceptor was irrelevant to the gigantic struggle on the Eastern Front, and attacks on Germany were as yet ineffectual and only carried out by night. So priority remained low, and Walter continued to have severe and dangerous motor problems.

Gradually more people joined the programme, although Lippisch himself took up another appointment in Vienna. A Luftwaffe officer, Rudolf Opitz, came to share the flying, and it is as well that he did because Dittmar stalled onto the poorly sprung skid and spent two years in hospital having his spine reassembled. On his first Me 163A flight Opitz almost met disaster, because he was far above dolly release height before he realised he was airborne. He kept the valuable dolly attached and landed back on it; by a miracle he did not swing and overturn (which usually meant a violent explosion). Opitz made the first Me 163B flight from Lechfeld on 26 June 1942, without propellants and towed by a Bf 110. It was to be almost a year later before, on 23 June 1943, powered flights began. Again Opitz had trouble, the dolly wrenching free during the tricky acceleration and the final part of the run being on the unsprung skid. A few seconds later the cockpit filled with choking, blinding peroxide fumes from a pipe fractured by the bumping. Opitz was on the point of baling out when the peroxide was at last all consumed by the motor.

First unit

In early 1943 a special Me 163B test squadron was formed at Karlshagen under Hauptmann Wolfgang Späte, but while this was still in its early stages Peenemunde was raided by the RAF and the unit, Erprobungskommando 16, was moved to Bad Zwischenahn. This was the centre for most Komet flying for the next year, and the aircraft became known to the Allies from high-flying reconnaissance photographs taken here in December 1943. By this time the programme had been further delayed by a raid of the very kind the Komet had been invented to prevent. The Messerschmitt factory at Regensburg was heavily hit by Boeing B-17s on 17 August 1943, many of the pre-production

batch being destroyed. The main production, however, was to be dispersed throughout Germany under the control of Klemm Technik, with final assembly at a secret Schwarzwald (Black Forest) centre and then guarded rail shipment to the flight-test base at Lechfeld.

This giant production plan suffered many further problems, and the flow did not begin to arrive at Lechfeld until February 1944. The production interceptor was designated **Me 163B-1a**, and although in many ways seemingly crude it was actually a very refined aircraft as a result of the prolonged experience with earlier variants. Nothing had been done, however, to cure the terrible danger of explosion, which was made all the more likely by the tricky and problem-ridden take-off dolly and landing skid.

Flying surfaces

The wing was smaller and simpler than those of the precursor aircraft, and although it appeared swept it was mainly its taper that gave a quarter-chord sweep angle of 23.3°. The wooden structure was simple, with two widely spaced spars and skin of fabric-covered ply usually 8 mm (0.31 in) thick. Outboard on the trailing edge were the only control surfaces, other than the rudder: large manual fabric-covered elevons used for both pitch and roll. The trim tabs were plain metal bent on the ground with pliers to give the required behaviour. Inboard were large, plain, hinged flaps which were lowered hydraulically by screw-jacks before landing, in unison with main landing flaps ahead of them on the underside of the wing. The landing flaps caused strong nose-up trim, and the trailing-edge flaps cancelled this out with equal nose-down trim. The small fuselage was light alloy, covered mainly with detachable panels to gain access to the densely packed interior. The largest item was the *T-stoff* tank of 1040-litre (229-Imp gal) capacity, which filled the space between the cockpit and the motor. Smaller *T-stoff* tanks filled each side of the cockpit. The *C-stoff* was housed in two 173-litre (38-Imp gal) tanks between the wing spars and two 73-litre (16-Imp gal) tanks in the leading edges.

The motor, which in production was called the HWK Type 509A-1, had a single chamber fed via two long straight pipes from the turbopump group located roughly in line with the trailing edge of the wing. Before each flight the entire system had to be drained and flushed

Probably seen at Lechfeld in the spring of 1941, the Me 163A V1 formed the link between the low-speed DFS 194 and the Me 163B Komet. Seen here on its take-off trolley, with flaps down, the V1 bore factory letter code KE+SW. Trials with the rocket engine began in July, this machine being the first to exceed 800 km/h (500 mph).

The Wolf Hirth Segelflugzeugbau (glider works) built a run of 10 Me 163A-0 pilot trainers, fitted with the dangerously temperamental R II-203b motor and a large sprung take-off dolly. This particular A-0 was fitted with wooden underwing racks each carrying 12 of the R4M air-to-air spin-stabilised rockets (a local addition).

An Me 163B (actually the Bertha prototype) makes a 'sharp start' at Bad Zwischenahn, home of the trials unit Erprobungskommando 16, which accepted its first Me 163B during May 1944. The jettisonable take-off trolley is clearly visible.

through with scrupulous care, using vast amounts of water. The motor was started with *T-stoff* fed from a separate starter tank in the top of the rear fuselage, while an electric motor cranked up the turbopumps. The tanks were pressurised, and once the feed reached the turbopumps the liquids were supplied under high pressure at the rate of 8 kg (17.64 lb) per second, combusting spontaneously on contact in the chamber. Sea-level thrust was about 14.71 kN (3,307 lb), rising with reducing atmospheric pressure to 16.61 kN (3,748 lb) at high altitude. The Type 509A could be throttled back to 0.98 kN (220 lb) idling rating, but it was inefficient at this level and could often stop entirely. The entire rear fuselage and motor could readily be detached. Although crude compared with later units, the Type 509A was a remarkable achievement and, although over 2.13 m (7 ft) long, weighed little over 100 kg (220 lb).

The cockpit was comfortable, although there was no system available for pressurisation other than a plain ram inlet at the front. The canopy was a flimsy Plexiglas moulding, hinged on the right side and with little ability to resist hail or birds at the speeds the Komet could attain. There was a hinged ventilation window on the left side of the hood, and another air inlet on the underside of the nose. Nose and back armour was provided, but the seat was not of the new ejection type and it was impossible to get out at high airspeeds. The nose was full of radio and other items, including the generator driven by the small windmill propeller, with access by hinging back the instrument panel. Armament comprised two cannon (one in the root of each wing between the spars). Most early armed Komets had the high-velocity 20-mm MG 151/20, but the standard production armament was the 30-mm MK 108, fed with 60 rounds housed above the main *T-stoff* tank. Compressed-air bottles cocked the guns, and gas pressure served most of the onboard auxiliary power services, including energising the flap hydraulics. The troublesome landing skid was hydraulically retracted on take-off, along with the neat steerable tailwheel. Retracting the skid automatically released the wheeled dolly, but this had a habit of bouncing up and smashing into the aircraft or even hooking on the front of the skid. If it failed to separate, a successful landing back on the dolly was not advised; it was only accomplished once. Even Hanna Reitsch tried it once, following total hang-up, and she was severely injured.

Special procedures

By learning in the most painful way, the Luftwaffe refined its Me 163B operating procedures and sloshed water everywhere during refuelling or ground running. Pilots and ground personnel wore special suits of non-organic asbestos and Mipolamfibre, although in a number of landings that ended inverted, the aircraft, even when not exploding, managed to inflict agonising corrosive injuries when the cockpit tanks spilt substantial amounts on to the pilot before he could be got out. No combat aircraft has ever demanded so much of its operators, and in particular the landing demanded a dead-stick approach at 210 km/h (130 mph) exactly into wind and on to an exact spot, with no opportunity for a second attempt, and always remembering to extend the skid and then return the lever to neutral to remove the hydraulic pressure and restore oleo springing.

Thus, early selected pilots were above average, and after initial experience flying a clipped-wing version of the Habicht glider they progressed to towed glides in the Me 163A, then glides in water-ballasted Me 163As, then powered flights in the Me 163A, and finally to the rather dreaded Me 163B. Production Komets were accepted by the Luftwaffe from May 1944. It had been Späte's plan to build up Komet forces at a dense ring of bases each about 100 km (62 miles) apart, so that each Komet could also glide home, but covering all approach routes for bombers from British bases. This never proved possible. Although a few combat missions were flown, often by development Komets, from Karlshagen, Zwischenahn, Wittmundhafen and Udetfeld, the first proper base selected was Brandis, near Leipzig, chosen to try to protect the largest concentration of oil refineries in Germany.

First enemy engagements

The unit was I/JG 400, under Oberleutnant Robert Olejnik and formed from Erprobungskommando 16 at Zwischenahn in May 1944 and finally equipped with aircraft in late July, at Brandis. Before this there had been many attempts by Komet pilots to engage the enemy, but these had always been frustrated, on one occasion by the cut-out of the motor by negative *g* just as the pilot was about to blast two unsuspecting Republic P-47s. The first major engagement was on 28 July 1944 when six Komets got airborne to try to interfere with 596 B-17s heading for the Leuna-Merseburg oil complex. No hits were scored, mainly because of high closing speeds, and the landings were hair-raising with many near-collisions.

The first major engagement came on 16 August 1944, when five Komets took on 1,096 USAAF heavies which had not yet been

1 Generator drive propeller
2 Generator
3 Compressed air bottle
4 Battery and electronics packs
5 Cockpit ventilation intake
6 Solid armour (15-mm) nose cone
7 Accumulator pressuriser
8 Direct cockpit air intake
9 FuG 25a radio pack
10 Rudder control assembly
11 Hydraulic and compressed air points
12 Elevon control rocker-bar
13 Control relay
14 Flying controls assembly box

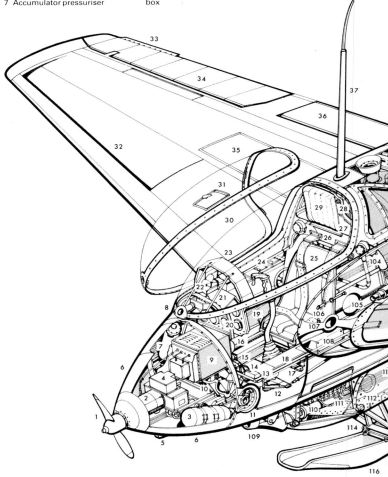

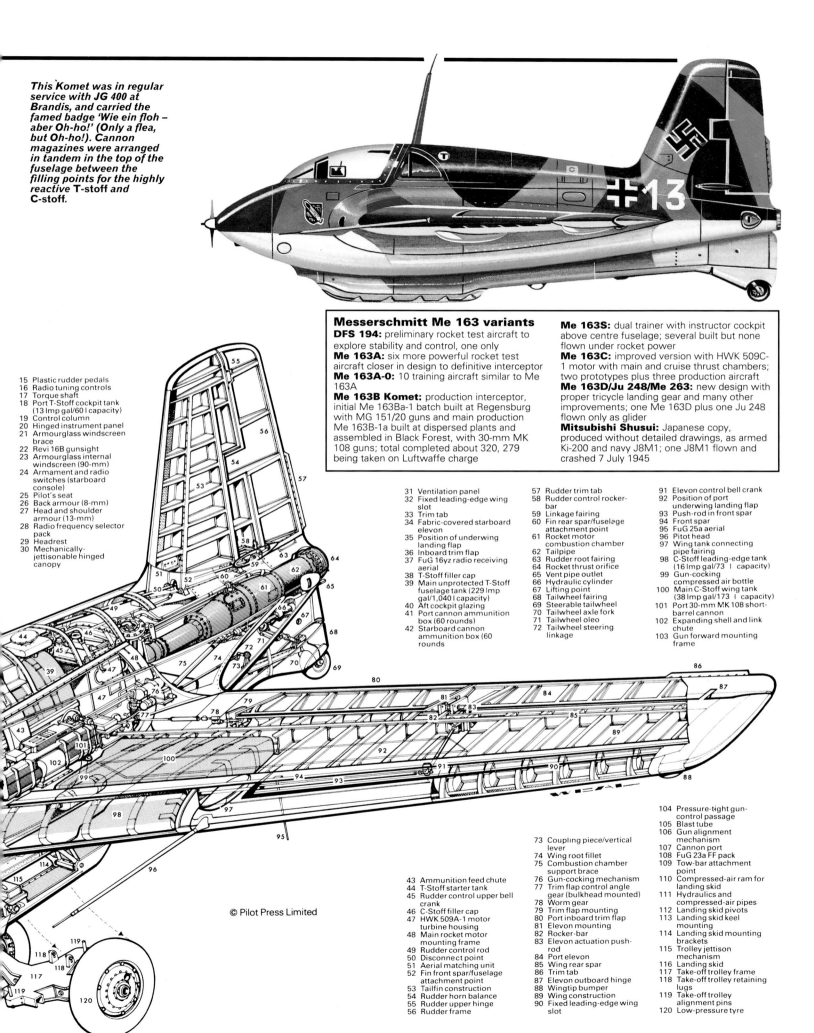

This Komet was in regular service with JG 400 at Brandis, and carried the famed badge 'Wie ein floh – aber Oh-ho!' (Only a flea, but Oh-ho!). Cannon magazines were arranged in tandem in the top of the fuselage between the filling points for the highly reactive T-stoff and C-stoff.

Messerschmitt Me 163 variants

DFS 194: preliminary rocket test aircraft to explore stability and control, one only
Me 163A: six more powerful rocket test aircraft closer in design to definitive interceptor
Me 163A-0: 10 training aircraft similar to Me 163A
Me 163B Komet: production interceptor, initial Me 163Ba-1 batch built at Regensburg with MG 151/20 guns and main production Me 163B-1a built at dispersed plants and assembled in Black Forest, with 30-mm MK 108 guns; total completed about 320, 279 being taken on Luftwaffe charge

Me 163S: dual trainer with instructor cockpit above centre fuselage; several built but none flown under rocket power
Me 163C: improved version with HWK 509C-1 motor with main and cruise thrust chambers; two prototypes plus three production aircraft
Me 163D/Ju 248/Me 263: new design with proper tricycle landing gear and many other improvements; one Me 163D plus one Ju 248 flown only as glider
Mitsubishi Shusui: Japanese copy, produced without detailed drawings, as armed Ki-200 and navy J8M1; one J8M1 flown and crashed 7 July 1945

15 Plastic rudder pedals
16 Radio tuning controls
17 Torque shaft
18 Port T-Stoff cockpit tank (13 Imp gal/60 l capacity)
19 Control column
20 Hinged instrument panel
21 Armourglass windscreen brace
22 Revi 16B gunsight
23 Armourglass internal windscreen (90-mm)
24 Armament and radio switches (starboard console)
25 Pilot's seat
26 Back armour (8-mm)
27 Head and shoulder armour (13-mm)
28 Radio frequency selector pack
29 Headrest
30 Mechanically-jettisonable hinged canopy

31 Ventilation panel
32 Fixed leading-edge wing slot
33 Trim tab
34 Fabric-covered starboard elevon
35 Position of underwing landing flap
36 Inboard trim flap
37 FuG 16yz radio receiving aerial
38 T-Stoff filler cap
39 Main unprotected T-Stoff fuselage tank (229 Imp gal/1,040 l capacity)
40 Aft cockpit glazing
41 Port cannon ammunition box (60 rounds)
42 Starboard cannon ammunition box (60 rounds

57 Rudder trim tab
58 Rudder control rocker-bar
59 Linkage fairing
60 Fin rear spar/fuselage attachment point
61 Rocket motor combustion chamber
62 Tailpipe
63 Rudder root fairing
64 Rocket thrust orifice
65 Vent pipe outlet
66 Hydraulic cylinder
67 Lifting point
68 Tailwheel fairing
69 Steerable tailwheel
70 Tailwheel axle fork
71 Tailwheel oleo
72 Tailwheel steering linkage

91 Elevon control bell crank
92 Position of port underwing landing flap
93 Push-rod in front spar
94 Front spar
95 FuG 25a aerial
96 Pitot head
97 Wing tank connecting pipe fairing
98 C-Stoff leading-edge tank (16 Imp gal/73 l capacity)
99 Gun-cocking compressed air bottle
100 Main C-Stoff wing tank (38 Imp gal/173 l capacity)
101 Port 30-mm MK 108 short-barrel cannon
102 Expanding shell and link chute
103 Gun forward mounting frame

© Pilot Press Limited

43 Ammunition feed chute
44 T-Stoff starter tank
45 Rudder control upper bell crank
46 C-Stoff filler cap
47 HWK 509A-1 motor turbine housing
48 Main rocket motor mounting frame
49 Rudder control rod
50 Disconnect point
51 Aerial matching unit
52 Fin front spar/fuselage attachment point
53 Tailfin construction
54 Rudder horn balance
55 Rudder upper hinge
56 Rudder frame

73 Coupling piece/vertical lever
74 Wing root fillet
75 Combustion chamber support brace
76 Gun-cocking mechanism
77 Trim flap control angle gear (bulkhead mounted)
78 Worm gear
79 Trim flap mounting
80 Port inboard trim flap
81 Elevon mounting
82 Rocker-bar
83 Elevon actuation push-rod
84 Port elevon
85 Wing rear spar
86 Trim tab
87 Elevon outboard hinge
88 Wingtip bumper
89 Wing construction
90 Fixed leading-edge wing slot

104 Pressure-tight gun-control passage
105 Blast tube
106 Gun alignment mechanism
107 Cannon port
108 FuG 23a FF pack
109 Tow-bar attachment point
110 Compressed-air ram for landing skid
111 Hydraulics and compressed-air pipes
112 Landing skid pivots
113 Landing skid keel mounting
114 Landing skid mounting brackets
115 Trolley jettison mechanism
116 Landing skid
117 Take-off trolley frame
118 Take-off trolley retaining lugs
119 Take-off trolley alignment pins
120 Low-pressure tyre

Specification
Messerschmitt Me 163B-1a
Type: rocket-powered target-defence interceptor
Powerplant: one Walter HWK 509A-1 or A-2 rocket motor pump-fed with hypergolic (spontaneously reacting) *T-stoff* and *C-stoff*, with high-altitude thrust of 16.67 kN (3,748 lb)
Performance: maximum speed about 830 km/h (510-520 mph) at low levels, rising to 960 km/h (597 mph) above 3000 m (9,845 ft); initial climb 4900 m (16,080 ft) per minute; service ceiling 12000 m (39,370 ft); maximum rocket endurance (allowing for periods at reduced thrust) 7 minutes 30 seconds; practical range about 130 km (80 miles) not allowing for combat
Weights: empty 1900 kg (4,190 lb); maximum take-off 4310 kg (9,502 lb)
Dimensions: span 9.40 m (30 ft 7 in); length 5.85 m (19 ft 2 in); height (on take-off dolly) 2.76 m (9 ft 0 in); wing area 18.50 m² (199.1 sq ft)
Armament: two 30-mm Rheinmetall MK 108 cannon each with 60 rounds

Powerplant
The Me 163B was powered by a single Hellmuth Walter Werke R II-211 rocket motor, with fuel for six minutes at full throttle. Derived from Von Braun's 2.89-kN (650-lb st) A 1 rocket engine of 1935, the engine was closely based on Walter's TP-1 and TP-2 'Cold' rockets using hydrogen peroxide (*T-stoff*) with an aqueous solution of sodium or calcium permanganate (*Z-stoff*) as a catalyst. Essentially the engine consisted of a steam generator into which the two fuels were sprayed using compressed air. This drove a turbine, which powered the pump that delivered *T-stoff* to the combustion chamber. The TP-2 was redesignated as the HWK (Hellmuth Walter Kiel) R I-203, and was developed progressively into the R II-203 which powered early Me 163 prototypes. Substitution of 30 per cent hydrazine hydrate, 57 per cent methyl alcohol, 13 per cent water and 17 per cent cupracyanide (*C-stoff*) for the *Z-stoff* resulted in a hot rocket engine with more thrust and greater reliability, which did not generate a white vapour trail. This was the R II-211, redesignated HWK 509A in production form.

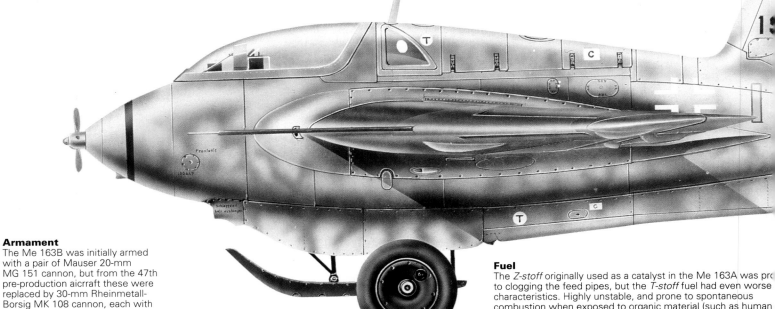

Armament
The Me 163B was initially armed with a pair of Mauser 20-mm MG 151 cannon, but from the 47th pre-production aicraft these were replaced by 30-mm Rheinmetall-Borsig MK 108 cannon, each with 60 rounds of ammunition.

Fuel
The *Z-stoff* originally used as a catalyst in the Me 163A was pro[ne] to clogging the feed pipes, but the *T-stoff* fuel had even worse characteristics. Highly unstable, and prone to spontaneous combustion when exposed to organic material (such as human flesh), *T-stoff* was also highly corrosive. The Me 163 pilot was surrounded by *T-stoff* tanks in flight, and had to wear a non-organic flying suit made of asbestos-Mipolamfibre. The *C-stoff* catalyst used in the Me 163 was also highly reactive, and had t[o] be stored in glass or enamelled containers.

Messerschmitt Me 163B-1a
3.Staffel, I/JG 400
Brandis

Between them, Willy Messerschmitt and Alexander Lippisch designed and built the fastest aircraft of World War II, the Me 163. It was an aircraft of last resort which was resurrected only when the streams of Allied bombers over Germany heralded the end of the war. Its performance was, quite literally, explosive, as its revolutionary engine made it dangerous and unpredictable. When it worked, it was a sight that few could have imagined as it streaked upwards into the sky at astonishing speed. However, it came too late to save the Reich. With elaborate plans for the Messerschmitt Me 163B to operate from two rings of bases covering west, north-west and northern Germany, the type could have proved one of the most important operational aircraft of World War II. In reality, this ambitious but unpredictable aircraft met with very limited success in the latter part of 1944 and early 1945. Evident in this illustration is the short oval-section fuselage and excellent view afforded to the pilot through the Plexiglas moulded canopy.

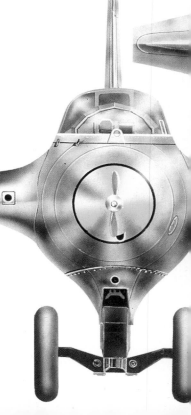

Take-off procedure
The Me 163 was usually started with the help of an external APU. The pilot placed the five-position throttle in the idle position, exposing the start button, which was then depressed. This activated the *T-stoff* steam turbine, which pumped *T-stoff* to the rocket motor. The starter button was released four to five seconds after the turbine started (at 40-50 per cent rpm). The throttle was then moved to the 1st Stage position, and then to the 2nd Stage position, instruments being carefully scrutinised at each stage. The 3rd Stage position caused the Komet to jump its tiny chocks and begin its take-off run. The dolly was jettisoned at a height of between 6 and 9 m (20 and 30 ft), and a steep climb was initiated when the speed reached 643 km/h (400 mph). The climb to 12192 m (40,000 ft) was undertaken at an airspeed of 800 km/h (498 mph), and took just under four minutes. At 12192 m, full throttle allowed acceleration from 402 to 965 km/h (250 to 600 mph) within seconds. Tactics were to climb to altitude, then make unpowered diving attacks slashing down through the enemy bomber formations, relighting the rocket engine to climb and position for another attack or to evade enemy fighters. Two minutes had to elapse between shutting down and relighting the engine.

Wing

Trials with the Me 163 V1 and V4 during October 1941 saw the aircraft reaching speeds of up to 885 km/h (550 mph), with maximum speed limited by fuel capacity. To get around this, Heini Dittmar had the Me 163 V4 fully tanked and then towed into the air behind a Bf 110C tug. Lighting the rocket, Dittmar accelerated to 1003.96 km/h (623.85 mph) (equivalent to Mach 0.84) when compressibility effects forced the aircraft into a steep dive, from which Dittmar recovered by cutting the engine. The sudden change in pitch stability was due to the fact that the Me 163 V4 had essentially retained the wing of the DFS 194, with considerable washout which caused wingtip compressibility stalls. On the Me 163B the wing was considerably redesigned, with reduced sweep on the trailing edge, constant sweep on the leading edge and with low drag fixed slots on the outer 40 per cent of the wing leading edge. These removed the danger of tip stalling, and also made the Me 163 unspinnable. Even with fully crossed controls, the aircraft would only sideslip.

Pitot probe

The Me 163's pitot static probe projected far out from the leading edge of the port wing, gathering data from the undisturbed air ahead of the aircraft. This location proved so successful that it was retained on the Me 163A, the Me 163B and the two-seat Me 163S.

Handling

Hauptmann Wolfgang Späte, reassigned from the Russian Front as Me 163 project officer, was one of the first Luftwaffe pilots to fly the Me 163. "I found this creation of Lippisch to be an aircraft with flight characteristics so beautifully balanced that I have seldom flown one like it, before or since." At speed, this was true enough, but the rudder and elevons required plenty of airspeed before they became effective, and there was a limited amount of directional control even at flying speed. Furthermore, the aircraft had a tendency to porpoise on take-off, which was a major problem since a heavy impact with the ground could cause a catastrophic explosion.

Airframe development

The Me 163 was derived from the Delta configuration developed by Alexander Lippisch in a series of pre-war light aircraft. After Walter's rockets had been flight tested in a number of Heinkel He 112 airframes, Heinkel designed and built the He 176 as the first rocket aircraft, but this proved disappointing, and in 1936 officials at the RLM visited Lippisch where they became convinced that the combination of tailless Delta and rocket engine might prove a winner. Building on experience gained with a number of tailless Delta designs, notably the DFS 40 Delta V pusher-engined flying wing, Lippisch began work on converting the DFS 194 to become a testbed for the R I-203 rocket engine. Joining the Messerschmitt AG at Augsburg, Lippisch formed Abteilung L, transforming his design into the Me 163.

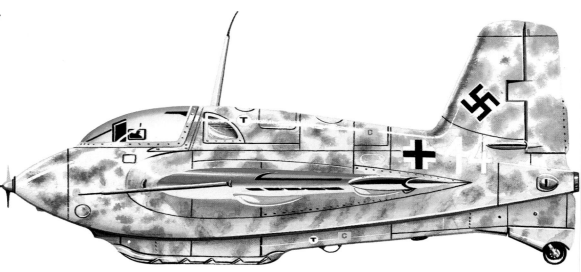

This colour scheme was used by the JG 400 Ergänzungsstaffel (training squadron) and also by operational elements of JG 400, to one of which the Me 163B-1a was assigned. This machine, operating from Brandis in early 1945, was unusual in having the white/yellow markings for C-stoff (hydrazine) and T-stoff (peroxide) added to the ventral drains.

Above and right: An Me 163 takes off, jettisoning its take-off dolly. If jettisoned too early these could bounce back into the departing Komet, and they sometimes refused to release at all but, by comparison with the hazards of landing the Me 163, take-offs were a picnic.

instructed to avoid Brandis. The first to reach a B-17 was hit by the bomber's tail gunner. Another Komet scored hits on a B-17 of the 305th BG, but was then destroyed by Lieutenant Colonel John Murphy's North American P-51. But, on 24 August, Feldwebel Siegfried Schubert destroyed two B-17s, and other Komets bagged two others. Such success was not to be repeated, and among the casualties was Schubert, who blew up on take-off because of the troublesome dolly. Never did the growing armada of Komets strike a telling blow, largely because of the difficulty of aiming accurately in the very brief firing time available. To overcome this the SG 500 (*Sondergeräte*, or special equipment) or *Jagdfaust* was devised, with 10 vertical barrels along the wingroots firing 50-mm projectiles upwards, triggered automatically by photocells sensing the reduced light input as the rocket interceptor flashed past beneath its target. SG 500 did well in tests, but was used just once, on 10 April 1945, before the final German collapse.

Messerschmitt AG built no fewer than 70 pre-production Me 163Bs at Regensburg, all assigned to particular operational or mechanical problems. Probably the most dangerous phase of each flight was the landing, which had to be perfect every time. Here the 35th Me 163B (V35), coded GH+IN, glides safely to a stop.

There were many ideas for improved Komets, including a far better version, the **Me 163D/Ju 248/Me 263**, which had a proper landing gear and a motor with main and cruise thrust chambers. Even the Soviet Union soon gave up development of this (as the **MiG Zh** or **I-270**) and the fairest overall assessment of the Me 163 is that 80 per cent of Komet losses occurred during take-off or landing, 15 per cent were due to loss of control in a compressibility dive or fire in the air, and the remaining five per cent were losses in combat. In 1945, with some 300 in front-line service, only I/JG 400 was able to engage the enemy; it claimed nine bombers but lost 14 aircraft in doing so.

Two of the Me 163B prototypes, V6 and V18, were later modified with prototypes of the HWK 509C-1 motor equipped with main and cruising thrust chambers, to give much better flight endurance. Here the V6 blows steam through its propellant lines in the summer of 1944. Note the repositioned retractable tailwheel.

Messerschmitt Me 261

In pre-war Nazi Germany, national pride was a matter of great importance. In all fields, Germans strived to gain world records, and the aviation industry was no different. Whereas most record-breaking attempts used modified versions of existing types, the **Me 261** was planned from the outset for distance records. In fact, the main goal was a vehicle to carry the Olympic torch non-stop from Berlin to Tokyo.

In 1937 Messerschmitt designed a large twin-engined aircraft with a huge wing, notable for having a very deep root, under the company project number **P 1064**. Although of conventional construction, the wing was sealed to form an integral tank, which at that time was a novel feature. The narrow fuselage housed two pilots seated side-by-side and a radio operator behind them in the forward compartment, with the flight engineer and naviagtor in a rear compartment, housed under a stepped glazed section. Access through the wing carry-through structure allowed passage between the two crew areas, and the rear compartment had rest bunks. Power for the aircraft was provided by two DB 606A-1/B-1 engines, with large radiator intakes mounted under the wing outboard of each nacelle. The DB 606 was actually a coupled engine, two DB 601s mounted side-by-side and driving a four-bladed propeller through a common gearbox. The undercarriage retracted rearwards into the nacelles, rotating through 90° to lie flat.

Construction of three prototypes was authorised, beginning in early 1939. However, the outbreak of hostilities in September brought work to a halt due to its non-strategic nature. It resumed in the summer of 1940, and the **Me 261 V1** flew for the first time on 23 December 1940, the **V2** following in the spring of 1941. The V2 differed from the first prototype by featuring smoother rear fuselage contours, and the stepped glazed portion was replaced by a smaller glazed blister. Consideration was given to using the Me 261 for long-range maritime patrols, but the difficulties of providing adequate defensive armament proved too great. The two prototypes were used for calibration work; they were damaged by Allied bombing at Lechfeld in 1944 and eventually scrapped.

In early 1943 followed a third aircraft, this time powered by the uprated DB 610 coupled engine and with accommodation for seven crew. In May, after repairs following a landing accident, the **V3** was handed over to the Aufklärungsgruppe des Oberbefehlshabers der Luftwaffe, the headquarters reconnaissance unit based at Oranienburg just outside Berlin. In Ob.d.L. hands it undertook several long-range reconnaissance missions.

Specification
Messerschmitt Me 261 V3
Type: ultra-long-range reconnaissance platform
Powerplant: one Daimler Benz DB 610A-1 (port) and one DB 610B-1 (starboard) 24-cylinder coupled engines, each rated at 2312 kW (3,100 hp)
Performance: maximum speed 620 km/h (385 mph) at 3000 m (9,840 ft); service ceiling 8260 m (27,100 ft); range at economical cruising speed 11025 km (6,850 miles)
Dimensions: wing span 26.87 m (88 ft 1¾ in); length 16.68 m (54 ft 8¾ in); height 4.72 m (15 ft 5¾ in)

By 1944, the Me 261 V2 was in poor repair, and was soon to be scrapped. Notable features were the huge main tyres, necessary to support the massive weight when the aircraft was fully fuelled.

Messerschmitt Me 262

Young German gunners, huddled around their light 20-mm and 37-mm flak weapons, could be excused for a slight lack of attention to their task at their first sight of the **Messerschmitt Me 262**s on the snow-covered expanses of Rheine-Hopsten air base in 1944. In every sense the sleek, shark-like fuselage, mottled ochre and olive green and beset with razor wings from which hung the huge turbojets, was a portent of the future. The noise, the high-pitched whine and howl of the Jumo 004B-1 turbines, the swirls of snow, the hot paraffin-tainted blast: all were of a different time. This was the present, however, and, beset by Allied air superiority on all sides, the skies over Westphalia were dangerous elements for operations of the Luftwaffe's dwindling strength. Black-helmeted pilots, crouched forward in the narrow cockpits of their Messerschmitt **Me 262A-2a** fighter-bombers, anxiously scanned the overcast skies for the first signs of the diving Hawker Tempests, North American P-51s or Supermarine Spitfires, as they coaxed throttles and jabbed brakes prior to take-off. Flak gunners trained their pieces along the approach paths, watched for the red Very lights that would bring them to instant action, and heard the thunder of the departing jets.

With such machines, how could Germany lose the war in the air? Such a thought must have raced through minds. The job of a flak gunner is humble, and he and his comrades could have had no insight into the extraordinary train of events and decisions that were instrumental in the denial in quantity of Germany's most potent air weapon of World War II. In the heady days of 1941, when the Messerschmitt Me 262 series was born, not one person in the Third Reich could foresee the desperate need for an outstanding aircraft with which to wrest air supremacy from the hands of the enemy. The Heinkel concern was already deeply involved in the development of a fighter powered by the new reaction-turbine engines when, on 4 January 1939, the Augsburg-based Messerschmitt AG received orders from the

The Me 262 V3 lands after its first flight at Leipheim on 18 July 1942. The smoke was caused by unburned fuel igniting in the jet pipes as it dripped out onto the runway. This was the first flight of the Me 262 using turbojet power alone, the first prototype having also had a nose-mounted piston engine.

Messerschmitt Me 262 Schwalbe

German air ministry (RLM, or Reichsluftfahrtministerium) to produce specifications for a similar type of aircraft. Two plans were drawn up by a team led by Dipl Ing Waldemar Voigt, one for a twin-boom configuration and the other for a pod-and-boom design. Neither of the two then-existing turbojet designs was considered to be powerful enough for a single-engined fighter, and as a result Voigt was forced to resort to the design of a twin-engined aircraft.

Early development

Heinkel had already turned to twin engines with the development of the promising He 280 series powered by the six-stage axial-flow BMW P 3302 engines, and Germany's first definitive jet fighter, the Heinkel He 280 V2 prototype, lifted off from Rostock-Marienehe's runway at 15.18 on 30 March 1941 with Fritz Schäfer at the controls. (Within six weeks of this maiden flight, the UK, too, flew its first jet aircraft: powered by a Whittle-designed W1X centrifugal-type turbojet of 3.82-kN (860-lb) thrust, the Gloster E.28/39 took to the air on 15 May.) At Augsburg, work had proceeded slowly on the design of what at first bore none of the hallmarks that graced the Heinkel product, or gave any hint of the fineness of line that was a characteristic of Messerschmitt's piston-engined fighters. The design was termed the Messerschmitt **P 1065 V1** and, in the absence of its twin jet engines,

was fitted with a 545-kW (730-hp) Junkers Jumo 210G driving a two-bladed propeller. This ugly duckling was then renamed the Messerschmitt **Me 262 V1**, and was taken into the air for the first time on 18 April 1941. Test pilots Karl Baur and Fritz Wendel reported no vices on subsequent flight programmes.

No urgency was attached to the flight development of the Me 262 V1 during that summer, for little priority had been assigned. Of far greater import for the Messerschmitt concern were the improvements to the Bf 109 and Bf 110 combat types, and the development of their replacements. The engines for the Me 262 V1 eventually arrived from Spandau in mid-November 1941, being BMW 003s each of 5.39 kN

This Messerschmitt Me 262B-1a/U1 under test at Wright Field in 1946 wears the USAAF codes of FE (Foreign Evaluation)-610. The aircraft was captured by the British following possible service with 10./NJG 11. The armament installed was two 30-mm MK 108A-3s and two 20-mm MG 151/20 cannon, and AI radar was an FuG 218 (Neptun V).

(1,213 lb) static thrust. On his first flight with the BMW 003s, Wendel suffered a double flame-out shortly after take-off and was forced to put PC+UA down with some damage.

Fortunately, an alternative to the touchy BMWs was available. This was the Junkers Jumo 004 which had been developed by Dr Anselm Franz's team since its award of a contract in July 1939 for a development specification. In their adherence to axial compressors, German engine designers showed much courage and foresight. This type of compressor was difficult to construct and balance, and was susceptible to vibration and could be damaged far more easily than the tough centrifugal type of compressor. It became apparent that the acceleration rates, fuel efficiency, power output, and drag coefficients of axial-flow turbojets far exceeded the figures produced by the tougher, and sometimes more reliable, centrifugal types. By August 1941, the Jumo 004 was giving 5.88 kN (1,323 lb) static thrust, and many of the earlier problems had been cured. Jumo 004s were installed on the Messerschmitt **Me 262 V3** (PC+UC), and this aircraft, bereft of the piston engine and still with tailwheel landing gear, left Leipheim's runway on the morning of 18 July 1942 in Wendel's experienced hands. It looked correct in every way, and it flew beautifully, and henceforth the fortunes of the Messerschmitt Me 262 were to rise at the expense of its nearest rival, the Heinkel He 280, which suffered a series of setbacks until its eventual cancellation in March 1943.

In the Luftwaffe's interest

Service test pilots of the Erprobungsstelle (test establishment) at Rechlin showed interest in the Me 262 from its earliest days. It was largely at their instigation that Messerschmitt received contracts to produce a number of prototypes for weapons and engine tests. The experienced Major Wolfgang Späte had already reported his enthusiastic findings when the General der Jagdflieger, Adolf Galland, flew the **Me 262 V4** on 22 May 1943 and become unequivocal in his constant praise for this revolutionary aircraft. At a conference in Berlin on 25 May, it was suggested that the piston-engined Messerschmitt Me 209A be cancelled and that all efforts be directed to the production of the Me 262; a production order for 100 followed in three days.

Other events then took a hand. On 17 August 1943 the US 8th Air Force's attack on Regensburg destroyed much of the embryonic Me 262 production lines, forcing Messerschmitt AG to move its jet development centres to Oberammergau, near the Bavarian Alps. The

Above: This Me 262A-1a belonged to III Gruppe of Ergänzungs-Jagdgeschwader Nr 2 (III/EJG 2). This powerful conversion unit, based at Lechfeld, flew many sorties against Allied aircraft in the spring of 1945; Leutnant Bell downed a P-38 Lightning with this particular aircraft on 21 March 1945. EJG 2 was formed on 2 November 1944.

Above: A female Luftwaffe auxiliary signals to the pilot of an EKdo 262 or EJG-2 Me 262A-1a. In the intercept role, the Me 262 could carry 24 underwing R4M rockets in addition to its built-in armament of four 30-mm MK 108 cannon. The aircraft had 100 rounds for each of the upper guns, and 80 for each of the lower pair.

Below: The Me 262 V3 was the first prototype to fly on turbojet power alone, the date being 18 July 1942. It was transferred to the German Aviation Experimental Establishment (DVL) in April 1944 for high-speed flight testing, and was written off on 12 September 1944 following damage in an air attack.

Messerschmitt Me 262 Schwalbe

In the quest for maximum rates of climb for point-defence work, some Messerschmitt Me 262s were modified for development programmes with liquid-fuelled Walter rockets. Illustrated is the Me 262C-1a first flown by Gerd Linder on 27 February 1945. The type arrived too late to enter service, although Major Heinz Bär of III/EJG 2 claimed a P-47 in this Me 262C-1a in the spring of 1945.

delay occasioned by the move was increased by a chronic shortage in the supply of skilled labour, and production slipped by many months. In the meantime, the **Me 262 V5** introduced the tricycle landing gear that was to become standard, only on this prototype the nose gear was fixed. The definitive **Me 262 V6** (Jumo 004Bs) flew on 17 October 1943: VI+AA featured a retractable tricycle landing gear, gun bays and blast ports, electrically operated tailplane, and a high-speed wing with automatic leading-edge slats and trailing-edge flaps.

Can it carry bombs?

By the autumn of 1943, Germany was on the defensive in the USSR and Italy, and was being subjected to furious aerial assault by day and by night. Not least of Hitler's concerns was when and where the Allies would strike in north-west Europe. During the amphibious invasions in North Africa, Sicily, Salerno and Reggio, Allied air power had kept the Luftwaffe and the German naval forces at bay, and had thus prevented the loss of shipping that could have jeopardised the entire extent of these operations. Therefore, nobody could have been surprised when many senior commanders, including Hitler, mooted the concept of the Messerschmitt Me 262 as a fighter-bomber as opposed to an interceptor, for the idea was tactically sound. It was at Insterberg, in East Prussia, on 26 November 1943, that Hitler watched the dove-grey VI+AA being put through its paces by Gerd Linder. Present was Professor Willy Messerschmitt, to answer the inevitable query from the fascinated Hitler: yes, indeed, the Me 262 could carry up to 1000 kg (2,205 lb) of bombs with uncomplicated

This Me 262A-2 has underwing pylons for the carriage of SC 250 (250-kg/ 551 lb) bombs. The fighter-bomber entered service with Kommando Schenck during the summer of 1944. This unit was formed from KG 51.

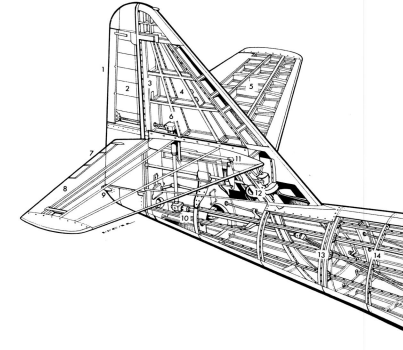

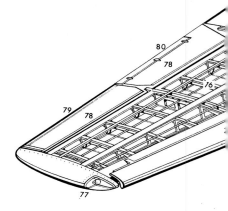

This Messerschmitt Me 262A-2a – 9K+FH (Nr 111625) – belonged to 1./KG 51. Command of Kampfgeschwader 51 came to Major Wolfgang Schenk in November 1944; during the summer of that year, Schenk took his Kommando into action with Me 262s on the Normandy war front.

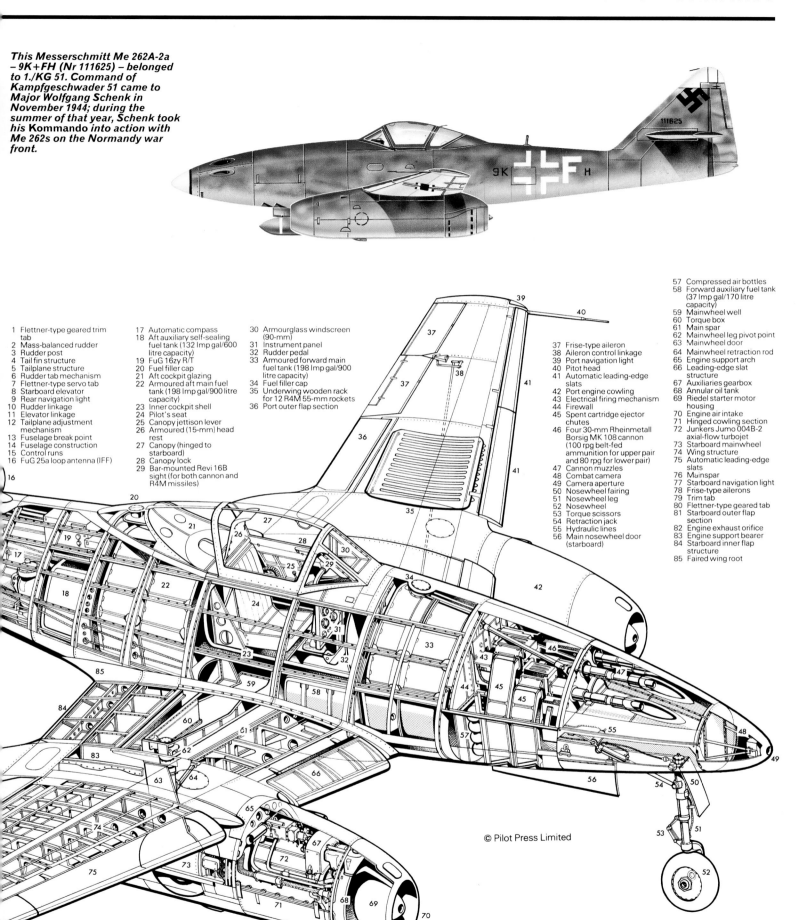

1 Flettner-type geared trim tab
2 Mass-balanced rudder
3 Rudder post
4 Tail fin structure
5 Tailplane structure
6 Rudder tab mechanism
7 Flettner-type servo tab
8 Starboard elevator
9 Rear navigation light
10 Rudder linkage
11 Elevator linkage
12 Tailplane adjustment mechanism
13 Fuselage break point
14 Fuselage construction
15 Control runs
16 FuG 25a loop antenna (IFF)

17 Automatic compass
18 Aft auxiliary self-sealing fuel tank (132 Imp gal/600 litre capacity)
19 FuG 16zy R/T
20 Fuel filler cap
21 Aft cockpit glazing
22 Armoured aft main fuel tank (198 Imp gal/900 litre capacity)
23 Inner cockpit shell
24 Pilot's seat
25 Canopy jettison lever
26 Armoured (15-mm) head rest
27 Canopy (hinged to starboard)
28 Canopy lock
29 Bar-mounted Revi 16B sight (for both cannon and R4M missiles)

30 Armourglass windscreen (90-mm)
31 Instrument panel
32 Rudder pedal
33 Armoured forward main fuel tank (198 Imp gal/900 litre capacity)
34 Fuel filler cap
35 Underwing wooden rack for 12 R4M 55-mm rockets
36 Port outer flap section

37 Frise-type aileron
38 Aileron control linkage
39 Port navigation light
40 Pitot head
41 Automatic leading-edge slats
42 Port engine cowling
43 Electrical firing mechanism
44 Firewall
45 Spent cartridge ejector chutes
46 Four 30-mm Rheinmetall Borsig MK 108 cannon (100 rpg belt-fed ammunition for upper pair and 80 rpg for lower pair)
47 Cannon muzzles
48 Combat camera
49 Camera aperture
50 Nosewheel fairing
51 Nosewheel leg
52 Nosewheel
53 Torque scissors
54 Retraction jack
55 Hydraulic lines
56 Main nosewheel door (starboard)

57 Compressed air bottles
58 Forward auxiliary fuel tank (37 Imp gal/170 litre capacity)
59 Mainwheel well
60 Torque box
61 Main spar
62 Mainwheel leg pivot point
63 Mainwheel door
64 Mainwheel retraction rod
65 Engine support arch
66 Leading-edge slat structure
67 Auxiliaries gearbox
68 Annular oil tank
69 Riedel starter motor housing
70 Engine air intake
71 Hinged cowling section
72 Junkers Jumo 004B-2 axial-flow turbojet
73 Starboard mainwheel
74 Wing structure
75 Automatic leading-edge slats
76 Mainspar
77 Starboard navigation light
78 Frise-type ailerons
79 Trim tab
80 Flettner-type geared tab
81 Starboard outer flap section
82 Engine exhaust orifice
83 Engine support bearer
84 Starboard inner flap structure
85 Faired wing root

© Pilot Press Limited

Messerschmitt Me 262A-1a
9./JG 7, Parchim,
March 1945

This Messerschmitt Me 262A-1a wears the markings of 9.Staffel of Jagdgeschwader 7, based at Parchim in early 1945 under 1.Jagddivision of I Jagdkorps operating in the defence of the Reich. After capture at the end of the war, this particular aircraft, Nr 500491, was given the code FE-111 by the technical branch of the USAAF for evaluation. In the course of 1979 the aircraft was stripped down, refurbished and rebuilt in over 6,000 hours of work, and placed on display at the National Air and Space Museum, Washington, DC, where it remains to this day. The illustration beautifully portrays the Me 262's sleek lines. The airframe alone, and in particular the wing design, was considered by the Allies to be far ahead of their own attainments in the field of high-speed flight.

Armament
The Me 262 carried four 30-mm MK 108 cannon in the nose, with 100 rpg for the upper guns and 80 for the lower. Armament was reduced to two MK 108s in the recce-configured Me 262A-5a and Me 262A-1a/U3, and some operational fighters and experimental variants had their cannon armament reduced or changed.

Cockpit
The Me 262 pilot enjoyed a superb all-round view, sitting high on the fuselage under a blown clear-view canopy. The aircraft was originally fitted with a Revi 16B reflector gunsight, but this was later replaced by the Askania EZ42 gyroscopic sight

Structure
The Me 262 was optimised for cheap and simple construction. High-strength alloys were avoided, and self-aligning bushes were used to eliminate the jigs usually necessary for reaming close-fitting bolt-holes. The fuselage was divided into four sub-assemblies: the nosecone housing guns and ammunition, the centre fuselage with cockpit and fuel tanks, the rear fuselage with radio bay and additional tanks, and the tail assembly. Virtually the entire wing formed a single torsion box, with lower wing panels screwed permanently in place. The oleos were of drawn seamless tubing, saving considerable man hours by comparison with the more usual forged undercarriage assemblies.

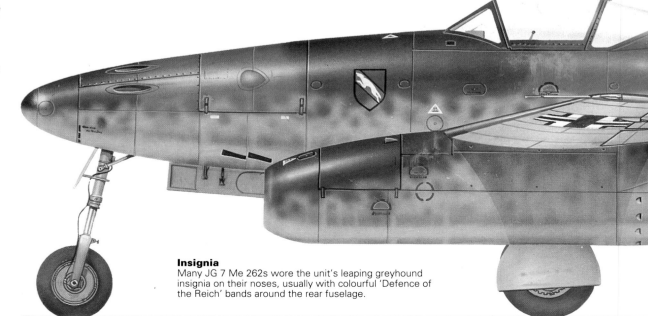

Insignia
Many JG 7 Me 262s wore the unit's leaping greyhound insignia on their noses, usually with colourful 'Defence of the Reich' bands around the rear fuselage.

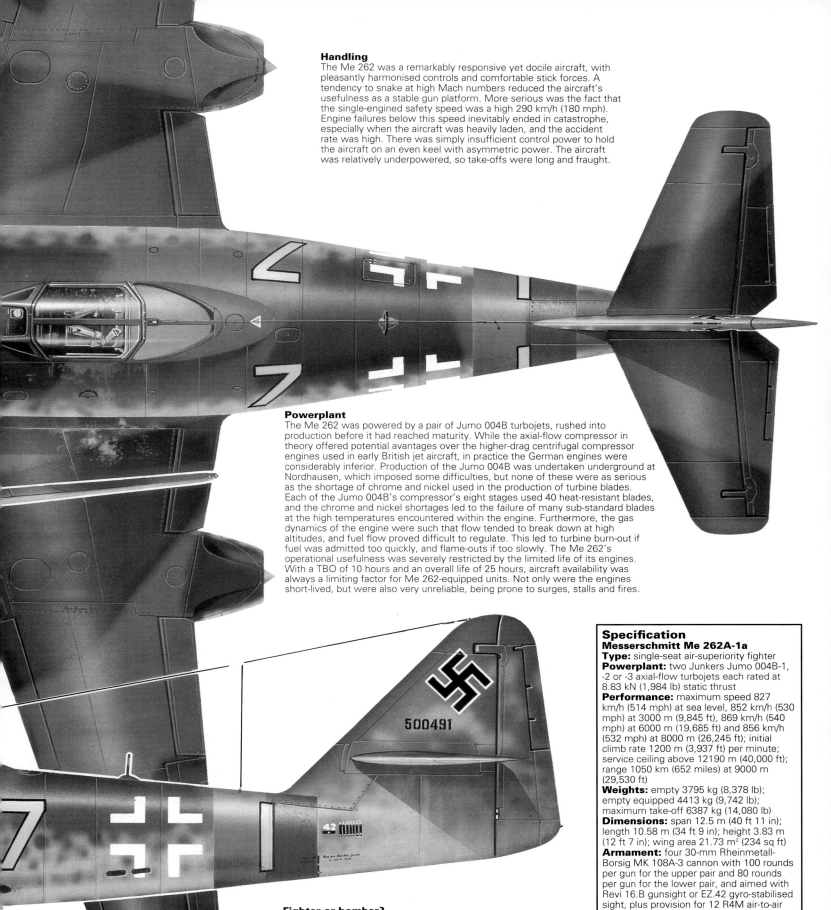

Handling

The Me 262 was a remarkably responsive yet docile aircraft, with pleasantly harmonised controls and comfortable stick forces. A tendency to snake at high Mach numbers reduced the aircraft's usefulness as a stable gun platform. More serious was the fact that the single-engined safety speed was a high 290 km/h (180 mph). Engine failures below this speed inevitably ended in catastrophe, especially when the aircraft was heavily laden, and the accident rate was high. There was simply insufficient control power to hold the aircraft on an even keel with asymmetric power. The aircraft was relatively underpowered, so take-offs were long and fraught.

Powerplant

The Me 262 was powered by a pair of Jumo 004B turbojets, rushed into production before it had reached maturity. While the axial-flow compressor in theory offered potential avantages over the higher-drag centrifugal compressor engines used in early British jet aircraft, in practice the German engines were considerably inferior. Production of the Jumo 004B was undertaken underground at Nordhausen, which imposed some difficulties, but none of these were as serious as the shortage of chrome and nickel used in the production of turbine blades. Each of the Jumo 004B's compressor's eight stages used 40 heat-resistant blades, and the chrome and nickel shortages led to the failure of many sub-standard blades at the high temperatures encountered within the engine. Furthermore, the gas dynamics of the engine were such that flow tended to break down at high altitudes, and fuel flow proved difficult to regulate. This led to turbine burn-out if fuel was admitted too quickly, and flame-outs if too slowly. The Me 262's operational usefulness was severely restricted by the limited life of its engines. With a TBO of 10 hours and an overall life of 25 hours, aircraft availability was always a limiting factor for Me 262-equipped units. Not only were the engines short-lived, but were also very unreliable, being prone to surges, stalls and fires.

Specification

Messerschmitt Me 262A-1a

Type: single-seat air-superiority fighter

Powerplant: two Junkers Jumo 004B-1, -2 or -3 axial-flow turbojets each rated at 8.83 kN (1,984 lb) static thrust

Performance: maximum speed 827 km/h (514 mph) at sea level, 852 km/h (530 mph) at 3000 m (9,845 ft), 869 km/h (540 mph) at 6000 m (19,685 ft) and 856 km/h (532 mph) at 8000 m (26,245 ft); initial climb rate 1200 m (3,937 ft) per minute; service ceiling above 12190 m (40,000 ft); range 1050 km (652 miles) at 9000 m (29,530 ft)

Weights: empty 3795 kg (8,378 lb); empty equipped 4413 kg (9,742 lb); maximum take-off 6387 kg (14,080 lb)

Dimensions: span 12.5 m (40 ft 11 in); length 10.58 m (34 ft 9 in); height 3.83 m (12 ft 7 in); wing area 21.73 m² (234 sq ft)

Armament: four 30-mm Rheinmetall-Borsig MK 108A-3 cannon with 100 rounds per gun for the upper pair and 80 rounds per gun for the lower pair, and aimed with Revi 16.B gunsight or EZ.42 gyro-stabilised sight, plus provision for 12 R4M air-to-air rockets under each wing

Fighter or bomber?

It has often been said that Hitler's initial insistence on using the Me 262 as a bomber seriously delayed the programme and reduced its impact on the Allied war effort. Certainly, in June 1944 Hitler insisted that testing and trials of the aircraft in the fighter role should do nothing to delay production of the bomber version, and in August would only reluctantly conceed that every 20th aircraft on the production line would be a fighter. However, the design of modifications for the bomber role were complete before he issued his edict and delays to Me 262 deliveries were imposed by engine shortages, not by having to incorporate modifications on the production line.

Keith Fretwell

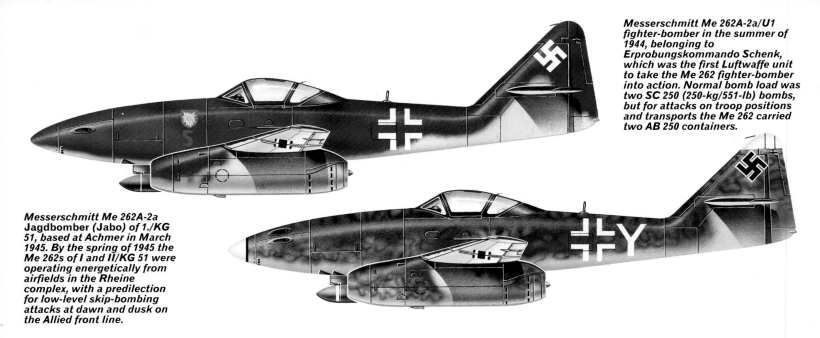

Messerschmitt Me 262A-2a/U1 fighter-bomber in the summer of 1944, belonging to Erprobungskommando Schenk, which was the first Luftwaffe unit to take the Me 262 fighter-bomber into action. Normal bomb load was two SC 250 (250-kg/551-lb) bombs, but for attacks on troop positions and transports the Me 262 carried two AB 250 containers.

Messerschmitt Me 262A-2a Jagdbomber (Jabo) of 1./KG 51, based at Achmer in March 1945. By the spring of 1945 the Me 262s of I and II/KG 51 were operating energetically from airfields in the Rheine complex, with a predilection for low-level skip-bombing attacks at dawn and dusk on the Allied front line.

conversion work completed within two weeks per unit. So, from that day the Messerschmitt Me 262 was destined to play a dual role, that of a fighter-bomber and that of a pure air-superiority fighter. Neither the role nor the aircraft could by then have had any influence on the outcome of the war. It was too late to start a major production scheme, as oil and aviation kerosene, precious alloys, and skilled airframe and engine specialists were all at a premium. The Messerschmitt Me 262 had been recognised in its full potential, but too late in the war.

Service conversion of the Me 262 was placed under Hauptmann Werner Thierfelder's Erprobungskommando 262 at Lechfeld, to where the unit moved on 21 December 1943, with pilots drawn from 8. and 9./ZG 26. The EKdo 262 was given a batch of pre-production **Me 262A-0** aircraft, and finally got into the swim of operations in the early summer of 1944. Thierfelder was killed in combat with 15th Air Force Mustangs over Bavaria on 18 July, and his place was taken by Hauptmann Neumeyer.

RAF discovers the Schwalbe

The RAF brought back its first confirmation of the Me 262's existence on 25 July, when a de Havilland Mosquito of No. 544 (PR) Squadron was intercepted near Munich, Flight Lieutenant A. E. Wall and his navigator Flying Officer A. S. Lobban escaping with difficulty. Equipped with Messerschmitt Me 262A-2a fighter-bombers, the Einsatzkommando Schenk (Major Wolfgang Schenk) was formed at Lechfeld in July, before posting to the Normandy invasion front. The unit was based at Châteaudun, Etampes and Creil, before pulling back to Juvincourt, near Reims, in late August. It was on 28 August 1944 that Allied fighter pilots downed the first Me 262 to be lost in combat: near Brussels, Major Joseph Myers and his wingman, Lieutenant M. D. Croy Jr, of the US 78th Fighter Group bounced Oberfeldwebel Lauer's Me 262 to force it down in a field. Operations by Einsatzkommando Schenk continued in a desultory manner until its incorporation into I Gruppe of Kampfgeschwader 51, which began combat operations from Rheine-Hopsten under Major Unrau in

October 1944. The value of the Me 262 as a reconnaissance aircraft was soon recognised, and a few went to the Einsatzkommando Braunegg, and to Nahaufklärungsgruppen 1 and 6.

Hitler's firm insistence on the Messerschmitt Me 262 being the property of the General der Kampfflieger (Marienfeld) denied Galland the opportunity of forming the first fighter unit until September 1944. One of Germany's finest fighter pilots, Major Walter Nowotny, formed the Kommando Nowotny based at Achmer and Hesepe near Osnabrück, to fly its first mission against Allied bombers and fighters on 3 October 1944. The Messerschmitt **Me 262A-1a** (two Jumo 004B-1 turbojets) formed the establishment of around 30. The armament was exceptionally potent and consisted of four Rheinmetall-Borsig MK 108A-3 30-mm cannon; the pilot was protected by 9-mm back armour, and a 90-mm armour-glass windscreen. With a maximum speed of 855 km/h (531 mph) at 8000 m (26,245 ft), the Me 262A-1a could outrun anything that the Allies had in their inventory, but proved to be vulnerable in the circuit pattern. Thus, several Me 262s succumbed to bold Allied fighter attacks during the approach and shortly after take-off. Initially, the Kommando Nowotny was given cover by III/JG 54 (Focke-Wulf Fw 190D-9s) from Varelbusch, but later some 120-140 Messerschmitt Bf 109G-10s and Bf 109K-4s and Focke-Wulfs were needed to protect I/KG 51's missions in the Rheine area, in addition to very strong flak defences.

Kommando Nowotny disbanded shortly after the death of its leader on 8 November 1944. The potent jet, the presence of which thoroughly alarmed Allied intelligence in the west, continued to be used in penny packets on bombing attacks (with AB 250 containers) on Allied front lines, reconnaissance missions, and an occasional foray against enemy fighters. In mid-November, Oberst Johannes Steinhoff formed the nucleus of Jagdgeschwader 7 at Brandenburg-Briest; III Gruppe was formed from the survivors of Kommando Nowotny, while I/JG 7 was later formed at Parchim. Four additional bomber units were formed on 30 January 1945, these comprising KG(J)6, KG(J)27, KG(J)54 and KG(J)55. Of these, only I/KG(J) 54 at

---

Messerschmitt Me 262 variants

Me 262 V1: first prototype (PC+UA) with single Junkers Jumo 210G piston engine; later fitted with two BMW 003 turbojets
Me 262 V2: test airframe for fitment of two BMW 003 turbojets
Me 262 V3: test airframe (PC+UC) with two Junkers Jumo 004 turbojets; first prototype to be flown by service test pilots
Me 262 V4: (PC+UD) fourth prototype of similar configuration
Me 262 V5: fitted with two Jumo 004s, PC+UE differed in having a fixed nosewheel, whereas previous prototypes had conventional tail wheels
Me 262 V6: definitive prototype (VI+AA) with lighter Jumo 004B-1 turbojets, and retractable tricycle landing gear; the **Me 262 V7**

(VI+AB) was similar but with redesigned cockpit canopy and cockpit pressurisation; many subsequent Versuchs prototypes evolved for testing of engines, radio, radar, and weapons systems
Me 262A-0: pre-production airframes based on the Me 262 V7 configuration; 23 produced; passed to test centre at Rechlin and to service trials detachment (EKdo 262) in late April 1944
Me 262A-1a: standard interceptor-fighter configuration with twin Jumo 004B-1 turbojets, four Rheinmetall-Borsig MK 108A-3 30-mm cannon, Revi 16.B gunsight, and FuG 16zY radio; the **Me 262A-1a/U1** designation covered three trials units with two MG 151, two MK 103 and two MK 108 cannon

Me 262A-2a: standard fighter-bomber configuration, similar to Me 262A-1a but with two Schloss 503A-1 bomb racks for two 250-kg (551-lb) bombs, and armament normally reduced to two 30-mm MK 108 cannon; the **Me 262A-2a/U2** was a trials development with Lotfe 7H bomb sight, glazed nose, and accommodation for prone bomb-aimer
Me 262A-3a: trials models intended for close-support role
Me 262A-5a: reconnaissance-fighter with either twin nose-mounted Rb 50/30 oblique cameras, or single Rb 20/30 or Rb 75/30 ; adapted to the reconnaissance role, the **Me 262A-1a/U3** was used by a number of units
Me 262B-1a: conversion trainer with dual flight controls under redesigned canopy; deletion of rear main fuel tank necessitated carriage of two 300-litre (66-Imp gal) drop

tanks on Schloss 503A-1 Wikingschiff racks
Me 262B-1a/U1: interim two-seat night-fighter with FuG 218 Neptun V airborne interception radar and FuG 350 ZC (Naxos) passive homer; fewer than a dozen in service by 1945
Me 262B-2a: definitive night-fighter with lengthened fuselage to contain additional fuel tanks; two produced
Me 262C-1a: point-defence interceptor-fighter with twin Jumo 004B-1s supplemented by tail-mounted Walter R II-211/3 (HWK 509) bi-fuel rocket motor to give outstanding rates of climb; one trials aircraft produced
Me 262C-2b: point-defence interceptor; twin BMW 003R power units each consisting of a BMW 003A turbojet and a BMW 718 bi-fuel rocket, fitted in place of conventional motors; one produced

Above: Although many Me 262s wore unit insignia, photos of such aircraft are very rare, and the majority of the German jets were extremely anonymous. These Me 262A-1as served with Kommando Nowotny.

Right: This Me 262A-1 was experimentally flown with a 50-mm Rheinmetall BK 5 cannon and was intended as a heavy bomber-destroyer. The modification was not adopted for production aircraft.

Giebelstadt, II/KG(J) 54 at Kitzingen and III/KG(J) 6 at Prague-Ruzyne played any part in operations, usually at reasonably high loss. The only occasions on which Jagdgeschwader 7 made any impact were during the battles of 18-21 March 1945 when, using Oranienburg and Parchim, a daily average of some 40 or more sorties was put up against American bombers. A new unguided air-to-air weapon, the R4M rocket, was used for the first time on Me 262A-1a fighters during these encounters. Final day operations fell to Generalleutnant Adolf Galland's Jagdverband 44 (JV 44) at München-Riem, to the aforementioned units, and to the night-fighting Messerschmitt Me 262B-1a/U1 aircraft of 10./NJG 11 at Burg.

Over the period March 1944 to 20 April 1945, the Luftwaffe took delivery of 1,433 Me 262s, but for the Allies the impact of this fine aircraft was largely psychological. On inspection after the war's end, it was acknowledged that in design of airframe and engine the Messerschmitt Me 262 was years ahead of aircraft of other nations, and its secrets permitted the Russians and the Anglo-Americans to accelerate development of jet fighter and bomber aircraft to the magic of Mach 1.0 and beyond over the ensuing years.

Right: An Me 262A-2a of 1./KG 51, during March 1945, carrying underfuselage bombs. A detachment of KG 51, operating as Kommando Schenck, began operations during August 1944, and the remainder of the Geschwader quickly began conversion to the new jet, with I and II Gruppen and the Geschwader Stab operational on the new type by the winter of 1944. Hitler himself was keen that the Me 262 be used in the bomber role.

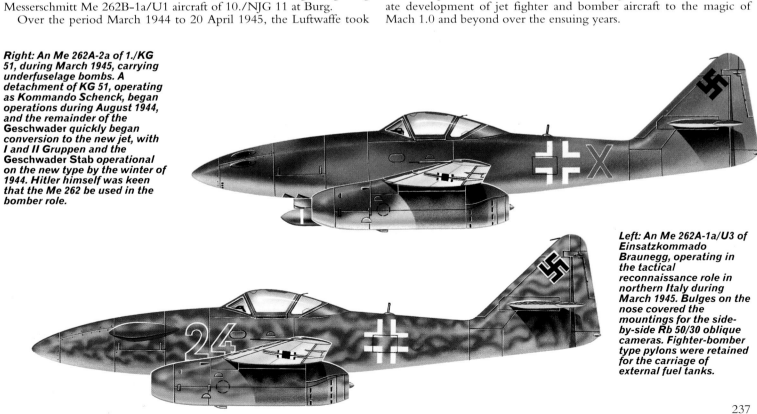

Left: An Me 262A-1a/U3 of Einsatzkommado Braunegg, operating in the tactical reconnaissance role in northern Italy during March 1945. Bulges on the nose covered the mountings for the side-by-side Rb 50/30 oblique cameras. Fighter-bomber type pylons were retained for the carriage of external fuel tanks.

Messerschmitt Me 321/323

O ne of the puzzles of aviation history is why Messerschmitt's Gigant (giant) family set such new standards in air transport capability. These machines were physically vast, but in terms of weight (under 45000 kg/99,208 lb) and power (about 4922 kW/ 6,600 hp) they were not particularly impressive. Moreover, they had an old-fashioned fabric-skinned structure, low flight performance and big doors only at the front. The real breakthrough came after World War II with the Lockheed C-130, which had far better payload provisions, a rear door which could be opened in flight, and high performance. It all makes one wonder why nobody built a stressed-skin airlifter of Gigant proportions, powered by four R-2800 Double Wasps.

Instead, the standard transports of World War II were the Junkers Ju 52/3m on the one hand and the Douglas DC-3 family on the other. Both had narrow, cramped fuselages which sloped steeply on the ground, with a side door. Troops, infantry weapons, spare parts, ammunition and, with difficulty, 250-litre (55-Imp gal) fuel drums or a motorcycle were possible loads. Anything really heavy or bulky had to go by surface means. The Soviets had airlifted trucks and even light tanks, although only by hanging them out in the slipstream underneath heavy bombers.

Slow realisation

This dismal state of affairs probably reflected an almost total disinterest on the part of the customers. Except on rare occasions, such as the hurried evacuation of Kabul in Afghanistan during the winter of 1928-29, there was little demand for air transport, and it was meekly accepted that transports, or 'bomber transports', were unable to carry anything heavy or bulky. Even Hitler's Luftwaffe failed to order any really capable transport, but nonetheless achieved fantastic success on 10 May 1940 in the invasion of Western Europe using Ju 52/3ms and even smaller gliders. When it came to the planned invasion of the UK, such airlift forces appeared inadequate. The initial plan for Operation Sealion envisaged that, with the RAF defeated, paratroops and gliderborne infantry could hold bridgeheads, while Ju 87B Stukas would demolish any opposing strongpoints. This plan was disrupted by the Luftwaffe's failure to eliminate the RAF. Hitler postponed Sealion, and planned the assault on the Soviet Union instead, which was expected to be over by the autumn of 1941. With a 'final solution' achieved in the East, Hitler then planned to occupy the UK.

More careful planning showed that it would be prudent to be able to bring in heavy armour, flak and other massive items with the very first airborne assault. With extraordinary suddenness, it was realised that there was an urgent need for transport aircraft with capability far greater than anything previously envisaged. Should they be powered machines or gliders? The instant choice fell upon gliders, even though these would be unlikely to make more than one mission each. The need was for large numbers of heavy assault gliders; a single one-way flight by the whole fleet ought to be enough. On 18 October 1940 Junkers and Messerschmitt were each given just 14 days in which to submit their outline designs for gliders, already given the designations Ju 322 and **Me 261w**, able to carry an 88-mm (3.46-in) gun and its half-track tractor, or a PzKpfW IV tank. This panic programme was called 'Warschau' (Warsaw), Junkers being 'Ost' (east) and the rival

Luftwaffe troops deplane from an Me 323D-1 during evaluation of the type in the air assault role. The Me 323D-1 was built from the start as a powered aircraft, and introduced two nose gun positions, two dorsal gun positions and a reduced number of cabin windows.

'Sud' (south). Of the Junkers Ju 322 Mammut, the less said the better: a colossal all-wing machine, it looked efficient and impressive but was a dismal failure. In complete contrast, Messerschmitt AG at Leipheim encountered no serious difficulty.

Under project leader Josef Frolich the design staff submitted its proposal on schedule on 1 November 1940, and by this time the company was frantically gathering materials for a production run of 200. The giant glider had a structure mainly of welded high-tensile steel tube, thousands of metres of which were produced in three weeks by Mannesmann AG. Unlike the Junkers offering, the Messerschmitt Me 261w, whose number changed to 263 and finally to **Me 321**, had a high wing on a conventional fuselage. The nose was gigantic, fully meriting the **Gigant** name, and it comprised left/right-hinged doors opened by a team of troops who then fitted ramps so that vehicles could drive out. Aft of the wing the fuselage tapered away to the tall strut-braced tail. Strong cross-beams could carry a PzKpfW IV tank, weighing around 20000 kg (44,092 lb) in most versions, or any other common front-line load. For carrying troops it was possible to add upper cross beams and planks to give double-deck capacity of at least 200, with the men's kit and weapons. The single-place cockpit was immediately ahead of the leading edge. The monster rolled on two Ju 90 main wheels and two Bf 109 nose wheels, at the corners of a dolly jettisoned after take-off; landing was effected on four skids. The entire trailing edge was occupied by vast hinged flaps and ailerons which were intended to be moved by Flettner servo tabs on the trailing edge.

The **Me 321 V1** (first prototype) was towed off at Leipheim behind a Junkers Ju 90 on 25 February 1941. Great physical effort was needed to fly the giant, and it was decided that from aircraft no. 101 off the line side-by-side dual control would be provided. Batteries and

The planned invasion of the British Isles, Operation Sealion, required heavy equipment to be airlifted with the first airborne assault. Although the invasion never took place, the Me 321 transport glider (originally designated Me 263) did reach production status; this is an Me 321A-1.

The tactical rudder code identifies this Me 323D-1 as serving with 1./TG 5, this unit being assigned to Lufttransportchef II and subordinated to Luftflotte 4 for service during the Crimean airlift. This particular Gruppe had flown more than 2,000 missions by May 1944, with primary bases in Poland, Hungary and Romania. Noticeable are the fewer windows and relocated sprung tailskid characteristic of the Me 323.

electric servo-motors were added to help de-dress the flaps, and later provision was made for up to eight auxiliary take-off rockets and a 20-m (66-ft) braking parachute for landing. Take-offs remained a problem. There was no aircraft of sufficient power available in numbers, and following rather discouraging model tests the *Troikaschlepp* was devised with three Messerschmitt Bf 110s all pulling one Me 321, the centre tug having a towline 20 m (66 ft) longer than those of the others. The rest of 1941 was punctuated by fantastic accidents, near-accidents and amazing escapes, on one occasion with the glider doing a tight turn away from the snapped-cable tugs, with rockets firing and one wingtip almost touching the ground. Another scheme was to fix the three twin-engined fighters to the glider itself, one above the fuselage and the others under the wings, disconnecting only near the destination.

Me 321s in action

In the event, Heinkel produced the five-engined He 111Z twin-fuselage tug, and Messerschmitt's Leipheim and Obertraubling factories delivered 50 Me 321As and 100 dual Me 321Bs. These saw much action (but never invaded Malta or many other planned targets, and were also too late to help at Stalingrad). The decision had been taken years earlier, in March 1941, to build a Gigant with engines. Inevitably this would carry much less, because its empty weight would be some 2.5 times greater. In many ways the glider was superior, but while it would have been ideal (with adequate tugs) for a one-time assault on the UK, it was less than satisfactory for the ongoing war in which it found itself, where trucking had to be done on a sustained basis from Marseilles to the Volga. There was no way an Me 321 could 'go round again' when approaching an overcrowded airfield, once at rest it was almost impossible to move, and staging points had to have special crews with masses of concentrated hydrogen peroxide for the rockets, drag chutes, tow cables and many other special items.

The powered **Me 323** was studied with many types of engine, and the choice fell on the least powerful, the French Gnome-Rhône 14N. This was because the engine installation and propeller of the Bloch 175 bomber was readily available and in production already, and could just be bolted to a strengthened Gigant wing. Six engines were needed, the left trio being GR14N 48s and the right trio GR14N 49s rotating in the opposite direction. A flight engineer cabin was added

An Me 321A-1 glider is towed into the air at Leipheim by a **Troikaschlepp** *of Bf 110C tugs. Note the Gigant's landing gear, jettisoned after take-off, and the booster rockets underwing.*

in each leading edge between the inner and middle engines, and a completely new multi-wheel permanent landing gear was added. This, like the aircraft itself, showed the way to the 'high flotation' gears of today: along each side were a tandem-wheel front truck and a main gear with three larger wheels. All wheels were sprung by massive levers and coil springs to hold the Me 323 level no matter what the load was on board. The tailskid was then off the ground, and with correct centre of gravity position a man could reach up and pull the tailskid down to the ground. Pictures show that often the centre of gravity was too far aft, the skid then being firmly on the ground. This excellent gear rode over atrocious front-line 'airfields', and pneumatic brakes could pull up a full-load landing in under 200 m (656 ft).

From four to six engines

The **Me 323 V1** first prototype had only four engines, and was the prototype of a proposed **Me 323C** which needed the *Troikaschlepp* or He 111Z at take-off with full load, but which could then fly back empty unaided. This remained a one-off, and the **Me 323 V2** with six engines proved the prototype of the **Me 323D** production version. Although the Me 323D was not easy to fly, its production was not delayed, and both Leipheim and Obertraubling were delivering by September 1942, just in time for the Tunisian campaign. Two Ju 52 *Gruppen* were converted into KGzbV 323, which at first led a charmed life despite having to shuttle between Sicily and North Africa in daylight. The only defensive armament in the **Me 323D-1** comprised two 7.92-mm (0.31-in) MG 15 machine-guns in cockpits on each side behind the wing, although troops could fire six MG 34 or MG 42 army weapons from the side windows. Once the aircraft reached the Mediterranean a lot more firepower was needed. The nose-door guns were changed for 13-mm (0.51-in) MG 131s and a second pair was added lower down in each door, and new aircraft received a forward dorsal cockpit with MG 15s firing to front and rear.

The supply of powerplants was augmented by adding those in production for the LeO 451 bomber, but the tight-fitting Mercier cowl and

Head-on view of the Me 323 V1, prototype of the four-engined Me 323C series which was not put into production. Use of only four of the GR 14N 48/49 engines did not provide sufficient power for take-off at full load and, although the **Troikaschlepp** *was not essential, a powerful tug would still have been required.*

One of the Me 323D-0 development aircraft (factory coded RD+QB) thunders into the air with the aid of eight hydrogen-peroxide-assisted take-off rockets of 4.9 kN (1,102 lb) thrust each. The rockets proved temperamental and also demanded protective clothing. 'Burn' time was 30 seconds.

Messerschmitt Me 321/323

Messerschmitt Gigant variants

Me 321A-1: initial production glider, with single pilot and various take-off rockets; up to six 1000-kg (2,205-lb) units

Me 321B-1: second production batch of gliders with side-by-side dual-control cockpit

Me 323 V1: prototype of Me 323C series with four GR 14N 48/49 engines

Me 323 V2: prototype of Me 323D series with six GR 14N 48/49 engines

Me 323C: planned four-engined 'powered glider' version; not built

Me 323D-0: first 10 pre-production aircraft, used for development; differed from V2 mainly in having fewer cabin windows, four MG 17 gun positions (and MG 34 or MG 42 sockets in windows) and smaller tailskid moved farther aft

Me 323D-1: first production version, as Me 323D-0 but subjected to many additions and modifications, especially to armament

Me 323D-2: troublesome production version with modified LeO 451 powerplants, initially with Ratier and later with Heine wooden two-bladed fixed-pitch propellers

Me 323D-6: Me 323D-2 modified with Chauvière propellers as on Me 323D-1, plus fore-aft MG 17 gun

positions above radio compartment

Me 323 V13: prototype of restressed heavier version with greater fuel capacity and improved armament

Me 323E-1: production V13 version, with left/right MG 131 guns in nose doors and rear-fuselage window mounts

Me 323 V14: prototype with four Jumo 211F-1 engines

Me 323 V15: prototype with two large HDL 151 turrets above wings

Me 323E-2: production version with two streamlined EDL 151 turrets, MG 131 gun for radio operator but rear dorsal cockpits removed

Me 323E-2/WT: special escort *Waffentrager* with HDL 151 nose turret, four EDL 151 wing turrets, six hand-held MG 151/20s and four MG 131s

Me 323 V16: prototype of planned **Me 323F** powered by six Jumo 211R engines and armament of Me 323E-2; gross weight 58000 kg (127,868 lb)

Me 323 V17: prototype of planned **Me 323G** with completely redesigned airframe stressed for greater weights, powered by six GR 14R engines

Ratier propeller caused many difficulties including overheating and vibration, and Me 323 sub-variants reached **D-6** before production of LeO installations could begin. Even then, the early LeO aircraft had reduced weights, cutting maximum payload to only 9525 kg (20,999 lb). At the same time, the Me 323 gave the Luftwaffe a tremendous airlift capability possessed by no other air force. Contrary to the insistent Afrika Korps rumour, the *Leukoplastbomber* (Elastoplast bomber) was neither fragile nor highly inflammable, but a tough giant capable of absorbing tremendous punishment. There are several RAF squadron combat reports which tell of a Gigant lumbering on its way after the British aircraft had expended all its ammunition.

Heavy losses

There were occasions, however, when Me 323Ds of various varieties were shot down in droves. The worst time for KGzbV 323 was April 1943 when it lost 43 aircraft, a single example surviving the final defeat in Tunisia in mid-May. Of these losses, at least 29 were shot down, the remainder being shot up on airfields. This drastically reduced the total number of Me 323s available, despite the fact that output at this time reached almost one per day, a level never again even approached. Operational experience led to numerous internal improvements, more secure payload positioning which facilitated attainment of the correct centre of gravity position, and the addition

A flypast by a late-model E-2 Gigant with the Nos 2 and 5 engines stopped. One of the drawbacks of the Gigant D-2 with LeO engines was the use of non-feathering two-bladed propellers, which also caused vibration. Throughout the Gigant story, most problems would have been solved by high-power engines.

of a retractable rear-fuselage support leg and a massive spade anchor under the tail to dig in after landing and shorten the run.

More basic changes resulted in new sub-types. A prototype with four 999-kW (1,340-hp) Jumo 211F (Ju 88 type) powerplants did not go into production, but the **Me 323E-1** became the new standard model by April 1943. This had slightly greater fuel capacity, a stronger airframe and enhanced armament. Although the original upper and lower front door gun positions were retained for a while (without guns), the forward armament was changed to two MG 131s at middle level in the extreme nose. A square window was added on each side of the rear fuselage with a pivoted MG 131 in the centre. Only a few Me 323E-1s were built before the **Me 323E-2** added a low-drag EDL 151 electric turret, with a 20-mm MG 151/20 cannon, in each wing behind the rear spar just inboard of the outer engines (tall HDL 151 turrets were flown on the **Me 323 V15** prototype, but drag was excessive). These isolated turrets dramatically increased firepower, but only in the upper hemisphere.

So complete had been the destruction of KGzbV 323 at the hands of Allied fighters and medium bombers that one Gigant, the **Me 323E-2/WT** (Waffentrager), was tested as a pure escort ship, rather like the US 8th Air Force Boeing YB-40. The WT had 11 MG 151/20 cannon and four MG 131s, manned by 12 gunners, and with 600 kg (1,323 lb) of extra armour. Five of the cannon were in turrets, one in the top of the sealed nose and the others along the top of the wings. This concept was judged inferior to fighter protection.

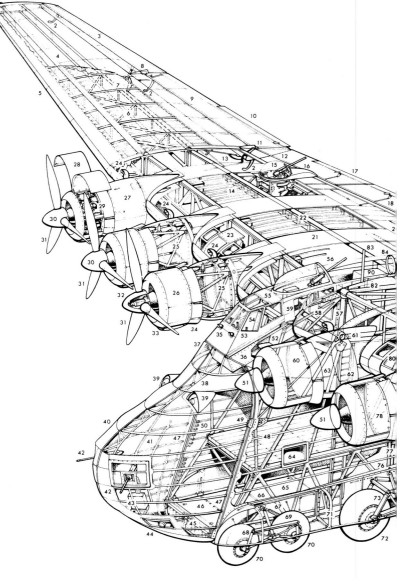

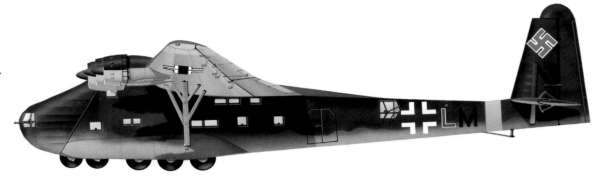

Messerschmitt Me 323E Gigant cutaway drawing key

1. Starboard navigation light
2. Aileron balance horns
3. Starboard aileron (outer)
4. Wing spars
5. Plywood leading-edge
6. Inter-spar cross bracing
7. Aileron control linkage
8. Actuator hinge bracing
9. Starboard aileron (inner)
10. Aileron Flettner tab
11. Aileron inner hinge
12. Aileron profile
13. Actuator hinge link
14. Inter-spar ribs
15. Starboard MG 151/20 electrically-operated turret (Me 323E-2)
16. Turret aerodynamic fairing
17. Flettner tab
18. Tab linkage
19. Starboard flap assembly
20. Flettner tab control
21. Wing skinning
22. Tubular spar member
23. Flight engineer's leading-edge station
24. Intakes
25. Engine bearer frames
26. Nacelle cowling panels
27. Starboard outer nacelle
28. Hinged servicing panels
29. 'LeO' type radial engine
30. Spinners
31. Three-blade propellers
32. Propeller hub
33. Chin intakes
34. Cowling gills
35. Flight deck intakes
36. Cockpit armoured box assembly
37. Nose door upper hinge frame
38. Door centre-line opening frame
39. Provision for nose door upper gun positions (Me 323E-2)
40. Nose door fabric covering
41. Nose door inner frames
42. MG 131 gun stations in nose door mid-sections (Me 323E-2)
43. Ammunition magazines
44. Provision for nose door lower gun positions (Me 323E-2)
45. Cargo floor forward sill
46. Cargo floor area
47. Fuselage forward frame
48. Provision for upper hold floor planking
49. Door upper hinge
50. Nose door multiple hinge assembly
51. Spinners
52. Pilot's seat
53. Control columns
54. Co-pilot's seat
55. Flight deck upper glazing
56. MG 15 dorsal forward gun station
57. Wing spar centre-section
58. Flight deck entry door
59. Cockpit box support frame
60. Port inner engine nacelle
61. Front spar/fuselage mainframe attachment
62. Flight deck crew entry ladder
63. Fuselage forward side frames
64. Cargo hold window
65. Main cargo floor tie-down points
66. Forward undercarriage attachment
67. Spring shock absorbers
68. Undercarriage forward assembly
69. Undercarriage fairing
70. Forward paired wheels
71. Undercarriage fairing frame member
72. Triple mainwheel assembly (in-flight position)
73. Shock absorbers
74. Mainwheel support frame
75. Strut members
76. Undercarriage/fuselage attachment
77. Mainframe member
78. Port mid engine nacelle
79. Firewall bulkhead
80. Intakes
81. Flight-engineer's leading-edge station
82. Main spar box frame
83. Aerial masts
84. D/F loop
85. Aileron control runs
86. Starboard flap inner section
87. Wing/fuselage decking
88. Wing centre-section aft frames
89. Wing control surface actuating linkage
90. Six main fuel cells
91. Wing spar framework
92. Cargo hold upper windows
93. Fuselage frame
94. Flight engineer's inspection crawlway
95. Cargo hold lower windows
96. Nacelle fairing
97. Undercarriage aft fairing
98. Landing light
99. Box spar frame
100. Turret aerodynamic fairing
101. Port MG 151/20 electrically-operated turret (Me 323E-2)
102. Cargo hold aft windows (provision for hand-held guns)
103. Fuselage formers
104. Flap inboard profile
105. Wing/fuselage decking fillet
106. Upper frames
107. Dorsal MG positions (Me 323E-1)
108. Ammunition magazine
109. Gunner's station
110. Rear entry (double) doors
111. Aft fuselage walkway
112. Fuselage structure
113. Starboard gunner's station
114. Port MG 131 gun position
115. Fuselage skinning
116. Dorsal aft decking
117. Frame structure
118. Cross frames
119. Control runs
120. Fuselage/tailfin fillet
121. Elevator control linkage
122. Rudder control linkage
123. Starboard tailplane ribs
124. Leading-edge ply
125. Elevator balance
126. Starboard elevator
127. Elevator hinge assembly
128. Tailplane upper brace strut
129. Elevator tab
130. Tailfin leading-edge
131. Tailfin spar
132. Tailplane brace strut attachment
133. Tailfin structure
134. Rudder balance
135. Flettner tabs
136. Rudder
137. Rudder hinge
138. Tailplane upper brace strut
139. Tab hinge fairing
140. Elevator cut-out
141. Flettner tab
142. Flettner tab hinge
143. Elevator balance horns
144. Port elevator

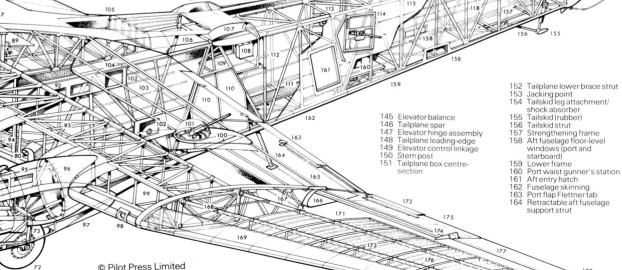

An Me 323 meets its end. This Me 323 is seen under attack by an RAF Martin Marauder. The Gigant's huge size and lumbering performance made it a sitting duck for Allied fighters, fighter-bombers, and even medium bombers like the B-26, although it could absorb a tremendous amount of punishment.

145. Elevator balance
146. Tailplane spar
147. Elevator hinge assembly
148. Tailplane leading-edge
149. Elevator control linkage
150. Stern post
151. Tailplane box centre-section
152. Tailplane lower brace strut
153. Jacking point
154. Tailskid leg attachment/shock absorber
155. Tailskid (rubber)
156. Tailskid strut
157. Strengthening frame
158. Aft fuselage floor-level windows (port and starboard)
159. Lower frame
160. Port waist gunner's station
161. Aft entry hatch
162. Fuselage skinning
163. Port flap Flettner tab
164. Retractable aft fuselage support strut
165. Hinge fairing
166. Flap outboard profile
167. Wooden aft-section wing rib structure
168. Tubular metal box spar frame
169. Leading-edge/rib attachment
170. Plywood leading-edge
171. Outer spar assembly
172. Aileron Flettner tab
173. Wing outboard rib stations
174. Aileron hinge fairing
175. Port aileron (inner)
176. Intermediate ribs
177. Aileron hinge line
178. Box spar end-section
179. Port aileron (outer)
180. Port navigation light

© Pilot Press Limited

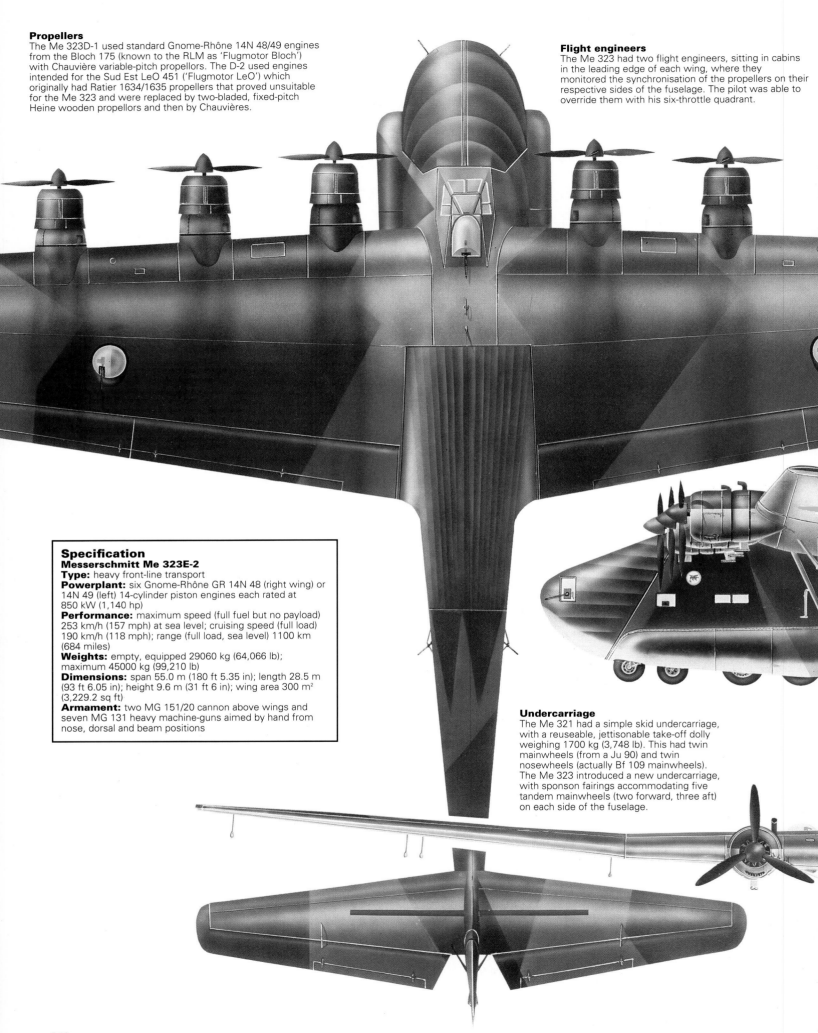

Propellers
The Me 323D-1 used standard Gnome-Rhône 14N 48/49 engines from the Bloch 175 (known to the RLM as 'Flugmotor Bloch') with Chauvière variable-pitch propellors. The D-2 used engines intended for the Sud Est LeO 451 ('Flugmotor LeO') which originally had Ratier 1634/1635 propellers that proved unsuitable for the Me 323 and were replaced by two-bladed, fixed-pitch Heine wooden propellors and then by Chauvières.

Flight engineers
The Me 323 had two flight engineers, sitting in cabins in the leading edge of each wing, where they monitored the synchronisation of the propellers on their respective sides of the fuselage. The pilot was able to override them with his six-throttle quadrant.

Specification
Messerschmitt Me 323E-2
Type: heavy front-line transport
Powerplant: six Gnome-Rhône GR 14N 48 (right wing) or 14N 49 (left) 14-cylinder piston engines each rated at 850 kW (1,140 hp)
Performance: maximum speed (full fuel but no payload) 253 km/h (157 mph) at sea level; cruising speed (full load) 190 km/h (118 mph); range (full load, sea level) 1100 km (684 miles)
Weights: empty, equipped 29060 kg (64,066 lb); maximum 45000 kg (99,210 lb)
Dimensions: span 55.0 m (180 ft 5.35 in); length 28.5 m (93 ft 6.05 in); height 9.6 m (31 ft 6 in); wing area 300 m² (3,229.2 sq ft)
Armament: two MG 151/20 cannon above wings and seven MG 131 heavy machine-guns aimed by hand from nose, dorsal and beam positions

Undercarriage
The Me 321 had a simple skid undercarriage, with a reuseable, jettisonable take-off dolly weighing 1700 kg (3,748 lb). This had twin mainwheels (from a Ju 90) and twin nosewheels (actually Bf 109 mainwheels). The Me 323 introduced a new undercarriage, with sponson fairings accommodating five tandem mainwheels (two forward, three aft) on each side of the fuselage.

Defensive armament
The Me 323D introduced two gun positions in the clamshell nose doors, each with a 7.9-mm MG 15 machine-gun, with two similarly equipped gun positions on each side of the wing trailing edge/fuselage junction. These could be augmented by up to six MG 34s firing from the cabin windows. In the Me 323E the door guns were replaced by less rudimentary gun positions lower down, on each side of the centreline, accommodating a 13-mm MG 131. Further MG 131s were also provided in new well-armoured positions on each side of the rear fuselage. The Me 323E-2 saw the abandonment of the overwing gun positions. In a novel scheme to provide an escort for Me 323s, one aircraft was modified as the Me 323E-2/WT, with five power-operated turrets in the nose and spread over the upper surface of the wing, each housing a single 20-mm MG 151 cannon. Six more MG 151s were provided in the forward and rear fuselage. The crew of 17 included 12 dedicated gunners, but the idea did not progress beyond the single flying prototype.

Messerschmitt Me 323E-2 I/TG 5 Russian Front, late 1943

The ultimate standard form of Gigant was the Me 323E-2; this is an E-2 of I/TG 5, which was desperately overworked on the Eastern Front from late 1943. This aircraft has a white stripe ahead of the tail instead of the expected yellow theatre band. The E-2 differed from earlier versions chiefly in defensive armament, the normal fit comprising two hand-aimed MG 131s low down in the front doors, another MG 131 firing aft from the radio compartment behind the cockpit, two 20-mm MG 151s in low-drag EDL 151 turrets behind the outboard engines, and four single MG 131s firing front and rear beam positions.

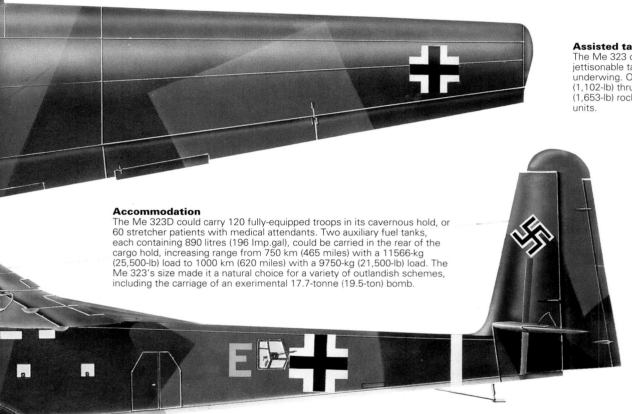

Assisted take off gear
The Me 323 could be fitted with jettisonable take-off assistance rockets underwing. Options included eight 4.9-kN (1,102-lb) thrust rockets, six 7.35-kN (1,653-lb) rockets or four 9.8-kN (2,205-lb) units.

Accommodation
The Me 323D could carry 120 fully-equipped troops in its cavernous hold, or 60 stretcher patients with medical attendants. Two auxiliary fuel tanks, each containing 890 litres (196 Imp.gal), could be carried in the rear of the cargo hold, increasing range from 750 km (465 miles) with a 11566-kg (25,500-lb) load to 1000 km (620 miles) with a 9750-kg (21,500-lb) load. The Me 323's size made it a natural choice for a variety of outlandish schemes, including the carriage of an exerimental 17.7-tonne (19.5-ton) bomb.

Flying controls
The entire trailing edge of the wing was hinged, the two-section outer portions functioning differentially as ailerons and the two inner sections as flaps. The tail surfaces incorporated conventional rudder and elevators. All of the control surfaces, except the outboard ailerons, incorporated trim tabs. The entire tail unit, together with the portion of the fuselage to which it was attached, could be hinged to change incidence between -5° and +2.5°.

Concept
When originally conceived, the powered version of the Me 321 was to have had four engines only, giving assistance during a loaded, towed take-off, but allowing the empty aircraft to take off under its own power for the return journey. The adoption of six engines transformed it into a conventional self-launching transport.

Powerplant
The Me 323 was powered by six Gnome-Rhône 14-cylinder radial piston engines, each driving a three-bladed Chauvière variable-pitch airscrew. The Me 323 V1 was an Me 321 glider fitted with four 849-kW (1,140-hp) Gnome-Rhône 14N 48/49 engines, but the second prototype added a fifth and sixth engine. The Gnome-Rhônes were stripped from French Bloch 175 bombers being built on German instructions at Mérignac. The prototypes were followed by a pre-production batch of 10 similarly powered Me 323D-0s and a production series of Me 323D-1s. In February 1942 there was a proposal to switch to six 1192-kW (1,600-hp) BMW 801A engines, but this was not followed up. A change of powerplant finally occurred with the Me 323E-1, which introduced uprated 894-KW (1,200-hp) Gnome-Rhône 14Rs, while the Me 323E-2/U1 introduced liquid-cooled inline Jumo 211s, each rated at 998 kW (1,340 hp), and some were later re-engined with the 1006-kW (1,350-hp) Jumo 211R. This gave the Me 323E a top speed of about 252 km/h (157 mph) empty.

Structure
Retaining the basic structure of the Me 321B-1 glider, the powered Me 323 had a reinforced steel tube girder wing spar with N braces and wooden former ribs, with new extensions to carry the engines. The fuselage was a rectangular framework of welded steel over a secondary structure of wood, all covered by doped fabric. The cargo hold floor was supported by substantial cross-girders and was stressed for loads of up to 20000 kg (44,090 lb).

An Me 323D-1 wears the fuselage codes of 5./TG 5 while operating on the Eastern Front, during the winter of 1943-44. Nicknamed the 'Elastoplast bomber', the Gigant could absorb a fair degree of punishment to the fabric-covered airframe, although the defensive armament was wholly inadequate for such a large, lumbering transport. The fixed nose armament and the twin dorsal turrets could be supplemented by six MG 34s fired from the fore and aft fuselage windows.

Flying in support of Afrika Korps and Luftwaffe operations in the Mediterranean theatre and North Africa, this Me 323D-2 served with KGzbV 323. Operating from Trapani and Castelvetrano, the Me 323s carried ammunition, fuel and other equipment, and flew out German casualties and empty fuel drums. Note the extra MG 131 armament in the lower nose loading doors.

With the German defeat in North Africa, nearly all Messerschmitt Me 323s were assigned to the Eastern Front, where they were heavily committed over a vast area. Much ingenuity was shown in creating servicing and engine-change platforms, one scheme having three truck-mounted rigs joined together under each wing. Production, however, faded from mid-1943 and, although Leipheim restarted building aircraft in early 1944, only 198 Me 323s of all types were built, the last appearing in April 1944. At this time, the whole programme had been transferred to the Zeppelin Luftschiffbau at Friedrichshafen, where the last variant to fly, the **Me 323 V16**, took to the air on about 11 December 1943. Powered by six Jumo 211Rs, it was intended to lead to the production **Me 323F**. The planned **Me 323G**, with six 984-kW (1,320-hp) GR14R engines, was halted when the **Me 323 V17** prototype was incomplete.

There were many planned developments, including an extraordinary proposal for a twinned Me 323 joined by a new centre-section and with nine BMW 801 engines. Unconnected with development of the aircraft itself was the brief project at Karlshagen armament establishment, which had a bomb weighing 17700 kg (39,022 lb). The Me 323 appeared to be the only aircraft able to carry it, and a single test flight was made in July 1944. How the bomb was carried is not recorded, but the Gigant (which is thought to have been damaged in a strafing attack beforehand) broke up in the air.

A staff command vehicle (an 8-tonne/8.8-ton load) is unloaded from an Me 323D-1 in Tunisia in late 1942. The Gigants did their first intensive sustained work in ferrying men and materiel to Tunisia, and KGzbV 323 (later redesignated TG 5) suffered severely at the hands of Allied fighters and medium bombers.

Messerschmitt Me 410

In February 1944, a *Staffel* of the Luftwaffe's II/KG 51, command-ed by Major Puttfarken, began flying intruder missions over England. Missions over the enemy country by long-range bomb-carrying night fighters had been almost unheard-of for more than a year. The aircraft used for the resumption was the **Messerschmitt Me 410**, and it was clear by this time that it was an outstanding air-craft: fast, heavily armed and a really formidable fighting machine. Puttfarken himself achieved five kills before he was shot down near Canterbury on 23 April.

All this was a great relief to Professor Dr Ing Willy Messerschmitt, because to everyone's surprise the development programme for this aircraft could hardly have been a greater disaster. This shattered the previously sky-high reputation of Messerschmitt AG, and also was of great concern to the Luftwaffe.

Back in 1938 the Reichsluftfahrtministerium was wisely taking a long-term view and planning well ahead to make sure that all the Luftwaffe's future requirements would be met in good time. There was nothing wrong with Messerschmitt's Bf 110 twin-engined long-range fighter, but the Luftwaffe high command regarded this *Zerstörer* class of aircraft as so overwhelmingly important that Messerschmitt was requested to prepare plans for a Bf 110 successor. The company's proposal was accepted in the summer of 1938, and contracts were placed for prototypes of rival designs, the Me 210 and Arado Ar 240, but the Arado submission was regarded as a mere backup. Messerschmitt's reputation was so high that the **Me 210** contract included provisions for mass production of long-lead parts, such as wing spars and landing gears, and an option on the first 1,000 aircraft off the assembly line.

A damning report

Messerschmitt's famed test pilot Dr Ing Hermann Wurster made the maiden flight of the first prototype Me 210 on 5 September 1939, just after the start of World War II. He reported that handling in both the yawing and pitching planes was totally unacceptable, in fact dangerous. Seldom has a first-flight test report been so damning. This was a big setback, because the Augsburg-Haunstetten design team had tried to create a world-beating multi-role aircraft able to fly the 'all can do' *Kampfzerstörer* missions as originally considered by the air staff in Berlin in 1934. These missions included air fighting, ground attack, dive bombing and reconnaissance. Now, it seemed, the new prototype was unfit even to fly.

Though it naturally made the maximum use of experience with the successful Bf 110, the Me 210 introduced many totally new features. One was that the nose was deep but very short. In fact the tip of the nose was well behind the propeller spinners. The pilot was right at the

Above: The business end of an Me 410B-2/U2/R4 of ZG 1, whose **Wespen** *emblem is painted on the nose. This* **Zerstörergruppe** *was operating against USAAF day bombers by the summer of 1944, when this photograph was taken.*

Below: With its neatly cowled engines and purposeful nose contours, the Messerschmitt Me 210 certainly looked the part, but it was plagued by vicious and unpredictable handling problems during its development. To rectify the matter the fuselage was considerably lengthened, as demonstrated by this aircraft.

Messerschmitt Me 410

In Luftwaffe service the Me 210 proved up to the job, although its performance was less than sparkling. Its main problem by the time it entered service was its appalling reputation, which was also to dog the Me 410 soon after.

front, the forward-firing armament of two of the new Mauser MG 151/20 cannon and two 7.92-mm MG 17 machine-guns being under the floor, instead of in front of the instrument panel as in the Bf 110. Even more remarkable, under the cockpit floor was a substantial bomb bay, with two doors, able to accommodate two SC 500 bombs of 500 kg (1,102 lb) each. Above and below the outer wings were large Venetian blind airbrakes for steep dive bombing attacks. A totally new feature was the very advanced rear defensive armament. In the fuselage just aft of the wing was a large drum mounted transversely, rotated up or down by an electric motor. On this drum's left and right ends were mounted single 13-mm MG 131 guns, pivoted so that they could swing out to the 90° abeam position. Each of these heavy machine-guns had 450 rounds. The whole FDL 131 assembly was under the control of the observer, who faced aft and had an optical sight and remote aiming pistol-grips. These barbettes promised good firepower over the entire rear hemisphere with very little drag.

The Me 210 introduced several other new features. The tandem cockpits were covered by a multi-panel glazed Plexiglas canopy which wrapped round at the sides to give the back-seater some vision downwards, so that he could fire at any fighter trying to find a 'blind spot' at six o'clock below and to the rear. The big main landing wheels were mounted inboard of single straight legs which during the retraction sequence turned to stow the wheels flat in the shallow rear of the nacelles, as in the Ju 88. The pilot and observer had hinged canopies, but instead of the roof opening up on transverse hinges each complete canopy section hinged to the right. A structural detail was that in the Bf 109 and 110 the engines were hung on bearers forged in solid Elektron (magnesium alloy), but the bearers in the Me 210 were hollow box-sections welded from steel sheet. The engines were Daimler-Benz DB 601A-1s virtually identical to those fitted to the 1939 Bf 109 and 110, but the new fighter was expected to be faster than either.

New styling

Immediately after the first flight the prototype was rebuilt with a huge single-fin tail and new tapered tailplane. This resulted in only a small improvement, and throughout 1940 the increasing number of prototypes (suddenly reduced by the crash of the second on 5 September 1940) was exhaustively flown by company pilots and the Rechlin test centre. With production building up it was imperative to find complete solutions, but these proved elusive. By 1941 **Me 210A-0s** and **A-1s** were coming off the assembly lines at Augsburg and Regensburg and from the MIAG plant at Braunschweig, but eventually, after prolonged arguments, it was decided that the whole programme had to be terminated. Manufacture stopped at the three factories between January and March 1942. One of the results was the enforced resignation of Willy Messerschmitt.

Despite its new designation, the Me 410 was very similar to its predecessor. This is the Me 410 V1, which had previously been one of the Me 210A-0 pre-production aircraft. Principal differences were the adoption of the DB 603A engine and a revised wing planform.

1 Starboard navigation light
2 Starboard detachable wingtip
3 Main spar
4 Wing leading-edge slat
5 Aileron control rods
6 External balance (underwing)
7 Starboard aileron
8 Tab (ground-adjustable only)
9 Aileron trim tab
10 Trim tab control
11 Slatted airbrakes (above and below wing)
12 Wing centre/outer section join
13 Starboard underwing radiator
14 Boundary layer bleed
15 Radiator flap section
16 Radiator flap motor (in flap section)
17 Starboard oil filter
18 Cowling panelling
19 Starboard engine supercharger intake
20 Starboard nacelle
21 Exhaust stub cover
22 Oil cooler intake (adjustable flap)
23 Auxiliary intake
24 Coolant filter access
25 Spinner
26 Three-bladed constant-speed VDM propeller
27 Starboard mainwheel
28 Bomb-bay doors (open)
29 Two 7.9-mm MG 17 machine-gun ports
30 Two 20-mm MG 151 cannon ports
31 Cabin air intake
32 Cabin air heater
33 Nose glazing
34 Rudder pedals
35 Instrument panel side sections
36 Instrument panel lower section
37 Control column
38 Pilot's heelboards
39 MG 151 cannon blast tube
40 Bomb bay
41 Bomb winch cable hoist
42 Port instrument console
43 Throttle quadrant
44 Pilot's seat
45 Starboard instrument console (weapons/oxygen)
46 Revi C/12D weapons sight
47 Armoured windscreen
48 Hinged cockpit canopy section
49 Pilot's armoured head/backrest
50 Canopy internal bracing
51 Ammunition magazines (1,000 rounds 7.9-mm/350 rounds 20-mm)
52 Pilot's entry handhold
53 Ammunition feed chutes
54 Port weapons breeches
55 Mainspar centre-section carry-through
56 Observer's seat
57 Electrical main distribution panel
58 Beam armament master switch and ammunition counter
59 Sighting head for FDSL beam barbettes
60 Hinged cockpit canopy section
61 Aerial mast (angled to starboard)
62 D/F loop aerial housing
63 Optically flat side windows
64 Barbette elevation input shaft
65 Barbette traverse input shaft
66 Observer's entry handhold
67 EZ2 D/F receiver remote control unit
68 FuG 10 radio receiver
69 EZ2 D/F receiver
70 FuG 10 radio transmitter
71 Rear spar centre-section carry-through
72 Wingroot fairing
73 Barbette electrics junction box
74 Access panel/handhold
75 Barbette torque amplifier
76 Barbette ring gears
77 Barbette centre rotating drum
78 Ammunition around drum (500 rpg)
79 Port beam gun fairing
80 13-mm MG 131 beam gun
81 Aerial unit
82 Rear fuselage access panel
83 FuG 25 IFF transformer
84 FuG 25 transponder
85 Aerial lead-in
86 Master compass
87 Fuselage frames
88 Course control drive

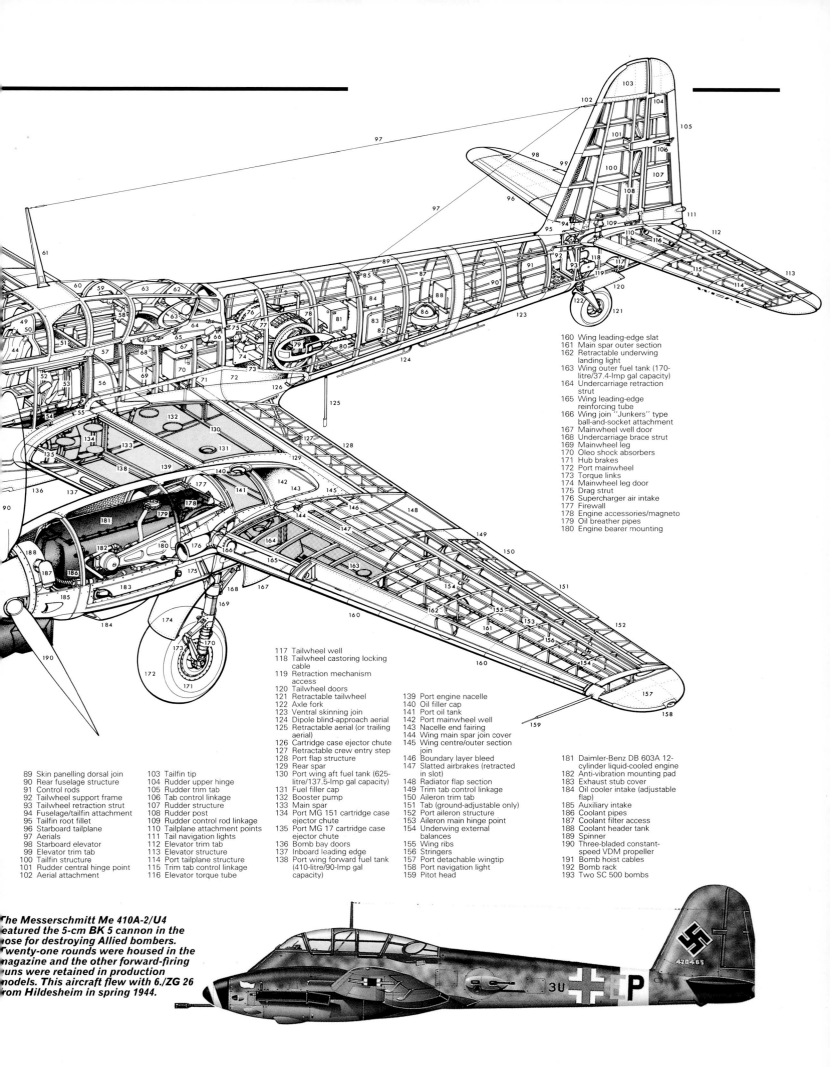

160 Wing leading-edge slat
161 Main spar outer section
162 Retractable underwing landing light
163 Wing outer fuel tank (170-litre/37.4-Imp gal capacity)
164 Undercarriage retraction strut
165 Wing leading-edge reinforcing tube
166 Wing join "Junkers" type ball-and-socket attachment
167 Mainwheel well door
168 Undercarriage brace strut
169 Mainwheel leg
170 Oleo shock absorbers
171 Hub brakes
172 Port mainwheel
173 Torque links
174 Mainwheel leg door
175 Drag strut
176 Supercharger air intake
177 Firewall
178 Engine accessories/magneto
179 Oil breather pipes
180 Engine bearer mounting

117 Tailwheel well
118 Tailwheel castoring locking cable
119 Retraction mechanism access
120 Tailwheel doors
121 Retractable tailwheel
122 Axle fork
123 Ventral skinning join
124 Dipole blind-approach aerial
125 Retractable aerial (or trailing aerial)
126 Cartridge case ejector chute
127 Retractable crew entry step
128 Port flap structure
129 Rear spar
130 Port wing aft fuel tank (625-litre/137.5-Imp gal capacity)
131 Fuel filler cap
132 Booster pump
133 Main spar
134 Port MG 151 cartridge case ejector chute
135 Port MG 17 cartridge case ejector chute
136 Bomb bay doors
137 Inboard leading edge
138 Port wing forward fuel tank (410-litre/90-Imp gal capacity)

139 Port engine nacelle
140 Oil filler cap
141 Port oil tank
142 Port mainwheel well
143 Nacelle end fairing
144 Wing main spar join cover
145 Wing centre/outer section join
146 Boundary layer bleed
147 Slatted airbrakes (retracted in slot)
148 Radiator flap section
149 Trim tab control linkage
150 Aileron trim tab
151 Tab (ground-adjustable only)
152 Port aileron structure
153 Aileron main hinge point
154 Underwing external balances
155 Wing ribs
156 Stringers
157 Port detachable wingtip
158 Port navigation light
159 Pitot head

89 Skin panelling dorsal join
90 Rear fuselage structure
91 Control rods
92 Tailwheel support frame
93 Tailwheel retraction strut
94 Fuselage/tailfin attachment
95 Tailfin root fillet
96 Starboard tailplane
97 Aerials
98 Starboard elevator
99 Elevator trim tab
100 Tailfin structure
101 Rudder central hinge point
102 Aerial attachment

103 Tailfin tip
104 Rudder upper hinge
105 Rudder trim tab
106 Tab control linkage
107 Rudder structure
108 Rudder post
109 Rudder control rod linkage
110 Tailplane attachment points
111 Tail navigation lights
112 Elevator trim tab
113 Elevator structure
114 Port tailplane structure
115 Trim tab control linkage
116 Elevator torque tube

181 Daimler-Benz DB 603A 12-cylinder liquid-cooled engine
182 Anti-vibration mounting pad
183 Exhaust stub cover
184 Oil cooler intake (adjustable flap)
185 Auxiliary intake
186 Coolant pipes
187 Coolant filter access
188 Coolant header tank
189 Spinner
190 Three-bladed constant-speed VDM propeller
191 Bomb hoist cables
192 Bomb rack
193 Two SC 500 bombs

The Messerschmitt Me 410A-2/U4 featured the 5-cm BK 5 cannon in the nose for destroying Allied bombers. Twenty-one rounds were housed in the magazine and the other forward-firing guns were retained in production models. This aircraft flew with 6./ZG 26 from Hildesheim in spring 1944.

Messerschmitt Me 410

Messerschmitt Me 410s served on Eastern, Mediterranean and Western fronts. This aircraft flew with I./SG 152 during the winter of 1943/44, when the unit was based at Deblin-Irena in Poland.

Testing continued at full pressure, and on 14 March 1942 an Me 210A-0 flew with a longer and deeper rear fuselage, slatted outer wings and various other changes. It proved a great improvement. Work accordingly was rushed ahead on a new aircraft embodying these changes, as well as revised outer wings with straight taper instead of 5° sweepback, and much more powerful DB 603 engines. To avoid the stigma attached to the number 210 this new aircraft was designated the **Me 410**.

Return to the Me 210

While this work went ahead, many modifications were made to the dozens of Me 210s that were available. Existing A-1 and **A-2** aircraft were fitted with the new rear fuselage and slats and issued to 16./KG 6 and later to III/ZG 1, the latter unit also receiving many A-1s and A-2s which Messerschmitt received permission to complete in late 1942. These saw action in Sicily, Tunisia and Sardinia. Following tests with an A-0 fitted with DB 605B engines, the Me 210C was put into production at Duna (Danube) aircraft works for both the Luftwaffe and Hungarian air force, using DB 605B engines made by Manfred Weiss. Meanwhile there were schemes to replace the MG 131 barbettes, which were troublesome, one featuring twin 20-mm MG 151 cannon fixed to fire to the rear and aimed by the pilot via a tall aft-facing periscopic sight. A few **Me 210B** reconnaissance aircraft were built, and Blohm und Voss fitted seven A-1s as tandem dual trainers (the back-seater, of course, facing forward).

In Hungarian service the **Me 210C-1** and **Ca-1** did well and were very popular. The Duna works delivered 267 aircraft before switching to the Bf 109G in March 1944, and the Hungarians used the speedy twin intensively on the Eastern Front.

Obviously the faults had been cured, and when the first Me 410 began flight testing in autumn 1942 it was the basis for an extremely useful aircraft. The new fuselage and new wing completely cured the previously terrible handling and tendency to flick into a spin, and the 1380-kW (1,850-hp) DB 603A engines resulted in outstanding performance. With the MG 131 barbettes now working well the Me 410A-1 *Schnellbomber* and Me 410A-2 *Zerstörer* began to come off the assembly lines in December 1942, and while production built up the Messerschmitt company and Luftwaffe armament and equipment centres developed a remarkable variety of schemes for different armament and mission equipment.

The basic models in production from January 1943 until September 1944 comprised the **Me 410A** series with DB 603A engines and the **Me 410B** with 1417-kW (1,900-hp) DB 603Gs and other minor

changes. The standard armament was the same as for the Me 210A series: two MG 151/20 and two MG 17 firing forward and the MG 131 barbettes at the rear. Aircraft with suffix /U1 had the MG 17s removed and a single vertical reconnaissance camera installed in the rear fuselage. Those designated /U2 were equipped for the *Zerstörer* role with two MG 151/20 cannon in the bomb bay, firing ahead. The /U2/R2 versions had the bomb bay fitted with two 30-mm MK 103 or MK 108 guns, the lower Plexiglas pane in the nose being replaced by a metal plate. The /U2/R5 conversion – like the others intended mainly for shooting down heavy bombers by day – installed four MG 151s in the bomb bay, giving six 20-mm cannon firing ahead. Equally heavy armament was provided by the /U2/R4, which added the two MG 151s in the bomb bay, in a *Waffenbehälter*, followed by two further MG 151s underneath in a *Waffentropfen*. The /U4 conversion fitted a single BK 5 50-mm gun. The first conversions had no other forward-firing armament. Newly built **A-2/U4**s followed with the BK 5 plus the twin MG 151s and twin MG 17s, and a further 100 field conversion kits were supplied comprising the BK 5 plus two 30-mm MK 103 and the associated ZFR 4a gunsight, the resulting designation again being **B-2/U4**. The rare **Me 410B-6** had the twin MK 103s in the bomb bay and two MG 131s in place of the MG 17s. Another rarity was the **B-5** torpedo bomber, which carried any of a variety of torpedoes slung under the left side of the fuselage. Forward-firing armament was reduced to just the two MG 151s, and most of these aircraft were fitted with FuG 200 Hohentwiel search radar. As well as the special Friedensengel gliding torpedo, B-5s tested the SB 800RS Kurt 800-kg (1,765-lb) rolling bomb for use against surface ships, and the SB 1000/410 blast weapon specially designed for external carriage by the B-5, with an elliptical low-drag cross-section and small drag chute to stabilise its fall. I/ZG 1 used the B-6 variant, which had twin MG 151/20s, twin MG 131s and two MK 103s plus Hohentwiel radar. They operated in the anti-ship role before being thrust into the anti-bomber battle, the radar then usually being removed.

Defence of the Reich

By mid-1944 almost all surviving Me 410s were engaged in the defence of the Reich against day bombers. With their speed and firepower they brought down many bombers, but overall the scoring rate was probably about even because the big twins were easy meat for escorting P-51s and P-47s. More fortunate were the **Me 410A-3** and **B-3** reconnaissance versions, which from December 1943 were built in numbers and, except over England, were fast enough to do much good work with modest attrition. Unlike the inadequate **A-1/U1** they

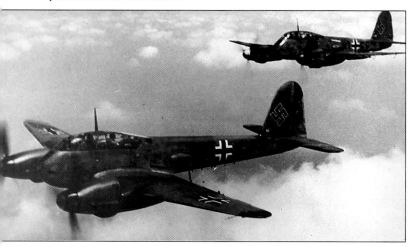

Test flights with the elongated fuselage revealed the Me 210 to be an adequate warplane, and the few that had been built were modified and cleared for service. Here a pre-production Me 210A-0 (background) formates on an Me 210A-1.

The lengthening of the fuselage and fitment of automatic wing slots mostly cured the instability problem, allowing some Me 210As to see action with the Luftwaffe. These aircraft are of III./ZG 1, seen operating in Tunisia during March/April 1943.

'Yellow 5' was an Me 410 serving with II/ZG76 in east Prussia during the autumn of 1944. The unit flew at the time from Seerappen.

had a properly designed installation of two Rb 20/30, 50/30 or 75/30 cameras in the deepened underside of the nose in what in other versions was the bomb or heavy gun bay.

The Me 410 had by 1944 fully established a good reputation in the Luftwaffe, and because of the wide publicity given to II/ZG 26 as the Hornissengeschwader, it became unofficially known as the Hornisse (Hornet). Many were used for special test and trials programmes. At least one tested the experimental rapid-fire 210-mm rocket launcher. Many Luftwaffe fighters had used the 210-mm rocket using clumsy Wfr.Gr.21 mortar tubes under the wings. The auto launcher was a big drum mounted inside the Me 410 weapon bay, tilted up at the usual angle and with the 'six o'clock' tube exposed underneath the aircraft. On lining up on a bomber the pilot could blast off all six rockets from the drum in less than two seconds. Initial trials seriously damaged the Me 410, but after much effort the system was made to work and it was subjected to combat trials in several Me 410Bs, though the results appear to have been lost.

Swan song

By early 1944 the Messerschmitt design team was busy with a stretched version, the **Me 410C**. This was intended to have much higher performance at high altitudes, even though it was intended to carry heavier loads of weapons and, in some versions, night interception radar. Two new wings were designed, with span increased to 18.25 m

Above: Festooned with nose-mounted antennas for the FuG 200 Hohentwiel radar, this former I/ZG 1 Me 410B-6 was used in the anti-shipping role, operating from Lorient, before the unit was withdrawn to Germany for air defence duties. Spiral painted spinners were a regular feature of the Me 410.

After some initial reservations regarding the aircraft's past, the Me 410 was found to be a potent warplane by Luftwaffe pilots, and achieved considerable success as a day-fighter against bomber formations. Against Allied fighters, however, it was cut to pieces.

(60 ft) or 20.45 m (67 ft). More powerful engines fitted with turbo-superchargers were to be used, either the DB603JZ, Jumo 213E/JZ or BMW 801TJ. All were to drive propellers with four very broad blades, and the Daimler-Benz engine was to have annular nose radiators replacing the usual ones under the rear part of the wings. At least two Me 410s tested the annular-cowled engines and the 410C's proposed revised forward fuselage and new main landing gears with twin wheels retracting straight to the rear without a 90° twist. Such were the problems afflicting the industry that before any 410C could be completed the programme was abandoned. In its place came the **Me 410D**, with the new twin-wheel gears, annular-cowled 603JZ engines and revised forward fuselage (which was expected to give better pilot view and lower drag). A further feature was outer wing panels which, though similar aerodynamically to those previously in production, were made of wood to conserve strategic materials.

Even this achieved nothing. Other wood programmes were in severe difficulty with adhesives and structural failures, and in summer 1944 the 410D was itself replaced by an interim **Me 410H** with no major change from the 410B-2 except the addition of extra untapered wing panels between the engines and the outer wings. These would have extended span to 23 m (75 ft), but the first conversion was never completed.

Below: This example of an Me 410A-3 was captured by US forces and evaluated after the end of the war. The 'F6' code signified its previous use by 2.(Fernaufklärungs)/122, which operated from Sardinia and other bases in the Mediterranean region. Reconnaissance was to be the last role for the Messerschmitt Me 410.

Specification
Messerschmitt Me 410A-1/U2
Type: two-seat heavy fighter (*Zerstörer*)
Powerplant: two Daimler Benz DB 603A inverted V-12 engines, each rated at 1305.5 kW (1,750 hp) for take-off, and 1380 kW (1,850 hp) at 2100 m (6,890 ft)
Performance: maximum speed 507 km/h (315 mph) at sea level, 624 km/h (388 mph) at 6700 m (21,980 ft) and 600 km/h (373 mph) at 8000 m (26,250 ft); maximum cruising speed 587 km/h (365 mph); range at maximum cruising speed 1200 km (746 miles); range at economical cruise 1690 km (1,050 miles)
Weights: empty equipped 7518 kg (16,574 lb); loaded 9651 kg (21,276 lb)
Dimensions: wing span 16.35 m (53 ft 7 in); length 12.48 m (40 ft 11 in); height 4.28 m (14 ft 0 in); wing area 36.20 m² (389.687 sq ft)
Armament: two 20-mm MG 151 cannon with 350 r.p.g. and four 7.9-mm (0.31-in) MG 17 machine-guns with 1,000 r.p.g. in lower fuselage firing forwards; two 13-mm (0.51-in) MG 131 machine-guns with 500 r.p.g. in remotely-controlled FDSL barbettes

Powerplant

While production Me 210s had been powered by a pair of 1005-kW (1,350-hp) DB 601F inverted V-12 inline engines, the Me 410A introduced the more powerful 1300-kW (1,750-hp) DB 603A, a more mature powerplant of the same configuration. The Me 410B had the DB603G, whose higher speed supercharger and increased compression ratio raised output to 1415 kW (1,900 hp). Most of the Me 210s problems had been solved by the time production was terminated, and the Me 410 was much more successful, since it was basically an up-engined derivative of the Me 210 with all necessary modifications incorporated.

Messerschmitt Me 410A-2/U2
9./Zerstörergeschwader 1
Germany, 1944

Although never rivalling the de Havilland Mosquito in terms of versatility or performance, the Me 410 did however introduce a welcome increase in performance over the Messerschmitt Bf 110 that had previously equipped the *Zerstörergeschwader*. ZG 1 was transferred back to Germany from the Mediterranean during 1943, adopting an air defence role. It is unclear whether the white fuselage band was a Defence of the Reich marking or merely the Mediterranean theatre band. III/ZG 1 became II/ZG 26, retaining Me 410s after other units withdrawn for air defence duties had converted to the Bf 110G-2. The aircraft was unofficially dubbed Hornisse.

Bomb bay
The bomb bay was mounted under the nose and forward cockpit. Able to take two bombs of up to 500-kg (1,102-lb) size, these were attached to a lowered rack which was then hoisted back into the bomb bay.

Iain Wyllie

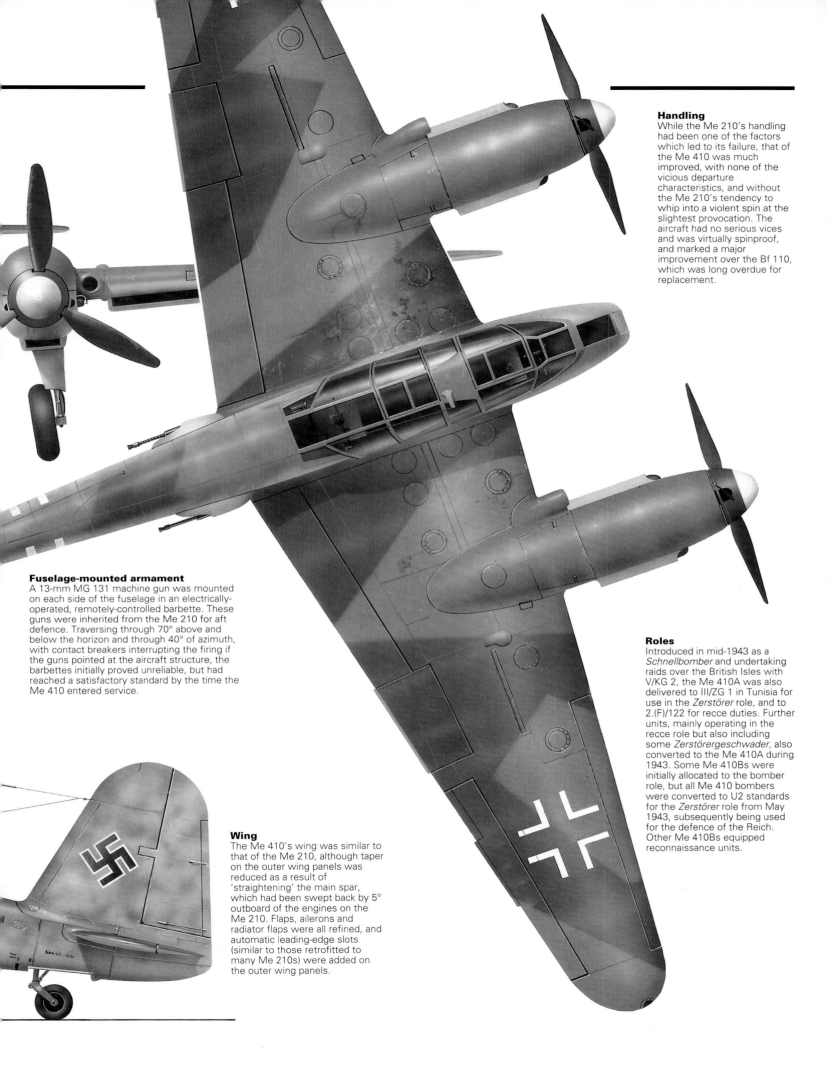

Handling
While the Me 210's handling had been one of the factors which led to its failure, that of the Me 410 was much improved, with none of the vicious departure characteristics, and without the Me 210's tendency to whip into a violent spin at the slightest provocation. The aircraft had no serious vices and was virtually spinproof, and marked a major improvement over the Bf 110, which was long overdue for replacement.

Fuselage-mounted armament
A 13-mm MG 131 machine gun was mounted on each side of the fuselage in an electrically-operated, remotely-controlled barbette. These guns were inherited from the Me 210 for aft defence. Traversing through 70° above and below the horizon and through 40° of azimuth, with contact breakers interrupting the firing if the guns pointed at the aircraft structure, the barbettes initially proved unreliable, but had reached a satisfactory standard by the time the Me 410 entered service.

Roles
Introduced in mid-1943 as a *Schnellbomber* and undertaking raids over the British Isles with V/KG 2, the Me 410A was also delivered to III/ZG 1 in Tunisia for use in the *Zerstörer* role, and to 2.(F)/122 for recce duties. Further units, mainly operating in the recce role but also including some *Zerstörergeschwader*, also converted to the Me 410A during 1943. Some Me 410Bs were initially allocated to the bomber role, but all Me 410 bombers were converted to U2 standards for the *Zerstörer* role from May 1943, subsequently being used for the defence of the Reich. Other Me 410Bs equipped reconnaissance units.

Wing
The Me 410's wing was similar to that of the Me 210, although taper on the outer wing panels was reduced as a result of 'straightening' the main spar, which had been swept back by 5° outboard of the engines on the Me 210. Flaps, ailerons and radiator flaps were all refined, and automatic leading-edge slots (similar to those retrofitted to many Me 210s) were added on the outer wing panels.

INDEX

Page numbers in **bold** refer to an illustration

40 (see DFS)
139 (see Martin)
175 (see Bloch)
194 (see DFS)
230 (see DFS)
1145-L (see CASA)
1402 Noroit (see Nord)

A

A-10 Thunderbolt II (see Fairchild)
A 20 (see Junkers)
AAC 1 Toucan (see Ateliers Aéronautiques de Colombes)
Aerocentre
  NC 270: 135
Ago
  Ao 225: 23
Aist, OKA-38 (see Antonov)
ANT-20 (see Tupolev)
Antonov
  OKA-38 Aist: 56, 60
Ao 225 (see Ago)
Anson (see Avro)
Ar 67 et seq (see Arado)
Arado
  Ar 67: 6
  Ar 68: 6, **6**, 198
  Ar 76: 62
  Ar 80: 197
  Ar 95: 6, **6**
  Ar 195: 6, 60
  Ar 196: 7-14, **7-14**, 107
  Ar 198: 63, 64, 69
  Ar 232: 15, **15**
  Ar 234 Blitz: 15-22, **15-22**, 176, 187
  Ar 240: 23, **23**, 245
  Ar 440: 23
Armstrong Whitworth
  Whitley: 98, 217
Ateliers Aéronautiques de Colombes
  AAC 1 Toucan: 152
Avro
  Anson: 62
  Lancaster: 28

B

B-17 Flying Fortress (see Boeing)
B-24 Liberator (see Consolidated)
B-26 Marauder (see Martin)
Ba 349 Natter (see Bachem)
Baby (see Porte)
Bachem
  Ba 349 Natter: 23, **23**, 54
Beaufighter (see Bristol)
Bellanca
  O-50: 55
Bf 108 (et seq) Taifun (see Messerschmitt)
Blackburn
  Skua: 163
Blenheim (see Bristol)
Blitz, Ar 234 (see Arado)
Bloch
  175: 242, 243
Blohm und Voss
  BV 138: 13, 14, 24, **24**, 25, **25**, 28, 34, 36, 110
  BV 141: 26, **26**, 27, **27**, 63, 64, 69
  BV 142: 27, **27**
  BV 222 Wiking: 28, **28**
  BV 238: 28, 29, **29**
  BV 250: 28, 29
  Ha 139: 26, **26**, 27
Boeing
  B-17 Flying Fortress: 74, 102, 107, 216, 223, 224, 228

YB-40: 240
Boulton Paul
  Defiant: 200
Bristol
  Beaufighter: 28, 92, 221
  Blenheim: 24, 32, 200
  Scout: 176
BV 138 et seq (see Blohm und Voss)

C

C-130 Hercules (see Lockheed)
C-352-L (see CASA)
Cap, K.65 (see Mraz)
CASA
  1145-L: 93
  C-352-L: 152
Catalina (see Consolidated)
Condor, Fw 200 (see Focke-Wulf)
Consolidated
  B-24 Liberator: 74, 188, 216
  Catalina: 10, 24
Criquet, M.S.502 (see Morane-Saulnier)
Curtiss
  Kittyhawk: 199, 200
  P-40 Warhawk: 203

D

D.520 (see Dewoitine)
DC-3 (see Douglas)
Defiant (see Boulton Paul)
de Havilland
  Mosquito: 15, 92, 128-130, 132-134, 220, 221, 236, 250
Dewoitine
  D.520: 212
DFS
  40: 227
  194: 222, 223, 225, 227
  230: 29, **29**, 33, 62, 94, 139, 151, 208
Do 15 et seq (see Dornier)
Dornier
  Do 15 Wal: 34, 36
  Do 17: 30-34, **30-33**, 38, **39**, 40, 43, 55, 86, 100, 104, 150, 171
  Do 18: 34-37, **34**, **35**, 97
  Do 19: 120
  Do 24: 36, **36**, 37, **37**, 97
  Do 24TT: 37
  Do 26: 38, **38**
  Do 215: 32, 33, **33**, 38, 40
  Do 217: 38-45, **38-45**, 104, 109, 129, 220
  Do 317: 41, 43, **43**, 180
  Do 318: 37
  Do 335 Pfeil: 46-53, **46-53**
  Militär-Wal 33: 34
Douglas
  DC-3: 85, 238
Drache, Fa 223 (see Focke-Achgelis)
Dragonfly, YO-51 (see Ryan)

E

E.28/39 (see Gloster)

F

F 13 (see Junkers)
F-16 Fighting Falcon (see General Dynamics)
F 24 (see Junkers)
F-86 Sabre (see North American)
Fa 61 et seq (see Focke-Achgelis)
Fairchild
  A-10 Thunderbolt II: 140
Fairey
  Swordfish: 10, 72
Falke, Fw 187 (see Focke-Wulf)
Fi 97 et seq (see Fieseler)
Fieseler
  Fi 97: 59

Fi 98: 136
Fi 103: 22, 54, **54**, 102, 105, 106
Fi 156 Storch: 54-60, **54- 60**
Fi 167: 60, **60**
Fi 256: 60
Fighting Falcon, F-16 (see General Dynamics)
Fl 265 et seq (see Flettner)
Flettner
  Fl 265: 61
  Fl 282 Kolibri: 61, **61**
Flying Fortress, B-17 (see Boeing)
Focke-Achgelis
  Fa 61: 61
  Fa 223 Drache: 56, 61, **61**
  Fa 225: 29
  Fa 266 Hornisse: 61
Focke-Wulf
  Fw 56 Stösser: 62, **62**
  Fw 58 Weihe: 62, **62**
  Fw 62: 6, 7
  Fw 159: 197
  Fw 186: 54
  Fw 187 Falke: 63, **63**
  Fw 189 Uhu: 26, 56, 63-70, **63-70**, 138, 140
  Fw 190: 15, 56, 59, 65, 69, 71-84, **71-83**, 93, 116, 165, 166, 168, 174, 177, **187**, 202, 208, 236
  Fw 191: 180
  Fw 200 Condor: 85-92, **85- 92**, 150, 191
  Ta 152: 80, 81, **81**, 83, 84, **84**, 177
  Ta 153: 80, 81, 84
  Ta 154 Moskito: 93, **93**, 115, 128
  Ta 254: 93
Fw 56 et seq (see Focke-Wulf)

G

G 23 (see Junkers)
G 24 (see Junkers)
G 31 (see Junkers)
G 38 (see Junkers)
General Dynamics
  F-16 Fighting Falcon: 128
Germany
  Kriegsmarine: 7, 10, 61, 97, 99
  Luftwaffe
    Aufklärungsführer Schwarzes Meer West: 14
    Aufklärungsgruppe
      (H)/14: 69, 139
      (F)/122: 30
      123: 157
      Oberbefehlshaber der Luftwaffe: 23, 38, 147, 156, 157, 229
    Aufklärungsstaffel
      (H)/31: 67, 95, 138
      (H)/32: 64, 65
      Oberbefehlshaber der Luftwaffe: 27, 33
      Oberost: 95
      See 222: 28
    Bordfliegergruppe 196: 8-11, 14
    Einsatzkommando
      Braunegg: 236, 237
      Schenk: 236, 237
      Ergänzungsjagdgeschwader 2: 230, 231, 232
    Ergänzungs-Transportgruppe: 15
    Erprobungskommando
      EKdo 16: 223, 224
      EKdo 25: 75
      EKdo 26: 143
      EKdo 162: 116, 118
      EKdo 188: 181
      EKdo 210: 213
      EKdo 262: 230, 236
      EKdo 335: 48, 50, 52
      EKdo Bonow: 22
      EKdo TA 152: 84
    Erprobungsstelle Rechlin: 26, 71, 98

Fallschirmjäger: 150, 155
Fernaufklärungsgruppe
  FAGr 5: 189-192, 194
  FAGr 122: 207, 249, 251
  FAGr 124: 180, 185
Fernkampfgruppe 2: 125
Fliegerführer Afrika: 219
Fliegergruppe Schwerin: 96
Fliegerkorps
  II: 213, 216
  IV: 163
  VII: 170
  VIII: 70, 212, 216
  X: 27, 170, 212
Grossraum-Lastenseglergruppe
  Me 321: 107
Grossraum-Transportgruppe: 195
Heeresaufklärungsstaffeln: 138
Jagddivision 30: 75
Jagdgeschwader
  JG 1: 72, 74, 76, 113-116, 118, 208
  JG 2: 6, 71, 72, 74, 83, 116, 130, 198, 199, 202, 203, 217
  JG 3: 75, 116, 201, 202, 206
  JG 4: 77
  JG 5: 23, 72, 74, 207
  JG 6: 83
  JG 7: 234, 237
  JG 20: 198
  JG 21: 198
  JG 26: 71, 72, 74, 83, 199, 202, 208
  JG 27: 196, 199, 200, 203, 207
  JG 51: 72, 74, 198, 202, 207
  JG 52: 6, 199, 200, 208
  JG 53: 6, 202, 208
  JG 54: 72, 74, 80, 83, 200, 202, 203, 206, 236
  JG 77: 63, 198, 203
  JG 101: 207
  JG 102: 207
  JG 104: 83, 207
  JG 106: 207
  JG 107: 207
  JG 108: 207
  JG 134: 6
  JG 300: 78, 208
  JG 301: 81, 84
  JG 400: 224, 226, 228
Jagdkorps I: 234
Jagdverband: 198
Jagdverband 44: 113, 118, 237
Kampfgeschwader
  KG 1: 99, 125, 156, 170, 177, 211
  KG 2: 30, 31, 33, 39-41, 185, 251
  KG 3: 30-33, 102, 106
  KG 4: 99, 100, 104, 106, 107, 125, 127, 170
  KG 6: 157, 181, 185, 187, 248
  KG 25: 172
  KG 26: 99, 100, 104, 185
  KG 27: 99, 102, 105-107
  KG 30: 113, 114, 118, 168, 170-172
  KG 40: 38, 39, 41, 86-89, 91, 92, 104, 105, 120-122, 124, 126, 127, 170, 188, 190,192
  KG 50: 125, 127
  KG 51: 170, 232, 233, 236, 237, 245
  KG 53: 31, 33, 99, 102, 106, 107
  KG 54: 100, 170, 171
  KG 55: 99-102, 105, 107
  KG 66: 39, 175, 185
  KG 76: 19, 31, 172
  KG 77: 171
  KG 100: 38, 39, 41-43, 105, 107, 124-127
  KG 152: 98, 99, 150, 156
  KG 154: 98
  KG 155: 98
  KG 157: 98, 99
  KG 200: 15, 39, 54, 75, 95, 185, 188, 190-192, 195
  KG 253: 98
  KG 257: 98
  KG 355: 98
  KG(J) 6: 236, 237
  KG(J) 27: 237

KG(J) 54: 237
KG(J) 55: 237
Kampfgeschwader zur besonderen
    Verwendung
  KGzbV 1: 150
  KGzbV 102: 151
  KGzbV 108 See: 24, 36, 97
  KGzbV 323: 239, 240, 244
Kampfgruppe
  KGr 88: 98, 99, 150
  KGr 100: 100, 101, 104
  KGr 806: 99
Kampfgruppe zur
    besonderen Verwendung
  KGrzbV 1: 150, 152, 155
  KGrzbV 2: 150
  KGrzbV 5: 105
  KGrzbV 20: 105
  KGrzbV 21: 157
  KGrzbV 22: 157
  KGrzbV 101: 150
  KGrzbV 102: 150
  KGrzbV 103: 150
  KGrzbV 104: 95, 150
  KGrzbV 105: 27, 86, 150
  KGrzbV 106: 95, 150
  KGrzbV 107: 150
  KGrzbV 108 See: 26
  KGrzbV 172: 152
  KGrzbV 200: 89, 92
Kommando
  Nowotny: 236, 237
  Schenck: 232
Kurierstaffel
  Oberkommando der Luftwaffe: 57
Küstenfliegergruppe
  KüFlGr 106: 35, 109, 110, 112
  KüFlGr 406: 24-26, 28, 35, 38, 110-
    112
  KüFlGr 506: 24, 35, 38, 107, 110
  KüFlGr 606: 110
  KüFlGr 706: 10, 110
  KüFlGr 906: 24, 35, 110, 112
Légion Condor: 6, 30, 55, 96, 98, 99,
    138, 150, 160, 162, 197, 198
Lehrgeschwader
  LG 1: 99, 156, 166, 168- 171, 211,
    212
  LG 2: 57, 72, 136, 137, 141, 199, 203,
    204
Luftflotte
  Nr 2: 43, 212
  Nr 3: 27, 102
  Nr 4: 64, 65, 239
  Reich: 219, 220
Luftlandegeschwader 1: 33, 139
Lufttransportchef II: 239
Lufttransportstaffel
  LTS 40: 61
  LTS 290: 188-190, 192
  LTS See 222: 28
Luftwaffe Kommando Don: 67
Luftwaffenkommando Südost: 13
Minensuchgruppe 1: 25, 37, 151-153
Nachtjagdgeschwader
  NJG 1: 129, 132, 134, 217, 218, 221
  NJG 2: 33, 179, 217
  NJG 3: 93, 174, 212, 221
  NJG 4: 219, 221
  NJG 5: 70, 220, 221
  NJG 6: 172, 216, 221
  NJG 10: 76
  NJG 11: 230, 237
  NJG 77: 201
  NJG 100: 40, 70
  NJG 101: 175
Nachtjagdgruppe 10: 130
Nachtschlachtgruppe
  NSGr 7: 95
  NSGr 11: 96
  NSGr 12: 139
Nahaufklärungsgruppe
  NAGr 1: 66, 236
  NAGr 6: 236
  NAGr 13: 71, 72, 206
  NAGr 15: 70

Oberbefehlshaber der Luftwaffe: 128
Oberkommando der Luftwaffe: 65
Ost-Flieger Gruppe: 93
Schlachtfliegergruppe 10: 136
Schlachtgeschwader
  SG 1: 72, 74, 75, 136, 137, 142, 165,
    206
  SG 2: 72, 73, 75, 137, 141, 142, 165
  SG 3: 164, 165
  SG 4: 77
  SG 9: 141, 143, 146, 164
  SG 77: 165
  SG 152: 248
Schleppgruppe 1: 107
Schleppgruppe 4: 104
Schnellkampfgeschwader
  SKG 10: 72, 74
  SKG 210: 206, 212, 213, 216
Seeaufklärungsgruppe
  SAGr 125: 6, 13, 14, 24, 25, 97, 107
  SAGr 126: 13, 14, 25, 97
  SAGr 127: 6, 97
  SAGr 128: 7, 14
  SAGr 129: 25, 28
  SAGr 130: 24, 25
  SAGr 131: 14, 24, 25
Seenotbereichskommando
  SBK III: 36
  SBK XI: 37
  SBK XII: 37
Seenotzentrale Ägaisches Meer: 97
Sonderkommando
  SdKdo Gotz: 19
  SdKdo Hecht: 19
  SdKdo Sommer: 19
  SdKdo Sperling: 19, 22
Stukageschwader
  StG 1: 159, 160, 162, 166
  StG 2: 162-164, 166
  StG 3: 161
  StG 51: 160, 166
  StG 77: 159, 162
  StG 162: 93, 136
  StG 163: 160, 162
Stürmkampfstaffeln: 93, 95
Transportfliegerstaffel: 15, 189
Transport Gruppe
  TGr 1: 153
  TGr 4: 15
  TGr 5: 239, 243, 244
  TGr 30: 107
Versuchskommando fur
    Panzerbekampfung:
    163
Versuchsstelle für Höhenfluge: 157
Versuchsverband
  Oberbefehlshaber der Luftwaffe: 19, 48,
    157, 195
Wustenotstaffeln: 56
Zerstörergeschwader
  ZG 1: 171, 198, 202, 211-213, 215,
    245, 248- 251
  ZG 2: 213
  ZG 6: 216
  ZG 26: 210, 212-214, 216, 218-220,
    236, 247, 249, 250
  ZG 52: 211, 213
  ZG 76: 211-213, 216, 217, 249
Reichsluftfahrtministerium
  (RLM): 7, 23, 26, 32, 38, 39, 46, 47,
    54, 60-63, 76, 81, 84, 86, 93,
    94, 115, 116, 128-130, 132,
    135, 147, 168, 180, 195, 197,
    210, 222, 227, 230
Gigant (see Messerschmitt Me 321 & Me
    323)
Gloster
  E.28/39: 230
Go 145 et seq (see Gotha)
Göppingen
  Gö 9: 46, **47**
Gotha
  Go 145: 93, **93**
  Go 229: 94, **94**
  Go 242: 33, 94, **94**, 95, 106, 151
  Go 244: 94, 95, **95**

Grasshopper, L-4 (see Piper)
Greif, He 177 (see Heinkel)
Grumman
  Martlet: 92
  Wildcat: 92

H

Ha 138 (see Hamburger Flugzeugbau &
    Blohm und Voss BV 138)
Ha 139 (see Blohm und Voss)
Ha 140 (see Hamburger Flugzeugbau)
HA 1110-K1L (see Hispano)
HA 1112-K1L (see Hispano)
Hamburger Flugzeugbau
  Ha 138: 24
  Ha 140: 108
  P.15: 26
Handley Page
  Victor: 22
HAS 1109-J1L (see Hispano)
Hawker
  Henley: 163
  Hurricane: 38, 71, 92, 140, 197, 199,
    200, 203, 213
  Sea Hurricane: 24
  Tempest: 229
  Typhoon: 71, 72, 74
He 45 et seq (see Heinkel)
Heinkel
  He 45: 29, 138
  He 46: 29, 63, 69, 95, **95**, 138
  He 49: 96
  He 50: 96, **96**
  He 51: 96, **96**, 150, 197
  He 59: 36, 37, 97, **97**
  He 60: 7, 9, 13, 97, **97**, 107
  He 66: 96
  He 70: 98, 108
  He 100: 98, **98**
  He 111: 23, 32, 33, 41, 54, 94, 98-107,
    98-106, 110, 129, 135, 150,
    156, 163, 170, 171, 211
  He 111Z: 105, 106, **107**, 239
  He 112: 98, 196, 197, 227
  He 114: 7, 107, **107**
  He 115: 108-112, **108-112**
  He 119: 120
  He 162 Salamander: 113- 119,
    113-119
  He 176: 222, 227
  He 177 Greif: 40, 85, 86, 104, 120-127,
    120-127, 135, 188
  He 178: 135
  He 219 Uhu: 93, 114, 128- 134, **128-
    134**
  He 274: 135, **135**
  He 277: 125, 135, **135**
  He 280: 135, **135**, 230, 231
Henley (see Hawker)
Henschel
  Hs 122: 138
  Hs 123: 96, 136, **136**, 137, **137**, 142,
    159
  Hs 126: 23, 63, 65, 66, 69, 95, 138,
    138, 139, **139**
  Hs 127: 168
  Hs 128: 147
  Hs 129: 70, 140-147, **140-147**, 166
  Hs 130: 147, **147**
Hercules, C-130 (see
    Lockheed)
Herkules (see Junkers Ju 352)
Hispano
  HA 1110-K1L: 209
  HA 1112-K1L: 209
  HAS 1109-J1L: 209
Ho IX (see Horten)
Hornisse, Fa 266 (see Focke-Achgelis)
Horten
  Ho IX: 94
Hs 122 et seq (see Henschel)
Hurricane (see Hawker)

I

I-16 (see Polikarpov)
Il-2 (see Ilyushin)
Ilyushin
  Il-2: 159, 208

J

J 1 (see Junkers)
J8M1 (see Mitsubishi)
J 10 (see Junkers)
J 21 (see Saab)
Ju 46 et seq (see Junkers)
Junkers
  A 20: 148
  F 13: 148
  F 24: 148
  G 23: 148
  G 24: 148
  G 31: 148
  G 38: 150
  J 1: 148
  J 10: 148
  Ju 46: 148
  Ju 52: 148
  Ju 52/3m: 15, 29, 85, 86, 105, 148-155,
    148-155, 188, 195, **218**,
    238, 239
  Ju 85: 168, 180
  Ju 86: 156, **156**, 157, **157**
  Ju 87: 60, 62, 75, 76, 96, 136, 142,
    143, 147, **158-167**, 159-167,
    238
  Ju 88: 31, 32, 40, 75, 104, 110, 129,
    134, 166, 168-179, **168-179**,
    180, 184, 185, 187, 208, 220,
    221, 246
  Ju 89: 120, 189, 191, 194
  Ju 90: 150, 189-191, **189- 191**, 193,
    238
  Ju 186: 157
  Ju 188: 40, 114, 129, 168, 173, 180-
    187, **180-187**, 195
  Ju 252: 152, 188, **188**, 195
  Ju 287: 188, **188**
  Ju 288: 168, 180, 184, 195
  Ju 290: 188-194, **190-194**
  Ju 322 Mammut: 238
  Ju 352 Herkules: 152, 188, 195, **195**
  Ju 388: 168, 182, 184, 187, 188, 195,
    195
  Ju 390: 194, **194**
  K 47: 159
  W 33: 148
  W 34: 148

K

K 47 (see Junkers)
K.65 Cap (see Mraz)
Kawasaki
  Ki-45 Toryu: 221
Ki-45 Toryu (see Kawasaki)
Ki-200 Shusui (see Mitsubishi)
Kittyhawk (see Curtiss)
Kolibri, Fl 282 (see Flettner)
Komet, Me 163 (see Messerschmitt)

L

L-1 Vigilant (see Vultee)
L-4 Grasshopper (see Piper)
LaGG-3 (see Lavochkin)
Lancaster (see Avro)
Lavochkin
  LaGG-3: 191
Liberator, B-24 (see Consolidated)
Lightning, P-38 (see Lockheed)
Lockheed
  C-130 Hercules: 238
  P-38 Lightning: 221, 231
Lysander (see Westland)

INDEX

M

M-20 (see Messerschmitt)
Mammut, Ju 322 (see Junkers)
Marauder, B-26 (see Martin)
Martin
  139: 36
  B-26 Marauder: **241**
Martlet (see Grumman)
Me 163 *et seq* (see Messerschmitt)
Messerschmitt
  Bf 108 Taifun: 197
  Bf 109: 55, 56, 71, 98, 114, 136, **174**,
    176, **187**, 196-210, **196-209**,
    213, 230, 236, 238, 246, 248
  Bf 110: 45, 63, 129, **149**, 163, 198,
    202, 210-223, **210-221**, 227,
    230, 239, **239**, 245, 246, 250,
    251
  Bf 162: 168
  Bf 163: 54
  M-20: 196
  Me 163 Komet: 222-228, **222-228**
  Me 209: 231
  Me 210: 216, 220, 245, 246, 248, **245**,
    246, 248, 250, 251
  Me 261: 229, **229**
  Me 261w: 238
  Me 262 Schwalbe: 16, 18, 84, 113,
    114, 118, 135, 176, 229-237,
    229-237
  Me 263: 238
  Me 321 Gigant: 106, 107, 238, **238**,
    239, **239**, 242, 243
  Me 323 Gigant: **238-244**, 239, 240,
    242-244
  Me 410: 37, 185, 245-251, **245-251**
MiG-15 (see Mikoyan-Gurevich)
MiG Zh [I-270] (see Mikoyan-Gurevich)
Mikoyan-Gurevich
  MiG-15: 113
  MiG Zh [I-270]: 228
Militar-Wal 33 (see Dornier)
Mistel composite: 75, 84, 172, **174**, 176,
  177, 208
Mitsubishi
  J8M1: 225
  Ki-200 ShuSui: 225
Morane-Saulnier
  M.S.406: 56
  M.S.500: 60
  M.S.501: 60
  M.S.502 Criquet: 60
Moskito, Ta 154 (see Focke-Wulf)
Mosquito (see de Havilland)
Mraz
  K.65 Cap: 60
M.S.406 *et seq* (see Morane-Saulnier)
Mustang, P-51 (see North American)

N

Natter, Ba 349 (see Bachem)
NC 270 (see Aerocentre)
Nord
  1402 Noroit: 187
Noroit, 1402 (see Nord)
North American
  F-86 Sabre: 113
  P-51 Mustang: 29, 74, 76, 80, 102, 107,
    202, 228, 229, 248

O

O-50 (see Bellanca)
OKA-38 Aist (see Antonov)
Operation
  Barbarossa: 31, 142, 151, 202, 213,
    216
  Bodenplatte: 80, 207, 208
  Merkur: 155, 166
  Rumpelkammer: 106
  Sealion (Seelöwe): 238
  Steinbock: 41, 124-127, 175
  Torch: 75
  Weserübung: 36, 110
  Yellow: 151

P

P.11 (see PZL)
P.15 (see Hamburger Flugzeugbau)
P-38 Lightning (see Lockheed)
P-40 Warhawk (see Curtiss)
P-47 Thunderbolt (see Republic)
P-51 Mustang (see North American)
Pfeil, Do 335 (see Dornier)
Piper
  L-4 Grasshopper: 55
Po-2 (see Polikarpov)
Polikarpov
  I-16: 198
  Po-2: 93
Porte
  Baby: 176
PZL
  P.11: 211

R

Republic
  P-47 Thunderbolt: 216, 224, 232, 248
Ryan
  YO-51 Dragonfly: 55

S

Saab
  J 21: 50
Sabre, F-86 (see North American)
Salamander, He 162 (see Heinkel)
Schwalbe, Me 262 (see Messerschmitt)
Scout (see Bristol)
SE 3000 (see Sud Est)
Sea Hurricane (see Hawker)
Short
  Stirling: 179
  Sunderland: 92
Shusui, Ki-200 (see Mitsubishi)
Siebel
  Si 201: 54
  Si 204: 70
Skua (see Blackburn)
SO 4000 (see Sud Ouest)
Spitfire (see Supermarine)
Stirling (see Short)
Storch, Fi 156 (see Fieseler)
Stösser, Fw 56 (see Focke-Wulf)
Sud Est
  SE 3000: 61
Sud Ouest
  SO 4000: 135
Sunderland (see Short)
Supermarine
  Spitfire: 71, 72, 74, 75, 102, 157, 170,
    198, 199, 200, 202, 203, 212,
    213, 229
Swordfish (see Fairey)

T

Ta 152 *et seq* (see Focke-Wulf)
Taifun, Bf 108 (see Messerschmitt)
Tempest (see Hawker)
Thunderbolt, P-47 (see Republic)
Thunderbolt II, A-10 (see Fairchild)
Toryu, Ki-45 (see Kawasaki)
Toucan, AAC 1 (see Ateliers
    Aéronautiques de
    Colombes)
Tupolev
  ANT-20: 29
Typhoon (see Hawker)

U

Uhu, Fw 189 (see Focke-Wulf)
Uhu, He 219 (see Heinkel)

V

V-1 flying bomb (see Fieseler Fi 103)
Vickers
  Wellington: 32, 198
Victor (see Handley Page)
Vigilant, L-1 (see Vultee)
Vultee
  L-1 Vigilant: 55

W

W 33 (see Junkers)
W 34 (see Junkers)
Wal, Do 15 (see Dornier)
Warhawk, P-40 (see Curtiss)
Weihe, Fw 58 (see Focke-Wulf)
Wellington (see Vickers)
Westland Lysander: 55
Whitley (see Armstrong Whitworth)
Wiking, BV 222 (see Blohm und Voss)
Wildcat (see Grumman)

Y

YB-40 (see Boeing)
YO-51 Dragonfly (see Ryan)